The Psychology of Adult Development and Aging

Editors

CARL EISDORFER and M. POWELL LAWTON

Published by
American Psychological Association
Washington, D.C.

Table of Contents

Preface

The recent upsurge of interest in the psychological aspects of aging represents one more instance of the current recognition of the pre-eminence of the individual as opposed to group stereotypes. This book amply illustrates the growing realization that the age group to which an adult belongs is a poor guide to his cognitive or emotional characteristics. As in the case of sex, ethnic, and other broad categories, age levels encompass too wide a range of individual differences —and the overlapping of age groups is too extensive—for the individual's chronological age to serve as a dependable basis for major life decisions. Does the attainment of a preestablished birthday change the worker instantaneously from an effective producer to an unproductive liability? Should knowledge about a patient's elderly status override all other considerations in the diagnosis of physical or mental disorders and automatically lead to the conclusion that his troubles are due simply to "old age"? These are the sorts of questions that society is beginning to face with candor and courage.

Another way in which developments in gerontological psychology exemplify contemporary trends in differential psychology as a whole is in the increasing identification of the contribution of experiential variables. There is less emphasis on how long the person has lived and more on what he has been doing during those years.

Representing the collaborative effort of outstanding leaders in the field, this book summarizes the state of psychological knowledge about aging. It may be regarded as a preliminary map of a recently discovered territory, not only surveying what is known but also outlining the unexplored and underdeveloped regions. It should thus prove to be an especially rich guide for gerontological research. Here can be found a vast collection of unanswered questions to suit the talents and tastes of investigators from almost every psychological specialty. Topical coverage is unusually broad, ranging from animal research and psychophysiological studies to problems of housing and transportation. Experimental, developmental, and clinical approaches are equally represented. In contrast to the traditional focus on the description of behavioral changes with aging, attention is given to several etiological models which provide a fruitful source of testable hypotheses for the gerontological researcher. The need for a problem-

v

centered, interdisciplinary approach is likewise emphasized. The importance of such an approach is becoming widely recognized in all fields of psychology as a means of ensuring that the results of basic research are translated into applied programs.

This volume constitutes a major product of the American Psychological Association's Task Force on Aging. The procedures followed by this task force in the preparation of the book, summarized in the Introduction, illustrate an effective pattern of group functioning that should be of interest in its own right. The coordination of so many authors, reviewers, critics, and discussants in all their complex collaborations and mutual interactions is an impressive undertaking. Especially noteworthy were the efforts to represent all major fields of psychology among the contributors and to obtain further inputs from a wide spectrum of APA divisions. The Task Force on Aging is to be congratulated both for the breadth and imaginativeness of its procedures and for the quality of its output.

Anne Anastasi
President
American Psychological Association

November 1972

Introduction

The American Psychological Association organized the Task Force on Aging in response to a request for representation at the White House Conference on Aging and a growing interest among its members in the aging processes and the problems of the aged. Carl Eisdorfer, then President of Division 20 (Adult Development and Aging), and M. Powell Lawton, President-Elect, were appointed cochairman. The purpose of the task force was to assemble a group of psychologists broadly representative of the association to prepare material reflecting current knowledge of the psychology of adult development and aging and to suggest directions for the future development of research, teaching, and services in the area. The White House Conference on Aging, scheduled for November 1971, gave additional impetus to these plans.

During the 1970 APA annual meeting in Miami, an organizational meeting of the task force was held, at which most of the association's divisions were represented. At that meeting plans were made to implement the association's goals. The following program of actions emerged and was successfully undertaken.

1. A series of papers covering the major areas of the psychology of aging were prepared by nationally prominent professionals in the field, and each one was assigned one or two critics. In many cases the papers were written by persons outside of the task force, and frequently expertise outside of psychology was obtained. The papers were organized into five categories: (a) foundations of gerontology, (b) clinical psychology, (c) experimental psychology, (d) developmental aspects of aging, and (e) social aspects of aging.

2. The resultant 18 invited papers along with a prepared critique for each were discussed in a two-day meeting held in June 1971; invited participants representing all of psychology and a few related scientific disciplines were in attendance. After extended discussion at a subsequent special task force meeting, the papers were revised and edited for publication in this volume, which is to serve as a sourcebook for academic and research workers in the field. This volume, covering the major topical areas of aging, represents the

state of psychological knowledge and the key issues in the psychology of aging at the close of 1971.

3. The results of the task force meeting were reported to the wider membership of APA through special programming at the 1971 annual meeting held in Washington, D.C. In addition to regular Division 20 programs, five presentations of the major topic areas were made at the annual meeting by the authors of the papers and new discussants. These meetings were exceptionally well attended.

4. The task force prepared a statement reflecting the expert knowledge that psychology is able to offer regarding normal aging, later life-span, and special assets and problems of the aged. This statement represents our unique contribution to national policy issues involving the aged population and was presented as the APA position statement at the 1971 White House Conference on Aging. This statement plus the official APA delegates, Leonard Gottesman and Jack Botwinick, constituted the association's explicit input to the conference, although a number of other APA members were delegates to the conference in other capacities.

One of the most valuable aspects of this venture was unquestionably the wide involvement of participants from many of the APA divisions. While most of the invited papers were written by gerontologists, the task force itself, the discussants, and the 1971 annual meeting included many people who had had little previous association with the subject matter of the study of aging, but who contributed strongly in terms of methodology, comparative content, and personally and socially motivated interest, from the vantage points of their own subareas.

The concurrence of the task force operation and the White House Conference year was not, of course, an accident. The production of a statement that would reflect explicitly psychological knowledge but still be useful in policy formulation was a difficult task, but a highly motivating one. The final statement was produced at the 1971 Washington meeting and was sent by APA President Kenneth M. Clark to Dr. Arthur Flemming, Chairman of the White House Conference on Aging. The text of the statement is as follows.

RECOMMENDATIONS TO THE WHITE HOUSE CONFERENCE ON AGING

APA Task Force on Aging

1. Alleged Loss of Intellectual Functioning

Many studies are now showing that the intelligence of older persons as measured is typically underestimated. For the most part, the observed decline in intellectual functioning among the aged is attributable to poor health, social isolation, economic plight, limited education, lowered motivation, or other variables not intrinsically related to the aging process. Where intelligence scores do decline, such change is associated primarily with tasks where speed of response is critical.

Recommendations. Far more attention should be given to understanding and eliminating the unnecessary causes of decline in intellectual function. The absence of intrinsic decline with age should also lead to serious questions concerning the appropriateness of any mandatory retirement age. Functional assessment, advisement programs, and training in alternative uses of skills at various stages of adult life should be incorporated into work situations. Federal departments such as Labor, Social Rehabilitation Services, and the Office of Education should establish sections with continuing responsibility for proposed and funding research and innovative programs in voluntary retirement, second-career training, leisure-time activity training, and better utilization of skills that do not change with age.

2. Education

It is evident that the majority of aged persons are seriously disadvantaged by past and current educational opportunities. Education should be conceived of as a continuing, lifelong activity. A more forceful implementation of adult education could do much to avoid not only intellectual deterioration among older persons but also the reduction of conflict between generations.

Recommendations. Some persons need retraining for second careers; many want the enrichment that comes from keeping up with recent advances; others want to raise their career goals; while still others want to develop leisure activities. Still others need educational assistance in the preservation of occupational, self-maintaining, and self-realizing skills. The federal Office of Education should institute a wide range of activities in the fields of adult education and counseling to meet these needs. The widest spectrum of the public and private sector, including state, county, and private educational systems, should develop educational systems for adults throughout the life-span.

3. Mental Health

There is a great unmet need for mental health services for the aged. At least three million older persons require mental health services. Of this number, a bare 20% have their needs met through existing psychiatric facilities. Although people 65 and over constitute 10% of the United States population, they comprise only 2% of the patients given outpatient mental health services, but 22% of the annual mental hospital admissions. Older Americans also tend to have mental and emotional symptoms for long periods of time, often years, before receiving help.

Recommendations. We recommend that federal agencies such as the National Institute of Mental Health pay much more explicit attention to the mental health problems of the elderly, whether in community agencies, comprehensive mental health centers, mental hospitals, or institutions for long-term care. Studies on the prevention and treatment of mental illness need to be accelerated. Alternatives to institutional care must be developed and evaluated for their effectiveness. An intensive research effort is needed to acquire more precise data on the effectiveness of existing services and additional services required to meet the need. In addition, more basic knowledge is required on the causes of specific mental disorders so that primary preventive techniques may be developed to reduce the incidence of mental disorders and their associated disabilities. A Center for the Mental Health of the Aged should be established within the National Institute of Mental Health, with the authority and funds for research, training, and innovative service programs for older people in the community and in hospitals.

4. Environments for the Elderly

Many of the psychological difficulties of older persons appear to result from lack of environmental supports, rather than from the aging process per se. Inadequate housing, deterioration of older neighborhoods, antitherapeutic institutions, poorly located services, inadequate transportation, and architectural barriers to mobility may act directly upon the emotional and physical state of any vulnerable individual, old or young. Psychological research has shown that improved housing brings new activities and friendships, better access to services provides a new sense of independence and well-being, and an improved community structure yields a heightened feeling of security, particularly for older people.

Recommendations. The federal government has the capability to improve the lives of elderly persons through subsidized programs for better housing, improved institutions, community-based service, delivery and leisure-time centers, and transportation systems. Appropriate government agencies, such as the Department of Housing and Urban Development and the Department of Transportation, should take responsibility for programs and research for environmental planning needs of the elderly. These departments should play leadership roles in initiating studies of housing, neighborhood planning, and transportation for older people and in investigating those factors of the physical and social environment that enhance the psychological and social well-being of older persons.

5. Institutions for the Aged

For some older people, the most appropriate place for care is a total custody institution. In contrast to the usual attitude of hopelessness about such patients, research has repeatedly demonstrated the effectiveness of rehabilitative and therapeutic programs in aiding institutionalized aged patients to live more satisfying lives in the institution and frequently enabling them to return to the community. New community and institutional service networks should be planned and evaluated.

Recommendations. Far more attention needs to be given to the development of innovative therapeutic services to institutionalized older persons. Federal agencies involved with planning and supporting institutional services should assume major responsibility for the dissemination of research knowledge and information regarding innovative programs to potential users. They should also assume responsibility for evaluation of the effectiveness of alternative forms of institutional and noninstitutional services.

6. Professional Manpower and Training

Based upon the most conservative projections of needs and available and future professional manpower it is clear that there is, and will continue to be, a striking shortage of psychologists to serve the public through direct clinical service, to perform basic research, and to educate others.

Recommendations. A minimum 10-year goal is that for every institution of higher learning concerned with graduate education there should be at least one psychologist competent to teach and conduct research on the psychological aspects of aging. It is also clear that we need at least several institutions that can function as major centers for teaching, research, and clinical activities with the aging. The magnitude of the problems related to the aging is so great that by 1980 the absolute minimum trained manpower should include 300 new academic psychologists, 600 applied psychologists, and 1,200 professional psychologists. Several surveys of manpower needs (see White House Conference Technical Paper on Training, 1971) have made quantitative projections and have documented the acute shortage of trained personnel. The most expert projections, based upon minimal estimates, indicate that the above estimate may be less than one-third of the actual requirement for the next decade, and that only 15 of 100 aged persons needing psychological help will be able to obtain it. Only the federal government, with at least a threefold increase in current funding levels for training in gerontology, can provide for these realistic manpower needs.

7. Research and Demonstration

The value of basic and applied research for extending and improving human lives has been amply demonstrated. Current and future research on aging can be expected to provide information relative to the management of the vital problems of the aged. A few examples are the psychological studies that have made significant contributions to understanding the mental and emotional disorders of aging persons; studies that have led to improvements in treatment and evaluation; studies that have elucidated the factors causing the apparent decline in learning and intelligence; and the social and personality factors that have implications for physical and environmental changes to improve life for older persons. Stereotyped attitudes of the public toward the aged and the negative attitudes of the elderly toward themselves have had detrimental effects on the lifestyle of the aged. Research is needed to determine effective methods of counteracting negative attitudes toward the aging and thereby promoting more constructive use of their skills. Behavioral scientists have information and tools to evaluate the impact of new programs on the feelings, attitudes, morale, and behavior of older persons. Yet, many of the federal programs seek little or no consultation with people who have specialized psychological knowledge relevant to planning.

Recommendations. Research and development in the behavioral sciences is still receiving meager support. It is most ironic that major budget cuts for federally supported research on aging were proposed during the year of the White House Conference on Aging. This pattern must be reversed and programs of basic and applied research in aging given much higher priority. This should be implemented by the creation of a National Institute of Gerontology, to be discussed in the section on government organization.

8. Government Organization

The administrative organization and funding of federal agencies relating to aging have shown little consistency in function or policy, despite the efforts of individual dedicated staff members. This has produced a public image of a lack of concern on the part of the federal government for its aging population. The absence of clear policies and stable organizations at the national level has contributed to vacillation and inefficiency on the part of local government and on the part of institutions which tie their programs into the federal establishment. In addition, the scientific community has had considerable difficulty in finding appropriate sources for funding its research and training.

Recommendations. In order to develop an administrative organization that will help improve the quality of life for older individuals and to maintain an adequate level of research and training support, highest priority should be given to establishing a National Institute of Gerontology within the Department of Health, Education, and Welfare, with assured adequate funding. Programs of other important federal agencies, that is, the National Institute of Mental Health and the Administration on Aging of the Social and Rehabilitation Service, and others previously mentioned, should be strengthened and would complement those in the Institute. It is also necessary that a Special Assistant to the White House on Aging be appointed to represent the concerns of older persons. This assistant should have direct access to departmental secretaries regarding their program of services, research, and training for the elderly and the authority to insure their implementation.

At the 1971 annual meeting in Washington, D.C., the task force voted to maintain its operation for another year in order to plan further feedback into the divisions, to make recommendations to APA regarding future activities it might wish to undertake in the field of aging, and to complete the preparation of this volume.

The executive committee of the task force consisted of James Birren, Wilma Donahue, Carl Eisdorfer, Frank Finger, Israel Goldiamond, Leonard Gottesman, M. Powell Lawton, Max Siegel, Rogers Wright, and Joseph Zubin.

Financial support for the operation of the task force was obtained from the National Institute of Child Health and Human Development, the Administration on Aging, and the National Institute of Mental Health. The project was administratively based in the APA Board of Professional Affairs, with the assistance of John McMillan and Gottlieb Simon of the Central Office staff. The editing and production of this book was the responsibility of the Separate Publications Department of APA. Thanks go to Estelle Mallinoff, Editor, Separate Publications, Patricia Walsh, Beth Forrester, Judy Smith, and Valerie Coleman, technical editors.

Carl Eisdorfer and M. Powell Lawton

Foundations of Gerontology

Foundations of Gerontology: History, Training, and Methodology

As one reviews the present status of gerontology as a science it becomes clear that far more effort has gone into descriptive gerontology than into etiological approaches to the field. Furthermore, as Riegel points out in his chapter, most workers have attacked the field from the point of view of their specific disciplines, leading to a piecemeal, unintegrated result. This discipline-centeredness leads to deeper and deeper knowledge of a particular area but fails to interconnect with the contributions of the other disciplines. To hope for an Einstein to come along and integrate the piecemeal findings seems misplaced. A shift from a discipline-centered to a problem-centered strategy is essential if progress in solving the problems of aging is to be achieved.

While gerontology, like psychology, has a long past, it has a short history, especially in the United States. In fact, the second quarter of the twentieth century appears to have marked the beginning of our formal definition of gerontology as an area of inquiry for psychology. While the percentage of the population aged 65 and over rose steadily from 2.7% in 1860 to 9.1% in 1970, the proportion of the aged males who were gainfully employed in the labor market dropped from 68% in 1890 to 26% in 1969, with the most rapid decline occurring between 1930 and 1940 (11.8%). Average life expectancy reached 66.7 years in 1946, and the dependency

Joseph Zubin received his PhD in psychology from Columbia University in 1932. His previous positions include Associate Research Psychologist, New York State Psychiatric Institute and Hospital, and Principal Research Scientist in Biometrics, New York State Department of Mental Hygiene. Currently he is Chief of Psychiatric Research (Biometrics), New York State Department of Mental Hygiene, and Professor Emeritus of Psychology, Columbia University. His major research interest is in the biometric approach to psychopathology.

ratio (ratio of the population of people 65 and over to the population in the working range 20–64) vacillated between 5 and 8% from 1830 to 1920 but then began to rise linearly until it reached 18% in 1970. Thus, while the problem of the aged has always been with us, its exacerbation in the 1930s and 1940s led to its recognition on a national level and to congressional action in the form of the Social Security Act and similar movements. We are, therefore, dealing with a relatively new phenomenon and need not be discouraged by the modest progress made thus far.

While the descriptive approach to the problem of aging, which accounts for much of the gerontological literature, is an important step in investigating the problem, there are few systematic conceptual links that would bridge the inevitable gap between research disciplines and the service specialties. We will not get any better integration of the field until we uncover the sources of the aging process. We must resort to certain strategies to overcome our ignorance of these sources. One of the most effective strategies when faced with abysmal ignorance is to construct scientific models. A brief survey of the field indicates that there are at least six such scientific models: ecological, developmental, learning theory, genetic, internal environment, and neurophysiological. Similarly, there are a variety of scientific models for therapeutic intervention: dyadic models, group models, public health models, and others, which are dealt with in the chapters in this section. In similar fashion, Birren discusses a variety of training models. It is clear that an imbrication of the vast variety of models in the four areas of description, etiology, therapy, and training is necessary for a successful attack on the aging problem.

DESCRIPTION OF CHANGES IN FUNCTIONING DUE TO NORMAL AGING

Naturalistic observations on changes in functioning with age go back to the ancient philosophers and continue into the present. The most popular form these observations take is a description of the stages of man. Those of Shakespeare, Freud, Piaget, and Eric Ericson are well known. Less well known are the stages described in the *Ethics of the Fathers* (Tractate Avoth). They include age 50—counsel; 60—old age; 70—hoary head; 80—heroics (special strength); 90—bending (beneath the weight of old age); and 100—"as though he were dead and had passed away and ceased from the world."

Such stages, interesting as they are, do not help in providing an assessment of man's functioning with age. Even the existence of stages that are qualitatively different from each other is debatable and may depend upon the level of abstraction that we are willing to entertain. For objective assessment we need to turn to systematic naturalistic studies, laboratory measurements, and observations under controlled conditions.

The descriptive approach deals primarily with methods for documenting signs of aging in terms of self-descriptive approaches, evaluations by others, psychodynamic investigations, and biometric investigations of the type to which I have already alluded. Systematic structured interviews, to which Gurland addresses himself, are one way of assessing the aged; self-administered personality inventories and attitude questionnaires are other descriptive approaches.

ETIOLOGY OF NORMAL AGING

Let us now turn to the causes that lie behind the waxing and waning of man's capacities. What models have been proposed? The ecological model postulates that the causes of aging are to be found primarily in the forces that impinge on the ecological niche that the aged occupies. Given a good supporting niche in which his needs are cared for and opportunities for continuing his active life prior to crossing the Rubicon are provided, there should be little or no reduction of function when the niche is favorable, except for those functions for which the physiological substrate itself is actually in decline. Most of the observed deterioration of functioning may be a product of the deleterious parameters of the niche. Research in this area has thus far depended upon rather crude analyses of the characteristics of the niche, such as socioeconomic status, education, socialization, and so on. There is need for a better taxonomy of the parameters of the ecological niche, that is, social network analysis, isolation history, and similar parameters.

The developmental model stipulates that the etiology of aging is to be sought in the transitional stage of passing from adulthood to the senium and the adjustment to the new stage of life which the person enters. You develop into aging just as you develop into childhood, adolescence, and adulthood. The reduction in performance in physiological, sensory, perceptual, psychomotor, and conceptual functioning that comes with age, the loss of friends, relatives, and family through death or mobility, the changes in self-image and goals accompanying retirement, threat of death, poverty, and changing sexual functioning all conspire to alter the functioning of the aged in a negative direction. These are the factors that we need to examine in our attempt to understand the causes of aging and the prevention of deteriorative trends that come with age.

The learning theory model stipulates that the changes in behavior observed in the aging are the result of learning. You learn to be old just as you learn anything else in life—through reinforcement. Given the proper types of reinforcement, no one need show the inroads of aging generally observed in our society. Even if there is physiological decline, we can learn to adapt to it; the negative consequences in affect and behavior are the result of the failure to adapt, and therapy based upon learning theory can eliminate them. Furthermore, institutionalization tends to reduce functioning because of the limitations of institutional life—a result of the formation of habits deleterious to welfare. This too can be prevented by proper application of learning theory principles, especially through such devices as friendly visiting services.

The lowered self-image of the aged is one of the most pervasive findings in gerontological surveys. It would be most useful to discover whether the lowered self-image is the cause of deteriorative aging or whether aging must inevitably produce a lowered self-image. If we could prevent a lowering of the self-image by proper behavioral therapy, perhaps much of the so-called aging effects on behavior could be prevented.

The genetic model stipulates that the limitation of functioning coming with age is a form of built-in obsolescence via our hereditary endowment. We must remember, however, that genetics is not an island unto itself; the environment must interact with the hereditary disposition in order for it to develop. Therefore, genetics must not be regarded as fate, and proper steps can be taken to prevent deleterious genetic tendencies and encourage benign tendencies.

The internal environment model stipulates that the sources of aging are to be sought in changes in the metabolic processes and contents of body fluids. Immunity to any proliferating tendency on the part of some cells has been implicated in the prevention of cellular breakdown and interference with this process, or autoimmunity has been postulated as the source of aging.

The neurophysiological model postulates that the source of aging is to be sought in information processing, which is mediated by the neurophysiology of the organism. The loss of brain cells or the creation of plaques may militate against the usual processing of information and bring about the changes that are characteristic of aging.

Thus, aging may be regarded as due to a series of subtle cortical insults that interfere with information processing.

Each of the above models has the virtue that it suggests hypotheses to test in order to determine the tenability of the model. For the ecological model, we must find techniques to test the role of ecological factors in the aging process. Since the ecological factors reflect the social-cultural-physical milieu of the niche in which the person is located, the best approach would be to apply culture-dependent techniques such as interviews or observational techniques. For example, in examining the subject's attitude toward work, his role as a worker can be examined. The information sought will be highly culture dependent since attitudes toward work vary so much from culture to culture.

The developmental and learning theory models can best be tested by culture fair techniques, which, though imbedded in the local culture, have cross-cultural equivalents. For example, the influence of isolation might be studied by means of greeting behavior or grieving behavior. Although these behaviors bear local color, they, nevertheless, have their equivalents in all cultures. The genetic, internal environment and neurophysiological models can best be tested by means of culture free techniques. Thus, the catecholamine balance in the internal milieu can be tested by laboratory techniques regardless of what ecological niche a person occupies. Though there may be local norms for these determinations, the method for making these determinations is independent of the culture of the milieu.

TRAINING MODELS

How to prepare research and clinical workers is discussed by Birren in a review that is both comprehensive and impressive. With regard to research training, there is a tendency to limit such programs to developmental psychology, with unfortunate consequences, since developmental psychology today is focused on the earlier ages of life. The majority of the funds, fellowships, and academic positions are in neonate and childhood studies. Theoretically, aging is part of development and should remain in this spectrum, but administratively and financially the developmental umbrella has been disastrous for gerontology. Perhaps administrative reorganization could improve the situation.

One area that Birren fails to stress is the training of nonpsychologists for gerontological work. It is high time we realized that we alone cannot cope with the problem and that training for this field requires the wide spectrum of approaches suggested by the various scientific models discussed earlier. One interesting question arises when we contemplate the gerontologist of the future. If he is to be conversant with ecology, development, learning, genetics, internal environment, and neurophysiology, can he remain a psychologist? The future belongs to those who prepare for it! If we can develop methods based upon psychological principles such as learning theory and developmental theory, but also provide knowledge in the other areas, the gerontologist of the future may be closer to psychology than to sociology or psychiatry, our two most closely related disciplines. However, I am hoping that each of the disciplines that has contributed to gerontology in the past as well as those that contribute to it now will so enrich gerontology that distinguishing between these influences will be an academic question.

Regarding the number of professionals needed to work with the aged, it is unfortunate that most of our estimates are based upon inpatient data. The number of aged individuals seeking outpatient care is notoriously low. With the development of population surveys it may become possible to estimate more accurately the service needs of the aged who now receive no care. The numbers required will be considerably larger than those now contemplated. I am reminded of the response of a Dutch psychologist to my comment that we need more service people to care for the aged. He said, "You are simply asking for more boys to place their finger in the cracking dyke!" The better way is prevention. By identifying the vulnerable high-risk population and supplying them with preventive attention, the flood tide of service can be halted. To permit the aged to break down and then bring in the repair man to put them together again is wasteful of personnel, funds, and human happiness.

One problem remains, the one which Riegel raises in his provocative chapter: How can we make our scientific and humane efforts more efficient? He roundly scolds current approaches to research and training as being too competitive and insufficiently cooperative and wants to revolutionize current procedures. I cannot help but empathize with his desires, but at the same time I am somewhat surprised at his attempt to substitute cooperative group effort for individual initiative. To introduce cooperative effort in research as a classroom exercise is one thing, but to limit research to cooperative efforts, even interdisciplinary efforts, is bound to reduce creativity.

His condemnation of collecting data for data's sake does not hold true for all scientific endeavor. No good scientist collects data for data's sake. Even those who disavow it carry models in their heads which dictate the kinds of experiments they do and the kind of data they collect.

As for the stress on historical research and the systematic retrieval of old findings, I again tend to agree that it is desirable, but special problems may arise depending upon the nature of the material. In my own studies, for example, in the world literature on prognosis in schizophrenia I discovered that nine-tenths of the articles reviewed were worthless for my purpose, and although I did manage to find some underlying currents, the tremendous effort expended was hardly recompensed by the results.

METHODOLOGICAL APPROACHES

Let me first point out that in order to deal adequately with the research problem in aging we need instruments geared to the task. Most of our instruments are culture bound, reflecting the particular milieu in which we find ourselves. This may be unavoidable in dealing with the ecological model. However, in dealing with research emanating from the developmental and learning theory models we need to develop culture fair techniques translatable from culture to culture. If attitudes toward self, labor, job, and family are the important areas for investigation of the developmental model, we must transcend the mores of our major society if we are to capture the essential problems of a subculture by providing culture fair measures. A puritan ethic can hardly be of use in a mañana culture! Then there is need for culture free indicators in studying the brain function, internal environment, and hereditary models. The development of such tools is a sine qua non.

One of the striking differentials in research findings is that which contrasts the results of longitudinal and cross-sectional studies. There is one advantage of longitudinal studies that needs to be kept in mind: their historical and follow-up values. Perhaps the best way to predict future behavior is to postdict past behavior, and for this purpose longitudinal studies, despite their selectivity, biases, and practice effects on testing, can never be surpassed by other approaches. The hope is that patterns of individual life progress can be found that characterize subgroups of individuals. These subgroup cohorts can provide prediction of future behavior, both adjusted and maladjusted, so that we can identify the high-risk populations for whom intervention is essential. In dealing with such data we are essentially dealing with time series, and fortunately the statistical treatment of such data has recently been fortified by powerful methods which should become part of our statistical lore.

THE FUTURE OF GERONTOLOGY

As one views the year 2000 with reference to the problems of the aged, it becomes quite clear that a larger and larger proportion of voters, consumers, and men of leisure, as well as workers, will be drawn from the age group beyond 65. What can one say that has not already been said regarding the changes this shift in population will bring? It will be as great if not greater than the shift from rural to urban centers, and its impact on education, industry, health, and business can only be guessed. How to prepare to serve such a tremendous population is a crucial issue. Certainly such areas as play, recreation, and continuing education will play an important part. But the greatest service that the psychologist can provide is to prevent the occurrence of *accidie,* the noonday demon of the monasteries of the Middle Ages, which arises from too much leisure, of boredom from too much education, and of isolation resulting from too much lonesomeness.

Academic and Professional Training in the Psychology of Aging

JAMES E. BIRREN and DIANA S. WOODRUFF

The purpose of this chapter is to examine the place of teaching and research on the psychological aspects of aging in the contemporary department of psychology. Also to be examined are the implications for training and service in the professional fields of psychology that have or will develop responsible roles in meeting the needs of an increasingly large population of retired and aged adults. Research on the psychological aspects of aging has implications as profound as those surrounding biological research on the nature of life, and teaching based upon research on aging can have great cultural impact. Such information has the potential for changing man's concept of himself not unlike the conceptual revolution following Darwin, in which man began to consider himself as having properties in common with other living things.

The subject matter of the psychology of aging may be defined as the systematic study and knowledge of the changes that occur in behavior in individuals in the second half of life. Alternatively, it might be defined as changes that occur in the organism after physical maturity. The former definition would take into account the changes

James E. Birren came to the University of Southern California after a distinguished career in government research in Washington, D.C. He received his PhD in psychology from Northwestern University in 1947, and spent a year at the University of Chicago in postdoctoral study. Positions he has held include Chief, Section on Aging, National Institute of Mental Health, 1953–64; Director, Aging Program, National Institute of Child Health and Human Development, 1964–65; and since 1965, Director, Andrus Gerontology Center, and Professor of Psychology, University of Southern California. His current research interests are the development of cognitive strategies with age and the biological bases of age changes in speed of behavior.

Diana S. Woodruff received her PhD in psychology from the University of Southern California in 1972, where she specialized in adult development

11

occurring after the ages 30 to 35, while the latter definition would place the beginning of the field at about age 18 or about college age.

This second view would leave within the scope of the psychology of aging about three-quarters of the life-span, for example, from 18 years old and upwards. In either case, the subject matter consists of the changes in the mature organism.

It takes no great scholar of the subject to be aware of the fact that the subject matter of the psychology of aging has been under-represented in the teaching and research programs of departments of psychology. This is somewhat surprising since most departments have a concern with developmental psychology. One might expect to see an interest in the transformations that occur in the behavior over the life-span rather than only in the development of children.

History

One of the earlier important figures in developmental psychology was G. Stanley Hall. His influence on psychology was considerable, particularly in the field of developmental psychology. Following his earlier emphasis on adolescence, he published, in 1922, a book entitled *Senescence: The Second Half of Life*. This book reflects his active interest in the developmental principles of behavior over the life-span. Recently, however, in a commentary on Hall, no mention was made of the fact that aging was an important aspect of his interest. Why the limited vision in developmental psychology with regard to changes in adults?

One historical fact may account for the almost exclusive pre-occupation of the developmental psychologist with the child—the fact that many persons had to be trained to become teachers of the young. Child psychology has been taught not only because it is a part of general psychology, but also because thousands of persons directly or indirectly involved in teacher training have to become knowledgeable about the basic principles of child development. The early departments of psychology were called on to teach courses about child development. Textbook after textbook on child psy-

and aging. She is currently an Assistant Research Psychologist at the University of California at Los Angeles. Brain–behavior relationships in the developing and aging nervous system are her major interest, and her research involves electrophysiology and biofeedback control. She also has a research interest in personality development over the life-span.

chology rolled off the presses of publishers. These books were, to varying degrees, responses to the educational needs of those persons who would be providing services to children. No parallel pressure was felt by departments of psychology in their early history to teach courses about the postadolescent person.

Another influence on developmental psychology that helped to restrict its interest to early-life phenomena was the fact that school children were attractive, captive populations for research purposes. The evolution of nursery schools also provided easy access to researchers interested in the development of behavior patterns. The massive numbers of adults at various stages of the life-span living under a wide variety of conditions have been less captive for research purposes. The master's candidate seeking a thesis or the quest for a doctoral dissertation was more practically met by choosing a developmental issue that could be studied in a captive population of children rather than one involving adults beyond college age.

Several historical reviews of the origins and trends in developmental psychology are available to the reader who wishes to consider the likelihood over the next decade of a substantial amount of attention being given to the adult portion of the life-span. Charles (1970), after reviewing the historical antecedents of developmental psychology, concluded:

> Child psychology and gerontology: May and December. How do they get together? Longitudinal studies seem to be, historically, the one source of concern for psychological characteristics and change from birth to old age. Though often lacking in methodological adequacy, they have focused our interests on the person as he grows, matures, and ages. At this point in time, we may be ready to develop research attacks on the intriguing problems that are revealed as the person moves through his life [p. 52].

In a related manner, Groffmann (1970) reviewed the history of life-span developmental psychology in Europe. One of his conclusions is highly relevant.

> Historians of psychology were typically not very interested in developmental psychology; historians of developmental psychology concentrated mainly on the origins of child psychology. As a result, one gains the impression that the historical roots of developmental psychology encompassed only child psychology. This impression is not quite correct [p. 67].

In a different vein, Riegel (pp. 37–68) looked at the history of developmental psychology as part of psychological gerontology. His quantitative analysis of publication led him to deemphasize the accumulation of science by individual publications and urged a sweeping reform of higher education. Birren (1961a, 1961b) also looked at the history of the psychology of aging, and his perspective suggests that the leadership in the developmental psychology of the adult has in many instances come from persons who earlier studied the child. Also, he found a relatively low publication volume of literature on the adult as compared with the literature on the child, but he forecasted an exponentially increasing amount of literature on adult development and aging.

In 1947, a report was issued by a commission established at Harvard University to examine the future of psychology (Gregg et al., 1970). The report was published under the title "The Place of Psychology in an Ideal University." It indicated that the basic components of psychology are the following: sensory processes, mechanisms of behavior, perception, memory, learning, motivation, thinking, personality development, individual differences, and gene-caused traits. The report also listed specializations in advanced areas of psychology, which should follow after the introductory course on the topics listed above. Among the specialized areas listed were the psychology of infancy, childhood, adolescence, maturity, and old age. Few departments during the 25 years since the Harvard report have shown an interest in a life-span developmental psychology.

Current Programs in Developmental Psychology

Brackbill (1971) made a survey of the four-year graduate training opportunities in developmental psychology. Of the 96 developmental programs described in her report, 10 psychology departments were apparently prepared to offer training in adulthood and old age as well as in the early phases of the life-span. Her report listed the University of Chicago, Duke University, Manitoba University, the University of Michigan, Pennsylvania State University, Syracuse University, Wayne State University, and the University of West Virginia as having specialized training programs in the psychology of adult development and aging. Other university psychology departments mentioned as offering content in aging were Catholic University of America, which provides opportunities for research training in adult thinking, and Temple University, which includes course work and research opportunities in adulthood and old age. The other 86 universities that listed opportunity for training in developmental psychology in the *Graduate Study in Psychology 1971–72* (APA, 1970) failed to include in their programs any consideration of development beyond adolescence. Not included in the survey were those programs, such as that of Washington University, that have specialized in the adult phase.

Just as the pragmatic need for scientific knowledge about principles in child development led to the establishment of positions in child development in every major university psychology department, so too may the present demand for knowledge about and services for the aging lead to the creation of courses and faculty positions in adult development and aging. Since 1900, almost 30 years have been added to the life expectancy of the average American, and the proportion of individuals over 65 in the population rose from 4.1% in 1900 to 9.5% in 1970. Declining birth rates, death rates, and low immigration have led to a dramatic increase in both the absolute and relative size of the older population.

Psychologists are becoming increasingly aware of the need to attend to the psychological and social issues that arise in a dynamic society. The emergence of an aged minority that represents almost 10% of the American population and the general trend toward aging of the total population are clearly issues to which psychologists must respond. The issues involve our retired and aged population, which is larger than the entire populations of most countries of Western Europe. Some innovative attempts of training in the psychology of aging have been initiated by the 10 adult development and aging programs mentioned in the APA *Division of Developmental Psychology (Division 7) Newsletter* (Brackbill, 1971). Several interdisciplinary gerontology programs not included in the survey (the University of Southern California, the University of California, San Francisco, and Washington University) also represent attempts to meet the emerging demand for the training of psychologists in the field of adult development and aging.

Funding sources. Most of the training for academic psychologists in the field of aging is funded by the National Institutes of Child Health and Human Development (NICHD). As of June 1970, 53 doctoral candidates were supported. Of these 53 students, 33 were trainees in psychology, and 20 were trainees in human development. Eleven different NICHD training grants support training programs in the psychology of aging; eight are housed in departments of psychology, two are in departments of human development, one is in a department of psychiatry (department of medicine), and one is in the Division of Behavioral Sciences (school of public health). This amount of training is small compared with that in the child portion of the life-span.

During the seven-year period since the first NICHD training programs in the psychology of aging were conceived, 49 PhDs and

4 MAs have been awarded, and there have been 8 postdoctoral graduates. The existing programs in adult development and aging have been successful inasmuch as 90% of those graduated from these programs are currently employed in academic and research positions. Since the existing programs have proved viable, they might be considered as useful models for the development of additional training programs in the psychology of aging.

Models for training. The life-span developmental approach is the emphasis of training programs at Syracuse University and at the University of West Virginia. Both programs are housed entirely within the psychology departments and offer doctoral degrees in psychology, with specialization in life-span developmental psychology. The basis for these programs is that the aged can only be understood as the end product of a lifelong process. Hence, the studies of childhood, adolescence, and adulthood are viewed as essential for the proper understanding of the status of the aged. At the University of West Virginia, a direct attempt is being made to unify the field of developmental psychology. Trainees are encouraged to explore the entire life-span and, hence, to tie together the bodies of information collected by specialists who have tended to isolate themselves in infant, child, adolescent, or adult development.

A multidisciplinary center such as the Gerontology Center at the University of Southern California provides another type of program for training psychologists specializing in adult development and aging. In this program, the student is first accepted for graduate study in the psychology department, and he may then choose to specialize in adult development and aging. In addition to fulfilling departmental requirements in psychology, trainees participate in courses, symposia, and summer institutes offered at the Gerontology Center. Psychology is one of seven areas in which the doctorate is available in the program, and psychology trainees interact with trainees in architecture, biology, physiology of exercise, public administration, social work, and sociology. This approach emphasizes the interdisciplinary nature of the research question in gerontology. Students learn the value of the contributions of other sciences and are especially equipped to undertake research of an interdisciplinary nature.

At the University of Chicago, the emphasis is on a broad concept of human development, and the multidisciplinary program is based in the departments of anthropology, psychology, and sociology. Most trainees obtain doctoral degrees in human development, but the doctorate is also offered in psychology. In this program, the students devote three quarters a year to course work and research, and a fourth quarter is spent in a field work or action setting. In this manner, an attempt is made to bridge the gap between theory, research, and application.

Washington University has long had a training program in the psychology of aging and has, in fact, produced the greatest number of doctorates in the subject of all the universities. Its program stresses both experimental and clinical aspects.

A means of introducing psychologists to the field of adult development and aging is through postdoctoral training. The Duke University Center for the Study of Aging and Human Development provides a two-year research training program for postdoctoral study. The program focus is on independent work in close collaboration with the faculty. The postdoctoral fellows participate in seminars, ongoing research projects, and independent research, and they are provided with specific skills in an area of the life cycle. This program is multidisciplinary, involving members in more than 10 departments of the university, including medicine, obstetrics and gynecology, pediatrics, political science, psychiatry, psychology, and sociology.

Training at the undergraduate level. Thus far, consideration has been given only to graduate training in the psychology of aging, where about two-thirds of the courses in aging are offered (United States Department of Health, Education, and Welfare, 1968). Many benefits also accrue from introducing the subject matter of aging into undergraduate courses. Since career decisions are made most often before the student enters graduate school, successful recruitment to meet the present and future personnel needs in research, teaching, and practice must start at the undergraduate level. The Gerontological Society report (United States Department of Health, Education, and Welfare, 1968) called for a 230% increase in the number of scientists in training in the field of aging, so the need for undergraduates to become interested in graduate training is great. In addition to attracting students to careers in adult development and aging, undergraduate courses in the psychology of aging might help to affect a change in the image of the aged within our culture. The misconceptions and negative stereotypes about aging should be altered in a society in which an increasing proportion of the population is growing old. Education in the psychology of aging at the college and junior college level could lead to increased compassion and understanding of the aged and to a generation of individuals who themselves are better prepared for the changes that occur with time. Also, consideration should be given to the training of paraprofessional personnel in the psychology of aging. It seems undesirable that we should train only for the PhD and also most unlikely that we could, by such an approach, supply the numbers of persons forecasted for employment.

Training centers. Most of the doctoral dissertations on problems in the psychology of aging have come from a relatively small number of universities. Twelve universities have produced 50% of the 209 dissertations identified as being in the field over the period 1934–69; 28 universities produced 75% of the dissertations. In the emergence of a new field such as the psychology of aging, it appears that most effort is not diffusely spread but is concentrated in a few schools that have adequate faculty and facilities. Those schools that have produced one or no dissertations per decade would appear on the surface to have insufficient depth in faculty and facilities to undertake major training efforts. Furthermore, in the early stages of expansion of efforts, centers of training might well be established in a limited number of universities that have already shown evidence of productivity so that maximum utilization of personnel might be achieved. The assumption is made that much activity in the 12 schools that have produced 50% of the dissertations on aging will be of greater advantage qualitatively and quantitatively than little effort in many institutions.

In view of the manpower needs, a goal of establishing a dozen training centers in the psychology of aging by the end of this decade would appear to be a conservative policy to recommend to public agencies to guide their support of training. Clearly, individual universities will, as they have in the past, elect to pioneer and begin innovative programs. However, data up to this point suggest that for a variety of reasons only a small number of institutions are likely to conduct programs in the psychology of aging and that these schools should be given special encouragement.

Literature

To undertake a program of training in the psychology of aging, sufficient materials must be available. The growth rate of psychological research on aging published in the United States is evidenced by the fact that while 15 to 20 years ago it was possible to know the whole literature, it is not possible today. A bibliographic search for publications in the psychology of aging in the period between 1963 and 1968 disclosed nearly 2,000 references (Botwinick, 1970).

While the research literature in the psychology of aging has grown markedly in the past two decades, textbooks integrating the material have just begun to appear. Several surveys were under-taken by the authors to ascertain the number of books published on adult development and aging in the past decade and to compare this number with the total number of books published in develop-mental psychology. The results of these surveys are presented in Table 1.

TABLE 1

Books Published in *Developmental Psychology* between 1960 and 1970

Phase	Survey I[a]		Survey II[b]	
	n	Percentage	n	Percentage
Childhood	207	66.8	227	63.4
Adolescence	47	15.2	59	16.5
Adulthood and old age	29	9.3	34	9.5
Childhood and adolescence	16	5.2	26	7.3
Life-span	11	3.5	12	3.3
Total	310	100.0	358	100.0

[a]Mail survey of publishers of psychological materials.

[b]Survey of books reviewed in *Contemporary Psychology*.

In one survey, publishers of psychological materials listed in the 1970–71 edition of the *Literary Market Place* were contacted by mail and asked to report all books in developmental psychology. Books in the categories of infancy, childhood, adolescence, young adulthood, maturity, old age, and aging were included. Replies were received from 54, or over two-thirds, of the 76 publishing houses that were contacted. Of the 310 books in developmental psychology reported by the publishers, 29 dealt with adult development and aging, and 11 covered the life-span from childhood to old age. Hence, slightly less than 13% of the books in developmental psychology included some content on adulthood and old age, and the content of 9.3% of the books consisted primarily of topics in adult development and aging.

Books reviewed in *Contemporary Psychology* between 1960 and 1970 were the data base for the second survey. All books in developmental psychology were counted and categorized in the headings of childhood, adolescence, adulthood and aging, childhood and adolescence, and life-span. Three hundred and fifty-eight books in developmental psychology were included, and the results of this survey were impressively consistent with the results of the survey of publishers. Nine and one-half percent of the books included dealt with adulthood and aging, and slightly over 3% covered the entire life-span. Hence, about 13% of the books in developmental psychology included some content on aging.

The results of both surveys indicate that 87% of the literature in developmental psychology deals with the first 25% of the life-span. The content relevant to the lives of 140 million adults or 70% of the population is represented in 13% of the developmental literature. Such an imbalance of attention to different phases of the life-span reflects the extent to which our youth-oriented culture has influenced advances in science. A more positive implication of this data is the great potential still to be realized in the developmental psychology of adult life. In the study of adulthood and aging, there is the opportunity for investigators to explore new areas that to date remain essentially untouched.

Developmental Psychology, the APA Journal devoted to development, also reflects the bias of psychologists to the study of childhood. Although in the editorial policy of the journal it is stated that "adolescence and the aging population appear to deserve particular attention at this time," some issues of the journal do not contain even 1 article on adulthood and aging. In 1970, a total of 138 articles were published in the journal. Table 2 shows the number of articles dealing with different phases of the life cycle. Only 5

TABLE 2

Articles Published in *Developmental Psychology* in 1970

Phase	Articles	
	n	Percentage
Childhood	113	81.9
Adolescence	9	6.4
Adulthood and aging	5	3.6
Childhood and adolescence	2	1.4
Life-span	9	6.4

articles appeared in the area of adult development and aging. There were 9 articles dealing with methodological or factual issues in life-span development, so a total of 14 articles (10%) had some relevance to development beyond adolescence. In striking contrast, 113 articles (81.9%) involved child development. This circumstance probably reflects the relatively small number of psychologists doing research in the area of adult development and aging rather than any selectivity on the part of the editors of *Developmental Psychology.*

Opportunities for Teaching and Research Careers

The scientific study of aging is just coming of age, and in this relatively new area, career opportunities are great. Several factors have combined to create at this point in time the current demand for researchers and teachers specializing in aging.

Current census data indicate that over 20 million Americans are age 65 or older, and politicians are suddenly becoming aware of the fact that 35% of the voting public are 50 years of age or more. Also, elderly voters vote more regularly in elections than young voters. This new awareness has undoubtedly been instrumental in focusing legislative and governmental attention on aging, and this fact, coupled with the trend toward funding applied research, has led to the increasing availability of research and training funds in the field of aging.

At a time when federal agencies such as NICHD are publicizing the availability of funds to support studies on the psychology of aging, few trained researchers exist to take advantage of the support. A recent survey of doctoral dissertations in aging indicated that since 1934, only .5% of the dissertations in the biological, medical, psychological, and social sciences have dealt with the topic of aging (Moore & Birren, 1971). In the 35-year period between 1934 and 1969, a total of 209 doctoral dissertations were completed in the psychology of aging. During that same period, a total of 15,964 dissertations were completed in psychology, so the dissertations in aging represent 1.3% of the output in psychology. These data are only approximations since not all universities exchanged information on doctoral dissertations in past years. Also, some errors are inherent in attempting to classify the content of dissertations by subject matter.

The relative scarcity of research data also represents an opportunity for future research contributions. Recent advances in research methodology in developmental psychology have opened new avenues for exploration. Interdisciplinary research has also been a frequent option of psychologists studying aging, and the potential for this type of endeavor is seemingly limitless.

Potentials for Professional Services

The enormous field of professional services to the retired and aged population has yet to be developed by psychologists. While there have been some beginnings, it is doubtful that in most major cities of the country, it is possible to obtain service or consultation by psychologists on most problems of aging. One possible reason for the slowness of the development is the fact that so many older people live on limited incomes and cannot pay for services themselves. Between one-third and one-half of the population of aged persons is at or below what would be defined as a poverty level for young adults. The services that would be taken for granted by a young adult population are deferred or done without by older persons. Another aspect is that professional services by psychologists, if available at all, tend to be delivered through private or public institutions. Hospitals, family service centers, and interdenominational homes for the aged are among the actual or potential providers of professional psychological services to the aged, rather than private practitioners.

One important area of public service to the aged lies in the control of the widespread confidence games and frauds perpetrated on older persons. Many of the frauds are made possible by the motivations of older persons and their attempts to obtain miracle cures and remedies for chronic diseases. Thus, magic cure-all pills, therapeutic belts, and other therapies advocated for arthritis bilk millions of dollars out of the pocketbooks of aged persons each year. In addition, home appliance and home repair frauds and con games single out vulnerable older people. Precisely why older persons are particularly vulnerable to such frauds has yet to be explored by psychologists, and the development of control measures has not even been considered.

There are many services that could be developed for the older adult by the main divisions of professional psychology, for example, clinical, counseling, community, industrial, educational, and consumer protection. The growth of private retirement systems in industry has sometimes been accompanied by preretirement counseling programs. Such programs should be organized by persons who have good insight into the psychological and social needs of the retiring individual.

It seems likely that in metropolitan areas there will be outpatient clinics for older persons established in local neighborhoods. The older patient frequently presents a mixture of social problems, psychological concerns, and physiological processes so that a psychologist is appropriately a member of a health team concerned with the health of the aged. In particular, new psychological diagnostic methods are needed to delineate more clearly the factors in health–behavioral relationships. For the healthy, moderately well-to-do retired person there are issues of where to live in retirement, what recreation to engage in, and other concerns that have a psychological component. At the present time, it is unlikely that private practitioners are or will be in a position to take the initiative in developing relevant consulting services. Economic reasons as well as the way in which services are traditionally organized suggest that leadership in professional services to the aged will begin with those institutions that deal directly with the aged and have a responsibility for their welfare. It is impossible at the present time to forecast a precise manpower estimate for such personnel in future decades. There is no doubt, however, that there is an enormous need for persons trained in specialized fields in professional services to the aged. Their basic training awaits leadership within psychology and the aid of administrators of institutions that employ psychologists. The need to supply a knowledge base on which rational services can rest implies a large cadre of active, trained investigators who are in a position to carry out research on aging.

Personnel Needs

A recent report by Cartter (1971) suggested that universities may be currently overproducing the number of PhDs that will be needed in the next 10 or 20 years. He essentially used a supply and demand model, with the demand being based upon current uses of PhDs in academic institutions. One of his arguments is the fact that the number of students in college will decrease in the next decade, reflecting the lowering birth rate in the population. There are alternative models to the one of supply and demand to be considered when estimating likely personnel needs for the future. One of these might be a "supply and need model," that is, the actual needs of the constituents of universities, government agencies, specialized research institutions, governmental organizations, and the public at large as forecast by professionals rather than available positions in the present job market. Still another model might be a "supply and want model," that is, one may take the view that society has a latent desire for more services than it can afford at a particular time. Thus, in a future, more affluent period, families may desire more psychological care for their children and adolescents than they can afford or would be available. They may want to seek more psychotherapy or other forms of care for themselves on family problems. Indeed, it is apparent in the distribution of professional services in this country that the higher the socioeconomic status of an area, the more demand there is for all types of professional services such as doctors, lawyers, dentists, psychiatrists, psychologists, and others. In 1968, New York had 29.9 psychologists per 100,000 population as compared with 4.6 psychologists for Mississippi (Cates, 1970). If one succumbs today to the lure of the tightly reasoned supply and demand model, society may be grossly ill equipped to meet the wants of a more affluent society 10 or 20 years from now when the current generation of college-aged students will carry forward expectations of a higher standard of living, particularly in the area of professional and educational services. It is unlikely that the educated college student of today will be content in his retirement with the same quantity and quality of services in our society that are now available to his parents or grandparents. It is with this thought in mind that we have to engage in academic planning and estimate future personnel needs by a variety of approaches in order to set the pattern for outcomes 10, 20, or more years from now.

In the developmental psychology of later life, psychology as a science has the obligation of providing knowledge, gained through research, on which professional services can be developed and through which an informed population can also help itself. The developmental psychology of aging is partly a cultural subject in which our research knowledge has a potential for dramatically changing our concepts about ourselves. Indeed, more cultural education about aging is called for because the falling birth rate will result in an increasingly higher percentage of aged in the total population. That is, with a lower birth rate, the older will become the average age of the population. At present, approximately 9.5% of the population, or 20 million individuals, are over the age of 65. The transition group now considering earlier retirement between the ages of 55 and 65 is another 8.7%, for a total of 48 million persons. If we take as our reference group the second half of life, that is, all persons over the age of 40, we have a total of about 35.8%, or 73.4 million persons. These figures are larger than the entire populations of most countries of the world. The number of persons over the age of 65 itself approximates the entire population of Canada.

Using an estimate of 30,000 psychologists as comprising the membership of APA, plus an estimated 30,000 additional persons who function as psychologists without holding membership in the APA, one may optimistically assume that there are about 60,000 individuals in varying degrees who are trained in psychology and/or teaching and who are doing research or rendering services. In view of the small number of dissertations on aging, the proportion of these individuals that have any training or knowledge of the processes of aging is very small. Thus, if one considers the size of the membership of the Division of Adult Development and Aging (Division 20), about 300, and adds to this another 300 who may be functioning as psychologists in the field of aging without being members of APA, one has a total of 600. If one also assumes that there are other persons in the APA with divisional membership who are functioning with regard to some aspect of aging but who do not belong to the division, one might liberally say that we have about 1,000 psychologists in this country who are engaged in an activity somewhat relevant to the issues of aging. This would be about 1 psychologist per 73,000 of the population over the age of 65. This figure compares with about 1 psychologist per 3,400 of the general population, for example, using a figure of 60,000 psychologists per 205 million population. From the work of Cates (1970), one derives an estimate of 1 psychologist per 5,888 of the general population. Apparently, whatever the basis of estimation, the number of psychologists is relatively low in the field of aging.

How many psychologists with knowledge of aging should there be? It would appear that eventually we might expect to have at least 1 psychologist in every major department of psychology in this country who will be teaching, doing research, and preparing students to specialize in the subject matter. In addition, professional components of psychology, such as counseling, clinical, and newer professional areas, also need teaching and research personnel. At present, most universities and departments of psychology do not have anyone producing in the subject matter.

A comprehensive survey of doctoral dissertations in the field of aging was undertaken for the period 1934 to 1969 (Moore & Birren, 1971). There were only 69 universities in this country that had awarded one or more degrees during that period with a dissertation identified as dealing with the psychology of aging. Many of the schools with single dissertations could have had a single, highly motivated student nominally encouraged by faculty members without much institutional support. That is, perhaps an institution should not be regarded as having placed any emphasis on or having any expertise in the psychology of aging unless it produced at least one doctoral dissertation on aging per decade. Only 31 schools would qualify, even at this low level.

There have been many states that have not produced a single dissertation in the psychology of aging within this period of the study, 1934 to 1969. We clearly have a gross underproduction at the source of our academic training. If all 300 members of Division 20 of the APA were in academic institutions doing research and preparing doctoral dissertations, we could graduate a student population of five times that number, assuming each professor could have five doctoral students in training. This would yield a figure of 1,500 PhDs in training. While it is not possible to know the actual figure, it is probably less than 100 at the present time. Thus, if we adopt the Cartter (1971) report that we have overproduced PhDs, we might miss the point that we have so grossly underproduced in this area that we might be led to ignore the needs rather than attempt to meet them.

What are the needs? The needs of science are difficult to estimate since they depend upon the motivation of the people in the field and the state of scientific development. It is reasonable that the smallest group of psychologists should be the basic researchers, with a larger number (about double) doing applied research, and about double that total engaging actively in professional training and professional services. Most research and graduate education will probably continue to be carried out only at the larger universities. Mayhew's survey of trends in higher education included a questionnaire sent to about 300 institutions in the United States (Mayhew, 1970). These were schools that offered some graduate education. It might be expected that we should eventually have an academic person in each one of these 300 institutions concerned with aging. When one considers that there are many more colleges and smaller schools that engage in education or training without necessarily having doctoral programs, the figure is double that or 600 persons doing applied research and teaching. If we doubled that figure to estimate the need for persons engaged in professional education and service, we would have 1,200, for a grand total of 1,900 basic, applied, and professional psychologists with a specialty in the processes of aging. Perhaps this should be our 10-year training goal. It might be questioned whether this figure is realistic for projection as a 10-year training goal. That is, is it realistic in terms of educational attainment, and is it realistic in terms of the needs of the population of the country? If we answer it in the latter sense, we are probably far short of a realistic figure. It would seem that the figure of 1,900 psychologists is more likely a 10-year academic goal, rather than a 10-year goal to meet the service needs of older persons in our society.

Kramer, Taube, and Redick (see pp. 428–528) have presented almost staggering projections of need for mental health specialists. Their work indicates that by the year 1975, 8,624 clinical psychologists will be needed to give only three hours of service per year, assuming a 2% need for care in the population. If one assumes a 10% need for care in the population and six hours per patient, the estimated number of psychologists is 86,235, far more than the total of all types of psychologists that exist today. About half of the patients may be assumed to fall within the second half of the life-span, wherein some knowledge and attention to the psychological issues of aging are relevant.

Psychological Disorders in Late Life

Wang (1969) reviewed the evidence on organic brain syndromes in later life. His evidence suggested that the incidence of severe psychological disorders requiring hospitalization was 941 per 100,000 of the population over 65 years of age. This is 3.3 times higher than the rate for those under the age of 65. His data for 1966 indicated that in the group over the age of 65, there were 35,964 first admissions plus 137,653 inpatient residents with chronic brain illnesses in institutions, for a total of 173,617 persons. If one assumes that a professional psychologist should expend at least 1 day per year in the care of each of these individuals and that there are 240 working days in the year (an overestimate), it would require about 700 psychologists to see each one of these patients for 1 day a year. Certainly in the standards of our society, this would be a minimum amount of psychological, diagnostic, and therapeutic services to this group. For many of these aging individuals the problems are so different from those of early life that a reorientation must take place in the training of clinical and other consulting psychologists.

Not all of the aged patients, of course, have irreversible organic syndromes. A large proportion of mental disability consists of affective states, particularly depression, that are reversible, and the individuals are able to return to community residence. The precision of the data in this area is limited, since institutions do not usually devote much time to the diagnosis and treatment of mental conditions in older patients even though there is a high prospect of recovery in the affective disorders. The conventional pattern is for outpatient clinics to devote their professional efforts to children and young adults. Existing evidence suggests that only 2% of the patients seen in psychiatric outpatient clinics were over the age of 64 (Wang, 1969). Community mental health programs also tend not to have the staff capability or interest to deal with older persons. The older patients get shunted off into residential facilities in which they have less access to professional attention, such as medical attention, physical therapy, and psychotherapy.

The development of retirement communities and an increase in specialized retirement associations involving millions of older persons will all result in an intelligent and inquiring audience that will expect psychologists to have something to say to them about aging in the light of research. More and more people are reaching the age of retirement with a greater sophistication and are expecting more of psychology and the other sciences. It seems appropriate that psychology as a science and as a profession has something to say to them about their position in life, something that may help to guide them in minimizing problems and maximizing life satisfaction. It is apparent that in the field of aging, as in many pioneering areas, it is difficult to estimate needs on an actuarial basis, yet it is precisely at this stage of development that our forecasts are most important. Certainly, our goal of having one senior investigator and teacher in every institution of higher learning by the end of this 10-year period is not an unrealistic or unjustified one. Such persons should be concerned with research on some aspect of aging, such as the neuropsychology of aging, genetic components, age changes in central nervous system (CNS) functioning and behavior, which range through the classical subject matter areas of perception, learning, memory, higher cognitive processes, social functioning, and personality. The range of scientific problems and their fundamental importance is so great that the subject matter should be seriously represented in every institution of higher learning.

Future Issues

Futurity is perhaps one of the least likely concepts to be associated with aging and the aged. However, the kinds of issues being raised by contemporary psychologists working in the field of aging suggest stimulating prospects for researchers and clinicians and for the group to which their investigation and efforts are directed. The nature and complexity of aging demand investigation for a broad variety of perspectives, and it is highly feasible that psychologists in all specialized areas have important contributions to make to the future of the psychology of aging as well as to the future cohorts of adult and aged individuals.

Since 1965, the strides in developmental research methodology have provided new means to describe and to explain behavior as a function of age. Such advances provide new approaches for developmentalists working at all stages of the life-span, and they serve to highlight the opportunity for quantitative psychologists in the area of life-span developmental psychology. Such advances led Birren (1970) to comment that the study of aging is moving from a descriptive to an experimental phase. Statisticians and methodologists have devised useful strategies for studying age–functional relationships, and investigators interested in adulthood and old age have led developmentalists in seeing the value of new research designs (Schaie, 1970). Until quite recently, the two basic research plans used to study age–functional relationships were the longitudinal method and the cross-sectional method. Reacting to the general awareness of the inadequacies of simple longitudinal and cross-sectional designs, Schaie (1965) and Baltes (1968) created several comprehensive models for studying developmental problems, which clarified the nature of age effects. More recently, Baltes and Goulet (1971) offered a new set of strategies for the study of age–functional relationships grouped under the heading "age simulation" designs. Equipped with sophisticated, new methodological tools, psychologists studying aging are better prepared to investigate the challenging issues faced by a society with an increasing proportion of aged individuals.

An emerging issue that must be attended to by psychobiologists and social psychologists alike is the increasing disparity in the life expectancy of men and women. A female child born today has a life expectancy of seven years longer than a male child, and as the average life expectancy increases, there seems to be further widening of the differential life expectancy of men and women. Are women biologically superior to men? Does the male role add stress, hence shortening the life expectancy for men?

While researchers are attempting to deal with the question of sex differences in life expectancy, clinical and counseling psychologists are needed to deal with one outcome of differential life expectancies—the problem of widowhood. There is a large and rising proportion of widows in contemporary society, resulting not only from the fact that women live longer but also because women tend to marry men who are older than they are. Widowhood after a long marriage is perhaps one of the greatest role changes experienced over the life-span, but the means to successful adjustment to this role have hardly been explored.

Indeed, many of the developmental tasks of the aged seem to revolve around rolelessness and the adoption of new roles. Retirement causes a loss of role that is frequently problematic for the older male, for his wife, and perhaps for their marriage. Another role about which there is little knowledge is that of the dying individual. A recent Gallup poll indicated that the topic of death and dying was the most taboo subject in American conversation, yet the elderly report a great need to talk about their impending death (Mathieu & Peterson, 1970). The role of a dying individual is difficult inasmuch as there is little socialization for such a role. Clinicians and counselors could make a great contribution in this area.

The number one cause of death in the United States is cardiovascular disease, and some data indicate that psychological measures may be useful predictors of candidates for coronaries. Can the personalities and life-styles of such individuals be changed to prevent heart attacks? Will somatic conditioning be useful in helping such individuals maintain more optimal heart rates and blood pressure? Such issues pose challenges for both experimental and applied psychology.

Somatic conditioning may be useful as a means for controlling a number of deleterious age changes. It has generally been thought that the aging processes are irreversible, but recent research in the area of the physiology of exercise suggests that a certain amount of a given capacity can be regained, even in the very elderly (deVries, 1970). Since a number of physiological processes have been demonstrated to come under conscious control of the subject (Bundzen, 1966; Carmona, 1967; Kamiya, 1962, 1968, 1969; Miller, 1969), it may be possible to train the aged to maintain certain physiological processes at optimal rates. The degree to which biofeedback can be used to compensate for deleterious age changes challenges the imagination. For example, such a prospect led Nowlis (1970) to speculate that the control of certain brain wave rhythms may help geriatric patients to maintain alertness over a longer period of time, thereby recovering deficits in cognitive functioning.

The potential usefulness of biofeedback as an age-simulation strategy is also being explored. Attempts are currently underway in our laboratory to manipulate the internal environment of young and old individuals in order to simulate different ages (Woodruff, 1971). Voluntary control of physiological processes such as heart rate, blood pressure, and electrical activity in the brain can be learned, and the rates of these processes are different in young and old individuals. It has been hypothesized that these physiological differences may cause age differences in behavior (Birren, 1965; Birren & Speith, 1962; Lacey & Lacey, 1958; Morris & Thompson, 1969; Surwillo, 1960, 1963, 1968; Szafran, 1965, 1966, 1968). Hence, by training young and old subjects to simulate old and young physiological rates and then measuring behavior, these hypotheses can be tested experimentally.

Training in adulthood and aging has altogether different implications for the educational psychologists. In a rapidly changing society in which a smaller and smaller proportion of the work force is required to maintain an optimal level of productivity, the desire and need for adult education are increasing. Methods developed for educating children and adolescents may be entirely inappropriate for educating adults returning to school after spending years away from an academic environment. Hence, educational psychologists may find the task of developing the means to motivate and teach adults even more challenging and demanding than the task of educating children.

Ethnicity is another area that has received little attention in the field of aging; yet, there are indications that aging may be very different for different ethnic groups. For example, the suicide rate among white males increases dramatically with age, while there appears to be only a slight increase with age in the suicide rate of nonwhite males. Do minority groups take better care of the psychological and social needs of their elderly? Are there genetic differences among the races that are expressed only in the period of later life? As psychologists become more interested in the behavioral similarities and differences among the various subcultures in society, information about the later life outcomes of these different life-styles will provide valuable insights into the impact of culture on behavior.

Summary and Conclusions

The psychology of aging appears ripe for a dramatic upsurge of activity in research and graduate training. There is not only a deepening interest on the part of a limited number of scholars in the theory and methods of the psychology of aging and a life-span developmental psychology, but in addition, there are obvious practical pressures for training of personnel to meet the needs of over 20 million retired and aged persons. The convergence of scientific interest and practical need should spur research and training activity within our universities.

An academic depression marks the beginning of the decade of the 1970s. There are not sufficient positions for the persons that have been recently trained in many of the traditional divisions of departments of psychology. This would suggest that psychology departments might encourage the movement of research, teaching, and graduate training programs toward both the scientific and the professional problems of aging.

One of the greatest deficiencies at the present time is the lack of sufficient, well-trained academic personnel equipped to teach and to do research on aging. Emphasis must therefore be given to the training of the "germinal" academic personnel who can create the research and knowledge base for university positions, for college and junior college teaching, and for professional and paraprofessional programs within our institutions of higher learning.

The number of dissertations produced on problems in the psychology of aging during the last 30 years has been alarmingly low. There have been 209 dissertations identified in the field during the period 1939–69. This is barely sufficient to keep the field supplied with replacement personnel let alone attempt to meet the projected manpower needs. Forecasts of manpower needs suggest a gross shortage of personnel that special emphasis and efforts must be made to increase training and also to recruit and train personnel from other less active subject-matter areas. Specific training goals are recommended to federal and state agencies so that the end of the decade will be marked by an ability to respond to scientific needs and to the needs of our nation of older persons.

Since the training of academic psychologists in aging has largely been carried out within a limited number of institutions, it seems advantageous at this early stage in the development of the field to encourage a small number of universities to expand their facilities and faculties and thereby create "training centers." The concentration of personnel and facilities in a limited number of training centers in the various geographic areas of the country appears more economical and has a greater promise of high quality of effort than a policy of expansion in which a little bit of training is done in many institutions. This latter approach appears to be a more desirable second phase of the field when sufficient, well-trained personnel would be available.

While the psychology of aging may be on the threshold of markedly increased activity in research and training, the level of training up until now has been minuscule as compared with other branches of psychology and with developmental psychology in particular. Developmental psychology has heavily concentrated on the child phase of the life-span. It is quite possible that this overriding interest in child psychology has been due to the need to give courses in child psychology in colleges for the general student and for teachers in training. Now that the population structure of the country has changed, there is a greater need for professional training to serve the personal needs of older adults and to consult on planning for the retired on a range of issues including housing, retirement counseling, marital counseling, physical and mental health problems, and the guidance of the growth of leisure time and adult education programs for our nation of the retired.

The emphasis in this chapter has been on the need to train a cadre of psychologists who will be able to establish a basis for training and research in the psychology of aging in our institutions of higher learning. Reasoning from limited data and projecting a conservative estimate, it would seem that by 1980, 300 academic psychologists, 600 applied psychologists, and 1,200 professional psychologists specializing in the field would be a desirable and realistic number.

In the field of mental health, forecasts have been made that are staggering in their implications for training. They indicate that by the year 1975, assuming a 2% need for psychiatric care in the population, 8,624 clinical psychologists would be needed to give only three hours of service per patient, per year. Assuming 10% of the population in need and six hours per patient, per year, the estimated number of psychologists would be 86,235, or more psychologists than all of the types that exist today. We may assume that about half of the patients in need would be in the second half of life, wherein some knowledge about and attention to the psychological issues of aging are relevant. These clinical psychologists can only be developed in the context of universities that have special interests and competence in the field. Perhaps collaboration between developmental psychologists doing research and teaching on adult life and aging and those engaged in existing clinical training programs can be instituted so that students can be versed in the theories and data of adult life in addition to acquiring professional skills.

While it has been recommended that the training over the next decade should be concentrated in a limited number of institutions, diversity in the training programs should be encouraged. It is not clear whether the most productive programs will be those that stress an interdisciplinary approach, a life-span developmental approach, or a mixture of basic and applied research, or if these programs will result in greater gains in knowledge and service to society. Experimentation in academic and professional training in the psychology of aging should be encouraged so that we do not inadvertently limit the capabilities of our training programs and the potential of meeting the needs of a changing society.

REFERENCES

American Psychological Association. *Graduate study in psychology: 1971–72.* Washington, D.C.: Author, 1970.

Appley, M. The place of psychology in the university. *American Psychologist,* 1970, **25**, 387–390.

Baltes, P. B. Longitudinal and cross-sectional sequences in the study of age and generation effects. *Human Development,* 1968, **11**, 145–171.

Baltes, P. B., & Goulet, L. R. Exploration of developmental parameters by manipulation and simulation of age differences in behavior. Unpublished manuscript, West Virginia University, 1971.

Birren, J. E. A brief history of the psychology of aging: Part 1. *Gerontologist,* 1961, **1**, 69–77. (a)

Birren, J. E. A brief history of the psychology of aging: Part 2. *Gerontologist,* 1961, **1**, 127–134. (b)

Birren, J. E. Age changes in speed of behavior: Its central nature and physiological correlates. In A. T. Welford & J. E. Birren (Eds.), *Behavior, aging, and the nervous system.* Springfield, Ill.: Charles C Thomas, 1965.

Birren, J. E. Toward an experimental psychology of aging. *American Psychologist,* 1970, **25**, 124–135.

Birren, J. E., & Spieth, W. Age, response speed, and cardiovascular functions. *Journal of Gerontology,* 1962, **17**, 390–391.

Botwinick, J. Geropsychology. *Annual Review of Psychology,* 1970, **21**, 239–272.

Brackbill, Y. (Ed.) *Division of Developmental Psychology (Division 7) Newsletter* (APA), 1971, Winter.

Bundzen, P. U. Autoregulation of functional state of the brain: An investigation using photostimulation with feedback. *Federal Proceedings Translation Supplement,* 1966, **25**, 551–554.

Carmona, A. B. Trial and error learning of the voltage of the cortical EEG activity. Unpublished doctoral dissertation, Yale University, 1967.

Carnegie Commission on Higher Education. *Less time, more options.* New York: McGraw-Hill, 1971.

Cartter, A. M. Scientific manpower for 1970–1985. *Science,* 1971, **172**, 132–140.

Cates, J. Psychology's manpower: Report on the 1968 National Register of Scientific and Technical Personnel. *American Psychologist,* 1970, **25**, 254–263.

Charles, D. C. Historical antecedents of life span developmental psychology. In L. R. Goulet & P. B. Baltes (Eds.), *Life span developmental psychology: Theory and research.* New York: Academic Press, 1970.

deVries, H. A. Physiological effects of an exercise training regimen upon men aged 52 to 88. *Journal of Gerontology,* 1970, **25**, 325–336.

Gregg, A., Barnard, C. I., Bronk, D. W., Carmichael, L., Dollard, J., French, T. M., Hilgard, E. R., Hunter, W. S., Thorndike, E. L., Thurstone, L. L., Whitehorn, J. C., & Yerkes, R. M. The place of psychology in an ideal university. *American Psychologist,* 1970, **25**, 391–410.

Groffmann, K. J. Life span developmental psychology in Europe: Past and present. In L. R. Goulet & P. B. Baltes (Eds.), *Life span developmental psychology: Theory and research.* New York: Academic Press, 1970.

Hall, G. S. *Senescence.* New York: Appleton-Century-Crofts, 1922.

Kamiya, J. Conditional discrimination of the EEG alpha rhythm in humans. Paper presented at the meeting of the Western Psychological Association, San Francisco, April 1962.

Kamiya, J. Operant control of EEG alpha rhythm and some of its reported effects on consciousness. In C. T. Tart (Ed.), *Altered states of consciousness.* New York: Wiley, 1969.

Lacey, J. I., & Lacey, B. C. The relationship of resting autonomic activity to motor impulsivity. *Proceedings of the Association for Research on Nervous and Mental Disease,* 1958, **36**, 144–209.

Literary Market Place, 1970–1971. New York: Bowker, 1970.

Mathieu, J. T., & Peterson, J. A. Death and dying: Some social psychological dimensions. Paper presented at the 23rd annual meeting of the Gerontological Society, Toronto, Canada, October 1970.

Mayhew, L. B. *Graduate and professional education 1980: A survey of institutional plans.* New York: McGraw-Hill, 1970.

Miller, L. B. Learning of visceral and glandular responses. *Science,* 1969, **163**, 434–445.

Moore, J. L., & Birren, J. E. Doctoral training in gerontology: An analysis of dissertations on problems of aging in institutions of higher learning in the United States: 1934–1969. *Journal of Gerontology,* 1971, **26**, 249–257.

Morris, J. D., & Thompson, L. W. Heart rate changes in a reaction time experiment with young and aged subjects. *Journal of Gerontology,* 1969, **24**, 269–275.

Nowlis, D. A. Implications of bio-feedback training. Unpublished manuscript, Stanford University, 1970.

Schaie, K. W. A general model for the study of developmental problems. *Psychological Bulletin,* 1965, **64**, 92–107.

Schaie, K. W. A reinterpretation of age-related changes in cognitive structure and functioning. In L. R. Goulet & P. B. Baltes (Eds.), *Life span developmental psychology: Theory and research.* New York: Academic Press, 1970.

Surwillo, W. W. Central nervous system factors in simple reaction time. *American Psychologist,* 1960, **15**, 419.

Surwillo, W. W. The relation of simple response time to brain-wave frequency and the effects of age. *Electroencephalography and Clinical Neurophysiology,* 1963, **15**, 105–114.

Surwillo, W. W. Timing of behavior in senescence and the role of the central nervous system. In G. A. Talland (Ed.), *Human aging and behavior.* New York: Academic Press, 1968.

Szafran, J. Decision processes and aging. In A. T. Welford & J. E. Birren (Eds.), *Behavior, aging, and the nervous system.* Springfield, Ill.: Charles C Thomas, 1965.

Szafran, J. Age differences in the rate of gain of information, signal detection strategy and cardiovascular status among pilots. *Gerontologia,* 1966, **12**, 6–17.

Szafran, J. Psychophysiological studies of aging in pilots. In G. A. Talland (Ed.), *Human aging and behavior*. New York: Academic Press, 1968.

United States Department of Health, Education, and Welfare, Public Health Service, National Institute of Child Health and Human Development. *Final report: A survey of training needs and mechanisms in gerontology.* St. Louis, Mo.: Gerontological Society, 1968.

Wang, H. S. Organic brain syndromes. In E. W. Busse & E. Pfeiffer (Eds.), *Behavior and adaptation in late life*. Boston: Little, Brown, 1969.

Woodruff, D. S. Biofeedback—Implications for gerontology. Paper presented at the 24th annual meeting of the Gerontological Society, Houston, October 1971.

On the History of Psychological Gerontology

KLAUS F. RIEGEL

This chapter consists of three parts. First, a quantitative analysis of the history of psychological gerontology will be given based upon the reconstructed flow of written information in reference networks. Second, this analysis will be supplemented by more traditional, idiographic interpretations, focusing especially on those "underdeveloped" areas not represented in the networks, and deducing conclusions from comparisons with the general area of developmental psychology. Third, in view of the enormous amount of wasted research efforts (noted in the first part) and the concurrent lack of investigations of significant issues (noted in the second part), questions need to be raised concerning our concepts of research and theory, communication and education, and, more generally, our conception of man, society, and their development.

QUANTITATIVE ANALYSIS OF THE HISTORY OF PSYCHOLOGICAL GERONTOLOGY

With the exception of recent reports by Birren (1961) and Munnichs (1966) on psychological gerontology and those by Charles

Klaus F. Riegel received his PhD in psychology at the University of Hamburg, West Germany, 1957. Since 1959, he has been a Professor of Psychology at the University of Michigan. His major interest and orientation are in cognitive changes during old age. Presently, the author is working on two books, one dealing with the acquisition of meaning and the other, with developmental and historical structuralism.

The analysis presented in the first part of this chapter was supported by the Institute of Gerontology, University of Michigan—Wayne State University. The author gratefully acknowledges the assistance and support of John Meacham, Jonathan Zerin, and Ruth M. Riegel.

37

(1970), Groffmann (1970), and Reinert (1970) on life-span developmental psychology, there have been few systematic inquiries into the history of this discipline (for related topics, see the symposium by Freeman & Webber, 1965; and reports by Burstein, 1965; Freeman, 1938; Grant, 1963; Moore & Birren, 1971; Nikitin, 1958). Most reviews, textbooks, and handbooks (especially, Birren, 1960; Goulet & Baltes, 1970) provide, however, brief sections of historical reconstructions. Moreover, nearly complete listings of the publications have been prepared under Shock's supervision and have been published regularly in the *Journal of Gerontology*. The following analysis is based, in part, upon this bibliography.

Method

The reference files of the present author on the literature of psychological gerontology prior to 1958 (Riegel, 1958, 1959) were supplemented by adding all entries that appeared under the heading "Psychological Processes" in Shock's classified bibliography of gerontology (1951, 1957) or in the *Journal of Gerontology* up to the last issue of 1970. Attention was given to journal articles. Abstracts of proceedings and unpublished reports were eliminated as well as articles on selected topics, especially those dealing with the statistics of suicides, employment, financial support, and the pathology of aging. The overriding criteria for inclusion were the occurrence of such terms as "age," "aging," "adult development," etc., in the title of the article and/or publication in appropriate journals, such as *Journal of Gerontology, Geriatrics,* or *Gerontologist.*

In an attempt to sample some divergent topics from the contemporary field of psychological gerontology, only three recent publications were originally chosen as *lead articles*. It soon became evident, however, that even a complete retrieval of the citations originating from these three publications would go far beyond the scope of the present investigation and the time and means available to the investigator. For this reason, only the single article listed below was retained at the top node, that is, at the most recent point in the publication network from which our search would start (see Figure 1). It would be desirable, of course, to extend the search process to articles representing several other topics. The procedures have been set up in such a manner that such an extension, possible with the aid of computers, can be performed.

Blum, J. E., Jarvik, L. F., & Clark, E. T. Rate of change on selective
tests of intelligence: A twenty-year longitudinal study of aging.
Journal of Gerontology, 1970, **25**, 171–176.

The article by Blum, Jarvik, and Clark (1970) represents a
top node point of a *root structure* going backwards in historical time.
In order to explore this structure, all the references made to earlier
publications that met the criteria mentioned above were coded and
transcribed onto the file card for the article by Blum et al. Notations
to the node publication of the following **generation** were made on

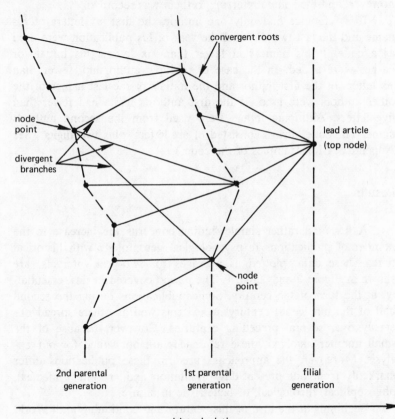

historical time

Fig. 1. Subsection of reference network for the description of technical
terms. (Note: The denotations "convergent" and "divergent" hold only
when the progression is considered as moving from left to right, i.e., forward in historical time. In case of a retrospective analysis, the terms become "divergent roots" and "convergent branches." In other words, these
denotations are dependent upon the interpretation applied.)

all the reference cards of the preceding parental generation. Some of the concepts used are demonstrated in Figure 1.

After the first generation of references were recorded on the file cards, each of the references became a new node point and the second generation of references were transcribed. This process was continued until the earliest period of retrievable references was reached, that is, the compounded period prior to 1919. Review articles, books, chapters in books, and dissertations were listed only as *terminal points* in the retrieval system; that is, references made in them were not transcribed onto the cards; the cards were retained in the file, however, and the source referring to them was recorded.

If a reference had only one author, the first six letters of his name and the last two digits of the year of his publication were used as a code. If his name had fewer than six letters, his initials or dashes were added. In the case of multiple authorship, fewer than six letters of the first author and the initials of the last names of the other authors were used. If the first author's name had fewer than five letters, additional letters were used from the second author's name. The code always consisted of six letters, plus two digits. (See Appendix A for examples of the code.)

Results

A first and rather simple finding concerns the increase in the number of publications in psychological gerontology with historical time. These data, plotted as averages for two-year intervals, are shown in Figure 2 and Table 1. The period covered begins, essentially, at the turn of the century. Some publications during the second half of the nineteenth century do exist as well as others spread unevenly over several preceding centuries. However, because of the small number involved, these references are not suited for our analysis. Moreover, the approaches used in these publications differ markedly from our present-day orientation and are either medical, philosophical, theological, or belletristic in nature.

Beginning at the turn of this century and continuing until World War II, a steady increase in the number of publications occurred. During a short period thereafter, further acceleration was halted, but with the end of the war a steep increase took place which has not yet faded completely. In 1968, the last year for which (at the present time) a rather complete estimate of the number of publications can be obtained from Shock's (1951, 1957) listings, a total of 235 publications in psychological gerontology were recorded that met the

Fig. 2. Number of publications per year in psychological gerontology.

criteria for inclusion. The total number of reference cards placed in the file equals 4,310, a figure which might increase slightly since a few items for the first four decades of this century are still being added to the file.

A second question concerns the percentages of items picked up through the retrieval analysis. Starting with only one lead article in 1970, we should expect a marked increase in percentages during the preceding decade. The further we go back in time, however, the more likely it should become that several writers converge upon the same source. In general, the detection of these key nodes and their sequential dependencies represents one of the major goals of our analysis. Within the present corpus of data, the convergence upon a limited set of such node items implies that the expansion in the number of references retrieved by going backward in historical time is limited within distinct boundaries. After an initial burst in the number of items retrieved during the latest decade, these percentages attain a level of a steady state characteristic for the topic of the lead

TABLE 1

Number of Reference Cards, Number and Percentage of Cards Retrieved, and Number of Retrievals as a Function of Time

Year	Reference card	Cards retrieved	Percentage of cards retrieved	Number of retrievals
1968-69	460	10	2.2	10
1966-67	418	14	3.4	22
1964-65	310	27	8.7	43
1962-63	299	49	16.4	104
1960-61	307	63	17.3	146
1958-59	282	91	32.3	261
1956-57	263	79	30.3	176
1954-55	230	62	27.0	187
1952-53	236	70	29.7	161
1950-51	200	47	23.5	155
1948-49	130	31	23.8	107
1946-47	94	28	29.8	79
1944-45	76	26	34.2	132
1942-43	82	22	26.8	60
1940-41	85	25	29.4	79
1938-39	76	19	25.0	29
1936-37	78	16	20.5	30
1934-35	58	11	19.0	36
1932-33	58	13	22.1	57
1930-31	55	11	20.0	32
1920-29	110	28	25.4	68
Before 1919	43	6	14.0	9
Total	4310	738		1983

article at the top node of the retrieval system. In other words, we should not expect a continued increase in the number of references retrieved the further we move backward in time because enough publications do not exist for the earlier periods to which an early author could refer and which would enter into the retrieval network under the criteria specified. As long as unrelated publications are excluded, the retrieval analysis should finally lead us to a few key papers representing the origin of psychological gerontology.

As shown in Figure 3 and Table 1, the whole decade of the 1960s represents the period during which our retrieval network shows a rapid expansion. A total of 261 references are made to 91 of the 282 publications of the two-year period of 1958–59; that is, many references are made to the same sources repeatedly. Fewer references are made to publications of the earlier years; that is, the curve is distinctly skewed to the right. However, these findings and interpretations require at least two modifications.

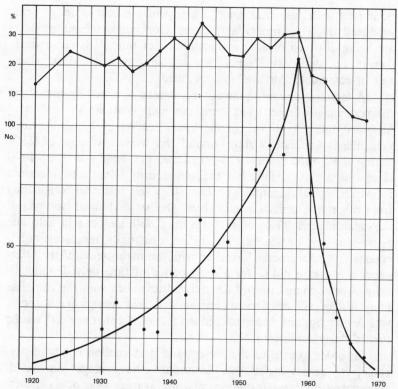

Fig. 3. Number and percentage of publications retrieved from the reference file as a function of time.

First, material is still in the process of being retrieved, especially for the first four decades of this century. Therefore, we should expect some future increase in the number of items picked up for these periods. Second, the shape of the curve shown in Figure 3 is dependent upon the citation habits of psychological gerontologists. For instance, we might expect that present-day behavioral scientists lack historical perspective and/or are forced by the editorial policies of some journals to make only a few and superficial references to closely related publications, most of which might precede the author's own publication only by a few years. In contrast, earlier behavioral scientists are often thought to be familiar and concerned with large portions of the literature and to be inclined to explore these sources thoroughly and exhaustively. Consequently, the average *citation span* might be longer for early authors and might have shrunk with historical time. As a further consequence, the length of the survival period, the "half-life" of publications (Price, 1965), might have decreased with historical time. Thus, while much more is being produced than in former days, larger proportions of our products are being disposed of after a short period of time. It is not unlikely then that a good deal of our efforts are being wasted and our channels of communication are being polluted.

A tentative answer to these issues can be obtained by computing the percentages of retrieved items per total items as a function of historical time. As shown in the upper section of Figure 3, these percentages fluctuate slightly around the overall average of 23% during the period from 1920–60. Thus, our lead article of 1970 directs us toward slightly less than one-fourth of the total literature in psychological gerontology. The study of retrievals originating from other lead articles would show whether additional portions of the unaccounted 77% of the literature will be brought into the retrieval system or whether this portion, essentially, represents publications that either never linked up with the mainstream of the references network or did so for a short period of time only. Parenthetically, a brief comparison of the retrived reference with the complete filing system will convince us immediately that foreign publications, with few exceptions, have suffered the fate of "benign neglect" on the part of "ugly Americans."

In order to analyze the present and past citation habits of psychological gerontologists, we determined the average number of references (meeting our criteria) and the average year of these citations per publication. When computed for two-year periods, the results of Figure 4 and Table 2 were obtained.

Contrary to our expectations, the number of citations per scientific article increased with historical time. Considerable upward deviations exist, however, for the publications during the 1940s, which might be attributable, in part, to the limited number of items for which, thus far, the retrieval has been completed. After a greater number of reference cards have been analyzed, these data points might follow a more consistent trend and might be interpreted with greater confidence.

In comparison, the results on the changes in the average citation span already show at this stage of analysis a highly consistent upward trend. As the number of references increases with historical time, the period covered through these references increases as well. Thus, contrary to our expectations, authors do not necessarily change their citation habits. Certainly, modern authors have not become more contemporaneous in their orientation than former scholars. Most likely, the increase in citation span has to be attributed to the historical growth of the repertoire (represented by our card file) from

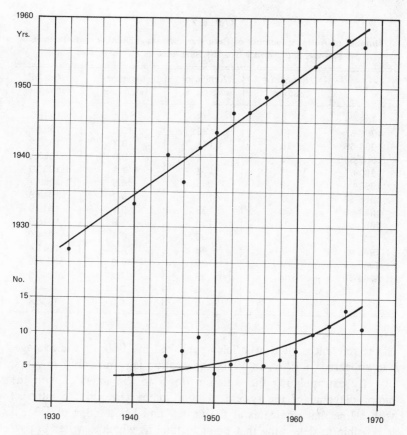

Fig. 4. Average number and years of publications cited as a function of time.

which authors can select their references. Former scholars had only a few relevant items to choose from; a modern writer can select from the total file of 4,310 items. It is conceivable to study changes in citation habits as a function of the growth of the reference systems. Such an analysis can be based upon previous work on the growth of linguistic repertoires (Riegel, 1966, 1968b) but is beyond the scope and means of the present inquiry.

The data points in the upper section of Figure 4 fall closely upon a straight line represented by the following regression equation:

$$y = .89x + 208.43.$$

The corresponding correlation coefficient equals .98. According to this equation, the citation lag equaled about eight years in 1960; that

TABLE 2

Number of Authors, Number of References, Average Number of References
per Author, and Average Year of Reference as a Function of Time

Year	Number of authors	Number of references	Average references	Year of references
1968-69	7	73	10.4	1955.9
1966-67	10	130	13.0	1957.1
1964-65	16	171	10.7	1956.2
1962-63	29	287	9.9	1953.3
1960-61	37	272	7.4	1955.9
1958-59	38	250	6.6	1950.7
1956-57	32	167	5.2	1948.5
1954-55	30	183	6.1	1946.9
1952-53	23	130	5.6	1946.3
1950-51	15	66	4.4	1944.0
1948-49	5	48	9.6	1941.4
1946-47	4	30	7.5	1936.3
1944-45	4	29	7.2	1940.1
1942-43	0	0	0	—
1940-41	4	16	4.0	1933.4

is, the references cited in articles published in 1960, on the average, had appeared in 1952. In 1940, the citation lag was only five years.

By extrapolating the equation down to the intersect with the major diagonal of the system of coordinates (i.e., to the intersect with a line that originates at the year 0 and has a slope of 1.0), it is possible to determine that point in time at which a writer in psychological gerontology would refer only to contemporaneous authors, most likely to himself. This point is found at the year 1895 and can be considered as the origin or zero-point of psychological gerontology. Searching through the few publications of the corresponding decade, we find the following entries:

> Richardson, B. W. (1891)
> Savage, G. H. (1893)
> Scott, C. A. (1896)

Galton collected his psychometric data at the World's Health Exhibit in 1885. However, these records were not thoroughly analyzed until the 1920s (Elderton, Moul, & Page, 1928; Ruger & Stoessiger, 1927).

Our retrieval analysis can be compared to the study of genealogies (Riegel, 1969). If we were to enumerate the number of ancestors of a present-day individual, we would, after a few generations, exhaust the number of all persons living at that period in history; the present-day individual, theoretically, would be a descendent of all the persons living a few hundred years ago (root structure). Conversely, if we choose one individual living about 800 years ago and if we determine the number of his present-day descendants for the case of two surviving offspring per generation, this number would exceed the world population of three billion (branch structure). Our examples demonstrate that neither the root structure model nor the branch structure model is sufficient, when taken alone, to describe the system of intergenerational relationships. We know, for instance, that a considerable degree of intermarriage must exist which, by going backward in time, converts divergent roots into convergent branches and generates a network of relationships closely similar to our retrieval system. The various references converge upon node points and thus prevent an exponential increase in the number of articles cited as we go backward in time. Rather, they generate a steady condition, which has already been demonstrated in the upper part of Figure 3.

In order to determine the interdependence of key node points, we proceed now in a reverse manner by picking those node articles upon which an exceptional number of references has converged and then we reconstruct, beginning with these node points, the historical, forward progression in psychological gerontology.

Out of the total of 4,310 references, 738 entered into the retrieval system. Among these, 52 were cited seven times or more, with the Wechsler Adult Intelligence Scale (combined 1939 and 1944 editions) leading the list with 66 citations. The 52 items were compared pairwise in terms of the number of shared publications that referred to them. For example, if two items were each cited seven times, and if five of these citations represented the same sources, the number five served as an index of the correlation between the two items. Since this figure is dependent upon the total number of citations per item, it had to be expressed in relative terms. Subsequently, these figures were transformed into lattice distances which attain a value of 0 if the two lists of citations are identical, and a value of 1 if they do not share a single source of citation. The data yielded one-half of a 52 × 52 matrix, which was analyzed by means of Johnson's (1967) hierarchical cluster analysis. The results are reported in Figure 5.

In the left section of Figure 5, the 52 items are plotted according to the years of their publication. (The full titles for the abbreviations can be found in Appendix A.) In the right section, the lines of various data points merge, dependent upon the distance between them. All items are ordered on the basis of the cluster analysis in such a way that those closely related to one another are also plotted closely together. Thus, the two entries on top of Figure 5, KLOPFE

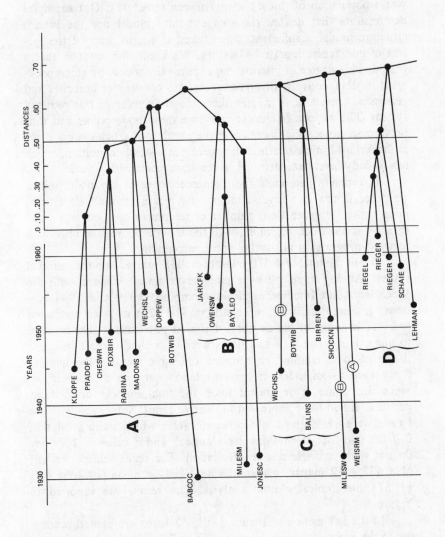

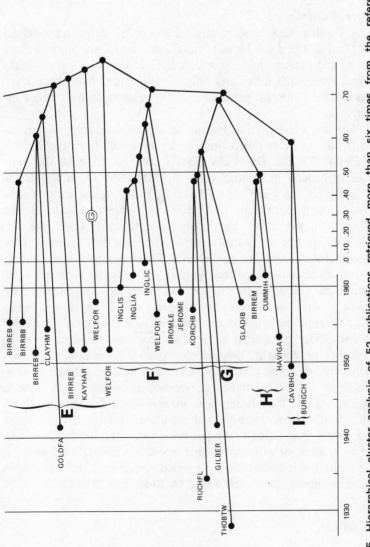

Fig. 5. Hierarchical cluster analysis of 52 publications retrieved more than six times from the reference file. (Encircled letters indicate a strong connection to other clusters.)

46 and PRADOF 47, have only a distance of .10 from one another. The next subcluster, CHESWR 49, FOXBIR 50, and RABINA 45, has a between-item distance of .33; it joins the first subcluster with an overall distance of .47.

Altogether, nine clusters denoted by capital letters were delineated. Most of them can be subdivided into several subclusters. Since some of the clusters join up with others at distances only slightly different from each other and only slightly larger than those characterizing their internal cohesion, rearrangements in their order are conceivable.

The first cluster, A, represents studies of intellectual deterioration. It also includes the revised Wechsler Adult Intelligence Scale (WECHSL 55 and DOPPEW 55). Cluster B contains the early studies of general intellectual changes (MILESM 32, JONESC 33, OWENSW 53, BAYLEO 55). Cluster C, including the early Wechsler Adult Intelligence Scale (WECHSL 44), extends Cluster B with a greater emphasis on vocabulary achievements (BALINS 41, WEISRM 36). Cluster D focuses still more strongly on verbal skills. It also includes Lehman's (LEHMAN 53) exceptional contribution.

In contrast to all preceding entries, Cluster E is based upon experimental studies of psychomotor skills rather than on psychodiagnostic testings. Both books by Welford (WELFOR 51 and WELFOR 58) enter into this cluster at the highest distances observed (.74 and .75). This assigns to them the most central location among the studies of concern, but, on the average, connects them only loosely with the other 50 items. Cluster F follows Cluster E conceptually by including studies on short-term retention and dichotic listening. Again, the cluster next in line, G, represents a closely related field, that is, learning and retention. A more distinct break occurs when progressing to the last two clusters, H and I. They characterize studies of adjustment and social variables. Undoubtedly, these topics are insufficiently represented in our analysis, a limitation due to the choice of our lead article by Blum et al. (1970).

Discussion

At the present time, our analysis is far from complete. It needs to be extended by emphasizing topics other than those of intellectual achievements. Through such extensions it would be possible to determine how many of the previous studies have become obsolete or have never entered into close and repeated connections with the mainstream of publications in psychological gerontology. In particular, it would be possible to determine how many of the 77% unaccounted publications would enter into the retrieval system. In order to maximize the possibility for inclusion, additional lead articles that are as divergent from one another as conceivable should be chosen.

But even if our retrieval system had been extended in such a manner, there is no certainty that some of the remaining publications, although insufficiently connected with the mainstream of psychological gerontology, do not represent significant topics of inquiry. All that we learn is that, thus far, they have not been recognized as important issues. Intuitively we might be convinced that, indeed, lack of recognition rather than irrelevance of the topics is often the prevailing condition that determines success in psychological gerontology as well as in psychology in general. All too often our activities and, more important, the recognition of these activities are guided by the well-established and documented trends in a given field; all too rarely are we sensitive enough to detect newly emergent trends and to support them intellectually, financially, and through our editorial decisions.

In order to identify such innovative activities at early dates, it remains necessary, at the present time, to retreat from our quantitative study of the history of psychological gerontology to approaches analyzing these issues in a more traditional manner. By inspection and evaluation of the existing literature and by comparing it with the area of psychology in general and with developmental psychology in particular, we might detect new trends, as well as identify "underdeveloped" and "overdeveloped" areas. Through additional quantitative studies of the type presented here, we might eventually succeed, however, in deriving such decisions without interpretative evaluations, or, at least, we might derive these decisions from a well-founded data base that is open to public inspection.

In order to achieve such a goal, our procedures need to be extended and mechanized, and more sophisticated methods and models have to be developed. The planning involved in such a task would also force us to perform the analysis (i.e., to study the history of psychological gerontology) in a prospective manner. Concretely speaking, our reference system would have to be supplemented as soon as new material appears in print rather than several years after its publication and by means of retrospective retrievals. Abstractly speaking, such an approach requires a new sense of history. As was forcefully emphasized by Lynd (1971), history for all too long has led us to contemplate the past but has done little to guide us into the future. Historical studies as described and envisaged here would lead us in this direction.

UNDERDEVELOPED AREAS IN PSYCHOLOGICAL GERONTOLOGY

Psychological gerontology has, in part, (a) recapitulated the history of general psychology, (b) been determined by contemporaneous movements and fads in psychology, and (c) initiated new research and interpretations well ahead of developmental and general psychology.

The psychology of the second half of the nineteenth century showed a strong preference for sensory and perceptual studies (Fechner, Helmholz, Hering, Wundt, and others). The same is true for psychological gerontology of the early part of the twentieth century. Much of the work was done outside of the psychological laboratories, however, and continues to be conducted in biological and medical research centers. Early psychology also showed a preference for the investigation of psychomotor skills (Cattell, Donders, and others). Here, psychological gerontology, through the psychometric studies initiated by Galton (see Elderton et al., 1928; Ruger & Stoessiger, 1927), has produced the oldest descriptive records of performance differences covering the full life-span. Today, the study of psychomotor performance represents one of the few areas in which, especially through the work of Welford (1951, 1958, 1960) and Birren (1964), psychological gerontology exacted a lasting influence on the general study of psychomotor processes.

The next periods in the history of general psychology saw the emergence of schools opposed to the psychophysics and physiological psychology of the earlier years. Some of these movements bypassed psychological gerontology altogether (as much as they bypassed general psychology in America), such as the act psychology of Brentano, the phenomenological psychology of Stumpf, Dilthey, and Spranger, and the psychology of sets and task attitudes of Külpe, Ach, Bühler et al. These trends have only recently influenced the thinking and research of psychological gerontologists. For instance, the latter topic, limited to the study of preparatory sets in reaction time, has been investigated by Botwinick (1967). The influence of Gestalt psychology was as modest and unsystematic in gerontology as it was for general psychology in America. Most surprisingly, the powerful movement of the study of verbal learning and associationism had until recently (Hultsch, 1971; Kausler, 1970) relatively little impact on psychological gerontology. However, it continues to dominate wide areas of American psychology.

Aside from the influence of sensoriperceptual and psychomotor psychology, the two decades between the world wars saw the overriding influence of the study of individual differences and child development on psychological gerontology. The extensive developmental records collected by Galton preceded all other investigations of individual differences by several decades. As a natural extension of these efforts (Riegel, 1972b), systematic explorations on the growth and decline of intellectual abilities began to appear (for a review, see Jones, 1960; Riegel & Riegel, 1972; but, especially, Baltes & Labouvie, pp. 157–219, this volume).

At about the same time, psychologists became seriously interested in theories of personality and pathology. Many of these activities, stimulated by Freud's work, were conducted outside of academic settings, in private practices, clinics, and institutions. Even though the clinical and social problems of aged persons in those days must have been almost as acute as they are presently, it took several decades until this type of work began to penetrate the psychology and the psychological management of the aged. No serious attempts were made until the mid-1930s, as documented in Hamilton (1942). Few of the important pacesetters—with the possible exception of Alfred Adler—devoted any attention to changes and problems of adulthood and later life (Riegel, 1960).

Studies and theories of social behavior, which had attracted increasing attention in psychology since the early 1930s, influenced psychological gerontology to a lesser extent. Selective emphasis, primarily on topics of adjustment, attitudes, interests, and role changes, did not develop until the 1950s. These topics were most extensively investigated at the University of Chicago under the influence of Burgess, Havighurst, Henry, Neugarten, and others. While the field of psychological gerontology began to be rounded out and, on the surface at least, began to represent all of the major areas of general psychology, there were, nevertheless, some topics that attracted considerable attention in psychology—especially in child psychology— but failed to be rigorously promoted through gerontological research and theorizing. These are the topics of language and cognitive development.

With the exception of some isolated work by the present author (Riegel, 1968a, 1968c, 1970), the first issue lacks attention altogether. The second issue has been approached from the traditional experimental viewpoint, for instance, by studying psychomotor and perceptual processes under increasingly complex conditions of set and preparation (Botwinick, 1967), or by adopting rather ingenious interpretations of the "psycho-logic" of operations as developed by Bourne (1970) and applied to gerontology by Arenberg (1968; see also pp. 74–97, this volume). Most surprisingly, however, the monumental work on cognition and cognitive development by Piaget and others (see Bruner et al., 1966; Elkind & Flavell, 1969; Flavell, 1963; Furth, 1969) as well as the equally impressive work in the Soviet Union by Luria, Leont'ev, and others on action and verbal control (see Cole & Maltzman, 1969) have completely bypassed the field of psychological gerontology. Only very recent developments seem to indicate a slow and hesitant shift in orientation (Flavell, 1970; Hooper, 1972; Piaget, 1972).

While psychological gerontology is thus very retarded in comparison to the developmental studies of children's cognitive and linguistic operations, there are other important areas in which it has outpaced the latter with ease. On the one hand, psychological gerontology has remained more closely connected than child psychology with neurological and physiological studies as well as with biomedical research in general. In part, this is reflected in the makeup of its scientific organizations (see Adler, 1958), laboratories, and publications (see Shock, 1951, 1957). With the exception of the study of early infancy, these connections have been lost in the investigations of child development.

On the other hand, psychological gerontology, in close affinity to sociological investigations, has made extraordinary advances in the analysis and conceptualization of developmental research designs, leaving the child psychologist far behind and still barely aware of the significance of these issues. More than the students of child development, psychological gerontologists have realized that during the long periods of time covered in their investigations, the society, that is, its social, educational, economic, and physical conditions, might change more markedly and rapidly than the individual himself. As explored by Schaie (1965) and Baltes (1968), neither the traditional cross-sectional nor the less common, although unduly emphasized, longitudinal designs allow the investigator to unconfound sociohistorical from individual changes. Only in conjunction with a design completely disregarded in psychology, that is, the time-lag design, is such an analysis possible.

Schaie (1965) also insisted that complex research designs allow us to estimate the relative contributions of biological and sociological components to the observed psychological changes. Thus, the analysis seems to dichotomize the field of developmental sciences in much the same manner as it had burdened child psychology ever since the nature–nurture controversy. Since the proposed analyses focus on changes and processes rather than on a static dichotomization (which ultimately relates to the equally static contrast of mind and body), essentially different perspectives are provided. These perspectives are similar to the dialecticism of modern Soviet psychology. Since these interpretations of individual and social changes touch on important issues concerning the future orientation of psychological gerontology (as well as the behavioral sciences in general), this topic is elaborated on in the following section.

CONCLUSIONS

Our quantitative analysis of the history of psychological gerontology can be regarded as an effort in futility. It represents both another addition to the legion of studies (4,310 of which were entered into our reference file), and it demonstrates that the vast majority of these studies represent nothing else than an enormous waste of our efforts (77% of which were never retrieved through our analysis and another large percentage of which never appeared in print in the first place, being rejected for publication by the journal editors). How can we prevent this pollution from spreading further? How can we make our human and scientific efforts more meaningful and efficient?

Numerous people and organizations have become deeply concerned about these problems. Not all of them are ready to admit, however, that any solution has to revolutionize the very basic conceptions of knowledge and science. Most of them still believe that with increased efforts and with the allocation of additional funds the problems can be resolved. In contrast to such optimistic views, I have to maintain that basic reformulations are necessary in our conceptions of knowledge and science, research and theory, education and implementation, and generally in our conception of man, society, and their development.

Criteria for Knowledge

In spite of the enormous increase in research output and in spite of our pride in the advancement of knowledge, superficially seen as the result of this increase, our concepts of research and theory have not advanced beyond viewpoints of the nineteenth century. As implied by most contributors to the discussion of communication in psychology in the April 1971 issue of the *American Psychologist* (Garvey & Griffith, 1971), we firmly believe that each of the many studies contributes at least a small bit to our stock of knowledge and, thereby, strips nature of another secret. These efforts are called the "collection of facts" and we wait patiently for some exceptional scientists to put these "facts" together and, thereby, "discover" another "law of nature." As clearly realized by the more thoughtful scholars, such a naive and mechanistic viewpoint is not only inadequate for the behavioral sciences but for all other disciplines as well. The prevailing conditions have been summarized by Heisenberg (1957):

> Thus was formed the solid framework of classical physics, and thus arose the conception of a material world in time and space comparable to a machine which, once set in motion, continues to run, governed by immutable laws. The fact that this machine as well as the whole of science were themselves only products of the human mind appeared irrelevant and of no consequence for an understanding of nature [p. 79].

The naive fact-finding attitude does not come to grips with the interaction of scientific advancements and the growth of society. Progress in knowledge and science is always codetermined by the nonscientific conditions and demands of the society in which they develop. Society, in turn, will be modified by the scientific progress made. By disregarding or rejecting these nonscientific influences, psychologists have remained safely hidden in their ivory towers and have escaped to the perceptual-structural criteria of knowledge (Riegel, 1972a, 1972c). "Truth" has been regarded as dependent upon the degree to which sensory impressions (both of the common sense and scientific-observational type) match or are congruent with systematic and, perhaps, formal models. By demonstrating such isomorphism, we continue to believe that we are describing and explaining nature as it "really is." Little do we recognize that both our observations as well as the theoretical models proposed are selectively dependent upon social, economic, and political conditions of the society in which we happen to live. Since considerations like these are outwardly rejected by most present-day psychologists, further development of our conceptualizations has been prevented and we have remained unable to discuss these issues in a systematic manner. At the same time, however, we do not hesitate to indoctrinate our students with our biased viewpoints, and it is only the new cohort of students that shows a growing sense of uneasiness in regard to our conceptions.

Goals of Higher Education

Students of psychology, upon entering university programs, are explicitly or implicitly forced to engage immediately in research activities and to accumulate sets of inappropriate techniques, for example, statistical techniques of parametric types. These activities may not be damaging as long as they are regarded as tasks, almost in a therapeutic sense, that provide the individual with opportunities for gaining scientific insights and human understanding (of course, the latter might be achieved more readily by sending the student into a school, into a home for the aged, or into a ghetto). These tasks can be harmful, however, if they induce upon the student precisely the same attitude toward science that we have criticized already, that is, the conviction that his activities are not merely of educational benefit for the student himself, but that they also contribute to the growing stock of scientific knowledge.

Perhaps students are selectively attracted to the behavioral sciences because of their preference for such conceptualization. Certainly this attitude is reinforced throughout undergraduate and graduate education. At least from the time of their admission and continuing throughout their whole academic careers, most psychologists seem to retain this attitude. The outcome is the enormous mass of research, compounded by rejection rates of up to 80% with which editors of leading psychological journals, with an ambivalent feeling of despair and pride, turn down the reports of the activities submitted to them—despair because with a brief notice they might destroy the ceaseless efforts and hopes of another individual and pride because the high rejection rate signals to them the exceptional attraction of their journal, the astounding activities of the field, and the high standards presumably attained. To the present author, however, these conditions, much like a continuing unemployment rate of 6% in the wealthiest nation on earth, indicate some very basic fallacies of the system of scientific activities that can be corrected only through major changes in our conceptualization of sciences and implemented through major modifications of our system of higher education.

Such modifications ought to be brought about by an emphasis on cooperation rather than competition between individuals, on quality rather than quantity of scientific products, and on integrative-structured rather than specialized-isolated achievements. Instead of setting each student and each scholar on his own track, they should be induced at the undergraduate and graduate levels to engage in group efforts, not in order to increase their productivity further but to direct them toward integration of efforts and to reduce the mass of separate contributions. Additional emphasis should be given to the reanalysis and reinterpretation of previous data, surveys of the literature, and historical studies.

As implied in these suggestions, advances in knowledge are not so much dependent upon the accumulation of additional data but upon the success in organizing those already available. As proposed by Looft (1971), a better psychology should be generated, but not a "psychology of more and more." Such a goal is not reached by inducing an overcompetitive attitude upon the young scholar but rather by fostering a contemplative reflective orientation. Competition does not assist but rather destroys thinking and merely represents an external, regulating condition that serves as a poor substitute for internal motivation.

Use of Technology

Within the established quarters of the behavioral and social sciences, the suggestions concerning undergraduate and graduate education might appear as antiscientific. By emphasizing the quality and integration of achievements rather than by evaluating progress through the number of studies produced, we do not want to deny, however, the usefulness of data collection. Indeed, our quantitative exploration of the history of psychological gerontology may serve as a demonstration of how quantitative comparisons can assist us in our tasks of achieving a fuller integration of research information and quick decisions regarding future directions.

This study represents a limited exploration of determinants and processes in the growth of sciences. For several years such explorations have been demanded by Birren (1961) and have been made possible through the systematic work by Shock (1951, 1957). This study is comparable to the well-known investigations by Asimov (1963), Garfield, Sher, and Torpie (1964), Price (1965), Xhignesse and Osgood (1967), and Garvey and Griffith (1971). These investigators have provided descriptive information on the growth of scientific disciplines as well as theoretical models that would allow for precise predictions and thus, assist in reasonable decisions. In general, these models further our conceptualization and understanding of the growth of social systems.

In the preceding section, a reduction in research output for the sake of structural, comprehensive integrations was emphasized. It was argued that such a reorientation has to be implemented through changes in the approach to and in the goals of higher education. In the present section, we are proposing the application of theories and techniques developed through research on computerized retrieval methods and on models of changing social systems. Such applications aim at coping more efficiently here and now with the information overload existing in most scientific disciplines, such as in psychological gerontology. The research and the models may enable us to develop a more rigorous form of conceptualization, to gain an understanding of the dynamics of growing scientific disciplines, and, concretely, to make us aware of newly emerging trends, of needs for consolidating different coexisting branches, or of splitting apart others that are, as yet, insufficiently differentiated.

Undoubtedly, the techniques for which these investigations of scientific information retrieval have become known do not solve the problems intrinsic to our rapidly expanding scientific disciplines. They may enable us, however, much like the recording devices for air or water pollution, to recognize points of saturation or catastrophy. The solutions for these problems, as we have stressed before, have to come through reorientations of the participating scientists and through reevaluations of our scientific discipline leading to a new conception of man, society, and their development.

Model of Man and Society

Traditionally, behavioral scientists have been bound to a conceptual model in which both the organism and the environment are regarded as passive. This model is the heritage of the sensualistic, elementaristic, and associationist tradition of British philosophy and has been most clearly preserved through the studies of verbal learning and behaviorism. As a theory of man, society, and their development, such a model is as insufficient as the modified version proposed by Skinner in which the experimenter actively manipulates and shapes the course of the individual's development. Since in this modified version, the organism remains to be regarded as a passive black box, and since the activities of the experimenter are arbitrary and idiosyncratic, but do not reflect the cultural–historical directions of society, this modification is as insufficient as is the model of the passive organism in a passive environment.

It is the outstanding achievement of Piaget, followed by Chomsky, to have returned activity to its origin, namely, into the organism. Learning and development are no longer considered as being brought about by the organism's exposure to and accumulation of bits and pieces of information and habits, but the organism is seen as actively and selectively exploring his environmental possibilities. While the organism thus learns only what he explores, this interpretation essentially fails to consider that the environment consists as well of individuals continuously interacting with the developing organism in an active manner. To Piaget and especially to Chomsky, the environment merely provides the necessary material from which the individual can make his selections; the environment does not impose its information on the organism. If individuals were living in a social vacuum they could not make such selections and, thus, could not develop.

Psychological gerontologists would have much to learn from Piaget and Chomsky because there is no doubt that the idea of an active, aging individual has not yet attained a respectable place in our thinking. But even more important, psychological gerontologists would have much to learn from Soviet psychology, where, for the first time, the sociocultural environment is also being considered as an active force in the individual's development.

The dialectic psychology initiated by Vygotskij (1929, 1962) and brought to its fruition by S. L. Rubinstein (see Payne, 1968) considers both the organism and the environment as active participants in a process of changes. Psychic activities or behavior are the outcomes of two interaction processes—one relating them to the internal biochemical processes, the other to external cultural–historical processes. The analysis of the first interaction process relies on Pavlov's work on the first and second signaling systems. The development of such a system of nervous activities does not emerge in a social vacuum, however. In the ontogenetic sense, it occurs for a particular individual in a particular social–educational setting; in the phylogenetic sense, Pavlov's theory itself is the product of a particular society in a particular cultural–historical setting. The psychic activities developing in the organism will change the cultural–historical conditions as much as cultural–historical developments will change the psychic activities of the individual. These changes characterize the second interaction system.

Since the cultural–historical conditions are the product of continuing efforts by generations and generations of individuals, it is not surprising that in his own development, an individual is bound to generate products essentially similar to those generated in society, for example, cognitive or syntactic structures. In other words, the problem of nativism–empiricism does not exist; ontogenetic and phylogenetic progressions converge. Similarly, the problem of consciousness versus behavior (mind–body) does not exist. Both are constructs emerging through the two types of interactions; one is founded in external cultural–historical conditions, the other in internal, biochemical conditions. Only in the mechanistic or idealistic views of Western philosophy do these two constructs appear as separate entities;

that is, they appear as behavior if the first system is emphasized at the expense of the second, and as consciousness if the reverse reasoning is applied.

Finally, behavior and consciousness, as seen from such a dialectic view, are psychic activities that are not only being changed by biochemical and cultural–historical conditions but that, in turn, might change both these conditions. This conclusion indicates far-reaching revisions, namely, the rejection of naive realism and the scientific fatalism that is insensitive to social issues and problems. Knowledge and science not only rely on sensoristructural truth criteria but also on those of social actions and consequences. If it were possible to conceptualize this problem distinctly, and if it could be applied to psychological gerontology successfully, then knowledge would be attained in the true and only sense of the word.

RECOMMENDATIONS

The results of this study lead to the following recommendations:

1. Deemphasize the ceaseless accumulation of research data that are more important for the competitive success of individuals than for the growth of knowledge, science, and society. Emphasize integrative and historical perspectives rather than the collection of bits and pieces of research guided by a naive, fact-finding attitude.

2. Implement these changes through an overhaul of our system of higher education. Rather than creating overambitious, competitive young scientists, often arrogant and elitistic in their thinking, foster an attitude of cooperation and sensitivity toward scientific issues, social problems, and people.

3. In order to cope with the present-day scientific pollution, make maximum use of modern technologies and models of the growth of science and society. Apply these tools for the benefit of scientific disciplines and society rather than having the fate of their participating members determined by and subordinated to the advances of these technologies.

4. In order to achieve such intellectual control, formulate a model of man in which his dialectic, developmental interdependence with the changing society is emphasized. Such a model overcomes the naive fact-finding orientation, the mechanistic reductionism, the static dichotomization into nature–nurture or body–mind, and the view of man and of society as passive aggregates shaped by blind external forces.

REFERENCES

Adler, M. History of the Gerontological Society. *Journal of Gerontology*, 1958, **13**, 94–100.

Arenberg, D. Concept problem solving in young and old adults. *Journal of Gerontology*, 1968, **23**, 279–282.

Asimov, I. *The genetic code.* New York: New American Library, 1963.

Baltes, P. B. Longitudinal and cross-sectional sequences in the study of age and generation effects. *Human Development*, 1968, **11**, 145–171.

Birren, J. E. (Ed.) *Handbook of aging and the individual: Psychological and biological aspects.* Chicago: University of Chicago Press, 1960.

Birren, J. E. A brief history of the psychology of aging. *Gerontologist*, 1961, **1**, 69–77, 127–134.

Birren, J. E. *The psychology of aging.* Englewood Cliffs, N.J.: Prentice-Hall, 1964.

Blum, J. E., Jarvik, L. F., & Clark, E. T. Rate of change on selective tests of intelligence: A twenty-year longitudinal study of aging. *Journal of Gerontology*, 1970, **25**, 171–176.

Botwinick, J. *Cognitive processes in maturity and old age.* New York: Springer, 1967.

Bourne, L. E., Jr. Learning and utilization of conceptual rules. In B. Kleinmuntz (Ed.), *Concepts and structure of memory.* New York: Wiley, 1970.

Bruner, J. S., et al. *Studies in cognitive growth.* New York: Wiley, 1966.

Burstein, S. The historical background of gerontology. *Geriatrics*, 1965, **10**, 183–193, 328–332, 536–540.

Charles, D. C. Historical antecedents of life-span developmental psychology. In L. R. Goulet & P. B. Baltes (Eds.), *Life-span developmental psychology: Research and theory.* New York: Academic Press, 1970.

Cole, M., & Maltzman, I. (Eds.) *A handbook of contemporary Soviet psychology.* New York: Basic Books, 1969.

Elderton, E. M., Moul, M., & Page, E. M. On the growth curves of certain characters in women and the interrelationship of these characters. *Annals of Eugenics*, 1928, **3**, 277–335.

Elkind, D., & Flavell, J. H. (Eds.) *Studies in cognitive development: Essays in honor of Jean Piaget.* New York: Oxford University Press, 1969.

Flavell, J. H. *The developmental psychology of Jean Piaget.* New York: Van Nostrand, 1963.

Flavell, J. H. Cognitive changes in adulthood. In L. R. Goulet & P. B. Baltes (Eds.), *Life-span developmental psychology: Research and theory.* New York: Academic Press, 1970.

Freeman, J. T. The history of geriatrics. *Annals of Medical History*, 1938, **10**, 324–355.

Freeman, J. T., & Webber, I. L. (Eds.) Perspectives in aging. *Gerontologist*, 1965, **5**(Pt. 2).

Furth, H. G. *Piaget and knowledge.* Englewood Cliffs, N.J.: Prentice-Hall, 1969.

Garfield, E., Sher, I. H., & Torpie, R. J. *The use of citation data in writing the history of science.* Philadelphia: Institute of Scientific Information, 1964.

Garvey, W. D., & Griffith, B. G. Scientific communication: Its role in the conduct of research and creation of knowledge. *American Psychologist,* 1971, **26,** 349–362.

Goulet, L. R., & Baltes, P. B. (Eds.) *Life-span developmental psychology: Research and theory.* New York: Academic Press, 1970.

Grant, R. L. Concepts of aging: A historical review. *Perspectives in Medical Biology,* 1963, **6,** 443–478.

Groffmann, K. J. Life-span developmental psychology in Germany: Past and present. In L. R. Goulet & P. B. Baltes (Eds.), *Life-span developmental psychology: Research and theory.* New York: Academic Press, 1970.

Hamilton, G. V. Changes in personality and psycho-sexual phenomena with age. In E. V. Cowdry (Ed.), *Problems of aging.* (2nd ed.) Baltimore: Williams & Wilkins, 1942.

Heisenberg, W. *Philosophic problems of nuclear science.* New York: Pantheon, 1952.

Hooper, F. H. Cognitive assessment across the life-span: Methodological implications of the organismic approach. In J. R. Nesselroade & H. W. Reese (Eds.), *Life-span developmental psychology: Methodological issues.* New York: Academic Press, 1973, in press.

Hultsch, D. F. Organization and memory in adulthood. *Human Development,* 1971, **14,** 16-29.

Johnson, S. C. Hierarchical clustering schemes. *Psychometrika,* 1967, **32,** 241–254.

Jones, M. E. Intelligence and problem-solving. In J. E. Birren (Ed.), *Handbook of aging and the individual: Psychological and biological aspects.* Chicago: University of Chicago Press, 1960.

Kausler, D. H. Retention–forgetting as a nomological network for developmental research. In L. R. Goulet & P. B. Baltes (Eds.), *Life-span developmental psychology: Research and theory.* New York: Academic Press, 1970.

Looft, W. R. The psychology of more. *American Psychologist,* 1971, **26,** 561–565.

Lynd, S. Historical past and existential present. In T. N. Guinsburg (Ed.), *The dimensions of history.* Chicago: Rand McNally, 1971.

Moore, J. L., & Birren, J. E. Doctoral training in gerontology: An analysis of dissertations on problems of aging in institutions of higher learning in the United States, 1934–1969. *Journal of Gerontology,* 1971, **26,** 249–257.

Munnichs, J. M. A. A short history of psycho-gerontology. *Human Development,* 1966, **9,** 230–245.

Nikitin, V. N. *Russian studies on age-associated physiology, biochemistry, and morphology: Historical sketch and bibliography.* Kharkov, USSR: A. M. Gorki Press, 1958.

Payne, T. R. *S. L. Rubinstein and the philosophical foundations of Soviet psychology.* New York: Humanities Press, 1968.

Piaget, J. Intellectual evolution from adolescence to adulthood. *Human Development,* 1972, **15,** 1–12.

Price, D. J. de Solla. Networks of scientific papers. *Science,* 1965, **149,** 510–515.

64   PSYCHOLOGY OF ADULT DEVELOPMENT AND AGING

Reinert, G. Comparative factor analytic studies of intelligence throughout the human life-span. In L. R. Goulet & P. B. Baltes (Eds.), *Life-span developmental psychology: Research and theory.* New York: Academic Press, 1970.

Richardson, B. W. Memory as a test of age. *Asclepiad,* 1891, **8**, 230–232.

Riegel, K. F. Ergebnisse und Probleme der psychologischen Alternsforschung: Teil I and II. *Vita Humana,* 1958, **1**, 52–64, 111–127, 204–243.

Riegel, K. F. Ergebnisse und Probleme der psychologischen Alternsforschung: Teil III. *Vita Humana,* 1959, **2**, 213–237.

Riegel, K. F. Personality theory and aging. In J. E. Birren (Ed.), *Handbook of aging and the individual: Psychological and biological aspects.* Chicago: University of Chicago Press, 1960.

Riegel, K. F. Development of language: Suggestions for a verbal fallout model. *Human Development,* 1966, **9**, 97–120.

Riegel, K. F. Changes in psycholinguistic performances with age. In G. A. Tallund (Ed.), *Human behavior and aging.* New York: Academic Press, 1968. (a)

Riegel, K. F. Some theoretical considerations of bilingual development. *Psychological Bulletin,* 1968, **70**, 647–670. (b)

Riegel, K. F. Untersuchungen sprachlicher Leistungen und ihrer Veränderungen. *Zeitschrift für allgemeine und angewandte Psychologie,* 1968, **15**, 649–692. (c)

Riegel, K. F. History as a nomothetic science: Some generalizations from theories and research in developmental psychology. *Journal of Social Issues,* 1969, **25**, 99–127.

Riegel, K. F. The language acquisition process: A reinterpretation of selected research findings. In L. R. Goulet & P. B. Baltes (Eds.), *Life-span developmental psychology: Research and theory.* New York: Academic Press, 1970.

Riegel, K. F. Developmental psychology and society: Some historical and ethical considerations. In J. R. Nesselroade & H. W. Reese (Eds.), *Life-span developmental psychology: Methodological issues.* New York: Academic Press, 1972, 1–23. (a)

Riegel, K. F. The influence of economic and political ideologies on the development of developmental psychology. *Psychological Bulletin,* 1972, **78**, 129–141. (b)

Riegel, K. F. Time and change in the development of the individual and society. In H. Reese (Ed.), *Advances in child development and behavior.* Vol. 7. New York: Academic Press, 1973, in press. (c)

Riegel, K. F., & Riegel, R. M. Development, drop and death. *Developmental Psychology,* 1972, **6**, 306–319.

Ruger, H. A., & Stoessiger, B. On the growth curves of certain characteristics in man (males). *Annals of Eugenics,* 1927, **2**, 76–111.

Savage, G. H. Symptoms of mental dissolution. *Transactions of the Medical Society (London),* 1893, **16**, 252–263.

Schaie, K. W. A general model for the study of developmental problems. *Psychological Bulletin,* 1965, **64**, 92–107.

Scott, C. A. Old age and death. *American Journal of Psychology,* 1896, **8**, 67–122.

Shock, N. W. *A classified bibliography of gerontology.* Stanford: Stanford University Press, 1951.

Shock, N. W. *A classified bibliography of gerontology: Supplement 1: 1949–1955.* Stanford: Stanford University Press, 1957.

Vygotskij, L. S. The problem of cultural development of the child. *Journal of Genetic Psychology,* 1929, **36,** 415–434.

Vygotskij, L. S. *Thought and language.* Cambridge: MIT Press, 1962.

Welford, A. T. *Skill and age: An experimental approach.* London: Oxford University Press, 1951.

Welford, A. T. *Aging and human skill.* London: Oxford University Press, 1958.

Welford, A. T. The measurement of sensory-motor performance: Survey and reappraisal of twelve years' progress. *Ergonomics,* 1960, **3,** 189–230.

Xhignesse, L. V., & Osgood, C. E. Bibliographical citation characteristics of the psychological journal network in 1950 and in 1960. *American Psychologist,* 1967, **22,** 778–791.

APPENDIX A

The following list defines the code for 52 node publications in the order shown in Figure 4.

KLOPFE 46
Klopfer, W. Personality pattern of old age. *Rorschach Research Exchange,* 1946, **10,** 145–166.

PRADOF 47
Prados, M., & Fried, E. G. Personality structure in the older age groups. *Journal of Clinical Psychology,* 1947, **3,** 113–120.

CHESWR 49
Chesrow, E. H., Wosika, P. H., & Reinitz, A. H. A psychometric evaluation of aged white males. *Geriatrics,* 1949, **4,** 169–177.

FOXBIR 50
Fox, C., & Birren, J. E. The differential decline of subtest scores of the Wechsler-Bellevue Intelligence Scale in 60–69 year old individuals. *Journal of Genetic Psychology,* 1950, **77,** 313–317.

RABINA 45
Rabin, A. I. Psychometric trends in senility and psychosis of the senium. *Journal of General Psychology,* 1945, **32,** 149–162.

MADONS 47
Madonick, M. J., & Solomon, M. The Wechsler-Bellevue Scale in individuals past sixty. *Geriatrics,* 1947, **2,** 34–40.

WECHSL 55
Wechsler, D. *Manual for the Wechsler Adult Intelligence Scale.* New York: Psychological Corporation, 1955.

DOPPEW 55
Doppelt, J. E., & Wallace, W. Standardization of the Wechsler Adult Intelligence Scale for older persons. *Journal of Abnormal and Social Psychology,* 1955, **51,** 312–330.

BOTWIB 51
Botwinick, J., & Birren, J. E. Differential decline in the Wechsler-Bellevue subtests in the senile psychoses. *Journal of Gerontology*, 1951, **6**, 365–368.

BABCOC 30
Babcok, H. An experiment in the measurement of mental deterioration. *Archives of Psychology*, 1930, **117**, 1–105.

JARKFK 57
Jarvik, L. F., Kallmann, F. J., Falek, A., & Klaber, N. M. Changing intellectual functions in senescent twins. *Acta Genetica et Statistica Medica*, 1957, **7**, 421–430.

OWENSW 53
Owens, W. A., Jr. Age and mental abilities: A longitudinal study. *Genetic Psychology Monographs*, 1953. **48**, 3–54.

BAYLEO 55
Bayley, N., & Oden, N. H. The maintenance of intellectual ability in gifted adults. *Journal of Gerontology*, 1955, **10**, 91–107.

MILESM 32
Miles, C. C., & Miles, W. R. The correlation of intelligence scores and chronological age from early to late maturity. *American Journal of Psychology*, 1932, **44**, 44–78.

JONESC 33
Jones, H. E., & Conrad, H. S. The growth and decline of intelligence: A study of a homogeneous group between the ages ten and sixty. *Genetic Psychology Monograph*, 1933, **3**, 223–298.

WECHSL 44
Wechsler, D. *The measurement of adult intelligence.* Baltimore: Williams & Wilkins, 1944.

BOTWIB 51
Botwinick, J., & Birren, J. E. The measurement of intellectual decline in the senile psychosis. *Journal of Consulting Psychology*, 1951, **15**, 145–150.

BALINS 41
Balinsky, B. An analysis of mental factors of various age groups from nine to sixty. *Genetic Psychology Monographs*, 1941, **23**, 192–234.

BIRREN 52
Birren, J. E. A factorial analysis of the Wechsler-Bellevue Scale given to an elderly population. *Journal of Consulting Psychology*, 1952, **16**, 399–405.

SHOCKN 51
Shock, N. W. Gerontology (later maturity). *Annual Review of Psychology*, 1951, **2**, 353–370.

MILESW 33
Miles, W. R. Age and human ability. *Psychological Review*, 1933, **40**, 99–123.

WEISRM 36
Weisenberg, T., Roe, A., & McBride, K. E. *Adult intelligence.* New York: Commonwealth Fund, 1936.

RIEGEL 59
Riegel, K. F. A study on verbal achievements of older persons. *Journal of Gerontology*, 1959, **14**, 453–456.

RIEGER 62
Riegel, K. F., & Riegel, R. M. Analysis of differences in test and item difficulty between young and old adults. *Journal of Gerontology,* 1962, **17**, 97–105.

RIEGER 59
Riegel, K. F., & Riegel, R. M. Standardisierung des Hamburg-Wechsler-Intellgenztests für Erwachsene (HAWIE) für die Altersstufenüber 50 Jahre. *Diagnostica,* 1959, **5**, 97–128.

SCHAIE 58
Schaie, K. W. Rigidity–flexibility and intelligence: A cross-sectional study of the adult life span from 20 to 70 years. *Psychological Monographs,* 1958, **72**(9, Whole, No. 462).

LEHMAN 53
Lehman, H. C. *Age and achievement.* Princeton: Princeton University Press, 1953.

BIRREB 55
Birren, J. E., & Botwinick, J. Speed of responses as a function of perceptual difficulty and age. *Journal of Gerontology,* 1955, **10**, 433–436.

BIRREB 55
Birren, J. E., & Botwinick, J. Age differences in finger, jaw, and foot reaction time to auditory stimuli. *Journal of Gerontology,* 1955, **10**, 429–432.

BIRREB 51
Birren, J. E., & Botwinick, J. The relation of writing speed to age and to the senile psychoses. *Journal of Consulting Psychology,* 1951, **15**, 243–249.

CLAYHM 54
Clay, H. M. Changes of performance with age on similar tasks of varying complexity. *British Journal of Psychology,* 1954, **45**, 7–13.

GOLDFA 41
Goldfarb, W. *An investigation of reaction time in older adults and its relationship to certain observed mental test patterns.* (Rep. No. 831). New York: *Teachers College Contributions to Education,* 1941.

BIRREB 51C
Birren, J. E., & Botwinick, J. Rate of addition as a function of difficulty and age. *Psychometrika,* 1951, **16**, 219–232.

KAYHAR 51
Kay, H. Learning of a serial task by different age groups. *Quarterly Journal of Experimental Psychology,* 1951, **3**, 166–183.

WELFOR 58
Welford, A. T. *Aging and human skill.* London: Oxford University Press, 1958.

WELFOR 51
Welford, A. T. *Skill and age: An Experimental approach.* London: Oxford University Press, 1951.

INGLIS 60
Inglis, J. Dichotic stimulation and memory disorder. *Nature,* 1960, **186**, 181–182.

INGLSA 61
Inglis, J., & Sanderson, R. E. Successive responses to simultaneous stimulation in elderly patients with memory disorder. *Journal of Abnormal and Social Psychology*, 1961, **62**, 709–712.

INGLIC 63
Inglis, J., & Caird, W. K. Age differences in successive responses to simultaneous stimulation. *Canadian Journal of Psychology*, 1963, **17**, 98–105.

WELFOR 56
Welford, A. T. Age and learning: Theory and needed research. In F. Verzar (Ed.), *Experimental research on aging*. (Experientia Suppl. 4) Basel, Switzerland: Birkhäuser, 1956.

BROMLE 58
Bromley, D. B. Some effects of age on short term learning and remembering. *Journal of Gerontology*, 1958, **13**, 398–406.

JEROME 59
Jerome, E. A. Age and learning—Experimental studies. In J. E. Birren (Ed.), *Handbook of aging and the individual*. Chicago: University of Chicago Press, 1959.

KORCHB 57
Korchin, S. J., & Basowitz, H. Age differences in verbal learning. *Journal of Abnormal and Social Psychology*, 1957, **54**, 64–69.

RUCHFL 34
Ruch, F. L. The differentiative effects of age upon human learning. *Journal of Genetic Psychology*, 1934, **11**, 261–268.

GILBER 41
Gilbert, J. G. Memory loss in senescence. *Journal of Abnormal and Social Psychology*, 1941, **36**, 73–86.

THOBTW 28
Thorndike, E. L., Bregman, E. O., Tilton, J. W., & Woodyard, E. *Adult learning*. New York: Macmillan, 1928.

GLADIB 58
Gladis, M., & Braun, H. W. Age differences in transfer and retroaction as a function of intertask response similarity. *Journal of Experimental Psychology*, 1958, **55**, 25–30.

BIRREM 61
Birren, J. E., & Morrison, D. E. Analysis of the WAIS subtests in relation to age and education. *Journal of Gerontology*, 1961, **16**, 363–369.

CUMMIH 61
Cumming, E., & Henry, W. *Growing old*. New York: Basic Books, 1961.

HAVIGA 53
Havighurst, R. J., & Albrecht, R. *Older people*. New York: Longmans, Green, 1953.

CAVBHG 49
Cavan, R. S., Burgess, E. W., Havighurst, R. J., & Goldhamer, H. *Personal adjustment in old age*. Chicago: Science Research Associates, 1949.

BURGCH 48
Burgess, W. E., Cavan, R. S., & Havighurst, R. J. *Your activities and attitudes*. Chicago: Science Research Associates, 1948.

Experimental Psychology

Experimental Studies

CARL EISDORFER

The following chapters summarize a good deal of the experimental activity in the psychology of aging. As such, the reviews represent a fair sample of the activity in the field. It is apparent that the major component of experimental work has been in the spheres of cognitive and intellectual functioning. The obvious decrements in performance that accompany advancing age past maturity have been noted, not only by the clinicians but by experimental psychologists as well, and with increasing activity in the field of aging, we are beginning to note the development of significant literature in these areas.

Of considerable consequence have been the results stemming from the longitudinal strategy. These data have enabled us to question the earlier concepts of cognitive decline that emerged from studies employing exclusively cross-sectional analyses of intelligence as measured by clinical tests. There is now reason to question the accuracy of many of our beliefs concerning the aged as well as the simple minded notion of a necessary age-linked decrement in all functions with age past maturity. As a result, investigators have become more interested and the experimental approaches of the last decade have begun to emphasize far more sophisticated analyses of the basis for behavioral change among the elderly. This period has also seen the beginnings of hypothesis formation concerning the basis for failures to learn and perform, and along with the psychophysiologic and psychobiologic studies cited in this section, they represent important additions to the literature of experimental psychology.

Carl Eisdorfer received his PhD in 1959 from New York University and his MD in 1964 from Duke University. President, 1972, of the Gerontological Society and of the Division of Adult Development and Aging of the APA. Formerly Professor of Psychiatry and Medical Psychology at Duke University Medical School, 1968–1972. Now Professor and Chairman of the Department of Psychiatry, and Adjunct Professor of Psychology, University of Washington.

Laboratory investigation of human and animal subjects is always fraught with difficulty. Developmental studies add a degree of complexity with time as an additional variable. These chapters, which reflect some of the more recent findings from the experimental psychology laboratory, describe complex biobehavioral interactions, subject-experimenter interactions, and a serious concern with such issues as the motivation of the subject and the relevance of the subject material. One important aspect of an experimental psychology of aging is that it clearly gets us away from dealing exclusively with rats or college student models.

While the chapters reflect a heavy emphasis of concern with the aging human, animal models are clearly important for the experimental and comparative developmental psychologist. Issues of relative longevity and maintenance of animals to advanced ages must be better understood. Still absent is an experimental developmental psychology which truly covers the age spectrum. Thus, we inevitably must deal with animal models. However, despite their advantages in longevity, often we are still faced with problems of cohorts of aged and younger subjects that may not give us an accurate estimation of behavior change through the life span, but rather a description of current behavioral patterns of organisms at various ages. This "cohort" variable may be a more serious problem for human studies where patterns of education, child care, nutrition, and the like differ from one generation to the next but animal models may not be immune to such differences, particularly as we become more sophisticated in handling, feeding, and environmental controls such that younger subjects may differ on far more than merely the age continuum. This concept of cohort differences is reflected in other writings in this volume but has important implication for all of experimental psychology.

Another aspect of these chapters is the attempt to integrate biologic with behavioral factors. As described in the works of Jarvik and Cohen and Thompson and Marsh, they do, I think, serve as important models for the psychology laboratory, and the hypotheses generated by Thompson and Marsh have implications for a wide spectrum of performance deficits apart from those found in the aged. Because investigators in gerontology are not working with captive groups of undergraduate college students, there must be a genuine concern with the parameters of the sample recruited and the precise nature of the variables. Thus, Arenberg's precise description of the nature of learning in the aged makes an important contribution in highlighting some of these factors as they contribute to aspects of cognitive functioning.

Certain subject areas were not included in this volume although they legitimately belong here. Such oversights were partly inadvertant due to the limited support available to the task force and were also, in part, secondary to the fact that the literature in many areas is woefully lacking. Thus, while studies of a decade or two ago in human perception had important implications for threshold phenomena, for constancy and for complex personality perception interaction, most of these leads have not been followed up and there is a scarcity of new information in this area. Such topics are fruitful areas for investigation. A review of the chapters in this section has a particular implication for the experimental psychologist, that is, to generate questions concerning the relevance of age as a hitherto ignored factor in much of the experimental work done to date. In the past there has been a relative lack of experimental data in contrast to clinical studies in aging. Clearly the base of information concerning the postmaturation adult and the processes of aging is small at this time, but the interest is emerging. It is a promising and fertile field for study and should offer insights as to the mechanisms of adaptation and behavior in humans as well as animals.

Cognition and Aging: Verbal Learning, Memory, and Problem Solving

DAVID ARENBERG

Prior to 1960, the literature on cognition and aging could have been reviewed exhaustively in two chapters. Today, even a review of selected literature could reach book-length proportions (see Botwinick, 1967). In this chapter, a comprehensive review will not be attempted. Instead, recent representative studies in verbal learning, memory, and problem solving will be reviewed to outline the developments in theory and research since the late fifties when two important syntheses of the available knowledge about cognition and aging were published (see Birren, 1959; Welford, 1958).

In this chapter, cognition is viewed as effectiveness in dealing with information. It will become increasingly apparent that time is a pervasive variable in cognition and aging. Response-time experiments have been designed that provide important knowledge about information processing and aging. Time to respond has been used as the dependent measure in a wide range of performance from simple reaction time to inductive reasoning and as an independent variable that contributes to age differences in psychometric performance and verbal learning. It would be surprising to find cognitive tasks in which age differences would not be affected by manipulating time in some way.

This chapter deals predominantly with the processes of registering, storing, and retrieving information and with manipulating information to solve a problem. Reaction time and response speed are

David Arenberg received his PhD in psychology from Duke University in 1960. He is currently a Research Psychologist at the Gerontology Research Center (Baltimore, Md.) of the National Institutes of Health, where he is Chief of the Section on Human Learning and Problem Solving. His research areas are problem solving, memory, and verbal learning with particular emphasis on gerontology.

measures that have been increasingly used in studies of information processing, but that literature will not be reviewed here.

Welford (1958) stated at the beginning of his chapter on learning and memory:

> It is clear that the decline of performance with age at most learning tasks must be accepted as well-established fact. What we need to know is the nature of the difficulty encountered by older people . . . [p. 225].

After reviewing the evidence available at that time, he concluded that (a) much of that difficulty is not due to a true incapacity to learn, but to the inability to deal with the presentation conditions, and that (b) where true learning or retention deficits with age can be demonstrated, they are due to increased interference with short-term retention.

Based upon the hypothesis of greater susceptibility to interference from other activity, Welford (1958) made further suggestions and predictions, some of which follow.

1. Age differences should be small for retention of subspan material, and they should increase as the amount to be learned increases beyond the immediate span.

2. Correcting earlier errors in learning should be more difficult for older people than for young people.

3. Learning by the "part" method should be particularly beneficial to older people, especially with frequent rest periods and distributed practice.

4. Incidental learning should be poorer for older people than for young people.

5. Older people should experience particular difficulty in learning when items arrive in close temporal proximity.

Although findings were available in 1958 that supported some of those points (as will be seen), others have been documented by subsequent experimental evidence.

Jerome (1959) carefully reviewed the experimental literature in an attempt to assess the validity of the popular belief that mental faculties, especially the ability to learn and to remember, deteriorate from early maturity to old age. At the end of an extensive review and excellent critique of procedures and findings, no general conclusions were presented. It is surmised that too many of the studies available at that time were contaminated by methodological difficulties to warrant general statements about aging, learning, and memory.

Kay (1959) considered the broad range of behaviors studied by psychologists interested in aging and learning and discussed those behaviors in terms of learning theory, which, he pointed out, has focused on a rather narrow range of behavior manipulable by experimental techniques in the laboratory. He concluded that studies of variables and techniques that have proved significant in nonaging experiments should prove valuable in gerontological learning research and proposed several that seemed most relevant. Among the proposals included were studies of short-term memory (with the advantage of experimental control of input conditions and readily measurable responses), rate of input transmission, ability to modify experiences, and transfer and interference.

VERBAL LEARNING

Pacing and Age

Recent age studies in verbal learning have usually included one or more other variables in order to determine conditions that affect age differences in performance. Pace variables have been particularly prevalent. For example, Eisdorfer, Axelrod, and Wilkie (1963) established that when the time to respond is increased in serial learning, the old benefit more than the young. The same effect has been found in paired-associate studies. Canestrari (1963) reported that paired-associate performance of the old improved more than that of the young when the pace was slowed. Furthermore, when given unlimited time to respond and to inspect the stimulus-response pair, "study time" was rarely extended, but the old frequently extended their time-to-respond interval with a concomitant reduction in errors.

In those studies, further age comparisons were made for errors of omission and errors of commission. It was found that errors of omission were responsible for the Age × Pace interaction. Taub (1967) reported similar results and also found that explicit instructions requiring a response to each stimulus presentation did not affect the Age × Pace interaction.

The increase in trials and errors for the old at a fast rate has been interpreted as a performance rather than a learning deficit; that is, the old learn as well under fast paced conditions as under slow paced conditions, but are less likely to respond in a short interval because they cannot or are reluctant to do so. Eisdorfer (1968) developed an intriguing concept of response suppression in an extensive series of serial-learning studies, mostly of groups of older people. The model merits substantial attention, particularly in view of recent findings of improved performance of the old when a drug is used to block autonomic arousal (Eisdorfer, Nowlin, & Wilkie, 1970). The argument is based upon the following facts and interpretations. Errors of omission account for the Age × Pace interaction (Eisdorfer et al., 1963). Mean response times when the old respond under a slower presentation rate indicate that they can respond fast enough to meet the requirements of faster presentation rates; therefore, responses are suppressed (Eisdorfer, 1965). Autonomic arousal, as measured by free fatty acid in plasma, is higher and more persistent during and after learning for the old than for the young. The autonomic arousal level of the old is beyond the optimal level for a learning task, particularly at a fast pace, and the result is response suppression and performance decrement (Eisdorfer, 1968). When a drug that blocked autonomic arousal was administered to old subjects, they made fewer errors in serial learning than a placebo group (Eisdorfer et al., 1970). Although some of the intermediate interpretations are not entirely data bound, the argument is impressive, and the studies exemplify how age deficits in verbal learning can be explored by experimental manipulation of other variables.

Paired-associate learning provides an even more manipulable experimental task than serial learning because time to respond and time to study a stimulus with its response can be paced independently. Arenberg (1965) varied the anticipation interval (time to respond) and found larger age differences at a short interval than at a longer interval. To explore the learning-performance question, self-paced test trials were alternated with paced acquisition trials in another study. The Age × Interval interaction was found for self-paced as well as for paced responses; that is, when the anticipation interval was short in acquisition trials, the age difference was not only large for responses during the paced acquisition trials, but was also large in the corresponding self-paced test trials when subjects had as much time to respond as they needed. The comparable age differences were smaller for the groups with a longer anticipation interval in acquisition trials. The self-paced evidence was interpreted as favoring the learning rather than the performance argument, but the arousal–response-suppression model could encompass the results without undue strain. If fast acquisition trials (short anticipation interval) induce higher arousal levels, response suppression could occur on the following trial despite the fact that it is self-paced. Unfortunately, the blood sampling in the experiments in which Eisdorfer (1968) measured free fatty acid probably masked possible differences in arousal due to pace; but an essential link in the arousal–

response-suppression argument is that when time to respond is short, arousal is particularly high and response suppression results.

In a recent study, Monge and Hultsch (1971) systematically varied both time to respond and time to inspect the stimulus and response elements together. They found that the trials required to learn a list decreased for the old and the young as either interval was lengthened, but only increasing the anticipation interval (time to respond) benefited the old more than the young. This finding was consistent with Arenberg's (1965) results and complemented Canestrari's (1963) finding that the older subjects tended to increase time to respond but not time to study when given the opportunity to do both.

Hulicka, Sterns, and Grossman (1967) reported a paired-associate study with findings somewhat at odds with the results mentioned thus far. They included all four combinations of paced and unpaced presentation (study trial) with paced and unpaced response time (test trial). The old and young groups recalled more correct response items when the presentation trial was unpaced than when it was paced. No gain for either group was found when the test trial was unpaced, unless the study trial was also unpaced.

Two points of procedure should be mentioned. In the instructions, the subjects were encouraged to form a mediation between stimulus and response elements of each pair. This probably contributed to the greater effectiveness of the pace condition for the study trial. The other procedural difference was the use of a single study trial and a single test trial per list. Paired-associate items are typically presented over many trials, and it seems reasonable that if increasing the anticipation interval increases the likelihood of rehearsal or increases the likelihood of successful search at the time of responding, the beneficial effects should result from repeated presentation and response opportunities. The limited effect of the anticipation interval in the Hulicka et al. (1967) results probably reflects the absence of repetition. The presentation of one study trial and one test trial is similar to short-term memory procedures, which are discussed in a later section.

Associative Strength and Age

The possibility that preexisting linguistic habits are stronger for the old than for the young or that such habits result in greater resistance to learning new verbal associations has been investigated in several recent studies of age and associative strength. Usually, paired-associate lists with word pairs of different associative strength are learned by different age groups. Associative strength is typically based upon word association norms. High associative strength is defined as a pair of words in which the response member is a high-probability response to the stimulus member when the stimulus is presented in a word association procedure.

Canestrari (1966) used 2 lists of 10 pairs of words with pairs of high associative strength in one list and pairs of low associative strength in the other. Each of the old and young subjects learned one of the two lists. In addition to an age difference, an interaction was found between age and list. The age difference for the high-strength items, which were likely to be consistent with established linguistic habits, was smaller than the age difference for the low-strength pairs, which may have been inconsistent with established habits.

Kausler and Lair (1966) reported similar results. They used mixed lists in which high, medium, and low associative strength pairs were presented within a single list. Again the Age $\times$ Strength inter-action was found. The old benefited more than the young from high-strength pairs.

Lair, Moon, and Kausler (1969) also investigated the effects of established linguistic habits on learning, but they used a list of zero-strength pairs and a list with high response competition. High response competition was obtained by breaking up high associative strength pairs and re-pairing each stimulus word with a response word from another pair. These newly created pairs were difficult to learn because for each stimulus there was a response word in the list that was consistent with established linguistic habits, but that response was incorrect and had to be suppressed. The difference between old and middle-aged groups was much larger for the response-competi-tion list than for the neutral list of zero associative strength.

Zaretsky and Halberstam (1968a) reported a study similar to that of Kausler and Lair (1966). Both the old and the young groups learned (and 15 minutes later relearned) five pairs of high or medium associative strength with few or no errors. Age differences were found, however, in learning and relearning five low associative pairs. Similar results were reported by Zaretsky and Halberstam (1968b) for hospitalized patients with and without brain damage.

Retroaction and Age

Retroaction is a prevalent method for studying interference in verbal learning. In a retroaction procedure, the experimental groups learn two lists and then relearn the first. Two early studies of retroaction and age reported disparate results. Gladis and Braun (1958) reported no differences among three age groups in recall or relearning after multiple covariance, including adjustments for original learning. Wimer and Wigdor (1958) found age differences in relearning covaried for original learning.

Among the many procedural differences between these two studies was the anticipation interval. Gladis and Braun (1958) used a four-second period for responding to each stimulus, whereas Wimer and Wigdor (1958) allowed one second to respond to each stimulus word. Arenberg (1967), who had previously demonstrated that a short anticipation interval was particularly detrimental to paired-associate learning for the older learners, investigated the role of the anticipation interval in retroaction. He found an interaction between age and interval when relearning (after an interpolated list) was covaried for original learning. An age difference in relearning was found at the short anticipation interval but not at the longer interval.

Hulicka (1967), in a carefully designed study with two learning conditions and control groups for each, investigated the effects of learning to a criterion and learning for a fixed number of trials on recall after an interpolated list. When the original list was learned to criterion, the age difference in recall was small and not statistically different from the control groups. This was similar to the early results of Gladis and Braun (1958) and to the results at the longer anticipation interval in Arenberg's (1967) study. (It should be noted that Hulicka also used a long anticipation interval.) However, when learning proceeded for a fixed number of trials, the age difference in recall for the groups with an interpolated list was larger than the age difference for the control groups.

These results need further comment. First, it should be pointed out that the groups who learned for a fixed number of trials did not differ in original learning; that is, the older groups learned with as few errors as the young did. If age differences in retroaction were predicted on the basis of less effective learning of the first list by the old for a fixed number of trials, this did not occur. Second, it should be noted that the older groups with an interpolated list had the same recall performance whether they learned the first list to criterion or for the fixed number of trials. Only the young groups with an interpolated list differed under the two learning conditions, and that difference accounted for the interaction between age and condition. Even with a well-designed study of retroaction such as this, the results are not unequivocal.

The most recent retroaction study of age available at this writing was reported by Traxler and Britton (1970), who used a different method to measure recall. Three retroaction paradigms known to produce differential interference in young adults were used with two age groups. In addition, two anticipation intervals were included. After two lists of paired associates were learned to criterion, stimulus words from both lists were provided, and the subjects wrote a response word for as many as they could recall. Age differences in recall of first-list responses were found in all conditions. The high interference paradigm resulted in greater retroaction effects for both age groups. The high interference paradigm was the procedure used in all the previously reported age studies of retroaction, and in the Traxler and Britton study, the interaction between age and anticipation interval was found under that condition. Larger age differences occurred when that interval was short than occurred when it was longer, confirming the findings of Arenberg (1967).

Retention after Learning

Surprisingly, the question of age deficits in retention at some interval after learning has received little attention among experimenters. Wimer and Wigdor (1958) reported data for the control groups in their retroaction study that showed little age difference in recall 15 minutes after learning to criterion. Hulicka and Weiss (1965) paired geometric designs with men's names and obtained retention measures 5 minutes, 20 minutes, and 1 week after learning. They found that groups who learned for a fixed number of trials showed age differences in retention, but retention was highly correlated with amount learned and reflected only differences in learning rather than retention. When learning was continued to a criterion of errorless performance, no retention difference in age was found at any interval. Similar results were reported by Hulicka (1965). Groups were matched on a preliminary learning task and then learned to match seven men's names with their faces. No age difference in learning or retention at 20 minutes or at 1 week was found. In view of the many studies of verbal learning that have reported age differences, matching according to previous learning performance probably contributed heavily to the fact that groups 76–89 years of age learned the sets of names and faces as well as groups 30–39 years of age in Hulicka's study.

Two other studies by Wimer (1960) and by Hulicka and Rust (1964) reported age differences in retention 24 hours after learning. It is interesting to note that both studies in which retention differences were found used nonsense equations as learning material. None of the studies that used meaningful words or names of people reported age differences in retention even a week after learning, when learning was continued until the subjects had learned all items in the list.

MEMORY

It has often been said that immediate memory and memory for events from the distant past are not affected by aging. Evidence for the former comes from the typical memory span findings in which a count is made of the longest sequence of digits, letters, or words a person can remember. Little if any age deficit has been found in this type of task. The evidence for extremely long-term memory is observational, because it does not lend itself to laboratory study. However, the question is often raised about rehearsal effects resulting from much retelling of the favorite memories that survive to old age. It is not feasible to evaluate such effects in a systematic way.

Memories that fall between immediate and distant memory are the ones that are apparently susceptible to decline with age, and they are the ones discussed here. Particular attention is paid to identifying loci of age deficits in registration, storage, and retrieval.

Talland (1965) used three sources of interference in variations of memory span procedures. Free recall requires a subject to report in any order as many words as he can. Responding can be a source of interference for items not yet recalled. When lists were 4 to 7 words in length, no age effect was seen from ages 20–69; only for lists of 9, 11, and 13 words did age differences emerge. In another variation, 4 to 7 words were presented and all but 1 were presented again. The subject was instructed to report the unrepeated word. This procedure imposes no response interference, but it does require search and matching of items in storage. Age differences were small under this condition. The third condition was like the second except that the subject was instructed to respond with all the repeated words and to save the unrepeated word until the end. Only under this condition were systematic age declines found from the 20s to the 60s. These data suggest that age deficits in immediate memory do not result from response interference alone or from search and matching stores with incoming items alone, but they do result from both sets of operations together.

It should be noted that for lists longer than seven words, recall decreased with increasing age. When the memory span is exceeded, more than response interference may be operating. It is possible that memory traces decay more rapidly for the old than they do for the young. (If so, it may be the only process that speeds up with age.) It is also possible that when the memory span is exceeded, additional input is interfering and more so for the old than for the young. For these reasons, the likelihood of material entering long-term storage would decrease with age when the memory span is exceeded.

Age and list length were included as variables in several studies (Craik, 1968) designed to investigate the effects of exceeding memory span. In one study, it was shown that the young recalled more words from 30-word than from 10-word lists (varying from unrelated words to meaningful text), but that the older subjects recalled about the same number of words at both list lengths. When lists of four to nine digits were used to test directly the age relation with list length, no interaction was found for either auditory or visual presentations. The fact that results for digit lists and the earlier word lists differed suggested to Craik that retrieval may be the source of some age deficits in memory. He reasoned that if all the material is in storage but items in a list form a small class, such as digits, little search is required. Even if search facility declines with age, performance effects would be small in such a task. When the class from which items are drawn is large, however, as with unrelated words, search deficits should be operative and large age differences should occur.

Craik (1968) explored his retrieval hypothesis in a study in which four classes of words were included: digits, county names, animals, and unrelated words. The interaction hypothesized between age and list length was found for all four classes of words; that is, age differences in recall increased with increasing list length. Although the increases in age differences were not statistically different, they were largest for animal names and unrelated words, the two largest classes in the study. That is consistent with the idea that age deficits in retrieval increase as the scope of search increases.

Craik (1968) then applied general ideas from two-storage memory models (see Atkinson & Shiffrin, 1968; Glanzer, 1968; Waugh & Norman, 1965) to his hypothesis of retrieval deficit with age. In typical two-storage models, items enter a primary storage where they are subject to rapid decay and interference. Some items also enter secondary storage, usually in coded form, where decay and interference from incoming items have little if any effect. Primary storage is quite limited. A telephone number approximately fills it (but for some of us, the fit is quite snug). Such a number can be recalled verbally or dialed, but without rehearsal, it is lost. (Note that frequently one must look up a strange number again when the line is busy.) Craik proposed that primary memory is little affected by age; it is in secondary storage that age deficits are found in both search and retrieval.

Age differences among lists of varying length support Craik's (1968) thesis. Subspan lists are recalled predominantly from primary storage and show little age differences. For longer lists, some items are retrieved from secondary storage, and that is where the age differences become prominent due to failure to enter secondary storage and to less effective search.

Craik (1968) further analyzed his data for the four classes of items in an attempt to estimate measures of primary and secondary memory. For the most part, here, too, the results fit the model. Age differences were not found for estimates of primary memory (except for unrelated words), whereas all the estimates of secondary memory were higher for the young than for the old. In addition, estimates of primary memory were similar across class of items, but secondary memory estimates decreased with size of class (from digits, to county names, to animal names, to unrelated words) for both age groups.

Other findings and interpretations will now be reviewed with the two-storage model in mind. When we look at Welford's (1958) suggestion that items arriving in close temporal contiguity should be particularly difficult for the old to remember, the two-storage model would predict no age effect so long as the capacity of the primary storage is not exceeded. Age deficits should only occur for fast inputs when primary storage is overloaded and excess items must enter secondary storage or be lost. Registration would be diminished with insufficient time to encode items into secondary storage.

Positive evidence for registration deficits with age was reported by Canestrari (1968). He displayed 10 paired-associate items for one second but varied the time (0, .5, or 5 seconds) between items. After five study trials without responding, one unpaced test trial was given. There was an interaction between age and presentation rate in which the oldest (the 60s) of four age groups showed the largest beneficial effect of increased time between items.

Some other points relevant to input difficulties are that (a) the old experience difficulty in developing associations between pairs of words (Riegel, 1965), and that (b) frequency of spontaneously developed mediators in paired-associate learning is low for the old (Hulicka & Grossman, 1967). These difficulties would impair encoding into secondary storage. Canestrari (1968) and Hulicka and Grossman (1967) showed that when mediators were provided performance in paired-associate learning improved, particularly for the old groups.

Craik (1968) and particularly Rabbitt (1968) investigated the effects of structure of the material on the memory of the old and the young. They reported that increasing structure facilitates retention more for the young than for the old. Encoding is an operation involved in entrance into secondary storage; decoding operates in retrieval from secondary storage. Structure should facilitate encoding and decoding. The fact that the old do not benefit as much as the young from structure suggests that they either fail to recognize cues provided by structure or fail to use them in encoding into and/or decoding from secondary storage.

Rabbitt and Clancy (1969) recently summarized evidence from several studies in which they explored age effects in registration, storage, and retrieval by manipulating codability of material. They concluded that the old are sometimes less sensitive to structure than the young, but not always. The age effect seems to vary to some extent with the memory processes involved in the task (registration, storage, and retrieval).

Earlier in this chapter some evidence was cited that was consistent with an age deficit in registration. There are other findings that do not fit such a deficit.

Dichotic listening is a memory procedure which has been widely used in age studies. In that procedure, two digits (or words) are presented simultaneously, one to each ear. According to Broadbent (1954) and many other experimenters in dichotic listening, when two or more pairs of digits are presented at a fast rate, order of response is by ear rather than by pairs as presented; that is, all digits to one ear are reported before any digits to the other ear. Of particular relevance to the question about whether or not registration is impaired with age is the fact that for the half-span reported first, age differences in recall have been small or nil, whereas age differences have consistently been demonstrated for the half-span reported second. In free recall, such results could occur due to (a) differential attention to the half-messages, possibly due to cerebral laterality differences, (b) acuity differences, (c) the likelihood that the better-stored half-span would be reported first, (d) increased decay of the second half-span from additional time in storage, or (e) interference from responding with the first half-span. The procedure has been modified to explore some of those possibilities. When the half-span to be recalled first is designated only after presentation, it is recalled more accurately than the second half-span, just as in free recall. That result was reported for old as well as for young subjects (Inglis, Sykes, & Ankus, 1968). Such a finding is not consistent with registration deficits in the aged. In order for the half-span designated first to be recalled correctly, the entire message must be available to the subject when recall begins because he does not know which half-span will be asked for first. Complete and accurate registration is required in order for the entire message to be available at the beginning of recall.

Similar results have been reported by Taub (1968a; Taub & Greiff, 1967) for visually presented sequences of letters. Half the letters were coded in one color and the other half in a different color to provide a "handle" for designating which half-messages to recall first. For various presentation conditions, the half-message designated first was recalled better by both the young and the old, and age differences were found only for the second half-message.

Other evidence that does not support an age deficit in registration comes from a recent paired-associate study by Monge and Hultsch (1971). They found that age interacted with the anticipation interval (time to respond) but did not interact with the inspection interval (study time). If the old suffer from registration difficulties, any additional time that reduces the rate of items should benefit the old more than the young; however, in their study, young and old benefited equivalently from an increase in time to view the stimulus and response words together.

There has been a long-standing belief that storage deficits occur with age. Fraser (1958) presented eight-digit items at two rates (40 per minute and 120 per minute) to a young and a middle-aged group and found that the slow rate had a deleterious effect on recall of the older subjects. (It should be noted that the digits were presented auditorily; unlike visual presentation, a decreased rate does not improve recall for auditory presentation of digits.) Fraser interpreted his data to mean that memory decays as auditory input rate increases, and the old are more susceptible to decay than the young.

In two-storage models, it is primary storage that is susceptible to decay. Craik (1968) argued from his list-length data that primary storage did not decline with age, and Taub's (1968b) free-recall data support Craik.

The early age findings from dichotic listening studies were also interpreted as storage deficits (Inglis & Caird, 1963; Mackay & Inglis, 1963). Inglis and his colleagues argued then that while the first half-span was recalled, the half-span yet to be reported was in storage and subject to decay. More recently, they have added an interference component to the decay argument. It was mentioned earlier that even when the half-span to be recalled first was determined by the experimenter and not known to the subject until after presentation, recall of the first half-span was accurate, and no age difference was found. The subjects could not anticipate which half-span would be called for first; therefore, the Broadbent (1954) model (with direct output of one half-span while the other is in temporary· storage) does not fit this situation. Both half-spans must be stored. In a more recent interpretation of his dichotic findings, Inglis (1965) stated that the first half-span is in storage a short time and is not subject to response interference; whereas the second half-span is in storage longer (more subject to decay) and is also interfered with by recall of the first half-span.

The dichotic data are similar to Talland's (1965) digit-span findings. In that study, no age difference was found for free recall of subspan lists or for recall of the one unrepeated digit; only when the unrepeated digit had to be stored while the repeated digits were recalled did an age difference emerge. In the dichotic procedure in which the half-span recalled first is designated after presentation, the task is to recall one part of the material (response interference) while storing the other part. One difference in these two sets of findings should be noted. In Talland's span data, both immediate recall of the repeated digits and deferred recall of the unrepeated digit were impaired with age; in the dichotic procedure, age differences were seldom found for the half-span recalled first, even when it was designated first after presentation. It is likely that determining which digits were repeated (in the Talland procedure) imposes greater search demands than determining which digits were presented to a particular ear (in the dichotic procedures).

A similar situation is seen for visual presentation. In the studies by Taub (1968a) and Taub and Greiff (1967), a list of letters was divided into two half-messages by assigning one of two colors to each letter. Letters of one color were called for before the letters of the other color. Age differences were found only in recall of the second half-messages. The color tag in these studies, like the ear tag in the dichotic studies, apparently required minimal search; age differences in recall of the first half-message were small or nil in either situation.

A study by Anders, Fozard, and Lillyquist (1972) also provided evidence for an age deficit in retrieval from primary storage. Lists of one, three, five, and seven digits were presented and followed by a test digit. The task was to press a "yes" or "no" key as quickly as possible. Yes and no response times were the same; this was interpreted to mean that the entire list is searched under both conditions. Times increased linearly with increasing list length for all age groups, but more steeply for the middle-aged, and even more for the old. Anders et al. interpreted the extremely low error rates to mean that all items were registered and stored accurately. Their data indicate that when the scope of search increases, more time is required, and the relative increase with age is a retrieval deficit.

Evidence of deficits in primary memory in the aged seems to be accumulating in one direction, that is, from a pure decay interpretation toward an interpretation in which responding interferes with recall of material yet to be searched and retrieved.

Other studies also provide substantial support for age deficits in retrieval from secondary storage. Schonfield and Robertson (1966) presented a list of 24 words in a free-recall task and found a monotonic decrease in recall across five age groups from the 20s to the 60s. When the task was changed to recognition of each list word among four distractors, not only did all age groups improve, but no age effect was found. In the recognition task, mean scores for the five age groups were nearly the same. Despite the additional time in storage imposed by the multiple-choice recognition procedure, storage deficits due to decay were not found. The essential difference between recall and recognition is the extent of the search. The fact that no age effect was found in recognition is therefore substantial evidence for a retrieval deficit with age which shows up in free recall.

Another free-recall study that supports the hypothesis of a retrieval deficit with age was reported by Laurence (1967). Two kinds of lists were used. One consisted of 12 nouns of the same category, for example, animal names; the other consisted of 12 unrelated nouns. She reported that the age difference in recall was greater for the unrelated nouns than for the related nouns. These results are consistent with Craik's (1968) findings mentioned previously. In both studies, age differences were largest for unrelated words. Again, when the scope of the search is increased, age differencs in recall increase—more evidence for the argument of a retrieval deficit with aging.

The trend in recent gerontological findings is to deemphasize registration and pure decay deficits and to emphasize storage deficits resulting from response interference and retrieval deficits. The evidence for age deficits in search and retrieval are consistent with a two-store model, but are equally consistent with an alternative model of one store and two retrieval systems (see Tulving, 1966).

PROBLEM SOLVING

When Jones (1959) reviewed the gerontological literature on intelligence and problem solving, not one experimental study of problem solving was included. This is particularly surprising in view of the widely held idea that despite the many deficits in microbehaviors typically studied in the laboratory, the behaviors that really count, such as thinking and reasoning, do not reflect such deficits, at least not until very late in life. A few studies of problem solving were cited by Welford (1958), but most of the experimental work in this area was published after 1960.

This is not to say that there is much to report now; the literature is still sparse. Few investigators have ventured into the area of problem solving, perhaps because of the difficulties in measuring performance. But a beginning has been made, and because problem solving is an important aspect of gerontology and has been reviewed infrequently, a disproportionate segment of this chapter is devoted to the experimental studies in this area.

In many of the early aging studies, performance on sorting tests was compared for two or more age groups, and the older subjects were found to be poorer sorters both quantitatively and qualitatively. (These studies will not be reviewed here, but for a recent and excellent study of sorting behavior see Bromley, 1967). Other measures of reasoning have also shown age differences in scores on tests of logical inference, generalization, and similar reasoning behavior measured psychometrically (see Friend & Zubin, 1958).

The few problem-solving experiments cited in Welford (1958) all showed age deficits in performance. In one of the early published experiments, Clay (1954) compared two age groups on tasks involving boards of three, four, five, and six squares per side. Marginal totals were given for each board, and the task was to fill the squares with markers of the values one, two, three, and four so that the rows and columns summed to the marginal totals specified. As the size of the board increased and the information to be dealt with increased exponentially, age differences increased substantially.

Jerome (1962) described an age study with a set of problems designed to investigate solution behaviors as well as the number of problems solved and the times to solution. (The problems were too involved to describe fully here.) The goal light was in the center of a circle of nine peripheral lights. Each peripheral light had a switch to turn it on. For each problem, a disk indicated which pairs of lights were directly related. Three logical relationships were possible between related pairs of lights. The direction of each relationship was indicated, but the specific relationship was not. A solution required lighting the goal light by a sequence of inputs in which only a subset of three switches could be pressed. Prior to the solution sequence, any switches could be pressed to investigate the relationships between lights.

A small group of subjects over the age of 60 experienced great difficulty in reaching solutions to these problems despite the fact that an effective solution strategy was presented and emphasized in every session. Not only did the older problem solvers reach fewer solutions when compared with a younger group, but their solution behaviors showed many more inputs (inquiries), particularly redundant (noninformative) inquiries. Despite the fact that the solution strategy provided by the experimenter emphasized identifying a subgoal condition (which in turn resulted in the goal light), the older group experienced great difficulty in applying the strategy. They seldom identified the subgoal condition early, and their search was unsystematic. Furthermore, after making many inquiries, they seemed unable to determine which pieces of information were relevant to the solution.

A later study by Young (1966), using problems of the same type, further investigated two points in Jerome's (1962) study. Although all of Jerome's subjects were encouraged to make notes and to use them to minimize memory demands of the task, the young seemed to benefit from their notes but the old did not. Young provided special training procedures involving the backward solution strategy and systematic note-taking techniques designed to decrease memory demands. Four levels of difficulty were included with three problems at each level. Whenever a subject failed to solve a problem, the solution strategy was applied in a session designed to demonstrate how the strategy could be used to solve that problem. All 10 young subjects were able to solve the third problem at the first three levels of difficulty, and 9 solved the last problem at the most difficult level. Only 4, 6, 6, and 3 of the 10 older subjects reached solutions for the four levels of difficulty, respectively. These results were quite similar to those of Jerome (1962). Despite the special training procedures and techniques for recording information, the old required many more inquiries even when they reached solutions, and their additional inquiries were mostly redundant. Although the old learned to identify the subgoal condition under instruction, they were unable to trace the chain back for each subgoal light; that is, they were unable to apply the solution strategy.

Unlike the results of the problem-solving studies cited thus far, in which age differences have been found consistently, studies of concept attainment have not all shown age differences. For example, Wetherick (1964), who has conducted several such studies, obtained mixed results in three problems for the same three groups of subjects. Four switches, each of which could be placed in three different positions, could be manipulated freely by the subject. The task was to determine the relevant switch positions required to allow a lamp to light when tested. One switch was relevant in the first problem, and two were relevant in the second. In the third problem, however, up to three switches could have been relevant, and the subjects were required to figure out how many as well as which switch positions made up the solution. All the subjects solved the first problem correctly, and age differences in effectiveness of their tests (inquiries) were negligible. In the second problem, the old not only solved the fewest problems correctly, but they made many more noninformative inquiries than the middle-aged and the young groups. Surprisingly, on the most difficult problem, the old reached as many correct solutions as the middle-aged and the young, and they made fewer noninformative inquiries. The reasons for this unexpected finding are not at all apparent, but it should be noted that subjects were matched on nonverbal intelligence (Raven's Progressive Matrices). Such matching has the general effect of selecting the better problem solvers from the pool of potential older subjects.

Wiersma and Klausmeier (1965) reported an age study of concept attainment. They also allowed the subjects to make "inquiries" to obtain information in order to identify correct solutions. Their primary performance measure was the time to identify a correct solution. Four problems (consisting of conjunctive concepts with two relevant dimensions) were solved more slowly by the oldest group (35–51) than by two younger groups. Also, the mean number of incorrect identifications prior to solution increased from the youngest to the oldest group, but the difference was not statistically significant. (Perhaps a directional statistical test of the age hypothesis would have yielded different results for incorrect identifications.) The longer times required by the oldest group to identify each concept could have resulted from an increase in time per inquiry, from an increase in number of inquiries, or from both. Unfortunately, the data reported provide no information about possible sources of the age differences in solution time.

It is rather interesting that selection procedures were used in two of the earliest age studies of concept attainment. In a selection paradigm, the subjects are permitted to select examples, and the experimenter then designates which ones are positive and which ones are negative examples of the concept. This general procedure has the advantage of eliciting selection behaviors to compare strategies and to evaluate effectiveness in obtaining information. A disadvantage of selection procedures is the possibility of fortuitous gains in information. Wetherick (1964) minimized that disadvantage by providing a positive example at the beginning of each problem. No information about initial examples was reported by Wiersma and Klausmeier (1965).

When the examples in a concept-attainment experiment are determined by the experimenter, he controls the amount of information available to the subject throughout a problem. Arenberg (1968) used such a reception procedure in five simple (one-attribute) problems to investigate whether certain types of information would elicit errors and whether such errors would be related to age. Concepts were "poisoned foods," and the task was not only to identify the poisoned food (solution) but to list all the viable solutions after each example (meal). In this way, the example that resulted in an error could be specified. Each type of problem was solved twice, and a smaller proportion of the old men than the young men solved both problems correctly for each type. Errors resulting from covertly redundant examples were clearly age related. Of the 21 old subjects, 9 committed at least one error immediately after a positive, redundant example; but none of the 21 young subjects committed such an error. A redundant example provides no information not already available from previous examples, but almost half of the old subjects performed as if they had new information. Surprisingly, in view of Wetherick's (1966) findings described below, no age difference was found for errors resulting from negative examples preceded by positive examples.

Wetherick (1966) described three studies of concept attainment in which each problem consisted of two to four groups of letters presented simultaneously. In some problems, the solution was a single letter; in others, it was a pair of letters together (conjunctive concept). Some problems consisted entirely of positive examples; others were mixed positive and negative.

In the first study, the positive examples were designated "Cat. I," and negative examples were designated "Cat. II." Three age groups with 10 men in each were matched for nonverbal intelligence. In all, 24 probems were presented to each subject. The results showed virtually no age differences in total problems solved correctly, but one type of error was prevalent in the oldest group—an error characterized by a failure to distinguish mixed (positive and negative) examples from all positive examples.

In the second study, five age groups of 10 men were matched for nonverbal intelligence. Each age group was further divided so that for half of the men the designations (Cat. I and Cat. II) of the first study were used, and for the other half the designations were "In" and "Not in." The results of the first study were replicated when the same designations were used. Virtually no age differences were found for number of correctly solved problems, but the oldest group committed many more errors of the type in which positive and negative examples were treated as though they were all positive. Such errors, however, were rare when the designations were In and Not in. Although subjects were not required to remember the examples and their designations (they were all in view simultaneously), it was necessary to remember that Cat. I was the positive designation and that Cat. II was the negative one. When that memory requirement was removed by using In and Not in as designations, errors in which positive and negative examples were both processed as positive were virtually eliminated.

In the third study, age groups were not matched. The number of correct solutions declined somewhat across three age groups, but no statistical comparison was reported. Errors in which mixed positive and negative examples were all treated as positive were again most frequent in the oldest group.

Wetherick's (1966) discussion of the prevalence of that type of error by the old was most intriguing and the argument was developed further in a later reference to those data (Wetherick, 1969). He proposed that such mishandling of information could lead to prejudice and rigidity—behaviors often attributed to the old. Negative evidence should be disconfirming, but when it is interpreted as positive, a belief or hypothesis is reinforced rather than disconfirmed. Furthermore, failure or inability to profit from disconfirming evidence could result in continuing behavior that is no longer appropriate. Such behavior is defined as rigidity. According to Wetherick's argument, failure to solve problems by the old is not attributable to the fact that the old are rigid and hold on to beliefs without evidence, but rather, it is the other way around. Due to an inability to handle disconfirming information, some old people cannot modify previous beliefs and continue to behave as if the negative evidence does not exist. Functionally, it does not.

In general, the findings from the studies of problem solving demonstrated age differences just as were found in many of the studies of verbal learning and memory. Studies that provided opportunities for the subjects to elicit information showed that the aged make more inquiries, especially noninformative inquiries. In addition, the old make less effective use of the information that they have requested or that has been presented by the experimenter. Both analysis (obtaining information) and synthesis (processing information to arrive at a solution) seem to be impaired with age.

RESPONSE TIME

Reaction-time experiments have not been reviewed here (see Thompson and Marsh's review—pp. 112–148 in this volume—of the relation of timed behavior to physiological measures). Response time has special relevance to the content of this chapter, and consequently some conclusions about response speed are presented here. In a discussion of information transmission and age, Rabbitt (1968) explored an intriguing analogy between senescent humans and obsolescent computers. His major thesis was that recognition and use of structure in transmitted information declines with age. He concluded that the old benefit little from a foresignal on a reaction time task. They seem unable to ignore the foresignal information when it is appropriate to do so. The old check their expectancies, are more slowed than the young when their expectancies are false, and process redundant information that results in slowing.

In conclusion, let us pass Rabbitt's provocative ideas on to you. He suggested that, like early computers, older humans are slow for each operation, they are less efficient (require more operations) than newer models, and they suffer from reduced information-handling capacity in dealing with multiple tasks.

REFERENCES

Anders, T. R., Fozard, J. L., & Lillyquist, T. D. The effects of age upon retrieval from short-term memory. *Developmental Psychology*, 1972, **6**, 214–217.

Arenberg, D. Anticipation interval and age differences in verbal learning. *Journal of Abnormal Psychology*, 1965, **70**, 419–425.

Arenberg, D. Age differences in retroaction. *Journal of Gerontology*, 1967, **22**, 88–91.

Arenberg, D. Concept problem solving in young and old adults. *Journal of Gerontology*, 1968, **23**, 279–282.

Atkinson, R. C., & Shiffrin, R. M. Human memory: A proposed system and its control processes. In K. W. Spence & J. T. Spence (Eds.), *Advances in the psychology of learning and motivation research and theory.* Vol. 2. New York: Academic Press, 1968.

Birren, J. E. (Ed.), *Handbook of aging and the individual.* Chicago: University of Chicago Press, 1959.

Botwinick, J. *Cognitive processes in maturity and old age.* New York: Springer, 1967.

Broadbent, D. E. The role of auditory localization in attention and memory span. *Journal of Experimental Psychology,* 1954, **47,** 191–196.

Bromley, D. B. Age and sex differences in the serial production of creative conceptual responses. *Journal of Gerontology,* 1967, **22,** 32–42.

Canestrari, R. E., Jr. Paced and self-paced learning in young and elderly adults. *Journal of Gerontology,* 1963, **18,** 165–168.

Canestrari, R. E., Jr. The effects of commonality on paired-associate learning in two age groups, *Journal of Genetic Psychology,* 1966, **108,** 3–7.

Canestrari, R. E., Jr. Age changes in acquisition. In G. A. Talland (Ed.), *Human aging and behavior.* New York: Academic Press, 1968.

Clay, H. M. Changes in performance with age in similar tasks of varying complexity. *British Journal of Psychology,* 1954, **45,** 7–13.

Craik, F. I. M. Short-term memory and the aging process. In G. A. Talland (Ed.), *Human aging and behavior.* New York: Academic Press, 1968.

Eisdorfer, C. Verbal learning and response time in the aged. *Journal of Genetic Psychology,* 1965, **107,** 15–22.

Eisdorfer, C. Arousal and performance: Experiments in verbal learning and a tentative theory. In G. A. Talland (Ed.), *Human aging and behavior.* New York: Academic Press, 1968.

Eisdorfer, C., Axelrod, S., & Wilkie, F. Stimulus exposure time as a factor in serial learning in an aged sample. *Journal of Abnormal and Social Psychology,* 1963, **67,** 594–600.

Eisdorfer, C., Nowlin, J., & Wilkie, F. Improvement of learning in the aged by modification of autonomic nervous system activity. *Science,* 1970, **170,** 1327–1329.

Fraser, D. C. Decay of immediate memory with age. *Nature,* 1958, **182,** 1163.

Friend, C. M., & Zubek, J. P. The effects of age on critical thinking ability. *Journal of Gerontology,* 1958, **13,** 407–413.

Gladis, M., & Braun, H. Age differences in transfer and retroaction as a function of intertask response similarity. *Journal of Experimental Psychology,* 1958, **55,** 25–30.

Glanzer, M. Storage mechanisms in free recall. *Transactions of the New York Academy of Sciences* (Series II), 1968, **30,** 1120–1129.

Hulicka, I. M. Age differences for intentional and incidental learning and recall scores. *Journal of the American Geriatrics Society,* 1965, **13,** 639–649.

Hulicka, I. M. Age differences in retention as a function of interference. *Journal of Gerontology,* 1967, **22,** 180–184.

Hulicka, I. M., & Grossman, J. L. Age group comparisons for the use of mediators in paired-associate learning. *Journal of Gerontology,* 1967, **22,** 46–51.

Hulicka, I. M., & Rust, L. D. Age-related retention deficit as a function of learning. *Journal of the American Geriatrics Society,* 1964, **12,** 1061–1065.

Hulicka, I. M., Sterns, H., & Grossman, J. Age-group comparisons of paired-associate learning as a function of paced and self-paced association and response time. *Journal of Gerontology,* 1967, **22,** 274–280.

Hulicka, I. M., & Weiss, R. L. Age differences in retention as a function of learning. *Journal of Consulting Psychology,* 1965, **29,** 125–129.

Inglis, J. Immediate memory, age and brain function. In A. T. Welford & J. E. Birren (Eds.), *Behavior, aging and the nervous system.* Springfield, Ill.: Charles C Thomas, 1965.

Inglis, J., & Caird, W. K. Age differences in successive responses to simultaneous stimulation. *Canadian Journal of Psychology,* 1963, **17,** 98–105.

Inglis, J., Sykes, D. H., & Ankus, M. N. Age differences in short-term memory. In S. Chown & K. F. Riegel (Eds.), *Interdisciplinary topics in gerontology.* Vol. 1. New York: Karger, 1968.

Jerome, E. A. Age and learning—Experimental studies. In J. E. Birren (Ed.), *Handbook of aging and the individual.* Chicago: University of Chicago Press, 1959.

Jerome, E. A. Decay of heuristic processes in the aged. In C. Tibbitts & W. Donahue (Eds.), *Social and psychological aspects of aging.* New York: Columbia University Press, 1962.

Jones, H. E. Intelligence and problem-solving. In J. E. Birren (Ed.), *Handbook of aging and the individual.* Chicago: University of Chicago Press, 1959.

Kausler, D. H., & Lair, C. V. Associative strength and paired-associate learning in elderly subjects. *Journal of Gerontology,* 1966, **21,** 278–280.

Kay, H. Theories of learning and aging. In J. E. Birren (Ed.), *Handbook of aging and the individual.* Chicago: University of Chicago Press, 1959.

Kay, H. Learning and aging. In K. W. Schaie (Ed.), *Theory and methods of research on aging.* Morgantown: West Virginia University Press, 1968.

Lair, C., Moon, W., & Kausler, D. Associative interference in the paired-associate learning of middle-aged and old subjects. *Developmental Psychology,* 1969, **1,** 548–552.

Laurence, M. W. A developmental look at the usefulness of list categorization as an aid to free recall. *Canadian Journal of Psychology,* 1967, **21,** 153–165.

Mackay, H. A., & Inglis, J. The effect of age on a short-term auditory storage process. *Gerontologia,* 1963, **8,** 193–200.

Monge, R., & Hultsch, D. Paired-associate learning as a function of adult age and the length of the anticipation and inspection intervals. *Journal of Gerontology,* 1971, **26,** 157–162.

Rabbitt, P. Age and the use of structure in transmitted information. In G. A. Talland (Ed.), *Human aging and behavior.* New York: Academic Press, 1968.

Rabbitt, P., & Clancy, M. Differential operation of coding processes on memory input, storage and retrieval in old and young. *Proceedings of the 8th International Congress of Gerontology,* 1969, **1,** 451–454. (Summary)

Riegel, K. F. Speed of verbal performance as a function of age and set: A review of issues and data. In A. T. Welford & J. E. Birren (Eds.), *Behavior, aging and the nervous system.* Springfield, Ill.: Charles C Thomas, 1965.

Schonfield, D., & Robertson, B. A. Memory storage and aging. *Canadian Journal of Psychology*, 1966, **20**, 228–236.

Talland, G. A. Three estimates of the word span and their stability over the adult years. *Quarterly Journal of Experimental Psychology*, 1965, **17**, 301–307.

Taub, H. A. Paired associates learning as a function of age, rate, and instructions. *Journal of Genetic Psychology*, 1967, **111**, 41–46.

Taub, H. A. Age differences in memory as a function of rate of presentation, order of report, and stimulus organization. *Journal of Gerontology*, 1968, **23**, 159–164. (a)

Taub, H. A. Aging and free recall. *Journal of Gerontology*, 1968, **23**, 466–468. (b)

Taub, H. A., & Greiff, S. Effects of age on organization and recall of two sets of stimuli. *Psychonomic Science*, 1967, **7**, 53–54.

Traxler, A. J., & Britton, J. H. Age differences in retroaction as a function of anticipation interval and transfer paradigm. *Proceedings of the 78th Annual Convention of the American Psychological Association*, 1970, **5**, 683-684. (Summary)

Tulving, E. Short and long term memory: Different retrieval mechanisms. Paper presented at the meeting of the 18th International Congress of Psychology, Moscow, August 1966.

Waugh, N. C., & Norman, D. A. Primary memory. *Psychological Review*, 1965, **72**, 89–104.

Welford, A. T. *Ageing and human skill*. London: Oxford University Press, 1958.

Wetherick, N. E. A comparison of the problem-solving ability of young, middle-aged and old subjects. *Gerontologia*, 1964, **9**, 164–178.

Wetherick, N. E. The inferential basis of concept attainment. *British Journal of Psychology*, 1966, **57**, 61–69.

Wetherick, N. E. The psychology of aging. *Occupational Therapy*, 1969, **32**, 15–17.

Wiersma, W., & Klausmeier, H. J. The effect of age upon speed of concept attainment. *Journal of Gerontology*, 1965, **20**, 398–400.

Wimer, R. E. Age differences in incidental and intentional learning. *Journal of Gerontology*, 1960, **15**, 79–81.

Wimer, R. E., & Wigdor, B. T. Age difference in retention of learning. *Journal of Gerontology*, 1958, **13**, 291–295.

Young, M. L. Problem-solving performance in two age groups. *Journal of Gerontology*, 1966, **21**, 505–509.

Zaretsky, H., & Halberstam, J. Age differences in paired-associate learning. *Journal of Gerontology*, 1968, **23**, 165–168. (a)

Zaretsky, H., & Halberstam, J. Effects of aging, brain-damage, and associative strength on paired-associate learning and relearning. *Journal of Genetic Psychology*, 1968, **112**, 149–163. (b)

Age and Animal Behavior

LEONARD F. JAKUBCZAK

My original task was to review the recent literature in the field of comparative psychology of aging. A preliminary search indicated that such a field does not exist. Almost all of the studies reviewed used the white rat as the subject, and no study made a direct comparison across species on behavioral tasks. Consequently, my task became one of reviewing the recent literature in the broader field of animal psychology of aging.

There are several reasons for using animal subjects in studies of behavioral aging, as Jerome (1959) pointed out. First, a great deal is known about age-related changes in the anatomy and the physiology of animal subjects. If one wants to test the behavioral implications of these changes, then one should use similar organisms. Second, certain experimental procedures may be carried out with animals that could not be carried out on man because of their danger or discomfort. Third, because of the relatively short life-span of animals and because of the possibility of genetic and experiential control and manipulation over the entire life-span, research with animals should make an important contribution to the understanding of the genetic, physiological, and experiential determinants of age-related changes in behavior. Fourth, if behavioral deterioration with age is a universal phenomenon, it should be found in a broad range of species. And fifth, it is easier to control motivation in animals than in humans. The working assumption in this area is that the basic mechanisms of behavioral aging are similar enough in man and

Leonard F. Jakubczak received his PhD in experimental psychology (gerontology) from Washington University, St. Louis, Missouri, in 1962. He is currently Research Psychologist and Coordinator of Research and Training in Psychology at the Veterans Administration Hospital, St. Louis, Missouri, as well as Research Associate in Gerontology, Washington University, St. Louis, Missouri. His major research interests center on age-related changes in motivation and their underlying physiological bases.

other mammals so that research on the latter will often generalize to man.

The last review of this area was made by Jerome (1959). The period covered by the present review is from 1960 to April 1971. To be included in this review, a study had to use animals as subjects and had to include *at least* two age groups: one representing early maturity and the other representing middle to late maturity. In rats and mice, for example, at least one group had to be younger than 7 months and another group had to be older than 12 months. A 24-month-old rat or mouse is considered senescent.

TABLE 1

Distribution of Animal Studies among Categories Based upon Types of Independent and Dependent Variables

Variables in addition to age	General behavior	Consummatory behavior	Instrumental behavior				Total
			Thorndikian		Avoidance		
			Unitary	Choice	Unitary	Choice	
None	4	5	7	6			22
Conditions of drive	6	2	2	2			12
Sex	3		4	4	3		14
Drugs	1	1	1		2	3	8
Radiation	2	1	1	3			7
Previous treatment	2		3				5
Task difficulty						4	4
Social grouping	1	1	2				4
Time factor				2		1	3
Stimulus intensity		2	1				3
Total	19	12	21	17	5	8	82

Table 1 provides an overview of the distribution of the animal studies among categories based upon types of independent and dependent variables. The studies were first grouped by three classes of behavior: (a) *general* (exploratory, running wheel, etc.), (b) *consummatory* (eating and drinking), and (c) *instrumental* (Thorndikian, avoidance). The instrumental behavior was categorized according to the scheme of Bitterman (1962, 1966). The essential factor in a Thorndikian situation is a contingency of some specific event on some measurable bit of behavior—a contingency arranged by an investigator who is interested in studying its effects on the animal. The essential feature of an avoidance task is that a sequence of two stimuli is scheduled, with the occurrence of the second stimulus contingent on the failure of the animal to make some specific response to the first. The studies were then grouped in terms of categories of independent variables other than age. The distribution of articles among the columns indicates the frequency with which different classes of behavior were studied in an aging context. Similarly, the distribution of studies among the rows indicates the frequency with which variables other than age were used in such context. Finally, the distribution of the articles among the "cells" of the table indicates the types of hypotheses relating age, other variables, and classes of behavior studied. As can be seen in Table 1, (a) the modal study did not use an independent variable other than age; (b) sex, conditions of drive, and drugs were the most frequently used "other" variables; (c) the most frequent task was Thorndikian in nature; and (d) the modal hypothesis was that performance on some unitary Thorndikian task is related to age. As can also be seen from Table 1, there are gaps in our knowledge of animal behavior as a function of age.

GENERAL ACTIVITY

The amounts of various types of activity decreased with increasing age beyond sexual maturity. There were age-related decrements in exploratory activity (Goodrick, 1966, 1967a), wheel-running activity (Jakubczak, 1967a, 1969a, 1970a), the number of active hours and the hourly rate of wheel-running activity (Jakubczak, 1969a), the frequency and duration of bursts of wheel-running activity (Jakubczak, 1971), home-cage activity (Hodge, Peacock, & Hoff, 1967; Jakubczak, 1961), locomotor activity both in rats (Furchtgott, Wechkin, & Dees, 1961; Goodrick, 1966; Werboff & Havlena, 1962) and in monkeys (Boer & Davis, 1968; Davis, 1962; Draper, 1966; Manocha, 1968), and web-spinning activity in spiders (Eberhard, 1971). In general, the greatest age differences were between growing and nongrowing animals. Taken together, these findings suggest that, like slowness of response, age-related decrements in amount of activity may be a universal characteristic of aging in animals.

Age affects the relationship between activity and various other factors, such as food deprivation, drugs, previous experience, etc. There were age-related decrements beyond sexual maturity in the effects of food deprivation on the amount of wheel running (Desroches, Kimbrell, & Allison, 1964; Jakubczak, 1967a), the number of active hours and the hourly rate of wheel running (Jakubczak, 1969a), the frequency and duration of bursts of wheel running (Jakubczak, 1971), and the amount of home-cage activity (Hodge et al., 1967). There were also age-related decrements in the effects of water deprivation on the wheel-running activity of rats (Jakubczak, 1970a). The results of these studies suggest that with increasing age beyond sexual maturity, the mechanisms that mediate behavioral arousal become less responsive to the changes in the internal milieu resulting from food and water deprivation.

Age also affects the relationship between activity and the effects of certain drugs. The effects of central nervous system (CNS) stimulating drugs on activity decrease with increasing age, while those of CNS-inhibiting drugs increase with increasing age. Amphetamine and Ritalin (methylphenidate) increased locomotor activity, as measured by photobeam interruptions, to a greater degree in young rats than in old rats (Farner, 1960, 1961b). Conversely, CNS-depressing drugs, such as hexobarbital and adrenergic blocking agents such as Regitin (phentolamine), decreased this form of activity to a lesser degree in young rats than in old rats. Farner (1960, 1961b), concluded that the excitability of the CNS decreases with age. However, these results might indicate that the CNS becomes hyperaroused with increasing age (cf. Eisdorfer, Nowlin, & Wilkie, 1970).

The relationship between previous social group and exploration is affected by age. For rats paired during testing, isolation reduced the exploration of young rats and increased the exploration of old rats in comparison with the scores of group-caged controls of the same age (Goodrick, 1965b). Goodrick suggested that these differences may have been due to age-related changes in dominance–subordination behavior.

Age does not affect the relationship between activity and certain other factors. Although the sex of the animal influences the level of activity, the effect is unrelated to age. Female rats explored and locomoted more than male rats, but these differences were invariant across age groups (Furchtgott et al., 1961; Goodrick, 1971; Werboff & Havlena, 1962). Similarly, X-irradiation did not augment the age-related decrease in activity in monkeys (Boer & Davis, 1968; Davis, 1962). Finally, previous wheel-running experience at the earlier age had no effect on the decrease in wheel running between 3 months and 15 months of age (Desroches et al., 1964).

Taken together, these results indicate that there are age-related decrements in the level of behavioral arousal and suggest that these decrements may be due to age-related changes in the capacity to detect and/or respond to internal and external factors that determine this level. The determination of the relative contribution of internal and external factors to the age-related decrease in behavioral arousal remains an important experimental problem (cf. Botwinick, 1959).

CONSUMMATORY RESPONDING

Although not as extensive as the literature on general activity, the available literature on food intake indicates that there are age differences in the amount of food eaten in response to the manipulation of conditions known to affect feeding (Teitelbaum, 1967), and the literature suggests that the mechanisms controlling eating become less efficient with age.

Normative data on the relationship between food consumption and age are sparse. The present evidence concerning this relationship is inconsistent. One study indicated no relationship between age and food intake (Osborn, Jones, & Kimeldorf, 1962), while another indicated a decrease in food intake with increasing age (Everitt, 1958), while still other studies indicated a nonmonotonic function (Farner, 1961a; Kibler & Johnson, 1966; Kibler, Silsby, & Johnson, 1963). All these studies used males as subjects. The inconsistent results of these studies are probably due to the measurement of food intake under varying environmental conditions.

Normative data on the relationship between water consumption and age are also sparse, but they are more consistent than those on food consumption. Water consumption increased with age as a monotonic function in the rat (Everitt, 1958; Goodrick, 1969b; Kibler et al., 1963; Osborn et al., 1962), and perhaps in the mouse (Goodrick, 1967b). Individual differences in water consumption in the rat also increased with age (Osborn et al., 1962). Experimental manipulation of factors that control water intake, such as osmotic pressure and volume of intravascular fluid, should result in a deeper understanding of the mechanisms of these age-related differences in water consumption.

As with activity, the consummatory responses are more difficult to energize and easier to inhibit with increasing age. Food deprivation (Jakubczak, 1969b) and water deprivation (Goodrick, 1969b) were more effective in increasing the consumption of the respective substances in young animals than in old animals. Similarly, adjustment to food deprivation was inversely related to age (Barrows & Roeder, 1965; Botwinick, 1967; Tacker & Furchtgott, 1963).

X-irradiation in *utero* magnified these age differences in adjustment to food deprivation (Tacker & Furchtgott, 1963). Young and old rats responded equally to the dilution of the caloric density of food with water by increasing total intake, thus regulating the number of calories eaten and body weight (Jakubczak, 1970c). However, addition of a bitter substance, quinine, to the food attenuated this increase in food intake to a greater degree in old rats than in young rats, with the result that the old rats did not maintain their weights as well as the young rats. Similarly, old mice drink less water diluted with alcohol than young mice (Goodrick, 1967a). Last, smaller doses of anorexigenic agents, such as amphetamine, are necessary to inhibit the consumption of food in old rats than in young ones (Farner, 1961a). Thus, with increasing age, food and water consumption become more difficult to energize but easier to inhibit.

The ability to make sensory discrimination decreases with age. Taste thresholds were higher with increasing age in rats (Goodrick, 1969b) and in mice (Goodrick, 1967b).

The effects of age on sexual behavior of animals was previously reviewed (Jakubczak, 1967b) and will not be reviewed herein. The major conclusions of the previous review were that (a) the observed age decrement in mating of male rodents may be due to *both* a decrease in the level of endogenous androgen and a decrease in the "responsiveness" of the neural target tissues to androgenic stimulation; and (b) the decrease in this "responsiveness" seems to occur prior to any marked decrease in androgen levels. The one or two articles (Drori & Folman, 1969; Larsson, 1969) that have appeared since then do not change the major conclusions of the previous review.

INSTRUMENTAL BEHAVIOR

The effects of age on the performance of unitary and choice, reward and escape Thorndikian tasks have been studied using a variety of reinforcers and experimental conditions. The evidence for age-related differences in learning performance is inconsistent, especially when the learning tasks are relatively easy.

Approximately half of the studies that used a unitary Thorndikian task and no additional independent variable demonstrated an age relationship. Young groups bar-pressed more than old groups for reinforcement with water (Solyom & Miller, 1965), and lowered temperature in rats (Rapaport, 1969), as well as light offset in mice (Goodrick, 1967b). There was an inverse relationship between age and speed of swimming in guinea pigs (Lisenby, 1968) and between age and shock escape in rats (Parè, 1969a). However, other studies have failed to find a reliable relationship between age and (a) bar pressing on a variable interval schedule for water reinforcement (Solyom, Enesco, & Beaulieu, 1967), (b) bar pressing for milk reinforcement (Goodrick, 1969a), (c) bar pressing for heat reinforcement in a cold environment (Jakubczak, 1966; Rapaport, 1967), or (d) bar pressing for light onset in mice (Goodrick, 1967b).

About half of the studies that used a choice Thorndikian task and no additional independent variable demonstrated a reliable age relationship; and those that did were relatively difficult tasks. Young mice swam faster and made fewer errors in an 8-unit multiple T-maze than old mice (Goodrick, 1967b); young rats learned a 14-unit multiple T-maze for food reinforcement more rapidly and with fewer errors than old rats (Goodrick, 1968); young rats made fewer errors in bar pressing for food reinforcement than young rats (Corke, 1964); and an old monkey required more trials to criterion on object-discrimination problems using the Wisconsin General Test Apparatus (WGTA) than younger monkeys required (Fletcher & Mowbray, 1962). Other studies failed to find a reliable relationship between age and reversal learning in rats on a single-unit Y maze (Botwinick, Brinley, & Robbin, 1962); or on a 4-unit Y maze (Botwinick et al., 1963), or a discrimination task either in rats (Dye, 1969; Kay & Sime, 1962), or in guinea pigs (Lisenby, 1968).

Several variables affect the relationship between performance on Thorndikian tasks and age. Previous experience influences this relationship. A longitudinal comparison of bar pressing for food rewards between the ages of 3 months and 15 months demonstrated an increase in performance in rats (Desroches et al., 1964). The increment in performance was due to the good retention of the response over the period of a year. In another study, previous life in groups had a beneficial effect on the performance of bar pressing for food in pairs in the case of old rats, while previous grouping and learning in pairs had an unfavorable effect on the performance of young rats (Rapaport & Bourliere, 1966). Taken together, these results emphasized the importance of prior experiences in obtaining and understanding age-related changes in performance.

Air ionization affects the relationship between age and performance on Thorndikian choice tasks. The learning of a multiple-unit T-maze for water escape was enhanced by air ionization to a greater degree in old rats than in young rats (Duffee & Koontz, 1965; Jordan & Sokoloff, 1959). Thus, air ionization may have a normalizing effect on CNS functioning, which is then reflected in performance on a complex task. In contrast, the effects of X-irradiation *in utero* were additive with the effects of age on the rat's ability to climb an inclined plane to escape heat (Wechkin, Elder, & Furchtgott, 1961) and on the perception of oddity by monkeys on the WGTA (Davis & McDonald, 1962).

The length of delay intervals affects the relationship between performance on WGTA and age. On a pattern reproduction task, old monkeys performed as well as or better than middle-aged monkeys on short-delay intervals but were significantly inferior to middle-aged monkeys on the longer delays (Medin, 1969).

With only one exception, the sex of the animal failed to influence the relationship between performance on Thorndikian tasks and age. Griew (1968) found that young female rats and old male rats adopted a maximizing strategy, while old females and young males matched their responses to the actual probabilities of escape from a water maze. In contrast, sex of the animal did not influence the relationship between age and climbing an inclined plane to escape heat (Wechkin et al., 1961), or bar pressing for food in a group (Oldfield-Box, 1969a, 1969b), or swimming a water maze (Birren, 1962).

The effects of food deprivation on the performance of Thorndikian tasks are proportional across age groups when the food deprivation results in equal percentage weight loss across age groups (Goodrick, 1965a, 1970). These results, taken together with those results obtained when activity is used as a dependent variable (Jakubczak, 1967a), suggest that the drive resulting from food deprivation can be equalized across age groups by depriving all groups so that they lose an equal percentage of their initial body weights.

Age differences in avoidance conditioning are more frequently found than age differences in Thorndikian learning. The age differences in the acquisition and retention of avoidance responses vary as a function of specific learning task requirements, such as task difficulty and massing in practice (Doty, 1966a, 1966b). Age differences are magnified by increases in task difficulty and massing of practice. The effects of handling on the acquisition and retention of avoidance responses were found to be related to age (Doty, 1968; Doty & O'Hare, 1966). Handling of the oldest groups brought their performance up to the level of young groups, suggesting that the oldest rats were lacking in sensory stimulation prior to handling.

The effects of drugs on avoidance conditioning are also related to age. A series of experiments using chlorpromazine (Doty & Doty, 1964), amphetamine (Doty & Doty, 1966), and eserine (Doty & Johnson, 1966) indicate that memory consolidation during the acquisition of the avoidance response is significantly slower in the old rats than in the young ones. Another series of experiments found that age-related deficits in avoidance learning can be ameliorated by drugs that were not stimulants and that were relatively selective for the oldest animals (Gordon, Tobin, Doty, & Nash, 1968).

Some work has been done on the relationship between age and Pavlovian conditioning. Young rats acquired the conditioned emotional response (CER) faster than old rats and showed more resistance to extinction (Solyom & Miller, 1965). Similarly, the rate of acquisition of a discriminative CER was a function of shock intensity and was inversely related to age (Parè, 1969b).

CONCLUSIONS

The area of age and animal behavior is as extensive and as varied as the parent area of animal psychology. Nevertheless, the literature represents a small portion of either the general field of animal psychology or of geropsychology. With notable exceptions, the area is not being worked systematically. Nevertheless, some conclusions may be drawn. (a) With increasing age beyond sexual maturity, the initial levels of various forms of general activity decrease in several species. These various forms of general activity, as well as consummatory responding, are more difficult to energize but easier to inhibit with increasing age. (b) Age differences in the acquisition of instrumental responses increase with the increasing difficulty of the tasks. These age differences in learning performance can be ameliorated to some degree by air ionization, certain drugs, increased sensory stimulation, and distributed practice.

Age-related decrements in short-term memory of human subjects are the subject of intensive research at present, and various theoretical constructs are being proposed to explain these decrements. As was seen in the above review, several studies of learning in animals have reported greater vulnerability of older animals to interference during the consolidation period, to massed practice, and to response delay. These reports suggest that an animal model of the age-related decrements in short-term retention is available. Thus, hypotheses based on the current theories concerning the age-related decrement in short-term retention may be tested in animals under strictly controlled conditions. Furthermore, new theories of explaining the deficit in short-term retention may result from the exploration of the relevant parameters of the deficit in animals and may be cross-validated in humans. This area of research has exciting possibilities for research during the next few years.

One of the central problems in the psychology of aging is whether the observed age decrements in performance are due to a loss of capacity to perform a task or are due to a loss of motivation to do so. The emphasis of the research in aging has been on age changes in capacities of various kinds. Little research has been done on the effects of age on motivational states per se, for example, hunger, thirst, sex, etc. This is surprising in view of the central position held by the concept of drive in behavior theory. Future research should be profitably concerned with the investigation of the effects of age on motivation, as well as with the effects of age on the relationship between motivation and performance. Research on animals will play a central role because with animals we have experimental control of such basic drives as hunger, thirst, etc.; while in the case of humans subjects we deal with complex acquired motives that are little understood. Systematic neurobehavioral studies are needed to determine the neural mechanisms that are involved in age changes in motivation. For example, it is known that the hypothalamus plays an important role in food- and water-seeking behavior. Consequently, what is the behavioral significance of the decrease in the number of cells in the hypothalamus with age? Is the functioning of the remaining cells changed in ways that would account for age changes in food intake, activity levels, and temperature regulation?

The next decade should take us further along the road toward an experimental psychology of aging. An experimental psychology of aging would attempt to reproduce the changes in organisms associated with age by manipulation of independent variables (Birren, 1970). Because of ethical as well as practical considerations, such manipulation is not feasible in humans but is feasible and practicable in animals. Perhaps the only experimental psychology of aging that will ever be available to geropsychologists will be an animal psychology of aging. If so, it is incumbent upon geropsychologists who use animals to develop a comparative psychology of aging, using organisms that are related to man by common ancestry or by common selection pressures. At present, in animal psychology of aging, as in animal psychology in general, the Snark is a Boojum (Beach, 1950).

REFERENCES

Barrows, C. H., & Roeder, L. M. The effect of reduced dietary intake on enzymatic activities and life span of rats. *Journal of Gerontology,* 1965, **20,** 69–71.

Beach, F. A. The snark was a boojum. *American Psychologist*, 1950, **5**, 115–124.

Birren, J. E. Age differences in learning a two-choice water maze by rats. *Journal of Gerontology*, 1962, **17**, 207–213.

Birren, J. E. Toward an experimental psychology of aging. *American Psychologist*, 1970, **25**, 124–135.

Bitterman, M. E. Techniques for the study of learning in animals: Analysis and classification. *Psychological Bulletin*, 1962, **59**, 81–93.

Bitterman, M. E. Animal learning. In J. B. Sidkowski (Ed.), *Experimental methods and instrumentation in psychology*. New York: McGraw-Hill, 1966.

Boer, A. P., & Davis, R. T. Age changes in the behavior of monkeys induced by ionizing radiations. *Journal of Gerontology*, 1968, **23**, 337–342.

Botwinick, J. Drives, expectancies, and emotions. In J. E. Birren (Ed.), *Handbook of aging and the individual*. Chicago: University of Chicago Press, 1959.

Botwinick, J. *Cognitive processes in maturity and old age*. New York: Springer, 1967.

Botwinick, J., Brinley, J. F., & Robbin, J. S. Learning a position discrimination and position reversals by Sprague-Dawley rats of different ages. *Journal of Gerontology*, 1962, **17**, 315–319.

Botwinick, J., Brinley, J. F., & Robbin, J. S. Learning and reversing a four-choice multiple T-maze by rats of three ages. *Journal of Gerontology*, 1963, **18**, 279–282.

Corke, P. P. Complex behavior in "old" and "young" rats. *Psychological Reports*, 1964, **15**, 371–376.

Davis, R. T. Supplementary report: Effects of age and radiation on gross behavior of monkeys. *Psychological Reports*, 1962, **11**, 738–740.

Davis, R. T., & McDonald, A. L. Perception of oddity by monkeys as a function of aging and radiation. *Psychological Reports*, 1962, **11**, 383–386.

Desroches, H. F., Kimbrell, G. M., & Allison, J. T. Effect of age and experience on bar pressing and activity in the rat. *Journal of Gerontology*, 1964, **19**, 168–172.

Doty, B. A. Age and avoidance conditioning in rats. *Journal of Gerontology*, 1966, **21**, 287–290. (a)

Doty, B. A. Age differences in avoidance conditioning as a function of distribution of trials and task difficulty. *Journal of Genetic Psychology*, 1966, **109**, 249–254. (b)

Doty, B. A. Effects of handling on learning of young and aged rats. *Journal of Gerontology*, 1968, **23**, 142–144.

Doty, B. A., & Doty, L. A. Effect of age and chlorpromazine on memory consolidation. *Journal of Comparative and Physiological Psychology*, 1964, **57**, 331–334.

Doty, B. A., & Doty, L. A. Facilitative effects of amphetamine on avoidance conditioning in relation to age and problem difficulty. *Psychopharmacologia*, 1966, **9**, 234–241.

Doty, B. A., & Johnston, M. M. Effects of post-trial eserine administration, age and task difficulty on avoidance conditioning in rats. *Psychonomic Science*, 1966, **6**, 101–102.

Doty, B. A., & O'Hare, K. M. Interaction of shock intensity, age, and handling effects on avoidance conditioning. *Perceptual and Motor Skills*, 1966, **23**, 1311–1314.

Draper, W. A. Free-ranging rhesus monkeys: Age and sex differences in individual activity patterns. *Science*, 1966, **151**, 476–478.

Drori, D., & Folman, Y. The effect of mating on the longevity of male rats. *Experimental Gerontology*, 1969, **4**, 263–266.

Duffee, R. A., & Koontz, R. H. Behavioral effects of ionized air on rats. *Psychophysiology*, 1965, **1**, 347–359.

Dye, C. J. Effects of interruption of initial learning upon retention in young, mature, and old rats. *Journal of Gerontology*, 1969, **24**, 12–17.

Eberhard, W. G. Senile web patterns in *Uloborus diversus (Araneae: Uloboridae)*. *Developmental Psychobiology*, 1971, **4**, 249–254.

Eisdorfer, C., Nowlin, J., & Wilkie, F. Improvement of learning by modification of autonomic nervous system activity. *Science*, 1970, **170**, 1327–1328.

Everitt, A. V. The change in food and water consumption and in faeces and urine production in ageing male rats. *Journal of Gerontology*, 1958, **2**, 21–32.

Farner, D. Die wirkung von Amphetamin und Hexobarbital auf junge und alte ratten. *Gerontologia*, 1960, **4**, 144–153.

Farner, D. Untersuchungen über die wirkung von pharmaka auf tiere verschiedenen alters. *Gerontologia*, 1961, **5**, 35–44. (a)

Farner, D. Untersuchungen über die wirkung von pharmaka auf tiere verschiedenen alters. *Gerontologia*, 1961, **5**, 45–54. (b)

Fletcher, H. J., & Mowbray, J. B. Note on learning in an aged monkey. *Psychological Reports*, 1962, **10**, 11–13.

Furchtgott, E., Wechkin, S., & Dees, J. W. Open-field exploration as a function of age. *Journal of Comparative and Physiological Psychology*, 1961, **54**, 386–388.

Goodrick, C. L. Operant level and light-contingent bar presses as a function of age and deprivation. *Psychological Reports*, 1965, **17**, 283–288. (a)

Goodrick, C. L. Social interactions and exploration of young, mature, and senescent male albino rats, *Journal of Gerontology*, 1965, **20**, 215–218. (b)

Goodrick, C. L. Activity and exploration as a function of age and deprivation. *Journal of Genetic Psychology*, 1966, **108**, 239–252.

Goodrick, C. L. Alcohol preference of the male Sprague-Dawley albino rat as a function of age. *Journal of Gerontology*, 1967, **22**, 369–371. (a)

Goodrick, C. L. Behavioral characteristics of young and senescent inbred female mice of the C57BL/6J strain. *Journal of Gerontology*, 1967, **22**, 459–464. (b)

Goodrick, C. L. Exploration of nondeprived male Sprague-Dawley rats as a function of age. *Psychological Reports*, 1967, **20**, 159–163. (c)

Goodrick, C. L. Learning, retention, and extinction of a complex maze habit for mature-young and senescent Wistar albino rats. *Journal of Gerontology*, 1968, **23**, 298–304.

Goodrick, C. L. Operant responding of non-deprived young and senescent male albino rats. *Journal of Genetic Psychology*, 1969, **114**, 29–40. (a)

Goodrick, C. L. Taste discrimination and fluid ingestion of male albino rats as a function of age. *Journal of Genetic Psychology*, 1969, **115**, 121–131. (b)

Goodrick, C. L. Light- and dark-contingent bar pressing in the rat as a function of age and motivation. *Journal of Comparative and Physiological Psychology*, 1970, **73**, 100.

Goodrick, C. L. Free exploration and adaptation within an open field as a function of trials and between-trial interval for mature-young, mature-old, and senescent Wistar rats. *Journal of Gerontology*, 1971, **26**, 58–62.

Gordon, P., Tobin, S., Doty, B., & Nash, M. Drug effects on behavior in aged animals and man: Diphenylhydantoin and procainamide. *Journal of Gerontology*, 1968, **23**, 434–444.

Griew, S. Age and sex differences in probability learning of rats in a swimming T-maze. *Gerontologia*, 1968, **14**, 197–203.

Hodge, M. H., Peacock, L. J., & Hoff, L. A. The effect of age and food deprivation upon the general activity of the rat. *Journal of Genetic Psychology*, 1967, **111**, 135–145.

Jakubczak, L. F. Age differences in sleep and activity of laboratory rats. *American Psychologist*, 1961, **16**, 371–372. (Abstract)

Jakubczak, L. F. Behavioral thermoregulation in young and old rats. *Journal of Applied Physiology*, 1966, **21**, 19–21.

Jakubczak, L. F. Age differences in the effects of terminal food deprivation (starvation) on activity, weight loss, and survival of rats. *Journal of Gerontology*, 1967, **22**, 421–426. (a)

Jakubczak, L. F. Age, endocrines and behavior. In L. Gitman (Ed.), *Endocrines and aging.* Springfield, Ill.: Charles C Thomas, 1967. (b)

Jakubczak, L. F. Effects of age and activity restriction on body weight loss of rats. *American Journal of Physiology*, 1969, **216**, 1081–1083. (a)

Jakubczak, L. F. Effects on injection of glucose on food intake of mature and old food-deprived rats. *Proceedings of the 77th Annual Convention of the American Psychological Association*, 1969, **4**, 723–724. (Summary) (b)

Jakubczak, L. F. Age differences in the effects of water deprivation on activity, weight loss and survival of rats. *Life Sciences*, 1970, **9**, 771–780. (a)

Jakubczak, L. F. Age, food deprivation, and the temporal distribution of wheel running of rats. *Proceedings of the 78th Annual Convention of the American Psychological Association*, 1970 **5**, 689–690. (Summary) (b)

Jakubczak, L. F. The effects of age, dilution, and quinine on food intake of rats. *Gerontologist*, 1970, **10**(3, Pt. 2), 27. (Abstract) (c)

Jakubczak, L. F. Burst frequency and burst duration of wheel running activity as a function of food deprivation and age of rats. *Gerontologist*, 1971, **11**(3, Pt. 2), 41. (Abstract)

Jerome E. A. Age and learning—Experimental studies. In J. E. Birren (Ed.), *Handbook of aging and the individual.* Chicago: University of Chicago Press, 1959.

Jordan, J., & Sokoloff, B. Air ionization, age, and maze learning of rats. *Journal of Gerontology*, 1959, **14**, 344–348.

Kay, H., & Sime, M. E. Discrimination learning with old and young rats. *Journal of Gerontology*, 1962, **17**, 75–80.

Kibler, H. H., & Johnson, H. D. Temperature and longevity in male rats. *Journal of Gerontology*, 1966, **21**, 52–56.

Kibler, H. H., Silsby, H. D., & Johnson, H. D. Metabolic trends and life span of rats living at 9 C. and 28 C. *Journal of Gerontology*, 1963, **18**, 235–239.

Larsson, K. The social, hormonal and neural control of sexual behavior. *Lakartidningen,* 1969, **66,** 4889–4893.

Lisenby, D. D. Chronological age, physiological change and performance in the mature guinea pig. Unpublished doctoral dissertation, Washington University, 1968.

Manocha, S. N. The effects of age on the behavior of rhesus monkeys: III. Free social behavior. *Journal of Genetic Psychology,* 1968, **112,** 249–254.

Medin, D. L. Form perception and pattern reproduction by monkeys. *Journal of Comparative and Physiological Psychology,* 1969, **68,** 412–419.

Oldfield-Box, H. Age differences in performance between rats in two experimental social organizations. *Journal of Gerontology,* 1969, **24,** 18–22. (a)

Oldfield-Box, H. A note on the performance of groups of laboratory rats of mixed ages in a social learning situation. *Gerontologia,* 1969, **15,** 1–6. (b)

Oldfield-Box, H. On analysing the formation of learning sets in young and old rats. *Gerontologia,* 1969, **15,** 302–307. (c)

Osborn, G. K., Jones, D. C., & Kimeldorf, D. J. Water consumption of the ageing Sprague-Dawley male rat. *Gerontologia,* 1962, **6,** 65–71.

Parè, W. P. Age, sex and strain differences in the aversive threshold to grid shock in the rat. *Journal of Comparative and Physiological Psychology,* 1969, **69,** 214–218. (a)

Parè, W. P. Interaction of age and shock intensity on acquisition of a discriminated conditioned emotional response. *Journal of Comparative and Physiological Psychology,* 1969, **68,** 364–369. (b)

Rapaport, A. L'adaptation du comportement du rat jeune, adulte et age aux variations de la temperature ambiante: I. Adaptation au froid. *Gerontologia,* 1967, **13,** 14–19.

Rapaport, A. L'adaptation du comportement du rat jeune, adulte et age aux variations de la temperature ambiante. *Gerontologia,* 1969, **15,** 288–292.

Rapaport, A., & Bourliere, F. La facilitation sociale de l'apprentissage d'une tache operationnelle chez le rat age. *Gerontologia,* 1966, **12,** 74–78.

Solyom, L., Enesco, H. E., & Beaulieu, C. The effect of RNA on learning and activity in old and young rats. *Journal of Gerontology,* 1967, **22,** 1–7.

Solyom, L., & Miller, S. The effect of age differences on the acquisition of operant and classical conditioned responses in rates. *Journal of Gerontology,* 1965, **20,** 311–314.

Tacker, R. S., & Furchtgott, E. Adjustment to food deprivation cycles as a function of age and prenatal X-irradiation. *Journal of Genetic Psychology,* 1963, **102,** 257–260.

Teitelbaum, M. Motivation and control of food intake. In, *Handbook of physiology:* Vol. 1. *Food and water intake.* Washington, D.C.: American Physiological Society, 1967.

Wechkin, S., Elder, R. F., Jr., & Furchtgott, E. Motor performance in the rat as a function of age and prenatal X-irradiation. *Journal of Comparative and Physiological Psychology,* 1961, **54,** 658–659.

Werboff, J., & Havlena, J. Effects of aging on open field behavior. *Psychological Reports,* 1962, **10,** 395–398.

Psychophysiological Studies of Aging

LARRY W. THOMPSON and GAIL R. MARSH

The impetus for this chapter stems from the fact that cross-sectional studies reveal a significant change in physiological and cognitive functioning in late adult years. Not only do both systems show significant decline with age, but it has also been well established that intra- and interindividual differences are increased in many physiological and behavioral measures. The question has been raised frequently whether or not changes in physiological measures seen with age might account for variations in cognitive processes. It has been repeatedly suggested that simultaneous investigation of physiological and cognitive measures in a variety of experimental designs would provide information regarding variables that are potentially relevant to the well-known age decrement in cognitive functioning (Birren, 1965; Obrist, 1965; Spieth, 1965; Welford, 1965). This chapter provides a broad review of electrophysiological and psychophysiological studies that fit within this general framework.

The topic of psychophysiology allows considerable latitude as to the choice of material, and, unless restrictions are posed, the magnitude of the task could become unwieldy. After a cursory review of studies involving both physiological and behavioral measures, the principal focus will be on studies that rely heavily on traditional bioelectric methods to reflect physiological functioning. Second, an emphasis will be placed on the relationships between physiological and behavioral indices rather than on a detailed analysis of the theory and techniques in either area.

Larry W. Thompson received his PhD in clinical psychology from Florida State University in 1961. He is currently a Professor of Medical Psychology at Duke University Medical Center. His major research interests center around electrophysiological correlates of behavior.

Gail R. Marsh received his PhD in physiological psychology from the University of Iowa in 1968. He is currently Assistant Professor in Medical Psychology in the Department of Psychiatry and also Research and Training Program Coordinator, Center for the Study of Aging and Human Development, at Duke University.

ELECTROENCEPHALOGRAPH MEASURES

Changes in the electroencephalograph (EEG) measures from young adulthood to senescence and their relationships to behavioral impairment in the elderly have been the subjects of numerous investigations. Many of the results have been fully and aptly discussed elsewhere (Obrist & Busse, 1965). However, it is desirable to summarize this general body of literature in some detail, even at the risk of being somewhat redundant.

Alpha Activity

Alpha rhythm is traditionally defined as waves in the range of 8 to 13 cycles per second (cps), which occur in greater abundance in the posterior regions of the head. They are most often apparent during relaxed states and tend to disappear or are attenuated by the presentation of a novel stimulus. Slowing of the alpha rhythm has been frequently reported as a function of age. The mean alpha frequency for normal young adults is approximately 10.2 to 10.5 cps (Brazier & Finesinger, 1944). In contrast to this, estimates of mean alpha frequency in normal elderly subjects (Busse & Obrist, 1963; Mundy-Castle, Hurst, Beerstecher & Prinsloo, 1954) and hospital patients (Friedlander, 1958; Harvald, 1958) have been consistently slower, ranging from 8.0 to 9.7 cps, with the slowest frequencies most often found in the oldest age groups. Longitudinal studies (Obrist, Henry, & Justiss, 1961; Wang & Busse, 1969) indicate that such changes are probably due to a continued downward trend in alpha frequency with advancing age as opposed to a sampling artifact resulting from a selective dropout of individuals with higher alpha frequencies.

Other reported changes in alpha activity pertain to its amplitude, general abundance, and topographical distribution. Mundy-Castle et al. (1954) found a decrease in percent-time alpha, particularly with evidence of increased dementia. Obrist and Henry (1958a, 1958b) also noted a pronounced decrease in the amount of alpha activity that was replaced by slower wave forms in elderly deteriorated patients. Gaches (1960) found a greater extension of alpha activity into the frontal and temporal areas with age and reported that it was correlated with the presence of cardiovascular disease.

The issue regarding the cause of alpha slowing with age remains unsettled. Obrist (1963, 1964) offered considerable evidence suggesting that vascular disease is an important factor. A comparison of age-matched arteriosclerotic and normal groups revealed lower alpha frequencies in the diseased group (Obrist & Bissell, 1955). A similar finding was observed in community male subjects with mild asymptomatic arteriosclerosis when compared with a group of highly selected elderly males who were as free of evidence of disease as possible (Obrist, 1963). Studies of cerebral circulation and metabolism on these same subjects revealed no significant differences between normal young controls and the superhealthy elderly group (Dastur, Lane, Hansen, Kety, Butler, Perlin, & Sokoloff, 1963). However, the group that exhibited mild asymptomatic disease showed a 10–16% decline in cerebral blood flow. Cerebral oxygen consumption was also decreased, but this difference was not statistically significant.

Obrist and Busse (1965) argued that such findings suggest that a declining alpha rate may be an early sign of vascular insufficiency. However, a slight but significant decrease in frequency can be seen in the extremely healthy group discussed above; this suggests that cardiovascular pathology is not the only contributing factor. Since EEG changes are decidedly related to health status, the possibility that even the healthy group may have minimal subclinical pathology which is responsible for the alpha slowing is plausible (Obrist, 1963). Nevertheless, the likelihood that there are at least two contributing factors (age and pathology), both of which have a similar effect on alpha frequency, cannot be discounted.

Fast activity. Fast activity includes waves with a frequency above the alpha range and usually in the range of 18 to 30 cps with diminished voltage ($25\mu v$ or less). Such activity is seen most often in the anterior regions of the head. The proportion of fast activity shows a significant increase in middle-aged normal subjects (Gibbs & Gibbs, 1950; Mundy-Castle, 1951) and psychiatric patients (Greenblatt, 1944) and is significantly more abundant in females than males during middle life and later years (Busse & Obrist, 1965). Fast activity is also readily apparent in the tracings of elderly people (Maggs & Turton, 1956; Markovich, 1962; Mundy-Castle, 1951; Obrist, 1954). Obrist and Busse (1965) conservatively estimated "that 50% of all elderly people show at least traces of low-voltage beta rhythm in one or more leads." The incidence of fast activity becomes less apparent in the elderly with advancing years (Busse, Barnes, Friedman, & Kelty, 1956; Silverman, Busse, & Barnes, 1955) and is decreased significantly in severely deteriorated senile patients (Barnes, Busse, & Friedman, 1956; Frey & Sjögren, 1959; Mundy-Castle et al., 1954; Obrist & Henry, 1958a).

Focal slow activity. Focal slow activity refers to localized episodic bursts of high-voltage waves in the delta (1 to 3 cps) and theta (4 to 7 cps) ranges. These are sometimes accompanied by focal sharp waves and amplitude asymmetries, particularly when the subject is in a drowsy state. A high incidence of focal slow activity has been reported in normal elderly volunteers ranging from 30–40% (Busse, Barnes, Silverman, Shy, Thaler, & Frost, 1954; Busse et al., 1956) to 50% (Mundy-Castle, 1962). These investigators and others (Busse & Obrist, 1963; Kooi, Guvener, Tupper, & Bagchi, 1964; Silverman et al., 1955) reported that such disturbances are seen predominantly in the left hemisphere (approximately 75% of the cases) and most often in the anterior temporal lobe. An increased incidence of temporal lobe foci has also been observed in the middle-aged range, again more often in the left than in the right hemisphere (Busse & Obrist, 1965; Kooi et al., 1964). Similar findings have been observed in hospital settings (Frey & Sjögren, 1959; Harvald, 1958), with some tendency for a wider distribution in the middle and posterior temporal regions (Barnes et al., 1956) as well as the involvement of frontal areas noted in patients with mental deterioration (Obrist & Henry, 1958a).

The occurrence of this focal slow activity in the elderly is particularly intriguing in that it is decidedly abnormal in appearance, yet has only minimal clinical or functional correlates. It is not related to handedness (Kooi et al., 1964; Silverman et al., 1955), aphasia, or seizures (Busse & Obrist, 1963; Frey & Sjögren, 1959). There is little evidence that it is related to gross measures of intellectual functioning, but this will be discussed in greater detail in a later section.

The underlying basis of these foci is unknown at present. With regard to physiological measures, a number of investigators have reported that some form of cardiovascular disease was encountered more often in subjects with foci (Kooi et al., 1964; Silverman et al., 1955). This, together with the predisposition of vascular disturbances in the temporal region, particularly in the left hemisphere (Hughes, 1960), raises the question that the temporal lobe focus may result from a differential impairment of blood supply. Obrist and Busse (1965) reviewed findings from a number of studies in which the appearance or disappearance of slow waves was noted during experimental manipulations of the cerebral hemodynamic picture (e.g., passive tilt, hyperventilation, carotid compression, inhalation of various O_2-CO_2 concentrations, etc.). Their interpretation of these data, in combination with their discussion of the relationship between foci and vascular disease, provides inferential evidence that localized vascular insufficiency may play an important role in the emergence of focal slow activity.

Diffuse slow activity. Diffuse slowing refers to the distribution of delta and theta waves in several areas of the brain as opposed to a specific focus. Such activity is seldom seen in community volunteers during early senescence. Obrist and Busse (1965) reported that ratings of diffuse slowing in their subjects under age 75 were comparable to those of healthy young adults. However, in subjects over age 75, 20% showed sufficient slowing to be rated as "S_1" according to Gibbs' classification. None of the subjects showed the degree of slowing that is seen in elderly samples of mental hospital patients. Diffuse slowing is highly associated with psychiatric diagnoses in elderly hospitalized patients, such that it is more prevalent in patients with organic brain syndrome than in patients with functional disorders (Hoch & Kubis, 1941; Liberson & Seguin, 1945; Luce & Rothschild, 1953; Obrist & Henry, 1958a). Elderly patients with diffuse slowing also tend to have a shorter life expectancy and less likelihood of being discharged from the hospital (McAdam & Robinson, 1962; Obrist & Henry, 1958a).

Data pertaining to the etiology of diffuse slowing are less obscure than for other EEG characteristics in the elderly. Obrist, Sokoloff, Lassen, Lane, Butler, and Feinberg (1963) reported that cerbral oxygen uptake was related negatively to percent-time occipital slowing ($r = -.78, p < .001$) and positively to peak frequency ($r = .74, p < .001$) in patients who have evidence of diffuse slowing. Lassen, Munck, and Tottey (1957) also observed significantly decreased cerebral oxygen consumption in 10 patients with senile dementia and diffuse slow activity. Significant correlations among percent-time slowing, cerebral blood flow, and vascular resistance have also been reported (Obrist et al., 1963). It is interesting to note that such relationships were not obtained in community subjects with minimal EEG changes (Obrist, 1963; Obrist et al., 1963).

A significant relationship between cerebral vascular insufficiency and diffuse slowing seems indisputable in the face of such evidence. However, as Obrist and Busse (1965) pointed out, there is some question as to whether circulatory or metabolic factors are the primary contributors to an endogenous aging process. In the one, circulatory deficits due to arteriosclerosis or other cardiovascular disorders are held responsible for EEG changes (Sokoloff, 1966). Such disorders may result in cerebral vascular insufficiency and hypoxia, which, after a protracted period of time, leads to tissue damage and a decline in oxygen utilization. On the other hand, Lassen (1966) emphasized endogenous factors that are accompanied by cortical atrophy. Decreases in cerebral blood flow primarily reflect an adjustment to the decreased metabolic demands of the cerebral tissue. Thus, changes in cerebral metabolism would account for the relationship between EEG characteristics and measures of cerebral blood flow.

In support of the circulatory impairment hypothesis, Obrist, Busse, and Henry (1961) found that elderly psychiatric patients with low blood pressure had significantly more diffuse slowing than patients with mildly elevated pressure. In patients with vascular disease and low blood pressure, over 70% of the EEGs showed diffuse slowing. This interaction of blood pressure and vascular disease led Obrist (1964) to suggest that "the observed EEG changes may represent the accumulative effects of chronic cerebral ischemia." He went on to speculate "that an adequate regulation of blood pressure, particularly in cases with vascular disease, is crucial for the maintenance of EEG normality in old age."

Hopefully, the implications of these findings may become more salient as the interrelationship of cardiovascular and EEG measures with behavior is considered in subsequent sections. Clearly, the severity of senile deterioration shows reliable variation both with indices of cerebral vascular impairment (Feinberg, Lane, & Lassen, 1960; Klee, 1964; Lassen et al., 1957; Obrist et al., 1970) and with the extent of diffuse slowing in the EEG (McAdam & Robinson, 1962; Mundy-Castle, 1954; Obrist, Chivian, Cronqvist, & Ingvar, 1970). Just as there seems to be little relationship between cerebral vascular measures and the EEG in healthy elderly subjects, consistent relationships between these and behavioral measures have been reported primarily in hospital patients or in subjects with suggested limiting pathology in the cardiovascular system, but not in community volunteers who are in relatively good health.

This finding suggests that variations of cortical function and physiological measures within the normal range are relatively independent. Extreme deviations of one, as a result of intervening pathological processes, however, may increase its effect on the other, thus resulting in a significant correlation. In response to these and other similar observations, Birren, Butler, Greenhouse, Sokoloff, and Yarrow (1963) advanced the "discontinuity hypothesis," which states that individual variations in cognitive functioning remain largely autonomous of somatic functions until critical or limiting levels are reached; these would most likely be a consequence of disease or trauma, which then results in a new set of relationships. While this hypothesis may be of limited usefulness in a broader range of psychophysiological studies, it emphasizes the significance of health status to cognitive processes in the elderly and underlines the importance of controlling for health factors when attempting to investigate age relationships.

Behavioral Correlates of Age-Related EEG Characteristics

In keeping with the hypothesis that cognitive impairment in the elderly can be attributed to central nervous system (CNS) changes (Gerard, 1959; Reitan, 1955; Welford, 1959), the question of a relationship between age-related EEG characteristics and behavioral measures is often posed. As mentioned earlier, such relationships have been found consistently in neuropsychiatric samples, in subjects who have undergone considerable deterioration or who otherwise show evidence of some limiting pathology.

Alpha activity. Slow alpha frequency, for example, has been associated with intellectual impairment in hospital patients (Bankier, 1967; Stoller, 1949) but not in subjects who show minimal evidence of intellectual deficit (Mundy-Castle, 1962; Obrist, 1963). On the other hand, Wang, Obrist, and Busse (1970) observed a significant relationship ($r = -.61$, $p < .01$) between alpha frequency and Verbal–Performance discrepancy on the Wechsler Adult Intelligence Scale (WAIS) in a homogeneous group of community volunteers. They did not find a significant relationship between frequency and either Verbal or Performance scores. In another study, Obrist, Busse, Eisdorfer, and Kleemeier (1962) investigated the relationship of alpha frequency to intelligence test scores in psychiatric patients, residents of a home for the aged, and elderly community volunteers. They found no relationship between alpha frequency and test scores in the community group. However, in the hospital and resident home sample, numerous significant correlations were obtained. The highest correlations were found between alpha slowing and subtests of the Performance scale of the WAIS, ranging from .20 to .45. When patients were grouped according to the presence or absence of arteriosclerosis, it became evident that this variable was contributing heavily to the relationship between EEG and test scores. Patients without arteriosclerosis showed no relationship between the two measures. The authors speculated that cardiovascular pathology is chiefly responsible for the observed results in this and other studies with similar findings.

Impaired memory function is also highly related to occipital frequency in patients (Hoagland, 1954) but not in community subjects (Obrist & Busse, 1965). Patients with chronic brain syndrome tend to have slower alpha frequencies than patients with functional disorders (Luce & Rothschild, 1953; Obrist & Henry, 1958b), with a prevalence for a dominant frequency as low as 7 cps (Frey & Sjögren, 1959).

Changes in the topographical distribution of alpha may also be correlated with behavioral changes. Justiss (1962) investigated the relationship between electrical activity in the frontal regions and degree of impairment of abstract function as reflected in the Grassi Block Design Test and the Porteus Maze Test. He noted that the amount of alpha activity in the frontal regions was negatively correlated ($r = -.424$, $p < .05$) with performance on the Porteus Maze Test in a sample of 30 elderly subjects especially selected to cover a wide range of functioning. Percentage frontal alpha showed no correlation with age, occipital alpha frequency, or performance on the Grassi test. The suggested relationship between increased frontal alpha and the occurrence of cardiovascular disease (Gaches, 1960) again raises the question of whether or not pathology might be largely responsible for the relationship seen in this study.

Fast activity. Several studies reported an absence or significant decrease of fast activity in elderly persons who show signs of deterioration (Barnes et al., 1956; Frey & Sjögren, 1959; Mundy-Castle et al., 1954; Obrist & Henry, 1958a). Obrist and Busse (1965) suggested that "because fast activity is most prevalent among intellectually well preserved subjects during early senescence, its presence in an elderly person's EEG can probably be regarded as a favorable sign [p. 191]."

Focal slow activity. By and large, attempts to correlate focal slowing with gross intellectual evaluations and psychiatric ratings have been unsuccessful (Busse et al., 1956; Mundy-Castle et al., 1954; Obrist et al., 1962; Thaler, 1956). The few exceptions to this should be interpreted as equivocal for the present in the face of overwhelming negative results. Obrist (1965) reported a relationship between resting temporal lobe abnormalities and choice reaction time in community volunteers, but recently pointed out that this finding is in need of confirmation before being considered reliable (W. D. Obrist, personal communication, 1964). Drachman and Hughes (1971) reported a relationship between temporal lobe abnormalities and Verbal–Performance scale discrepancies on the WAIS. In view of the fact that the ages of their subjects ranged from 51 to 69 and that the nature of the reported deficit is frequently observed as a concomitant of aging, one might raise the question of whether or not some other age-related factor may be contributing heavily to the relationship. In this regard, Wang et al. (1970) found no significant difference in verbal–performance discrepancy between subjects with temporal lobe foci and those without, when the two groups were made comparable with respect to age and socioeconomic status.

However, Wang et al. did find a significant decline in verbal scores over a 3.5-year period in the subjects who had foci at the time of the first testing. The authors speculated that the origin of the focus may be temporal cortex, since the observed foci in their subjects involved predominantly the left temporal region and since lesions in this area frequently are associated with impairment of verbal functioning. This is an interesting observation that deserves further study. Although the two groups were comparable on relevant predictor variables, the possibility remains that mean differences could be spurious. Another approach to this problem might be to partial out the variance in the dependent measures that can be accounted for by these related measures and then test for differences between the two groups. An additional point regarding methodology could be made here: if their finding proves to be reliable with repeated testing, this would argue for the efficiency of a longitudinal approach in clarifying causal factors in functional relationships.

In view of the well-established association between temporal lobe lesions and learning and memory disorders (Milner, 1962), one might expect to see a similar relationship in elderly patients with abnormal focal slowing in the temporal lobe. Drachman and Hughes (1971) were unable to obtain any relationship between learning measures and foci. In a recent, well-controlled study, Obrist (1971) compared a group of 20 subjects with extremely large temporal lobe foci with a control group matched for age, socioeconomic status, and education. He found no differences between the groups on verbal learning and memory performance, IQ scores, verbal–performance discrepancy, or longevity index. As Obrist and Busse (1965) pointed out, the question of whether or not such focal abnormalities have a specific behavioral correlate remains an attractive research problem.

Diffuse slow activity. As mentioned earlier, diffuse slow wave activity is highly associated with severe intellectual impairment in elderly subjects. Obrist and Busse (1965) pointed out that this "more than any other EEG variable is related to senile intellectual deterioration." Not only are lower intelligence test scores associated with diffuse slowing in patient samples (Barnes et al., 1956; Obrist et al., 1962; Silverman, Busse, Barnes, Frost, & Thaler, 1953; Thaler, 1956), but gross assessments of functioning using rating scales have shown a similar relationship (McAdam & Robinson, 1962; Mundy-Castle et al., 1954; Weiner & Schuster, 1956).

The consistent failure to find EEG correlates of cognitive functioning in healthy community volunteers poses interesting challenges for future research. One could take the position that the discontinuity hypothesis or some modification thereof is sufficient to explain most of the findings, but it is difficult to envision its heuristic value with respect to continued theory construction. One obvious and extremely practical direction would involve continued attempts to isolate critical physiological variables and delineate acceptable limits of variation in order to maintain adequate levels of functioning. It follows then to determine the mechanisms responsible for aberrant processes and to develop methods of early detection and correction.

The argument could also be raised that much of the present information and speculation concerning EEG behavior relationships is encumbered by the limitations of the measures generally used. The psychological assessment procedures typically employed, for example, may not be sufficiently refined to provide reliable estimates of the minimal impairment in normal elderly subjects. It is interesting to note that two of the studies reporting significant relationships in community subjects used the verbal–performance discrepancy as a behavioral index (Drachman & Hughes, 1971; Wang et al., 1970), a measure that is frequently felt to be more sensitive to structural changes in the brain than the Verbal or Performance scale individually. Similarly, the reaction time test, which was related to foci in community subjects (Obrist, 1965), has not been used often in the studies reviewed so far. It would seem that a careful review and revision of the traditional assessment procedures employed in such studies is in order. The application of "newer" theories related to cognitive processes, which have come from the experimental psychologists, might prove to be extremely productive in the development of sensitive and appropriate instruments. Certainly, this has been the case in other areas of gerontology (Craik, 1968; Rabbitt, 1968; Szafran, 1968).

Along this same line, the standard clinical evaluation of the EEG does not lend itself to quantification and therefore may not reflect subtle changes in CNS functioning. It goes without saying that tremendous industry is being applied in attempting to solve technical and theoretical problems encountered in developing practical analytic systems for the quantification of the EEG. Considerable progress has been made, but many of the techniques are not yet available to the scientist who is in a position to conduct EEG–behavior research in a clinical setting.

Electrocortical Reactivity and Aging

Aside from problems of quantification, the clinical resting EEG may be limited in its sensitivity to minimal changes in cerebral function and in its contribution to theoretical developments in the study of brain–behavior relationships. Research concerned with EEG arousal responses to sensory stimulation (evoked alpha blocking) and the possible role of the reticular system in behavior arousal (Lindsley, 1958; Magoun, 1958; Morruzzi & Magoun, 1949; Sharpless & Jasper, 1956) raises a question concerning the relationship between some EEG index of cortical reactivity and behavioral impairment in the elderly. According to activation theory, desynchronization or alpha blocking as a result of sensory input represents a state of heightened cortical excitability by virtue of reticular system influences. During this state, transfer of neuronal information is facilitated. If this is true, one might expect to find some association between efficiency of information processing at the behavioral level and the extent to which the EEG reacts to sensory stimulation.

The notion that this response may provide a useful index of cerebral dysfunction was introduced by Liberson (1944). Decreased EEG reactivity to sensory stimulation has been reported in brain-damaged subjects (Wells, 1962, 1963) and in elderly subjects (Andermann & Stoller, 1961; Verdeaux, Verdeaux, & Turmel, 1961). A comparison of arousal responses to repeated photic stimulation in healthy young and old community volunteers of superior intelligence revealed decreased EEG reactivity and more rapid habituation in the old (Obrist, 1965; Wilson, 1962).

Surprisingly enough, there has been very little work in this general area. Again, problems in quantifying the EEG may be largely responsible, since it is virtually essential to quantify appropriate portions of the EEG tracing in order to obtain a reliable measure of reactivity and habituation. Thompson and Wilson (1966) completed a manual frequency analysis of parietal occipital tracings during photic stimulation on two groups of high-IQ elderly subjects. Both groups were in good health and comparable with respect to age, socioeconomic status, and IQ. However, one group demonstrated extremely good verbal-learning ability, which was comparable to bright young controls, while the other group did poorly on the paired-associate learning task, in spite of the fact that they all were in the superior range of intellectual functioning as measured by the WAIS. The results were consistent with activation theory in that the good learners showed greater cortical reactivity to sensory input than the poor learners, although there was no difference between the groups on the resting EEGs. The generality of these findings, however, is questionable in view of the select nature of the subjects and their small number (seven and eight subjects in each group, respectively).

A somewhat related approach has been to look at EEG changes and behavioral measures simultaneously to determine if within-subject variations in the behavior investigated change in EEG amplitude during a complicated vigilance task. Some tendency has been observed for high-voltage alpha bursts to occur with errors in the elderly subjects that would be consistent with an interpretation of decreased cortical arousal during lapses in attention.

Birren (1965) observed no relationship between variations in reaction time and several EEG measures in elderly subjects. Reaction times were grouped according to whether the stimulus occurred during the presence or absence of alpha, whether the alpha frequency was greater or lesser than the mean, or whether voltages were greater or lesser than the mean for each individual. Thompson and Botwinick (1968) also found no relationship between measures of EEG arousal and reaction time in either young or old subjects and concluded that EEG changes in their study could not account for the slowing in old age. Failure to find a relationship in those two studies is somewhat discouraging, but methodological problems in both indicate that further work along these lines is warranted.

In contrast to these findings, Surwillo (1963b) reported that a large proportion of the slowing in response speed in the elderly can be explained by changes in EEG period (EEG period, as defined by Surwillo, is the reciprocal of alpha frequency). In a more recent paper, Surwillo (1968) presented evidence from a number of investigations, many of them his own work, that supports the hypothesis that time in the domain of the CNS is reckoned in terms of the alpha frequency present. An "alpha generator" may have a function somewhat analogous to a pulse generator or gating clock in timing events that occur in the brain. He reviewed studies using elderly subjects that show the relationships of EEG alpha slowing to increased reaction time (Surwillo, 1963b), increased variability in reaction time (Surwillo, 1963a), increased decision time (Surwillo, 1964b), and slowness of involuntary responses as reflected in latency of alpha blocking (Surwillo, 1966a). These relationships were obtained after chronological age had been partialed out, which suggests that alpha gating may be a powerful mediating factor in response speed irrespective of age. Efforts to modify response speed by altering EEG frequency with a photic stimulator provided further tentative, but not conclusive, evidence of the role of the "alpha generator" as a time-base generator (Surwillo, 1964a).

Surwillo's position that slowing of this timing mechanism can account for many of the age-related behavioral changes is advanced in a cogent and systematic fashion. This provocative formulation is one of the few attempts to provide an orderly model of EEG–behavior relationships in the elderly and should prove to be very useful in generating new hypotheses for future research ventures. There are considerable limitations in his model, however, since the supporting data were necessarily obtained only from behavioral situations during which well-developed wave forms (usually alpha) were present in the EEG tracings. As Surwillo (1968) succinctly pointed out, "any procedure that involves arbitrary selection of data imposes restrictions of interpretation that cannot be ignored." Nevertheless, at the very least, he left little doubt in the reader's mind that significant EEG correlates of response speed can be obtained in healthy elderly subjects.

Sleep Patterns in the Aged

In view of the obvious changes in sleep patterns with age, it is puzzling that this area of investigation has received so little attention. Feinberg (1969) pointed out that effects of age on EEG activity during sleep are markedly greater than any other age-related EEG characteristic. Briefly, his data suggested that total sleep time remains fairly stable throughout the adult years with some decrease in later adulthood (Kales, Wilson, Kales, Jacobson, Paulson, Kollar, & Walter, 1967). The number of arousals during the night, however, increases linearly during the adult years. The percentage of rapid eye movement (REM) sleep maintains a plateau throughout adulthood and early senescence with evidence of a marked drop during the eighth and ninth decades (Feinberg, 1969). Whereas total sleep and REM sleep remain fairly constant during adult years, the amount of high-voltage Stage-4 sleep shows a constant and substantial decline during this period (Agnew, Webb, & Williams, 1967; Feinberg, 1969).

Feinberg (1969) felt that such pronounced changes (50–100%) are a result of changes in CNS function and are not secondary to alterations in other physiological systems. He further contended that one could expect such significant variations to have profound implications for behavioral functions. Parallel changes in sleep patterns of the aged and patients with organic brain disease have been reported (Feinberg & Carlson, 1968; Feinberg, Koresko, & Heller, 1967). Although the comparable variations in the two sets of measures may result from their relationship to a third factor such as structural brain changes, an interesting alternative hypothesis (the sleep cognitive hypothesis) suggests that certain brain processes during sleep are essential to adequate cognitive functioning (Feinberg, 1969). To date, support for this position is only indirect, but continued work in this area should be extremely fruitful in developing a clearer understanding of brain–behavior relationships.

Average Evoked Response and Senescence

The study of average evoked responses from scalp recordings became an effective and practical means of investigating electrocortical activity with the application of computer technology to the oscilloscope-trace technique (Dawson, 1951, 1954). Essentially, this involves summing brief intervals of an EEG tracing immediately following the presentation of specific stimuli. After repeated presentations of the stimulus, spontaneous EEG activity, which is unrelated to the specific sensory input, tends to average to zero voltage, whereas electrical activity that is time locked to the stimulus becomes enhanced. Typically, this is a complex wave form consisting of several positive and negative components.

Since the development of this technique, there has been a phenomenal proliferation of investigations in this area, producing a nearly incomprehensible literature at this point. Although these phenomena appear to be reliable, this body of literature demonstrates, perhaps above all else, that there are marked individual differences in the measureable characteristics of these wave forms (Whipple, 1964). Variations within subjects as a function of level of attention and/or alertness have also been noted (Ciganek, 1967; Davis, 1964; Goff, Allison, Shapiro, & Rosner, 1966; Gross, Begleiter, Tobin, & Kissin, 1965; Haider, Spong, & Lindsley, 1964; Satterfield, 1965; Spong, Haider, & Lindsley, 1965). The relevance of these measures to efficient psychological performance attests to the potential utility of the study of evoked responses in aging. To date, only a few studies investigating age relationships have been reported.

In spite of the tremendous variability of this response, there are consistent trends reported in the few studies pertaining to aging. In general, amplitude of the earlier wave forms during the first 100 milliseconds following the stimulus tends to increase with age for visual (Dustman & Beck, 1969; Schenkenberg, 1970; Straumanis, Shagass, & Schwartz, 1965), somatosensory (Luders, 1970; Shagass & Schwartz, 1965), and auditory (Schenkenberg, 1970) stimulation. Amplitude of later portions of the evoked response, up to approximately 400 milliseconds following the stimulus, tends to decrease with age for all three sensory modalities (Dustman & Beck, 1969; Luders, 1970; Schenkenberg, 1970). Such changes become apparent during middle age and are increasingly pronounced with the onset of senescence (Luders, 1970; Schenkenberg, 1970). Increased latency of wave peaks during the first 200 milliseconds of the evoked response has also been reported with age for visual, auditory, and somatosensory stimuli (Dustman & Beck, 1969; Kooi & Bagchi, 1964; Luders, 1970; Schenkenberg, 1970; Straumanis et al., 1965). Age differences are not as apparent in latencies after 200 milliseconds (Luders, 1970; Straumanis et al., 1965). However, a comparison of patients with chronic brain syndrome and old controls revealed that the peak latency for waves occurring after 120 milliseconds was significantly longer for patients than for controls (Straumanis et al., 1965).

There is general agreement among the investigators that the changes in evoked responses with age are due primarily to CNS factors. Straumanis et al. (1965) considered three possibilities for the increase in amplitude and latency of early wave forms in the visual-evoked response. These were increased neural excitability, decreased neural inhibition, and decreased variability in latency of neural response. They speculated that decreased neural inhibition may be the most likely factor. Such diminished inhibition, they felt, would be consistent with decreased precision of CNS functioning. Luders (1970) interpreted the variations in amplitude of early components in the somatosensory-evoked response as reflecting alterations in postsynaptic activity of cells in the somatosensory cortex. The second of four components described by Luders (1970) includes waves that occur from 40 to 80 milliseconds following the stimulus. He cited several investigations dealing with sleep, drugs, and pathology that supported his argument that changes in this portion of the wave form may reflect modifications in the associational pathways with age.

Schenkenberg (1970) suggested that the decrease in amplitude seen in the postprimary portion of later components of the evoked response is due to decreased effectiveness of the reticular activating system. An alternative suggestion by Schenkenberg focuses on possible decreased responsivity of the cortex following the primary volley. In this regard, it is interesting to note that in our laboratory, amplitude changes in the later components of the evoked response (200–400 milliseconds following the stimulus) are not readily associated with age (Marsh & Thompson, 1972). The principal difference between our experimental designs and those in the literature is that the stimuli are always of some consequence to the subjects, and therefore subjects are more likely to be more highly alerted throughout the stimulus presentation period. This suggestion of decreased age differences in the later components with increased levels of attention or activation is in need of further investigation. Although such tentative results are consistent with the hypothesis that age changes in later components are due to reticular system influences, they offer little toward the determination of any specific anatomical structure as a primary contributor to the age changes.

Many criticisms have been raised regarding the problems of interpreting average evoked potentials and the complications of averaging techniques. There is, nevertheless, considerable evidence to indicate that, under carefully controlled experimental conditions, reliable measures can be obtained that show functional relationships with other critical measures. Future work on aging using this technique should prove fruitful. A welcome addition to this procedure would be an index of variability for the average of each time-sampling point. Such a measure is becoming less difficult to obtain with increased analogue to digital capabilities interfaced with digital computers.

Careful consideration must be given to a number of factors that can influence the evoked response. The levels of attention and motivation have already been mentioned. A factor that is persistently overlooked is the possible contribution of background activity. This is particularly important in aging research in view of the documented changes in EEG characteristics. Significant Sex × Age (Schenkenberg, 1970; Shagass & Schwartz, 1965; Straumanis et al., 1965) as well as Personality Factor × Age interaction effects (Shagass & Schwartz, 1965) have been reported. Luders (1970) also cited two Japanese studies that reported Sex × Age differences (Ikuta, 1969; Inanga, Ishikawa, Tachibana, Shirakawa, Kotorii, & Hirozaki, 1969). Consistent trends and interpretations for such interaction effects are not yet available, but the data clearly indicate that such individual differences as sex, personality, and intelligence should be considered in future investigations of evoked responses.

Contingent Negative Variation

Cooper, Aldridge, McCallum, Walter, and Winter (1964) reported a slow-rising negative potential at the vertex in experimental situations employing an S_1-S_2 paradigm. Using DC amplifiers, they recorded a slow rise in negativity during the S_1-S_2 interval that tends to reach its peak immediately before the presentation of S_2 and then to shift in a positive direction following the presentation of S_2. This evoked slow potential response was labeled the contingent negative variation (CNV) because it appeared to be contingent upon the first stimulus signaling the occurrence of a second stimulus that required a response and because it varied in the negative direction.

The size of this response has been reported to be positively associated with the level of attention or arousal as reflected in reaction time performance (Hillyard & Galambos, 1967; J. I. Lacey & B. C. Lacey, 1970; Waszak & Obrist, 1969), amount of effort required in a motor act (Rebert, McAdam, Knott, & Irwin, 1967), and response to tone pips at threshold level (Hillyard, 1969; Low, Borda, Frost, & Kellaway, 1966; Rebert et al., 1967). The CNV has been regarded as a correlate of various psychological constructs, such as expectancy (Walter, 1965), conation (Low et al., 1966), motivation (Irwin, Knott, McAdam, & Rebert, 1966; Rebert et al., 1967), and attention (Tecce & Scheff, 1969). In view of the relevance of such constructs to age-related decrements in performance, it would seem reasonable to investigate possible age differences in CNV and their relationship to measures of performance.

To date, the effects of age on CNV measures remain relatively unexplored. Thompson and Nowlin (in press) investigated the interrelationship of heart rate deceleration and CNVs in a traditional reaction time task. They reported no significant overall age difference in CNVs. There was a significant Age × Response Speed interaction effect, such that the size of the CNV was positively associated with speed of response in the group of young subjects but less so in the group of old subjects. Marsh and Thompson (in press) also failed to find a significant age effect on the CNV in a pitch discrimination task. Tentative results in a recent study dealing with the perception of verbal and nonverbal visual stimuli presented tachistoscopically further revealed an absence of age differences (Marsh & Thompson, in press). Thus, the meager available data indicate that healthy elderly males develop CNVs during increased attentive states that are comparable to the changes seen in young subjects. Since virtually no data have been collected on female elderly subjects, the possibility remains that an Age $\times$ Sex interaction may be obtained.

Cardiovascular Disease and Intellectual Decline in the Elderly

In pointing out the relationship between cardiovascular disease and EEG changes earlier, we also suggested the potential relevance of cardiovascular disorders to intellectual impairment. An impressive array of investigations offers further documentation of the significance cardiovascular problems such as coronary artery disease and hypertension may have in the development of cognitive deficits (Apter, Halstead, & Heimburger, 1951; Birren et al., 1963; Enzer, Simpson, & Blankstein, 1942; Krasno & Ivy, 1950; Reitan, 1954; Simonson & Enzer, 1941; Spieth, 1965). By and large, such studies implicate circulatory insufficiency as an important factor in the age-related decline observed in cross-sectional studies. Recent results from a longitudinal study provide additional confirmation of this notion (Wilkie & Eisdorfer, 1971). Whereas normotensive subjects showed a slight decline and hypertensive subjects showed a marked decline in intellectual functioning, mild elevations of blood pressure in early senescent subjects resulted in no change or a slight improvement. The authors interpreted their findings as supporting Obrist's (1964) contention that mild increases in blood pressure may be essential to the maintenance of adequate cerebral circulation.

An interesting series of papers by Szafran, which focused on the early detection of deterioration in professional flying personnel, revealed that the cardiopulmonary status of pilots who are in good health is related to choice reaction times, sequential decision making, and the rate at which information can be processed under conditions of information overload (Szafran, 1963, 1965, 1966a, 1966b). In attempting to develop useful ways of describing, classifying, and conceptualizing his data, the author has borrowed heavily from the formulations of information theory and signal detection theory—a trend that should be richly rewarding in future psychophysiological studies on aging.

In a more recent systematic review of his work, Szafran (1968) discussed his data in the context of evaluating reserve channel capacity under conditions of task overload and reduced signal to noise ratio. He emphasized cardiovascular–behavioral relationships, pointing out that decreased cardiovascular function may, by virtue of its effect on cerebral circulation, increase neural noise, which, in turn, would decrease efficient information processing. Perhaps more importantly, he argued convincingly that the functional loss so frequently referred to in the literature is "not a necessary feature of the performance of a professionally successful and healthy middle-aged or older adult."

Such evidence forces one to appreciate the difficulties and significance for gerontology of differentiating effects of aging and those of minimal pathology. Appropriate to this line of thinking, Spieth (1965) presented a stimulating paper in which he developed a model to account for cross-sectional age decrements on the basis of pathology. Taking the facts that health status is positively correlated with performance (in this case response speed) and that both the incidence and degree of impaired health increase during the adult years, he portrayed the performance distributions one could expect to obtain at different age levels, assuming that age, per se, had no effect. Interestingly enough, a search of the literature revealed a study on writing speed (Birren & Botwinick, 1951) that fit the model beautifully.

Although, as Spieth pointed out, "there is undoubtedly a great deal more to aging than cardiovascular or other particular diseases," the need for detailed information regarding health status of subjects has been undeniably demonstrated. In agreement with Szafran (1966a, 1966b), one could argue that studies which clearly define health and occupational states of subjects may result in radical revisions of our conceptions regarding the effects of aging and the functional capabilities of healthy persons in late adulthood.

MEASURES OF AUTONOMIC NERVOUS SYSTEM AROUSAL

Age differences in autonomic nervous system structure and function have been readily apparent in the literature for a considerable length of time. The relevance of such differences to behavioral changes in the elderly have been briefly discussed in more recent papers (Cohen & Shmavonian, 1967; Shmavonian & Busse, 1963). A cursory review of the literature, however, revealed a paucity of studies dealing with indexes of autonomic reactivity in the elderly and their relationship to behavioral functioning.

Galvanic Skin Response Studies on Aging

The galvanic skin response (GSR) measures have been recorded in both conditioning and vigilance studies. Botwinick and Kornetsky

(1959, 1960) used a conditioning paradigm in which a tone was the conditioned stimulus (CS) and a shock was the unconditioned stimulus (US). Prior to the initiation of conditioning, the CS was repeatedly presented alone until the GSR was habituated. They reported that elderly subjects showed more rapid habituation to the CS alone, conditioned less readily, and extinguished more quickly than young subjects. In the total sample, the number of conditioned responses was correlated with the number of responses in the habituation ($r = .62$) and extinction ($r = .60$) periods. They concluded that autonomic reactivity as reflected in their measure appeared to be a general process and that it was considerably less evident in older subjects.

Shmavonian (Shmavonian, Miller, & Cohen, 1968, 1970; Shmavonian, Yarmat, & Cohen, 1965) recorded GSR, vasomotor reactivity, and EEG during a trace-conditioning procedure in which the CS was a tone, and the US was a shock. Their GSR measure reflected the change in conductance from pre- to post-CS during 10 acquisition trials and 10 extinction trials. They also looked at basal conductance at the time of CS onset. Their data indicate that the magnitude of conditioned GSR responses (in micromhos) is substantially less for the old than for the young. Further, the basal measure indicates that the level of general activation is significantly higher for the young than for the old throughout the acquisition and extinction trials. A similar finding was apparent for their plethysmograph measure, which suggests that vasomotor reactivity was considerably less for the old than for the young. Interestingly enough, their EEG measure showed greater reactivity for the old than for the young; this finding will be discussed in a later section.

Surwillo (1966b) investigated changes in skin potential (Tarchanoff effect), skin temperature, and heart rate during a vigilance task. Subjects were required to monitor a Mackworth clock for 60 minutes and to note irregular movements of the hand by pushing a key. The author hypothesized that the measures of autonomic activity would change at a different rate for the elderly during an hour-long vigilance task. In the case of the heart rate and skin potential, his hypothesis was not confirmed. Although the increase in the number of errors was greater with time for the old than for the young, the rate of change for heart rate and skin potential was similar for both age groups. The overall measures of skin potential and heart rate, however, were higher for the young than for the old. Changes in skin temperature were in support of the hypothesis. During the last 45 minutes, skin temperatures decreased in the young but increased in the old ($p < .001$). Surwillo argued that since a decrease in skin temperature has been correlated with mental work and stress, and an increase in temperature has been associated with sleep, then this measure may predict differential changes in arousal and vigilance behavior.

Latency of skin potential responses to critical stimuli in the vigilance test was reported to be longer in the elderly than in the young (Surwillo & Quilter, 1965a). However, there was no significant difference in key-press speed between young and old subjects; a middle-aged group was significantly faster than the other two. The authors pointed out the difference between the speed set in this and a traditional reaction time test and emphasized that differences in motivation, which favored the older subjects, may compensate for physiological decrements.

The frequency of spontaneous skin potential changes during psychological experiments is also decreased in the elderly (Silverman et al., 1959; Surwillo & Quilter, 1965b). Both of these investigations reported a positive relationship between some index of efficiency of performance and the number of spontaneous skin responses occurring in a given time segment, temporally associated with the performance measure. Such findings are consistent with the interpretation that decreased incidence of spontaneous skin potential responses in the elderly may reflect a decreased level of autonomic arousal with age (Shmavonian & Busse, 1963; Silverman et al., 1959; Surwillo, 1965b).

Heart Rate and Blood Pressure Changes during Reaction Time

In recent years, considerable interest has been generated in the relationship between heart rate changes and the level of attentive states. Contrary to other traditional indexes of activation, the direction of heart rate fluctuations is somewhat dependent upon the nature of the experimental task. Situations requiring an internal direction of attention are associated with heart rate acceleration, whereas an external direction of attention is accompanied by a decrease in heart rate (J. I. Lacey, Kagan, Lacey, & Moss, 1963). J. I. Lacey (1967) hypothesized that heart rate deceleration may facilitate environmental intake and related behavioral functioning by virtue of its influence on afferent feedback to the CNS. Support for this position is apparent in studies that report beat-by-beat deceleration during fixed foreperiods in a traditional reaction time task (B. C. Lacey & J. I. Lacey, 1965). Slowing of the heart rate reaches its lowest point at or shortly before the presentation of the response signal, followed by rapid acceleration over the next several heart beats. Further, the rate of deceleration is correlated with response speed, such that the greater the rate of change, the faster the response.

Since elderly subjects tend to have altered heart rate patterns as well as decreased response speed, the question could be raised whether any of the age-related slowing could be accounted for by variations in heart rate. Morris and Thompson (1969) investigated the effects of age on heart rate deceleration and respiration in fixed foreperiod intervals of 4, 9, and 14 seconds. They reported that old subjects decelerated less than one beat per minute (bpm) in all three conditions, but that the observed changes were statistically significant. Young subjects showed significantly more deceleration (approximately 3.5–4.0 bpm) in all three conditions. There was also some suggestion of a relationship between rate of change and response speed in the young, but not in the old.

The age differences in heart rate during reaction time performance pose questions concerning concomitant changes in other cardiovascular measures such as blood pressure. It has been suggested that increased blood pressure during the foreperiod may account for the deceleration. For example, sympathetic arousal during the task may result in increased pressure, which may act homeostatically to decrease heart rate through baroreceptor reflex systems to the heart via the vagus nerve (Heymans & Neil, 1958). On the other hand, J. L. Lacey's (1967) hypothesis would be consistent with a decrease in blood pressure concomitant with cardiac deceleration, the argument being that afferent feedback from peripheral arterial baroreceptor systems may have an inhibitory effect on cortical and psychomotor functioning. Systematic animal studies have suggested a possible mechanism for such action (Heymans & Neil, 1958). A third explanation would be that cardiac deceleration is simply a part of an active inhibitory process to diminish irrelevant somatic activity during preparation to respond. (P. A. Obrist, Webb, Sutterer, & Howard, 1970), and hence one might expect a secondary decrease in blood pressure.

Nowlin, Eisdorfer, and Thompson (1970a) recorded heart rate, respiration, and intra-arterial blood pressure during reaction time procedures with fixed foreperiods of 4 and 9 seconds. The observed heart rate deceleration prior to the imperative stimulus and subsequent acceleration was in agreement with the results reported by B. C. Lacey and J. I. Lacey (1965). The investigators also reported a significant relationship between extent of deceleration in the 4-second foreperiod condition and reaction time ($r = -.54$; $p < .05$). For young subjects, changes in diastolic pressure tended to parallel the heart rate changes: as heart rate slowed, diastolic pressure dropped, reaching its lowest point simultaneously with the slowest heart beat. Systolic blood pressure also showed a gradual decrease followed by an increase, but this change lagged behind heart rate and diastolic changes and was approximately two beats out of phase. There were no significant relationships between pressure measures and reaction time. A similar pattern of blood pressure response was observed for the elderly, but the changes were considerably less in magnitude (Nowlin et al., 1970b). As with the young, there was no significant relationship between blood pressure and response speed in the elderly group.

The results of these studies clearly indicate that there are systematic changes in cardiovascular responsivity with changes in level of attention as reflected in reaction time. It is also apparent that the changes for the elderly are markedly reduced, with no suggestion of a relationship to reaction time in any of the conditions. The absence of an increase in pressure during cardiac deceleration demonstrates that the characteristic heart rate change is not a homeostatic reflex reaction to increasing pressure. The possible role of respiration has also been considered and discounted as a principal factor in all of the studies reported here.

A reasonable interpretation of such findings would, in some manner, implicate CNS processes associated with increased levels of arousal as being principally responsible for the systematic patterning of cardiac responses. A likely pathway for the mediation of these processes via the autonomic nervous system has been well established though not developed in complete and specific detail (Folkow, Heymans, & Neil, 1965).

In general, the data reported in this section are consistent with the hypothesis that the elderly have less autonomic reactivity than young subjects during states of focused attention and increased activation. This can be seen in decreased heart rate and blood pressure change, decreased skin potential responses, decreased vasomotor reactivity, and increased skin temperature. A major problem, which is in need of further elaboration, is the possible uncoupling with age of peripheral sites from CNS functioning. Changes in end-organ reactivity due to such factors as skin changes or arteriosclerosis, for example, may contribute heavily to the observed age differences in bioelectric measures. There is evidence of structural changes in the CNS that would support the hypothesis of decreased central autonomic reactivity in the elderly (Andrew, 1956; Nelson & Gelhorn, 1957, 1958), but the picture is by no means clear at the present time. There is also the possibility that decreased sympathetic-adrenal reactivity, stemming particularly from functional changes in the adrenal medullary system, may be a determinant in the age changes reported (Cohen & Shmavonian, 1967). The importance of this controversy is increased when one contrasts the differential age effects in measures of central and autonomic nervous system activation (see below).

Free Fatty Acid Mobilization

Increased mobilization of free fatty acid (FFA) into blood plasma has been related to increased levels of autonomic nervous system activity (Bogdonoff, Estes, Friedberg, & Klein, 1961). In contrast to the above findings, investigations of FFA mobilization during learning and vigilance studies suggest that elderly subjects are more highly aroused than young subjects in experimental settings involving assessment of cognitive skills (Powell, Eisdorfer, & Bogdonoff, 1964; Troyer, Eisdorfer, Wilkie, & Bogdonoff, 1966). Consideration of these results in conjunction with other learning studies led Eisdorfer (1968) to hypothesize that, contrary to the general impression, older subjects may generally be in a state of high arousal. In attempting to account for the association between learning and FFA in the elderly, Eisdorfer relied heavily on Malmo's activation hypothesis, which holds that the functional relationship between performance and arousal is best described by the familiar inverted U. Therefore, if elderly subjects are in a high-arousal state, their performance levels are more likely to decline than are those of the young as a result of increased stress. As support for this contention, he cited several learning studies that indicated that the number of omission errors in a serial-learning task increases for the old as the presentation interval decreases, while the number of commission errors shows relatively little change. This occurs even though the older subject has ample time to generate a response within the shortest presentation interval, which in turn increases autonomic arousal to detrimental levels.

In a further elaboration of this hypothesis, Eisdorfer, Nowlin, and Wilkie (1970) postulated that feedback to the CNS from the peripheral effects of autonomic arousal might be one of the factors negatively influencing verbal learning in older persons under stress.

This was tested by the administration of propranolol immediately before subjects participated in a learning experiment. Propranolol produces a blockade of autonomic beta-adrenergic receptor sites in peripheral end organs, but apparently has minimal effect on CNS processes. Thus, such effects as heart slowing with some decreased blood pressure and blood flow, slight pupillary dilatation, and constriction of bronchi should result. Two groups of elderly subjects, comparable with respect to age, socioeconomic status, and general level of intellectual functioning, performed in a serial-learning task immediately after the administration of propranolol or a placebo. Measures of GSR, heart rate, and FFA level were also obtained during the experiment.

The experimental group made significantly fewer errors ($p < .05$), had lower FFA levels ($p < .001$), and slower heart rates ($p < .01$) than the control group. The GSR was also lower in the experimental group, but this difference was not statistically significant. The authors concluded (a) that learning in older subjects can be improved by modification of the autonomic nervous system with pharmacologic agents and (b) that a state of high rather than low "autonomic end-organ arousal" can account for a large portion of the learning deficit observed in elderly subjects. These results have important implications for psychophysiological research and theory construction in aging that make early replication highly desirable.

At first glance, the discrepancies between studies measuring FFA and those involving other measures of autonomic reactivity are difficult to reconcile. Not only are other peripheral autonomic responses decidedly lower and fewer in number in the elderly than in the young, but also at least one measure of autonomic reactivity (frequency of spontaneous GSRs) tends to be positively correlated with efficiency of performance in both old and young (Shmavonian & Busse, 1963; Silverman, Cohen, & Shmavonian, 1959; Surwillo & Quilter, 1965a). In the face of such evidence, it is difficult to comprehend how a further lowering of end-organ arousal state could facilitate performance. The difficulty becomes less burdensome, however, if one accepts the notion that in the elderly traditional autonomic measures may no longer adequately reflect the extent of autonomic nervous system arousal. It must also be borne in mind that the different end organs controlled by the autonomic nervous system may show differential age effects, and thus different autonomic nervous system measures may show increasing divergence with increasing age.

Since stimulation of the sympathetic nervous system is an important factor in FFA mobilization, autonomic arousal could be interpreted as high in stress situations when FFA is high. In such instances, the speculation could be raised that the depressed level of autonomic reactivity in the elderly as reflected in GSR, vasomotor, and heart rate responses is due partially to deterioration, specifically in the cardiovascular system and in the end organs producing the GSR. If this were true, then it is conceivable that a high level of downward discharges from CNS to autonomic effectors could occur, but the extent of this state would not be reflected in all peripheral systems. As a consequence, the normal feedback relationships from peripheral effectors to CNS could be distorted to such an extent that while some systems undergo minimal change, others (e.g., FFA) may' disproportionately modulate the level of CNS activation. Thus, in stressful situations, elderly subjects may be sufficiently activated centrally to impair performance without this being reflected in some peripheral measures (e.g., GSR). An alternative model could argue for an increased sensitivity by the CNS to those systems that fluctuated less with increasing age. Thus, only slight changes in these systems could have disproportionately greater negative feedback effects on the CNS.

Keeping the first model above in mind, one could argue that propranolol improves performance in the elderly by *increasing* the level of CNS activation. If one conceptualizes autonomic feedback as being part of a complex regulatory system to maintain appropriate levels of activation, then it is easy to construct a model where, within limits, feedback from peripheral sites may serve to modulate reciprocally the downward and upward discharges from the autonomic components of the CNS. As end-organ activity increases, such discharges, which are probably hypothalamic in origin (Cohen & Shmavonian, 1967), would be increasingly inhibited, resulting in decreased activation both cortically and autonomically. Conversely, if afferent input from peripheral autonomic systems decreased, particularly in the face of perceived stress, then CNS activity would be facilitated with a concomitant increase in cortical arousal. If this were the case, then propranolol, by virtue of its mitigating effect on end-organ feedback, may actually enhance CNS activation. Experiments designed to assess the effects of stress and such blocking agents on performance, CNS activity, autonomic responses, and their interrelationship would seem to be indicated. Regardless of whether or not the application of a feedback model holds, the significance of altering performance in the elderly by modifying autonomic activity may be difficult to overestimate.

CENTRAL AND AUTONOMIC NERVOUS SYSTEM RELATIONSHIPS

During the development of this chapter, it has been increasingly difficult to ignore the potential significance of central–autonomic interrelationships to age-related changes in behavior. Age discrepancies in measures of CNS reactivity are minimal when comparing young with healthy elderly volunteers, and may even be difficult to demonstrate if the measures are obtained while subjects are actively engaged in behavioral tasks. On the other hand, marked age differences have been reported in autonomic nervous system responsivity in stressful situations.

Studies in which simultaneous recordings of cortical and autonomic measures have been made reveal significant correlations between the two in young subjects (e.g., J. I. Lacey & B. C. Lacey, 1970), while such relationships are not obvious in older subjects. Thompson and Nowlin (1971), for example, recorded heart rate and CNV during a reaction time task and failed to find an overall age difference in CNV, but the old showed significantly less cardiac deceleration than the young in both conditions. Further, there was a significant relationship between CNV and response speed for the young group, but not for the old. If the CNV reflects level of attention or arousal, then the results indicate that the old were attending and were as aroused as the young. However, this was not reflected in performance measures, in that the old had longer reaction times, and there was no association between the CNV and response speed. Although the data suggest comparable alertness for young and old with respect to this cortical measure, the elderly were significantly less reactive at the autonomic level.

Similar results were reported by Shmavonian et al. (1965) in a conditioning experiment. Old subjects had markedly lower GSR and vasomotor reactivity than the young, but activation in the EEG was greater for the old group. Such studies raise the question: "Are antagonistic influences between the two systems, even if only momentary, responsible for impairment seen in the elderly?" Cohen and Shmavonian (1967) emphasized the importance of an optimal balance among central, autonomic, and hormonal effects to integrative sensory motor functioning. Aged subjects, they argue, show a less-integrated total response, which may account for some of the decline in adaptive abilities.

Such findings and interpretations encourage research investigations that would determine the relationship between measures of autonomic and central nervous system reactivity at varying levels of performance. Appropriate investigations are not readily apparent in the literature at the present time. Thompson and Nowlin (1971) made a crude comparison that fits into this general context. Between-subject correlations were calculated for CNV and cardiac deceleration for both fast and slow reaction time trials in 3- and 6-second foreperiod conditions. For the young, they found the highest degree of correlation in the condition that yielded the fastest reaction times ($r = .929$, $p < .05$). Correlation coefficients in other conditions were smaller and nonsignificant. Correlation coefficients for the old subjects, on the other hand, tended to be negative, and the largest was obtained in the condition that yielded the slowest reaction times ($r = -.670$, ns). Though such findings must be viewed as tentative for the moment, they nevertheless suggest that efficient performance is associated with high concordance between autonomic and central nervous system reactivity, while a lack of congruence may be associated with poorer performance.

Although the processes and structures that underlie the change in central–autonomic interrelationships with age are not clearly understood at the present time, evidence is accumulating that some optimally harmonious interaction between the two systems may be essential for the maintenance of maximally efficient adaptive responses during late adulthood. The potential relevance of the concept of feedback is implicit in this line of reasoning. It appears that autonomic nervous system activity may play a different and perhaps more important role in cognitive functioning than originally thought, as a result of its afferent input systems to the brain (Heymans & Neil, 1958; J. I. Lacey, 1967; J. I. Lacey & B. C. Lacey, 1970). In view of the obvious changes in autonomic reactivity over the life-span, even in healthy elderly individuals, this would seem to be a likely point of departure for future research. Continued investigation and comparison of pharmacologic agents that modify either central or peripheral autonomic nervous system activity should prove to be extremely fruitful in the study of brain–behavior relationships in the elderly.

REFERENCES

Agnew, H. W., Webb, W. B., & Williams, R. L. Sleep patterns in late middle age males: An EEG study. *Electroencephalography and Clinical Neurophysiology*, 1967, **23**, 168–171.

Andermann, K., & Stoller, A. EEG patterns in hospitalized and non-hospitalized aged. *Electroencephalography and Clinical Neurophysiology*, 1961, **13**, 319.

Andrew, W. Structual alterations with aging in the nervous system. *Journal of Chronic Diseases*, 1956, **3**, 575–596.

Apter, N. S., Halstead, W. G., & Heimburger, R. F. Impaired cerebral functions in essential hypertension. *American Journal of Psychiatry*, 1951, **107**, 808–813.

Bankier, R. G. A correlative study of psychological and EEG findings in normal, physically ill and mentally ill seniles. *Electroencephalography and Clinical Neurophysiology*, 1967, **22**, 189–190.

Barnes, R. H., Busse, E. W., & Friedman, E. L. The psychological functioning of aged individuals with normal and abnormal electroencephalograms: II. A study of hospitalized individuals. *Journal of Nervous and Mental Diseases*, 1956, **124**, 585–593.

Birren, J. E. Age changes in speed of behavior: Its central nature and physiological correlates. In A. T. Welford & J. E. Birren (Eds.), *Behavior, aging, and the nervous system*. Springfield, Ill.: Charles C Thomas, 1965.

Birren, J. E., & Botwinick, J. The relation of writing speed to age in the senile psychosis. *Journal of Consulting Psychology*, 1951, **15**, 243–249.

Birren, J. E., Butler, R. N., Greenhouse, S. W., Sokoloff, L., & Yarrow, M. R. Interdisciplinary relationships: Interrelations of physiological, psychological and psychiatric findings in healthy elderly men. In, *Human Aging: A biological and behavioral study*. (USPHS Publ. No. 986) Washington, D.C.: United States Government Printing Office, 1963.

Bogdonoff, M. D., Estes, E. H., Jr., Friedberg, S. J., & Klein, R. F. Fat mobilization in man. *Annals of Internal Medicine*, 1961, **55**, 328–338.

Botwinick, J., & Kornetsky, C. Age differences in the frequency of the GSR during a conditioning experiment. *Journal of Gerontology*, 1959, **14**, 503.

Botwinick, J., & Kornetsky, C. Age differences in the acquisition and extinction of the GSR. *Journal of Gerontology*, 1960, **15**, 83–84.

Brazier, M. A. B., & Finesinger, J. E. Characteristics of the normal electroencephalogram: I. A Study of the occipital cortical potentials in 500 normal adults. *Journal of Clinical Investigation*, 1944, **23**, 303–311.

Busse, E. W., Barnes, R. H., Friedman, E. L., & Kelty, E. J. Psychological functioning of aged individuals with normal and abnormal electroencephalograms: I. A study of non-hospitalized community volunteers. *Journal of Nervous and Mental Diseases*, 1956, **124**, 135–141.

Busse, E. W., Barnes, R. H., Silverman, A. J., Shy, G. M., Thaler, M., & Frost, L. L. Studies of the process of aging: Factors that influence the psyche of elderly persons. *American Journal of Psychiatry*, 1954, **110**, 897–903.

Busse, E. W., & Obrist, W. D. Significance of focal electroencephalographic changes in the elderly. *Postgraduate Medicine*, 1963, **34**, 179–182.

Busse, E. W., & Obrist, W. D. Pre-senescent electroencephalographic changes in normal subjects. *Journal of Gerontology*, 1965, **20**, 315–320.

Ciganek, L. The effects of attention and distraction on the visual evoked potential in man: A preliminary report. *Electroencephalography and Clinical Neurophysiology*, 1967, Suppl. 26, 70–73.

Cohen, S. I., & Shmavonian, B. M. Catecholamines, vasomotor conditioning and aging. In L. Gitman (Ed.), *Endocrines and aging.* Springfield, Ill.: Charles C Thomas, 1967.

Craik, F. I. M. Short-term memory and the aging process. In G. A. Talland (Ed.), *Human aging and behavior.* New York: Academic Press, 1968.

Dastur, D. K., Lane, M. H., Hansen, D. B., Kety, S. S., Butler, R. N., Perlin, S., & Sokoloff, L. Effects of aging on cerebral circulation and metabolism in man. In, *Human aging: A biological and behavioral study.* (USPHS Publ. No. 986) Washington, D.C.: United States Government Printing Office, 1963.

Davis, J. Enhancement of evoked cortical potentials in humans related to a task requiring a decision. *Science,* 1964, **145**, 182–183.

Dawson, G. D. A summation technique for detecting small signals in a large irregular background. *Journal of Physiology,* 1951, **115**, 2–3.

Dawson, G. D. A summation technique for the detection of small evoked potentials. *Electroencephalography and Clinical Neurophysiology,* 1954, **6**, 65–84.

Drachman, D. A., & Hughes, J. R. Memory and the hippocampal complexes: III. Aging and temporal EEG abnormalities. *Neurology,* 1971, **21**, 1–14.

Dustman, R. E., & Beck, E. C. The effects of maturation and aging on the wave form of visually evoked potentials. *Electroencephalography and Clinical Neurophysiology,* 1969, **26**, 2–11.

Eisdorfer, C. Arousal and performance: Experiments in verbal learning and a tentative theory. In G. A. Talland (Ed.), *Human aging and behavior.* New York: Academic Press, 1968.

Eisdorfer, C., Nowlin, J., & Wilkie, F. Improvement of learning in the aged by modification of autonomic nervous system activity. *Science,* 1970, **170**, 1327–1329.

Enzer, N., Simpson, E., & Blankstein, S. S. Fatigue of patients with circulatory insufficiency, investigated by means of fusion frequency of flicker. *Annals of Internal Medicine,* 1942, **160**, 701–707.

Feinberg, I. Effects of age on human sleep patterns. In A. Kales (Ed.), *Sleep physiology and pathology.* Philadelphia: Lippincott, 1969.

Feinberg, I., & Carlson, V. R. Sleep variables as a function of age in man. *Archives of General Psychiatry,* 1968, **18**, 239–250.

Feinberg, I., Koresko, R. L., & Heller, N. EEG sleep patterns as a function of normal and pathological aging in man. *Journal of Psychiatric Research,* 1967, **5**, 107–144.

Feinberg, I., Lane, M. H., & Lassen, N. A. Senile dementia and cerebral oxygen uptake measured on the right and left sides. *Nature,* 1960, **188**, 962–964.

Folkow, B., Heymans, C., & Neil, E. Integrated aspects of cardiovascular regulation. In W. F. Hamilton & P. Dow (Eds.), *Handbook of physiology: Circulation.* Vol. 1. Baltimore: Waverly Press, 1965.

Frey, T. S., & Sjögren, H. The electroencephalogram in elderly persons suffering from neuropsychiatric disorders. *Acta Psychiatrica Scandinavica,* 1959, **34**, 438–450.

Friedlander, W. J. Electroencephalographic alpha rate in adults as a function of age. *Geriatrics,* 1958, **13**, 29–31.

Gaches, J. Etude statistique sur les traces "alpha largement developpe" en fonction de l'age. *Presse médicale,* 1960, **68,** 1620–1622.

Gerard, R. W. Aging and organization. In J. E. Birren (Ed.), *Handbook of aging and the individual.* Chicago: University of Chicago Press, 1959.

Gibbs, F. A., & Gibbs, E. L. *Atlas of electroencephalography.* Vol. 1. *Methodology and controls.* Cambridge, Mass.: Addison-Wesley, 1950.

Goff, W. R., Allison, T., Shapiro, A., & Rosner, B. S. Cerebral somatosensory responses evoked during sleep in man. *Electroencephalography and Clinical Neurophysiology,* 1966, **21,** 1–9.

Greenblatt, M. Age and electroencephalographic abnormality in neuro-psychiatric patients: A study of 1593 cases. *American Journal of Psychiatry,* 1944, **101,** 82–90.

Gross, M. M., Begleiter, H., Tobin, M., & Kissin, B. Auditory evoked response comparison during counting clicks and reading. *Electroencephalography and Clinical Neurophysiology,* 1965, **18,** 451–454.

Haider, M., Spong, P., & Lindsley, D. B. Attention, vigilance, and cortical evoked-potentials in humans. *Science,* 1964, **145,** 180–182.

Harvald, B. EEG in old age. *Acta Psychiatrica Scandinavica,* 1958, **33,** 193–196.

Heymans, C., & Neil, E. *Reflexogenic areas of the cardiovascular system.* Boston: Little, Brown, 1958.

Hillyard, S. A. The CNV and the vertex evoked potential during signal detection. In E. Donchin & D. B. Lindsley (Eds.), *Current research problems in the study of averaged evoked potentials.* (NASA SP-191) Washington, D.C.: National Aeronautics and Space Administration, 1969.

Hillyard, S. A., & Galambos, R. Effects of stimulus and response contingencies on a surface negative slow potential shift in man. *Electroencephalography and Clinical Neurophysiology,* 1967, **22,** 297–304.

Hoagland, H. Studies of brain metabolism and electrical activity in relation to adrenocortical physiology. In G. Pincus (Ed.), *Recent progress in hormone research.* Vol. 10. New York: Academic Press, 1954.

Hoch, P. H., & Kubis, J. Electroencephalographic studies in organic psychoses. *American Journal of Psychiatry,* 1941, **98,** 404–408.

Hughes, J. R. A statistical analysis on the location of EEG abnormalities. *Electroencephalography and Clinical Neurophysiology,* 1960, **12,** 905–909.

Ikuta, T. Sex differences of the somatosensory evoked potentials. *Clinical Electroencephalography* (Tokyo), in press.

Inanaga, K., Ishikawa, K., Tachibana, H., Shirakawa, N., Kotorii, S., & Hirozaki, H. The effect of maturation on the wave form of the visual evoked potential. *Clinical Electroencephalography* (Tokyo), 1969.

Irwin, D. A., Knott, J. R., McAdam, D. W., & Rebert, C. S. Motivational determinants of the "contingent negative variation." *Electroencephalography and Clinical Neurophysiology,* 1966, **21,** 538–543.

Justiss, W. A. The electroencephalogram of the frontal lobes and abstract behavior in old age. In H. T. Blumenthal (Ed.), *Medical and clinical aspects of aging.* New York: Columbia University Press, 1962.

Kales, A., Wilson, T., Kales, J. D., Jacobson, A., Paulson, M. J., Kollar, E., & Walter, R. D. Measurements of all-night sleep in normal elderly persons: Effects of aging. *Journal of the American Geriatrics Society,* 1967, **15,** 405–414.

Klee, A. The relationship between clinical evaluation of mental deterioration, psychological test results and the cerebral metabolic rate of oxygen. *Acta Neurologica Scandinavica*, 1964, **40**, 337–345.

Kooi, K. A., & Bagchi, B. K. Visual evoked responses in man: Normative data. *Annals of the New York Academy of Sciences*, 1964, **112**, 254–269.

Kooi, K. A., Guvener, A. M., Tupper, C. J., & Bagchi, B. K. Electroencephalographic patterns of the temporal region in normal adults. *Neurology*, 1964, **14**, 1929–1035.

Krasno, L. R., & Ivy, A. C. The response of the flicker fusion threshold to nitroglycerine and its potential value in the diagnosis, prognosis, and therapy of subclinical and clinical cardiovascular disease. *Circulation*, 1950, **1**, 1267–1276.

Lacey, B. C., & Lacey, J. I. Cardiovascular and respiratory correlates of reaction time. (Appended Preprint No. 3, Progress Report) Bethesda, Md.: National Institute of Mental Health, June 1965.

Lacey, J. I. Somatic response patterning and stress: Some revisions of activation theory. In M. H. Appley & R. Trumbull (Eds.), *Psychological stress: Issues and research*. New York: Appleton-Century-Crofts, 1967.

Lacey, J. I., Kagan, J., Lacey, B. C., & Moss, H. A. The visceral level: Situational determinants and behavioral correlates of autonomic response patterns. In P. H. Knapp (Ed.), *Expression of the emotions in man*. New York: International Universities Press, 1963.

Lacey, J. I., & Lacey, B. C. Some autonomic-central nervous system inter-relationships. In P. Black (Ed.), *Physiological correlates of emotion*. New York: Academic Press, 1970.

Lassen, N. A. Cerebral blood flow and metabolism in health and disease. In C. H. Millikan (Ed.), *Cerebrovascular disease (Research Publications Association for Research in Nervous and Mental Disease)*. Vol. 41. Baltimore: Williams & Wilkins, 1966.

Lassen, N. A., Munck, O., & Tottey, E. R. T. Mental function and cerebral oxygen consumption in organic dementia. *Archives of Neurology and Psychiatry*, 1957, **77**, 126–133.

Liberson, W. T. Functional electroencephalography in mental disorders. *Diseases of the Nervous System*, 1944, **5**, 357–364.

Liberson, W. T., & Seguin, C. A. Brain waves and clinical features in arteriosclerotic and senile mental patients. *Psychosomatic Medicine*, 1945, **7**, 30–35.

Lindsley, D. B. Psychophysiology and perception. In, *Current trends in the description and analysis of behavior*. Pittsburgh: University of Pittsburgh Press, 1958.

Low, M. D., Borda, R. P., Frost, J. D., Jr., & Kellaway, P. Surface-negative, slow-potential shift associated with conditioning in man. *Neurology*, 1966, **16**, 771–782.

Luce, R. A., Jr., & Rothschild, D. The correlation of electroencephalographic and clinical observations in psychiatric patients over 65. *Journal of Gerontology*, 1953, **8**, 167–172.

Luders, H. The effects of aging on the wave form of the somatosensory cortical evoked potential. *Electroencephalography and Clinical Neurophysiology*, 1970, **29**, 450–460.

Maggs, R., & Turton, E. C. Some EEG findings in old age and their relationship to affective disorder. *Journal of Mental Science,* 1956, **102,** 812–818.

Magoun, H. W. *The walking brain.* Springfield, Ill.: Charles C Thomas, 1958.

Markovich, S. E. Electroencephalographic patterns in elderly patients: A longitudinal study. In H. T. Blumenthal (Ed.), *Medical and clinical aspects of aging.* New York: Columbia University Press, 1962.

Marsh, G. R., & Thompson, L. W. Age differences in evoked potentials during an auditory discrimination task. Paper presented at the 25th Annual Meeting of the Gerontological Society, San Juan, Puerto Rico, December 1972.

Marsh, G. R., & Thompson, L. W. Effects of age on the contingent negative variation in a pitch discrimination task. *Journal of Gerontology,* in press.

McAdam, W., & Robinson, R. A. Diagnostic and prognostic value of the electroencephalogram in geriatric psychiatry. In H. T. Blumenthal (Ed.), *Medical and clinical aspects of aging.* New York: Columbia University Press, 1962.

Milner, B. Laterality effects in audition. In V. B. Mountcastle (Ed.), *Interhemispheric relations and cerebral dominance.* Baltimore: Johns Hopkins University Press, 1962.

Morris, J. D., & Thompson, L. W. Heart rate changes in a reaction time experiment with young and aged subjects. *Journal of Gerontology,* 1969, **24,** 269–275.

Moruzzi, G., & Magoun, H. W. Brain stem reticular formation and activation of the EEG. *Electroencephalography and Clinical Neurophysiology,* 1949, **1,** 455–473.

Mundy-Castle, A. C. Theta and beta rhythm in the electroencephalograms of normal adults. *Electroencephalography and Clinical Neurophysiology,* 1951, **3,** 477–486.

Mundy-Castle, A. C. Central excitability in the aged. In H. T. Blumenthal (Ed.), *Medical and clinical aspects of aging.* New York: Columbia University Press, 1962.

Mundy-Castle, A. C., Hurst, L. A., Beerstecher, D. M., & Prinsloo, T. The electroencephalogram in the senile psychoses. *Electroencephalography and Clinical Neurophysiology,* 1954, **6,** 245–252.

Nelson, R., & Gellhorn, E. The action of autonomic drugs on normal persons and neuropsychiatric patients. *Psychosomatic Medicine,* 1957, **19,** 486–494.

Nelson, R., & Gellhorn, E. The influence of age and functional neuropsychiatric disorders on sympathetic and parasympathetic functions. *Journal of Psychosomatic Research,* 1958, **3,** 12–26.

Nowlin, J. B., Eisdorfer, C., & Thompson, L. W. Cardiovascular response during reaction time performance. Unpublished manuscript, Duke University Medical Center, 1970. (a)

Nowlin, J. B., Eisdorfer, C., & Thompson, L. W. Effects of age on cardiovascular responses during reaction time performance. Unpublished manuscript, Duke University Medical Center, 1970. (b)

Obrist, P. A., Webb, R. A., Sutterer, J. R., & Howard, J. L. Cardiac deceleration and reaction time: An evaluation of two hypotheses. *Psychophysiology,* 1970, **6,** 695–706.

Obrist, W. D. The electroencephalogram of normal aged adults. *Electroencephalography and Clinical Neurophysiology,* 1954, **6,** 235–244.

Obrist, W. D. The electroencephalogram of healthy aged males. In, *Human aging: A biological and behavioral study.* (USPHS Publ. No. 986) Washington, D.C.: United States Government Printing Office, 1963.

Obrist, W. D. Cerebral ischemia and the senescent electroencephalogram. In E. Simonson & T. H. McGavack (Eds.), *Cerebral ischemia.* Springfield, Ill.: Charles C Thomas, 1964.

Obrist, W. D. Electroencephalographic approach to age changes in response speed. In A. T. Welford & J. E. Birren (Eds.), *Behavior, aging, and the nervous system.* Springfield, Ill.: Charles C Thomas, 1965.

Obrist, W. D. EEG and intellectual function in the aged. Paper presented at the 25th Annual Meeting of the American EEG Society, Minneapolis, September 1971.

Obrist, W. D., & Bissell, L. F. The electronencephalogram of aged patients with cardiac and cerebral vascular disease. *Journal of Gerontology,* 1955, **10,** 315–330.

Obrist, W. D., & Busse, E. W. The electroencephalogram in old age. In W. P. Wilson (Ed.), *Applications of electroencephalography in psychiatry: A symposium.* Durham: Duke University Press, 1965.

Obrist, W. D., Busse, E. W., Eisdorfer, C., & Kleemeier, R. W. Relation of the electroencephalogram to intellectual function in senescence. *Journal of Gerontology,* 1962, **17,** 197–206.

Obrist, W. D., Busse, E. W., & Henry, C. E. Relation of electroencephalogram to blood pressure in elderly persons. *Neurology,* 1961, **11,** 151–158.

Obrist, W. D., Chivian, E., Cronqvist, S., & Ingvar, D. H. Regional cerebral blood flow in senile and pre-senile dementia. *Neurology,* 1970, **20,** 315–322.

Obrist, W. D., & Henry, C. E. Electroencephalographic findings in aged psychiatric patients. *Journal of Nervous and Mental Diseases,* 1958, **126,** 254–267. (a)

Obrist, W. D., & Henry, C. E. Electroencephalographic frequency analysis of aged psychiatric patients. *Electroencephalography and Clinical Neurophysiology,* 1958, **10,** 621–632. (b)

Obrist, W. D., Henry, C. E., & Justiss, W. A. Longitudinal study of EEG in old age. *Excerpta medica (International Congress Series),* 1961, No. 37, 180–181.

Obrist, W. D., Sokoloff, L., Lassen, N. A., Lane, M. H., Butler, R. N., & Feinberg, I. Relation of EEG to cerebral blood flow and metabolism in old age. *Electroencephalography and Clinical Neurophysiology,* 1963, **15,** 610–619.

Opton, E. M., Jr. Electroencephalographic correlates of performance lapses on an attention task in young and old men. Unpublished doctoral dissertation, Duke University, 1963.

Powell, A. H., Eisdorfer, C., & Bogdonoff, M. D. Physiologic response patterns observed in a learning task. *Archives of General Psychiatry,* 1964, **10,** 192–195.

Rabbitt, P. Age and the use of structure in transmitted information. In G. A. Talland (Ed.), *Human aging and behavior.* New York: Academic Press, 1968.

Rebert, C. S., McAdam, D. W., Knott, J. R., & Irwin, D. A. Slow potential change in human brain related to level of motivation. *Journal of Comparative Physiology*, 1967, **63**, 20–23.

Reitan, R. M. Intellectual and affective changes in essential hypertension. *American Journal of Psychiatry*, 1954, **110**, 817–824.

Reitan, R. M. The distribution according to age of a psychologic measure dependent upon organic brain functions. *Journal of Gerontology*, 1955, **10**, 338–340.

Satterfield, J. H. Evoked cortical response enhancement and attention in man: A study of responses to auditory and shock stimuli. *Electroencephalography and Clinical Neurophysiology*, 1965, **19**, 470–475.

Schenkenberg, T. Visual, auditory, and somatosensory evoked responses of normal subjects from childhood to senescence. Unpublished doctoral dissertation, University of Utah, 1970.

Shagass, C., & Schwartz, M. Age, personality, and somatosensory cerebral evoked responses. *Science*, 1965, **148**, 1359–1361.

Sharpless, S., & Jasper, H. Habituation of the arousal reaction. *Brain*, 1956, **79**, 655–680.

Shmavonian, B. M., & Busse, E. W. Psychophysiological techniques in the study of the aged. In R. H. Williams, C. Tibbitts, & W. Donahue (Eds.), *Processes of aging*. New York: Atherton Press, 1963.

Shmavonian, B. M., Miller, L. H., & Cohen, S. I. Differences among age and sex groups in electro-dermal conditioning. *Psychophysiology*, 1968, **5**, 119–131.

Shmavonian, B. M., Miller, L. H., & Cohen, S. I. Differences among age and sex groups with respect to cardiovascular conditioning and reactivity. *Journal of Gerontology*, 1970, **25**, 87–94.

Shmavonian, B. M., Yarmat, A. J., & Cohen, S. I. Relationships between autonomic nervous system and central nervous system in age differences in behavior. In A. T. Welford & J. E. Birren (Eds.), *Behavior, aging and the nervous system*. Springfield, Ill.: Charles C Thomas, 1965.

Silverman, A. J., Busse, E. W., & Barnes, R. H. Studies in the processes of aging: Electroencephalographic findings in 400 elderly subjects. *Electroencephalography and Clinical Neurophysiology*, 1955, **7**, 67–74.

Silverman, A. J., Busse, E. W., Barnes, R. H., Frost, L. L., & Thaler, M. B. Studies on the process of aging: 4. Physiological influences on psychic functioning in elderly people. *Geriatrics*, 1953, **8**, 370–376.

Silverman, A. J., Cohen, S. L., & Shmavonian, B. M. Investigation of psychophysiologic relationships with skin resistance measures. *Journal of Psychosomatic Research*, 1959, **4**, 65–87.

Simonson, E., & Enzer, N. State of motor centers in circulatory insufficiency. *Archives of Internal Medicine*, 1941, **68**, 498–512.

Sokoloff, L. Cerebral circulatory and metabolic changes associated with aging. In C. H. Millikan (Ed.), *Cerebrovascular disease (Research Publications Association for Research in Nervous and Mental Disease)*. Vol. 41. Baltimore: Williams & Wilkins, 1966.

Spieth, W. Slowness of task performance and cardiovascular diseases. In A. T. Welford & J. E. Birren (Eds.), *Behavior, aging, and the nervous system*. Springfield, Ill.: Charles C Thomas, 1965.

Spong, P., Haider, M., & Lindsley, D. B. Selective attentiveness and cortical evoked responses to visual and auditory stimuli. *Science,* 1965, **148,** 395–397.

Stoller, A. Slowing of the alpha rhythm of the electroencephalogram and its association with mental deterioration and epilepsy. *Journal of Mental Science,* 1949, **95,** 972–984.

Straumanis, J. J., Shagass, C., & Schwartz, M. Visually evoked cerebral response changes associated with chronic brain syndromes and aging. *Journal of Gerontology,* 1965, **20,** 498–506.

Surwillo, W. W. The relation of response-time variability to age and the influence of brain wave frequency. *Electroencephalography and Clinical Neurophysiology,* 1963, **15,** 1029–1032. (a)

Surwillo, W. W. The relation of simple response time to brain-wave frequency and the effects of age. *Electroencephalography and Clinical Neurophysiology,* 1963, **15,** 105–114. (b)

Surwillo, W. W. Some observations on the relation of response speed to frequency of photic stimulation under conditions of EEG synchronization. *Electroencephalography and Clinical Neurophysiology,* 1964, **17,** 194–198. (a)

Surwillo, W W. The relation of decision time to brain wave frequency and to age. *Electroencephalography and Clinical Neurophysiology,* 1964, **16,** 510–514. (b)

Surwillo, W. W. On the relation of latency of alpha attenuation to alpha rhythm frequency and the influence of age. *Electroencephalography and Clinical Neurophysiology,* 1966, **20,** 129–132. (a)

Surwillo, W. W. The relation of autonomic activity to age differences in vigilance. *Journal of Gerontology,* 1966, **21,** 257–260. (b)

Surwillo, W. W. Timing of behavior in senescence and the role of the central nervous system. In G. A. Talland (Ed.), *Human aging and behavior.* New York: Academic Press, 1968.

Surwillo, W. W., & Quilter, R. E. The influence of age on latency time of involuntary (galvanic skin reflex) and voluntary responses. *Journal of Gerontology,* 1965, **20,** 173–176. (a)

Surwillo, W. W., & Quilter, R. E. The relation of frequency of spontaneous skin potential responses to vigilance and to age. *Psychophysiology,* 1965, **1,** 272–276. (b)

Szafran, J. Age differences in choice reaction time and cardiovascular status among pilots. *Nature,* 1963, **200,** 904–906.

Szafran, J. Age differences in sequential decisions and cardiovascular status among pilots. *Aerospace Medicine,* 1965, **36,** 303–310.

Szafran, J. Age, cardiac output and choice reaction time. *Nature,* 1966, **209,** 836. (a)

Szafran, J. Age differences in the rate of gain of information, signal detection strategy and cardiovascular status among pilots. *Gerontologia,* 1966, **12,** 6–17. (b)

Szafran, J. Psychophysiological studies of aging in pilots. In G. A. Talland (Ed.), *Human aging and behavior.* New York: Academic Press, 1968.

Tecce, J. J., & Scheff, N. M. Attention reduction and suppressed direct-current potentials in the human brain. *Science,* 1969, **164,** 331–333.

Thaler, M. Relationships among Wechsler, Weigl, Rorschach, EEG findings and abstract concrete behavior in a group of normal aged subjects. *Journal of Gerontology*, 1956, **11**, 404–409.

Thompson, L. W., & Botwinick, J. Age differences in the relationship between EEG arousal and reaction time. *Journal of Psychology*, 1968, **68**, 167–172.

Thompson, L. W., & Nowlin, J. B. Cortical slow potential and cardiovascular correlates of attention during reaction time performance. In L. Jarvik, C. Eisdorfer, & J. Blum (Eds.), *Aging: Psychological and somatic changes*. New York: Springer, in press.

Thompson, L. W., & Wilson, S. Electrocortical reactivity and learning in the elderly. *Journal of Gerontology*, 1966, **21**, 45–51.

Troyer, W. G., Jr., Eisdorfer, C., Wilkie, F., & Bogdonoff, M. D. Free fatty acid responses in the aged individual during performance of learning tasks. *Journal of Gerontology*, 1966, **21**, 415–419.

Verdeaux, G., Verdeaux, J., & Turmel, J. Etude statisique de la frequence et de la reactivite des electroencephalogrammes chez les suyets ages. *Journal of the Canadian Psychiatric Association*, 1961, **6**, 28–36.

Walter, W. G. Brain responses to semantic stimuli. *Journal of Psychosomatic Medicine*, 1965, **9**, 51–61.

Walter, W. G., Cooper, R., Aldridge, V. J., McCallum, W. C., & Winter, A. L. Contingent negative variation: An electrical sign of sensorimotor association and expectancy in the human brain. *Nature*, 1964, **203**, 380–384.

Wang, H. S., & Busse, E. W. EEG of healthy old persons—A longitudinal study: I. Dominant background activity and occipital rhythm. *Journal of Gerontology*, 1969, **24**, 419–426.

Wang, H. S., Obrist, W. D., & Busse, E. W. Neurophysiological correlates of the intellectual function of elderly persons living in the community. *American Journal of Psychiatry*, 1970, **126**, 1205–1212.

Waszak, M., & Obrist, W. D. Relationship of slow potential changes to response speed and motivation in man. *Electroencephalography and Clinical Neurophysiology*, 1969, **27**, 113–120.

Weiner, H., & Shuster, D. B. The electroencephalogram in dementia: Some preliminary observations and correlations. *Electroencephalography and Clinical Neurophysiology*, 1956, **8**, 479–488.

Welford, A. T. Psychomotor performance. In J. E. Birren (Ed.), *Handbook of aging and the individual*. Chicago: University of Chicago Press, 1959.

Welford, A. T. Performance, biological mechanisms and age: A theoretical sketch. In A. T. Welford & J. E. Birren (Eds.), *Behavior, aging and the nervous system*. Springfield, Ill.: Charles C Thomas, 1965.

Wells, C. E. Response of alpha waves to light in neurologic disease. *Archives of Neurology*, 1962, **6**, 478–491.

Wells, C. E. Alpha wave responsiveness to light in man. In G. H. Glaser (Ed.), *EEG and behavior*. New York: Basic Books, 1963.

Whipple, H. E. Sensory evoked response in man. *Annals of the New York Academy of Science*, 1964, **112**.

Wilkie, F., & Eisdorfer, C. Intelligence and blood pressure in the aged. *Science*, 1971, **172**, 959–962.

Wilson, S. Electrocortical reactivity in young and aged adults. Unpublished doctoral dissertation, George Peabody College for Teachers, 1962.

The Developmental Psychology of Aging

Developmental Processes and Aging

K. WARNER SCHAIE

An attempt to integrate the chapters related to developmental processes is faced with a paradox: The common theme of the chapters in this section is the apparent absence of convincing findings on the nature of developmental processes in adulthood and the observation that directionality of age changes is in considerable doubt. Nevertheless, it is this very paradox that makes these chapters particularly relevant to possible recommendations of changes in public policy, for they tell us that what we think we know about the aged and aging is in need of serious revision, revision of the kind that will invalidate policies based upon some of today's assumed certainties.

Perhaps one of the most striking commonalities among these chapters is the recognition that it is quite unlikely that uniform aging processes can be identified and consequently that many different paradigms for age changes in behavior must be considered. Thus, it becomes necessary to consider models of aging that, in addition to the now prevalent "irreversible decrement" paradigm, may permit consideration of processes that imply either behavioral stability or, alternately, decrement with co-occurring compensation (cf. Schaie, 1972).

The strongest remaining support for the irreversible decrement model may be found in Jarvik and Cohen's summary statement, which calls attention to the impressive cumulative evidence of a significant association between mortality and decrement on the

K. Warner Schaie received his PhD in clinical and developmental psychology from the University of Washington in 1956. He is currently Chairman and Professor of Psychology at West Virginia University, where he also serves as Director of the Life-Span Developmental Psychology Training Program. He is President-Elect of Division 20 of APA and Chairman of the Developmental Behavior Sciences Study Section, National Institutes of Health. His major research interests are in life-span developmental methodology and age changes in cognitive behavior in adulthood.

Vocabulary, Similarity, and Digit Span subtests of the Wechsler Adult Intelligence Scale. But even these data must be seen in the context of a possibly impaired population. That is, these data may be predictive for a population in which significant vascular changes have occurred and in which in terms of the concepts used by Klee-meier (1961) many of its members may have been assessed just prior to death (cf. Reimanis & Green, 1971; Riegel & Riegel, 1972). Other support for the decrement model may be seen in the data reported by Jarvik and Cohen on the increasing percentage of hypodiploid cells in older persons functioning at a suboptimal level. It is impressive to note that the effects of chromosome breakdown seem to apply primarily to rather specific memory decrement rather than to more complex behavior patterns. Currently emerging data on generational shifts in age gradients, however, suggest that these findings too may offer only temporary explanations. That is, just as in the case of cultural change, there may also be change in the rate of chromosome loss with advancing age from one cohort to the next.

In their chapter, Baltes and Labouvie properly take the validity of the irreversible decrement model to task and point out that this stand, among other consequences, has led to a reluctance to consider the utility of modification research for problems of aging. Attention is called to the fact that intelligence generally has been considered from the point of view of performance criteria rather than the study of antecedents. As a first step it seems important to shift from the view of intelligence as a one-sided construct (Gewirtz, 1969) to a multidimensional conceptualization that might have greater explanatory power.

Baltes and Labouvie note that the evidence for generational differences is now overwhelming and that much of the variance in developmental phenomena can be accounted for by such differences particularly when experimental mortality is taken into account (cf. Baltes, Schaie, & Nardi, 1971; Schaie, 1971a). But the argument is taken a good step farther by claiming that in the absence of good research or theory on cause–effect relationships in the interaction between biological substrates in intelligence, the most parsimonious position would be that decrements in intellectual functions reflect environmental limitations and educational deficits. It follows then that recommendations for future research should include attempts to obtain control of age functions by manipulative research. Such research must address itself to the environmental and learning parameters associated with intellectual ontogeny. Some of this research, as it pertains to the environmental ontogeny of intelligence, could and should obviously be intervention research.

The lack of utility and the implausibility of unitary models of developmental change in adulthood were emphasized further in Lowenthal and Chiriboga's chapter on socialization and Neugarten's chapter on personality development. With some justification, Lowenthal and Chiriboga call for the use of process-oriented concepts. They argue persuasively that we may have difficulty in understanding the behavior of older people unless we have charted the dynamic course of their previous life experience. Their example indicating that retired women and widowers seem to experience greater social stress than women who have had no careers and men who are still married in advanced age suggests that some of the primary stresses of aging may relate not to phenomena inherent in aging but to other concomitant developmental factors, which might produce difficulties at any life stage.

Although the data reviewed by Lowenthal and Chiriboga do not bear directly on the issue of generational shifts in age-related experiences of the elderly, they do hint that such factors must be investigated in the future. For example, the evidence on a cross-sex shifting in value systems of older people obtained from cross-sectional data could be more parsimoniously explained in terms of changed social perception of what values older people of the different sexes are supposed to display. Such a view would be particularly relevant in view of the very stable sex differences maintained over the entire adult age range found for both cognitive and personality variables (Schaie & Strother, 1968a, 1968b; Schaie, 1971a, 1971b).

As a response to the apparent morass of contradictory evidence and insufficient models in the area of personality, Neugarten appears to caution us to step back and start all over again. She tells us that we must cease to follow the blind alley of vain attempts to extend theories of personality to aging where such theories do not contain relevant concepts applicable to aging. She enjoins us as well to be wary of trying to quantify and apply standardized measures to the study of age change where such measures do not really fit the data obtained. She points out that we really do not know anything about the consistency of adult personality, or if there were consistency, what the antecedents therefore might be. While I share Neugarten's position on the primitive state of knowledge of adult personality (cf. Schaie & Marquette, 1972), it is nevertheless difficult to agree with all of her prescriptions for change. There can be no question that it is important to study age-related changes as well as specific age functions, but the latter cannot be completely disregarded if we are to apply our knowledge to concrete problems of social significance. Though I am a relatively "soft" behaviorist who believes in the validity of introspective data as a permissible source of evidence, I still am not convinced that turning to such data would yield the sought-for panacea. Perhaps we can understand Neugarten's interest in introspective sources of information better if we consider her position as arguing for the increase of complexity of personality in old age. Since there is not now convicing evidence that this is so (in fact structural analyses of objective data long ago suggested the contrary, cf. Cohen, 1957), support for this position requires the assumption that we have in the past ignored important data sources. Much more compatible with my own views is Neugarten's proposition that age per se may not account for much variance in the study of personality to begin with. This may be a heretical statement to those who firmly believe that the phenomena of aging are basically biological in nature. But if the heated discussions following Jensen's (1969) controversial article have taught us anything, it is that if there is indeed relative homogeneity in the biological characteristics of a population sub-group, then it becomes even more important to consider other parameters that may be modifiable even, or especially, if they account for only a relatively small proportion of the total variance.

The apparent consensus of the developmental age change chapters on the lack of utility of unitary developmental models for old age leaves us with important conclusions relevant to public policy. The first conclusion is that the notion of a fixed retirement age is contrary to the public interest and that the concept of a fixed retirement age is not based upon any assumptions for which scientific facts can be adduced that are applicable to more than a single point in time. In fact, the arguments presented in the chapters on development and aging suggest that under certain circumstances chronological age may be an irrelevant concept for determining the necessity or desirability of retirement practices. Next, it appears equally obvious that different kinds of research strategies will be required to obtain data on development and aging that can be basic to public policy decisions (Schaie, 1972). Thus, we must continue to rely exclusively on cross-sectional surveys of the present status of population groups of different ages if we wish to determine ways in which these groups differ on contemporaneous, socially significant variables, and where we wish to address ourselves to socially required special-privilege decisions. But these data will have no utility in long-range planning. We know that the level of performance of comparable age groups at different points in time is changing, and we know further that the rate of change (i.e., slope of age-change gradients) for those variables where maturational processes are involved is changing. Therefore, it becomes necessary to follow several generations of individuals in short-term longitudinal studies to develop data for long-range programming. It also becomes necessary to replicate one's cross-sectional studies continuously to determine current facts for current policy decisions.

A further public policy implication of the data on personality and social development seems to be the indication that the adjustment mechanisms used in old age may represent individual responses to environmentally programmed conditions required of older people rather than maturationally required responses. If this is indeed the case, public policy discussions might well involve a deliberation as to what roles for the elderly are optimal for society, on the assumption that positive as well as negative changes in adjustment may be expected from experimental intervention in the behavior of the elderly as well as at other age levels. Obviously, this involves some serious investigation of the needs of the older person from his point of view, as well as an investigation of the roles that those of us who are now in the middle years expect to play when we reach old age.

In summary, it appears that unitary models for age changes in cognitive and personality variables may be less useful than was previously expected and that stability and compensation models of aging must be considered in addition to the overworked decrement model. Because of generational differences and observed changes in rate of aging, it further appears that data thought to be appropriate for decisions on retirement and special programs for the aging must now be subjected to intensive and continuing review. Social mechanisms for such review should be urgently sought.

REFERENCES

Baltes, P. B., Schaie, K. W., & Nardi, A. H. Age and experimental mortality in a seven-year longitudinal study of cognitive behavior. *Developmental Psychology,* 1971, **5,** 18–26.

Cohen, J. The factorial structure of the WAIS between early adulthood and old age. *Journal of Consulting Psychology,* 1957, **21,** 283–290.

Gewirtz, J. L. Levels of conceptual analysis in environmental–infant interaction research. *Merrill-Palmer Quarterly,* 1969, **15,** 7–47.

Jensen, A. How much can we boost IQ and achievement? *Harvard Educational Review,* 1969, **39,** 1–123.

Kleemeier, R. W. Intellectual changes in the senium or death and IQ. Paper presented at the annual meeting of the American Psychological Association, New York, September 1961.

Reimanis, G., & Green, R. F. Imminence of death and intellectual decrement in the aging. *Developmental Psychology,* 1971, **5,** 270–272.

Riegel, K. F., & Riegel, R. M. Development, drop, and death. *Developmental Psychology*, 1972, **6**, 306–319.

Schaie, K. W. Cultural change and repeated assessment in the study of the adult personality. Paper presented as part of a symposium on "Personality assessment of the aged" at the annual meeting of the American Psychological Association, Washington, D. C., September, 1971. (a)

Schaie, K. W. Generational vs. ontogenetic components of change: A second follow-up. Paper presented as part of a symposium on "Intellectual development in adulthood and old age" at the annual meeting of the American Psychological Association, Washington, D. C., September 1971. (b)

Schaie, K. W. Methodological problems in descriptive developmental research on adulthood and aging. In J. R. Nesselroade & H. W. Reese (Eds.), *Life-span developmental psychology: Methodology*. New York: Academic Press, 1972.

Schaie, K. W., & Marquette, B. W. Personality in maturity and old age. In R. M. Dreger (Ed.), *Multivariate personality research: Contributions to the understanding of personality in honor of R. B. Cattell*. Baton Rouge, La.: Claitor's Publishing Division, 1972.

Schaie, K. W., & Strother, C. R. A cross-sequential study of age changes in cognitive behavior. *Psychological Bulletin*, 1968, **70**, 671–680. (a)

Schaie, K. W., & Strother, C. R. The effect of time and cohort differences upon age changes in cognitive behavior. *Multivariate Behavioral Research*, 1968, **3**, 259–294. (b)

Adult Development of Intellectual Performance: Description, Explanation, and Modification

PAUL B. BALTES and GISELA V. LABOUVIE

During the formative stages of behavioral gerontology, intellectual and/or cognitive functioning was at the core of research as shown in a variety of historical reviews (e.g., Botwinick, 1967; Bromley, 1966; Charles, 1970; Jones, 1959; Riegel, 1958). Although recent decades have seen behavioral gerontology attain a much wider horizon, aging research in intellectual abilities has managed to preserve its frontier character in a number of respects.

The main aims of this chapter are to elucidate the type of issues that are apt to guide future research in the area defined by the topic and to highlight various implications for research in other behavioral domains. This endeavor will be facilitated by a number of recent reviews which provide an exhaustive coverage of the field (e.g., Botwinick, 1967; Horn, 1970; Riegel & Riegel, 1972; Schaie, 1970). The present review conceptualizes intelligence as a construct that needs explication in terms of its empirical referents within a framework of antecedent–process–consequent relationships. Moreover, in line with the frequently stated major objectives of any comprehensive scientific endeavor in the behavioral sciences, the available

---

Paul B. Baltes received his Diploma (1963) and his PhD (1967) in psychology from the University of Saarland, Saarbrücken, West Germany. Currently he is an Associate Professor of Human Development and Director of the Division of Individual and Family Studies in the College of Human Development at Pennsylvania State University. He taught at the University of Saarland and was an Associate Professor of Psychology at West Virginia University prior to his present appointment. His primary research interests are in developmental research methodology, the analysis of cultural change patterns, and in personality development throughout adulthood and old age.

Gisela V. Labouvie began her training in psychology at the University

evidence will be organized around three perspectives: (a) description, (b) explanation, and (c) modification. These headings, of course, are not mutually exclusive but are useful didactic vehicles.

In addition to this evaluative summary of the current state of research, we will focus on four propositions and themes which, although in the center of research approaches in the area of intellectual functioning, transcend the latter domain and deserve more serious consideration by researchers interested in other behavioral processes. Although these propositions will not serve as explicit organizational criteria, they are an implicit characteristic of the present writing. Specifically, the four propositions are (a) the usefulness of considering multivariate models in the examination of complex aging phenomena, (b) the necessity for formulating and applying more adequate research strategies and models in order to separate ontogenetic from historical change components, (c) the need for experimental intervention research aimed at specifying antecedent–consequent relationships and the mechanisms underlying descriptive age changes, and (d) the potential advantages inherent in a life-span look at aging phenomena.

The latter positions are not new but they have appeared in a number of recent papers dealing with the developmental analysis of change phenomena. Some have been written primarily within the context of substantive aging research (e.g., Birren, 1970; Chown, 1968; Riegel & Riegel, 1972; Schaie, 1970), some within the context of life-span development al psychology (e.g., Baltes, 1968; Baltes & Goulet, 1970; Baltes & Nesselroade, in press; Bayley, 1963; Neugarten, 1969; Wohlwill, 1970c), others within the framework of experimental infancy and child psychology (e.g., Baer, 1970; Bijou, 1968; Gewirtz, 1969a, 1969b; Goulet, 1970), and still others within the context of measurement and design (e.g., Cronbach & Furby, 1970; Harris, 1963; Nesselroade, 1970; Schaie, 1972). An attempt will be made to illustrate the implications of these relatively independent trends for the examination of adult changes in cognitive functioning.

The final emphasis in this chapter will be on highlighting some of the implications of aging changes in intelligence for aspects of

of Saarland, Saarbrücken, West Germany, where she received a Prediploma in psychology in 1967. After obtaining a PhD in life-span developmental psychology from West Virginia University in 1972, she joined the University of Wisconsin as an Assistant Professor in Educational Psychology. Her major research interests are in intellectual development over the life-span and in interage social interaction patterns.

societal and educational planning. Specifically, it will be shown that the existing body of literature reflects ontogenetic changes for a very particular set of aging cohorts that is "deficient" from various social and educational viewpoints (e.g., Charles, 1971; Granick & Friedman, 1970; Kuhlen, 1963; Pressey, 1956). Moreover, it will be argued that the search for any "true" fixed aging process follows an erroneous "stability" model of research. Thus, it is asserted that as a reflection of rapidly changing environmental and biological contexts, we should expect aging phenomena to be highly labile and subject to dramatic modifications. In other words, contrary to the often-found belief in the predictability and irreversibility of the aging process, we will espouse the notion that the nature of informal and formal educational intervention associated with cultural change defines, at least to a substantial degree, the future nature of the organism–environment interchanges that are involved in the shaping of aging phenomena.

DESCRIPTIVE ONTOGENY OF INTELLECTUAL ABILITIES

Definition and Objectives

In certain respects it seems futile to add to the rich, albeit vague, body of literature dealing with the definition of intelligence or intellectual abilities. Defining the concept simply exemplifies the problems inherent in delineating a rather global concept in a nomological net of antecedent–intervening–consequent relationships. Most of the definitions proposed stress selectively one or another component of this network, indicating that the search for a comprehensive definition of intelligence as yet is an unsuccessful one. In light of these difficulties, most researchers, in line with a position attributed to Boring, tend to settle for a definition of intelligence as that class of behaviors that is measured by available assessment devices (for a current discussion, see Bijou, 1971; Humphreys, 1971). We will first concentrate on this performance or product (consequent) aspect of the intelligence construct and neglect those areas of research that are primarily aimed at conceptualizing intelligence as an inferred process-construct as is most convincingly illustrated, for example, by Piagetian and learning approaches (see also ch. 6 by Arenberg). In later sections, however, it will be shown how process- and antecedent-oriented research is necessary to explicate the ontogeny of age–performance functions.

The performance aspect of intelligence is, of course, intrinsically tied to two somewhat related historical trends, that is, the proliferation of intelligence tests aimed at specifying individual differences in cognitive performance and the numerous attempts of factor analysts to develop multidimensional models (e.g., Burt, Cattell, Guilford, Spearman, Thurstone, Vernon, and others) suited for the analysis of the interrelationships (structure) among the products of intelligence. It is the type of research that explicitly or implicitly uses multiple test batteries, particularly if in correspondence with a multidimensional conception of intelligence, that constitutes the subject matter of this review.

The bulk of research on the relationship between aging and intelligence consisted of the search for what might be called the "true" or "normal" aging function of intelligence. In recent years, however, the investigation of such aging functions has drawn attention to a number of perspectives which suggest that most conventional interpretations involving aging and intelligence are in serious need of reevaluation. The following discussion of various developments will center around three sources of concern: (a) the distinction between quantitative and structural change derivable from factor-analytic models of intelligence, (b) age-related changes in population and sample composition, and (c) the interaction of ontogenetic (individual) with generational (historical) change.

Models of Intelligence

Earlier researchers showed a tendency to apply intelligence tests without strong consideration for the underlying theoretical models; however, more recent research has focused on exploring the implications of existing models for the assessment of ontogenetic change. Thus, increasingly, it is being realized that the nature of interpretations is intrinsically tied to the model applied in that many of the conclusions drawn are dictated more by the nature of the model characteristics than by the data themselves. A good example of this dilemma is the use of the Wechsler Adult Intelligence Scale, which, on the basis of its underlying model, provides only a meager framework for the analysis of developmental phenomena. Thus, it might be useful to explore briefly the type of changes that, in principle, could occur under a given set of model assumptions.

Factor-analytic models. Since organizational models of intellectual performance have been closely tied to the development of factor analysis as a tool for organizing individual differences, the factor-analytic model will be briefly described and then used as a sample case. The logic of factor analysis is most easily understood when the model is expressed in the "specification equation" (Cattell, 1966; Nesselroade, 1970) which states the relationship (in an additive and linear framework) between a given observed performance (P) and a number of inferred components (factor loadings, factor scores) into which the observed performance may be decomposed:

$$P_{ji} = b_{j1} F_{1i} + b_{j2} F_{2i} + \ldots + b_{jk} F_{ki} + S_{ji}$$

This equation states that an individual's (i) performance (P) in a given task (j) is a weighted (bj) sum of the individual's scores on a number of factors ($F_{1,2} \ldots {}_k$). The weights (factor loadings) indicate the contribution of each factor to the particular performance. The element S_{ji} represents that part of the individual's P_j score that cannot be expressed in terms of a combined contribution of the set of factors and is thus specific to the individual's performance. One important feature of this model is that the factor loadings are subscripted without reference to individuals and individual differences. They convey subject-invariant relationships between performances (tests) and factors (e.g., Nesselroade, 1970). Conversely, the factor scores are subscripted without reference to variables, thus indicating test-invariant individual variations on the set of factors.

Note that factor analysis, when stated in this form, is simply a *descriptive model* attempting to identify a parsimonious set of inter-individual-differences dimensions. The exact nature of the model to be preferred (i.e., the number of factors and the interrelationship among factors assumed optimal), however, is not a strictly empirical issue, since variations in the model considered acceptable will occur as a function of the nature of the subjects sampled, the items used to mark the intelligence domain, the method of data analysis, and the preferred level of conceptualization. Moreover, factor analysis can be used not only as a descriptive model but also as a model that provides a basic theory of behavior, that is, with explanatory information about the antecedents (factors) and mechanisms (linear, additive combinations) that underlie the directly observed performances studied.

Factor-analytic research on intelligence illustrates very nicely the close interaction between a model of data analysis and the type of information about developmental change that can be obtained. For example, there are a variety of models available (e.g., Guilford, Spearman, Thurstone, Vernon) which differ markedly as to content (e.g., type of tests), number of dimensions (e.g., Spearman's g factor versus Guilford's structure of intellect), and the nature of the structural relationships among those dimensions (e.g., orthogonal versus oblique, horizontal versus hierarchical). In the view of the present writers, as is true for models in general (Reese & Overton, 1970), none of these models is necessarily true or false. On the contrary, each of the models may be useful depending upon the assumptions and restrictions one is willing to accept and upon the questions one is asking. However, it is important to recognize that the use of a particular factor-analytic model by necessity will lead to specified outcomes. Consider, again, for example, the "misuse" of the Wechsler Adult Intelligence Scale, which is largely based upon Spearman's notion of a general factor, in the examination of differential age functions and structural change characteristics (for a discussion, see Reinert, 1970).

Factor models and ontogeny: Structural versus quantitative change. The original conceptualization of factor models of intelligence was not explicitly guided by developmental theorizing. In fact, for the most part, it seems fair to state that the original formulations, assuming subject-invariant, fixed-factor-loading patterns, were contrary to a developmental approach. In principle, the only indices of the specification equation that are explicitly stated as exhibiting individual differences, whether age-related or not, are the factor scores that are subscribed for individuals. However, there are some initial implications for ontogenetic analyses inherent in the classical factor-analytic model and the specification equation upon which it is based:

1. The emphasis is on *structured measurement* involving a close correspondence between theoretical constructs (factors) and associated measurement instruments (tests).

2. The emphasis is on the *multidimensional* nature of intelligence involving the charting of separate age–performance functions for each of the factors involved.

The literature abounds with evidence for the usefulness of such a multidimensional conception of intelligence. It has been shown, for example, that a global measure of intelligence such as the IQ is ill suited for a developmental analysis. Moreover, in a related vein, it has been found that the developmental functions differ markedly for different dimensions (factors) of intellectual performance. A classical example is the differential ontogenetic trend obtained for fluid and crystallized abilities (Horn, 1967, 1970; Horn & Cattell, 1966) with fluid intelligence showing an earlier peak and a steeper decline during late adulthood and old age.

Stimulated by earlier suggestions (e.g., Burt, 1954; Garrett, 1946), however, we have witnessed a growing interest in utilizing all developmental aspects inherent in factor models of intelligence. Thus, recent discussions have pointed to additional implications for the study of change. Some of these trends reflect substantive advances dictated by data (e.g., Anastasi, 1970; Horn, 1968; Horn & Cattell, 1966; Reinert, 1970); others represent attempts at formulating richer models that explicitly deal with the examination of change in multiple-response systems (e.g., Baltes & Nesselroade, 1970, in press; Cattell, 1969; Corballis & Traub, 1970; Emmerich, 1968; Nesselroade, 1970). Since the substantive developments will be reviewed later, some pertinent methodological developments will be highlighted first.

The examination of factor models from a developmental perspective (e.g., Baltes & Nesselroade, in press; Cattell, 1969) suggests that there are three aspects of the underlying specification equation that may be subject to change during ontogeny: *(a) factor-loading patterns, (b) factor intercorrelations, and (c) factor scores.*

Since changes in the factor-loading pattern and the factor intercorrelations refer to differences in the structural relationships among responses (between variables and between factor constructs), it has been proposed that such differences should be considered to be of the *structural* type (Baltes & Nesselroade, 1970, in press; Cattell, 1969). The conventional differences in factor scores or other composite scores, in contrast, are labeled as being of the *quantitatve* type. Formal illustrations of such structural and quantitative differences are contained in the various references mentioned above.

The distinction between quantitative and structural change characteristics is indeed an important one, since it has significant implications for adequate measurement (e.g., Baltes & Nesselroade, 1970; Bentler, in press; Nunnally, 1972; Schaie, 1972) and the systematic formulation of theoretical models of ontogenetic change patterns (e.g., Baltes & Nesselroade, in press; Coan, 1966; Emmerich, 1968). Particularly, the *simultaneous* treatment of structural and quantitative change aspects opens a new avenue to examining a variety of theoretical issues. To illustrate, these factor change models appear useful in operationalizing a number of change concepts such as differentiation, integration, or the trait–state distinction, that have continuously been emphasized in the developmental literature.

Note again that, particularly in the aging literature, the emphasis has been solely on quantitative ontogenetic changes in factor scores or some other kind of composite (IQ, subtests, etc.) scores. Such an approach, however, as will be shown later, is not apt to fully represent the complexity of the changes occurring during the later part of the life-span.

Normative Developmental Patterns

In the following two sections, highlights of the main findings with regard to the description of both structural and quantitative changes in intellectual performance will be discussed. The organizational distinction between structural and quantitative change characteristics, of course, is an arbitrary one, since both aspects are to be considered simultaneously in obtaining a comprehensive picture of adult ontogeny. It should also be recognized that the ontogenetic functions presented are preliminary and should be taken neither as fixed nor as final. On the contrary, in later discussions an effort will be made to present alternative models of interpretation and to focus on extraordinary specificity of age functions with regard to both the universe of subjects and times of measurement involved. In particular, the accumulated evidence on the impact of generational change components (e.g., Nesselroade, Schaie, & Baltes, 1972; Riegel, 1969; Rosler, 1967; Schaie & Strother, 1968a, 1968b) suggests that many of the reported age functions might be less indicative of cohort-specific ontogenetic changes than of cross-cohort historical changes.

Structural changes. The potential importance of structural changes in the organizational pattern of intelligence was recognized quite early both for the first (e.g., Burt, 1954; Garrett, 1946) and the second part of the life-span (e.g., Balinsky, 1941; Lienert & Crott, 1964; Schaie, 1962). Unfortunately, the period of late adulthood and old age is least investigated, although certain changes in old age (such as terminal drop, selective survival) would suggest that the structure of intellect also may undergo substantial transformation during this age segment.

Although the accumulated evidence on structural changes during ontogeny is far from being unequivocal (e.g., Anastasi, 1970; Reinert, 1970), some preliminary conclusions appear justified. Figure 1 summarizes the main contentions found in the literature. The general trend seems best described by an *integration-differentiation-reintegration* sequence. Increasing differentiation is indicated by the factor structures showing a greater number of factors, less of a dominant general factor, and lower factor intercorrelations.

In childhood the major trend is one of "emergence" of structure such that originally relatively specific performances become more and more interrelated (correlated), resulting in a strong first (g) factor and positive manifold. Subsequent ontogeny during late childhood and adolescence appears to be characterized by an increasing differentiation of this integrated ability system into a set of

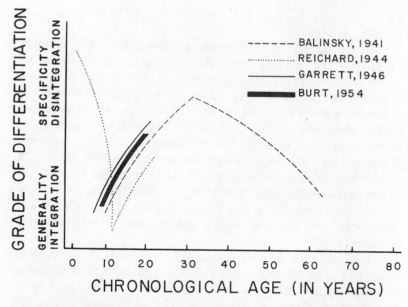

Fig. 1. Direction and age levels for changes in factor structure according to the major age-differentiation hypotheses of intelligence. (Reprinted by permission of the publisher from G. Reinert, "Comparative Factor Analytic Studies of Intelligence throughout the Human Life Span." In L. R. Goulet & P. B. Baltes [Eds.], *Life-Span Developmental Psychology*. New York: Academic Press, 1970.)

relatively independent major dimensions. The course of structural change throughout adulthood and old age, as mentioned before, is least known, although there is speculation to describe it as one of reintegration or dedifferentiation. Moreover, there is some indirect evidence (e.g., terminal drop, selective survival) to suggest that the rate of structural change may accelerate in old age, whereas the major period of adulthood may exhibit a relatively high degree of stability. In a later section, those antecedents and mechanisms that might mediate the ontogeny of structural transformations in the organizational pattern of intelligence will be explored in detail. In the view of the present writers, however, it is premature to conceive of the structural transformations in childhood and old age as representing homologous but reversed processes.

Quantitative age changes. In line with a multidimensional conception of intelligence, most researchers, agreeing on the superficiality of a single universal age function for intelligence, emphasize the notion of age functions being distinct (direction, rate, values of maxima and minima) for different dimensions. Recently, however, the notion of differential age functions has taken an even more extreme perspective.

Earlier suggestions (for reviews, see Botwinick, 1967; Bromley, 1966; Horn, 1970; Jones, 1959; Riegel & Riegel, 1972) elaborated on the need for specifying distinct functions for separate behavioral domains (memory, perception, reasoning, etc.); however, it has been postulated that age functions are also different for various subgroups within cohorts (e.g., ability level, social class, survivorship, etc.) and for subgroups that are members of different cohorts or generations. If one adds the possibility of Age, Social Class, Ability Level, and Survivorship × Cohort interactions to this picture, the potential net of ontogenetic paths is indeed labyrinthine. Nevertheless, a few signal results will be presented to give a flavor of the numerous sources and components that are confounding conventional, descriptive aging research.

1. *Fluid versus crystallized intelligence.* One of the major deficiencies of most descriptive research is that the tests used (e.g., the Wechsler Adult Intelligence Scale) are not an intrinsic part of a developmental theory of intelligence. The major exception is the work by Cattell (1963) and Horn (1967, 1968, 1970) who have proposed a model of intelligence that is closely tied to developmental considerations. In addition to an ontogenetic interpretation of hierarchical conceptions of intelligence (e.g., Vernon, 1961) and the assumption that "the formal structure of abilities is partly developmentally determined [Cattell, 1963, p. 1]," two major (second-order) dimensions of intelligence, *fluid* and *crystallized,* are distinguished.

The dimensions of fluid intelligence are assumed to be tied primarily to neurophysiological antecedents reflecting gene-related differences. Fluid intelligence, however, is not a measure of hereditary differences alone. It also represents that part of intelligence that results from the interaction of basic physiological capacity with a set of subject- and culture-invariant experiential antecedents. Conversely, crystallized intelligence is assumed to be a precipitate out of experience (Horn, 1967) and is largely due to subject-related differences in experiential processes associated with the course of acculturation. Since both types of intelligence share some common hereditary and experiential elements, they are assumed to exhibit a certain degree of correlation which, however, should diminish as age increases.

The interesting implication for the quantitative study of ontogeny is that Cattell and Horn postulate, and offer, some cross-sectional data suggesting that the developmental functions for fluid and crystallized intelligence are markedly different, as shown in

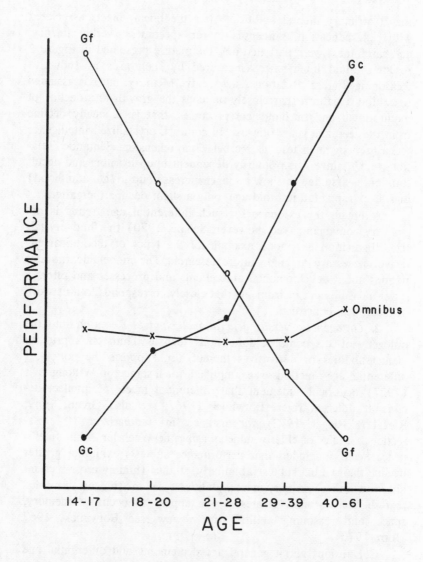

Fig. 2. Intellectual performance as a function of age with sex, education, visualization, and fluency statistically controlled. (Reprinted by permission of the publisher from J. L. Horn, "Organization of Data on Life-Span Development of Human Abilities." In L. R. Goulet & P. B. Baltes [Eds.], *Life-Span Developmental Psychology*. New York: Academic Press, 1970.)

Figure 2. The data presented are based upon a large-scale cross-sectional study by Horn and Cattell (1967) which involved scores for 20 primary mental abilities. After the linear effects associated with sex, education, perceptual-motor speediness, verbal fluency, and carefulness were partialed out, the picture presented in Figure 2 resulted. Fluid intelligence (measured by such tests as Inductive Reasoning, Figural Relations, Associative Memory, etc.) is assumed to exhibit a pattern that closely matches the growth and decline of maturational and/or biological processes, that is, a steady decline from the teen-age years onward. In contrast, crystallized intelligence (measured by such tests as Verbal Comprehension, Semantic Relations, etc.), since it is primarily dependent upon learning and acculturation, is assumed to show a longer increase (up to late adulthood) and, if extrapolated into old age, only a slight decline thereafter.

Although the evidence for such differential age trends is not yet very convincing (see, however, Schaie, 1970) the fluid–crystallized distinction is a good example of the types of theoretical endeavor necessary to guide future research. The model incorporates notions about developmental antecedents and processes and offers a set of measurement instruments that closely corresponds to a network of theoretical constructs.

2. *Ontogenetic versus generational change.* Research into the ontogeny of less complex dimensions such as Thurstone's primary mental abilities or derivatives thereof also supports the notion of differential age functions as exemplified, for instance, in Willoughby's (1927) historical statement that differential facets of intellect decline at different rates. Botwinick (1967; see also Green, 1969; Riegel & Riegel, 1972), for instance, in summarizing 10 cross-sectional studies of elderly subjects using the Wechsler Adult Intelligence Scale concluded that performance subtests exhibit a greater decline than verbal subtests. Similarly, studies (mainly cross-sectional) with other primary-mental-abilities-type instruments revealed that the earliest and greatest losses appear to occur in memory, space, and reasoning abilities (for review, see Botwinick, 1967 Horn, 1970).

Conclusions about general age decrements and differential age functions, however, were seriously challenged when gross discrepancies between cross-sectional and longitudinal outcomes were reported (e.g., Bayley, 1968, 1970; Bayley & Oden, 1955; Glanzer & Glaser, 1959; Owens, 1953, 1966; Schaie & Strother, 1968a, 1968b). By and large, cross-sectional studies of intelligence produced age functions pointing to an early performance decrement, whereas longitudinal studies suggested maintenance or even stability into late adulthood. In line with earlier, less formal propositions both from within psychology (e.g., Anastasi, 1958; Bell, 1953; Birren,

1959; Kuhlen, 1940, 1963) and from other social sciences (e.g., Ryder, 1965; Whelpton, 1954), it was primarily Schaie (1965) who reexamined both the cross-sectional and longitudinal method in light of the relationship between historical (generational) and individual (ontogenetic) change components.

The main argument was that cross-sectional studies sample age groups from different cohorts or generations, whereas longitudinal studies are cohort-specific in that they observe a sample from a single cohort. Consequently, if members of different generations differ as to their genetic potential and experiential backgrounds (e.g., amount of education), one should not expect that cross-cohort (cross-sectional) and within-cohort (longitudinal) age comparisons will result in comparable outcomes. Schaie (1965) and Baltes (1968) proposed somewhat differing strategies, consisting of the sequential and simultaneous application of cross-sectional and longitudinal designs, which can be used to disentangle ontogenetic from generational change components.

Thus far, empirical evidence on the significance of generational change is restricted to a few studies (e.g., Nesselroade et al., 1972; Riegel, Riegel, & Meyer, 1967; Rosler, 1967; Schaie & Strother, 1968a, 1968b). The evidence presented, however, is unequivocal, since all studies clearly substantiate the importance of cohort differences. Consider, for example, the multivariate reanalysis of the Schaie and Strother (1968a, 1968b) data presented in Figure 3.

Figure 3 summarizes the main findings by contrasting cross-sectional (solid lines) with seven-year longitudinal (broken lines) results of the Schaie-Strother study covering the age range 21–77. The study (see Nesselroade et al., 1972) is based upon 301 male and female subjects who were given a total of 13 measures of cognitive functioning (Primary Mental Abilities, Test of Behavioral Rigidity) in 1956 and again in 1963. Thus, two cross-sectional (1956, 1963) and a total of eight seven-year longitudinal comparisons could be performed. Using factor analysis and cross-occasion factor matching, four second-order dimensions resulted and were labeled Crystallized Intelligence, Cognitive Flexibility, Visuo-Motor Flexibility, and Visualization.

Overall, the data clearly substantiate the need for considering generational change components, since the variance components associated with generation differences turned out to be much greater than those associated with cohort-specific age changes. In fact, the statistical analyses suggested that two of the four dimensions (Cognitive Flexibility, Visualization) did not exhibit any mean age changes at all but remained stable over the age range investigated.

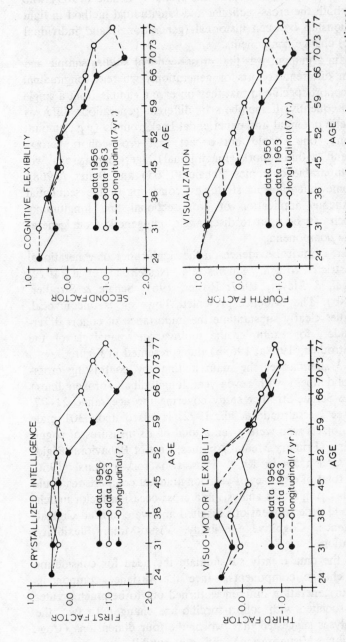

Fig. 3. Differential age functions for four second-order factors of intelligence based on two cross-sectional (1956, 1963) and eight seven-year (1956-63) longitudinal studies. (Reprinted by permission of the publisher, the Gerontological Society, from J. R. Nesselroade, K. W. Schaie, & P. B. Baltes, "Ontogenetic and Generational Components of Structural and Quantitative Change in Adult Cognitive Behavior." *Journal of Gerontology*, 1972, **27**, 222-228.)

Interestingly enough, the remaining two dimensions showed divergent age functions. Whereas Crystallized Intelligence showed an increase in performance through the oldest age group, Visuo-Motor Flexibility exhibited negative age changes starting in young adulthood. In addition, with regard to the impact of generational differences, the outcome suggested that the strength of such historical change components is differential both for the age levels investigated and the intelligence dimensions sampled. Note also that, in a strict sense, the outcome applies only to a specific set of cohorts measured at specified times of measurement.

The significance of generational change for the interpretation of previous simple cross-sectional or longitudinal studies can hardly be underestimated, especially if Age $\times$ Cohort interactions are considered. Recognize, for example, that the differential age functions typically reported for performance and verbal tests indeed may not be indicative of ontogenetic change differentials but of cross-cohort differences in environmental inputs. In a similar vein, the often reported effect of selective survival or social class membership on the nature of age functions, to be discussed next, might also be partially monitored by cross-cohort differences rather than ontogenetic differentials.

Alternative interpretations and components. In addition to the presence of generational change components, the literature is replete with other contradictory designs. For example, most designs used are preexperimental (Campbell & Stanley, 1963) and exhibit such a lack of control that the interpretation of differences resulting from age and cohort comparisons as being indicative of age and cohort effects can rarely be clearly justified (for extensive discussions, see Baltes, 1968; Nunnally, in press; Schaie, in press; Wohlwill, 1970c). Among the design fallacies affecting both cross-sectional and longitudinal comparisons are age and cohort differences in volunteering behavior, test sophistication, measurement validity, experimental mortality, and biological survival. Although space does not permit a full presentation, some of these rival interpretations will be highlighted, since they have received a fair amount of attention in the recent literature.

1. *Sample and population composition.* Within the behavioral sciences, issues involving age- and cohort-related changes in the composition of parent populations and the resulting samples have been examined, again primarily in the area of intellectual development (e.g., Baltes, Schaie, & Nardi, 1971; Birren, 1959; Davies, 1954; Jarvik & Blum, 1971; Jarvik & Falek, 1963; Kleemeier, 1962; Riegel & Riegel, 1972; Riegel et al., 1967).

Two separate issues are relevant in this context: (a) age and cohort differences in selection and experimental mortality due to psychological and/or social reasons, and (b) age and cohort differences in survival due to biological reasons (Baltes et al., 1971). One could argue that these imply two different types of "mortality" curves, that is, a psychological and a biological one. Whereas "psychological" mortality results in potential biases of the various age and cohort samples investigated, biological mortality introduces age- and cohort-related biases both in the underlying parent population and the samples included in a given study. Such changes in the underlying parent population will be discussed in somewhat greater detail.

In principle, the survival question is a reflection of the mortality curve which suggests a higher death frequency in old age (for an excellent discussion, see Davies, 1954). The basic argument is that, due to individual differences in length of life, a given population with increasing age becomes more and more homogeneous, at least with regard to the length of life variable itself. The survival factor, however, also becomes relevant for other target (dependent) variables, if it is shown that a correlation exists between length of life and performance in the target variable under consideration. If this correlation is positive (as appears to be true for some intelligence dimensions), there is a greater probability for superior subjects to remain in the testable population and the effect is to contribute a positive

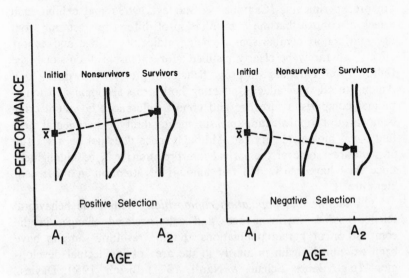

Fig. 4. The effect of selective survival on mean age functions: Hypothetical examples for positive and negative selection.

"change" component to an averaged age function (see Figure 4). If the correlation is negative (as is apparently true for weight), the effect is the opposite, that is, to contribute a negative "change" component to the average weight–age function. It is important to realize that such selective survival effects may suggest change where, on the intraindividual level, there is no change since selective survival per se does not refer to changes in behavior but in the composition of the population only.

Stimulated by a variety of earlier sources, Riegel and Riegel (1972; for recent contributions, see also Jarvik & Blum, 1971; Palmore, 1969; Pfeiffer, 1970), in particular, have elaborated on the general implications of such survival effects. Specifically, they have suggested that it is necessary to develop formal models and that the strength of survival effects may indeed be such that it represents a major source of error to be reckoned with in the interpretation of cohort-specific age functions. The resulting picture will probably be fairly complex, since such effects have been shown to differentially affect distinct classes of performance. Moreover, Baltes et al., (1971; see also Davies, 1954) alerted researchers to the disconcerting fact that the analysis of such survival effects is further complicated by the possibility of cohort differences in survival processes which can only be assessed by means of longitudinal sequences and the application of fairly complex control group designs.

2. *Terminal change.* There is a second issue associated with longevity differences or the mortality curve which involves predeath-specific changes. Similar to the frequently cited greater rate of development in early infancy, it is maintained that "natural" death is preceded and/or indicated by an accelerated decline or increase in certain functions (e.g., Davies, 1954; Jarvik & Blum, 1971; Jarvik & Falek, 1963; Kleemeier, 1962; Lieberman, 1966; Riegel & Riegel, 1972; Riegel et al., 1968; see also pp. 178–199 of this chapter). In the context of intelligence, the focus has been on a selective drop or deterioration in performance manifesting itself in the years immediately preceding death.

Figure 5 simulates this effect using a hypothetical situation and making a number of simple assumptions (linearity, randomness, homogeneity in rate and length) which may turn out to be gross oversimplifications. The example shows how, with increasing age, a greater proportion of the people investigated pass through the period of terminal change (in this case terminal drop) which produces an average age function exhibiting a continuous but increasing rate of decrement.

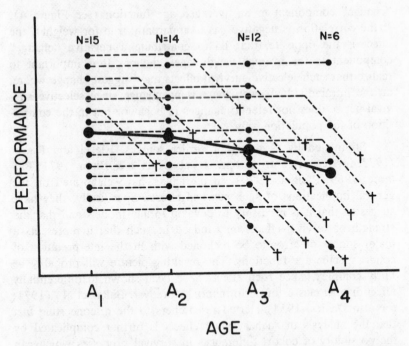

Fig. 5. The effect of age-related increase in frequency of terminal change patterns on mean age functions: Hypothetical example. (Note. t = time of death, • = individual raw score, ● = mean performance.)

Note that this average function does not give a good representation of the "true" intraindividual change patterns (for additional examples, see Davies, 1954). In this context, it seems necessary to set apart the process of terminal change from the effects of selective survival (see also Riegel & Riegel, 1972). Although both concepts are tied to the mortality curve, terminal change refers to a developmental process involving "true" ontogenetic change aspects, whereas selective survival "fallaciously" suggests that change occurs when, on an intraindividual level, it does not ever exist. This distinction is important and needs to be incorporated in future attempts at model building in this area. Note also that both the terminal change and selective survival hypotheses can only be investigated by application of repeated-measurement designs which, in order to disentangle ontogenetic from generational components, should be incorporated in sequential models.

3. *Age and cohort specific validities.* One further issue obliterating the interpretation of conventional age–performance functions

as indicating ontogenetic change is related to the problems of age and/or cohort-related changes in measurement validity (e.g., Schaie, in press). Ideally, measurement instruments should indicate identical attributes and processes across all segments of the life-span. With the exception of occasional warnings (e.g., Pressey & Kuhlen, 1957), however, it is often overlooked that conventional intelligence tests have been developed for the purpose of academic selection and de-selection. Accordingly, they are validated against scholastic achieve-ment criteria in younger samples. As a result, the various aspects of validity (content, concurrent, predictive, construct) are not neces-sarily applicable to distant age and cohort groups.

So far there has been little research on the age and cohort specificity of validity characteristics of intelligence tests. Looft (1970), for example, reported differences between young and old subjects (equated for educational level) in the degree of understand-ing and supplying definitions of individual items of the Wechsler Adult Intelligence Scale Vocabulary subtest. According to Looft, such differences suggest considerable generational change in the availability of specific items of information. Moreover, studies dem-onstrating changing interrelationships among ability and learning or problem-solving performance at different stages of task profi-ciency (for summaries, see Fleishman & Bartlett, 1969; Roberts, 1968–69) suggest that similar validity differentials may apply on an ontogenetic level as well.

The issue of age and cohort differentials in measurement va-lidity reflects, of course, the dilemma inherent in working with an intelligence concept that is more strongly rooted in pragmatic con-siderations (i.e., tied to available measurement devices) than in theoretical model assumptions. Specifically, what is lacking is a model of intelligence, including the corresponding measurement instruments, that explicitly incorporates notions about both structural and quantitative change characteristics (e.g., Baltes & Nesselroade, in press).

Future research will therefore have to concentrate on more systematic attempts toward construct validation of measurement de-vices across all age and cohort groups. This may require the identifi-cation of single-measurement instruments (tasks or items) that show age or cohort invariance in terms of their validities, although, in line with the distinction between a physical and a functional stimulus, it will probably be necessary to use nonidentical instruments in order to measure equivalent attributes and processes across the life-span. In the latter case, it is possible to examine validities by systematically cross-linking measurement instruments between age and cohort groups to obtain continuous coverage of all age and cohort groups. Such cross-linking may, for instance, proceed by the use of overlapping tasks and marker systems at specific age levels. Examples of such cross-linking are Bayley's (1955) use of overlapping measurement instruments at some age levels and the use of comparative and interbattery factor techniques (e.g., Baltes & Nesselroade, 1970; Browne & Kristof, 1969; Nesselroade, 1970).

4. *Other modifiers of aging functions.* There is a host of additional subject- and response-related characteristics "modifying" (Botwinick, 1967) the nature of age functions which deserve consideration. Although space limitations prevent a thorough analysis, a few comments are in order. A first class of modifiers refers to the effects of individual differences in initial ability (e.g., Bayley & Oden, 1955; Birren & Morrison, 1961; Owens, 1966; Riegel et al., 1967, 1968) and in educational and occupational level (e.g., Fozard & Nuttall, 1971; Granick & Friedman, 1970; Green, 1969; Lorge, 1955; Nuttall & Fozard, 1970; Owens, 1966). Such studies, however, appear to suffer from serious deficiencies.

On the one hand, since they deal with naturally assigned variables, such studies are of the quasi-experimental type; a weakness which precludes unambiguous inferences about the direction of causality. On the other hand, most researchers do not pay sufficient attention to the many pitfalls inherent in change data (e.g., Cronbach & Furby, 1970; Harris, 1963). With regard to the Ability Level $\times$ Aging interaction model, for example, Baltes, Nesselroade, Schaie, and Labouvie (1972) have demonstrated that differential age functions associated with initial ability differences may very well represent statistical regression artifacts. Thus, more refined designs and controls are necessary before sound inferences about such differences in developmental functions are warranted.

Another class of modifiers concerns the distinction between ability-specific and ability-extraneous but performance-related components. Heeding the frequently espoused distinction between competence and performance (e.g., Bandura, 1969) or potential ability and actual ability (Botwinick, 1967), the question is whether ontogenetic differences are solely a function of changes in the processing abilities themselves, or whether other ability-extraneous but performance-related factors (e.g., personality variables, sensory and response variables, etc.) contribute a major share to ontogenetic variance. Resolution of this issue hinges on the definition of intelligence, particularly the type of antecedents and processes taken as being an intrinsic part of the intelligence construct. In later sections on the explanation and modification of intellectual ontogeny, this issue will be considered again.

Concluding commentary on descriptive age functions. The evidence accumulated is not sufficient to make precise statements about the nature of ontogenetic changes in intellectual performance, but it is certainly rich enough to seriously challenge the often-stated stereotype of a general performance decrement during late adulthood and old age.

From a substantive viewpoint, a first set of conclusions reflects the general disregard for utilizing existing models of intelligence and for the arsenal of designs and controls available for the analysis of change phenomena. Consideration of factor-analytic models of intelligence, for example, provides an explicit framework for examining intelligence as a multidimensional construct whose ontogeny involves both structural and quantitative change characteristics. Such an approach is in sharp contrast to the simple application of available tests, such as the Wechsler Adult Intelligence Scale, which, at best, are only vaguely tied to a theoretical network concerning intellectual performance. In a similar vein, an evaluation of the research designs used clearly indicates that the vast majority of studies lacks the type of control that would permit such research to make an unambiguous contribution to our knowledge about the nature of ontogeny in adulthood and old age.

The second major conclusion centers around the evasiveness, or the lack of universality and stability, of age functions (see also Riegel & Riegel, 1972). Intellectual age–performance functions, reflecting the operation of a multitude of antecedents and organism–environment interchanges, cannot be seen as being fixed but must be viewed as continuously changing, on both the levels of individual and historical analysis. In addition to the recognition of such cohort-specific factors as educational, occupational, and ability levels (e.g., Botwinick, 1967), it was primarily the recent evidence on the impact of generational change components (Kuhlen, 1963; Schaie, 1970) that set the stage for reevaluation. The search for "normal" aging phenomena, therefore, resembles a Sisyphean task to the extent that age–performance functions are subject to continuous alterations. Thus, although prediction is the major goal of research, one appears to be caught in an endless sequence of postdictive analyses.

Some of these disconcerting limitations, of course, are intrinsic to any descriptive approach. Recognition of the futility involved in chasing invariant age functions, however, leads to focusing on a different type of descriptive research. In line with Wohlwill's (1970a) persuasive position, we argue that, except for a few large-scale studies, developmental research should cease to treat age as the major independent variable. In contrast, the age parameter should be considered as a dependent variable which is an intrinsic part of the developmental function. Conversely, such a change in focus, of course, leads to more intensive concerns with process-oriented, analytical research aimed at explicating ontogenetic changes in terms of explanatory, causal mechanisms (e.g., Baer, 1970, in press; Baltes & Goulet, 1971; Birren, 1970, Wohlwill, 1970a, 1970c). However, in order to arrive at a set of historical change parameters, this shift in focus stimulates a much more careful analysis of the ecosystems that provide the setting for organism–environment interchanges (e.g., Bloom, 1964). Both of these latter aspects will be dealt with in the following sections.

DEVELOPMENTAL ANTECEDENTS AND EXPLANATORY MODELS

As is true for any class of responses, the ontogeny of intelligence reflects, and ultimately must be explained in terms of, past and present genetic and environmental sources and their interaction as manifested in maturational and experiential (learning) processes. In other words, explanatory research aims at specifying the antecedents and processes operating in producing ontogenetic change phenomena.

Ideally, such research should be addressed to a synchronized analysis of both psychological and biological components involved in the generation of age functions. In general, however, the multidisciplined search for the developmental history of intelligence has proceeded along relatively independent routes. Thus, it is often difficult to establish cross-domain linkages and to decide the direction of mutual effect sequences. This deficiency in cross-linking is even characteristic of efforts within psychological research on intelligence. Although there is, for example, a wealth of research dealing with each of the segments of the intelligence construct (antecedents, processes, consequents), there is a conspicuous lack of cross-segment matching.

Crudely speaking, there are three basic explanatory classes of learning-maturation-interaction models that have reached popularity in the area of intellectual development—the maturational model, the cognitive-developmental model, and the learning model (e.g., Gagne, 1968; Hunt, 1961, 1964; Kohlberg, 1968, 1969).

Of these three basic models, the cognitive-developmental model with its heavy emphasis on universal developmental sequences (e.g.,

Flavell, 1963, 1970; Hooper, in press; Kohlberg, 1969; Langer, 1970; Reese & Overton, 1970) has not yet become popular in the literature of adult development and aging. Possibly this is due to an increasing diversification of environmental inputs once maturity is reached and the corollary that it is difficult to make a strong case for a universal set of experiences in adult development (e.g., see Flavell, 1970).

More attention has been paid to maturational models and the relationship between biological ontogeny and intelligence during the second part of the life-span (e.g., Birren, 1964; Birren & Szafran, 1970; Botwinick, 1967; Horn, 1970; Schaie, 1970; Welford, 1958, 1965). With regard to learning models, there is a considerable amount of recent literature focusing on the ontogeny of the learning process itself (e.g., Gagne, 1968; Goulet, 1970, in press; Kausler, 1970; Kay, 1968; Kendler & Kendler, 1970; Stevenson, 1970). Little emphasis, however, has been placed on interlocking the evidence accumulated in this area with the ontogeny of ability systems. Thus, most of the available discussion involving the relationships between learning and intelligence (e.g., Anatasi, 1970; Baltes & Nesselroade, in press; Ferguson, 1954, 1956; Horn, 1970; Longstreth, 1968; Roberts, 1968–69; Whiteman, 1964) is exploratory and speculative.

Before reviewing the landmarks of the literature dealing with the antecedents and processes of intellectual ontogeny, it may be useful to further specify the status of such evidence in the present context. In this chapter we are not interested in the ontogeny of maturational or learning changes per se which, in principle, could be organized around the same headings (description, explanation, modification) used in summarizing information on the ontogeny of intelligence. Rather, we are interested in the type of evidence that has been presented to "explain" the ontogeny of intelligence. Since much of the available body of information is not based upon manipulative but rather upon correlational research strategies, it is often difficult to assess whether maturational (biological) and experiential (learning) changes represent antecedents, correlates, or consequents of the ontogeny of intelligence. In fact, it is largely the theoretical model underlying (either implicitly or explicitly) the research endeavors that specifies the direction of analysis and interpretation. Good examples of this situation are Piagetian propositions (e.g., Montada, 1970; Piaget, 1970) to account for learning phenomena in terms of developmental processes as contrasted with the behavioristic focus on representing developmental phenomena in terms of cumulative learning sequences (see Baer, 1970; Sutton-Smith, 1970).

Similar issues mark the relationship between biological and psychological explanations.

Molar Sources of Development: Heredity– Environment Interactions

A first class of explanatory studies is addressed to examining the relative contribution of molar genetic and environmental differentials to individual differences in general, and ontogenetic differences, in particular. Nature–nurture research, however misunderstood and defamed, is a very potent vehicle in the initial study of developmental phenomena. In other words, despite numerous criticisms aimed at demonstrating the futility of such research, recent papers have demonstrated its usefulness provided the underlying model assumptions are understood and considered when interpretations are advanced (e.g., Burt, 1969; Cattell, in press; Jensen, 1969; McClearn, 1968, 1970; Vandenberg, 1966, 1969).

Ideally, of course, the developmental analysis of molar genetic and environmental contingencies follows an experimental tack by means of manipulating both genetic (e.g., inbreeding) and environmental (e.g., enrichment versus deprivation, cross-fostering) variables. Since on the human level such intervention research is often impracticable and controversial, classical nature–nurture research has circumvented this difficulty by utilizing naturally occurring variations in the degree of hereditary (e.g., identical twins, fraternal twins/siblings, unrelated children) and environmental (reared together versus reared apart) homogeneity. The present section will deal with this aspect of nature–nurture records only. Explanatory models concerned with the explication of the age-related, cumulative processes mediating genetic and environmental differentials will be highlighted in subsequent sections.

There is by now an impressive body of research to suggest that, in general, a major share of the variance in intellectual abilities is genetically determined. Note, however, that the strength of this genetic contribution shows marked differences when various dimensions of intelligence are contrasted (e.g., Jensen, 1969; Vandenberg, 1966). From a developmenal perspective, however, two issues are particularly relevant when evaluating these data.

First, there is the issue that the resulting nature–nurture ratios are sample statistics (e.g., Jensen, 1969) which do not indicate the contribution of hereditary and environmental differences in a definite sense but only represent the state of affairs in a specific sample at a given point in time. Thus, nature–nurture ratios are of the *fixed-effect* type and they can vary with the degree of environmental and genetic homogeneity sampled (see the controversy between Hebb, 1970, and Jensen, 1971a). It would seem that most studies deal with rather restricted samples of the universe of environmental variation thus necessarily reflecting relatively small contributions of environmental differentials. In fact, Longstreth's (1968) conclusion that the effects of environmental treatments are substantial if artificially manipulated along a wider range of environmental deprivation and enrichment presents a convincing case in point.

In a similar vein, it is surprising that the bulk of heredity–environment research has not incorporated age or age-correlated treatments as design parameters (see Cattell, in press). With the exception of the work by Kallman, Jarvik, and collaborators (e.g., Jarvik & Blum, 1971; Jarvik, Blum, & Varma, 1971; Kallman, 1961), practically no research into the ontogeny of intelligence has utilized subjects older than their thirties. Yet developmental processes are under *continuous* genetic and environmental control, with different heredity–environment systems effective or activated at different stages of development (e.g., Ginsburg, 1971; McClearn, 1970). In fact, such concepts as critical and sensitive periods (Kessen, 1968; Thompson & Grusec, 1970) explicitly call for a consideration of Age $\times$ Gene $\times$ Environment interactions.

The recognition of heredity–environment interchanges as being in constant flux (both on the level of individual and historical analysis) further accentuates the notion of nature–nurture ratios being of a fixed type and subject to continuous alterations. It appears of prime significance to examine the ontogeny of such nature–nurture ratios through adulthood and old age. The results of Jarvik et al. (1971), for example, obtained by contrasting identical with fraternal twins (however, without controlling for environmental homogeneity), suggest that genetic effects on ability systems are maintained into old age.

Further, it is important to realize that classical nature–nurture research is not very promising concerning the distinction between quantitative and structural ontogeny of intelligence (e.g., Baltes & Nesselroade, in press; Carroll, 1966; Tryon, 1935). Inquiries into the genetic antecedents and correlates of a multidimensional construct such as intelligence would seem to require more specific information about the dimensionality of the gene structure than is contained in a continuum of hereditary similarity (identical twins, siblings, etc.). Knowledge about structural aspects of the gene structure, however, both with regard to its transmission and its ontogeny is so scarce (e.g., McClearn, 1968; Vandenberg, 1969) that specific linkages between gene patterns and intelligence dimensions are not yet possible. In summary, then, while there is evidence for the important role of gene structures and genetic mechanisms in the ontogeny of intelligence, knowledge about the linkage and interaction systems involved in the emergence of quantitative and structural change characteristics is extremely meager.

Biological Correlates and Antecedents

Status of biological age functions. The importance of biological processes in cognitive aging changes derives from the assumption that behavioral changes may reflect, to a considerable degree, decline processes in neurophysiological and neuroanatomical structures (e.g., Birren, 1964, Birren & Szafran, 1970; Horn, 1970; Schaie, 1970). These changes themselves have been linked to two sets of processes. "In theory, these changes could be the inevitable result of an intrinsic maturational process which is built into the organism. Alternatively, such changes may result from a series of external events the frequency of which accumulates with age [Horn, 1970, p. 450]." This distinction between intrinsic and external causes is similar to that between determinate and ancillary aging processes (Strehler, 1962), or normal and pathogenic causes of aging (e.g., Birren, 1964, 1965, 1970; Botwinick, 1967; Chinn, 1970). The former group of changes are assumed to be lawfully and inevitably linked to the passage of time and to reflect the normal species trend of aging (e.g., Birren, 1968, 1970; Strehler, 1962). The latter, however, imply the operation of unpredictable environmental influences and are seen as a (pathological, but in principle modifiable) departure from normal aging processes.

This explanatory approach to the study of biological changes also parallels recent trends in developmental psychology (e.g., Wohlwill, 1970c) to look at age not as an independent variable but, rather, to incorporate it into the specification of developmental functions which then are to be explicated in terms of antecedents and processes. Interestingly enough, due to the mutual cross-disciplinary relationships, aspects of biological ontogeny may be antecedents, correlates, or consequents of psychological ontogeny and vice versa. In fact, the nature of the relationships reported strongly suggests the consideration of multiple and mutual cause–effect sequences.

Biological ontogeny and intelligence. Reviews of neurophysiological and neuroanatomical changes in later adulthood (e.g., Birren,

1964; Birren & Szafran, 1970; Chinn, 1970; Hicks & Birren, 1970; Horn, 1970; Magladery, 1959; Strehler, 1962; Surwillo, 1968; Szafran & Birren, 1970; Welford & Birren, 1965) reveal a host of alterations that potentially affect the efficiency of brain functioning and therefore may impose direct limitations on complex integrative activities. In many cases, however, the association between neurophysiological and cognitive decline syndromes is merely a surmise, being based upon extremely few and largely descriptive demonstrations of intrasubject correlation of the two sets of decline patterns.

Some recent studies, however, have suggested that the assumption of a cause–effect sequence has some justification. Of particular importance in this context is the information accumulating on the importance of cerebrovascular disease. Thus, Wang, Obrist, and Busse (1970) demonstrated that decreased cerebral blood flow (and the resulting limitation of oxygen supply) is associated with decline in Wechsler Adult Intelligence Scale performance, while Jacobs, Winter, Alvis, and Small (1969) found a dramatic improvement in cognitive functioning as a result of a hyperoxygenation treatment. Other research has suggested that EEG changes, particularly slowing of the dominant frequency, are correlated with intellectual impairment (e.g., Obrist, 1969; Obrist, Busse, Eisdorfer, & Kleemeier, 1962; Surwillo, 1968; Wang et al., 1970). Thus, present evidence seems to point to a syndrome of cerebral metabolic rate reduction and possibly a very general slowing of the central nervous system (e.g., Birren, 1970; Chown, 1968; Hicks & Birren, 1970). However, this should not be interpreted as suggesting a simple one-to-one relationship of one major biological factor, or group of factors, with cognitive performance. On the contrary, the rather global level of analysis obviates such an inference.

The above evidence is corroborated on a more molar level by studies comparing cognitive functioning in elderly subjects differing in health characteristics (e.g., Birren, Butler, Greenhouse, Sokoloff, & Yarrow, 1963; Botwinick & Birren, 1963) and, in particular, by the relationship between survival and maintenance of cognitive functioning alluded to in an earlier section (e.g., Birren, 1968; Blum, Clark, & Jarvik, 1968; Goldfarb, 1969; Granick & Birren, 1969; Jarvik, 1962, 1967; Jarvik & Blum, 1971; Jarvik & Falek, 1963; Kleemeier, 1962; Palmore, 1969; Riegel & Riegel, 1972; Riegel et al., 1967, 1968). Such data clearly suggest the decisive role of various age-correlated pathological syndromes, most importantly, the high incidence of arteriosclerotic disease and its relationship to cerebral dysfunctioning.

Matching biological changes and intelligence dimensions. As was true for the alignment of genetic with intelligence structures, a major deficiency of the existing work is that little effort has been made to interlock the dimensions of biological and intellectual ontogeny.

On a theoretical level, such biological decline should show a particularly strong correlation with that class of cognitive abilities that depends highly upon the integration abilities that Cattell (1963) and Horn (1968, 1970) termed fluid abilities, and Hebb (1949) and Vernon (1969) referred to as "Intelligence A." Unfortunately, however, directly pertinent data are not available.

On a data level, there is the suggestive evidence contained in studies of survival and terminal change to indicate that predeath change may affect selectively specific aspects of intellectual functioning. Thus, Birren (1968) and Jarvik and Blum (1971) reported that tests of verbal abilities and information storage did display a death-related drop, while no such relationship was found for tests containing a highly speeded component; rather, the latter seemed to continuously decline over later adulthood. From this evidence, they concluded that decline on speeded tasks represents a normal concomitant of biological aging, while differential decrements in cognitive functions of the crystallized type reflect different pathological syndromes (Birren, 1968, 1970; Jarvik, 1967; Jarvik & Blum, 1971). Let us note, however, that it would be highly desirable to collect similar data using measurement instruments that closely parallel multidimensional models of intelligence. Such a strategy would permit the investigator to classify the subtests chosen on an a priori basis, for example, as to their speed versus power component, rather than leave him with this disconcerting task during the strenuous phase of interpretation.

Concluding commentary on biological ontogeny and intelligence. It appears, then, that an evaluation of research aimed at examining the biological correlates of intellectual ontogeny results in the impression that, except for the general conclusion of a correlation between biological and psychological aging, the evidence presented does not yet allow the specification of detailed antecedent–consequent relationships. Specifically, research in this area is afflicted with three deficiencies: (a) it relies largely on nonmanipulative strategies, (b) it tends to consider the relationship between primary biological aging and intelligence to be of a fixed and irreversible nature, and (c) it places little emphasis on a model-oriented, structured measurement of intelligence.

As long, however, as the core of such research does not make use of intervention programs, it seems reasonable to argue that (a) the extent of the modifiability of biological age functions is unexplored, and (b) the direction of cause–effect sequences is left to personal bias rather than sound inference. In fact, we suggest that, similar to the fruitlessness of trying to detect the "true" and "normal" age function of intelligence, an attempt to uncover a "true" and "normal" biological aging component is a futile enterprise. Just as normal aging is defined relative to a particular environment, so we should expect that our definition of normality will vary with alterations of the environment. In this context, it is of interest to recall the data of Schaie and associates, mentioned in an earlier section, that show a systematic cohort-related displacement of growth curves for speed-related tasks, which are typically taken as rather pure indicators of maturational-biological components. Similar generational change components (e.g., Damon, 1965) may apply to biological age functions and their relationship to intellectual ontogeny in old age.

Thus, in the absence of a set of well-defined causal mechanisms relating biological to psychological attributes, it will be necessary to continually redefine the universe of both "normal" biological and psychological age functions. Recognition of the need for intervention research and the incorporation of historical change components, however, is increasing as shown in recent advances in the cellular biology of aging (e.g., Comfort, 1970; see also pp. 220–280 by Jarvik & Cohen), in developmental genetics (e.g., Ginsburg, 1971; McClearn, 1970), as well as in attempts at reversing changes that, for a long time, have been considered normal maturational concomitants of aging (e.g., DeVries, 1970; Jacobs et al., 1969). Consequently, progress in the knowledge of biological factors of aging suggests, as Comfort (1970) concluded, "the possibility of not only slowing aging, but of reversing it [p. 139]." The domain of intelligence should be a prime target for such biological intervention research.

Psychological Explanations of Intellectual Ontogeny

Psychological interpretations of aging phenomena in intellectual behavior focus on the cumulative effects of Organism $\times$ Environment interactions in terms of learning sequences. Needless to say, such learning sequences can result both in increments and decrements of performance (facilitating versus inhibitory effects).

In line with a learning-oriented explanation, psychological interpretations have also stressed the essential modifiability of ontogeny by means of systematic intervention programs. The position implied is that cognitive performance decline in old age need not reflect, in many cases, a restriction in biologically based *competence,* or what Botwinick (1967) has termed "potential ability." Further, there has been a tendency to be too ready to attribute an impairment to maturational factors without seriously considering the possibility of environmental deficits, or the operation of performance-inhibitory behavior components that have developed in response to, and are maintained by, environmentally based contingencies. First, evidence will be summarized to illustrate the effect of environmentally based differentials for both the structural and quantitative ontogeny of intelligence. Second, an attempt will be made to specify more explicitly the learning processes involved in Organism $\times$ Environment interactions that may underlie the emergence and structural transformation of ability systems. We shall also speculate on the ontogenetic changes in learning processes that may account for the type of ontogeny found in old age.

Molar environmental antecedents and correlates. Ignoring various model differences, the dominant concern of learning approaches to behavior change has been to repeatedly present selected stimulus conditions to organisms according to specific contingencies so as to observe the effect on subsequent performance. Although the prime interest of research has been on specifying the mechanisms of the learning process itself (transfer, schedules of reinforcement, and so on), the implicit focus on environmentally based input has resulted in a great number of studies that compare criterion groups which differ in terms of global environmental stimulation.

In a life-span perspective, this emphasis on environmental determination of intellectual ontogeny has been most persuasively argued by Bloom (1964) who noted that "the environment is a determiner of the extent and kind of change taking place in a particular characteristic [p. 209]." In the aging literature (probably due to the implicit focus on maturational components), particularly, there is a dearth of empirical data relating environmental input systems to behavior, although a number of recent articles have called attention to the need for ecological approaches (e.g., Duncan, 1968; Lawton, 1970; Schooler, 1970). Thus, most of the conclusions presented follow from research on the first part of the life cycle but are easily generalizable to the period of late adulthood and old age.

1. *Quantitative and structural ontogeny.* There are three major types of research that have been used in examining the effects of environmental differentials on intellectual ontogeny (e.g., Bayley, 1970; Longstreth, 1968). These approaches are (a) attempting to establish correlational links between individual differences in envi-

ronmental patterns (e.g., parental behavior) and individual differences in intellectual performance at a later stage of development, as illustrated in various longitudinal studies (e.g., Bayley & Schaefer, 1964; Honzik, 1967; Kagan & Moss, 1962); (b) a variation of the first in that naturally occurring criterion groups are utilized (for a review, see Longstreth, 1968) which presumably differ as to their molar environmental input (e.g., high versus low social class, institutionalization versus noninstitutionalization); and (c) examining the effects of either naturally occurring or systematically introduced environmental interventions (e.g., adoption, institutionalization, educational intervention, etc.) on subsequent intellectual ontogeny. The emphasis in the latter approach is not only on assessing the cumulative effect of existing environmental differentials but also on specifying the key variables of environmental systems, the key conditions for modification, and the nature of Age × Environment interaction systems (for discussion, see Fowler, 1969; Gewirtz, 1968; White, 1969).

The vast amount of evidence accumulated on this problem has been aptly summarized in other places (e.g., Bayley, 1970; Bloom, 1964; Botwinick, 1967; Horn, 1970; Jensen, 1969; Longstreth, 1968; Reese & Lipsitt, 1970). Thus, a great wealth of largely correlational data has been presented over the last decades on the importance of parental behavior and family conditions on intellectual ontogeny (e.g., Baumrind & Black, 1967; Bayley, 1968, 1970; Bayley & Schaefer, 1964; Bloom, 1964; Honzik, 1967; Horn, 1970; Pedersen & Wender, 1968; Sontag & Baker, 1958; Wolf, 1964).

It has been suggested, for example, that the effects of environmental enrichment and deprivation accumulate with increasing age (e.g., see Longstreth, 1968), although Schultz and Aurbach (1971) contend that this evidence should not be taken as indicating that long-term deprivation effects are irreversible. From a long-term perspective, studies by Bayley and Schaefer (1964), Honzik (1967), and Owens (1966) are particularly impressive. Honzik, for example, reported substantial correlations, but marked sex differences, when relating variables describing differences in early parent–child relationships and family environments to later intellectual performance in 18-year-olds. Similarly, Owens, examining intellectual development from age 50 to 60 found that life history variables associated with patterns of living moderate the quantitative ontogeny in late adulthood. Likewise, there has been an increasing amount of data to show the accelerating or decelerating effects of specialized environmental treatments, both experimental and naturalistic (e.g., Bloom, 1964; Gray & Klaus, 1970; Hunt, 1961; Jensen, 1969;

LaCrosse, Lee, Letman, Ogilvie, Stodolsky, & White, 1970; Longstreth, 1968; Miller, 1970; Skeels, 1966).

In fact, the evidence is much too voluminous to be summarized here. Suffice it to state at this point that the body of data is generally consistent with the view that there is a high degree of correspondence between environmental differences and ontogenetic differences as well as between environmental change and ontogenetic change. However, efforts to substantiate that the final product of intellectual ontogeny, at any stage in the life history, is largely defined by the accumulating history of Organism $\times$ Environment interactions still leave unanswered many crucial questions: What are the limits of modifiability? What are the environmental antecedents for structural transformations? How can age-specific environmental patterns be determined and studied? In many ways, statements about such complex interchange systems require a much more precise knowledge about the dimensions of the environment itself.

2. *Measuring and structuring the environment during ontogeny.* The quest for a stronger environmental orientation, of course, has been a prime feature of the researchers who have heralded the need for and rise of ecological psychology (e.g., Barker, 1968; Bloom, 1964; Craik, 1970; Proshansky, Ittelson, & Rivlin, 1970; Willems, in press; Wohlwill, 1970b). What is conspicuously evident in the context of intellectual ontogeny, however, is the increasing recognition of the fact that complex response systems such as intelligence are one-sided constructs (e.g., Gewirtz, 1969b) unless they are tied to relatively complex systems of antecedents (in the present context) of the environmental type. In fact, in its most extreme form, the argument may be advanced that the key antecedents for any quantitative or structural ontogeny of behavior lie in quantitative and structural changes of the environment. In good behavioristic tradition, such a proposition appears self-evident. Nevertheless, it is surprising that developmental psychology has made comparatively little effort to gain systematic information about life-span correlates of environmental input systems.

On the one hand, it may be argued that conventional behaviorism, although explicitly manipulating stimulus aspects of the environment, has not focused on structuring the environment in any comprehensive manner. On the other hand, one wonders whether the principles developed within the framework of classical behaviorism, due to their largely univariate and molecular nature, might be ill suited for organizing the antecedents involved in the ontogeny of such molar response systems as intelligence (e.g., Baltes & Nesselroade, in press). In other words, what may be necessary to explain the ontogeny of molar constructs is an equivalent level of analysis as to both antecedents and consequents. Thus we would like to suggest that significant advances in the area of complex intellectual ontogeny are most likely to occur if more efforts are invested in formulating two-sided constructs by analyzing antecedents and consequents on conceptually equivalent dimensions (see Gewirtz, 1969).

As mentioned earlier, Bloom (1964) was one of the first to address himself to this issue and to conclude that the arsenal of environmental measures is at best very crude. One may hope, however, that recent attempts at exploring and specifying environmental dimensions (e.g., Beattie, 1970; Dogan & Rokkan, 1969; Duncan, 1968; Lawton, 1970; Reichardt, 1970; Schooler, 1970; Schwartz & Proppe, 1970, etc.) will stimulate coordinated research into the environmental antecedents for the acquisition and maintenance of intellectual functioning in old age.

In a discussion of the potential antecedent conditions for quantitative and structural change sequences, Baltes and Nesselroade (in press) have summarized some of the questions that are of immediate interest in the assessment of molar organism–environment interchanges. First, it will be necesary to arrive at a structured measurement approach by not only exploring the dimensionality of environmental fields (e.g., Reichardt, 1970; Schooler, 1970) but also by examining ontogeny-related changes in such environmental fields. Specifically, it will be helpful to delineate the environmental universe by developing taxonomies of environmental variables (e.g., Sells, 1963) that are prevalent for the elderly.

It will also be desirable to collect observations on environmental patterns not only by means of appropriate sampling techniques (e.g., Wright, 1960), but also by systematically integrating observational procedures within a theoretical framework that explicitly recognizes the dynamic interaction between environmental patterns and behavioral products. Schwartz and Proppe (1970), for instance have argued convincingly for the use of person–environment transaction research that explicitly focuses on specifying those transactions resulting in performance decrements. People of the operant tradition similarly emphasize the need for assessing the effects of environmental manipulations—natural or contrived—as they relate functionally to changes in behavioral repertoires (e.g., Bijou, 1971; Bijou, Peterson, & Ault, 1968; Lindsley, 1964). If such attempts at assessing environmental patterns for the elderly proceed in conjunction with the assessment of intellectual ontogeny and the use of manipulative intervention strategies, they will have significant implications for "testing the limits" (e.g., Schmidt, 1970) of intellectual performance in old age. Such knowledge will be particularly helpful in specifying optimum environments for maintaining, or even increasing, intellectual performance in the elderly (e.g., Lindsley, 1964).

As of now, knowledge about the average environment of the elderly is rather fragmentary, although researchers uniformly conclude that it is characterized by being intellectually and socially impoverished. With regard to intellectual stimulation, for example, a census report on enrollment in adult education classes (after Granick & Friedman, 1970) shows only 2.8% of 60–74-year-olds and 1.1% of age 75 and over participating. Similarly, there is evidence to suggest that most family settings and institutions for the elderly offer few of the conditions that have been specified as being conducive to the shaping and maintenance of cognitive repertories (Gewirtz, 1968; Wolf, 1964). Finally, Neugarten's (1968) suggestions as to age-graded societal expectations leaves the impression that maintaining intellectual performance, particularly in conventional intelligence tests, is not one of the target goals specified for the period of old age. Undoubtedly, the existing environmental fields (Tryon, 1935) in which most aged persons live are a reflection of such societal expectations.

Learning processes and intellectual ontogeny. It would be comforting if it were possible to point to a rich empirical testimony specifying the learning mechanisms linking developmental organism–environment interchanges to intellectual ontogeny. Unfortunately, however, the areas of intelligence (at least as defined in this chapter) and learning have developed rather independently. As Whiteman (1964) observed, psychometric, learning, and cognition people rarely talked to one another about intelligence.

Thus cross-linking the domains of learning tasks to conventional ability systems is as yet an unsolved problem (e.g., Dunham, Guilford, & Hoepfner, 1968; Jensen, 1968; Roberts, 1968–69). In fact, since the magnitude of observed cross-domain correlations is surprisingly low and in continuous flux (depending upon the stages of the learning process), much of the following attempt to discuss learning processes as the major class of antecedents for intellectual ontogeny may not be compelling; hopefully, at least it will be persuasive. This situation, however, reflects one of the most conspicuous dilemmas of classical ability research, in that abilities are not tied to a system of antecedent conditions and mechanisms.

The major approach to the explanation of intellectual ontogeny in terms of learning is to consider learning concepts as building elements whose cumulative and interactive combination results in performance increases. Such a strategy is helpful in specifying the processes that are basic for acquisition and maintenance and, of course, if applications are at stake, for intervention and modification. From a developmental perspective, however, the situation becomes more complex since there are continuous, mutual interactions between once "acquired" ability systems and the nature of subsequent learning processes. Such Developmental Level $\times$ Learning interactions (e.g., Goulet, 1970, in press; Jensen, 1971b; Roberts, 1968–69), although largely unexplored, may be at the core of developmental theorizing.

1. *Associative processes and quantitative ontogeny.* When considering the usefulness of learning processes as building elements for the acquisition of intellectual abilities, the first conclusion is that most learning models traditionally have been intraproblem oriented; that is, they have concentrated on the growth aspects (speed, frequency, intensity, etc.) of specific responses in specific stimulus settings (see Goulet, 1970, in press). Thus the most simple model would state that growth in intellectual performance represents a cumulative gain in the specific response units that are emphasized by our educational setting. Such a model has been applied, for instance, to the increase in vocabulary noted over the life-span (e.g., Riegel, 1966). Most authors now agree, however, that such essentially "rote" processes are not sufficient to explain the development of intelligence in general, and that a more satisfactory account should consider the development of higher order skills which, having intersituational applicability, are thus a prerequisite for the highly efficient processing of information that is the basic characteristic of mature intelligence (e.g., Gagne, 1968; Goulet, in press; Horn, 1970; Jensen, 1971b; Kausler, 1970).

An example of the development of such "higher order skills" or, in Horn's (1970) terms, "generalized solution instruments," is the development of learning sets (Harlow, 1949, 1959). The development of learning sets or of "learning how to learn" allows the subject to approach new discrimination tasks with extreme quickness and what seems to be efficient, strategic behavior. Harlow's emphases on transferable intersituational elements has since been incorporated into a number of models more specifically addressed to intellectual ontogeny. For instance, Ferguson (1954, 1956), in a significant but often overlooked contribution, proposed to explain the development of intellectual abilities in terms of the acquisition of sets of skills that transfer across a relatively wide range of tasks. According to Ferguson, the development of such skills eventually reaches an asymptote, resulting in a stabilization of abilities in adulthood.

More recently, Gagne (1968) proposed a somewhat more complete model picturing the ontogeny of cognitive behavior as a hierarchically organized sequence of the learning of progressively more complex sets of rules. More specifically, he describes ontogeny as the sequential acquisition of simple stimulus–response connections, motor and verbal chains, multiple discriminations, concepts, simple rules, and, finally, complex rules, in that order. Simpler forms of learning are thought to form building blocks for more complex behavior. Moreover, the acquisition of progressively more complex rules is facilitated by the mechanisms of transfer and generalization. Thus, even highly complex expressions of intelligence are explained in terms of experience, or in Gagne's words, intelligence is "conceived as the building of increasingly complex and interacting structures of learned capabilities [p. 190]." Note also that in line with other positions (e.g., Baer, 1970; Goulet, 1970), the role of chronological age is secondary in such a frame of reference. As Gagne pointed out, stages of development "are not related to age, except in the sense that learning takes time [p. 190]." Likewise, stages are not related to a normal sequence of maturational processes, "except in the sense that the combining of prior capabilities in new ones carries its own inherent logic [p. 190]."

In this context, the interaction between acquired performance or ability level and the nature of subsequent learning phenomena becomes apparent. Developmental progression in the complexity of associative functioning, for example, expresses itself in different levels of conceptual ability. Thus, it has been pointed out that children advance from an associative to a conceptual level of problem solving (e.g., Goulet, 1970, in press; Kendler & Kendler, 1962, 1970; Reese, 1962, White, 1965). Jensen (1968, 1969, 1971b), similarly, has commented on socioeconomic class differences in what he called Level I (associative) and Level II (conceptual or mediated) learning. According to Jensen (1971b) it may well be that both developmental and socioeconomic class differences in conceptual ability reflect differences in the richness and complexity of associative context transferable to any new problem situation. In general, these positions imply that there is a complex ontogenetic interaction between learning and ability domains. Unfortunately, however, developmental analyses have not yet attended sufficiently to the task of simultaneously considering both behavior systems (Roberts, 1968–69), especially as they apply to the latter segment of the life-span.

2. *Operant models and quantitative ontogeny.* Operant-learning positions focus on organism–environment interchanges without intensive consideration for the processes that link antecedents to conse-

quents. Although operant researchers have rarely addressed themselves to intellectual ontogeny per se, they have generated a set of principles which have direct bearing on interpreting intellectual ontogeny.

First of all, from the operant position, development is seen as reflecting changes in *performance* due to a few pervasive principles such as reinforcement, discrimination, generalization, and extinction (e.g., Bijou, 1970a, 1971; Bijou & Baer, 1961; Gerwirtz, 1969b). In particular, both the emphasis on response systems as *operants* (which alter environmental conditions) and on *reinforcement schedules* (which are largely environmentally based) argue for viewing intellectual ontogeny in a dynamic interchange of organism–environment interactions. For example, response systems become progressively more complex (such as in response chains) as they are differentially reinforced so as to be brought under the control of more differentiated stimulus and reinforcement contingencies. Moreover, more complex behaviors may develop and be maintained because they are efficient in bringing about reinforcing consequences in the environment. Thus, an important implication of the operant approach is the close functional interdependence between response systems, on the one hand, and their environmental setting or conditions, on the other. In fact, operant theory has most explicitly recognized the need for a conjoint, two-sided description of environmental and response characteristics in order to explicate ontogenetic change sequences.

The stress on the interactive relationships between environmental and response systems inherent in operant theorizing illustrates from another angle the relevance of systematic environmental analyses for explanation of intellectual ontogeny. From an operant perspective, for example, deficient intellectual performance does not necessarily imply a biological condition. In contrast, deficiencies in intellectual performance may either reflect poor acquisition due to inadequate programming of reinforcement and discriminative stimuli, or they may result from poor maintenance conditions associated with loss of stimulus control, extinction, random reinforcement, and similar contingencies (e.g., Bijou, 1971; Lindsley, 1964). It follows that, due to the dramatic significance of stimulus and reinforcement control, the performance of an elderly person cannot be taken as a good indicator of his intellectual potential. Thus, in addition to the practice deficiency notion espoused by associative learning models, the average environment of the elderly may exhibit both *general and specific reinforcement deficits* that could account for a major share of the age decrements reported in various dimensions of intellectual behavior.

An interesting analysis of potential changes in reinforcement patterns has been offered by Lindsley (1964). He claimed that reinforcement deficits may be particularly disruptive for behavioral repertories that typically are maintained by potent long-range conditioned reinforcers. As a result of their fragility and uncertain life expectancy, the elderly might, therefore, become more dependent on idiosyncratic and immediate reinforcers. Similar attempts to specify the reinforcement patterns characteristic of environmental fields during old age should receive high priority in future research (for methodological suggestions, see Bijou et al., 1968; Willems, in press).

3. *Learning processes and structural ontogeny.* Various authors recently have viewed the contributions of learning models to the understanding of structural ontogeny (Anastasi, 1970; Baltes & Nesselroade, in press; Horn, 1970). There are a multitude of studies, although often methodologically deficient (for further discussion, see e.g., Corballis, 1965; Reinert, 1970), which substantiate the effects of educational, occupational, and familial differentials on the "emergence of structure" (Horn, 1970, p. 438) in conjunction with the process of acculturation. Similarly, there are models of life-span socialization (e.g., Brim, 1966; Neugarten, 1968) suggesting continuous changes in socializing agents, goals, and mechanisms which accentuate the notion that structural change extends into old age. In fact, Baltes and Nesselroade (in press), utilizing only three distinct age-graded, environmental differentials (general and response-specific environmental differences and environmental stability versus lability), were successful in simulating the type of structural ontogeny (integration, differentiation) typically found in developmental research on intelligence.

Few facts, however, are available which would allow us to specify the exact learning conditions and mechanisms that operate in the production of such structural change. Two lines of research and theory are particularly relevant in this context. One refers to short-term manipulation of structural patterns of intelligence. The second involves more general attempts to speculate on the key learning mechanisms associated with the emergence of structure and its subsequent transformation.

Short-term manipulation of structural change patterns, primarily using practice as a treatment variable, has shown that a given learning performance changes its factorial composition with increasing trials and practice (e.g., Dunham et al., 1968; Frederiksen, 1969; Labouvie, Baltes, Goulet, & Frohring, in press). Moreover, research into the effect of practice and selective reinforcement on ability patterns suggests that ability structures, as a result of practice, become more complex, that is, more differentiated (for a review, see e.g., Fleishman & Bartlett, 1969). Such research is of interest to long-term developmentalists if it is viewed as potentially "simulating" (Baltes & Goulet, 1971) the type of learning processes that may operate throughout the life-span. As Anastasi (1970) stated: "The investigator thus tries to reproduce the process of trait formation that can be inferred from the observation of age changes [p. 906]." In this context, then, different amounts of practice would be seen as paralleling the cumulative effects involved in the ontogenetic learning history. In fact, such an interpretation is attractive, since the factor changes obtained (increased differentiation) indeed parallel the kind of structural changes exhibited in long-term (but descriptive) intellectual ontogeny during the first part of the life-span.

With regard to more general learning-oriented explanations of structural change patterns in ability systems, Ferguson's (1954, 1956) discussion is of both historical and theoretical significance. In line with Hebb's (1949) discussion of the relationships between learning, transfer, and development, Ferguson focuses on transfer as the prime process underlying the acquisition and transformation of ability systems. He views intellectual abilities as overlearned response systems which stabilize in early adulthood after having reached a crude limit of performance. Differentiation of response systems occurs due to differential amounts of positive and negative transfer operating throughout ontogeny.

In a similar vein, Whiteman (1964) utilized the concept of area-specific learning sets as components for the establishment of clusters of response classes exhibiting stable individual differences. Additional suggestions were offered by Carroll (1966) who enumerated four sources for the "co-occurrence" of response units and the resulting factor patterns. In addition to genetic components, he focused on overlap, transfer, and simultaneous learning of multiple responses as antecedent processes for the formation of ability systems. In fact, he argued that "given a series of behaviors, one could arrange a training situation so as to obtain any particular factor structure that one might desire [p. 408]." Such statements, however, are not conclusive but only suggestive of the type of research programs necessary to specify the learning conditions involved in structural ontogeny.

Thus far, the contributions of operant theory to the understanding of emerging behavior systems (e.g., Gewirtz, 1969b) are similarly general. Accordingly, even though one tends to agree with Gewirtz's demands for a careful analysis of the different conditioning histories that result in the emergence of different "functional response classes" and for a detailed analysis of the sequential flow of discriminative and reinforcing stimuli which operate in shaping response classes and their maintenance, such propositions as yet are untested.

Implications for explaining intellectual ontogeny in old age. The fact that most of the explanatory conceptions advanced have their primary roots in child psychology has resulted in only occasional mention of research and theorizing directly related to the process of aging. Therefore, it appears desirable to attempt a brief recapitulation with an explicit focus on the implications for intellectual ontogeny in late adulthood and old age.

First of all, notwithstanding biological and maturational components, there is the compelling conclusion that whatever changes occur throughout later life could be due to a host of psychological antecedents and/or cumulative, experiential histories. Indeed, the number of potential psychological explanations is proliferating at such a rate that it is difficult to assign priorities for future research. In general, it is most unfortunate that, due to the widespread acceptance of performance deficits, most psychological models advanced to date deal with decrement-related explanations only. It should be kept in mind that such a decline-oriented position may seriously misrepresent the nature of intellectual ontogeny during old age.

There is the tremendous need for elucidating the nature of *age-graded environmental changes* and their functional relationship to ability systems. Here, for example, we can point to Ferguson's notion that the ontogeny of particular abilities will closely reflect what might be called the adaptive utility of certain abilities in specified environments. Lindsley's (1964) notion of a loss in the potency of long-range personal and social reinforcers in old age is also of relevance in this context. In a related vein, LeVine (1969) drew attention to a Darwinian "variation-selection" model which may be powerful in organizing the type of adaptation processes required of the elderly. Further, the notions of age-grading systems (e.g., Bengtson, 1970; Neugarten, 1968) and developmental tasks (e.g., Havighurst, 1953) explicitly postulate the existence of systematic age-correlated changes in the environment. Thus, it appears likely that the average environment of the elderly is deficient not only in terms of social and physical components but also in terms of its opportunity for educational and intellectual interchanges and the availability of reinforcement systems (e.g., Havighurst, 1970; Riley, Foner, Hess, & Toby, 1969).

Such *environmental "deficits"* or *differentials"* may represent powerful explanations both for general and differential intellectual decrements in old age. Consider, for example, that the age-graded nature of the educational system deemphasizes formal training in efficient information processing and complex problem solving in the aged. Moreover, consider that age differences in a given study might not only reflect the effect of age-specific deprivation or enrichment that differentiates older and younger subjects but also the differential distance from the time of formal schooling (compare the often reported age-decrement functions with retention curves). Further, note that the measurement instruments used when comparing age groups may not at all adequately sample the universe of task conditions that define the maintenance systems for the elderly. Finally, recognize that environmental differentials combine both ontogenetic (individual) and generational (historical) change components. Indeed, the overpowering effect of cohort differences found in recent studies (e.g., Schaie, 1970) assigns high probability to the conclusion that cross-sectional age decrements in cognitive functioning are less indicative of biological aging phenomena than of changes in cultural input systems.

On the other hand, there is a host of *process-related* explanations that, taken alone or in their interaction, could underlie performance differentials between young and old persons. Again, the emphasis unfortunately is on decrement, although there is increasing realization that certain aspects of learning efficiency do not show marked decrements if the age samples are matched for irrelevant, extraneous performance variables (e.g., Goulet, 1972).

Thus, the elderly person may lack general test sophistication or related practice when compared with the young (e.g., Chown, 1968; Goulet, 1972; Jones, 1959). He might differ in test-taking attitudes; for example, he might be more cautious in his responding, the result being that he takes more time in order either to avoid errors (e.g., Arenberg, 1967; Birren, 1970; Botwinick, 1966, 1969; Brinley, 1965; Canestrari, 1963, 1968; Eisdorfer, 1965; Eisdorfer, Axelrod, & Wilkie, 1963) or to search for original answers (e.g., Riegel, 1965). His general rigidity may hamper him in complex problems that require quick information search and flexible processing strategies under rapidly changing task conditions, thus causing him to adhere to familiar but inappropriate strategies (e.g., Brinley, 1965; Chown, 1961, 1968; Schaie, 1958). He may neglect the deliberate, planned organization of material in order to increase his memory capacity (e.g., Goulet, 1970; Hultsch, 1969; Kausler, 1970) or, in a related vein, he may exhibit learning set deficiencies (e.g., Monge, 1969). Or the elderly could be unable to inhibit the interference from overlearned familiar habits in tasks that call for novel approaches (e.g., Botwinick, 1967; Brinley, 1965; Goulet, 1972; Kausler, 1970).

It is difficult to choose, however, from the potpourri of potential experiential sources when explaining changes in ability systems. First, as Goulet (1972) argued, more sophisticated designs are necessary to delineate the ontogeny of each of these process components. Thus, it is increasingly emphasized that, as is true for various intelligence dimensions, different components of learning behavior exhibit differential ontogenetic changes.

Goulet (1972), for example, differentiated between Class I and Class II learning skills, with Class I skills referring to skills directly relevant to task mastery (such as mnemonics and mediational mechanisms) and Class II behavior to skills which permit the subject to inhibit response tendencies that are detrimental to task mastery. Both classes of skills interact in producing a given performance but are assumed to exhibit differential age changes. With regard to the elderly, for example, Goulet claimed that there is "not one whit of evidence to suggest that the decline in learning efficiency after middle adulthood is attributable to 'forgetting' of Class I skills [p. 25]." He suggested, however, that decline in learning efficiency in the aged may be due to Class II components' gaining in strength, with increasing age thus (by generalization) inhibiting Class I skills. Since the majority of learning studies in late adulthood are univariate, however, extremely little is known about the covariation of various learning components and the degree of their conjoint ontogeny.

A second, related drawback of the utilization of such process-oriented factors for the explanation of intellectual ontogeny also reflects the lack of a multidimensional conception of learning phenomena. Although there are a few recent contributions to a multivariate analysis of learning (e.g., Dunham et al., 1968; Frederiksen, 1969; Jensen, 1969), it is still pure speculation as to which components of learning align with which components of intelligence or vice versa. Dunham et al. (1968), for example, demonstrate that problem-solving behavior is an affair involving complex factor composition that shifts as learning proceeds. Correspondingly, when considering long-term links between learning and intelligence, one should assume that such cross-domain relationships are not fixed but continuously shifting. Thus, although one may be tempted to hypothesize, for example, that Goulet's Class I skills and Cattell's crystallized intelligence are differential representations of similar processes, or that Goulet's Class II skills could be linked to what

Nesselroade et al. (1972) call flexibility factors, such attempts are clearly speculations that need careful analysis.

From a theoretical perspective, therefore, it would be of great advantage if future research in this area would aim more explicitly at examining the interactive, mutual relationships linking learning to ability systems. Such approaches, particularly if conducted on equivalent (matched) levels of analysis, would provide us with the type of information that is an imperative prerequisite for a complete analysis of learning–intelligence relationships in a framework of antecedent–process–consequent events. Without such interlocking studies we are left with the conclusion that age-correlated changes in learning components represent sufficient but not necessary explanations for intellectual ontogeny in old age.

Despite the "shaky" evidence regarding the interactive relationships between learning and intelligence, consideration of experiential determinants of intellectual ontogeny, of course, is heuristically profitable. On the one hand, their enumeration counteracts the predominant use of biological interpretations. Thus, although many of the processes and factors mentioned may have a biological component or interact with biological aging, in the view of the present writers, it appears fruitful to conceive of response speed, storage and processing capacity, and so on, as process variables that are largely dependent upon learning histories. On the other hand, the focus on experiential determinants of ability systems further clarifies the distinction between performance and competence, and lays the groundwork for attempts at intervention and modification. For example, while it has been suggested that elderly subjects are relatively poor in the unprompted use of mediational skills, there is also evidence to suggest that elderly subjects profit from training in the use of such skills in subsequent learning and memory tasks (e.g., Canestrari, 1968; Grimm, 1970; Hultsch, 1969). Such evidence will be reviewed and utilized in the following section.

PROSPECTS: INTERVENTION AND MODIFICATION

This inquiry into the description and explanation of intellectual ontogeny may be somewhat disheartening to those who look for decisive answers. Indeed, the current scarcity of sound analytical research necessitates some tolerance for ambiguity. Nevertheless, there are signs heralding the development of the prototheoretical models necessary to guide theoretical and practical endeavors.

On the one hand, the major conclusions regarding the descriptive ontogeny of intelligence (e.g., that the notion of a fixed-age function should be challenged) indicate that clear-cut relationships have not yet been established. Moreover, the number of rival explanatory interpretations is such that it is difficult to place reasonable bets. Yet, on the other hand, we feel that this state of affairs is exciting in that it offers substantial evidence for arguing against universal and irreversible aging phenomena in the area of intellectual ontogeny. In fact, in line with our argument that a large portion of intellectual ontogeny is dependent upon experiential histories and specific cultural settings, we see a rich variety of challenging issues both with regard to theoretical analyses and potential applications.

Specifically, from a theoretical perspective, there is a need for manipulative intervention research that would permit the (a) cross-linking of developmental antecedents, processes, and products; (b) specification of the direction of effect sequences; and (c) pinpointing of the key developmental determinants. Furthermore, from an applied perspective, the intricate relationship between societal conditions and the nature of aging alerts us to the fact that there is little justification in the search for "normal" aging. On the contrary, this position dictates that efforts should be concentrated on exploring the biological and psychological fundamentals involved in "redesigning the aging process [Kastenbaum, 1968, p. 280]" and transforming the environment of the elderly (Lindsley, 1964).

Need for Manipulative and Analytical Research

It is imperative that the proliferation of ex post facto hypotheses about particular antecedents and processes involved in producing ontogenetic changes eventually be supplemented by programmatic hypothesis-testing research. Such research, by necessity, will have to rely on various kinds of manipulative strategies (e.g., Campbell & Stanley, 1963) which contribute to demonstrating cause–effect sequences.

The rationales for manipulative research, of course, are too numerous to be discussed at length in the present chapter. The scarcity of manipulative experiments in behavioral gerontology, however, warrants some comments, especially since a variety of recent papers (e.g., Baer, 1970, in press; Baltes & Goulet, 1971; Baltes & Nesselroade, in press; Biren, 1970; Goulet, 1970; Wohlwill, 1970a, 1970c) have addressed themselves to formulating strategies aimed at explicating age functions by systematic intervention research. The major tenet underlying the use of manipulative experimentation is that, once developmental functions have been described, research should concentrate on identifying key antecedents and processes by strategies which explicitly involve *alterations* and *modifications* of the *developmental functions* considered. Thus, experimental manipulation of assumed key antecedents becomes the crux of construct validation. Such validation could proceed, for example, by demonstrating the differential effects of key treatments (designed to simulate naturalistic processes) on subjects differing in age and/or in age-associated preexperimental treatment conditions (e.g., Baltes & Goulet, 1971; Goulet, in press).

In the area of intellectual ontogeny during old age, there are only a few studies signaling the rise of manipulative experimentation. Thus, most of the guidance will have to come from other developmental specialties (e.g., Gewirtz, 1968; Goulet, 1970; McGaugh & Dawson, 1971; Rohwer, 1970; Starr, 1971; White, 1969). Directly illustrative are two studies, one by Jacobs et al. (1969) mentioned earlier and another by Kamin (1957). Jacobs et al., interested in specifying biological antecedents, examined the effect of hyperoxygenation on tests geared to measure recent memory and conceptual efficiency and concluded that the applied treatment led to significant performance increases. Focusing on experiential antecedents, Kamin hypothesized that age differences in intelligence test performance reflect practice differentials. Consequently, young and old subjects were given practice on Primary Mental Ability subtests; however, it was impossible to remove the existing preexperimental age differentials.

Other available research is related, although only indirectly, to manipulating intellectual ontogeny in that it deals with processes that can be potentially linked to ability systems. There are several studies, for example, that suggest that age decrements in learning efficiency are considerably smaller when subjects are prompted to use mediators (e.g., Canestrari, 1968; Crovitz, 1966; Hulicka & Grossman, 1967; Hultsch, 1969). Similarly, Coleman (1963) found flexibility in task approach to be enhanced by appropriate reinforcement contingencies in a sample of geriatric subjects. Further, Bry and Nawas (1969), although using college students, reported data which show that problem-solving efficiency can be enhanced by application of reinforcement schedules aimed at increasing response speed.

In general, however, the gamut of biological and environmental sources and interactions potentially effective in shaping gerontological ontogeny in intelligence is largely unexplored. As stated earlier, what seems of prime urgency at this point is that such manipulative research programs be tied more closely both to theories of intelligence and theories about the functional relationships involved in onto-genetic organism–environment interchanges. Moreover, the inherent complexity of ability systems will also require the application of more complex intervention programs, probably embedded in naturalistic settings, in order to consider the multiple determinancy of intellectual ontogeny. In any case, however, it is apparent that such manipulative designs are a "must" in advancing our knowledge about the antecedents and processes underlying the aging product associated with intelligence. Otherwise, to paraphrase a review title by White (1969), we will continue to be left with "an edifice without a foundation [p. 49]." Indeed, if ability researchers do not respond to the call for manipulative experimentation, the whole area may be in danger of losing whatever remains of its former glamour.

Need for Programmed Intervention

Unprecedented amounts of money and effort have been invested in designing educational and social intervention programs for the young aimed at accelerating the rate of ontogeny; however, similar investments in modifying or monitoring the intellectual ontogeny of the aged are at best minikin (e.g., Charles, 1971; Eklund, 1969; Granik & Friedman, 1970; Pressey & Kuhlen, 1957). Although it is beyond the scope of the present chapter to evaluate the desirability and relative merits of planned educational programming, the present writers feel that a major aspect of educational reform should consist of *redistributing educational programs throughout the life-span*. Similar contentions, of course, have been espoused more and more frequently during the last decades for a variety of reasons. What are some of the implications of the present review for this issue?

The conscientious researcher, when pressed to contribute to socially relevant issues of application, tends to be conservative due to the preliminary and uncertain character of basic research (e.g., LaCrosse et al., 1970; Watson, 1971). With sufficient caution, however, it seems justifiable to conclude that research has yielded a strong case for the essential plasticity of intellectual ontogeny during late adulthood and old age. In fact, the recognition that (a) intellectual aging is modifiable and (b) a significant portion of the gerontological ontogeny in intelligence reflects societal expectations and associated environmental settings allocates a major responsibility for innovation and change to society as a whole.

Implications of ontogenetic and generational differentials for educational planning. A major implication is that the demand for redistribution of educational efforts does not only follow from purely ontogenetic considerations which suggest that performance deficits in the elderly could be due to environmental deficits that are largely programmed by societal expectations. On the contrary, the dramatic cohort differences in abilities reported in recent years (Nesselroade et al., 1972; Rosler, 1967; Schaie, 1970) suggest that the major source for the intellectual performance deficits of the elderly does not lie in ontogenetic but, rather, in historical change components.

Earlier centuries, characterized by a high degree of environmental stability, were able to program life-span ontogeny by a relatively short period of formal socialization, without the aging individual being in serious danger of losing his capacity for intellectual adaptation to rapid cultural progress. Our century, however, faces such a tremendous rate of cultural change that the intellectual proficiency of older generations acquired through formal socialization and education may be offset, in a relatively short period of time, by the younger generations' continuous exposure to more effective and longer training programs.

Although there is evidence (e.g., Schaie, 1970) that not all facets of cultural change proceed conjointly toward either increasing or decreasing intellectual performance, one is justified in stating that the majority of recently studied cultural change components are positive, that is, disfavor the aged. Thus, the aged not only suffer from potential ontogenetic environmental deficits but also from deficits that are due to generational change components. Such deficiencies characterizing the cultural milieu of the aged population, corresponding to already recognized situations involving disadvantaged children and minority groups (e.g., Bloom, Davis, & Hess, 1965; Grotberg, 1969; Hess & Bear, 1968; Hunt, 1969), need immediate counteraction. One vehicle is to focus on a concept of education that is not structured around massive age-specific blocks but on educational interventions that are systematically distributed across the life-span and pay heed to the unique developmental tasks and attributes that characterize all age groups. As Pressey and Kuhlen (1957) concluded 15 years ago: "This country, with its lengthening life span plus its rapid change, especially needs educational programming throughout life [p. 212]."

Matching developmental theory and educational programming. A second proposition, deriving from our review and our belief in the necessity of conjoint research and application, is that modification attempts should be guided by our basic knowledge of the developmental principles involved in shaping gerontological ontogeny. Thus, particularly during exploratory phases, educational interaction should be continuously monitored and related to existing theoretical networks. In fact, as Watson (1971) stated when discussing the applicability of infancy research in the seventies: "Our decisions will not only need to be relevant, they will need to be right [p. 150]." In other words, the probability that mutual cross-disciplinary benefits will accrue from modification research is conditional on the way in which such attempts are integrated, for example, both into psychological and educational theory (e.g., Rohwer, 1970).

The interaction between basic researchers in the behavioral sciences and educators can be very fruitful. Bruner's (1966) discussion of the differential objectives underlying theories of instruction and theories of learning and development is a case in point. According to Bruner, theories of instruction focus on prescription and cannot be satisfied with postdictive description and explanation of the natural or normal course of intellectual ontogeny. On the contrary, theories of instruction aim at specifying the optimal conditions for acquisition and maintenance. Recognition of the "prescriptive" nature of educational programming alerts the developmentalist toward expanding his conventional arsenal by exploring a richer variety of conditions, and the educator, in turn, benefits from the more rigorous technologies and designs the developmentalist has to offer.

With regard to the area of intellectual ontogeny, this means, for example, that ability researchers explicitly should focus not only on the study of relatively specific stimulus determinants, but should more vigorously attack the problem of specifying the psychological properties of more complex environmental fields (e.g., Beattie, 1970; Lawton, 1970). Similar conclusions have already been drawn in the area of mental retardation, where Gewirtz (1968) and Bijou (1970a; see also, Weisberg, 1971), for example, have called for the analysis of reinforcement schedules in the natural ecology of the developing organism. Of particular importance in this context is Lindsley's (1964) plea for attempting to localize and utilize those stimulus and reinforcement conditions that control the behavior of the elderly (see also Bijou, 1970b).

Conversely, the quest for matching developmental theory with educational intervention forces the educator to consider specifying teaching objectives (Bloom, 1956) in terms of psychological models of intelligence (e.g., Guilford's structure of intellect) and teaching strategies in terms of the acquisition processes (e.g., optimal sequencing, optimal timing of stimulus material and reinforcement, and so on) that have been shown to be most effective at a particular level of ontogeny. Rohwer (1970), for example, summarized some of the implications that derive from Gagne's (1968) hierarchical, cumulative learning model (containing the seven varieties of learning mentioned earlier) for curriculum development. Similarly, he discussed the potential usefulness of applying Guilford's (1967) structure-of-intellect model as a framework for the formulation of educational objectives in attempts to modify intellectual ontogeny.

The increasing awareness of the need for such interdisciplinary commerce, theoretical and applied, is one of the major reasons for the optimistic outlook the present writers have about the future of intellectual ontogeny in old age. It is our belief that a concerted program of intervention will allow us to control large segments of intellectual aging to a greater degree than is commonly supposed.

SUMMARY

Research and theory in intellectual ontogeny is reviewed with a focus on the second part of the life-span and the description, explanation, and modification of multidimensional ability systems.

It is concluded that accurate *description* of intellectual ontogeny suffers from numerous methodological deficiencies resulting primarily from the use of simple cross-sectional and longitudinal designs and the failure to utilize structured measurement systems associated with current models of intelligence which suggest, for example, a distinction between quantitative and structural aspects of ontogeny. Whatever interpretable data are available, they not only point to large individual differences in intraindividual ontogeny but also to differential age functions for different ability dimensions. In particular, findings on terminal change patterns and the import of generational change components indicate that ontogenetic changes during late adulthood and old age are surprisingly small when contrasted with both short-term changes preceding death and nondevelopmental differences between successive generations. The latter findings point to the need for reevaluating the often-stated decrement model and suggest that performance differentials between young and old do not reflect ontogenetic (individual) but, rather, historical (generational) processes. It is emphasized that the descriptive search for "true" or "normal" age functions is a futile attempt, if there is failure to recognize that age functions are not fixed but, being specific for a given point in history, fluctuate in conjunction with a complex network of factors that characterize societal change. In fact, the perpetually changing cultural contingencies dictate a continual monitoring of the rate and direction of intellectual ontogeny.

The review of *explanatory* research reveals that few details are known about the specific genetic and experimental antecedents and processes that control long-term intellectual ontogeny. However, both the data on environmental (learning) and biological (maturational) intervention research suggest that intellectual ontogeny is highly alterable, even during old age. Although previous fads have been to assign biological components a dominant role in controlling intelligence in the aged, preliminary analyses of the gerontological ecosystems strongly imply that the elderly live in environmental fields that are conspicuously deficient of contingencies that are conducive to intellectual acquisition and maintenance. Further, it is argued that for the domain of intellectual ontogeny to remain a viable area of research, more emphasis needs to be placed on using manipulative experimentation in order to cross-link developmental antecedents and processes with the ontogeny of ability systems.

Since this review resulted in the conclusions that intellectual ontogeny is alterable and that cross-sectional performance decrements are largely due to environmental deficits, the final section deals with implications for *societal* and *educational planning*. It is argued that the rapidity of cultural change calls for a redistribution of educational efforts throughout the life-span. Moreover, it is stressed that large-scale intervention programs should be closely tied to developmental research and theory.

REFERENCES

Anastasi, A. *Differential psychology*. New York: Macmillan, 1958.

Anastasi, A. On the formation of psychological traits. *American Psychologist*, 1970, **25**, 899–910.

Arenberg, D. Regression analysis of verbal learning on adult age at two anticipation intervals. *Journal of Gerontology*, 1967, **22**, 411–414.

Baer, D. M. An age-irrelevant concept of development. *Merrill-Palmer Quarterly*, 1970, **16**, 239–245.

Baer, D. M. The control of the developmental process: Why wait? In J. R. Nesselroade & H. W. Reese (Eds.), *Life-span developmental psychology: Methodological issues*. New York: Academic Press, in press.

Balinsky, B. An analysis of the mental factors of various age groups from nine to sixty. *Genetic Psychology Monographs*, 1941, **23**, 191–234.

Baltes, P. B. Longitudinal and cross-sectional sequences in the study of age and generation effects. *Human Development*, 1968, **11**, 145–171.

Baltes, P. B., & Goulet, L. R. Status and issues of a life-span developmental psychology. In L. R. Goulet & P. B. Baltes (Eds.), *Life-span developmental psychology*. New York: Academic Press, 1970.

Baltes, P. B., & Goulet, L. R. Exploration of developmental variables by manipulation and simulation of age differences in behavior. *Human Development*, 1971, **14**, 149–170.

Baltes, P. B., & Nesselroade, J. R. Multivariate longitudinal and cross-sectional sequences for analyzing ontogenetic and generational changes. *Developmental Psychology*, 1970, **2**, 163–168.

Baltes, P. B., & Nesselroade, J. R. The developmental analysis of individual differences on multiple measures. In J. R. Nesselroade & H. W. Reese (Eds.), *Life-span developmental psychology: Methodological issues.* New York: Academic Press, in press.

Baltes, P. B., Nesselroade, J. R., Schaie, K. W., & Labouvie, E. W. On the dilemma of regression effects in examining ability-level-related differentials in ontogenetic patterns of intelligence. *Developmental Psychology*, 1972, **6**, 78–84.

Baltes, P. B., Schaie, K. W., & Nardi, A. H. Age and experimental mortality in a seven-year longitudinal study of cognitive behavior. *Developmental Psychology*, 1971, **5**, 18–26.

Bandura, A. Social-learning theory of identificatory processes. In D. A. Goslin (Ed.), *Handbook of socialization theory and research.* Chicago: Rand McNally, 1969.

Barker, R. C. *Ecological psychology.* Stanford: Stanford University Press, 1968.

Baumrind, D., & Black, A. E. Socialization practices associated with dimensions of competence in preschool boys and girls. *Child Development*, 1967, **38**, 291–327.

Bayley, N. On the growth of intelligence. *American Psychologist*, 1955, **10**, 805–818.

Bayley, N. The life span as a frame of reference in psychological research. *Vita Humana*, 1963, **6**, 125–139.

Bayley, N. Cognition and aging. In K. W. Schaie (Ed.), *Theory and methods of research on aging.* Morgantown: West Virginia University Library, 1968.

Bayley, N. Development of mental abilities. In P. H. Mussen (Ed.), *Carmichael's manual of child psychology.* New York: Wiley, 1970.

Bayley, N., & Oden, M. H. The maintenance of intellectual ability in gifted adults. *Journal of Gerontology*, 1955, **10**, 91–107.

Bayley, N., & Schaefer, E. S. Correlations of maternal and child behaviors with the development of mental abilities: Data from the Berkeley Growth Study. *Monographs of the Society for Research in Child Development*, 1964, **29**, (6, Whole No. 97).

Beattie, W. M. The design of supportive environments for the life-span. *Gerontologist*, 1970, **10**, 190–193.

Bell, R. Q., Convergence: An accelerated longitudinal approach. *Child Development*, 1953, **24**, 145–152.

Bengtson, V. L. Adult socialization and personality differentiation: The social psychology of aging. In J. E. Birren (Ed.), *Contemporary gerontology: Issues and concepts.* Los Angeles: Gerontology Center, University of Southern California, 1970.

Bentler, P. R. Assessment of developmental factor change at the individual and group level. In J. R. Nesselroade & H. W. Reese (Eds.), *Life-span developmental psychology: Methodological issues.* New York: Academic Press, in press.

Bijou, S. N. Ages, stages, and the naturalization of human development. *American Psychologist,* 1968, **23,** 419–427.

Bijou, S. W. Reinforcement history and socialization. In R. A. Hoppe & G. A. Milton (Eds.), *Early experiences and the process of socialization.* New York: Academic Press, 1970. (a)

Bijou, S. W. What psychology has to offer education—now. *Journal of Applied Psychology,* 1970, **3,** 65–71. (b)

Bijou, S. W. Environment and intelligence: A behavioral analysis. In R. Cancro (Ed.), *Contributions to intelligence.* New York: Grune & Stratton, 1971.

Bijou, S. W., & Baer, D. M. *Child development: A systematic and empirical theory.* Vol. 1. New York: Appleton-Century-Crofts, 1961.

Bijou, S. W., Peterson, R. F., & Ault, M. H. A method to integrate descriptive and experimental field studies at the level of data and empirical concepts. *Journal of Applied Behavioral Analysis,* 1968, **1,** 175–191.

Birren, J. E. Principles of research on aging. In J. E. Birren (Ed.), *Handbook of aging and the individual.* Chicago: University of Chicago Press, 1959.

Birren, J. E. *The psychology of aging.* Englewood Cliffs, N.J.: Prentice-Hall, 1964.

Birren, J. E. Age changes in speed of behavior: Its central nature and physiological correlates. In A. T. Welford & J. E. Birren (Eds.), *Behavior, aging, and the nervous system.* Springfield, Ill.: Charles C Thomas, 1965.

Birren, J. E. Increments and decrements in the intellectual status of the aged. *Psychiatric Research Reports,* 1968, **23,** 207–214.

Birren, J. E. Toward an experimental psychology of aging. *American Psychologist,* 1970, **25,** 124–135.

Birren, J. E., Butler, R. W., Greenhouse, S. W., Sokoloff, L., & Yarrow, M. R. (Eds.), *Human aging: A biological and behavioral study.* Washington, D.C.: United States Government Printing Office, 1963.

Birren, J. E., & Morrison, D. F. Analysis of the WAIS subtests in relation to age and education. *Journal of Gerontology,* 1961, **16,** 363–369.

Birren, J. E., & Szafran, J. Behavior, aging, and the nervous system. In J. E. Birren (Ed.), *Contemporary gerontology: Issues and concepts.* Los Angeles: Gerontology Center, University of Southern California, 1970.

Bloom, B. S. (Ed.), *Taxonomy of educational objectives: The classification of educational goals: Handbook 1. Cognitive domain.* New York: Longmans, Green, 1956.

Bloom, B. S. *Stability and change in human characteristics.* New York: Wiley, 1964.

Bloom, B. S., Davis, A., & Hess, R. *Compensatory education for cultural deprivation.* New York: Holt, Rinehart & Winston, 1965.

Blum, J. E., Clark, E. C., & Jarvik, L. F. Longitudinal changes with advancing age: Report of follow-up study. Paper presented at the annual meeting of the American Psychological Association, San Francisco, September 1968.

Botwinick, J. Cautiousness in advanced age. *Journal of Gerontology,* 1966, **21,** 347–353.

Botwinick, J. *Cognitive processes in maturity and old age.* New York: Springer, 1967.

Botwinick, J. Disinclination to venture response versus cautiousness in responding: Age differences. *Journal of Genetic Psychology,* 1969, **115**, 55–62.

Botwinick, J., & Birren, J. E. Cognitive processes: Mental abilities and psychomotor responses in healthy aged men. In J. E. Birren, R. N. Butler, S. W. Greenhouse, L. Sokoloff, & M. R. Yarrow (Eds.), *Human aging: A biological and behavioral study.* Washington, D. C.: United States Government Printing Office, 1963.

Brim, O. G. Socialization through the life cycle. In O. G. Brim & S. Wheeler (Eds.), *Socialization after childhood.* New York: Wiley, 1966.

Brinley, J. F. Cognitive sets, speed, and accuracy of performance in the elderly. In A. T. Welford & J. E. Birren (Eds.), *Behavior, aging, and the nervous system.* Springfield, Ill.: Charles C Thomas, 1965.

Bromley, D. B. *The psychology of human aging.* Baltimore: Penguin Books, 1966.

Browne, M., & Kristof, W. On the oblique rotation of a factor matrix to a specific pattern. *Psychometrika,* 1969, **34**, 237–248.

Bruner, J. *Toward a theory of instruction.* Cambridge, Mass.: Harvard University Press, 1966.

Bry, P. M., & Nawas, M. M. Rigidity: A function of reinforcement history. *Perceptual and Motor Skills,* 1969, **29**, 118.

Burt, C. The differentiation of intellectual abilities. *British Journal of Educational Psychology,* 1954, **24**, 76–90.

Burt, C. Intelligence and heredity: Some common misconceptions. *Irish Journal of Education,* 1969, **3**, 75–94.

Campbell, D. T., & Stanley, J. C. Experimental and quasi-experimental designs for research on teaching. In N. L. Gage (Ed.), *Handbook of research on teaching.* Chicago: Rand McNally, 1963.

Canestrari, R. E., Jr. Paced and self-paced learning in young and elderly adults. *Journal of Gerontology,* 1963, **18**, 165–168.

Canestrari, R. E., Jr. Age changes in acquisition. In G. A. Talland (Ed.), *Human aging and behavior.* New York: Academic Press, 1968.

Carroll, J. B. Factors of verbal achievement. In A. Anastasi (Ed.), *Testing problems in perspective.* Washington, D.C.: American Council on Education, 1966.

Cattell, R. B. Theory of fluid and crystallized intelligence: A critical experiment. *Journal of Educational Psychology,* 1963, **54**, 1–22.

Cattell, R. B. The meaning and strategic use of factor analysis. In R. B. Cattell (Ed.), *Handbook of multiviariate experimental psychology.* Chicago: Rand McNally, 1966.

Cattell, R. B. Comparing factor trait and state scores across ages and cultures. *Journal of Gerontology,* 1969, **24**, 343–360.

Cattell, R. B. Heredity–environment issues in a developmental framework. In J. R. Nesselroade & H. W. Reese (Eds.), *Life-span developmental psychology: Methodological issues.* New York: Academic Press, in press.

Charles, D. C. Historical antecedents of life-span developmental psychology. In L. R. Goulet & B. P. Baltes (Eds.), *Life-span developmental psychology.* New York: Academic Press, 1970.

Charles, D. C. The older learner. *Educational Forum,* 1971, **35,** 227–233.

Chinn, A. B. Physiology of human aging. In J. E. Birren (Ed.), *Contemporary gerontology: Issues and concepts.* Los Angeles: Gerontology Center, University of Southern California, 1970.

Chown, S. M. Age and the rigidities. *Journal of Gerontology,* 1961, **16,** 353–362.

Chown, S. M. Experimental psychology and the problems of aging. In G. P. Powers & W. Baskin (Eds.), *New outlooks in psychology.* New York: Philosophical Library, 1968.

Coan, R. W. Child personality and developmental psychology. In R. B. Cattell (Ed.), *Handbook of multivariate experimental psychology.* Chicago: Rand McNally, 1966.

Coleman, K. K. The modification of rigidity in geriatric patients through operant conditioning. *Dissertation Abstracts,* 1963, **24,** 2560–2561.

Comfort, A. Biological theories of aging. *Human Development,* 1970, **13,** 127–139.

Corballis, M. C. Practice and the simplex. *Psychological Review,* 1965, **72,** 399–406.

Corballis, M. C., & Traub, R. E. Longitudinal factor analysis. *Psychometrika,* 1970, **35,** 79–98.

Craik, K. H. Environmental psychology. In, *New directions in psychology.* Vol. 4. New York: Holt, Rinehart & Winston, 1970.

Cronbach, L. J., & Furby, L. How should we measure "change"—Or should we? *Psychological Bulletin,* 1970, **74,** 68–80.

Crovitz, E. Reversing a learning deficit in the aged. *Journal of Gerontology,* 1966, **21,** 236–238.

Damon, A. Discrepancies between findings of longitudinal and cross-sectional studies in adult life: Physique and physiology. *Human Development,* 1965, **8,** 16–22.

Davies, D. F. Mortality and modbidity statistics: I. Limitations of approaches to rates of aging. *Journal of Gerontology,* 1954, **9,** 186–195.

DeVries, H. A. Physiology of exercise and aging. In J. E. Birren (Ed.), *Contemporary gerontology: Issues and concepts.* Los Angeles: Gerontology Center, University of Southern California, 1970.

Dogan, M., & Rokkan, S. (Eds.), *Quantitative ecology analysis in the social sciences.* Cambridge, Mass.: MIT Press, 1969.

Duncan, L. E., Jr. Ecology and aging. *Gerontologist,* 1968, **8,** 80–83.

Dunham, J. L. Guilford, J. P., & Hoepfner, R. Multivariate approaches to discovering the intellectual components of concept learning. *Psychological Review,* 1968, **75,** 206–221.

Eisdorfer, C. Verbal learning response time in the aged. *Journal of Genetic Psychology,* 1965, **107,** 15–22.

Eisdorfer, C., Axelrod, S., & Wilkie, F. L. Stimulus exposure time as a factor in serial learning in an aged sample. *Journal of Abnormal and Social Psychology,* 1963, **67,** 594–600.

Eklund, L. Aging and the field of education. In M. W. Riley, J. W. Riley, Jr., M. E. Johnson, A. Foner, & B. Hess (Eds.), *Aging and society.* Vol. 2. *Aging and the professions.* New York: Russell Sage Foundation, 1969.

Emmerich, W. Personality development and concepts of structure. *Child Development,* 1968, **39,** 671–690.

Ferguson, G. A. On learning and human ability. *Canadian Journal of Psychology*, 1954, **8**, 95–112.

Ferguson, G. A., On transfer and the abilities of man. *Canadian Journal of Psychology*, 1956, **10**, 121–131.

Flavell, J. H. *The developmental psychology of Jean Piaget*. Princeton, N.J.: Van Nostrand, 1963.

Flavell, J. H. Cognitive changes in adulthood. In L. R. Goulet & P. B. Baltes (Eds.), *Life-span developmental psychology*. New York: Academic Press, 1970.

Fleishman, E. A., & Bartlett, C. J. Human abilities. *Annual Review of Psychology*, 1969, **20**, 349–380.

Fowler, W. The effect of early stimulation: The problem of focus in developmental stimulation. *Merrill-Palmer Quarterly*, 1969, **15**, 157–170.

Fozard, J. L., & Nuttall, R. L. General Aptitude Test Battery scores for men differing in age and socioeconomic status. *Journal of Applied Psychology*, 1971, **55**, 372–379.

Frederiksen, C. H. Abilities, transfer, and information retrieval in verbal learning. *Multivariate Behavioral Research Monographs*, 1969, Vol. 4 (Whole No. 2).

Gagne, R. H. Contributions of learning to human development. *Psychological Review*, 1968, **75**, 177–191.

Garrett, H. E. A developmental theory of intelligence. *American Psychologist*, 1946, **1**, 372–378.

Gewirtz, J. L. On designing the functional environment of the child to facilitate behavioral development. In L. L. Dittman (Ed.), *Early child care: The new perspectives*. New York: Atherton Press, 1968.

Gewirtz, J. L. Levels of conceptual analysis in environment–infant interaction research. *Merrill-Palmer Quarterly*, 1969, **15**, 7–47. (a)

Gewirtz, J. L. Mechanisms of social learning: Some roles of stimulation and behavior in early human development. In D. A. Goslin (Ed.), *Handbook of socialization theory and research*. Chicago: Rand McNally, 1969. (b)

Ginsburg, B. E. Developmental genetics of behavioral capacities: The nature–nurture problem re-evaluated. *Merrill-Palmer Quarterly*, 1971, **17**, 187–202.

Glanzer, M., & Glaser, R. Cross-sectional and longitudinal results in a study of age-related changes. *Educational and Psychological Measurement*, 1959, **19**, 89–101.

Goldfarb, A. I. Predicting mortality in the institutionalized aged. *Archives of General Psychiatry*, 1969, **21**, 172–176.

Goulet, L. R. Training, transfer, and the development of complex behavior. *Human Development*, 1970, **13**, 213–240.

Goulet, L. R. The interfaces of acquisition: Models and methods for studying the active, developing organism. In J. R. Nesselroade & H. W. Reese (Eds.), *Life-span developmental psychology: Methodological issues*. New York: Academic Press, in press.

Granick, S., & Birren, J. E. Cognitive functioning of survivors versus non-survivors: 12-year follow up of healthy aged. Paper presented at the 8th International Congress of Gerontology, Washington, D.C., August 1969.

Granick, S., & Friedman, A. S. The influence of education on the maintenance of intellectual functioning in the aged. Paper presented at the annual meeting of the American Psychological Association, Miami Beach, September 1970.

Gray, S. W., & Klaus, R. A. The Early Training Project: A seventh-year report. *Child Development,* 1970, **41,** 909–924.

Green, R. F. Age–intelligence relationships between ages sixteen and sixty-four: A rising trend. *Developmental Psychology,* 1969, **1,** 618–627.

Grimm, B. A developmental study of interference in paired-associate learning. Unpublished master's thesis, West Virginia University, 1970.

Grotberg, E. (Ed.), *Critical issues in research related to disadvantaged children.* Princeton, N.J.: Educational Testing Service, 1969.

Guilford, J. P. *The nature of human intelligence.* New York: McGraw-Hill, 1967.

Harlow, H. F. The formation of learning sets. *Psychological Review,* 1949, **56,** 51–65.

Harlow, H. F. Learning set and error factor theory. In S. Koch (Ed.), *Psychology: A study of a science.* Vol. 2. New York: McGraw-Hill, 1959.

Harris, C. W. (Ed.), *Problems in measuring change.* Madison, Wis.: University of Wisconsin Press, 1963.

Havighurst, R. J. *Human development and education.* New York: Longmans, Green, 1953.

Havighurst, R. J. Minority subcultures and the law of effect. *American Psychologist,* 1970, **25,** 313–322.

Hebb, D. O. *Organization of behavior.* New York: Wiley, 1949.

Hebb, D. O. A return to Jensen and his social science critics. *American Psychologist,* 1970, **25,** 568.

Hess, R. D., & Baer, R. M. (Eds.) *Early education.* Chicago: Aldine, 1968.

Hicks, L. H., & Birren, J. E. Aging, brain damage, and psychomotor slowing. *Psychological Bulletin,* 1970, **74,** 377–396.

Honzik, M. Environmental correlates of mental growth: Predictions from the family setting at 21 months. *Child Development,* 1967, **38,** 337–364.

Hooper, F. H. Cognitive assessment across the life-span: The transition from theoretical description to operational reality. In J. R. Nesselroade & H. W. Reese (Eds.), *Life-span developmental psychology: Methodological issues.* New York: Academic Press, in press.

Horn, J. L. Intelligence—Why it grows, why it declines. *Trans-Action,* 1967, **4,** 23–31.

Horn, J. L. Organization of abilities and the development of intelligence. *Psychological Review,* 1968, **75,** 242–259.

Horn, J. L. Organization of data on life-span development of human abilities. In L. R. Goulet & P. B. Baltes (Eds.), *Life-span developmental psychology.* New York: Academic Press, 1970.

Horn, J. L., & Cattell, R. S. Refinement and test of the theory of fluid and crystallized intelligence. *Journal of Educational Psychology,* 1966, **57,** 253–270.

Horn, J. L., & Cattell, R. B. Age differences in fluid and crystallized intelligence. *Acta Psychologica,* 1967, **26,** 107–129.

Hulicka, I. M., & Grossman, J. L. Age-group comparisons for use of mediators in paired-associate learning. *Journal of Gerontology,* 1967, **22,** 46–51.

Hultsch, D. F. Adult age differences in the organization of free recall. *Developmental Psychology,* 1969, **1,** 673–678.

Humphreys, L. G. Theory of intelligence. In R. Cancro (Ed.), *Contributions to intelligence.* New York: Grune & Stratton, 1971.

Hunt, J. McV. *Intelligence and experience.* New York: Ronald Press, 1961.

Hunt, J. McV. The implications of changing ideas of how children develop intellectually. *Children,* 1964, **11,** 83–91.

Hunt, J. McV. *The challenge of incompetence and poverty.* Urbana: University of Illinois Press, 1969.

Jacobs, E. A., Winter, P. M., Alvis, H. J., & Small, S. M. Hyperoxygenation effect on cognitive functioning in the aged. *Proceedings of the 77th Annual Convention of the American Psychological Association,* 1969, **4,** 721–722. (Summary)

Jarvik, L. F. Biological differences in intellectual functioning. *Vita Humana,* 1962, **5,** 195–203.

Jarvik, L. F. Survival and psychological aspects of aging in man. *Symposia of the Society for Experimental Biology,* 1967, **21,** 463–482.

Jarvik, L. F., & Blum, J. E. Cognitive declines as predictors of mortality in discordant twin pairs: A twenty-year longitudinal study of aging. Unpublished manuscript, Columbia University, 1971.

Jarvik, L. F., Blum, J. E., & Varma, A. D. Genetic components and intellectual functioning during senescence: A twenty-year study of aging twins. Unpublished manuscripts, Columbia University, 1971.

Jarvik, L. F., & Falek, A. Intellectual stability and survival in the aged. *Journal of Gerontology,* 1963, **18,** 173–176.

Jensen, A. R. Social class and verbal learning. In M. Deutsch, I. Katz, & A. R. Jensen (Eds.), *Social class, race, and psychological development.* New York: Holt, Rinehart & Winston, 1968.

Jensen, A. R. How much can we boost IQ and scholastic achievement? *Harvard Educational Review,* 1969, **39,** 1–123.

Jensen, A. R. Hebb's confusion about heritability. *American Psychologist,* 1971, **26,** 394–395. (a)

Jensen, A. R. The role of verbal mediation in mental development. *Journal of Genetic Psychology,* 1971, **118,** 39–70. (b)

Jones, H. E. Intelligence and problem-solving. In J. E. Birren (Ed.), *Handbook of aging and the individual.* Chicago: University of Chicago Press, 1959.

Kagan, J., & Moss, H. A. *Birth to maturity: A study in psychological development.* New York: Wiley, 1962.

Kallman, I. J. Genetic factors in aging: Comparative and longitudinal observations on a senescent twin population. In P. H. Hoch & J. Zubin (Eds.), *Psychopathology of aging.* New York: Grune & Stratton, 1961.

Kamin, L. J. Differential changes in mental abilities in old age. *Journal of Gerontology,* 1957, **12,** 66–70.

Kastenbaum, R. Perspectives on the development and modification of behavior in the aged: A developmental-field perspective. *Gerontologist,* 1968, **8,** 280–283.

Kausler, D. H. Retention-forgetting as a nomological network for developmental research. In L. R. Goulet & P. B. Baltes (Eds.), *Life-span developmental psychology.* New York: Academic Press, 1970.

Kay, H. Learning and aging. In K. W. Schaie (Ed.), *Theory and methods of research in aging.* Morgantown: West Virginia University, 1968.

Kendler, H. H., & Kendler, T. S. Vertical and horizontal processes in human concept formation. *Psychological Review,* 1962, **69**, 1–18.

Kendler, H. H., & Kendler, T. S. Developmental processes in discrimination learning. *Human Development,* 1970, **13**, 65–89.

Kessen, W. Comparative personality research. In E. F. Borgatta & W. W. Lambert (Eds.), *Handbook of personality theory and research.* Chicago: Rand McNally, 1968.

Kleemeier, R. W. Intellectual change in the senium. *Proceedings of the Social Statistics Section of the American Statistical Association,* 1962, 290–295.

Kohlberg, L. Early education: A cognitive-developmental view. *Child Development,* 1968, **39**, 1013–1062.

Kohlberg, L. Stage and sequence: The cognitive-developmental approach to socialization. In D. A. Goslin (Ed.), *Handbook of socialization theory and research.* Chicago: Rand McNally, 1969.

Kuhlen, R. G. Social change: A neglected factor in psychological studies of the life-span. *School and Society,* 1940, **52**, 14–16.

Kuhlen, R. G. Age and intelligence: The significance of cultural change in longitudinal vs. cross-sectional findings. *Vita Humana,* 1963, **6**, 113–124.

Labouvie, G. V., Baltes, P. B., Goulet, L. R., & Frohring, W. The differential validity of a recall task at various stages of learning and as a function of two experimental conditions. *Journal of Educational Psychology,* in press.

LaCrosse, E. R., Lee, P. C., Letman, F., Ogilvie, D. M., Stodolsky, S. S., & White, B. L. The first six years of life: A report on current research and educational practice. *Genetic Psychology Monographs,* 1970, **82**, 161–266.

Langer, J. Werner's theory of development. In P. H. Mussen (Ed.), *Carmichael's handbook of child psychology.* New York: Wiley, 1970.

Lawton, M. P. Assessment, integration, and environments for older people. *Gerontologist,* 1970, **10**, 38–46.

LeVine, R. A. Culture, personality, and socialization: An evolutionary view. In D. A. Goslin (Ed.), *Handbook of socialization theory and research.* Chicago: Rand McNally, 1969.

Lieberman, M. A. Observations on death and dying. *Gerontologist,* 1966, **6**, 70–72.

Lienert, G. A., & Crott, H. W. Studies on the factor structure of intelligence in children, adolescents and adults. *Vita Humana,* 1964, **7**, 147–163.

Lindsley, O. R. Geriatric behavioral prosthetics. In R. Kastenbaum (Ed.), *New thoughts on old age.* New York: Springer, 1964.

Longstreth, L. *Psychological development of the child.* New York: Ronald Press, 1968.

Looft, W. R. Note on WAIS Vocabulary performance by young and old adults. *Psychological Reports,* 1970, **26**, 943–946.

Lorge, I. Capacities of older adults. In W. T. Donahue (Ed.), *Education for later maturity: A handbook.* New York: Whiteside, 1955.

Magladery, J. W. Neurophysiology of aging. In J. E. Birren (Ed.), *Handbook of aging and the individual.* Chicago: University of Chicago Press, 1959.

McClearn, G. E. Behavioral genetics: An overview. *Merrill-Palmer Quarterly,* 1968, **14,** 9–24.

McClearn, G. E. Genetic influences on behavior and development. In P. H. Mussen (Ed.), *Carmichael's handbook of child psychology.* New York: Wiley, 1970.

McGaugh, J. L., & Dawson, R. G. Modification of memory storage processes. *Behavioral Science,* 1971, **16,** 45–63.

Miller, J. O. Cultural deprivation and its modification. In C. H. Haywood (Ed.), *Social-cultural aspects of mental retardation.* Boston: Appleton-Century-Crofts, 1970.

Monge, R. H. Learning in the adult years—Set or rigidity. *Human Development,* 1969, **12,** 131–140.

Montada, L. *Die Lernpsychologie Jean Piaget's.* Stuttgart, W. Germany: Klett, 1970.

Nesselroade, J. R. Application of multivariate strategies to problems of measuring and structuring long-term change. In L. R. Goulet & P. B. Baltes (Eds.), *Life-span developmental psychology.* New York: Academic Press, 1970.

Nesselroade, J. R., Schaie, K. W., & Baltes, P. B. Ontogenetic and generational components of structural and quantitative change in adult cognitive behavior. *Journal of Gerontology,* 1972, **27,** 222–228.

Neugarten, B. L. (Ed.), *Middle age and aging.* Chicago: University of Chicago Press. 1968.

Neugarten, B. L. Continuities and discontinuities of psychological issues into adult life. *Human Development,* 1969, **12,** 121–130.

Nunnally, J. C. Research strategies and measurement methods for investigating human development. In J. R. Nesselroade & H. W. Reese (Eds.), *Life-span developmental psychology: Methodological issues.* New York: Academic Press, in press.

Nuttall, R. L., & Fozard, J. L. Age, socioeconomic status, and human abilities. *Aging and Human Development,* 1970, **1,** 161–169.

Obrist, W. D. Cerebral physiology and behavior in the aged. Paper presented at the meeting of the 8th International Congress of Gerontology, Washington, D.C., August 1969.

Obrist, W. D., Busse, E. W., Eisdorfer, C., & Kleemeier, R. W. Relation of the electroencephalogram to intellectual function in senescence. *Journal of Gerontology,* 1962, **17,** 197–206.

Owens, W. A., Jr. Age and mental abilities: A longitudinal study. *Genetic Psychology Monographs,* 1953, **48,** 3–54.

Owens, W. A., Jr. Age and mental abilities: A second adult follow-up. *Journal of Educational Psychology,* 1966, **51,** 311–325.

Palmore, E. B. Physical, mental, and social factors in predicting longevity. *Gerontologist,* 1969, **9,** 103–108.

Pedersen, F. A., & Wender, P. H. Early social correlates of cognitive functioning in six-year-old boys. *Child Development,* 1968, **39,** 185–193.

Pfeiffer, E. Survival in old age: Physical, psychological, and social correlates of longevity. *Journal of the American Geriatrics Society,* 1970, **18,** 273–285.

Piaget, J. Piaget's theory. In P. H. Mussen (Ed.), *Carmichael's manual of child psychology.* New York: Wiley, 1970.

Pressey, S. L. Major problems—and the major problem—Motivation, learning, and education in the later years. In J. E. Anderson (Ed.), *Psychological aspects of aging*. Washington, D.C.: American Psychological Association, 1965.

Pressey, S. L., & Kuhlen, R. G. *Psychological development through the life span*. New York: Harper & Row, 1957.

Proshansky, H. M., Ittelson, W. H., & Rivlin, L. G. (Eds.) *Environmental psychology: Man and his physical setting*. New York: Holt, Rinehart & Winston, 1970.

Reese, H. W. Verbal mediation as a function of age level. *Psychological Bulletin*, 1962, **59**, 502–509.

Reese, H. W., & Lipsitt, L. P. *Experimental child psychology*. New York: Academic Press, 1970.

Reese, H. W., & Overton, W. F. Models of development and theories of development. In L. R. Goulet & P. B. Baltes (Eds.), *Life-span developmental psychology*. New York: Academic Press, 1970.

Reichardt, R. Approaches to the measurement of environment. *International Social Science Journal*, 1970, **22**, 661–671.

Reinert, G. Comparative factor analytic studies of intelligence throughout the human life span. In L. R. Goulet & P. B. Baltes (Eds.), *Life-span developmental psychology*. New York: Academic Press, 1970.

Riegel, K. F. Ergebnisse und Probleme der psychologischen Alternsforschung: I and II. *Vita Humana*, 1958, **1**, 52–64, 204–243.

Riegel, K. F. Ergebnisse und Probleme der psychologischen Alternsforschung. *Vita Humana*, 1959, **2**, 213–237.

Riegel, K. F. Speed of verbal performance as a function of age and set: A review of issues and data. In A. T. Welford & J. E. Birren (Eds.), *Behavior, aging, and the nervous system*. Springfield, Ill.: Charles C Thomas, 1965.

Riegel, K. F. Development of language: Suggestions for a verbal fallout model. *Human Development*, 1966, **9**, 97–120.

Riegel, K. F. Research designs on the study of aging and the prediction of retest-resistance and death. Paper presented at the meeting of the 8th International Congress of Gerontology, Washington, D.C., August 1969.

Riegel, K. F., & Riegel, R. M. Development, drop, and death. *Developmental Psychology*, 1972, **6**, 306–319.

Riegel, K. F., Riegel, R. M., & Meyer, G. A study of the drop-out rates in longitudinal research on aging and the prediction of death. *Journal of Personality and Social Psychology*, 1967, **4**, 342–348.

Riegel, K. F., Riegel, R. M., & Meyer, G. The prediction of retest resisters in research on aging. *Journal of Gerontology*, 1968, **23**, 370–374.

Riley, M. W., Foner, A., Hess, B., & Toby, M. L. Socialization for the middle and later years. In D. A. Goslin (Ed.), *Handbook of socialization theory and research*. Chicago: Rand McNally, 1969.

Roberts, D. M. Abilities and learning: A brief review and discussion of empirical studies. *Journal of School Psychology*, 1968–69, **7**, 12–21.

Rohwer, W. D., Jr. Implications of cognitive development for education. In P. H. Mussen (Ed.), *Carmichael's manual of child psychology*. New York: Wiley, 1970.

Rosler, H. D. Akzeleration und Intelligenzleistung im Erwachsenenalter. In F. Klix, W. Gutjahr, & J. Mehl (Eds.), *Intelligenzdiagnostik.* Berlin: E. Germany: Deutsche Verlag der Wissenschaften, 1967.

Ryder, N. The cohort as a concept in the study of social changes. *American Sociological Review,* 1965, **30,** 843–861.

Schaie, K. W. Rigidity–flexibility and intelligence: A cross-sectional study of the adult life span from 20 to 70 years. *Psychological Monographs,* 1958, **72,** (9, Whole No. 462).

Schaie, K. W. A field-theory approach to age changes in cognitive behavior. *Vita Humana,* 1962, **5,** 129–141.

Schaie, K. W. A general model for the study of developmental problems. *Psychological Bulletin,* 1965, **64,** 92–107.

Schaie, K. W. A reinterpretation of age-related changes in cognitive structure and functioning. In L. R. Goulet & P. B. Baltes (Eds.), *Life-span developmental psychology.* New York: Academic Press, 1970.

Schaie, K. W. Methodological problems in research on adulthood and aging. In J. R. Nesselroade & H. W. Reese (Eds.), *Life-span developmental psychology: Methodological issues.* New York: Academic Press, in press.

Schaie, K. W., & Strother, C. R. A cross-sectional study of age changes in cognitive behavior. *Psychological Bulletin,* 1968, **70,** 671–680. (a)

Schaie, K. W., & Strother, C. R. The effects of time and cohort differences on the interpretation of age changes in cognitive behavior. *Multivariate Behavior Research,* 1968, **3,** 259–294. (b)

Schmidt, L. R. Testing the limits im Leistungsverhalten: Möglichkeiten und Grenzen. Vol. 2. In E. Duhm (Ed.), *Praxis der Klinischen Psychologie.* Göttingen, W. Germany: Hogrefe, 1970.

Schooler, K. K. Effect of environment on morale. *Gerontologist,* 1970, **10,** 194–197.

Schultz, C. B., & Aurbach, H. A. The usefulness of cumulative deprivation as an explanation of educational deficiencies. *Merrill-Palmer Quarterly,* 1971, **17,** 27–39.

Schwartz, A. N., & Proppe, H. G. Toward person-environment transactional research in aging. *Gerontologist,* 1970, **10,** 228–232.

Sells, S. B. (Ed.) *Stimulus determinants of behavior.* New York: Ronald Press, 1963.

Skeels, H. M. Adult status of children with contrasting early life experiences. *Monographs of the Society for Research in Child Development,* 1966, **31,** (3, Whole No. 105).

Sontag, L. W., & Baker, C. T. Personality, familial, and physical correlates of change in mental ability. In L. W. Sontag, C. T. Baker, & V. L. Nelson (Eds.), *Mental growth and personality development: A longitudinal study. Monographs of the Society for Research in Child Development,* 1958, **23,** (2, Whole No. 2).

Starr, R. H., Jr. Cognitive development in infancy: Assessment, acceleration and actualization. *Merrill-Palmer Quarterly,* 1971, **17,** 153–186.

Stevenson, H. W. Learning in children. In P. H. Mussen (Ed.), *Carmichael's manual of child psychology.* New York: Wiley, 1970.

Strehler, B. L. *Time, cells, and aging.* New York: Academic Press, 1962.

Surwillo, W. W. Timing of behavior in senescence and the role of the central nervous system. In G. A. Talland (Ed.), *Human aging and behavior*. New York: Academic Press, 1968.

Sutton-Smith, B. Developmental laws and the experimentalist's ontogeny. *Merrill-Palmer Quarterly*, 1970, **16**, 253–259.

Szafran, J., & Birren, J. E. Perception. In J. E. Birren (Ed.), *Contemporary gerontology: Issues and concepts*. Los Angeles: Gerontology Center, University of Southern California, 1970.

Thompson, W. R., & Grusec, J. Studies of early experience. In P. H. Mussen (Ed.), *Carmichael's manual of child psychology*. New York: Wiley, 1970.

Tryon, R. C. A theory of psychological components—an alternative to "mathematical factors." *Psychological Review*, 1935, **42**, 425–454.

Vandenberg, S. G. Contributions of twin research to psychology. *Psychological Bulletin*, 1966, **66**, 327–352.

Vandenberg, S. G. Human behavior genetics: Present status and suggestions for future research. *Merrill-Palmer Quarterly*, 1969, **15**, 120–154.

Vernon, P. E. *The structure of human abilities*. London: Methuen, 1961.

Vernon, P. E. *Intelligence and cultural environment*. London: Methuen, 1969.

Wang, H. S., Obrist, W. D., & Busse, E. W. Neurophysiological correlates of the intellectual function of elderly persons living in the community. *American Journal of Psychiatry*, 1970, **126**, 1205–1212.

Watson, J. S. Cognitive-perceptual development in infancy: Setting for the seventies. *Merrill-Palmer Quarterly*, 1971, **17**, 139–152.

Weisberg, P. Operant procedures with the retardate: An overview of laboratory research. *International Review of Research in Mental Retardation*, 1971, **5**, 113–145.

Welford, A. T. *Aging and human skill*. London: Oxford University Press, 1958.

Welford, A. T. Performance, biological mechanisms, and age: A theoretical sketch. In A. T. Welford & J. E. Birren (Eds.), *Behavior, aging, and the nervous system*. Springfield, Ill.: Charles C Thomas, 1965.

Welford, A. T., & Birren, J. E. (Eds.) *Behavior, aging, and the nervous system*. Springfield, Ill.: Charles C Thomas, 1965.

Whelpton, P. K. *Cohort fertility (native white women in the United States)*. Princeton, N.J.: Princeton University Press, 1954.

White, B. L. Child development research: An edifice without a foundation. *Merrill-Palmer Quarterly*, 1969, **15**, 49–79.

White, S. H. Evidence for a hierarchical arrangement of learning processes. In L. P. Lippsitt & C. C. Spiker (Eds.), *Advances in child development and behavior*. Vol. 2. New York: Academic Press, 1965.

Whiteman, M. Intelligence and learning. *Merrill-Palmer Quarterly*, 1964, **10**, 298–309.

Willems, E. P. Behavioral ecology and experimental analysis: Courtship is not enough. In J. R. Nesselroade & H. W. Reese (Eds.), *Life-span developmental psychology: Methodological issues*. New York: Academic Press, in press.

Willoughby, R. R. Family similarities in mental-test abilities. *Genetic Psychology Monographs*, 1927, **2**, 235–277.

Wohlwill, J. I. The age variable in psychological research. *Psychological Review*, 1970, **77**, 49–64. (a)

Wohlwill, J. F. The emerging discipline of environmental psychology. *American Psychologist*, 1970, **25**, 303–312. (b)

Wohlwill, J. F. Methodology and research strategy in the study of developmental change. In L. R. Goulet & P. B. Baltes (Eds.), *Life-span developmental psychology*. New York: Academic Press, 1970. (c)

Wolf, R. M. The identification and measurement of environmental process variables related to intelligence. Unpublished doctoral dissertation, University of Chicago, 1964.

Wright, H. F. Observational child study. In P. H. Mussen (Ed.), *Handbook of research methods in child development*. New York: Wiley, 1960.

A Biobehavioral Approach to Intellectual Changes with Aging

LISSY F. JARVIK AND DONNA COHEN

However elegant and memorable, brevity can never, in the nature of things, do justice to all the facts of a complex situation. On such a theme one can be brief only by omission and simplification. Omission and simplification help us to understand—but help us, in many cases, to understand the wrong thing, for our comprehension may be only of the abbreviator's neatly formulated notions, not of the vast, ramifying reality from which these notions have been so arbitrarily abstracted.

But life is short and information endless; nobody has time for everything. In practice we are generally forced to choose between an unduly brief exposition and no exposition at all. Abbreviation is a necsary evil and the abbreviator's business is to make the best of a job, which, though intrinsically bad, is still better than nothing. He must learn to simplify, but not to the point of falsification. He must learn to concentrate upon the essentials of a situation, but without ignoring too many of reality's qualifying side-issues.

Aldous Huxley

We are indebted to Corsellis (1962) for leading us to a lucid expression of our thoughts in tackling an overview of a virgin territory —the psychobiology of age-correlated intellectual changes.

The most clearly observable, and perhaps most salient manifestation of the psychobiological changes that occur with advancing age is the gradual enfeeblement of mind and body. This enfeeblement

Lissy F. Jarvik received her PhD in psychology from Columbia University in 1950 and her MD from Western Reserve University in 1954. She is currently Professor of Psychiatry at the University of California, Los Angeles, and Chief of the Psychogenetics Unit at the Brentwood Veterans Administration Hospital, Los Angeles, California. Her research interests include human genetics and gerontology, specifically the psychological, psychiatric, chromosomal, and other genetic aspects of aging.

Donna Cohen received her BS in zoology from Duke University in 1969, and is currently a doctoral student in psychology at the University of progresses relentlessly and the older the person, the more consistent is its appearance; hence, our image of the very oldest as a shrunken, shriveled shell, sheltering the shadow of a formerly active mind. Yet, there are notable exceptions—persons relatively vigorous in health and strength, functioning at a high intellectual level. Among these come to mind Pablo Casals, who at the age of 94 still gives concerts and conducts an annual summer festival in Puerto Rico, and Picasso, who at the age of 90 is the envy of many a younger artist.

If enfeeblement is not an inevitable concomitant of old age, then any number of questions arise—questions that remain unanswered even to this day although they have been posed throughout the history of science and philosophy, from Hellas till now. Among the most cogent ones are: To what extent are the undesirable features seen in very old persons the result of pathology and to what degree are they preventable? What are the factors responsible for the marked differences existing between individuals in the rate and degree of physical and mental decline? What are the factors retarding such decline?

In an attempt to summarize the information available to date that has a bearing on the above questions, this chapter will concentrate on the following issues related to intellectual functioning during the later years:

1. What, if any, are the intellectual changes that are associated with advancing chronological age?

2. What, if any, are the biological changes that are associated with advancing chronological age?

3. What changes *invariably* accompany aging, and which of them reflect pathological processes?

4. Which biological events are antecedents, or correlates, of intellectual alterations?

5. What are the endogenous and exogenous factors that seem to accelerate or retard aging?

6. What studies should be formulated that would have meaning for the research worker interested in underlying causes?

Southern California. She is also on the staff of the Psychogenetics Unit at the Brentwood Veterans Administration Hospital, Los Angeles, California.

This research was supported by National Institute of Child and Human Development Grant HD-01615.

The authors would like to thank Vincent Cristofalo, Wistar Institute, for his critical review of the manuscript and Connie Weil, New York State Psychiatric Institute, for her help in the final preparation of the manuscript.

Since mental functioning depends upon the organization of the nervous system, a biobehavioral approach is necessary to understand these complex phenomena of intellectual changes with age. Most of the research is still at the descriptive level of scientific inquiry, however, and few investigators have attempted to bridge the gap between mental events and the biological substrate. Obviously, this is a difficult endeavor. Still, sufficient observations have been collected to suggest several research strategies for the detection of underlying determinants of behavior.

Intellectual functioning in the organism may be looked upon as the result of processes determined by allometric changes at the different levels of organization. Somehow, the molecular–genetic matrix must be related to adaptive enzyme systems and humoral factors, to cell, tissue, and organ system interactions, and to the behavioral constructs we designate as intelligence, learning, and memory.

The following discussion is intended to highlight the reported data on the aging organism. It is our bias that the whole organism is the crucial unit of observation. It will be helpful, however, to maintain a constant mental image of the living system as an integrated hierarchy of regulatory systems. In order to visualize where interference with aging processes might be essayed, a highly simplified schema has been constructed (Figure 1). Such a hierarchy of biobehavioral levels of organization incorporates the suggestion that any higher order statement of biological processes contains the lower processes of macromolecular organization as units (Weiss, 1969), and further, that the higher order statement of the repertoire of human behaviors contains biological statements as units.

BEHAVIORAL CHANGES ASSOCIATED WITH ADVANCING AGE

The term intellectual is used in this review in its broad sense and includes perception, cognition, learning, and memory. Changes in these areas have been studied intensively and extensively, usually by comparing the performance of young and old persons. Scrutiny of the results obtained for various psycholog'cal functions creates the overwhelming impression that declines with age are few. By far the most consistent modification in behavior noted with advancing age is a decline in performance on speeded tasks, and it has been regarded by some as one primary aspect of aging (Birren, 1964, 1970). This slowness has been observed in almost all situations—on

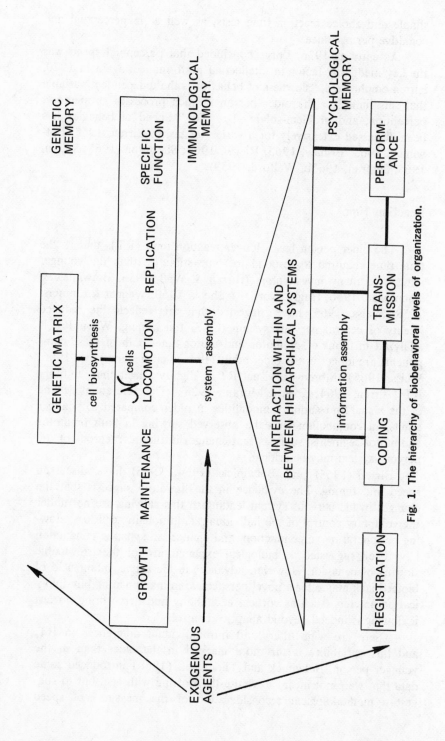

Fig. 1. The hierarchy of biobehavioral levels of organization.

simple and choice reaction time tests, as well as in perceptual and cognitive performance.

As early as 1936, Lorge concluded that perceptual speed was the key mediating factor in intellectual performance; again in 1970, Birren emphasized, "slowness of behavior is the independent variable that sets limits for the older person in such processes as memory, perception, and problem-solving [p. 126]." Speed of behavior has been discussed extensively for a variety of tasks (Birren, 1965; Botwinick, 1965; Brinley, 1965; Riegel, 1965; Simonson, 1965; Spieth, 1965; Szafran, 1965b; Welford, 1959).

Reaction Time

The older person has a longer reaction time (RT), that is, the total time required to respond to some stimulus, than the younger adult, and many investigators (Birren & Wall, 1956; Botwinick & Thompson, 1966; Hugin, Norris, & Shock, 1960; Wagner & Emmers, 1958; Weiss, 1965) have suggested that this reflects the reduced fidelity of central nervous system (CNS) functioning. When RT is analyzed in terms of premotor and motor time, both of these components are longer in the older adult (Botwinick & Thompson, 1966; Weiss, 1965). Moreover, visual RT is slightly longer than auditory RT (Birren, 1964; Koga & Morant, 1923). The differential decline of the visual and auditory modalities in older compared to younger adults, in conjunction with the observed slowing in both premotor and motor segments, suggests that changes in the interneurons of the nervous system may be critical.

Birren (1965) and Botwinick (1964, 1965) have discussed speed and timing. The evidence in the literature suggests that the changes in the nervous system leading to this slowing are not under the voluntary control of the individual. Traditionally, cell loss, slowing peripheral nerve conduction, and changes in synaptic conduction have been suggested as biological explanations for the irreversible slowing of behavior. However, advances in the active, infant field of biofeedback may offer a novel perspective in manipulating physiological parameters, such as cortical excitability and nerve firing, to test if slowing is indeed beyond adaptive control.

There are wide inter- and intraindividual differences in RT, and this variability is far more marked in the older than in the younger person. Botwinick and Thompson (1968) introduced some data that were not meant to refute the slowing with age, but to suggest a methodological reconsideration of the measures of speed changes. They compared the RTs of old and young adults by dividing the young adults into athletic and nonathletic populations; even though the older group was slower than the younger groups, the RT of the old adults was closer to the nonathletic young adults than it was to the athletic group.

In subpopulations, exercise, genetics, nutrition, and other factors are confounded in a single measure of central tendency. If certain exogenous influences should turn out to be key determinants of individual change in CNS activity, they may constitute the means to devise a life-style during young adulthood which will optimize intellectual functioning during the later years. It is important, therefore, that the crucial parameters be examined.

Sensory and Perceptual Changes

There is a large literature on alterations in sensation and perception with aging. Since adequate discussions are available (Braun, 1959; Comalli, 1967, 1970; Corso, 1971; Szafran & Birren, 1968; Weiss, 1959), this chapter is limited to only a few representative reviews and studies. The evidence clearly indicates that there is a decline in sensory and perceptual functioning, and that the onset and rate of decline vary across modalities.

Corso (1971), who has published the most recent review of sensory changes, concluded that "the underlying mechanisms which are involved in these changes may show neural and non-neural modifications with time." He further posited that the neuronal losses were irreversible primary changes and "noncompensable modifications of the nervous system." Loss of neurons is irreversible, and it is generally assumed that there must be some functional reorganization in the peripheral and CNS as a result of this change. However, very little, if anything, is known about the compensatory abilities of neuronal feedback networks. Healthy tissue in a supportive environment could reorganize and continue functioning. Even if some networks are lost eventually, the possibility of applying biofeedback procedures to transfer the lost functions to another network is an intriguing area for research.

Little work has been done on sensory adaptation with the exception of dark adaptation (Comalli, 1967). Measurements of threshold levels and recovery time from experimentally induced flash blindness (Szafran, 1968) suggest that pilots may be a more experienced and efficient group of observers than the population at large. Their threshold is lower than that of the general population, and they seem to be able "to extract information more efficiently even at very low levels of signal-to-noise ratio." Szafran emphasized Weale's (1963) caution that any explanation of age changes must consider the level of perceptual skill of the individual, as well as the integrity of the peripheral receptor system. The elegance of Szafran's study resides in its consideration of the energy properties of th estimulus, and its implications for speculating about the information-extracting abilities of the retina in a pathology-free and highly select population.

Szafran's (1963, 1965a, 1966) further psychophysiological studies on pilots indicated that these well-trained individuals were able to maintain a high discrimination ability if free from pathology. Cardiovascular status rather than age per se seemed to be related to this type of performance. Slowness and errors in performance did appear with fatigue. Yet, when slowing occurred, it did not necessarily signify a complete inability to cope with environmental events.

There is evidence that critical flicker frequency decreases with advancing age, that older persons are slower than younger persons in processing visual input (Eisdorfer & Axelrod, 1964), and that they seem to have a registration deficiency (Kline, 1970). The ability to recall a visual stimulus varies as a function of the interval between the original and the following stimulus to a greater extent in younger than older people.

Corso (1971) has suggested that research be directed toward the investigation of functioning across modalities to explore neural coding, sensory input storage, and interference effects. According to Arenberg (1967c), data in the psychological literature suggest that the older person may have an impairment in converting visual stimuli into auditory storage, and, therefore, should benefit most in learning and retaining information by techniques that facilitate auditory maintenance of the trace as it is being processed. Differential susceptibility to certain illusions, a decreased ability to abstract information from embedded figures, difficulties in handling irrelevant stimuli, and changes in information processing and signal detection seem to occur in the older person, and measure processes beyond simple perceptual functioning.

In summary, the capabilities for operative vigilance, the adaptation of CNS functioning to sensory organization and vice versa, and the behavioral adaptation to nervous reorganization may all be determined by critical processes functioning across modalities. Very little is known about these matters. In studying perceptual changes with aging, persons suffering from visual and auditory impairment have to be excluded. Since in the highest age groups auditory impairment becomes nearly universal, its psychological consequences need to be investigated. The area of sensory deprivation, however, is beyond the scope of the present report.

Cognition

Jones (1959) critically analyzed the literature through 1959, and Botwinick (1967) summarized subsequent studies through 1967. Baltes and Labouvie (pp. 157–219) have set an excellent perspective on research through the 1970s. With regard to intellectual performance, as measured by the Wechsler Adult Intelligence Scale (WAIS), the Wechsler-Bellevue, Raven's Progressive Matrices, and other tests, cross-sectional data have long suggested a decline with age (Doppelt & Wallace, 1955; Jones & Conrad, 1933; Miles & Miles, 1932; Wechsler, 1958). During the past 10 years, however, longitudinal studies have become available and their results suggest that, except for speeded performance tasks, there may be no change, or even a slight increase on cognitive tasks, at least in the age group up to the eighth decade. Jarvik, Eisdorfer, and Blum (in press) presented a summary of the longitudinal studies. This dissociation of cognitive stability from psychomotor deterioration was described a decade ago by Eisdorfer, Busse, and Cohen (1959); it occurred regardless of age group (between 60–75 years), irrespective of intelligence level, and without reference to the two levels of socioeconomic status investigated or residential situation (hospital or community).

The range has now been extended below 60. Honzik and Macfarlane (in press) reported that decline on speeded motor tasks begins between the ages of 18 and 40 years, at a time when verbal scores are still increasing. Although Eichorn's (in press) data tended to show gains in both performance and verbal scores between the ages of 16 and 36 years, the greatest and most consistent gains occurred in vocabulary—a verbal test. Scrutiny of the subtest scores at the upper end of the age scale showed specifically that no significant declines were observed between the seventh and eighth decades of life in vocabulary knowledge, abstract reasoning (similarities), memory for digits, or block design (Jarvik, Kallmann, & Falek, 1962). Stability rather than decline in scores has also characterized the healthy noninstitutionalized groups examined by Granick and Birren (1969) and Eisdorfer (1963), and supplemented the original studies of Bayley and Oden (1955) and Owens (1953, 1966) pertaining to gains rather than losses through the fifth decade of life. Indeed, cognitive decline exhibited on tests lacking a speed component may be pathognomic of disease, with such a decline showing a positive association with mortality (Baltes, Schaie, & Nardi, 1971; Berkowitz & Green, 1963; Goldfarb, 1969; Jarvik, Kallmann, Falek, & Klaber, 1957; Kleemeier, 1961; Lieberman, 1965; Palmore, 1969; Riegel, 1969; Riegel & Riegel, 1972; Riegel, Riegel, & Meyer 1967, 1968; Sanderson & Inglis, 1962; Wilkie & Eisdorfer, 1971). In the healthy older person, cognitive decline may be a myth.

Intelligence is an extremely complex variable to measure. The WAIS and Wechsler-Bellevue subtests, as mentioned earlier, have been used in most of the cross-sectional, longitudinal, and mixed-model studies, but they are only vaguely related to the multidimensional concepts of intelligence (Baltes & Nesselroade, 1971). Other factor change models with multiple measures of factor scores, factor patterns, and changes in intercorrelations in intellectual functioning may yield more information on intellectual decline. Horn and Cattell (1966) examined intelligence on two dimensions—fluid and crystallized—and gave evidence that assessed abilities of crystallized intelligence maintain themselves or even increased in the 59–61 age range. Performance with fluid abilities decreased.

Baltes, Nesselroade, Schaie, and Labouvie (1972) and Nesselroade, Schaie, and Baltes (1972) derived four second-order factors from 13 measurement variables to describe cognitive changes—crystallized intelligence (CI), cognitive flexibility (CF), visuomotor flexibility (VMF), and visualization (VIS). The CI and VIS measures were relatively stable, and CF and VMF showed the predicted decline in older age groups. There are several methodological problems to be confronted in any assessment of performance score changes. Baltes and Goulet (1970) argued that sophisticated models of change over the entire life-span of the individual should be developed. For example, there are problems in measuring initial levels of mental functioning in a test-retest design using any number of subgroups (healthy and diseased categories, etc.), and it is necessary to consider regression toward the mean as a statistical artifact that may exaggerate age differences. These considerations engender arguments for the controversy surrounding differential decline of intellectual functioning with different ability levels.

Learning and Memory

Just as intelligence is a potential ability inferred from psychometric performance, so learning and memory are inferred from some change in the behavior of the organism:

For some organisms certain experiences leave an after-effect which manifests itself in changed behavior at a later time. This change in behavior indicates that learning has occurred and has left a memory trace somewhere, presumably in the brain, but not necessarily [Jarvik, in press].

The understanding of cellular and tissue changes underlying learning and memory, as well as immunological reactions, drug responses, and enzyme activity are extremely complex. The design of current drug research attempting to elucidate the physicochemical basis of memory assumes that similar biochemical mechanisms may be working in all the above-named processes, mechanisms intimately associated with the DNA–RNA–protein assembly matrix (Jarvik, in press). However, to date, these ideas still lack experimental proof.

The psychological literature on learning and memory is extensive; Kay (1959) and Jerome (1959) reviewed the early studies, Botwinick (1967) and Chown and Riegel (1968), the more recent ones. Jakubczak (pp. 98–111) discusses the animal studies on age-related learning.

The general impairment observed in older versus younger persons is again most pronounced in terms of speed. In verbal learning studies, compensation for the slowness of the aged greatly reduces their disadvantage where the time variable has been manipulated. Older people need time to respond and adequate pacing is one mechanism by which age differences may be reduced. Since interference effects seem to assume greater prominence as age increases, any manipulation reducing interference tends to keep age differences to a minimum. Older persons may have difficulty acquiring stimuli (Canestrari, 1968b) as suggested in the literature on conditioning and perception. Classical conditioning is difficult in both old animals and old people; however, increasing the unconditioned stimulus intensity may improve the acquisition of the appropriate response (Botwinick & Kornetsky, 1960; Braun & Geiselhart, 1959; Kimble & Pennypacker, 1963; Shmavonian et al., 1968; Solyom & Barik, 1965). Further, more time seems to be required by the old than by the young to learn the initial discriminations (Birren, 1962; Doty, 1966; Doty & Doty, 1964). Age decrements in task performance may be improved by clearer instructions and explanation of concepts and by operant conditioning techniques (Baltes & Goulet, 1970). Reinforcement given to an individual for responding faster results in rapid and more accurate performance (Hoyer, Labouvie, & Baltes, 1971).

The areas of concept formation, decision-making behavior, and problem solving in the elderly have not been adequately explored. If decision-making ability depends on an accumulation of experience as Guilford (1969) suggested, and if intellectual decline in the healthy aging person is a myth, there is good reason to expect effective cognitive functioning with advancing age.

The study of linguistic processes is one unusual and valuable tool to examine cognition in the aging person as an interactional phenomenon. Riegel (1968, 1970) and Palmero (1970) reviewed some of the research efforts in the field of language acquisition and psycholinguistic changes with age, and Riegel (1971) suggested that language is a kind of labor. He developed the thesis that the growth of linguistic and monetary systems are analagous histories of processes evolving to more abstract and symbolic levels. Gerontologic research could build on the ideas of Chomsky (1965), Piaget (1970), and Riegel (1971) by considering the interaction between language, the behavioral substrate, and the historical-cultural tradition. "Language . . . is an activity, founded through the two interactions [Riegel, 1971, p. 14]." The study of language as a process revealing significant information on the evolving intellectual status of people should prove to be an exciting research area.

The state of an organism—often discussed in the psychological literature with such constructs as set and expectancy, vigilance and attention, motivation and arousal—is a crucial variable in evaluating cognitive behavior, and it has not been adequately considered in learning experiments. State variables in the living system would affect attentiveness, ability to process stimuli and responses to them, and essentially define the receptiveness of the organism on which higher mental processes depend. One such variable, arousal, assessed with such measures as heart rate, blood pressure, and catecholamine plasma assays, has been shown to be related to performance with an inverted-U function, for example, maximum performance with moderate arousal and deteriorating performance with under- or over-arousal.

Troyer, Eisdorfer, Bogdonoff, and Wilkie (1967), Hulicka and Weiss (1965), and Eisdorfer (1968a) demonstrated the influence of arousal upon performance. Eisdorfer's results have been interpreted to suggest that the older person is autonomically overaroused and, therefore, does not learn as well. When arousal is indexed by free fatty acid (FFA) levels in the blood plasma during a paced serial learning task, older persons are seen to have higher levels than younger adults (Eisdorfer, 1968a). They also make more errors. Since FFA levels are considered an index of autonomic arousal, a higher FFA level suggests a more activated state. Attempts to reduce arousal by blocking lipid mobilization through drug modification (interference via the autonomic nervous system; ANS) resulted in improved learning, at least in the single experiment reported so far (Eisdorfer, Nowlin, & Wilkie, 1970).

Others have proposed that the aging organism is underaroused rather than overaroused. Support for this position stems from the conditioning literature demonstrating the difficulty to classically condition the older person (perhaps due to less activated and less receptive systems), and from electroencephalographic data generally suggesting a lowered cortical excitability.

A lively controversy revolves around the state of activation of the old organism: Is the old person over- or underaroused? Arguments are persuasive on both sides of the issue, and they may possibly be integrated if arousal is regarded as a phenomenon subject to regional variability due to selective changes in the feedback patterning between peripheral receptors and central nerve centers (Eisdorfer, 1971).

As mentioned, psychophysiological indices of arousal—heart rate, galvanic skin response, and FFA assays, and measures such as the electroencephalogram (EEG) and conditionability—have been used to make inferences about the ability of the organism to receive and transduce stimuli, and have led to contradictory conclusions. The various operational measures may not be extracting the same information about the condition of the organism, and for this reason may yield opposing results on the state of arousal. For example, FFAs presumably index autonomic arousal while EEG patterns are indications of CNS activity.

But there is perhaps a more crucial issue to confront than the equivalence of information obtained from different operations. Different regions of the body may be more or less activated from CNS–ANS interaction; for example, the organism could be centrally underaroused and, at the same time, autonomically overaroused. Innervations and hormonal secretions are different across the organism, and may effect differential activation, so that electrical indices suggesting lowered cortical excitability and FFA assays indicating increased autonomic arousal may both be correct. Consequently, it does not simply follow that the organism must be either under- or overaroused; it may be both.

The response behavior of older persons in the verbal learning studies is intriguing: Older people tend to make errors of omission rather than errors of commission. This error performance may be evidence of some response inhibition or may be interpreted as a general cautiousness or conservatism. On audiometric measures the older person also performs more poorly, and this has generally been interpreted as an impaired ability to detect the stimulus. However, application of signal detection theory to the analysis of audiometric measures obtained from young and old subjects showed no significant differences in detectability; it did show that older adults established higher criterion values than younger adults. Consequently, they were reluctant to affirm the presence of low-intensity inputs even though their performance in a detection task affirmed their sensitivity to these stimuli. Rees and Botwinick (1971) suggested that "the magnitudes of auditory deficits in later life may be overestimated due to either cautiousness or conservatism on the part of elderly adults."

It is also appropriate to question whether the enhanced learning ability of rats raised in enriched environments (Krech, Rosenzweig, & Bennett, 1962, 1966) could have an analogue in the maintenance of functional abilities by senescent organisms. The interaction between cortical development and catecholamine concentration in enriched versus deprived environments has been extensively investigated in immature animals (Krech et al., 1962, 1966; Rosenzweig, 1966; Rosenzweig, Krech, Bennett, & Diamond, 1968). From these anatomical and chemical changes, it is plausible to infer that changes must be occurring at the molecular level with selective enzyme activation.

More recently, Bondareff, Horotsky, and Routtenberg (1971) obtained data suggesting that the spread of catecholamines—dopamine and norepinephrine—in the brain tissue of old rats is only about one-half that of young rats. Animals raised in active, stimulating environments might maintain a less obstructed flow of extracellular catecholamines during aging. The relation between intrastriatal spread and the ability of the rat to function in the environment needs to be investigated.

The forgetfulness of the aged is proverbial, yet unequivocal scientific validation is missing. "Old people remember what interests them. . . . Besides, I never heard of an old man forgetting where he buried his money." Thus spake Cicero some 2,000 years ago, expediently dismissing the loss of memory attributed to advanced age. Nonetheless, the literature today continues to be quite controversial when investigators attempt to describe specific kinds of memory loss or the underlying mechanisms of memory and forgetfulness. Various aspects of the experimental work are discussed by Botwinick (1967), Craik (1968), Inglis (1965, 1970), Inglis, Sykes, and Ankus (1968), Talland (1965), and Jarvik (in press). Arenberg (pp. 74–97) presented a recent compilation of contributions to the field of gerontology.

One may assume numerous perspectives when attempting to elucidate the gradual impairment of memory, which, traditionally, has been regarded as a deficit in registration, retention, retrieval, or any combination of these. One useful outlook is to regard memory as a time-related process that may be classified as proceeding from the time of registration onward: immediate, short-term, intermediate, and long-term memory storage.

Although this taxonomy does not explicate the mechanism for the preservation of individual experiences, it does provide a sufficient set of labels for time-related phases of the phenomenon of memory. The researcher can thus test time relations in the continuum of stimulus acquisition and storage, and can seek to localize where interference effects may become manifest.

It is generally accepted that immediate memory is impaired with aging. Such impairment may represent a registration deficit due to the inability to encode a trace (receptor dysfunction) or an interference effect from the pattern of nerve activity. Most investigators also agree that short-term memory worsens with aging and this may also be an interference phenomenon. Both immediate and short-term memory decline in the visual and auditory modalities, but visual memory seems to be more affected than auditory storage, perhaps due to a breakdown in the conversion of visual stimuli into an auditory memory storage (Arenberg, 1967c).

In contrast to the general agreement on immediate and short-term memory, the results on intermediate and long-term storage in healthy older persons are conflicting, with some investigators finding a decline while others do not.

Even more controversial than the data are the interpretations. There have been many theoretical considerations of the memory process, but the critical problem is the mechanism for the preservation of experiences. There is a growing literature on the physico-chemical and physiological basis of memory. Intraneuronal or chemical approaches seem to implicate molecular coding in the DNA–RNA matrix. Whether the nucleic acids contribute directly to the coding or indirectly to cell functioning, has not yet been determined. Although the neuron is in a process of dynamic organization (Weiss, 1959), and nerve stimulation is associated with changes in protein activity (Schlesinger, in press), the direct involvement of DNA and RNA in memory storage is questionable. Work with older people has taken a clinical approach, investigating patient populations rather than concentrating on basic research on primary molecular processes.

In summary, major behavioral changes appear to be a slowing in performance, a deficiency in the registration of the raw stimulus, and a change in the ability of the individual to handle input. These changes characterize the behavior of old persons who are ostensibly in good health, and must be clearly distinguished from the behavioral changes seen in the psychopathology associated with senescence. Gerontologists would probably benefit most from the study of changes that generally occur with the passage of time in healthy individuals, and from investigations of why these events do not occur at the same time or at the same rate in all individuals. The greatest deficit appears to be in knowledge of age changes in the absence of disease. Research on age-related diseases will have important, although secondary gains for gerontology. Before examining those biological variations that may underlie the psychological phenomena outlined above, a brief survey of the biological events has been compiled.

BIOLOGICAL CHANGES ASSOCIATED WITH ADVANCING AGE

Age-related changes may be due to selective changes in the genome and to changes in cell responses to other factors such as hormones.

The literature on age-correlated biological changes is extensive. Discussions on molecular and macromolecular aspects of aging have been given by Barrows (1971), Deyl (1968), Frolkis (1968), von Hahn (1970a, 1970b), Strehler (1962), and Verzar (1963). Bourne (1961) has provided a text on structural changes; cell, tissue, and organ changes have been discussed by Balazs (1970), Franks (1970), Goldman (1970), and Strehler (1962).

Perhaps all aging may be reduced to a collection of errors in the genetic matrix which generates the many physicochemical systems supporting cell biosynthesis and homeostatic regulation. However, it remains to be clarified how endogenous and exogenous events produce the errors which eventually disrupt the homeostatic balance and interfere with the integrity of the living system. These external and internal events may exert both acute and chronic stresses on the functioning organism.

Molecular Aspects of Aging

Enzymatic protein synthesis is a crucial underlying process controlling the other biochemical pathways in the organism; any change in the synthesis of structural and enzymatic proteins with aging would logically affect fat and carbohydrate metabolism. Perhaps, alterations in the formation of protein and the cumulative effects are critical determinants of what happens in the aged individual. Since the

DNA–RNA–protein assemblies for any number of protein products affect the functional integrity of the organism, the genetic–molecular information system underlies biological and behavioral change. Medvedev (1967), Deyl (1968), and H. W. Woolhouse (personal communication, 1971) developed the thesis that the synthesis network from gene to protein has the potential to generate, accumulate, and repair errors at a number of stages including DNA replication, trancription (formation of RNA from DNA), translation (protein assembly with RNA), and the active process of positioning and maintaining the protein in the cell. An accumulation of errors over time— "creeping error" (H. W. Woolhouse, personal communication, 1971) —could conceivably determine changes in the senescent organism. Mutations, the formation of thymine dimers (Setlow & Carrier, 1964), cross-linkages, incorrect transcription of gene sequences, etc., are just a few examples of events that, over a lifetime, could introduce elements of creeping error in the cell system contributing to the production of anamolous protein. Orgel (1963) has argued strongly that cumulative errors in protein synthesis during translation are a major source of changes leading to senescence.

The cell has numerous mechanisms for eliminating error as well as for generating it. For example, most molecules are degraded after some functional lifetime and then resynthesized. Therefore, even if anomalous protein is produced, it may be degraded before having a chance to introduce lethal consequences at the cellular level. The problem of turnover rates—breakdown and synthesis of systems in the cell—is an important area to be considered in aging research (H. W. Woolhouse, personal communication, 1971). A lethal accumulation of errors leading to the deletion of cells is less significant probably in dividing cells than in nondividing ones. However, since all cells are in a state where components are in a dynamic turnover and reorganization, even nondividing systems, such as neurons, will perpetuate the effects of creeping error.

Given the many possibilities for error at the molecular level, there must be at least just as many sources of potential for error at other levels of biological organization. Important unanswered questions that need research are:

1. What happens to genes and their behavioral expression during aging?

2. What do changes in protein indicate about the function of the living organism?

3. What lies in the vast gap between protein synthesis and organismic behavior?

For the present we can only assume that changes in protein metabolism are crucial. Perusal of Table 2 shows that very little can be said about biochemical changes with aging in DNA, RNA, and protein. The literature is sparse and, although there are many investigations on age changes in protein, their results are contradictory and fragmentary. Medvedev (1967) warned that contradictions are to be expected in living organisms because they contain many enzyme systems, each liable to many variations. Structural proteins—collagen and elastin—show definite age changes, while other proteins and protein complexes—enzymes, globulins, histones, and albumins—show no evident pattern of alteration.

Perhaps we should look for a profile of changes across tissues. For example, the protein context of cells and the rates of protein synthesis with aging are reported by different investigators to increase, decrease, or remain the same. Gordon (1971), in a discussion of drug effects, protein synthesis, and deteriorating function, suggested that we should expect different tissues to show synthesis changes in both directions with the increase of entropy in the body with aging. This entropy increase could affect ribosome-protein interaction which may well eventually control the rates of synthesis in different protein systems.

Given some accumulation of errors in DNA, RNA, and proteins—errors in the most fundamental cell machinery—we should expect considerable mosaicism in cells, even within the same tissue (e.g., differences between cells in electrolyte composition, antibody binding, hormonal circulation, and enzyme activity). Bellamy (1970) argued from a molecular–cellular perspective that each tissue probably ages differently and should be studied separately and systematically. He also pointed out that only Kirk and his colleagues have done this with human tissues—the blood vessels—in people ranging from the first through the ninth decade (Kirk, 1959a, 1959b, 1959c, 1960a, 1960b, 1960c, 1961a, 1961b, 1962a, 1962b, 1962c, 1962d, 1965, 1966; Kirk & Dyrbye, 1956a, 1956b; Kirk & Ritz, 1967; Kirk & Sorenson, 1956; Kirk, Wang, & Brandstrup, 1959). The data suggested that enzyme activity increases at a steady rate from ages 20–40, but that different enzymes reach maximal activity in different decades and decrease at varying rates. Even in the ninth decade, 50% of the 30 enzymes studied maintained a very high level of activity (90% of their activity recorded in the first years of life). Barrows (1965) reported that of 41 enzymes studied in the rat liver, 78% were not affected by age, and of 31 examined in the rat kidney, 86% were not affected. Enzymes in animal brain tissues have not shown marked age changes either (Epstein & Barrows, 1969; Hollander & Barrows, 1968).

The genetic blueprint ultimately provides the cell with a large number of adaptive enzymes, hormones, globular and structural proteins, and other complexes that influence cell biosynthesis and tissue and organ function. Enzymes are degraded and resynthesized at various rates, and perhaps scrutiny of the turnover rates will clarify how and why specific enzyme groups change their activity with aging. The modification of rate-limiting enzymes could affect any number of biochemical steps that maintain the biochemical integrity of the cell. For example, the activity of the enzyme lipase seems to decline with advancing age (Kipshidze & Tkeshelashvili, 1966), and this decline may be associated with age changes in fat metabolism (Hrüza, 1967). Also, if the reader will indulge speculation, fat metabolism may play a greater role in the consolidation of memory than has been ascribed to it thus far (Gaito, 1966). If this indeed should be the case, we may someday be able to describe the links in the chain between the enzyme lipase and the behavior defined as memory impairment.

How does one translate the results of protein synthesis into brain function and behavior? Obviously, any answer at this time must be speculative. However, several profitable directions may be taken in gerontological research to lay the groundwork for understanding cognitive changes; among these are synapse conduction and membrane physiology, neural–glial relationships, enzyme activity, and hormonal influences on metabolism, and their relationships to slowing of behavior and specific memory impairments.

We have already suggested that in the healthy organism, metabolism—turnover of proteins, lipids, and carbohydrates—is related to cell integrity. For example, data on the turnover of mitochondrial lipids are inconclusive (Huemer, Bickert, Lee, & Reeves, 1970). Since the mitochondria are sites of energy production for the cell, any changes here could be extremely important. The relations between the turnover of components in the organelles, the synthesis of energy-rich adenosine triphosphate, cell metabolism, and the ability of the whole organism to run, talk, think, eat, and love may someday be clarified.

More specifically, enzyme activity in the nerve pathways is an important observation post for rate-limiting steps directly related to learning and memory. Receptor sites for neurotransmitters are found around the synaptic nerve terminal, and the specific enzyme for destroying or inactivating the transmitter is located in the synaptic cleft. Any changes in enzyme synthesis and activity would have definite effects on synaptic transmission, but, to date, the changes in synaptic enzymes have not been thoroughly evaluated. Post-mortem examination of 5–57-year-old accident victims revealed decreased action of tyrosine hydroxylase (McGeer & McGeer, 1971). Choline acetylase and glutamic acid decarboxylase, which are important in the synthesis of other transmitters, showed no change with age. These are sparse data and more research is needed. It also seems that a given neuron usually produces only one transmitter, although it may have several receptor sites (Horridge, 1968). Research needs to be directed toward understanding the fast chemical events at the synapse as well as the slower action of hormones, and relating them to the slowing of behavior. While transmitters tend to be specific, no single hormone has a specific effect on one or several neurons; endocrine secretions have a generalized effect on the nervous system and exert their influence on many other aspects of body function as well.

The hormonal system may be regarded as a second information system in the body working along with the nervous system. Thus, hormones may affect protein synthesis; for example, thyroid has a primary binding site on mitochondria. Some aged mitochondria in the brain lose the ability to bind thyroid hormone according to Sokoloff (see Lajtha, 1970), and it is appropriate to question the significance of this change and to ask what other differences might exist between mature and immature cerebral organelles, and further, what changes mature organelles undergo with advancing age.

Protein breakdown and synthesis could influence neurotransmitter efficiency and ultimately the balance of central-autonomic nervous activity. Evidence suggests that the postsynaptic membrane is composed of a high proportion of insoluble protein (Lajtha, 1970). Membrane composition may vary along the course of the nerve according to different functions of the axon, dendrite, and cell body, and this alteration may be necessary for optimal functioning. Membrane stabilization would be a key area for research. Any change in molecular transport of neurotransmitters, whether brought about by changes in metabolism and ribosome stability or vascular influences, are likely to be centered at the membrane. Molecular and ionic events underlie nerve mechanisms; however, to date, little can be said to explain the deterioration of nervous coordination and higher intellectual processes in old age. Changes in the blood-brain barrier with aging permitting the leakage of certain substances may ultimately affect behavior (J. Walker, personal communication, 1972).

We have speculated that changes in protein metabolism probably underlie brain activity. Ribosomes in the cell are the sites for the assembly of amino acids composing specific proteins. In vitro research using homogenates of neural and glial ribosomes—both membrane bound and free in the cytoplasm—from animals of different ages, and perhaps reared in different environments, may yield valuable data on the stability of ribosomal functioning. The assumption is that ribosome stability is related to neuron stability. In vitro studies of the dividing and nondividing systems are worthwhile, although it is extremely difficult to relate the results of in vitro systems to in vivo aging. However, there is no evidence so far to suggest that learning and memory mechanisms are dependent upon changes in the synaptic membrane. Electrophysiological studies localizing changes that occur with learning (e.g., hippocampus) in both young and old organisms could eventually lead into ribosomal and membrane studies in these nerve tissues.

Currently, it is impossible to draw any clear connection between the accumulation of errors in the molecular–genetic matrix of events and the changes in learning and memory. Much research will have to be completed before the bridge can be spanned. Meanwhile, we share the view of Busse (1970) that changes in the amounts of DNA, RNA, and proteins specific to the CNS (e.g., s-100) may be important elements in learning and memory.

Functional Aspects of Aging

The universal physical change, perhaps analogous to behavioral slowing, is a decrease in muscular strength with advancing age. It is noteworthy that Quetelet recorded this in 1836 (Simonson, 1965). However, there is now a growing literature suggesting that through physical reconditioning *some* of the muscle changes seen in aging may in part be counteracted (Barry, Daly, Pruett, Steinmetz, Page, Birkhead, & Rodahl, 1966; Brunner & Jokl, 1970; DeVries, 1969). To advance this area of prophylaxis and rehabilitation, basic research into the underlying causes of cell loss and enfeeblement is necessary.

Cell loss. The progressive loss of nondividing or slowly dividing cells, although unequal across tissues, is one of the most widely accepted general age changes. However, as more attention is given to the scrutiny of healthy brain tissue, the actual occurrence of cell loss, in the absence of vascular disease, is being questioned (C. Finch, personal communication, 1972). Cell loss is most marked in the brain, skeletal muscles, and kidneys, and is less pronounced in the liver. It is commonly assumed that this loss in the organism is responsible for decreased muscular strength, disturbed homeostasis, and some impairment of brain function. This is an assumed relationship, and although a logical expectation, cell loss may be only one possible functional tie to physiological decline: others, such as changes in enzyme and hormone activity, may be more important in determining the efficiency of metabolic pathways in cell functioning.

For example, cell loss (substantia nigra through the caudate and putamen) is insufficient to account for the impaired brain function often seen in Parkinson's disease (McGeer & McGeer, 1971). By pondering the pallor of the substantia nigra it has been discovered that the nerve cells that were present were unable to synthesize dopamine and maintain normal catecholamine metabolism (McGeer, 1971). Although the specific reason for the breakdown in tyrosine metabolism is unknown, the administration of l-dopa (a precursor of dopamine) changes the course of the disease (Barbeau & McDowell, 1970). If nerve cells were irreversibly damaged, as previously held, it is difficult to conceive how such effects could occur.

With aging, there is a decrease in brain weight—averaging 200 grams by the eighth decade—which is usually attributed to cell loss; we commonly assume such loss must contribute to altered functioning. However, this may be too simple an explanation of observed behavior in aging individuals. Indeed, cell loss may have important consequences if it leads to specific lesions—lesions in the lateral hypothalamus, for example, can cause a lack of appetite. As discussed later, however, the correlation between cerebral pathology and prior mental functioning has been far from perfect.

Without bypassing the consequences of cell loss for efficient organ function, it is important to consider alternative shifts in essential chemical activity. The dopaminergic, noradrenergic, and serotonergic pathways are just a few examples of biochemical systems where disturbances may lead to behavior changes long before any important cell loss has taken place. Indeed, the changes in mood, appetite, and sleep exhibited by old persons may be directly related to the chemical functionings of brain centers.

Cell and tissue aging. The results of in vitro experiments have been summarized by Hay (1967), Walford (1969), and Holeckova and Cristofalo (1970). They suggested that (a) there is a change in the growth potential of cell cultures, (b) the time required to initiate mitotic events—the latent period—is increased and is longest in brain and cardiac cells, and (c) there may not be a limit to the total number of cell divisions. All three findings may be modified with the development of better laboratory techniques, making it difficult and perhaps inappropriate to interpret them as real changes.

An impression of current knowledge can be gained from Cristofalo's (in press) and Hayflick's (1965, 1968, 1970) analyses of the potentials for cell growth and division, and from Krohn's (1966) review of the transplantation literature. Franks (1970) summarized the basic question about cellular aging to which we are only beginning to approach very tentative answers:

1. Is there a finite lifespan for cells?
2. Is the lifespan affected by cellular organization, i.e., do tissues have a different lifespan from free cells?
3. If there is a finite lifespan, is it the same for all cells and tissues?
4. Are there species differences in cell or tissue lifespan?
5. Are there specific "age changes" in cells and tissues?
6. If there are specific "age changes" are they the same in all cells and tissues? [p. 281]

His article implied that the result of any number of specific cell events may be an increased susceptibility to disease. There are really no determinate set of changes that can be regarded as age changes. Even though many cells show an accumulation of age pigments, one such pigment, lipofuscin, appears to be more a function of vitamin E in the diet than age (Pentschew & Schwartz, 1962).

Amyloid accumulates in the intracellular spaces with advancing age, and has been identified in senile plaques in brain tissue (Nikaido, Austin, Rinehart, Treub, Hutchinson, Stukenbrok, & Miles, 1971; Schwartz, 1965, 1969). It has been associated with autoimmune disorders, infections, advanced malignancy, and Alzheimer's disease; the relationships between these disorders remains to be explored and may significantly provide for research into aging processes. Specifically, the analysis of deposits in Alzheimer's plaques may afford vital clues to the deterioration of vital tissues (Amyloidosis, 1970).

Somatic mutation may not lead directly to cell damage and consequent cell and tissue aging, but instead may indirectly lead into autoimmune processes that regulate the damage. The cell recognition system in different tissues may break down, or autoimmune clones (amyloid deposits) may disrupt organ function (Burnet, 1970; Walford, 1969).

Changes in the immunologic system and its activity are an important research area in aging. Walford (1967, 1969) and Makinodan, Perkins, and Chen (1971) have written syntheses and analyses of the research activities with animals and men. The latter even discussed the possible outcomes of altering the immune system in the aging individual. Antibody response decreases gradually after adolescence and natural antibody titer decreases. Older individuals are not as responsive to antigens contacted early in life.

The nature of the defect is not clear, but it seems to be due to both intrinsic and extrinsic factors such that the general level of immune activity decreases but long before the onset of pathology. Any changes in the immune system as well as other systems would affect life-span as well as behavioral functioning. Current research efforts are aimed at elucidating the intrinsic and extrinsic factors and assessing the effect of the ablation of lymph organs and chemical stimulants on immunologic activity and life-span.

Among other changes prominent in the aging organism are changes in connective tissue, shifts in cell H_2O and changes in some electrolytes. Exchangeable potassium, for instance, declines markedly after the age of 40. There also appears to be an accumulation of free radicals and a leakage of lysosomes. Bellamy (1970), Sobel (1968), and Walford (1969) provided information in these areas. Organ weight generally decreases, and there is an increasing diversity in cell size and arrangement. Age pigments accumulate in various cells, but are unequal across cells, as is cell loss across tissues. Apparently there is no relation between cell loss and pigment accumulation. Pigments have been viewed as lesions, or bulk waste products, interfering with cell activity, but there is little substantiating evidence. Pigment induction experiments (Chio, Reiss, Fletcher, & Tappel, 1969) suggest that pigment accumulation may be responsible, at least in part, for indications of aging. Zeman (1971) suggested that persons afflicted with Batten-Vogt syndrome or the disorders known as neuronal ceroid-lipofuscinoses, may provide the conditions for studying the functional consequences of pigment accumulation.

There are, however, changes in almost every organ system ranging from general demineralization of the skeleton through respiratory, cardiovascular, neurological, integumental, gastroitestinal, excretory, and urogenital changes. These changes alter the system, making it weaker and less efficient in handling input from the external and internal environments.

Uniform change with aging appears to be a less efficient homeostasis, a decreased rate of adjustment to various stimuli when placed under stress, either psychological or biological. (For a discussion of nervous-hormonal adjustment mechanisms, see Gutmann, 1970; for a general consideration of homeostasis, see Comfort, 1970). Indeed, Shock (1967) has proposed that age changes are clearly evidenced only when the organism is stressed to its maximum performance.

Changes in the Nervous System

Looking more closely at the particular findings in the nervous system, the most striking impression is the lack of clear-cut change. Perhaps the most constant changes, as already mentioned, are neuronal atrophy, pigment accumulation, unequal neuron loss accompanied by glial infiltration, and a decrease in brain weight.

The EEG shows a shift to slower frequencies and some temporal focal slowing in the older age groups. Even greater changes are observed in EEG activity during sleep—the older person spending a reduced amount of time in Stage-4 sleep (the last or deepest stage). After age 60, the evoked potential shows an increase in amplitude and delay changes in some of the early components, possibly indicating a loss of inhibitory control with aging. Furthermore, there appear to be autonomic changes with age, but, to date, these have been systematically studied only in animals and only by a single investigator (Frolkis, 1968). Bondareff (1959), Brody (1970), Perez and Moore (1970), Himwich and Himwich (1959), Magladery (1959), and Thompson and Marsh (pp. 112–148) offered discussions of neuroanatomical, neurochemical, and neurophysiological changes with aging. Blumenthal (1970), Wang (in press), and Troyer (in press) provided details on CNS and ANS activity. Thompson and Marsh's chapter is a thorough critical review of psychophysiological studies of aging.

BIOBEHAVIORAL CHANGES ASSOCIATED WITH ADVANCING AGE

In the preceding pages two questions have been reviewed with the purpose of integrating behavioral and biological changes with advancing years: What are the cognitive alterations associated with aging? What biological events can be identified as preceding or accompanying such intellectual changes? This review has made it abundantly clear that the information collected so far should be supplemented by data concerning the integrative hormonal and nervous systems, the structural–functional network of other body systems, and the natural life-span of populations.

Intellectual Function and Biological Changes

Longitudinal observations. Significant indications of psychobiological relationships have been the fruition of a few longitudinal studies of aging persons. These studies demonstrated that intellectual loss was not as pronounced as previously suggested by cross-sectional studies, that it varied across individuals, and that a general decline occurred only on tests with a speed component. Some cross-sectional studies have confirmed the longitudinal findings (Schaie, Rosenthal, & Perlman, 1953). Only a few investigators to date have attempted to probe the interaction unearthed in longitudinal studies of healthy older persons between mental changes, biological functioning, and mortality. Though scant, this work has generally yielded positive correlations between behavioral and biological variables, and is of great importance because it has clinical as well as experimental applicability.

A positive relationship has emerged between survival during senescence and performance on certain tests of intellectual functioning. In all the lognitudinal studies carried out so far it has been observed that those persons who died prior to the retest, or for other reasons were lost to follow-up, had obtained lower scores at first testing than those who had survived. The lower initial scores of the nonsurvivors compared to survivors are probably attributable to their more rapid decline rather than to lower abilities in early life, since it has been noted that rapid cognitive decline frequently precedes death. Computation of a "Critical Loss" factor, based on a specified rate of decline in certain intellectual subtests has been found to be a good predictor of high-risk versus low-risk persons (Jarvik & Blum, 1971).

As a concession to practical realities, research is restricted to survivors; it should be kept in mind that selective bias operates when one deals with survivors only (Riegel, 1969; Riegel & Riegel, 1972).

Since most nonsurvivors died as a result of cardiovascular or cerebrovascular disease (the most common cause of death in the upper age group), it has been postulated that cognitive decline may be an early indicator of cerebrovascular dysfunctioning (Jarvik & Falek, 1963; Wilkie & Eisdorfer, 1971). Vascular changes influencing cerebral functioning are crucial in the evaluation of cognitive decline, and the relationships between vascular alterations, brain electrical activity, cerebral blood flow, and intelligence are discussed by Thompson and Marsh (pp. 112–148) and Wang (in press).

The extent of change in mental function occurring after the age of 60 may be clarified by further prospective longitudinal studies. Tests of cognitive function may offer a new means of diagnosing minute biological changes which presage mortality, and which, if detected early enough, might at some future time be therapeutically aborted. In further evaluating the diagnostic sensitivity of intellectual tests, it is important to determine their predictive validity for persons at an earlier age and for persons in the pathological extremes.

By identifying several subgroups in the vast aggregate comprising the mental decline ordinarily ascribed to the aging process, it may be possible to do in aging what was accomplished in the field of mental deficiency. Once, nearly all individuals attaining an IQ below some specified level were placed in a single category and labeled mentally defective. Today, well over 100 inborn errors of metabolism have been identified, and in a few of these, it has already been possible through timely diagnosis and treatment to prevent mental deficiency.

Cerebral blood flow. Cerebral blood flow (CBF) declines in individuals with cerebral arteriosclerosis or chronic brain syndromes, and cognitive impairment generally correlates with this reduced blood flow or oxygen concentration. In a recent study (Wang, in press), low regional CBF measured by an isotope inhalation technique was associated with a decline in scores on the WAIS, especially on the Performance scale. Twenty-four men and women, community volunteers between 71–87 years old, were tested at the beginning and end of a 12-year interval on the WAIS; the CBF measures were taken only upon retest. The results suggested that the metabolic health of the brain assessed by blood flow is important for the intellectual functioning of healthy older people. Altered blood flow, however, has not been traced to specific brain areas; senile dementia patients show decreased blood flow scattered across the frontal, temporal, and parietal lobes of the brain (Wang, Obrist, & Busse, 1970).

Hypertension. It is reasonable to assume that healthy tissue is probably a necessary precursor to efficient neural processing, yet basal metabolism does not seem to change with aging when water loss and cell volume changes are controlled. At this time, however, there is a lack of adequate information on changes in protein metabolism, carbohydrate metabolism (although there is a definite change in carbohydrate tolerance), and lipid metabolism. It is conceivable that relatively small shifts in essential biochemical activities may have little effect on cognitive functioning, but that cumulative compensations to stressors may at some point lead to impairment of higher mental abilities. For example, it is possible that repeated arousal from biological as well as psychosocial stressors and the continuous demands on the general defense alarm system (nervous–endocrine response preparatory for fight-or-flight) may lead to essential hypertension (Henry & Cassel, 1969). This has already been demonstrated in mice (Henry, Meehan, & Stephens, 1967). However, the precise biological changes accompanying chronic arousal or anxiety have not been specified.

Hypertension is correlated with intellectual decline. Data collected from the Duke longitudinal study (Wilkie & Eisdorfer, 1971) over a 10-year period (with age groups 69–79) showed an association between a decrease in WAIS scores and death for hypertensives, while normotensives maintained cognitive stability. Even though elevation of blood pressure marked enough to be diagnosed as hypertension is negatively related to psychometric performance and survival, a mild elevation of blood pressure may, as Obrist (1964) argued, be adaptive in maintaining brain circulation to overcome increased cerebral–vascular resistance in the aging person.

Aneuploidy. Cerebrovascular changes have been suggested as a major cause of intellectual decline and death. Some of the observable age changes in mental characteristics, however, seem to be associated with karotypic changes rather than arteriosclerosis. It has been hypothesized that one common factor between intelligence and biological changes may be the gradual accumulation of aberrant cells with the eventual attainment of a level where homeostatic mechanisms can no longer maintain survival (Jarvik, 1963). Experimental support for this postulate evolves from the observation of a statistically significant increase in the proportion of aneuploid cells (i.e., cells containing other than the normal diploid count of chromosomes) with increasing age (Hamerton, Taylor, Angell, & McGuire, 1965; Jacobs, Brunton, & Brown, 1964; Jacobs, Brunton, Brown, Doll, & Goldstein, 1963; Jacobs, Court-Brown, & Doll, 1961). Even though Bloom, Archer, and Awa (1967) were not able to demonstrate this increase in aneuploidy, several laboratories report a significantly higher proportion of hypodiploid cells (cells having lost one or more chromosomes) for older women than for younger women or older men (Court-Brown, Buckton, Jacobs, Tough, Kuenssberg, & Knox, 1966; Jarvik, & Kato, 1970; Sandberg, Cohen, Rim, & Levin, 1967). Nielsen (1968, 1970) and Goodman, Fecheimer, Miller, and Zartman (1969) confirmed the increase in hypodiploidy in elderly women.

Chromosome monitoring techniques may offer a novel approach to exploring mental changes. The relation between chromosome loss and memory loss is an intriguing one, but has been described so recently that it remains as yet unconfirmed. Briefly, a significant positive correlation has been found between the Graham-Kendall Memory-For-Designs Test (Graham & Kendall, 1960) and the percentage of cells having lost one or more chromosomes (Jarvik & Kato, 1969). Moreover, a higher proportion of women with the diagnosis of senile dementia—a disorder characterized by loss of memory, as well as confusion—showed a chromosome loss than did women of a comparable age without mental disturbance (Nielsen, 1968, 1970). An increased frequency of chromosome loss has also been established in older persons who functioned well enough to continue living in the community, rather than in institutions, but showed sufficient memory impairment to be diagnosed as suffering from organic brain syndrome in mild or moderate degrees (Jarvik, Altschuler, Kato, & Blumner, 1971). Chromosome loss also has been associated with cognitive impairment as measured by performance on the Stroop Color-Word test (Bettner, Jarvik, & Blum, 1971) and on Reitan's Trail-Making Test (unpublished data).

Longitudinal data are lacking, as are chromosome counts in other dividing cell systems. The assumption is being made that with advancing age chromosomes are lost in the glial cells and that this may interfere with neuronal functioning. While Horridge (1968) argued that beyond a nutritive role glial functioning may have little bearing on neuronal activity, other researchers claimed both a metabolic and integrative role for glial cells. These claims open several avenues for research. For example, if we could make some measurements on enzyme systems or metabolic by-products in the dividing glial cells, and relate these to a loss of function, we might be closer to a molecular explanation of the changes underlying mental changes. However, currently, it is extremely difficult to separate glial and neuronal fractions from each other. Glial cells seem to proliferate in rats even at advanced ages (Dalton, Homes, & Leblond, 1968; Grinker & Bucy, 1969), but in all the descriptive work conducted the types of glial cells observed have not been specified. Whether this cell growth maintains or hinders cerebral function remains to be determined.

Genetic factors in survival and intellectual functioning. That hereditary factors play a role in survival has been generally accepted. Variations in life-span from a maximum of four days in the housefly and 177 years in the Galapagos tortoise are powerful examples of interspecies differences based on genetic variability. In man, twin studies have confirmed the potency of genetic factors on longevity. Mean differences in the life-span of monozygotic twin partners were consistently smaller than those of dyzygotic co-twins (Jarvik, Falek, Kallmann, & Lorge, 1960; Kallman, 1953). Since both life-span and intelligence are known to reflect genotypic differences (Cohen, 1964; Erlenmeyer-Kimling & Jarvik, 1963; Glass, 1960; Kallmann & Jarvik, 1959) it is possible that common mechanisms underlie the observed relationships between cognitive stability and survival, or, conversely, between cognitive deterioration and mortality.

As discussed earlier, intelligence is a construct with many dimensions. Yet, much of the variance in measured intellectual abilities is genetically determined (Erlenmeyer-Kimling & Jarvik, 1963; Wilson & Harpring, in press), and performance viewed over the lifespan must be under continuous genetic and environmental control. Only a single group of investigators (Jarvik & Blum, 1971; Jarvik & Falek, 1963; Jarvik et al., 1957, 1960; Kallmann, 1961) has accumulated data on genetic factors in intellectual abilities as manifested during senescence. And the results have shown that genetic control of intellectual performance seems to be carried into the seventh and eighth decades of life.

Intellectual functioning in monozygotic twins was significantly more similar than in dizygotic partners on a variety of tests administered between the ages of 60–95 years (Feingold, 1950). Since these twins had been away from formal educational training for many decades, the continued expression of genetic similarity was impressive. In the presence of pathology, however, the intellectual performance of monozygotic co-twins deviated markedly. Thus, if one of a pair of identical twins showed a specific cognitive decline ("Critical Loss") and the other did not, it was always the twin with the cognitive decline who died first (Jarvik & Blum, 1971).

The importance of heredity in various types of pathology affecting the aged, such as hypertension, hyperlypemia, and coronary heart disease, is well known (Jarvik, 1970). In mental disorders associated with aging, whatever studies have been done have generally confirmed that genetic determinants are of crucial importance in the presenile brain atrophies, as well as in senile and arteriosclerotic psychoses (Kallmann, 1953; Larsson, Sjogren, & Jacobson, 1963).

Psychopathology and Behavior Change

Studying the extremes of pathology sometimes provides us with information on normal functioning. Thus, psychoanalytic theory of "normal" behavior had its origin exclusively in Freud's astute observations of pathological deviation. Similarly, the memory impairment which is the hallmark of presenile and senile dementia may provide clues to the etiology of the memory loss so prevalent among many nonpsychotic aged persons. Also referred to as senile psychosis or senile brain disease, and included in the category of organic brain syndrome, senile dementia is characterized neuroanatomically by cerebral atrophy, senile plaque formation, neurofibrillary tangles, and lipid accumulation. The mechanism of how plaques might hinder brain function is unknown, although it may indicate an autoimmune breakdown. The neurofibrillary tangles, especially marked in Alzheimer patients, are obvious evidence of nerve degeneration (Nikaido et al., 1971). Clinically, senile dementia is diagnosed by mild to severe memory impairment, spatiotemporal disorientation, and confusion. Discussions of the genetic and environmental influences, ultrastructures, clinical descriptions, and relations to other diseases are provided by Mayer-Gross, Slater, and Roth (1965), Müller and Ciompi (1968), Zerbin-Rudin (1967), Kallmann (1953), and Larsson et al. (1963).

It has been difficult to differentiate diagnostically processes of brain deterioration in senile dementia and in arteriosclerotic dementia. Usually, behavioral impairment begins more abruptly in cerebral arteriosclerosis and general physical and mental decline is less diffuse (Busse, 1959). Recent isotope inhalation techniques employed in regional cerebral circulation studies are beginning to be used to study brain deterioration due to vascular changes. Obrist, Chivian, Cronqvist, & Inguar (1970) and Simard, Aleson, Paulson, Lassesn, & Skinhoj (1971) have demonstrated that reduced CBF correlates with the degree of dementia. In senile patients reductions were prominent in the gray and white matter, whereas, in presenile patients, low blood flow was observed only in the areas of gray matter. Conditions of brain cell damage and vascular changes do overlap, but the causal relations remain to be explored. Behavioral deficits may be due primarily to vascular changes, or may be a function of alterations in the metabolism of brain tissue. Simard et al. found normal vasomotor functioning in their 15 patients with senile dementia, and suggested that dementia is not due to chronically decreased blood circulation, but rather to a sudden occlusion or primary deterioration of tissues.

The relationship between degree of pathology and intellectual impairment is far from clear, although Wang (in press) reviewed some of the evidence for the hypothesis of a positive association. Rothschild (1937) argued for the importance of environmental stresses, in the presence of concomitant brain deterioration, as the key factors in the etiology of senile mental impairment. Others hold that brain damage is the primary factor in intellectual decline, and that environmental stressors serve as precipitating crises. Corsellis (1962) in a postmortem study of over 300 cases and Malamud (1965) in a study of 400 cases concluded that mental impairment is fairly well correlated with the presence of brain tissue alterations. Even persons exhibiting functional disorders, such as depression and psychoneurotic reaction patterns, show vascular changes in the large and small vessels, the presence of senile plaques, and some neurofibrillary tangles. Roth, Tomlinson, and Blessed (1967) counted the number of plaques in 60 senile patients in postmortem studies, and compared these counts to the intensity of dementia. There was a significant relation between the number of senile plaques and the clinical assessment of dementia.

There is a general relation between the results of histological observations of brain sections (changes in gross and microscopic structures) and the clinical assessment of individuals as presented in Corsellis' and Malamud's observations. In rats, too, the number of brain lesions in sections analyzed from animals sacrificed at different ages has been related to the onset of a variety of diseases. Dayan (1970a, 1970b) suggested that a similar relationship exists in man between the brain pathology and both life-span and susceptibility to disease.

It is worthwhile to note, however, that Dayan (1971) in a review of brain alterations in 113 old animals, representing 47 vertebrate species, reported that there are no consistent trends in brain alterations between man and animals except for a decrease in brain weight. The neuronal loss contributing to the decreased mass has been traditionally regarded as the biological underpinning of intellectual deficits in man, but this has not been sufficiently substantiated.

Although the more favorable prognosis for patients with psychogenic disorders when compared to organic brain syndrome is well known (Roth, 1955; Trier, 1966), the high frequency of depression in the older population is not generally recognized. Roth pointed out that depression that was once attributed to aging and its symptoms—apathy, mild memory impairment, and slight confusion—were incorrectly diagnosed as organic senile psychosis; it is now recognized as related to functional psychiatric illness. It is very difficult to evaluate the psychological test results of a depressed patient and to determine whether the performance has been diminished by lack of motivation, apathy, and retardation symptomatic of the disease itself, or by intellectual impairment.

The literature regarding memory deficits is basically descriptive. Caird (1966) summarized details on regressive memory loss, and Inglis (1970) and Talland (1965) provided general discussions about memory disorder. Jarvik, Gritz, and Schneider (in press) recently reviewed drug use to reverse memory deficits in the aged. Genetic, environmental, nutritional, hormonal, vascular, and metabolic factors have all been implicated in senescent memory loss. In terms of general patient care, very little is offered beyond basic caretaking.

Speed of Behavior and Biological Changes

Behavioral slowing is the most consistent accompaniment of advancing age and has been correlated with respiratory functioning, EEG slowing, evoked potential amplitude, and decreased critical flicker fusion (CFF) frequency, rather than the general health status of the individual (Birren, 1965; Jalavisto, 1965). The slowing of the alpha frequency of the EEG and its role as a central timing mechanism for the CNS has yet to be elucidated (Surwillo, 1968). Manipulation of the EEG through physiological feedback techniques and concomitant testing of RT should be approached to test Surwillo's hypothesis (D. Woodruff, personal communication, 1971). This type of research, however, is only one avenue to elucidating the slowing of behavior.

The changes in the nervous system underlying this general slowing are complex. When considering biobehavioral organization we can best regard the general state of the organism as one limiting factor, and the nervous system as a second limiting factor. This is not to suggest that nervous system function is impaired differently from that of other organ systems, but that the nervous system has an integrating role with the endocrine organs, which propagates the effects of impairment beyond the confines of the nervous system itself.

Temporal disorganization. Samis (1968) has suggested that aging is the progressive loss of temporal organization, such that with any set of biological changes, tissues and organs have to compensate in their normal rhythms of activity. Even though this compensation is, on the one hand, a healthy adaptive response, it induces, on the other hand, a desynchronization of activity, which in turn may result in slowing of organizational functioning. Disorganization, then, is seen as an inherent property of the system, implying that instead of a single set of events, an infinite set of possible events may produce aging phenomena whether stemming from a genetic program, cellular interactions, or from exogenous influences. Thus, slowing may be the inevitable outcome of cellular reorganization in response to temporal disorganization.

A change in the temporal organization of the system implies a change in the ability to receive internal or external stimuli and to support information handling and processing. Immunological, endocrine, ANS, and CNS activities are all networks of communicating changes from the cellular to the organismic level. Systematic study of the interaction of hierarchical regulatory processes integrating stimuli from internal and external sources is urgently needed to understand biobehavioral organization.

Decreased sensory input. Sensory input and the subsequent neural transformations heavily influence the full spectrum of CNS activity, and also affect the homeostatic balance imposed by other organ systems through the mediation of the autonomic system; sensory stimuli probably effect a change in the state of the organism. A registration deficiency reported in old persons, possibly due to reduced central inhibitory influences or impaired receptors, suggests a decrease in sensory input. This occurrence, in addition to disorganization of hierarchical processes, may explain some of the changes in speed and timing in the behavior of the aging organism. In any behavioral task—involving either intellectual or work performance—the older person will make errors and magnify deficits.

Impaired synaptic transmission. The loss of neurons in the CNS, particularly those with fast conducting fibers, and the slight slowdown in peripheral nerve conduction, may provide a partial explanation of slowing. Synaptic transmission probably plays a more significant role. Lipofuscin grains accumulate postsynaptically (Müller & Ciompi, 1968) and may be instrumental in altering synaptic transmission and reducing resultant threshold changes. Research should be designed to clarify changes in groups of synapses in the brain especially in the polysensory areas, such as the premotor area of the frontal lobe and portions of the parietal and temporal lobes. It is possible that changes in a single synapse have no significant consequences but that the pattern of synapses and their changes are crucial in the slowing observed with aging.

Decreased autonomic activity. As mentioned earlier, very little is known about the reorganizational abilities of the nervous system in adapting to cell loss and possible glial interference. Small phasic fibers are lost preferentially to larger, tonic fibers in the ANS (Botar, 1961), and this is reflected in the decreased reactivity of the ANS in handling sensory stimuli requiring immediate attention and organismic response. Basic autonomic changes seem to contribute to an elevated synaptic threshold, possibly resulting in slowing (Troyer, in press). Troyer pointed out that along with changes in autonomic functioning, there are psychological correlates of such changes as illustrated in Eisdorfer's verbal learning studies (Eisdorfer et al., 1970), and that there are autonomic effects on general physiological functioning. Some target organ tissues change in their sensitivity to endocrine activity, just as receptors and autonomic nerve centers in animals have been shown to change in their sensitivity to neurotransmitters (Frolkis, 1968). These nervous–hormonal events may result in slowing of behavior.

Cell and membrane changes. Aside from changes in the nervous system there are general modifications in cells which have been considered as the biological substrate of the cognitive changes we see. The issue of molecular transport of nutrients involves cell and membrane changes, connective tissue alterations (in collagen, elastin, and ground substance), and circulatory functioning (Sobel, 1968). Sobel referred to McFarland's position that lack of oxygen by whatever mechanism is a key element of biological functioning that may prevent effective psychological as well as metabolic performance. He concluded however, that the "evidence in support of the hypothesis that changes in connective tissue result in reduced rate of delivery of oxygen to cells, has no more experimental support now than when it was first proposed." And connective tissue is perhaps the most intensively studied tissue!

General remarks. Slowing does not have to imply inability of the organism to make adequate responses to the environment. As mentioned earlier, the aging organism is capable of responding to sensory and perceptual stimuli, and motor coordination remains relatively good (Simonson, 1965). Fatigue and motivation will affect performance on any task, and it is interesitng to note that when hypnosis was used with track athletes their running time improved to a level not otherwise attained (Simonson, 1965). Simonson said that he did not propose that hypnosis can affect oxygen transport, but he did suggest that the CNS can improve the organism's tolerance to physicochemical changes.

Jakubczak (1967), in a discussion of psychophysiological changes with aging, suggested that age changes in inhibitory and excitatory processes of nervous regulation need to be investigated in behavioral research:

> Age-related deterioration in the CNS may be reflected not only in a decrease of neural activity and the speed of initiation of response, but also in an increase in erratic responses due to a decreased central inhibitory control.

He attempted to explain Rabbitt's (1965) finding that the older person appears less able to deal with irrelevant stimuli, by suggesting that inhibitory control of some brain regions specific in blocking sensory processes are weakened.

Exogenous Agents Affecting Survival and Intellectual Functioning

Although numerous agents can shorten life-span, our greatest interest is in those substances which can inhibit or retard the aging process and prolong the life-span. Radiation provides the classical example of an exogenous agent accelerating the aging process, inducing chromosomal abberations, cellular abnormalities, lysosome damage, suppression of the immune response, and a shortening of the life-span. Nonetheless, radiation applied to the appropriate organism in the appropriate dose ranges, and at the appropriate time, can actually prolong the life-span. Similarly, variations in nutrition depending upon the type and amount of nutrients, can either reduce or enhance length of life; in poikilotherms, so can manipulation of temperature.

Among the other agents reported to retard aging are antibiotics, antioxidants, anticross-linking agents, immunosuppressives, and hormones (Table 2). These agents interact with each other and their effects have been summarized by Walford (1969). None, however, to our knowledge has been investigated with regard to its effect on mental functioning.

There is another group of exogenous agents, however, for which the claim is made that they improve cognitive performance in the aged. Historically, the earliest is probably procaine. Unfortunately, attempts to reproduce the original claims have not been successful and in controlled studies it has not been possible to distinguish the effects of procaine from those of a placebo. Nonetheless, the drug is used clinically in Europe. It is possible that differences due to different manufacturers, dosages, and administration methods might explain the equivocal findings.

Among the newer remedies is hyperbaric oxygen treatment (Goldfarb, Hochstadt, Jacobson, & Weinstein, 1970; Jacobs, Small, & Alvis, 1970), and, again, the original claims have not been substantiated.

The use of RNA extracts in treating memory deficits has evolved in the consideration of metabolic factors in memory loss. Memory improvement has been reported in several studies with DNA and later RNA; the greatest improvement was reported for arteriosclerotic patients, followed by people with presenile dementia, and lastly, those with senile dementia (Cameron, 1958; Cameron & Solyom, 1961; Cameron, Solyom, & Beach, 1963; Cameron, Solyom, Sved, & Wainrib, 1963; Cameron, Sved, Solyom, Wainrib, & Barik, 1963). Other experimeters report negative or nodefinitive results with their patients (Dalderup, Van Haard, Keller, Dalmeijer, Frijda, & Elshout, 1970).

If nucleic acids do affect learning and memory, then drugs affecting RNA synthesis would be expected to influence performance. Such experiments are beginning to be carried out and have yielded conflicting results with a few drugs. Talland and McGuire (1967) found magnesium pemoline to be only a general CNS stimulant with little or no effect on general performance and Eisdorfer, Conner, and Wilkie (1968) found a slight improvement in embedded figure recognition, but no improvement in learning and memory. Talland, Mendelson, Koz, and Aaron (1965) found no improvement in memory performance in patients treated with tricyanoaminopropene, which is also supposed to enhance brain RNA synthesis.

The involvement of RNA in memory deficits in the aged needs to be explored further. The initial enthusiasm has not been verified, and the RNA hypothesis does not seem to be viable at this time. Some studies report improvement, but the changes have been small.

Continued efforts in drug research are merited; the example of the early futile attempts to relieve the symptoms of Parkinson's disease is historic. The imaginative approach of changing the streoisomer to l-dopa, drastically altering the dose and schedule of administration, resulted in the first successful reversal of a far advanced neuropathological condition.

CONCLUSION

The questions posed at the beginning of this review have only begun to be investigated. The process of discovery, replication, and validation characterizing the scientific method is slow and often yields a plethora of isolated facts. It is distressing when we seek to elevate accumulated data to a precise statement and find we cannot augment the wisdom expressed in Greek antiquity by Plato: "An old man can no more learn much than he can run fast (*Republic*, VII, 536)." The eyeball method of science tells us that old persons *can* learn and *can* run, although the speed and amount of their activity lag behind that of younger persons. It is an important mandate that gerontologists determine how to narrow the gap.

To date, researchers have been largely concerned with the investigation of diseases which characteristically occur in the upper age groups. In this way, many changes have been shown to be pathological age alterations rather than the concomitants of physiological aging. If man is to enjoy a "long and happy life," the time has come to concentrate on those events or processes which appear to be independent of pathology and maintain cognitive functioning. The most pronounced change is a slowing of behavior. The precise biological events underlying this are still obscure, but may result from an accumulation of waste products or an inefficient repair system.

Nearly all events accompanying aging described in this chapter can be regarded as the cumulative effect of errors in all levels of biological organization, whether it be the accumulation of mitotic errors or the overloading of the memory system from the accumulation of a lifetime of experiences. Once consolidated, there may be only a slight decay. The interaction and sequence of events have yet to be elucidated.

It is distressing to attempt to assess the fruits of labor in a foundling field and to find that we are unable to draw any conclusions. Perhaps there is solace—and perhaps not—from Jeans' (1966) attempt to integrate two disciplines:

> But the plain fact is that there are no conclusions of any kind. . . . This may seem a disappointing harvest to have gathered from so extensive a field of new scientific activity, and from one, moreover, which comes so close to the territory of philosophy. Yet, we may reflect that physics and philosophy are at most a few thousand years old, but probably have lives of thousands of millions of years stretching away in front of them. They are only just beginning to get under way, and we are still, in Newton's words, like children playing with pebbles on the seashore, while the great ocean of truth rolls unexplored, beyond our reach. It can hardly be a matter for surprise that our race has not succeeded in solving any large part of its most difficult problems in the first millionth part of its existence. Perhaps life would be a duller affair if it had, for to many it is not knowledge but the quest for knowledge that gives the greater interest to thought—to travel hopefully is better than to arrive. [p. 217].

Only patience may relieve the despair of our slow endeavors to understand aging processes as we look forward to a long and stimulating journey toward new knowledge of biobehavioral interactions.

BIBLIOGRAPHY

Amyloidosis of Alzheimer's disease: A clue to ageing. *Lancet,* 1970, 598–599.

Agnew, H. W., Webb, W. B., & William, R. L. Sleep patterns in late middle age males: An EEG study. *Electroencephalography and Clinical Neurophysiology,* 1967, **23,** 168–171.

Andrew, W. Structural alterations with aging in the nervous system. *Journal of Chronic Diseases,* 1956, **3,** 575–596.

Arenberg, D. Anticipation interval and age differences in verbal learning. *Journal of Abnormal Psychology,* 1965, **70,** 419–425.

Arenberg, D. Verbal learning and retention. *Gerontologist,* 1967, **7,** 10–13.

Asdell, S. A., Doornenbal, H., Joshi, S. R., & Sperling, G. A. The effects of sex steroid hormones upon longevity in rats. *Journal of Reproduction and Fertility*, 1967, **14**, 113–120.

Balázs, A. Organismal differentiation, aging and rejuvenation. *Experimental Gerontology*, 1970, **5**, 305–312.

Baltes, P. B., & Goulet, L. R. Status and issues of a life-span developmental psychology. In L. R. Goulet & P. B. Baltes (Eds.), *Life-span developmental psychology: Research and theory*. New York: Academic Press, 1970.

Baltes, P. B., & Goulet, L. R. Exploration of developmental variables by manipulation and simulation of age differences in behavior. *Human Development*, 1971, **14**, 149–170.

Baltes, P. B., & Nesselroade, J. R. The developmental analysis of individual differences on multiple measures. Paper presented at the West Virginia Conference on Life-Span Developmental Psychology: Methodological Issues, 1971.

Baltes, P. B., Nessleroade, J. R., Schaie, K. W., & Labouvie, E. W. On the dilemma of regression effects in examining ability-level-related differentials in ontogenetic patterns of intelligence. *Developmental Psychology*, 1972, **6**, 78–84.

Baltes, P. B., Schaie, K. W., & Nardi, A. H. Age and experimental mortality in a seven-year longitudinal study of cognitive behavior. *Developmental Psychology*, 1971, **5**, 18–26.

Barbeau, A., & McDowell, F. H. (Eds.) L-dopa and Parkinsonism. Philadelphia: F. A. David, 1970.

Barber, A., & Bernheim, F. Lipid peroxidation: Its measurement, occurrence, and significance in animal tissues. In B. L. Strehler (Ed.), *Advances in gerontological research*. Vol. 2. New York: Academic Press, 1967.

Barrows, C. H., Jr. Cellular metabolism and aging. *Federation Proceedings*, 1956, **15**, 954–959.

Barrows, C. H., Jr. Changes in enzyme levels and patterns. In A. M. Brues & G. A. Sacher (Eds.), *Aging in levels of biological organization*. Chicago: University of Chicago Press, 1965.

Barrows, C. H., Jr. The effect of age on protein synthesis. Paper presented at the 8th International Congress of Gerontology, Washingotn, D.C., 1969.

Barrows, C. H., Jr. The challenge—mechanisms of biological aging. *Gerontologist*, 1971, **115**, 5–11.

Barrows, C. H., Jr., & Roeder, L. M. Effect of age on protein synthesis in rats. *Journal of Gerontology*, 1961, **16**, 321–325.

Barrows, C. H., Jr., Roeder, L. M., & Falzone, J. A., Jr., Effect of age on activities of enzymes and concentrations of nucleic acids in tissues of female wild rats. *Journal of Gerontology*, 1962, **17**, 144–147.

Barrows, C. H., Jr., Yiengst, M. J., & Shock, N. Senescence and the metabolism of various tissues of rats. *Journal of Gerontology*, 1959, **13**, 351–355.

Barry, A. J., Daly, J. W., Pruett, E. D. R., Steinmetz, W. R., Page, H. F., Birkhead, N.C., & Rodahl, K. The effects of physical conditioning in older individuals. *Journal of Gerontology*, 1966, **21**, 182–191.

Bayley, N., & Oden, M. H. The maintenance of intellectual ability in gifted adults. *Journal of Gerontology*, 1955, **10**, 91–107.

Beauchene, R. E., Fanestil, D. D., & Barrows, C. H., Jr. The effect of age on active transport and Na-K-activated-ATP use activity in renal tissues of rats. *Journal of Gerontology,* 1965, **20,** 306–316.

Beauchene, R. E., Roeder, L. M., & Barrows, C. H., Jr. The interrelationships of age, tissue protein synthesis and proteinuria. *Journal of Gerontology,* 1970, **25,** 359–363.

Bellamy, D. Long-term action of prednesdone phosphate on a strain of short-lived mice. *Experimental Gerontology,* 1968, **4,** 327–334.

Bellamy, D. Aging and endocrine responses to environmental factors: With particular reference to mammals. In, *Symposium on hormones and the environment, University of Sheffield, 1969.* Cambridge, England: Cambridge University Press, 1970.

Bender, A. D. Effect of age on intestinal absorption: Implications for drug absorption in the elderly. *Journal of the American Geriatrics Society,* 1968, **16,** 1331–1339.

Bender, A. D., Kormendy, C. G., & Powell, R. Pharmacological control of aging. *Experimental Gerontology,* 1970, **5,** 97–129.

Berg, B. N., & Simms, H. S. Nutrition and longevity in the rat: II. Longevity and onset of disease with different levels of food intake. *Journal of Nutrition,* 1960, **71,** 255–263.

Berg, B. N., & Simms, H. S. Nutrition and longevity in the rat: III. Food restriction beyond 800 days. *Journal of Nutrition,* 1961, **74,** 23–32.

Berkowitz, B., & Green, R. F. Changes in intellect with age: Longitudinal study of Wechsler-Bellevue scores. *Journal of Genetic Psychology,* 1963, **103,** 3–21.

Bertolini, A. M. *Gerontologic metabolism.* Springfield, Ill.: Charles C Thomas, 1961.

Bettner, L. G., Jarvik, L. F., & Blum, J. E. Stroop Color-Word-Test, non-psychotic organic brain syndrome and chromosome loss in aged twins. *Journal of Gerontology,* 1971, **26,** 458–469.

Birren, J. E. Age differences in learning a two-choice water maze by rats. *Journal of Gerontology,* 1962, **17,** 207–213.

Birren, J. E. *The psychology of aging.* Englewood Cliffs, N.J.: Prentice-Hall, 1964.

Birren, J. E. Age changes in speed of behavior: Its central nature and physiological correlates. In A. T. Welford & J. E. Birren (Eds.), *Behavior, aging, and the nervous system.* Springfield, Ill.: Charles C Thomas, 1965.

Birren, J. E. Age and decision strategies. In A. T. Welford & J. E. Birren (Eds.), *Interdisciplinary topics in gerontology.* Vol. 4. Basel, Switzerland: Karger, 1969.

Birren, J. B. Toward an experimental psychology of aging. *American Psychologist,* 1970, **25,** 124–135.

Birren, J. E., & Botwinick, J. The relation of writing speed to age and to the senile psychoses. *Journal of Consulting Psychology,* 1951, **55,** 243–249.

Birren, J. E., & Botwinick, J. Age differences in finger, jaw and foot reaction time to auditory stimuli. *Journal of Gerontology,* 1955, **10,** 429–434. (a)

Birren, J. E., & Botwinick, J. Speed of response as a function of perceptual difficulty and age. *Journal of Gerontology,* 1955, **10,** 433–436. (b)

Birren, J. E., Butler, R. N., Greenhouse, S. W., Sokoloff, L., & Yarrow, M. R. Interdisciplinary relationships: Interrelations of physiological, psychological, and psychiatric findings in healthy elderly men. In J. E. Birren, R. N. Butler, S. W. Greenhouse, L. Sokoloff & M. R. Yarrow (Eds.), *Human aging.* (USPHS No. 986) Washington, D.C.: United States Public Health Service, 1963.

Birren, J. E., Cardon, P. V., & Phillips, S. L. Reaction time as a function of the cardiac cycle in young adults. *Science,* 1963, **140,** 195–196.

Birren, J. E., & Jeffries, D. Bibliography on learning and memory, 1967. Unpublished manuscript, University of Southern California, 1967.

Birren, J. E., & Kay, H. Swimming speed of the albino rat: Age and sex differences. *Journal of Gerontology,* 1958, **13,** 374–377.

Birren, J. E., Riegel, K. F., & Morrison, D. F. Age differences in response speed as a function of controlled variations of stimulus conditions: Evidence of a general speed factor. *Gerontologia,* 1962, **6,** 1–18.

Birren, J. E., & Wall, P. D. Age changes in conduction velocity, refractory period, number of fibers, connective tissue space and blood vessels in sciatic nerve of rats. *Journal of Comparative Neurology,* 1956, **104,** 1–16.

Bjorksten, J. Aging: Present status of our chemical knowledge. *Journal of the American Geriatrics Society,* 1962, **10,** 125–139.

Bloom, A. D., Archer, P. G., & Awa, A. A. Variation in the human chromosome number. *Nature,* 1967, **216,** 487–489.

Blumenthal, H. T. (Ed.), *Interdisciplinary topics in gerontology.* Vol. 7. Basel, Switzerland: Karger, 1970.

Bondareff, W. Morphology of the aging nervous system. In J. E. Birren (Ed.), *Handbook of aging and the individual.* Chicago: University of Chicago Press, 1959.

Bondareff, W., Horotsky, R., & Routtenberg, A. Intrastriatal spread of catecholamines in senescent rats. *Journal of Gerontology,* 1971, **26,** 163–167.

Botar, J. *The autonomic nervous system: An introduction to its physiological and pathological histology.* Budapest: Akademiai Kiado, 1961.

Botwinick, J. Research problems and concepts in the study of aging. *Gerontologist,* 1964, **4,** 121–129.

Botwinick, J. Theories of antecedent conditions of speed of response. In A. T. Welford & J. E. Birren (Eds.), *Behavior, aging, and the nervous system.* Springfield, Ill.: Charles C Thomas, 1965.

Botwinick, J. *Cognitive processes in maturity and old age.* New York: Springer, 1967.

Botwinick, J. Geropsychology. *Annual Review of Psychology,* 1970, **21,** 239–272. (a)

Botwinick, J. Learning in children and in older adults. In L. R. Goulet & P. B. Baltes (Eds.), *Life-span developmental psychology: Research and theory.* New York: Academic Press, 1970. (b)

Botwinick, J., & Birren, J. E. Mental abilities and psychomotor responses in healthy aged men. In J. E. Birren, R. N. Butler, S. W. Greenhouse, L. Sokoloff, & M. R. Yarrow (Eds.), *Human aging,* (USPHS No. 986) Washington, D.C.: United States Public Health Service, 1963.

Botwinick, J. & Kornetsky, G. Age differences in the acquisition and extinction of the GSR. *Journal of Gerontology,* 1960, **15,** 83–85.

Botwinick, J., & Thompson, L. W. Components of reaction time in relation to age and sex. *Journal of Genetic Psychology,* 1966, **108,** 175–183.

Botwinick, J., & Thompson, L. W. Practice of speeded response in relation to age, sex and set. *Journal of Gerontology*, 1967, **22**, 72–76.

Botwinick, J., & Thompson, L. W. Individual differences in reaction time in relation to age. *Journal of Genetic Psychology*, 1968, **112**, 73–75.

Boulankin, I. N., & Parina, E. V. Changes in protein synthesis with age. In, *Physiology and biochemistry of aging*. Jerusalem: Israel Program for Scientific Translation, 1963.

Bourne, G. *Structural aspects of aging*. New York: Hafner, 1961.

Brandt, R. L. Increased prevalence of diminished carbohydrates tolerance in an aged population. In H. T. Blumenthal (Ed.), *Aging around the world*. Vol. 4. *Medical and clinical aspects of aging*. New York: Columbia University Press, 1962.

Braun, H. W. Perceptual processes. In J. E. Birren (Ed.), *Handbook of aging and the individual*. Chicago: University of Chicago Press, 1959.

Braun, H. W., & Geiselhart, R. Age differences in the acquisition and extinction of the conditioned eyelid response. *Journal of Experimental Psychology*, 1959, **57**, 386–388.

Brinley, J. F. Cognitive sets, speed and accuracy of performance in the elderly. In A. T. Welford & J. E. Birren (Eds.), *Behavior, aging, and the nervous system*. Springfield, Ill.: Charles C Thomas, 1965.

Brizzee, K. R., Cancilla, P. A. Sherwood, N., & Timeras, P. S. The amount and distribution of pigments in neurons and glia of the cerebral cortex, autofluorescent and ultrastructural studies. *Journal of Gerontology*, 1969, **24**, 127–135.

Broadbent, D. E., & Heron, A. Effects of a subsidiary task on performance involving immediate memory by younger and older men. *British Journal of Psychology*, 1962, **53**, 189–198.

Brock, M. A., & Strehler, B. L. Studies on the comparative physiology of aging: IV. Age and mortality of some marine cnidaria in the laboratory. *Journal of Gerontology*, 1963, **18**, 23–28.

Brody, H. Organization of the cerebral cortex: III. A study of aging in human cerebral cortex. *Journal of Comparative Neurology*, 1955, **102**, 511–556.

Brody, H. Structural changes in the aging nervous system. In H. T. Blumenthal (Ed.), *Interdisciplinary topics in gerontology*. Vol. 7, Basel, Switzerland: Karger, 1970.

Brooke, M. S. Immunological paralysis in mice exposed to sublethal irradiation or treated with 6-mercaptopurine. *Transplantation*, 1966, **4**, 1–7.

Brunner, D., & Jokl, E. (Eds.), *Physical activity and aging*. Baltimore: University Park Press, 1970.

Burnet, F. M. An immunological approach to ageing, *Lancet*, 1970, 358–360.

Busse, E. W. Psychopathology. In J. E. Birren (Ed.), *Handbook of aging and the individual*. Chicago: University of Chicago Press, 1959.

Busse, E. W. Summary. In H. T. Blumenthal (Ed.), *Interdisciplinary topics in gerontology*. Vol. 7, Basel, Switzerland: Karger, 1970.

Caird, W. W. Aging and short-term memory. *Journal of Gerontology*, 1966, **21**, 295–299.

Callaway, E. Response speed, the EEG alpha cycle, and the autonomic cardiovascular cycle. In A. T. Welford & J. E. Birren (Eds.), *Behavior, Aging, and the nervous system*. Springfield, Ill.: Charles C Thomas, 1965.

Cameron, D. E. The use of nucleic acid in aged patients with memory impairment. *American Journal of Psychiatry,* 1958, **114,** 943.

Cameron, D. E., Kral, V. A., Solyom, L., Sved, S., Wainrib, B., Beaulieu, C., & Enesco, H. RNA and memory. In J. Gaito (Ed.), *Macromolecules and behavior.* New York: Appleton-Century-Crofts, 1966.

Cameron, D. E., & Solyom, L. Effects of ribonucleic acid on memory. *Geriatrics,* 1961, **16,** 74–81.

Cameron, D. E., Solyom, L., & Beach, L. Further studies upon the effects of the administration of ribonucleic acid in the aged patients suffering from memory (retention) failure. *Neuropsychopharmacology,* 1963, **2,** 351–355.

Cameron, D. E., Solyom, L., Sved, S., & Wainrib, B. Effects of intravenous administration of ribonucleic acid upon failure of memory for recent events in presenile and aged individuals. In J. Wortis (Ed.), *Recent advances in biological psychiatry.* Vol. 5. New York: Plenum Press, 1963.

Cameron, D. E., Sved, S., Solyom, L., Wainrib, B., & Barick, H. Effects of ribonucleic acid on memory defect in the aged. *American Journal of Psychiatry,* 1963, **120,** 320–325.

Canestrari, R. E. Paced and self-paced learning in young and elderly adults. *Journal of Gerontology,* 1963, **18,** 165–168.

Canestrari, R. E. Age differences in spatial-stimulus generalization. *Journal of Genetic Psychology,* 1965, **106,** 129–135.

Canestrari, R. E. The effects of commonality of paired-associate learning in two age groups. *Journal of Genetic Psychology,* 1966, **108,** 3–7.

Canestrari, R. E. Research in learning. *Gerontologist,* 1967, **7,** 61–66.

Canestrari, R. E. Age changes in acquisition. In G. A. Talland (Ed.), *Human aging and behavior.* New York: Academic Press, 1968. (a)

Canestrari, R. E. Age differences in verbal learning and verbal behavior. In S. Chown & K. F. Riegel (Eds.), *Interdisciplinary topics in gerontology.* Vol. 1. Basel, Switzerland: Karger, 1968. (b)

Carlson, L. D., Scheyer, W. J., & Jackson, B. H. The combined effects of ionizing radiation and low temperature on the metabolism, longevity and soft tissues of the white rat: I. Metabolism and longevity. *Radiation Research,* 1957, **7,** 190–197.

Chapanis, A. Relationship between age, visual acuity, and color vision. *Human Biology,* 1950, **22,** 1–31.

Chinn, A. B., Lavik, R. S., & Cameron, D. B. Measurement of protein digestion and absorption in aged persons by a test meal of I131 labelled protein. *Journal of Gerontology,* 1956, **11,** 151–153.

Chio, K. S., Reiss, U., Fletcher, B., & Tappel, A. L. Peroxidation of subcellular organelles: Formation of lipofuscinlike fluorescent pigments. *Science,* 1969, **166,** 1535–1536.

Chlebovsky, O., Praslika, M., & Horak, J. Chromosome abberations: Increased incidence in bone marrow of continuously irridated rats. *Science,* 1966, **153,** 195–196.

Chomsky, N. *Aspects of the theory of syntax.* Cambridge, Mass.: MIT Press, 1965.

Chown, S., & Heron, A. Psychological aspects of aging in man. *Annual Review of Psychology,* 1965, **16,** 417–450.

Chown, S., & Riegel, K. F. Psychological functioning in the normal aging and senile aged. In S. Chown & K F. Riegel (Eds.), *Interdisciplinary topics in gerontology.* Vol. 1. Basel, Switzerland: Karger, 1968.

Clark, J. M., & Smith, M. J. Independence of temperature on the rate of aging in *Drosophila subobscura. Nature,* 1961, **190**, 1027–1028.

Clark, J. M., & Smith, M. J. Increase in the rate of protein synthesis with age in *Drosophila subobscura. Nature,* 1966, **209**, 627–629.

Cohen, B. H. Family patterns of mortality and lifespan. *Quarterly Review of Biology,* 1964, **39**, 130–181.

Cohen, L. D., & Axlerod, S. The performance of young and elderly persons on embedded figure tasks in two sensory modalities. Paper presented at the 5th International Congress of Gerontology, San Francisco, 1960.

Comalli, P. E., Jr. Cognitive functioning in a group of 80–90 year old men. *Journal of Gerontology,* 1965, **20**, 14–17.

Comalli, P. E., Jr. Perception and age. *Gerontologist,* 1967, **7**, 73–78.

Comalli, P. E., Jr. Life-span changes in visual perception. In L. P. Goulet & P. B. Baltes (Eds.), *Life-span developmental psychology: Research and theory.* New York: Academic Press, 1970.

Comalli, P. E., Jr., Wapner, S., & Werner, H. Perceptual verticality in middle and old age. *Journal of Psychology,* 1959, **41**, 259–266.

Comfort, A. The effect of age on growth-resumption in fish *(Lebistes)* checked by food restriction. *Gerontologia,* 1960, **4**, 177–186.

Comfort, A. Effect of delayed and resumed growth on the longevity of a fish *(Lebistes reticulatus,* Peters) in captivity. *Gerontologia,* 1963, **8**, 150–155.

Comfort, A. The prevention of aging in cells. *Lancet,* 1966, **2**, 1325–1329.

Comfort, A. Physiology, homeostasis, and aging. *Gerontologia,* 1970, **14**, 224–234.

Corsellis, J. A. *Mental illness and the aging brain.* London: Oxford University Press, 1962.

Corso, J. F. Sensory processes and age effects in normal adults. *Journal of Gerontology,* 1971, **26**, 90–105.

Court-Brown, W. M., Buckton, K. E., Jacobs, P. A., Tough, I. M., Kuenssberg, E. V., & Knox, J. D. E. *Chromosome studies on adults.* London: Cambridge University Press, 1966.

Craik, F. I. M. Short-term memory and the aging process. In G. A. Talland (Ed.), *Human aging and behavior.* New York: Academic Press, 1968.

Cristofalo, V. J. Animal cell cultures as a model system for the study of aging. In B. L. Strehler (Ed.), *Advances in gerontological research.* Vol. 4. New York: Academic Press, 1972.

Critchley, M. Neurologic changes in the aged. *Journal of Chronic Diseases,* 1956, **3**, 459–477.

Crovitz, E. Reversing a learning deficit in the aged. *Journal of Gerontology,* 1966, **21**, 236–238.

Curtis, H. J., & Tilley, J. The life-span of dividing mammalian cells in vivo. *Journal of Gerontology,* 1971, **26**, 1–7.

Dalderup, L. M., Van Haard, W. B., Keller, G. H., Dalmeijer, J. F., Frijda, N. H., Elshout, J. J. An attempt to change memory and serum composition in old people by a daily supplement of dried Baker's yeast. *Journal of Gerontology,* 1970, **4**, 320–324.

Dalton, M. N., Homes, O. R., & Leblond, C. P. Correlation of glial proliferation with age in mouse brain. *Journal of Comparative Neurology,* 1968, **134**, 397–399.

Das, B. C., & Bhattacharya, S. K. Changes in human serum protein fractions with age and weight. *Canadian Journal of Biochemistry and Physiology,* 1961, **39,** 569–579.

Dastur, D. K., Lane, M. H., Hansen, D. B., Kety, S., Perlin, S., Butler, R. N., & Sokoloff, L. Effects of aging on cerebral circulation and metabolism in man. In J. E. Birren, R. N. Butler, S. W. Greenhouse, L. Sokoloff, & M. R. Yarrow (Eds.), *Human aging.* (USPHS No. 986) Washington, D.C.: United States Public Health Service, 1963.

Davis, P. A. The electroencephalogram in old age. *Diseases of the Nervous System,* 1941, **2,** 77.

Dayan, A. D. Quantitive histological studies on the aged human brain: I. Senile plaques and neurofibrillary tangles in "normal" patients. *Acta Neuropathologia,* 1970, **16,** 85–94. (a)

Dayan, A. D. Quantitive histological studies on the aged human brain. II. Senile plaques and neurofiriallary tangles in senile dementia. *Acta Neuropathologia,* 1970, **16,** 95–102. (b)

Dayan, A. D. Comparative neuropathology of aging—Studies on the brains of 47 species of vertebrate. *Brain,* 1971, **94,** 31–42.

DeDuve, C., & Wattiaux, R. Functions of lysosomes. *Annual Review of Physiology,* 1966, **28,** 435–492.

DeVries, H. A. Physiology of exercise and aging: Issues and concepts. Unpublished manuscript, University of Southern California, 1968.

Deyl, Z. Macromolecular aspects of aging. *Experimental Gerontology,* 1968, **3,** 91–112.

Doppelt, J. E., & Wallace, W. L. Standardization of the Wechsler Adult Intelligence Scale for older persons. *Journal of Abnormal and Social Psychology,* 1955, **51,** 312–330.

Doty, B. A. Age and avoidance conditioning in rats. *Journal of Gerontology,* 1966, **21,** 287–290.

Doty, B. A., & Doty, L. A. Effects of age and chlorpromazine on memory consolidation. *Journal of Comparative and Physiological Psychology,* 1964, **57,** 331–334.

Dustman, R. E., & Beck, E. C. The effects of maturation and aging on the wave form of visually evoked potentials. *Electroencephalography and Clinical Neurophysiology,* 1969, **26,** 2–11.

Eichorn, D. H. The Institute of Human Development studies. In L. F. Jarvik, C. Eisdorfer, & J. E. Blum (Eds.), *Intellectual functioning in adults: Some psychological and biological influences.* New York: Springer, in press.

Eisdorfer, C. The WAIS performance of the aged: A retest evaluation. *Journal of Gerontology,* 1963, **18,** 169–172.

Eisdorfer, C. Verbal learning and response time in the aged. *Journal of Genetic Psychology,* 1965, **107,** 15–22.

Eisdorfer, C. New dimensions and a tentative theory. *Gerontologist,* 1967, **7,** 14–18.

Eisdorfer, C. Arousal and performance: Verbal learning. In G. A. Talland (Ed.), *Human aging and behavior.* New York: Academic Press, 1968. (a)

Eisdorfer, C. Intellectual changes with advancing age: A 10-year follow-up of the Duke sample. Paper presented at the symposium on Longitudinal Changes with Advancing Age, American Psychological Association, San Francisco, September 1968. (b)

Eisdorfer, C. Intellectual and cognitive change in the aged. In E. W. Busse, & E. Pfeiffer (Eds.), *Behavior and adaptation in late life*. Boston: Little, Brown, 1969.

Eisdorfer, C. Autonomic changes in behavior. In C. Gaitz (Ed.), *Aging and the brain*. New York: Plenum, 1972.

Eisdorfer, C., Axelrod, S. Senescence and figural after effects in two modalities: A correction. *Journal of Genetic Psychology*, 1964, **104**, 193–197.

Eisdorfer, C., Axelrod, S., & Wilkie, F. Stimulus exposure time as a factor in serial learning in an aged sample. *Journal of Abnormal and Social Psychology*, 1963, **67**, 594–600.

Eisdorfer, C., Busse, E. S., & Cohen, L. D. The WAIS performance of an aged sample: The relationship between verbal and performance IQ's. *Journal of Gerontology*, 1959, **14**, 197–201.

Eisdorfer, C., Conner, J. F., & Wilkie, F. The effect of magnesium pemoline on cognition and behavior. *Journal of Gerontology*, 1968, 283–288.

Eisdorfer, C., Nowlin, J., & Wilkie, F. Improvement of learning in the aged by modification of autonomic nervous system activity. *Science*, 1970, **170**, 1327–1329.

Eisner, D., & Schaie, K. W. Age changes in response to visual illusions from middle to old age. *Journal of Gerontology*, 1971, **26**, 146–150.

Elens, A., & Wattiaux, R. Age correlated changes in lysosomal enzyme activities: An index of aging? *Experimental Gerontology*, 1969, **4**, 131–135.

Epstein, M. H., & Barrows, C. H., Jr. The effects of age on the activity of glutamic acid decarboxylase in various regions of the brains of rats. *Journal of Gerontology*, 1969, **24**, 136–139.

Erlenmeyer-Kimling, L., & Jarvik, L. F. Genetics and intelligence: A review. *Science*, 1963, **142**, 1477-1479.

Evans, R. B. Age and simple reaction time: A longitudinal study over 50 years. *Dissertation Abstracts*, 1967, **28**(Pt. B), 2156-2157.

Everitt, A. V. The effect of pituitary growth hormone on the aging male rat. *Journal of Gerontology*, 1959, **14**, 415–424. (a)

Everitt, A. V. The effect of prolonged thyroxine treatment on the aging male rat. *Gerontologia*, 1959, **3**, 37–54. (b)

Fanestil, D. D., & Barrows, C. H., Jr. Effect of nutrition on longevity and enzyme content of rotifers. *Federation Proceedings*, 1964, **23**, 503.

Fanestil, D. D., & Barrows, C. H., Jr. Aging the rotifer. *Journal of Gerontology*, 1965, **20**, 462–469.

Feifel, H. Judgment of time in younger and older persons. *Journal of Gerontology*, 1957, **12**, 71–74.

Feinberg, I. Aging, brain plasticity, and sleep. Paper presented at the 8th International Congress of Gerontology, Washington, D.C., 1969.

Feinberg, I., & Carlson, V. R. Sleep variables as a function of age in man. *Archives of General Psychiatry*, 1968, **18**, 239–250.

Feinberg, I., Koresko, H. L., & Heller, N. EEG sleep patterns as a function of normal and pathological aging in man. *Journal of Psychiatric Research*, 1967, **5**, 107–144.

Feinberg, I., Koresko, H. L., & Schaffner, I. R. Sleep electroencephalographic and eye movement patterns in patients with chronic brain syndrome. *Journal of Psychiatric Research*, 1965, **3**, 11–26.

Feingold, L. A psychometric study of senescent twins. Unpublished doctoral dissertation, Columbia University, 1950.

Finch, C. E., Foster, J. R., & Mirsky, A. E. Aging and the regulations of cell activities during exposure to cold. *Journal of General Physiology*, 1969, **54**, 690–712.

Flavell, J. H. Cognitive changes in adulthood. In L. R. Goulet & P. B. Baltes (Eds.), *Life-span developmental psychology*. New York: Academic Press, 1970.

Franks, L. M. Cellular aspects of aging. *Experimental Gerontology*, 1970, **4**, 281–290.

Fraser, D. C. Decay of immediate memory with age. *Nature*, 1958, **182**, 1163.

Friedlander, W. J. Electroencephalographic alpha rate in adults as a function of age. *Geriatrics*, 1958, **13**, 29–31.

Friedman, S. M., & Friedman, C. L. Prolonged treatment with posterior pituitary powder in aged rats. *Experimental Gerontology*, 1964, **1**, 37–48.

Frolkis, V. V. Neuro-humoral regulations in the aging organism. *Journal of Gerontology*, 1966, **21**, 161–167.

Frolkis, V. V. Regulatory process in the mechanism of aging: Introductory lecture: Verbatim report. *Experimental Gerontology*, 1968, **3**, 113–123.

Gaito, J. *Molecular biology*. Springfield, Ill.: Charles C Thomas, 1966.

Galton, F. *Inquiries into human faculty and its development*. New York: Macmillan, 1883.

Gardner, E. D. Decrease in human neurons with age. *Anatomical Record*, 1940, **77**, 529–436.

Gilbert, J. C., & Levee, R. F. Patterns of declining memory. *Journal of Gerontology*, 1971, **26**, 70–75.

Gilbert, J. G. Memory loss in senescence. *Journal of Abnormal and Social Psychology*, 1941, **36**, 73–86.

Glass, B. Genetics of aging. In N. Shock (Ed.), *Aging: Some social and biological aspects*. (No. 65) Washington, D.C.: American Association for the Advancement of Science, 1960.

Goerttler, K., Haag, D., & Tschahargone, C. Differences with age in nucleic acid content of cell nuclei in human skin. In, *Die Naturwissenschaften*. Berlin, W. Germany: Springer-Verlag, 1970.

Goldfarb, A. I. Predicting mortality in the institutionalized aged: A seven-year follow-up. *Archives of General Psychiatry*, 1969, **21**, 172–176.

Goldfarb, A. I., Hochstadt, N., Jacobson, J. H., & Weinstein, E. Hyperbaric O_2 treatment of organic mental syndrome in aged persons. Paper presented at the 23rd annual meeting of the Gerontological Society, Toronto, 1970.

Goldman, R. Decline in organ functioning with aging. In I. Rossman (Ed.), *Clinical geriatrics*. New York: Lippincott, 1970.

Goodman, R. M., Fechheimer, N. S., Miller, F., & Zartman, D. Chromosomal alterations in three age groups of human females. *American Journal of Medical Science*, 1969, **258**, 26–31.

Gordon, P. Molecular approaches to the drug enhancement of deteriorated functioning in the aged. In B. L. Strehler (Ed.), *Advances in gerontological research*. Vol. 3. New York: Academic Press, 1971.

Goulet, L. R., & Baltes, P. B. (Eds.), *Life-span developmental psychology: Research and theory*. New York: Academic Press, 1970.

Grad, B., & Kral, V. The effect of senescence on resistance to stress: Response of young and old mice to cold. *Journal of Gerontology*, 1957, **12**, 172–181.

Graham, F. K., & Kendall, B. S. Memory-for-Designs Test: Revised general manual. *Perceptual and Motor Skills,* 1960, **11,** 147–188.

Granick, S., & Birren, J. E. Cognitive functioning of survivors vs. non-survivors: 12-year follow-up of healthy aged. Paper presented at the 8th International Congress of Gerontology, Washington, D.C., 1969.

Granick, S., & Friedman, A. S. The effect of education on the decline of psychometric performance with age. *Journal of Gerontology,* 1967, **22,** 191–195.

Gregory, J. G., & Barrows, C. H. The effect of age on renal functions of female rats. *Journal of Gerontology,* 1969, **24,** 321–323.

Grinker, R. R., & Bucy, P. C. *Neurology.* Springfield, Ill.: Charles C Thomas, 1969.

Guilford, J. P. Intellectual aspects of decision making. In A. T. Welford, & J. E. Birren (Eds.), *Interdisciplinary topics in gerontology.* Vol. 4. Basel, Switzerland: Karger, 1969.

Gutmann, E. Nervous and hormonal mechanisms in the aging process. *Experimental Gerontology,* 1970, **5,** 357–366.

Haferkamp, O., Schlettwein-Gsell, D., Schwick, H. G., & Storiko, K. Serum protein in an aging population with particular referenec to elevation of immune globulins and antibodies. *Gerontologia,* 1966, **12,** 30–38.

Hall, D. A. Connective tissue metabolism. Paper presented at the 8th International Congress of Gerontology, Washington, D.C., 1969.

Hamerton, J. L., Taylor, A. I., Angell, R., & McGuire, V. M. Chromosome investigations of a small isolated human population: Chromosome abnormalities and distribution of chromosome counts according to age and sex among the population Tristan Da Cunna. *Nature,* 1965, **206,** 1232–1234.

Harmon, D. Aging: A theory based on free radical and radiation chemistry. *Journal of Gerontology,* 1956, **11,** 298–300.

Harmon, D. Prolongation of the normal life span by radiation protection chemicals. *Journal of Gerontology,* 1957, **12,** 257–263.

Harmon, D. Prolongation of the normal life span and inhibition of spontaneous cancer by antioxidants. *Journal of Gerontology,* 1961, **16,** 247–254.

Harmon, D. Free radical theory of aging: Effect of free radical reaction inhibitors on the mortality rate of male LAF mice. *Journal of Gerontology,* 1968, **23,** 476–482.

Hay, R. J. Cell and tissue culture in aging research. In B. L. Strehler (Ed.), *Advances in gerontological research.* Vol. 2. New York: Academic Press, 1967.

Hayflick, L. The limited in vitro lifetime of human diploid cell strains. *Experimental Cell Research,* 1965, **37,** 614–636.

Hayflick, L. Human cells and aging. *Scientific American,* 1968, **218,** 32–37.

Hayflick, L. Aging under glass. *Experimental Gerontology,* 1970, **5,** 291–304.

Hayflick, L., & Moorehead, P. S. The serial cultivation of human diploid cell strains. *Experimental Cell Research,* 1961, **25,** 585–621.

Heilbrunn, L. V. Colloidal changes in aging cells. *Journal of Gerontology,* 1958, **13**(Suppl. No. 2), 2–6.

Henry, J. P., & Cassel, J. C. Psychosocial factors in essential hypertension: Recent epidemiologic and animal experimental evidence. *American Journal of Epidemiology,* 1969, **90,** 171–200.

Henry, J. P., Meehan, J. P., & Stephens, P. M. The use of psychosocial stimuli to induce prolonged hypertension in mice. *Psychosomatic Medicine,* 1967, **29,** 408–432.

Himwich, H. E., & Himwich, W. A. Brain metabolism in relation to aging. *Journal of Chronic Diseases,* 1956, **3,** 487–498.

Himwich, W. A. Neurochemistry of aging. *Postgraduate Medicine,* 1962, **31,** 195.

Himwich, W. A., & Himwich, H. E. Neurochemistry of aging. In J. E. Birren (Ed.), *Handbook of aging and the individual.* Chicago: University of Chicago Press, 1959.

Holeckova, E., & Cristofalo, V. J. *Aging in cell and tissue culture.* New York: Plenum Press, 1970.

Hollander, J., & Barrows, C. H., Jr. Enzymatic studies in senescent rodent brains. *Journal of Gerontology,* 1968, **23,** 174–179.

Honzik, M. P., & Macfarlane, J. W. Personality development and intellectual functioning from 21 months to 40 years. In L. F. Jarvik, C. Eisdorfer, & J. E. Blum (Eds.), *Intellectual functioning in adults: Some psychological and biological influences.* New York: Springer, in press .

Horn, J. L., & Cattell, R. B. Age differences in primary mental ability factors. *Journal of Gerontology,* 1966, **21,** 210.

Horridge, G. A. *Interneurons.* San Francisco: W. H. Freeman Press, 1968.

Hoyer, H. F., Labouvie, T. V., & Baltes, P. B. Operant modification of age decrements in intellectual performance. Symposium on Intellectual Development in Adulthood and Old Age, American Psychological Association, Washington, D.C., September 1971.

Hrachovec, J. P. Age changes in amino acid incorporation by rat liver microsomes. *Gerontologia,* 1969, **15,** 52–63.

Hrůza, A. Changes in lipid metabolism with aging. *Symposia of the Society for Experimental Biology,* 1967, **21,** 375–402.

Huemer, R. P., Bickert, C., Lee, K. D., & Reeves, A. E. Mitochondrial studies in senescent mice: I. Turnover of brain mitochondrial lipids. *Experimental Gerontology,* 1970, **6,** 259–265.

Hugin, F., Norris, A. H., & Shock, N. W. Skin reflex and voluntary reaction time in young and old males. *Journal of Gerontology,* 1960, **15,** 388–391.

Hulicka, I. M. Age differences for intentional and incidental learning and recall. *Journal of the American Geriatrics Society,* 1965, **13,** 639–649.

Hulicka, I. M. Age changes and age differences in memory functioning. *Gerontologist,* 1967, **7,** 46–54. (a)

Hulicka, I. M. Age differences in retention as a function of interference. *Journal of Gerontology,* 1967, **22,** 180–184. (b)

Hulicka, I. M., & Grossman, J. L. Age-group comparisons for the use of mediators in paired-associate learning. *Journal of Gerontology,* 1967. **22,** 46–51.

Hulicka, I. M. & Weiss, R. L. Age differences in retention as a function of learning. *Journal of Consulting Psychology,* 1965, **29,** 125–129.

Inglis, J. Immediate memory, age and brain function. In A. T. Welford & J. E. Birren (Eds.), *Behavior, aging and the nervous system.* Springfield, Ill.: Charles C Thomas, 1965.

Inglis, J. Memory disorder. In C. G. Costello (Ed.), *Symptoms of psychopathology.* New York: Wiley, 1970.

Inglis, J., & Ankus, M. Effects of age on short-term storage and serial rote learning. *British Journal of Psychology*, 1965, **56**, 183–195.

Inglis, J., & Caird, W. K. Age differences in successive response to simultaneous stimulation. *Canadian Journal of Psychology*, 1963, **17**, 98–105.

Inglis, J., Sykes, D. H., & Ankus, M. Age differences in short-term memory. In M. F. Lowenthal & A. Zilli (Eds.), *Interdisciplinary topics in gerontology*. Vol. 3. Basel, Switzerland: Karger, 1968.

Jacobs, E. A., Small, S. M., & Alvis, H. A. Effect of hyperbaric oxygen on cognition in aged males. Paper presented at the 23rd annual meeting of the Gerontological Society, Toronto, 1970.

Jacobs, P. A., Brunton, M., & Brown, W. M. C. Cytogenetic studies in leucocytes on the general population: Subjects of ages 65 years and more. *Annals of Human Genetics*, 1964, **27**, 353–362.

Jacobs, P. A., Brunton, M., Brown, W. M. C., Doll, R., & Goldstein, H. Changes of human chromosomes count distribution with age: Evidence for a sex difference. *Nature*, 1963, **197**, 1080–1081.

Jacobs, P. A., Court-Brown, W. M., & Doll, A. Distribution of human chromosome count in relation to age. *Nature*, 1961, **191**, 1178–1180.

Jakubczak, L. F. Psychophysiological aging. *Geronologist*, 1967, **7**, 67–72.

Jalavisto, E. On the interdependence of circulatory-respiratory and neuralmental variables. *Gerontologia*, 1965, **10**, 31–37.

Jarvik, L. F. Senescence and chromosomal changes. *Lancet*, 1963, **1**, 114–115.

Jarvik, L. F. Chromosome changes and aging. In R. Kastenbaum (Ed.), *Contributions to the psychology of aging*. New York: Springer, 1965.

Jarvik, L. F. Genetics and aging. In I. Rossman (Ed.), *Clinical geriatrics*. New York: Lippincott, 1970.

Jarvik, L. F. Genetics and aging. In I. Rossman (Ed.), *Clinical geriatrics*. New York: Lippincott, 1970.

Jarvik, L. F., Altschuler, K. Z., Kato, T., & Blumner, B. Organic brain syndrome and chromosome loss in aged twins. *Diseases of the Nervous System*, 1971, **32**, 159–170.

Jarvik, L. F., & Blum, J. E. Cognitive declines as predictors of mortality in twin pairs: A twenty-year longitudinal study of aging. In, E. Palamore & F. Jeffers (Ed.), *Prediction of lifespan*. Lexington, Mass.: Heath, 1971.

Jarvik, L. F., Eisdorfer, C., & Blum, J. E. (Eds.), *Intellectual functioning in adults: Some psychological and biological influences*. New York: Springer, in press.

Jarvik, L. F., & Falek, A. Intellectual stability and survival in the aged. *Journal of Gerontology*, 1963, **18**, 173–176.

Jarvik, L. F., Falek, A., Kallmann, F. J. & Lorge, I. Survival trends in a senescent twin population. *American Journal of Human Genetics*, 1960, **12**, 170–179.

Jarvik, L. F., Kallmann, F., & Falek, A. Intellectual changes in aged twins. *Journal of Gerontology*, 1962, **17**, 289–294.

Jarvik, L. F., Kallmann, F. J., Falek, A., & Klaber, M. Changing intellectual functions in senescent twins. *Acta Genetica et Statistica Medica*, 1957, **7**, 421–430.

Jarvik, L. F., & Kato, T. Chromosomes and mental changes in octogenarians. *British Journal of Psychiatry*, 1969, **115**, 1193–1194.

Jarvik, L. F., & Kato, T. Chromosome examinations in aged twins. *American Journal of Human Genetics*, 1970, **22**, 562–573.

Jarvik, M. E. Effects of chemical and physical treatments on learning and memory. *Annual Review of Psychology*, in press.

Jarvik, M. E., Gritz, E., & Schneider, N. Drugs and memory disorders of the aged. *Communications in Behavioral Biology*, in press.

Jeans, J. *Physics and philosophy*. Ann Arbor, University of Michigan Press, 1966.

Jerome, E. A. Age and learning—experimental studies. In J. E. Birren (Ed.), *Handbook of aging and the individual*. Chicago: University of Chicago Press, 1959.

Jones, D. C. L., & Kimeldorf, D. J. Effect of age at irradiation on life span in the male rat. *Radiation Research*, 1964, **22**, 106–115.

Jones, H. E. Intelligence and problem-solving. In J. E. Birren (Ed.), *Handbook of aging and the individual*. Chicago: University of Chicago Press, 1959.

Jones, H. E., & Conrad, H. S. The growth and decline of intelligence: A study of a homogenous population between the ages of ten and sixty. *Genetic Psychology Monographs*, 1933, **13**, 233–298.

Joseph, N. R. *Physical chemistry of aging*. In N. R. Joseph (Ed.), *Interdisciplinary topics in gerontology*. Vol. 8. Basel, Switzerland: Karger, 1971.

Kales, A., Wilson, T., Kales, J. D., Jacobson, A., Paulson, M. J., Kollar, E., & Walter, R. D. Measurements of all-night sleep in normal elderly persons: Effects of aging. *Journal of the American Geriatrics Society*, 1967, **15**, 404–414.

Kallmann, F. J. *Heredity in health and mental disorders*. New York: Norton, 1953.

Kallmann, F. J. Genetic factors in aging: Comparative and longitudinal observations on a senescent twin population. In P. H. Hoch, & J. Zubin (Eds.), *Psychopathology of aging*. New York: Grune & Stratton, 1961.

Kallmann, F. J., & Jarvik, L. F. Individual differences in constitution and genetic background. In J. E. Birren (Ed.), *Handbook of aging and the individual*. Chicago: University of Chicago Press, 1959.

Kay, H. Learning and retraining verbal material. *British Journal of Psychology*, 1955, **46**, 81–100.

Kay H. Theories of learning and aging. In J. E. Birren (Ed.), *Handbook of aging and the individual*. Chicago: University of Chicago Press, 1959.

Kimble, G. A., & Pennypacker, H. W. Eyelid conditioning in young and aged subjects. *Journal of Genetic Psychology*, 1963, **103**, 283–289.

Kipshidze, N. N., & Tkeshelashvile, L. K. Characteristics of some enzyme activity in blood serum at different ages. Paper presented at the 7th International Congress of Gerontology, Vienna, 1966.

Kirk, J. E. The adenylpyrophosphatase, inorganic pyrophosphatase and phosphomonoesterase activities of human arterial tissue in individuals of various ages. *Journal of Gerontology*, 1959, **14**, 181–188. (a)

Kirk, J. E. The 5-nucleotidase activity of human arterial tissue in individuals of various ages. *Journal of Gerontology*, 1959, **14**, 288–291. (b)

Kirk, J. E. The ribose-5-phosphate isomerase activity of arterial tissue in individuals of various ages. *Journal of Gerontology*, 1959, **14**, 447–449.

Kirk, J. E. The glyoxylase-1 activity of arterial tissue in individuals of various ages. *Journal of Gerontology*, 1960, **15**, 158–162. (a)

Kirk, J. E. The isocitric dehydrogenase and TPN-malic enzyme activities of arterial tissue in individuals of various ages. *Journal of Gerontology*, 1960, **15**, 262–266. (b)

Kirk, J. E. The leucine aminopeptidase activity of arterial tissue in individuals of various ages. *Journal of Gerontology*, 1960, **15**, 136–141. (c)

Kirk, J. E. The aconitase activity of arterial tissue in individuals of various ages. *Journal of Gerontology*, 1961, **16**, 25–28. (a)

Kirk, J. E. The purine nucleoside phosphorylase activity of arterial tissue in individuals of various ages. *Journal of Gerontology*, 1961, **16**, 243–246. (b)

Kirk, J. E. The cathepsin activity of arterial tissue in individuals of various ages. *Journal of Gerontology*, 1962, **17**, 158–162. (a)

Kirk, J. E. The diaphorase and cytochrome C reductase activities of arterial tissue in individuals of various ages. *Journal of Gerontology*, 1962, **17**, 276–280. (b)

Kirk, J. E. The glycogen phosphorylase activity of arterial tissue in individuals of various ages. *Journal of Gerontology*, 1962, **17**, 154–157. (c)

Kirk, J. E. Variation with age in the creatine phosphokinase activity of human aortic tissue. *Journal of Gerontology*, 1962, **17**, 369–372. (d)

Kirk, J. E. The glutamic dehydrogenase and glutathione reductase activities of arterial tissue in individuals of various ages. *Journal of Gerontology*, 1965, **20**, 357–362.

Kirk, J. E. The phosphoglucomutase, phosphoglyceric acid mutase and phosphomannose isomerase activities of arterial tissue of various ages. *Journal of Gerontology*, 1966, **21**, 420–525.

Kirk, J. E., & Dyrbye, M. Hexosamine and acid hydrolyzable sulphate concentrations of the aorta and pulmonary artery in individuals of various ages. *Journal of Gerontology*, 1956, **11**, 273–281. (a)

Kirk, J. E., & Dyrbye, M. The betaglucuronidase acitivity of aortic and pulmonary artery tissue in individuals of various ages. *Journal of Gerontology*, 1956, **11**, 33–37. (b)

Kirk, J. E., & Laursen, T. J. S. Changes with age in diffusion coefficients of solutes for human tissue membranes. In G. E. W. Wolstenholme & M. P. Cameron (Eds.), *CIBA Foundation colloquia on aging*. Vol. 2. *Ageing in transient tissues*. Boston: Little, Brown, 1955.

Kirk, J. E., & Ritz, E. The glyceraldehyder-3-phosphate and a glycerophosphate dehydrogenase activities of arterial tissue in individuals of various ages. *Journal of Gerontology*, 1967, **22**, 427–438.

Kirk, J. E., & Sorensen, L. B. The aldolase activity of aortic and pulmonary artery tissue in individuals of various ages. *Journal of Gerontology*, 1956, **11**, 373–378.

Kirk, J. E., Wang M. S., & Brandstrup, N. The glucose-6-phosphate and 6-phospho-gluconate dehydrogenase activities of arterial tissue in individuals of various ages. *Journal of Gerontology*, 1959, **14**, 25–31.

Kleemeier, R. W. Intellectual changes in the senium or in death and the I.Q. Presidential Address, Division of Maturity and Old Age, presented at the annual meeting of the American Psychological Association, New York: September 1961.

Kline, D. W. Age differences in backward monoptic masking. Paper presented at Gerontological Society Meetings, Toronto, 1970.

Koga, Y., & Morant, G. M. On the degree of association between reaction times in the case of different senses. *Biometrika*, 1923, **15**, 346–372.

Korchin, S. J., & Basowitz, H. Age differences in verbal learning. *Journal of Abnormal and Social Psychology*, 1957, **54**, 64–69.

Korenchevsky, V. *Physiological and pathological aging.* New York: Hafner, 1961.

Krech, D., Rosenzweig, M. R., & Bennett, E. L. Relations between brain chemistry and problem-solving among rats raised in enriched and impoverished environments. *Journal of Comparative and Physiological Psychology*, 1962, **55**, 801–807.

Krech, D., Rosenzweig, M. R., & Bennett, E. L. Environmental impoverishment, social isolation, and changes in brain chemistry and anatomy. *Physiology and Behavior*, 1966, **1**, 99–104.

Krohn, P. L. *Topics in biology of aging.* New York: Wiley, 1966.

LaBella, F. Pharmacological retardation of aging. *Gerontologist*, 1966. **6**, 46–50.

LaBella, F., & Paul G. Structure of collagen from human tendons as influenced by age and sex. *Journal of Gerontology*, 1965, **20**, 54–59.

Lajtha, A. (Ed.), *Protein metabolism of the nervous system.* New York: Plenum, 1970.

Lamb, M. J., & Smith, J. M. Radiation and aging in insects. *Experimental Gerontology*, 1964, **1**, 11–20.

Landowne, M. Characteristics of impact and pulse wave propagation in brachial and radial arteries. *Journal of Applied Physiology*, 1958, **12**, 91–97.

Landowne, M., & Stanley, J. Aging of the cardiovascular system. In N. W. Shock (Ed.), *Aging: Some social and biological aspects.* (No. 65) Washington, D.C.: American Association for the Advancement of Science, 1960.

Larsson, T., Sjogren, T., & Jacobson, G. *Senile dementia.* Copenhagen: Munksgaard, 1963.

Leith, J. D., Jr. On steroid hormones, cellular aging and cell nuclei. **Gerontologist**, 1967, **7**, 244–246.

Leto, S., Kokkoman, G. C., & Barrows, C. H., Jr. Age changes in various biochemical measurements of C_{57} BL/6V female mice. *Journal of Gerontology*, 1970, **26**, 24–27.

Lieberman, M. A. Psychological correlates of impending death. *Journal of Gerontology*, 1965, **20**, 181–190.

Liu, R. K., & Walford, R. L. Increased growth and life span with lowered ambient temperature in the annual fish, *Cynolebias adloffi. Nature*, 1966, **212**, 1277–1278.

Looft, W. R. Note on WAIS Vocabulary performance by young and adults. *Psychological Reports*, 1970, **20**, 943–946.

Lorenz, E., Jacobson, L. O., Heston, W. E., Shimkin, M., Eschenbrenner, A. B., Deringer, M. K., Doniger, J., & Schweisthal, R. Effects of long-continued total-body gamma irradiation on mice, guinea pigs, and rabbits: III. Effects on life span, weight, blood picture, and carcinogenesis and the role of the intensity of radiation. In R. E. Zirkle (Ed.), *Biological effects of external X and gamma radiation.* New York: McGraw-Hill, 1954.

Lorge, I. Learning, motivation and education. In J. E. Anderson (Ed.), *Psychological aspects of aging.* Washington, D.C.: American Psychological Association, 1956.

Ludere, H. The effects of aging on the wave form of the somatosensory cortical EP. *Electroencephalography and Clinical Neurophysiology*, 1970, **29**, 450–460.

Luse, S. A., & Smith, K. R. The ultrastructure of senile plaques. *American Journal of Pathology*, 1964, **44**, 553–563.

MacArthur, J. W., & Baillie, W. H. T. Metabolic activity and duration of life: I. Influence of temperature on longivity in *Daphnia magna*. *Journal of Experimental Zoology*, 1929, **53**, 221–242.

Mackay, H. A., & Inglis, J. The effect of age on a short-term auditory storage process. *Gerontologia*, 1963, **8**, 193–200.

Magladery, J. W. Neurophysiology of aging. In J. E. Birren (Ed.), *Handbook of aging and the individual*. Chicago: University of Chicago Press, 1959.

Makinodan, T., Perkins, E. H., & Chen, M. Immunologic activity of the aged. In B. L. Strehler (Ed.), *Advances in gerontological research*. Vol. 3. New York: Academic Press, 1971.

Malamud, N. A comparative study of the neuropathologic findings in senile psychoses and in normal elderly. *Journal of the American Geriatrics Society*, 1965, **13**, 113–117.

Mayer-Gross, W., Slater, W., & Roth, M. *Clinical psychiatry*. London: Cassell, 1965.

McCay, C. M. Chemical aspects of aging and the effects of diet upon aging. In A. I. Lansing (Ed.), *Cowdry's problems of aging*. Baltimore: Williams & Wilkins, 1952.

McCay, C. M., Dilley, W. E., & Crowell, M. F. Growth rates of brook trout reared upon combinations of cereal grains. *Journal of Nutrition*, 1929, **1**, 233–246.

McGeer, P. L. The chemistry of mind. *American Scientist*, 1971, **59**, 221–229.

McGeer, P. L., & McGeer, E. G. Cholinergic enzyme systems in Parkinson's disease. *Archives of Neurology*, 1971, **25**, 265–268.

McGhie, A., Chapman, J., & Lawson, J. S. Changes in immediate memory with age. *British Journal of Psychology*, 1965, **56**, 69–75.

Medvedev, Z. A. Molecular aspects of aging. *Symposia of the Society for Experimental Biology*, 1967, **21**, 1–28.

Miles, C. C., & Miles, W. R. The correlation of intelligence scores and chronological age from early to late maturity. *American Journal of Psychology*, 1932, **44**, 44–78.

Miller, J. H., & Shock, N. W. Age differences in renal tubular response to antidiuretic hormone. *Journal of Gerontology*, 1953, **8**, 446–450.

Misiak, H. Age and sex differences in critical flicker frequency. *Journal of Experimental Psychology*, 1947, **37**, 318–332.

Monagle, R. D., & Brody, H. A Study of the lipofuscin deposition pattern in three human brain stem nuclei. *Gerontologist*, 1968, **8**, 19.

Monge, R. H., & Hultsch, D. F. Paired-associate learning as a function of adult age and the length of the anticipation and inspection intervals. *Journal of Gerontology*, 1971, **26**, 157–162.

Müller, C. H., Ciompi, L. *Senile dementia*. Stuttgart: Hans Huber, 1968.

Mundy-Castle, A. C., Hurst, L. A., Beerstecher, D. M., & Prinsloo, T. The electroencephalogram in the senile psychosis. *Electroencephalography and Clinical Neurophysiology*, 1954, **6**, 245–252.

Nehrke, M. F., & Coppinger, N. W. The effect of task dimensionality on discriminative learning and transfer of training in the aged. *Journal of Gerontology*, 1971, **26**, 151–156.

Nesselroade, J. R., Baltes, P. B., & Labouvie, E. W. Evaluating factor invariance in oblique space: Baseline data generated from random numbers. *Multivariate Behavioral Research*, 1971, **6**, 233–241.

Nesselroade, J. R., Schaie, K. W., & Baltes, P. B. Ontogenetic generational components of structural and quantitative change in adult cognitive behavior, *Developmental Psychology*, in press.

Neurath, P., DeRemer, K., Bell, B., Jarvik, L. F., & Kato, T. Chromosome loss compared with chromosome size, age, and sex of subjects. *Nature*, 1970, **225**, 281–232.

Nielsen, J. Chromosomes in senile dementia. *British Journal of Psychiatry*, 1968, **114**, 303–330.

Nielsen, J. Chromosomes in senile, presenile, and arteriosclerotic dementia. *Journal of Gerontology*, 1970, **25**, 312–315.

Nikaido, T., Austin J., Rinehart, R., Treub, L., Hutchinson, J., Stukenbrok, H., & Miles, B. Studies in aging of the brain. *Archives of Neurology*, 1971, **25**, 198–211.

Norris, A. A., & Shock, N. Exercise in the adult years with special reference to advanced years. In W. L. Johnson (Ed.), *Science and medicine of exercise and sports*. New York: Harper, 1960.

Norris, A. H., Shock, N. W., Landowne, M., & Falzone, J. A., Jr. Pulmonary function studies: Age differences in lung volumes and bellow functions. *Journal of Gerontology*, 1956, **4**, 379–387.

Obrist, W. D. Simple auditory reaction time in aged adults. *Journal of Psychology*, 1953, **35**, 259–266.

Obrist, W. D. The electroencephalogram of normal aged adults. *Electroencephalography and Clinical Neurophysiology*. 1954, **6**, 235–244.

Obrist, W. Cerebral ischemia and the senescent electroencephalogram. In E. Simonson, & T. H. McGavack (Eds.), *Cerebral ischemia*. Springfield, Ill.: Charles C Thomas, 1964.

Obrist, W. D. Electroencephalographic approach to age changes in response to speed. In A. T. Welford, & J. E. Birren (Eds.), *Behavoir, aging and the nervous system*. Springfield, Ill.: Charles C Thomas, 1965.

Obrist, W. D., Busse, E. W., Eisdorfer, C., & Kleemeier, R. W. Relation of the electroencephalogram to intellectual function in senescence. *Journal of Gerontology*, 1962, **17**, 197–206.

Obrist, W. D., Chivian, E., Cronqvist, S., & Ingvar, D. Regional cerebral blood flow in senile and presenile dementia. *Neurology*, 1970, **20**, 315–322.

Obrist, W. D., & Henry, C. E. Electroencephalographic findings in aged psychiatric patients. *Journal of Nervous and Mental Disease*, 1958, **126**, 254–267.

Obrist, W. D., & Henry, C. E. Electroencephalographic frequency analysis of aged psychiatric patients. *Electroencephalography and Clinical Neurophysiology*, 1958, **10**, 621–632.

Orgel, L. E. The maintenance of the accuracy of protein synthesis and its relevance to aging. *Proceedings of the National Academy of Science*, 1963, **49**, 517–523.

Otomo, E. Electroencephalography in old age: Dominant alpha pattern. *Electroencephalography and Clinical Neurophysiology*, 1966, **21**, 489–491.

Owens, W. A. Age and mental abilities: A longitudinal study. *Genetic Psychology Monographs*, 1953, **48**, 3–54.

Owens, W. A. Age and mental abilities: A second adult follow-up. *Journal of Educational Psychology*, 1966, **57**, 311–325.

Packer, L., Deamer, D. W., & Heath, R. L. Regulation and deterioration of structure in membranes. In B. L. Strehler (Ed.), *Advances in gerontological research*. Vol. 2. New York: Academic Press, 1967.

Palermo, D. S. Research on language acquisition: Do we know where we are going? In R. L. Goulet & P. B. Baltes (Eds.), *Life-span developmental psychology: Research and theory*. New York: Academic Press, 1970.

Palmore, E. B. Physical, mental an dsocial factors in predicting longevity. *Gerontologist*, 1969, **9**, 103–108.

Peak, D. T. Changes in short-term memory in a group of aging community residents. *Journal of Gerontology*, 1968, **23**, 9–16.

Peak, D. T. A replication study of changes in short-term in a group of aging community residents. *Journal of Gerontology*, 1970, **25**, 316–319.

Pentschew, A., & Schwartz, K. Systemic axonal dystrophy in vitamin E deficient adult rats. *Acta Neurophysiologia*, 1962, **1**, 313–334.

Perez, V. J., & Moore, B. W. Biochemistry of the nervous system in aging. In H. T. Blumenthal (Ed.), *Interdisciplinary Topics in Gerontology*, Vol. 7. Basel, Switzerland: Karger, 1970.

Pfeiffer, E. Survival in old age: Physical, psychological and social correlates of longevity. *Journal of the American Geriatric Society*, 1970, **18**, 273–285.

Piaget, J. *Structuralism*. New York: Basic Books, 1970.

Polland, W. S. Histamine test meals: An analysis of 988 consecutive tests. *Archives of International Medicine*, 1933, **51**, 903–919.

Pyhtila, M. J., & Sherman, F. G. Influence of age on rat liver and kidney chromatin. *Gerontologia*, 1969, **15**, 321–327.

Rabbitt, P. M. A. Age and discrimination between complex stimuli. In A. T. Welford, & J. E. Birren (Eds.), *Behavior, aging and the nervous system*. Springfield, Ill.: Charles C Thomas, 1965.

Rees, J., & Botwinick, J. Detection and decision factors in auditory behavior of the elderly. *Journal of Gerontology*, 1971, **26**, 133–136.

Reichel, W., Hollander, J., Clark, J. H., & Strehler, B. L. Lipofuscin-pigment accumulation as a function of age and distribution in rodent brain. *Journal of Gerontology*, 1968, **23**, 71–78.

Riegel, K. F. Speed of verbal performance as a function of age and set: A review of issues and data. In A. T. Welford, & J. E. Birren (Eds.), *Behavior, aging, and the nervous system*. Springfield, Ill.: Charles C Thomas, 1965.

Riegel, K. F. Changes in psycholinguistic performance with age. In G. A. Talland (Ed.), *Human behavior and aging*. New York: Academic Press, 1968.

Riegel, K. F. Research designs in the study of aging and the prediction of retest-resistance and death. Paper presented at the meeting of the 8th International Congress of Gerontology, Washington, D.C., 1969.

Riegel, K. F. The language acquisition process: A reinterpretation of selected research findings. In L. R. Goulet & P. B. Baltes (Eds.), *Life-span developmental psychology: Research and theory*, New York: Academic Press, 1970.

Riegel, K. Language as labor: A comparison between the linguistic and monetary systems. Unpublished manuscript, 1971.

Riegel, K. F., & Riegel, R. M. Development, drop and death. *Developmental Psychology*, 1972, **6**, 306–319.

Riegel K. F., Riegel, R. M., & Meyer, G. A study of the drop-out rates in longitudinal research on aging and the prediction of death. *Journal of Personality and Social Psychology*, 1967, **4**, 343–348.

Riegel, K. F., Riegel, R. M., & Meyer, G. The prediction of retest-resisters in longitudinal research on aging. *Journal of Gerontology*, 1968, **23**, 370–374.

Riese, W. The cerebral cortex in the very old human brain. *Journal of Neuropathology and Experimental Neurology*, 1945, **5**, 160–164.

Rockstein, M. Differential gerontomimetic effects of X-irradiation to pupae or male and female house flies. In P. J. Lindop, & G. A. Sacher (Eds.), *Radiation and aging*, London: Taylor & Francis, 1966.

Rosenzweig, M. R. Environmental complexity, cerebral change, and behavior. *American Psychologist*, 1966, **21**, 321–332.

Rosenzweig, M. R., Krech, D., Bennett, E. L., & Diamond, M. C. Modifying brain chemistry and anatomy by enrichment or impoverishment of experience. In G. Newton, & S. Levine (Eds.), *Early experience and behavior*. Springfield, Ill.: Charles C Thomas, 1968.

Ross, M. H. Protein, calories and life expectancy. *Federation Proceedings*, 1959, **18**, 1190–1211.

Roth, M. The natural history of mental disorder in old age. *Journal of Mental Science*, 1955, **101**, 281–301.

Roth, M. Tomlinson, B. E., & Blessed, G. The relationship between quantitative measures and of degenerative changes in the cerebral gray matter of elderly subjects. *Proceedings of the Royal Society of Medicine*, 1967, **60**, 254–260.

Rothschild, D. Pathological changes in senile psychoses and their psychobiologic significance. *American Journal of Psychiatry*, 1937, **93**, 757–788.

Rudzinska, M. A. The use of a protozoan for studies on aging: III. Similarities between young overfed and old normally fed *Tokophrya infusionum:* A light and electron microscope study. *Gerontologia*, 1962, **6**, 206–226.

Russell, A. P., Dowling, L. E., & Herrmann, R. L. Determination of age-related DNA by hybridization on DNA columns. Paper presented at the 7th International Congress of Gerontology, Vienna, 1966.

Rust, J. H., Robertson, R. J., Staffeldt, E. F., Sacher, G. A., Grahn, D., & Fry, R. J. M. Effects of lifetime periodic gamma ray exposure on the survival and pathology of guinea pigs. In P. J. Lindop, & G. A. Sacher (Eds.), *Radiation and aging.* London: Taylor & Francis, 1966.

Sacher, G. A. Effects of X-rays on the survival of *Drosophila imagoes. Physiological Zoology*, 1963, **36**, 295–311.

Samis, H. V. Aging: The loss of temporal organization. *Perspectives in Biology and Medicine*, 1968, **12**, 95–102.

Samis, H. V., Falzone, J. A., & Wulff, V. J. H^3-thymidine incorporation and mitotic activity in liver of rats of various ages. *Gerontologia*, 1966, **12**, 79–88.

Samis, H. V., & Wulff, V. J. The template activity of rat liver chromatin. *Experimental Gerontology*, 1969, **4**, 111–118.

Samorajski, T., Ordy, J. M., Zeman, W., & Curtis, H. J. Brain irradiation and aging. In H. T. Blumenthal, (Ed.), *Interdisciplinary topics in gerontology.* Vol. 7. Basel, Switzerland: Karger, 1970.

Sandberg, A. A., Cohen, M. M., Rim, A. A., & Levin, M. L. Aneuploidy and age in a population survey. *American Journal of Human Genetics,* 1967, **19**, 633–643.

Sanderson, R. E., & Inglis, J. Learning and mortality in elderly psychiatric patients. *Journal of Gerontology,* 1961, **16**, 357–376.

Schaiberger, G. E., Sallman, B., & Giegel, J. L. A metabolic study of aging in the bacterial cell. *Journal of Gerontology,* 1965, **20**, 23–28.

Schaie, K. W., Rosenthal, F., & Perlman, R. Differential mental deterioration in alter maturity. *Journal of Gerontology,* 1953, **8**, 191–196.

Schaie, K. W., & Strother, C. R. Cognitive and personality variables in college graduates of advanced age. In G. A. Talland (Ed.), *Human aging and behavior.* New York: Academic Press, 1968.

Schenkenberg, T. Visual, auditory, and somatosensory evoked response to normal subjects from childhood to senescence. Unpublished doctoral dissertation, University of Utah, 1970.

Schlesinger, K. Intelligence and behavior genetics. In H. J. Jerison (Ed.), *Perspectives on the nature of intelligence.* In press.

Schonfield, D. Memory loss with age: Acquisition and retrieval. *Psychological Reports,* 1967, **20**, 223–226.

Schwartz, P. Senile cerebral, pancreatic insulin, and cardiac amyloidosis. *Transactions of the New York Academy of Sciences,* 1965, **27**, 393–413.

Schwartz, P. Amyloidosis: Cause and manifestation of senile deterioration. Springfield, Ill.: Charles C Thomas, 1969.

Setlow, R. B., & Carrier, W. L. The disappearance of thymine dimers from DNA: An error-correction mechanism. *Proceedings of the National Academy of Sciences,* 1964, **51**, 226–231.

Shmavonian, B. M., Miller, L. H., & Cohen, S. I. Differences among age and sex groups in electrodermal conditioning. *Psychophysiology,* 1968, **5**, 119–131.

Shmavonian, B. M., Miller, L. H., & Cohen, S. I. Differences among age and sex groups with respect to cardiovascular conditioning and reactivity. *Journal of Gerontology,* 1970, **25**, 87–94.

Shock, N. W. Aging changes in renal function. In A. I. Lansing (Ed.), *Cowdry's problems of aging.* Baltimore: Williams & Wilkins, 1952.

Shock, N. W. The role of the kidney in electrolyte and water regulation in the aged. In G. E. W. Wolstenholme & M. O'Connor (Eds.), *CIBA Foundation colloquia on aging.* Vol. 4. *Water and electrolyte metabolism in relation to age and sex.* Boston: Little, Brown, 1958.

Shock, N. W. The beginning of deterioration. In W. L. Marxer & G. R. Cowgill (Eds.), *The art of preventive medicine.* Springfield, Ill.: Charles C Thomas, 1967.

Silberberg, R. Jarret, S. R., & Silberberg, M. Longevity of female mice kept on various dietary regimens during growth. *Journal of Gerontology,* 1962, **17**, 239–244.

Silverman, A. J, Busse, E. W., & Barnes, R. H. Studies in the processes of aging: Electroencephalographic findings in 400 elderly subjects. *Electroencephalography and Clinical Neurophysiology,* 1955, **7**, 67–74.

Silverman, A. J., Cohen, S. I., & Shmavonian, B. M. Investigation of psycho-physiological relationships with skin resistance measures. *Journal of Psychosomatic Research,* 1959, **4,** 65–87.

Simard, D., Oleson, J., Paulson, O. B., Lassesn, N. A., & Skinhoj, E. Regional cerebral blood flow and its regulation in dementia. *Brain,* 1971, **94,** 273–281.

Simms, H. S., Berg, B. N., & Davies, D. F. Onset of disease and longevity of rat and man. In G. E. W. Wolstenholme & M. O'Connor (Eds.), *CIBA Foundation colloquia on aging.* Vol. 5. *The lifespan of animals.* Boston: Little, Brown, 1959.

Simonson, E. Performance as a function of age and cardiovascular disease. In A. T. Welford & J. E. Birren (Eds.), *Behavior, aging and the nervous system.* Springfield, Ill.: Charles C Thomas, 1965.

Sinex, F. M. The role of collagen in aging. In B. S. Gould (Ed.), *Biology of collagen.* New York: Academic Press, 1968.

Smith, A. N. Cross-sectional and longitudinal studies of aging: Aging in bone as a model. *Experimental Gerontology,* 1970, **5,** 273–280.

Sobel, H. Aging of connective tissue and molecular transport. *Gerontologia,* 1968, **14,** 235–254.

Solyom, L., & Barik, H. C. Conditioning in senescence and senility. *Journal of Gerontology,* 1965, **20,** 483–488.

Spieth, W. Slowness of task performance and cardiovascular disease. In A. T. Welford & J. E. Birren (Eds.), *Behavior, aging, and the nervous system.* Springfield, Ill.: Charles C Thomas, 1965.

Spoor, A. Presbycusis values in relation to noise-induced hearing loss. *International Audiology,* 1967, **6,** 48–57.

Straumanis, J. J., Shagass, C., & Schwartz, M. Visually evoked cerebral response changes associated with chronic brain syndromes and aging. *Journal of Gerontology,* 1965, **20,** 498–506.

Strehler, B. L. Studies on the comparative physiology of aging: II. On the mechanism of temperature life-shortening in *Drosophila melanogaster. Journal of Gerontology,* 1961, **16,** 2–12.

Strehler, B. L. *Time, cells and aging.* New York: Academic Press, 1962.

Strehler, B. L. On the histochemistry and ultrastructure of age pigment. In B. L. Strehler (Ed.), *Advances in gerontological research.* Vol. 1. New York: Academic Press, 1964. (a)

Strehler, B. L. Studies on the comparative physiology of aging: III. Effects of X-radiation dosage on age-specific mortality rates of *Drosophila melanogaster* and *Campanularia flexuosa. Journal of Gerontology,* 1964, **19,** 83–87. (b)

Sulkin, N. M., & Kuntz, A. Histochemical alterations in automatic ganglion cells associated with aging. *Journal of Gerontology,* 1952, **7,** 533–543.

Surwillo, W. W. Age and the preception of short intervals of time. *Journal of Gerontology,* 1964, **19,** 322–324.

Surwillo, W. W. Timing of behavior in senescence and the role of the central nervous system. In G. A. Talland (Ed.), *Human aging and behavior.* New York: Academic Press, 1968.

Szafran, J. Age differences in choice reaction time and cardiovascular status among pilots. *Nature,* 1963, **200,** 904–906.

Szafran, J. Age differences in sequential decisions and cardiovascular status among pilots. *Aerospace Medicine,* 1965, **36,** 303–310. (a)

Szafran, J. Decision processes and aging. In A. T. Welford & J. E. Birren (Eds.), *Behavior, aging, and the nervous system.* Springfield, Ill.: Charles C Thomas, 1965. (b)

Szafran, J. Age differences in the rate of gain of information, signal detection strategy and cardiovascular status among pilots. *Gerontologia,* 1966, 12, 6–17.

Szafran, J. Psychophysiological studies of aging in pilots. In G. A. Talland (Ed), *Human aging and behavior.* New York: Academic Press, 1968.

Szafran, J., & Birren, J. E. Perception. In J. E. Birren (Ed.), *Contemporary gerontology: Issues and concepts.* Los Angeles: Gerontology Center, University of Southern California, 1968.

Talland, G. A. The effect of age on speed of simple manual skill. *Journal of Genetic Psychology,* 1962, 100, 69–76.

Talland, G. A. *Deranged memory.* New York: Academic Press, 1965.

Talland, G. A. Age and immediate memory span. *Gerontologist,* 1967, 7, 4–9.

Talland, G. A., & McGuire, M. T. Tests of learning and memory with Cylert. *Psychopharmacologia,* 1967, 10, 445–351.

Talland, G. A., Mendelson, J. H., Koz, G., & Aaron, R. Experimental studies of the effects of tricyanoaminopropene on the memory and learning capacities of geriatric patients. *Journal of Psychiatric Research,* 1965, 3, 171–179.

Taub, H. A., & Walker, J. B. Short-term memory as a function of age and response interference. *Journal of Gerontology,* 1970, 25, 177–183.

Tkach, J. R., & Yoshitsugi, H. Autoimmunity in chronic brain syndrome. *Archives of General Psychiatry,* 1970, 23, 61–64.

Toth, S. E. Review article: The origin of the lipofuscin age pigments. *Experimental Gerontology,* 1968,3, 19–30.

Trier, T. R. Characteristics of mentally-ill aged: A comparison of patients with psychogenic disorders and patients with organic brain syndrome. *Journal of Gerontology,* 1966, 21, 354–364.

Troyer, W. G. Mechanisms of brain-body interaction in the aged. In L. F. Jarvik, C. Eisdorfer, & J. E. Blum (Eds.), *Intellectual functioning in adults: Some psychological and biological influences.* New York: Springer, in press.

Troyer, W. G., Eisdorfer, C., Bogdonoff, M. D., & Wilkie, F. Experimental stress and learning in the aged. *Journal of Abnormal Psychology,* 1967, 72, 65–70.

Verzar, F. *Lectures on experimental gerontology.* Springfield, Ill.: Charles C Thomas, 1963.

Viidik, A. Age-correlated changes in the physical properties of collagen. Paper presented at the 8th International Congress of Gerontology, Washington, D.C., 1969.

von Fieandt, K., Atuhtala, A., Kullberg, P., & Saari, K. Personal tempo and phenomenal time at different age levels. (Report No. 2) Psychological Institute, University of Helsinki, 1956.

von Hahn, H. P. The regulation of protein synthesis in the aging cell. *Experimental Gerontology,* 1970, 5, 323–334. (a)

von Hahn, H. P. Structural and functional changes in nucleoprotein during the aging of the cell. *Gerontologia,* 1970, 16, 116–178. (b) von Hahn, H. P., & Fritz, E. Age-related alterations in the structure of DNA: III. Thermal stability of rat liver DNA related to age, histone, content and ionic strength. *Gerontologia*, 1966, **12**, 237–250.

von Hahn, H. P., Miller, J., & Eichorn, G. L. Age-related alterations in the structure of nucleoprotein: IV. Changes in the composition of whole histone from rat liver. *Gerontologia*, 1969, **15**, 293–301.

Wagner, M. J., & Emmers, R. Spinal synaptic delay in young and aged rats. *American Journal Physiology*, 1958, **194**, 403–405.

Walford, R. L. The general immunology of aging. In B. L. Strehler (Ed.), *Advances in gerontological research*. Vol. 2. New York: Academic Press, 1967.

Walford, R. L. *The immunologic theory of aging*. Baltimore: Williams & Wilkens, 1969.

Wang, H. S. The brain and intellectual function in senescence. In L. F. Jarvik, C. Eisedorfer, & J. E. Blum (Eds.), *Intellectual functioning in adults: Some psychological and biological influences*. New York: Springer, in press.

Wang, H. S., Obrist, W. D., & Busse, E. W. Neurophysiological correlates of the intellectual function of elderly persons living in the community. *American Journal of Psychiatry*, 1970, **126**, 1205–1212.

Wapner, S., Werner, H., & Comalli, P. E., Jr. Perception of part-whole relationships in middle and old age. *Journal of Gerontology*, 1960, **15**, 412–416.

Weale, R. A. *The ageing eye*. London: H. K. Lewis, 1963.

Weale, R. A. On the eye. In A. T. Welford, & J. E. Birren (Eds), *Behavior, aging and the nervous system*. Springfield, Ill.: Charles C Thomas, 1965.

Wechsler, D. *The measurement and appraisal of adult intelligence*. Baltimore: Williams & Wilkins, 1958.

Wechsler, D. Intelligence, memory and the aging process. In P. H. Hoch & J. Zubin (Eds.), *Psychopathology of aging*. New York: Grune & Stratton, 1961.

Weiss, A. D. Sensory functions. In J. E. Birren (Ed.), *Handbook of aging and the individual*. Chicago: University of Chicago Press, 1959.

Weiss, A. D. The locus of reaction time change with set, motivation and age. *Journal of Gerontology*, 1965, **20**, 60–64.

Weiss, P. A. The life history of the neuron. *Research Publication Association for Research in Nervous and Mental Diseases*, 1955, **35**, 8–18.

Weiss, P. A. The living system: Determinism stratified. In A. Koestler & J. R. Smythies (Eds.), *Beyond reductionism*. New York: Macmillan, 1969.

Welford, A. T. Psychomotor performance. In J. E. Birren (Ed.), *Handbook of aging and the individual*. Chicago: University of Chicago Press, 1959.

Wetherick, N. E. Changing an established concept: A comparison of the ability of young, middle-aged, and old subjects. *Gerontologia*, 1965, **11**, 82–95.

Wiersman, W., & Klausmeir, H. T. The effect of age upon speed of concept attainment. *Journal of Gerontology*, 1965, **20**, 398–400.

Wilkie, F., & Eisdorfer, C. Intelligence and blood pressure in the aged. *Science*, 1971, **172**, 959–962.

Wilson, R. S., & Harpring, E. B. Twins: Early mental development. *Child Development*, in press.

Wimer, R. E., & Wigdor, B. Age differences in retention of learning. *Journal of Gerontology*, 1958, **13**, 291–295.

Woodford-Williams, E., Alvarez, A. S., Webster, D., Landless, B., & Dixon, M. P. Serum protein patterns in "normal" and pathological aging. *Gerontologia,* 1964–1965, **10,** 86–99.

Wulff, V. J. An investigation of RNA metabolism in relation to age. Paper presented at the 8th International Congress of Gerontology, Washington, D.C., 1969.

Wulff, V. J., Samis, H. V., & Falzone, J. A. The metabolism of ribonucleic acid in young and old rodents. In B. L. Strehler (Ed.), *Advances in gerontological research.* Vol. 2. New York: Academic Press, 1967.

Yiengst, M. J., Barrows, C. H., Jr., & Shock, N. W. Age changes in the biochemical composition of muscle and liver in the rat. *Journal of Gerontology,* 1959, **14,** 400–404.

Youhotsky-Gore, I., & Pathmanathan, K. Some comparative observations on the lysosomal status of muscle from young and old mice. *Experimental Gerontology,* 1968, **3,** 281–286.

Young, M. L. Problem solving performance in two age groups. *Journal of Gerontology,* 1966, **21,** 505–510.

Yuan, G. C., Chang, R. S., Little, J. B., & Cormil, G. Prolongation of post meiotic life-span of primary human amnion cells in vitro by hydrocortisone. *Journal of Gerontology,* 1967, **22,** 174–179.

Zeman, W. The neuronal ceroid-lipofuscinoses-Batten-Voyt syndrome. In B. L. Strehler (Ed.), *Advances in gerontological research.* Vol. 3. New York: Academic Press, 1971.

Zerbin-Rudin, E. Hirntrophische prozesse. *Humangenetik,* 1967, **2,** 84–157.

Zimkina, A. M., Asofov, B. D., Kiseliva, A. M., & Makkaveiskiy, P. A. Peculiarities of the electroencephalogram in elderly and aged persons. *Electroencephalography and Clinical Neurophysiology,* 1965, **18,** 107, (Abstract)

Social Stress and Adaptation: Toward A Life-Course Perspective

MARJORIE FISKE LOWENTHAL and DAVID CHIRIBOGA

This chapter focuses on the necessity for new approaches to concepts of stress and adaptation directed toward making the paradigm more useful in studies of the adult life course. For the time being, we are limiting our definition of stress to social stress in real-life situations. We shall also seek clearer distinctions between the concept of social stress (or stressors) and circumstances that may more properly be examined as mediators or as consequences of stress. Experimental studies of stress are not an integral part of this chapter. Physiological responses to stress, while obviously of considerable significance both as second-order stressors in themselves (Selye, 1956) and as prerequisites for coping with stress (Levine & Scotch, 1970), are also beyond the scope of this chapter. This is not to say, however, that the approach we are proposing has no relevance for these other important areas of stress research. On the contrary, signs of dissatisfaction with the simple S–R model proliferate in experimental, physiological, and clinical studies, and we have learned much from them. We hope that our further specification of mediating factors,

---

Marjorie Fiske Lowenthal is Professor of Social Psychology in Residence at the University of California, San Francisco. Trained at Mt. Holyoke, Harvard, and Columbia, she is now Director of the Training and Research Program in Human Development at Langley Porter Neuropsychiatric Institute. Her present research interests are in the psychosocial characteristics associated with growth, stabilization, and retrogression at transitional stages of adult life.

David Chiriboga received his PhD in human development from the University of Chicago in 1972. He is currently a research psychologist with the Human Development Group of the Langley Porter Neuropsychiatric Institute, the University of California, San Francisco. His major research interests center on an adult life perspective on stress, adaptation, and temporal orientations.

as well as our efforts to operationalize and explore adaptation as a process, may prove of interest to investigators in these related fields.

The shortcomings of most social stress models stem from the considerable variation among investigators in assigning particular indicators to the independent, mediating, and outcome parameters. On the adaptation side, the limitations of the usual approaches reflect the often static and rigid nature of most concepts of mental health. When applied to cross-sectional studies of mental health, the use of diagnoses or "degree of impairment" ratings as principal criteria of adaptation often results in misleading profiles of the functional capabilities of the populations studied. Such models prove even less illuminating in the analysis of adaptive processes throughout the adult life course and especially in old age.

Our aim in this chapter is to suggest ways of clarifying the stress and mediating domains of the model and of adding flexibility and a process orientation to the adaptation side. We shall first review the more relevant concepts and findings in the sociological, sociopsychological, and psychiatric literature[1] and some of our own studies on aging, both of which prompted us to work toward clarification and elaboration of the paradigm. In the two ensuing sections, we make concrete suggestions to this end and conclude with illustrative findings from ongoing research.

THE AMBIGUITIES OF STRESS AND ADAPTATION

The works of Lowenthal (1968), Lowenthal, Berkman, and Associates (1967), and others (Dodge & Martin, 1970; Langner & Michael, 1963; Rahe, McKean, & Arthur, 1967) suggest a rather impressive relationship between social stress and mental or physical health. The indicators of stress used in such studies, however, are often a mixture of externally imposed events (past and present) over which the individual has little control, and circumstances with which the individual himself has been inextricably involved. While many of these, such as interpersonal conflict or a socially isolated life-style, are no doubt stressful, they have frequently developed as a consequence of entrenched personality characteristics, in themselves possible responses to early life stress. In short, items are included on the stressor side of the paradigm that, regardless of

---

[1] The authors are indebted to Thomas Lonner and Phyllis Olsen for invaluable editorial assistance in preparing the reference list.

how adaptation is measured, almost certainly introduce a tautological component into the stress–adaptation correlations.

Such mixtures of external and what we might call equivocal or second-order stressors are found not only in sociopsychological field studies but in research on patient populations as well.[2] When such items as "worries for no reason," divorce, job problems, or a low level of social interaction are considered stressors in these studies, we should not be surprised to find the authors reporting significant correlations between indicators of stress and indicators of adaptation. Investigators who have differentiated such stresses from those that were externally imposed often report little difference between patient and nonpatient populations (Berkman, 1971; MacFarlane, 1964; Renaud & Estess, 1961; Schofield & Ballan, 1959).

Similar ambiguities appear in clinicians' definitions of "situational" or "environmental" stress as a precipitant of mental illness. For example, Leff, Roatch, and Bunney (1970) categorized threats to sexual identity, changes in marital relationship, and various kinds of work difficulties as stressful "environmental events" causatively associated with hospital admission for depressive breakdown. Another study (Smith, 1971) included hospitalization in a mental institution (which no doubt is stressful) in a stress index. Not surprisingly, it correlates highly with indicators of maladaptation.

Specific, episodic social stresses, such as residential moves or retirement, are often included in stress indices without distinction as to whether they were voluntary or involuntary. Some measures (cf. Holmes & Rahe, 1967) also include both incremental, or positive, and decremental, or negative, changes in the same index. Dohrenwend and Dohrenwend (1969) distinguished between "security" and "achievement" changes in their sophisticated social stress model, but they too intermingled external and internal, voluntary and involuntary, and negative and positive stressors. As Levin (1966), Croog (1970), and especially Scott and Howard (1970) pointed out, there is bound to be a degree of arbitrariness in making such distinctions, but our point is that only if each dimension is analyzed separately will we make headway in understanding the dynamics of stress and adaptation from a life-course perspective.

Another shortcoming of many stress indices is that in addition to childhood and recent stress, they also combine chronic and epi-

---

[2] Paykel et al. (1969), Murphy, Kuhn, Christensen, and Robins (1962), Gordon, Singer, and Gordon (1961), Mechanic and Volkart (1961), Antonovsky and Kats (1967), and Rahe et al. (1967).

sodic and multiple and cumulative stressors as well. Both Langner and Michael (1963) and Berkman (1971) in his replication study made a significant step in differentiating between childhood and later stress, but they could not, with the data at hand, assess their comparative importance for successive adult life stages. As we shall illustrate in the next section, the relevance of such time dimensions varies with the stage of the life course, and it is therefore necessary to distinguish between them. Timing of stress, in terms of the stage of the life cycle at which it occurs, as well as in terms of duration of the stressor, is also highly relevant but has, on the whole, been neglected. Timing is implicit in the work of Blau (1961), and duration of the stressor as well as duration of the anticipation of it has been studied in the experimental work of Lazarus (1966); Neugarten (1969) also noted the significance of being on or off schedule in normative events of the adult life course.

Turning to intervening or ameliorating factors, we should note that only recently have psychologists and sociologists begun to pay attention to individual variations in the perception of what is or is not stressful as a critical intervening factor between sociostructural, sensory, or physical stress and adaptation. Lazarus (1966; Lazarus, Opton, & Averill, 1968) increasingly emphasized the significance of cognitive appraisal, and Janis (1958) reported that the relationship between anticipated and perceived loss is crucial for postsurgical adaptation. Thurlow (1971), in a study of industrial workers, noted that a person's subjective appraisal of changes in his social circumstances is more significantly related to illness than are objective measures of such change. Henley and Davis (1967), in a study of the chronically ill aged, also concluded that the individual's perception of a situation is more relevant to his morale than the actual condition. A cross-cultural study by Hinkle, Christenson, Kane, Ostfeld, Thetford, and Wolff (1958) reported no direct association between life stress and illness among Chinese and American samples, and the authors concluded that a major consideration may be a predisposition to view life as threatening. Such predispositions may well originate in early life (see Jaco's, 1970, review). However, as Winnik (1968) suggested, catastrophic stress in later life may result in drastically increased susceptibility to stress, even among persons who experienced the most benign of childhood influences. Korchin (1965) presented, with some support from the research literature, the provocative possibility that the complex, creative person may be more stress prone and that stress resistance may develop at the expense of other, more desirable qualities.

Similarly, while many models have included social structure and social networks as potential stressors or ameliorators of stress, little attention has been paid to individual variations in the perception of such structures and networks. This neglect has been singled out by Katz (1967), who directed his fellow social psychologists to attend to the neglected area of the individual's perceptions of various levels of his social reality. Maddox (1970), among sociologists, and Clark (1971), among anthropologists, recently pointed out that the individual's social perceptions have been neglected in the assessment of the relationship between sociocultural factors and behavior. This is to say, for example, that it is not enough to identify someone as being old, or black; one must know whether he accepts, rejects, or is conflicted about the elderly or blacks as reference groups. Also relevant to the perceptual issue is whether the individual himself sees those circumstances that he considers stressful as imposed on him by others or by "fate," or whether he believes he, himself, has been involved in bringing them about (Biderman, 1967; Ruff, 1967).

Just as there should be both greater differentiation and more flexibility in the examination of stressors and mediating factors and characteristics, so, if we wish to adopt an adult life-course perspective, we must be more flexible in our concepts of adaptation. In particular, as psychologists and sociologists have pointed out, there is a need for a model in which psychological resources as well as impairments are assessed (Barron, 1963; Clausen, 1969; Jahoda, 1958; Smith, 1969).

The issue of physical health status as an indicator of adaptation is complex. Many investigators view self or clinical appraisal of physical illness or impairment only as a stressor, while others, such as Holmes and Rahe (1967), view physical symptoms and illnesses as outcome or dependent variables. In between, of course, is the vast and rather inconclusive literature of psychosomatic medicine in which the emphasis tends to be on the personality characteristics of cohorts susceptible to various types of illness (e.g., see the review of Mai, 1968). Ideally, physical health status characteristics should be subdivided among those that are hereditary or given, those that are universal under certain environmental conditions, and those that are neither and, thus are potential reactions to social stress. Since such a typology seems at present an unrealizable goal, for the time being, indicators of physical health should be alternatively assessed both as potential stressors and as outcomes. When change in physical health status is examined as the dependent variable, the significance of friendship and intimacy patterns should be further explored as mediating factors, since the data thus far reported tend to conflict (Kissel, 1962; Lowenthal & Haven, 1968; Volinn & Spielholz, 1969).

IMPLICATIONS OF RECENT RESEARCH IN AGING

Our research on normal and abnormal aging[3] sharpened our awareness of the inadequacies of most stress and adaptation models for studies of older persons as well as for studies with an adult life-course perspective. Our research also served to reinforce our conviction that the collaboration of several disciplines is required for such studies because the relevance of such concepts as roles, reference groups, self-image, and ethnic identity changes as individuals move through the adult life course.

Paradoxes of Social Stress

Beginning with the sociostructural concepts and variables prevalent in sociological theory and research, one can discover several paradoxical or unexpected findings in their association with adaptation if one adopts a life-course perspective. For example, widowhood and retirement are not clearly and unequivocally associated with either subjective or objective indications of maladaptation in later life. When such an association does exist, it is often the reverse of what one might expect on the basis of traditional theories of sex roles—retirement may result in greater maladaptation among women, while men may suffer excessively from widowerhood. Similarly, low socioeconomic status is more closely associated with mental illness among men than among women (Lowenthal, 1968; Lowenthal et al., 1967). Among women, the development of psychiatric disorder in later life is often associated with low levels of self-esteem. There is also an association between low levels of social interaction and low self-esteem among women in nonpatient populations (Clark & Anderson, 1967). Panel analysis indicates that such correlations may *decrease* with age (Lowenthal et al., 1967). Findings such as these suggest the possibility of life-course changes in the salience of problems and conflicts relating to normative sex roles and goals. The decreasing importance of economic achievement among men, their often more severe reaction to loss of a spouse, and the decreasing

---

[3] National Institute of Mental Health Grant MH 09145, 1958–69.

stress of living alone among women lend some support to the Neugarten and Gutmann (1964) thesis, drawn from projective data, that men's interests become more interpersonal and women's more instrumental with advancing age. This thesis is finding further support in our own recent findings from nonprojective data (Thurnher, 1971) of age- or stage-linked shifts from instrumentality to expressivity among men and the obverse among women. Women whose main lifetime goals have been instrumental, for example, those who have had careers, may experience value or goal shifts similar to those of men. Those among them who combined work with marriage and parenthood may have had little time to develop friendships. Thus, when they face retirement, like the men who become widowers, they have few resources for pursuing interpersonal objectives that may have become increasingly important to them.

Another paradox is found in the apparently changing salience of social isolation for adaptation in later life. While many clinicians and social scientists will consider an isolated life-style in itself a major indicator of maladaptation, our earlier work has indicated that lifelong isolation is not necessarily associated with maladaptation in later life (Lowenthal, 1964b). This is true regardless of whether the indicators of maladaptation are subjective, or whether we look at elderly first admissions to a psychiatric screening ward. These findings suggest the possibility that the former self, rather than reference groups or individuals, may increasingly become the salient yardstick for the sense of relative deprivation in old age; that is, the lifelong isolate does not suffer from age-linked social losses because he has never had social ties. A pattern of successive marginal social relationships, however, is associated with poor adaptation in later life, including serious mental illness (Lowenthal, 1965).

Both the extremely isolated and the marginal social life-styles appear to be associated with parental deprivation in childhood (Lowenthal, 1968). Such early loss of social support apparently generates extreme sensitivity and conflict about interpersonal relationships. A socially isolated life-style protects the individual from such involvements. Conversely, those who try to live a more conventional social life and do not succeed may well endure excessive strain, a strain that perhaps increases with age. While we know, for instance, that the presence of an old friend or confidant greatly helps to mitigate the social stresses accompanying the aging process (Lowenthal & Haven, 1968), just as the presence of a friend reduces reactions to laboratory stress (Kissel, 1962), the socially marginal life-style, characterized by disruptions in social and work relationships, usually precludes continuity of friends or spouse. Borderline all along, people adopting this style constitute a population at serious risk when they confront age-linked losses. In terms of our suggested elaboration of the stress paradigm, the marginal life-style, a response to early life stress, thus becomes a second-order stressor, while the extremely isolated style becomes an ameliorating factor between the stresses of later life and adaptation.

In short, imposed social stresses and the equivocal or second-order stresses appear to vary in their salience for adaptation, depending upon age or, perhaps more properly, upon life stage. The time dimensions of stress, in short, are essential to a life-course perspective, especially in studies of elderly populations.

As the research reviewed in the first part of this chapter amply illustrates, most studies that assess imposed and second-order social stresses in relation to adaptation show a moderate relationship in the expected direction. Even in the most rigorous of such studies, these relationships, however, are neither impressive nor consistent with each other. "Deviant" cases abound. This appears to be as true for sociocultural factors and crises (low socioeconomic status, economic depression, minority group membership) as for more idiosyncratic losses or catastrophes. Holding any particular presumptive stress constant to the extent possible, the subjects tend to scatter along any adaptive continuum an investigator cares to use. Similarly, cumulative- or multiple-stress indices produce wide distributions on adaptive indicators. Clearly, a stressful circumstance for one may be a challenge or even a palliative to another, while a third person many not notice it at all. These findings, plus the fact that persons who have experienced little presumptive stress may rank high on indicators of maladaptation, suggested the salience of a stress proneness concept (Lowenthal et al., 1967). A step toward operationalizing stress proneness and some preliminary findings from our current application of this typology will be reported in the last two sections.

Life-Course Changes in the Salience of Adaptive Criteria

The need for flexibility in the appraisal of adaptive indicators is clearly demonstrated by findings that suggest that the young person's psychological "impairment" may be the old person's "resource" and vice versa. To mention a few, there may be a change in the relationship between intra- versus extrapunitiveness and other indicators of adaptation in the adult life course (J. Britton, personal communication, 1971; Lowenthal, 1968). Dependency and counter-dependency may show reverses in their salience for adaptation in young adulthood as compared with old age, though, as yet, there is little agreement on this hypothesis (Clark, 1969; Goldfarb, 1969; Perlin, 1958). Some degree of obsessiveness may prove adaptive in the retirement stage (Perlin & Butler, 1963). Whereas goodness of fit between real and ideal self-image has long been considered a significant indicator of adaptation, it may well be that stability of the self-concept becomes increasingly crucial as the individual ages (M. Lieberman, personal communication, 1969; Lowenthal, 1968; Rosner, 1966).

Finally, for many older people, maintaining a sense of continuity, especially in the value system, appears to be a significant part of the adaptive process (Clark & Anderson, 1967; Lowenthal, Spence, & Thurnher, in press). Indeed, in later life, the importance of such stability may account for the restructuring and reinterpretation of one's "biography," noted both in literary autobiographies and clinical material (Butler, 1963; Lewis, 1971). One of the major hypotheses of our current research on transitional stages of adulthood is that maintaining continuity in values and in the perceived goodness of fit between values and goals (or past achievements) is in itself a critical adaptive process (Clark & Anderson, 1967; Lowenthal, 1971). It may well prove to be an essential component of stability in the self-concept.

CLARIFICATION OF THE STRESS AND ADAPTATION PARAMETERS

It seems clear then, at the present state of our knowledge, that any stress–adaptation paradigm will have some components whose placement in one or another parameter is arbitrary. Our present aim is to refine these specific components so that they may, where logical, be examined alternatively as causative, mediating, or outcome variables. These alternatives hold for most indicators except those that can be clearly defined as external and beyond the individual's control.

Imposed Social Stress

In defining this latter type of presumed or "objective" stress, probably the best we can do at this juncture is to specify certain circumstances that a wide variety of judges in a given culture would consider to be both superimposed and stressful. These circumstances would include certain characteristics of the interpersonal and extrapersonal social environment that the individual was born into, such as parental deprivation or extreme poverty; sociohistorical events, such as economic depressions, wars, or natural catastrophes; and involuntary role and status losses, such as bereavement, unemployment due to factors beyond the individual's control, or forced retirement. While logic would dictate that such circumstances always be examined from the stressor side of the paradigm, they should, however, be labeled as *presumptive* stressors. As the classical studies of Durkheim (1951) made clear, even so relatively unambiguous a superimposed stress as loss of spouse may produce reactions that vary dramatically by culture, political circumstances, sex, life stage, and family constellation.

Equivocal and Second-Order Stressors

As we have noted, depending upon the investigator, other interpersonal and social circumstances such as divorce, isolation, deviance, and occupational instability are variously examined in the stressor, mediating, or adaptation domains of the paradigm. Since the individual is, himself, usually involved in the development of such circumstances and since the possibility exists that they are consequences of prior stress, in the ideal developmental model they should first be assessed in relation to early, or continuing, *imposed* stress. Positive or incremental changes in which the individual himself also plays some role (such as marriage, parenthood, promotion) would be included in the list of second-order potential stressors, but they should be assessed separately from circumstances that are presumptively "negative." The next step would then be to assess these positive and negative second-order stressors in relation to subjective and objective indicators of adaptation. Finally, some circumstances, such as a socially isolated life-style, should be assessed as intervening variables between recent stresses imposed later in life (such as retirement or widowhood) and adaptation.

This degree of differentiation among equivocal second-order stressors would provide the basis for grouping and describing the types of people who are susceptible to particular categories of social stress, an important step toward prediction and planning. For example, we all know people who cope magnificently with imposed catastrophe (risers to the occasion) but who have great difficulty in thinking through and carrying out a voluntary change in their lives.

Similarly, some people are more threatened by incremental or positive changes (voluntary or involuntary) than by negative ones. We need to know how and for whom these variations in stress susceptibility arise.

Adaptation

Three approaches to the adaptive parameter will help to make it more useful for assessing mental health in later life: (a) assessment not of degree of impairment but of the *balance* between resources and impairments and between particular types of resources and impairments; (b) a *process* orientation, involving an examination of stability or change in the component dimensions and in the ratio between them; and (c) *flexibility* in the labeling of impairments and resources (a characteristic that may be an impediment at one life stage may prove to be a resource at another).

A still-to-be-charted field in the assessment of adaptation from an adult life-course perspective is the changing relationship between reported or observed symptoms, on the one hand, and clinical assessments of mental health status, on the other. While reported symptoms tend to increase with age and psychiatrists assessing such symptoms (blinded for age) may rate the old more "sick" than the young (Neugarten, 1964), these differences tend to be wiped out when age is known to the clinician. Though not fully explicated, it is clear that clinicians (as do laymen) consider some symptoms to be "normal" in the later stages of life (Lowenthal, 1964a; Lowenthal & Berkman, 1964), hence, the importance of assessing psychological resources and deficits both from the clinician's viewpoint and from the subject's, and each of these at successive life stages. Each of these assessments, in turn, should then be compared with behavioral measures of level of functioning.

In short, while the emphasis in regard to presumptive and second-order stressors is on the need for more specification of their components and time dimensions, the emphasis in the adaptive sphere (while specificity is also required), is on flexibility and the suspension of stereotyped judgments as to what characteristics, symptoms, and processes are and are not adaptive in later life.

RESEARCH STRATEGY FOR KEY CONCEPTS

A life-cycle approach to problems of stress and adaptation, then, requires the introduction of at least three concepts into the traditional paradigm: the time dimensions of stress, the individual's perceptions of stress and of his social networks, and a flexible process orientation to the adaptive domain.

Time Dimensions of Stress

Infancy and childhood stress. There is, of course, a vast body of significant work on the concurrent effects of social deprivation during infancy and childhood (e.g., Bowlby, 1958; Harlow & Zimmermann, 1959; Spitz & Wolf, 1946). Our primary concern with this early period, however, is limited to the changing relationship between early deprivation and adaptation at successive stages of the adult life course. The significance of these early life influences for adaptation at particular stages or circumstances of adult life has been explored in a large body of significant research, clinical and otherwise. Much of this work has been influenced by Freudian and neo-Freudian concepts (e.g., Erikson, 1959; Grinker & Spiegel, 1945; Janis, 1958; Keniston, 1965; Paykel, Myers, Dienelt, Klerman, Lindenthal, & Pepper, 1969; Winnik, 1968). Although implicit in the work of White (1963), to the best of our knowledge there has been little if any concern with the changing significance of such early influences at successive stages of adulthood and old age.

Cumulative and multiple stress. Thus far in the mental health literature, beginning with the classical suicide studies of Durkheim (1951) and continuing through the recent epidemiological literature, little distinction has been made among chronic, cumulative (i.e., a series of acute stresses), and multiple-concurrent stress. Our proposal is to specify these dimensions as clearly as possible and to assess their comparative relationship to adaptation at successive adult stages. A persistent and very low socioeconomic status, for example, may be operationally defined as a chronic stress, but, as we have seen, it may have varying effects on adaptation at different life stages. If stresses, chronic or acute, pile up in the course of a lifetime, some individuals may reach a breaking point, while others may be strengthened to face multiple-concurrent stresses or losses in old age.

Precipitating stress. Though the concept of a single precipitating stress as a trigger for mental illness or other forms of maladaptation has not thus far proven to be a very fruitful one, within a time dimension framework it can readily be tested further. Specific recent changes or losses in roles and status, such as bereavement, social exclusion, retirement, loss of income, residential moves, and geographic moves of close others, should be separately assessed and compared (though of course they may then be combined into an index of concurrent stress). As in studying the other time dimensions of stress, we must maintain distinctions between voluntary and involuntary changes, as well as between those that are on versus off schedule in terms of normative expectations. Whether or not a sudden perception of one's self as "old" ever falls into the category of a precipitating stress is also an important area for exploration. When and if such sudden perceptions develop, it will be particularly important to determine whether or not the trigger was an internal clue (such as failure of strength or of faculties) or a reaction to a social situation.

Anticipatory stress. While laboratory studies of stress as well as field studies of the armed forces during World War II have taken anticipation of stress into account, relatively few of the more recent sociopsychological studies have done so. Exceptions include the works of Lieberman (1970; Chiriboga & Liebermann, 1970) at the University of Chicago and of Streib and Schneider (1971) at Cornell University. The next important step is to assess poststress adaptation in relation to the nature and intensity of anticipated stress, as Janis (1958) did with surgical patients.

Finally, the above time dimensions of stress should be assessed from the standpoint of whether there are life-stage differences in their significance for adaptation. For example, do the deprivations of infancy and early childhood have their maximum impact during the identity crises of adolescence and young adulthood? Do they re-emerge as relevant in periods of catastrophe? Do they generally assume increasing salience in late adulthood and old age? Do current and precipitating stresses of various types decrease or increase in salience as cumulative stress increases? Does anticipated stress have a greater impact in earlier or later life stages, and is it associated with amount of presumed or perceived stress in prior stages?

A highly efficient way of assessing the time dimensions of stress is via a life chart, originally developed by Jean MacFarlane at the Institute for Human Development, University of California, Berkeley. Respondents plot each year of their lives on a 9-point scale, 9 being "absolute tops" and 1 being "rock bottom." The completed chart, in conjunction with questions focused on significant changes, provides content for the analysis of major social stress during the life course. For example, in an analysis of middle-aged men and women whose youngest child was about to leave the home, consideration of scalar shifts in the life chart and of corresponding interview responses gave us evidence that the so-called "empty nest" period rarely invokes the kind of mid-life stress reaction widely conjectured in the psychoanalytic literature (Lowenthal & Chiriboga, 1972).

Perceptual Variations

A *typology of stress perception* is proving, in our own work, to be a fruitful means of operationalizing a factor that is obviously a critical mediator between presumptive stress and adaptation.

If one envisages a fourfold table with presumably stressful real events or circumstances (losses, discontinuities, other trauma) as one dimension and the perception of stress as manifest in the presentation of self (in this case in life-history interviews) as the other, four modes of stress perception are derived (see Table 1).

At present, we are using an adaptation of the Holmes and Rahe (1967) schedule for our measure of presumptive stress. As this chapter was being prepared, this schedule was being subdivided and pruned in order to separate out the various dimensions proposed earlier in this chapter, such as positive and negative change, voluntary and involuntary, imposed and equivocal or second-order stressors. Stress perception is currently derived from ratings of life-history protocols by an interdisciplinary team. The next step will be to structure the perceptual dimension, so that it can be applied to studies where no life-history narratives are available.

In passing, we might mention methods of operationalizing the other closely related perceptual area that we believe to be essential in studying psychosocial aspects of aging, namely, that of variations in social perceptions. Such a typology will be derived from the individual's perceptions of himself in comparison with objective indicators of his roles, statuses, networks, and social structures. A simple example would be a measure of economic status in conjunction with the individual's perception of himself as rich or poor. Another would

TABLE 1

A Social Stress Typology

Exposure to presumptive stress	Perception of stress	
	Thematic	Not thematic
Frequent and/or severe	+ + (overwhelmed)	+ − (challenged)
Infrequent and/or mild	− + (self-defeated)	− − (lucky)

be an assessment of frequency and scope of interaction in comparison with self-assessment as isolated or socially integrated. Finally, means for measuring perceptions of continuity in the value system and consistency between values and goals are also being developed (Thurnher, 1971). These perceptions, which we believe are also crucial mediators between stress and adaptation, are derived from very detailed interviews, but they show promise of lending themselves to structured instrumentation.

The Adaptive Process

Thus far, two methods have been developed for operationalizing a concept of adaptation that focuses on the relationship between positive and negative indicators. The first method is a measure of the relationship between recent positive and negative affect, on the one hand, and self-appraisal of happiness, on the other (Bradburn, 1969; Bradburn & Caplovitz, 1965). The second is an assessment of the ratio between psychological resources and psychological impairments, which in turn may be compared (a) with self-appraisal of morale or life satisfaction and (b) with psychiatrists' ratings of mental health (Chiriboga & Lowenthal, 1971). These measures, applied to cross-sectional studies of different life stages as well as in longitudinal studies, will add a more flexible, process-oriented approach to the psychology of aging. Further, by measuring change in the specific "resource" and "impairment" attributes, such as denial, intra- versus extrapunitiveness, and stability and change in self-image in relation to other indicators of adaptation, we will be able to further transcend the static and frustrating stringencies of diagnostic and "degree of impairment" models.

THE CHALLENGE OF A LIFE-COURSE PERSPECTIVE

A study of transitional stages of adulthood[4] is beginning to yield findings from the perspectives suggested above, which may help further to unravel some of the stress–adaptation paradoxes. The community-based sample consists of 52 high school seniors facing such transitions as first job, college, or marriage; 50 newlyweds facing

---

[4] National Institute of Child Health and Human Development, Grant HD 03051.

the transition of parenthood; 54 middle-aged parents facing the departure of their youngest child from the home; and 60 preretirees, persons within three years of anticipated retirement. Interviews and testing averaged nine hours per subject and covered life history, values, current and projected goals, social networks and social perceptions, projective tests, and a variety of indicators of adaptation.[5]

In this section, there will be a report first on the time dimensions and on negative and positive aspects of presumptive stress in relation to self-reports of morale. Next, preliminary data will be offered to illustrate how the addition of a stress perception factor helps to explain the deviant cells in the presumptive stress–morale paradigm. Moving from subjective to objective indicators of adaptation, we will then briefly describe a psychological balance typology, which, in turn, will be assessed in terms of its association with presumed actual stress and with the typology of stress perception.

Time Dimensions of Presumptive Stress and Their Relation to Current Morale

The measures of recent and cumulative stress thus far operationalized are still inadequate by the standards we have recommended and are based on an additive model. They derive from the Holmes and Rahe (1967) Social Readjustment Scale which, while it comingles imposed external events with those that the individual himself may have brought about, will ultimately allow the inclusion of an empirically derived system for weighing the relative severity, as well as the frequency, of stressors. In its original form, the schedule includes 42 common life events requiring some readjustment, such as marriage, death of spouse, and loss of job. We have added 16 events in order to increase the schedule's applicability to the youngest and oldest sample groupings and have also added positive and negative dimensions to some of the events, such as major improvement in work conditions, as well as deterioration. Although we have made distinction among stresses experienced during the first, second, third, and fourth years immediately prior to the inter-

---

[5] The theoretical framework for the study is described in Lowenthal (1971). Preliminary reports of findings will be found in Lowenthal and Chiriboga (1972), Spence and Lonner (1971), Thurnher (1971), and Thurnher, Spence, and Lowenthal "Value Confluence and Behavioral Conflict in Intergenerational Relations" (publication pending).

view, here we shall combine the four years to provide a recent stress measure to compare with all prior stress.

Despite methodological shortcomings (which we plan to rectify as the analysis proceeds), the data show promise. The relationship between recent stress and stress accumulated from birth up to four years prior to the interview was slight. In other words, respondents who had very stressful lives in the past as measured in terms of presumptive stress are not necessarily the same as respondents who had considerable recent exposure to presumptive stress. As one might expect, the recent stress score was significantly higher for the two younger groups, particularly the newlyweds, while scores on life-course stress were higher for the two older groups.

The association between recent exposure to stress and current morale[6] is equivocal. Those who experienced much recent stress felt lonely, depressed, and bored and restless in the week prior to testing more often than did those with little recent presumptive stress (see Table 2). However, they also reported themselves to have felt elated, excited, pleased, and proud more often during the prior week. Altogether, they reported more of *both* positive and negative experiences than did the unstressed. Among those ranking high on cumulative past stress, on the other hand, there was little relationship with morale or affect, except that those with high scores on actual cumulative stress felt less bored and less lonely than others. In other words, while recent stress is associated with current affective complexity, past stress seems to have little to do with it.

Positive versus Negative Presumptive Stress and Morale

As we have noted, in a considerable body of the sociopsychological research on stress, any major change in life circumstances has often been included in the stress index, with no analytic distinctions drawn between positive and negative changes. Our preliminary analyses of the varying consequences of positive and negative stressors have produced mixed results. On the one hand (see Table 2), those high on presumptive stress, whether positive or negative, report more positive affect and more negative affect than those with low

---

[6] Measures of morale are drawn from Bradburn (1965) and consist of responses to the question, "In general, how happy are you these days?" as well as to questions probing the frequency of 12 positive and negative affective experiences during the past seven days.

TABLE 2

Correlations between Indices of Stress and Morale for the Total Sample

Feeling	Recent stress			Cumulative stress			Perceived stress
	Posi-tive	Nega-tive	Com-bined	Posi-tive	Nega-tive	Com-bined	
On top of the world	.26	.13*	.25				−.14
Excited	.19		.22				
Pleased	.16		.18				
Proud	.24		.21				
Lonely			.25	−.13*	−.16	−.15	
Angry				−.12*			
Could not get going							
Depressed	.12*	.20	.18				
Bored	.23		.28	−.14	−.24	−.23	
Restless	.14		.18			−.12*	
More to do than could							
Uneasy		.18					
Overall happiness	.12*						−.13*

Note. For all measures, a higher score indicates more of the construct assessed. N = 216.

*$p \leq .10$; all other correlations: $p \leq .05$.

rankings on presumptive stress. Changes then, may have similar consequences whether they are positive or negative, although there is some evidence that positive stress, particularly when recent, is more related to high morale than is negative stress. Those high on recent positive stress were more apt to report affective experiences, particularly positive ones, during the prior week; they also tended to report themselves as happier. Those high on negative stress reported fewer such experiences. The two significant correlations indicated lower morale, namely, feelings of depression and uneasiness.

Combining people of various ages or at various life stages may also obscure the differing consequences of positive and negative stress. For example, middle-aged persons who had lived through many negative experiences throughout their past lives reported themselves to be happier than did those who had not. Preretirees highly exposed to negative stress over their life-span, on the other hand, were less happy than those not so exposed. We do not know yet whether these provocative differences are associated with a greater sense of futurity among middle-aged persons, with relief that their child-rearing stage is about to conclude, or with other factors. Among the preretirees, we also do not know whether their unhappiness is related to additional stresses accumulated since they were in the pre-empty-nest stage, whether they are anticipating retirement with more dread than the middle-aged persons anticipate the postparental stage, or whether, because they are chronologically older,[7] they are primarily reacting to a shortened sense of futurity, which may become one more negative stress.

Perceived Stress and Current Morale

Our data, then, suggest that presumptive social stress, whether recent or cumulative, positive or negative, may be associated with high morale, at least at some life stages. Conversely, some persons with little stress exposure have low morale.

Our exploration of such paradoxical findings began with the introduction of a rating of the degree of preoccupation with stress, based on the life-history section. Although only two correlations showed evidence of a trend, both appear reasonable. Those ranking low on stress perception were more likely to report feeling on top of the world during the prior week and also to report themselves as generally happier than did those who were more preoccupied with stress.

We then cross-referenced the stress perception dimension with the stress exposure dimension (see Table 1) and found that those high on stress exposure and high on preoccupation with stress had the lowest current morale and that those low on both had the highest morale. However, those high on stress exposure and having little preoccupation with it had far better morale than those with little stress exposure but considerable preoccupation with what they did have. Thus, the justification for the labels given to these latter two groups: the challenged and self-defeated, respectively. These distinctions hold both for the typology built on the basis of exposure to recent stress and for the typology built on the basis of past cumulative stress. On both typologies, it should be added, there were more men than women with high actual stress scores but low rankings on stress perception.

---

[7] The preretirees averaged nearly 10 years older than those in the pre-empty-nest stage.

One of our next major inquiries will be into the question of whether or not persons with a tendency to deny stress show any decrease on our morale indicators as they grow older, particularly, as they move into the retirement stage. In short, the question we are raising is whether or not the category that we have labeled as the challenged actually includes deniers as well.

The concept of stress perception, then, helps considerably to explain some of the anomalies of a model based on actual stress exposure alone and helps to account for those with low-stress scores who have low morale and those with high-stress scores who have high morale. There is, of course, need for further refinement of the perceptual dimension. For example, we have not yet had time to differentiate between individual variations in susceptibility to particular types of stressors and variations in what might be called a stress proneness syndrome, that is, a tendency to be preoccupied with stress regardless of type.

The Adaptive Equation

Most stress research to date has assessed the relationship between various stresses and indicators of degree or type of impairment. In an earlier part of this chapter, we advocated the addition of psychological resources to the adaptive domain. Some resource indicators may represent stable personality characteristics, with a continuing potential for mediating between stressor and stress reaction. Others may fluctuate in response to variations in real or perceived stress. While we hope, in a four-year follow-up study, to be able to differentiate between the more and the less stable of the psychological resources, for the time being we shall assess all of them as potential segments of the adaptive equation.

The 13 resource indicators focus on qualities relevant to concepts of positive mental health. They consist of ratings of parts or all of the interview. Resources include familial and extrafamilial mutuality, contextual and life-cycle perspective, growth, competence, insight, perceived and judged encroachment, hope, satisfaction with interpersonal and intrapersonal competence, and self-satisfaction.[8]

---

[8] These indicators were developed during a series of consultations and work seminars with psychoanalysts Robert Butler and Leonard Micon. A satisfactory level of reliability was attained for all measures.

The five indicators of psychological deficits are drawn from a 42-item symptoms inventory and (independently) from three-judge evaluations of the entire protocol (exclusive of the symptoms lists and other psychological tests and checklists). Included here also is a total count of symptoms mentioned, a psychiatrist's rating of the degree of psychopathology implicit in the total response set, and a count of the number of "severe" ratings on individual symptoms for each respondent. The rating of overall psychological impairment, the direction of impairment (i.e., decreasing or increasing), and the ratings of resources were made by an interdisciplinary team of social scientists.

For this preliminary analysis, subjects were divided into high, low, and intermediate groups on both numbers of resources and numbers of deficits. Reading down the diagonal from upper left to lower right (see Table 3), we move from the psychologically most complex persons to the psychologically simplest or most-constricted persons.

Among those with many resources, the happiest, again as measured by the Bradburn (1969) measure, were those who also had many deficits. In fact, they were the second happiest of all the nine groups (the happiest of all had moderate resources and few deficits). The third happiest group were those having few resources and few deficits, and whose psychological makeup, in short, appears to be quite simple. Those intermediate on *both* resources and deficits were the least happy—even less so than those with few resources and many deficits. In other words, those with a wealth of resources can cope with many deficits better, or at least more happily, than those with only moderate resources can cope with few deficits.

Life-stage variations in the balance typology may help to explain these seeming paradoxes. The happiest teen-agers were complex,

TABLE 3

A Psychological Balance Typology

Resources	Deficits		
	Many	Intermediate	Few
Many	+ + (complex)	+ 0	+ −
Intermediate	0 +	0 0 (bland)	0 −
Few	− +	− 0	− − (simple)

Note. Where "+" equals many, "−" equals few, and "0" equals intermediate on each of the two balanced dimensions.

high on both resources and deficits; the happiest newlyweds were those with many resources and few deficits; the happiest middle-aged parents were those with moderate resources and few deficits; the happiest preretirees were those with the simplest adaptive equation: few resources but also few deficits. Indeed, among these oldest members of our sample, the most complex were the least happy—less happy even than those low on resources and with many deficits, exactly the converse of the high school seniors. In other words, "complex" teen-agers seem to face their fairly unstructured future with aplomb. Young adults, most of whom were planning for a first child in the near future, tend to be happy only if they have many resources. Among the two older groups, however, resources appear not to continue to contribute to a sense of well-being. For them, having many deficits is associated with unhappiness and having a high rank on resources does not compensate, perhaps because those who have many resources become increasingly frustrated in their attempts to realize their maximum potential.

Stress and the Adaptive Equation

Looking at the stress measures in the light of psychological resources and deficits, we are finding that persons with many actual stresses tend to have high ranks on resources but, surprisingly, they exhibit no definite ranking on deficits (see Table 4). This is particularly true for cumulative stress. In general, those ranking high on presumed stress tend to have a broader perspective on both themselves and society—to be more growth oriented, insightful, and competent. They also tend to encroach on others more than others encroach on them.

Persons with the lowest ranks on the indices of both recent and cumulative stress tend to be the psychologically simple, that is, low on both resources and deficits. Again, variations in the perception of stress, as in preoccupation with it, help to explain both the common patterns and the deviations from these patterns. Persons low on presumptive stress but high on stress perception are more likely to be rated psychologically impaired by the psychiatrist than those high on actual stress but low on stress perception.[9] Perceived stress, indeed, manifests the most consistent associations with adaptive

---

[9]The psychiatrist's ratings were based only on the symptoms list; the stress proneness ratings were based only on the life history section of the interview.

TABLE 4

Correlations between Indices of Stress, Resources, and Deficits for the Total Sample

Resources and deficits	Recent stress			Cumulative stress			Perceived stress
	Positive	Negative	Combined	Positive	Negative	Combined	
Resources							
Intrafamilial mutuality				.15			−.14
Extrafamilial mutuality				.22			
Contextual perspective		.15		.34	.21	.30	
Life-cycle perspective				.26	.16	.27	
Growth	.25	.19	.27				
Competence	.18			.32	.16	.27	
Insight				.20		.18	
Perceived accommodation	−.18			−.12*			.19
Judged accommodation					−.26	−.22	
Hope	.17		.17	−.12*	−.15	−.16	−.26
Satisfaction with competence				.20		.18	−.18
Satisfaction with interpersonal competence				.12*			−.18
Satisfaction with self	.13			.14			−.27
Deficits							
Symptoms total			.19				.22
Number of severe symptoms		.14	.13				.22
Psychiatrist's ratings of symptoms list							.17
Psychological impairment				−.174			.23
Direction of impairment							

Note. For all measures, a higher score indicates more of the construct assessed. $N = 216$.

*$p \leq .10$; all other correlations: $p \leq .05$.

indicators. Regardless of their ranking on presumptive stress, those high on perceived stress are rated as less apt to have a capacity for mutuality in close interpersonal relationships, more apt to be passive and accommodating, less apt to be hopeful concerning the future, and less apt to be satisfied with their competence, their social effectiveness, and themselves in general. They also exhibit greater psychiatric symptomatology and general psychological impairment.

Looking back over Tables 2 and 4, then, we can see a high association between recent stress and current morale and little association between cumulative stress and morale. We find no consistent association between exposure to stress and current morale, unless we add the dimension of stress perception. When this dimension is added, there is a strong relationship on both the subjective and objective measures. Those with high stress exposure and low stress perception report themselves as happier than those with low stress exposure. They also report a greater richness in recent affective experiences. Their morale, as self-reported, is, in short, high. At the same time, they are rated as psychologically more complex by an interdisciplinary rating team, and they are assessed as mentally and emotionally healthier by a psychiatrist who reviewed and rated their symptoms (blinded for the rest of the protocol).

In summary, we have seen that recent stress correlates more highly with morale than with psychological resources and deficits. Cumulative stress, on the other hand, correlates highly with the adaptive equation but not with morale. Finally, there is much less of a relationship between perceived stress and morale than between perceived stress and psychological resources and deficits.

CONCLUSION

A life-course perspective on the relationship between stress and adaptation has implications for both policy and planning. It also, we believe, holds promise for a gradual development of workable theories of the middle range (see Merton, 1957).

We have seen that the happiest preretirees are those who rank low on both resources and deficits. From a practical perspective, it would appear that those whom Korchin (1965) might call the dull may be those most likely to grow old gracefully and happily in our culture. The more complex preretirees, with possibly a greater potential for contributing to society, perhaps because they have such a potential, are not as happy as they face a life stage in which the absence of social demands may in itself become a genuine stress. By cutting off those persons about to retire from challenge and opportunity, and, yes, even from social stress, we may enable the dull to continue to be happy; but the complicated and possibly the most gifted are likely to become objectively maladapted and subjectively miserable unless they transcend social prejudices and strictures.

From a theoretical point of view, the application of a life-cycle perspective to the stress–adaptation paradigm holds much promise, in part because it requires an integration of concepts and data from a number of social science disciplines. As Neugarten points out (see ch. 10), personal change in adult life must be studied in the context of biological, sociohistorical, and socialization theories as a minimum.

More particularly, within a stress–adaptation paradigm, to understand the dynamics of the time dimensions of stress, for example, we need to draw on both psychoanalytic theory and epidemiological data. To assess the significance of the varying thresholds between too much and too little stress at successive life stages, we must draw on physiological and psychophysiological studies of physical stress and of sensory deprivation. To further refine the concept of stress perception, and in particular the perception of social stresses and supports, we hope that, just as Havighurst (see ch. 18) has contributed a life-cycle perspective to role theory, sociologists will also begin to apply such a perspective to reference groups, to alienation concepts and research, and in particular, to the individual's perceptions of his social networks and structures.

Of special importance in this connection, especially for our time and our place, is the potential of anthropology for providing insights into the significance of ethnic identity as an ameliorator as well as a source of stress at successive stages of the life cycle. Finally, if we hope to understand such critical issues as whether or not the tendency of the males of our culture to deny stress is causally related to the increase in their suicide, morbidity, and mortality rates with advancing age, we need the skills and insights of those psychoanalysts and other clinicians who have adopted a life-course perspective.

REFERENCES

Antonovsky, A., & Kats, R. The life crisis history as a tool in epidemiological research. *Journal of Health and Social Behavior,* 1967, **8,** 15–21.

Barron, F. *Creativity and psychological health.* Princeton, N.J.: Van Nostrand, 1963.

Berkman, P. L. Life stress and psychological well-being: A replication of Langner's analysis in the Midtown Manhattan Study. *Journal of Health and Social Behavior,* 1971, **12,** 35–45.

Biderman, A. D. Life and death in extreme captivity situations. In M. H. Appley & R. Trumbull (Eds.), *Psychological stress: Issues in research.* New York: Appleton-Century-Crofts, 1967.

Blau, Z. S. Structural constraints on friendship in old age. *American Sociological Review,* 1961, **26,** 429–439.

Bowlby, J. The nature of the child's tie to his mother. *International Journal of Psycho-Analysis,* 1958, **39,** 350–373.

Bradburn, N. *The structure of psychological well-being.* Chicago: Aldine, 1969.

Bradburn, N. M., & Caplovitz, D. *Reports on happiness: A pilot study of behavior related to mental health.* Chicago: Aldine, 1965.

Butler, R. N. The life review: An interpretation of reminiscence in the aged. *Psychiatry,* 1963, **26,** 65–76.

Caudill, W. *Effects of social and cultural systems in reacting to stress.* (Pamphlet No. 14) New York: Social Science Research Council, 1958.

Chiriboga, D. A., & Lieberman, M. A. Relocation stress in the aged: A replication study. Paper presented at the 23rd Annual Meeting of the Gerontological Society, Toronto, Canada, October 1970.

Chiriboga, D., & Lowenthal, M. F. Psychological correlates of perceived well-being. *Proceedings of the 79th Annual Convention of the American Psychological Association,* 1971, **6,** 603–604. (Summary)

Clark, M. M. The anthropology of aging: A new area for studies of culture and personality. *Gerontologist,* 1967, **7,** 55–64.

Clark, M. M. Cultural values and dependency in later life. In R. Kalish (Ed.), *The dependencies of old people.* (Occasional papers in Gerontology No. 6) Ann Arbor: Institute of Gerontology, University of Michigan-Wayne State University, 1969.

Clark, M. M. On the relationship between cultural anthropology and studies of adult development and aging. Paper presented at the Conference on Anthropology and Mental Health, Center for Advanced Study in the Behavioral Sciences, Stanford, California, October 15–16, 1971.

Clark, M., & Anderson, B. G. *Culture and aging: An anthropological study of older Americans.* Springfield, Ill.: Charles C Thomas, 1967.

Clausen, J. A. Methodological issues in the measurement of mental health of the aged. In M. F. Lowenthal & A. Zilli (Eds.), *Interdisciplinary topics in gerontology: Colloquium on health and aging of the population.* Vol. 3. New York: Karger, 1969.

Croog, S. H. The family as a source of stress. In S. Levine & N. A. Scotch (Eds.), *Social stress.* Chicago: Aldine, 1970.

Dodge, D. L., & Martin, W. T. *Social stress and chronic illness.* Notre Dame: University of Notre Dame Press, 1970.

Dohrenwend, B. P., & Dohrenwend, B. S. *Social status and psychological disorder: A causal inquiry.* New York: Wiley, 1969.

Durkheim, E. (Trans. by J. A. Spaulding & G. Simpson; Ed. by G. Simpson) *Suicide, a study in sociology.* Glencoe, Ill.: Free Press, 1951.

Erikson, E. H. Identity and the life cycle. *Psychological Issues,* 1959, **1**(1, Whole No. 1).

Goldfarb, A. I. The psychodynamics of dependency and the search for aid. In R. A. Kalish (Ed.), *The dependencies of old people.* (Occasional Papers in Gerontology No. 6) Ann Arbor: Institute of Gerontology, University of Michigan-Wayne State University, 1969.

Gordon, R. E., Singer, M. B., & Gordon, K. K. Social psychological stress. *Archives of General Psychiatry,* 1961, **4,** 459–470.

Grinker, R. R., & Spiegel, J. P. *Men under stress.* Philadelphia: Blakiston, 1945.

Harlow, H. F., & Zimmermann, R. R. Affectional responses in the infant monkey. *Science,* 1959, **130,** 421–432.

Henley, B., & Davis, M. S. Satisfaction and dissatisfaction: A study of the chronically-ill aged patient. *Journal of Health and Social Behavior,* 1967, **8,** 65–75.

Hinkle, L. E., Christenson, W. N., Kane, F. D., Ostfeld, A., Thetford, W. N., & Wolff, H. G. An investigation of the relation between life experience, personality characteristics, and general susceptibility to illness. *Psychosomatic Medicine,* 1958, **20,** 278–295.

Holmes, T. H., & Rahe, R. H. The social readjustment rating scale. *Journal of Psychosomatic Research,* 1967, **11,** 213–218.

Horvath, F. Psychological stress: A review of definitions and experimental research. *General Systems: Yearbook of Society for General Systems Research,* 1960, **4,** 203–230.

Jaco, E. G. Mental illness in response to stress. In S. Levine & N. A. Scotch (Eds.), *Social stress.* Chicago: Aldine, 1970.

Jahoda, M. *Current concepts of positive mental health.* New York: Basic Books, 1958.

Janis, I. L. *Psychological stress: Psychoanalytic and behavioral studies of surgical patients.* New York: Wiley, 1958.

Katz, D. Group process and social integration. *Journal of Social Issues,* 1967, **23**(1), 3–24.

Keniston, K. *The uncommitted: Alienated youth in American society.* New York: Harcourt, Brace & World, 1965.

Kissel, S. Social stimuli and reduction of stress. *Dissertation Abstracts,* 1962, **22**(12), 4407.

Korchin, S. J. Some psychological determinants of stress behavior. In S. Z. Klausner (Ed.), *The quest for self-control.* New York: Free Press of Glencoe, 1965.

Langner, T. S., & Michael, S. T. *Life stress and mental health: The Midtown Manhattan Study.* New York: Free Press of Glencoe, 1963.

Lazarus, R. S. *Psychological stress and the coping process.* New York: McGraw-Hill, 1966.

Lazarus, R. S., Opton, E. M., Jr., & Averill, J. R. The management of stressful experiences. Paper presented at the Foundations' Fund for Research in Psychiatry Conference on Adaptation to Change, Dorado, Puerto Rico, June 1968. (Mimeo)

Lecky, P. *Self consistency: A theory of personality.* (Edited and interpreted by F. C. Thorne) Hamden, Conn.: Shoe String Press, 1961.

Leff, M. J., Roatch, J. F., & Bunney, W. E., Jr. Environmental factors preceding the onset of severe depressions. *Psychiatry,* 1970, **33,** 293–311.

Levin, S. Toward a classification of external factors capable of inducing psychological stress. *International Journal of Psycho-Analysis,* 1966, **47,** 546–551

Levine, S., & Scotch, N. A. (Eds.) *Social stress.* Chicago: Aldine, 1970.

Lewis, C. N. Reminiscing and self-concept in old age. *Journal of Gerontology,* 1971, **26,** 240–243.

Lieberman, M. A. Vulnerability to stress and the process of dying. *Proceedings of the 7th International Congress of Gerontology, Vienna, Austria.* Vol. 7. Vienna, Austria: Egerman, 1966.

Lieberman, M. A. Crises of the last decade of life: Reaction and adaptations. Invited paper presented at Symposium on Mental Health of the Aged, University of Southern California, Los Angeles, June 1970.

Lowenthal, M. F. *Lives in distress: The paths of the elderly to the psychiatric ward.* New York: Basic Books, 1964. (a)

Lowenthal, M. F. Social isolation and mental illness in old age. *American Sociological Review,* 1964, **29,** 54–70. (b)

Lowenthal, M. F. Antecedents of isolation and mental illness in old age. *Archives of General Psychiatry,* 1965, **12,** 245–254.

Lowenthal, M. F. Social adjustment in the aged. *Proceedings of the 7th International Congress of Gerontology, Vienna, Austria.* Vol. 8. Vienna, Austria: Verlag des Wiener Medizinischen Akademie, 1966. (Suppl.)

Lowenthal, M. F. The relationship between social factors and mental health in the aged. In A. Simon & L. J. Epstein (Eds.), *Aging in modern society.* (Psychiatric Research Report 23) Washington, D.C.: American Psychiatric Association, 1968.

Lowenthal, M. F. Intentionality: Toward a framework for the study of adaptation in adulthood. *Aging & Human Development,* 1971, **2**(2), 79–95.

Lowenthal, M. F., & Berkman, P. L. The problem of rating psychiatric disability in a study of normal and abnormal aging. *Journal of Health and Human Behavior,* 1964, **15,** 40–44.

Lowenthal, M. F., Berkman, P. L., & Associates. *Aging and mental disorder in San Francisco: A social psychiatric study.* San Francisco: Jossey-Bass, 1967.

Lowenthal, M. F., & Chiriboga, D. Transition to the empty nest: Crisis, challenge, or relief? *Archives of General Psychiatry,* 1972, **26,** 8–14.

Lowenthal, M. F., & Haven, C. Interaction and adaptation: Intimacy as a critical variable. *American Sociological Review,* 1968, **33,** 20–30.

Lowenthal, M. F., Spence, D. L., & Thurnher, M. Interplay of personal and social factors at transitional stages. Discussion in I. Rosow, *Socialization to old age.* Washington, D.C.: National Institute of Child Health and Human Development, in press.

Maddox, G. L. Themes and issues in sociological theories of human aging. *Human Development,* 1970, **13,** 17–27.

MacFarlane, J. W. Perspectives on personality consistency and change from the guidance study. *Vita Humana,* 1964, **7,** 115–126.

Mai, F. M. M. Personality and stress in coronary disease. *Journal of Psychosomatic Research,* 1968, **12,** 275–287.

Mechanic, D., & Volkart, E. H. Stress, illness-behavior, and the sick role. *American Sociological Review,* 1961, **26,** 51–58.

Merton, R. K. *Social theory and social structure.* Glencoe, Ill.: Free Press, 1957.

Murphy, G. E., Kuhn, N. O., Christensen, R. F., & Robins, E. Life stress in a normal population: A study of 101 women hospitalized for normal delivery. *Journal of Nervous and Mental Disorders,* 1962, **134,** 150–161.

Neugarten, B. L. Summary and implications. In B. L. Neugarten & Associates, *Personality in middle and late life.* New York: Atherton, 1964.

Neugarten, B. L. Continuities and discontinuities of psychological issues into adult life. *Human Development,* 1969, **12,** 121–130.

Neugarten, B. L., & Gutmann, D. L. Age-sex roles and personality in middle age: A thematic apperception study. In B. L. Neugarten & Associates, *Personality in middle and late life.* New York: Atherton, 1964.

Paykel, E. S., Myers, J. K., Dienelt, M. N., Klerman, G. L., Lindenthal, J. J., & Pepper, M. P. Life events and depression. *Archives of General Psychiatry,* 1969, **21,** 753–760.

Perlin, S. Psychiatric screening in a home for the aged: I. A follow-up study. *Geriatrics,* 1958, **13,** 747–751.

Perlin, S., & Butler, R. N. Psychiatric aspects of adaptation to the aging experience. In J. E. Birren, R. N. Butler, S. W. Greenhouse, L. Sokoloff, & M. R. Yarrow (Eds.), *Human aging: A biological and behavioral study.* (USPHS Publ. No. 986) Washington, D.C.: United States Government Printing Office, 1963.

Rahe, R. H., & Holmes, T. H. Life crisis and disease onset: I. Qualitative and quantitative definition of the life crisis and its association with health change. II. A prospective study of life crises and health changes. Seattle: Department of Psychiatry, School of Medicine, University of Washington, 1966.

Rahe, R., McKean, J. D., Jr., & Arthur, R. J. A longitudinal study of life-change and illness patterns. *Journal of Psychosomatic Research,* 1967, **10,** 355–366.

Renaud, H., & Estess, F. Life history interviews with one hundred normal American males: "Pathogenicity" of childhood. *American Journal of Orthopsychiatry,* 1961, **31,** 786–802.

Rosner, A. Stress and the maintenance of self-concept in the aged. *Proceedings of the 7th International Congress of Gerontology, Vienna, Austria.* Vol. 8. Vienna, Austria: Verlag der Wiener Medizinischen Akademie, 1966.

Ruff, G. E., & Korchin, S. J. Adaptive stress behavior. In M. H. Appley & R. Trumbull (Eds.), *Psychological stress: Issues in research.* New York: Appleton-Century-Crofts, 1967.

Schofield, W., & Ballan, L. A comparative study of the personal histories of schizophrenics and nonpsychiatric patients. *Journal of Abnormal and Social Psychology,* 1959, **59,** 216–225.

Scott, R., & Howard, A. Models of stress. In S. Levine & N. A. Scotch (Eds.), *Social stress.* Chicago: Aldine, 1970.

Selye, H. Stress and psychiatry. *American Journal of Psychiatry,* 1956, **113,** 423–427.

Smith, M. B. *Social psychology and human values.* Chicago: Aldine, 1969.

Smith, W. G. Critical life-events and prevention strategies in mental health. *Archives of General Psychiatry,* 1971, **25,** 103–109.

Spence, D. L., & Lonner, T. D. The empty nest: A transition in motherhood. *Family Coordinator,* 1971, Oct., 369–375.

Spitz, R. A., & Wolf, K. M. Anaclitic depression. In, *Psychoanalytic study of the child*. Vol. 2. New York: International Universities Press, 1946.

Streib, G. F., & Schneider, C. J. *Retirement in American society: Impact and process*. Ithica: Cornell University Press, 1971.

Thurnher, M. Values and goals in later middle age. Paper presented at the annual meeting of the Gerontological Society, Houston, Texas, October 1971.

Thurlow, H. J. Illness in relation to life situation and sick-role tendency. *Journal of Psychosomatic Research*, 1971, **15**, 73–88.

Tyhurst, J. H. The role of transition states—including disasters—in mental illness. In, *Symposium on preventive and social psychiatry, April 15–17, 1957*. Washington, D.C.: United States Government Printing Office, 1957.

Volinn, I. J., & Spielholz, J. B. Relating health and social contacts to the morale of elderly persons. *Public Health Reports*, 1969, **84**, 1013–1020.

White, R. W. Ego and reality in psychoanalytic theory. *Psychological Issues*, 1963, **3**(3, Whole No. 2).

Winnik, H. Z. Contribution to symposium on psychic traumatization through social catastrophe. *International Journal of Psycho-Analysis*, 1968, **49**, 298–301.

Personality Change in Late Life: A Developmental Perspective

BERNICE L. NEUGARTEN

From the perspective of a developmental psychologist, aging should be studied within the broader context of the life cycle or the life course. Old age is neither a separate nor a disjunctive period of life. Although it has its unique characteristics, it is to be seen within the same complex of biological and sociocultural dimensions that provide the framework for studying behavior at all age periods.

While a psychology of old age depends upon a psychology of the life cycle, the latter has been slow to appear. A number of texts and readers have been published in the past two decades in which the authors have attempted to bring together findings regarding childhood, adulthood, and old age (notably, Lidz, 1968; Perlman, 1968; Pressey & Kuhlen, 1957), but these attempts have not been altogether successful. In part this is because the quantity of research in child development outbalances that in adult development, particularly with regard to systematic observations of individuals studied over time. While a few sets of personality data have been reported for persons followed from adolescence into adulthood (Block, 1971; Havighurst, Bowman, Liddle, Matthews, & Pierce, 1962; Hess, 1962; Honzik, 1966; Kagan & Moss, 1962; Tuddenham, 1959), we have only a few fragments of data for individuals followed from young adulthood into middle age (Kelly, 1955; Terman & Oden, 1959),

Bernice L. Neugarten is Professor of Human Development and Chairman, Committee on Human Development, University of Chicago, and has been Director of the Graduate Training Program in Adult Development and Aging since 1958. She received the Gerontological Society's Kleemeier Award in 1971 for outstanding contributions to research on aging. Her major research interests relate both to psychology and to sociology: to personality change and to intergenerational and age group relations.

The author is indebted to Charles Taylor, who read this chapter in first draft and made a number of valuable suggestions.

no personality data for middle age to old age, and only a few studies of long-term adult outcomes for individuals on whom childhood data are available (Baller, Charles, & Miller, 1967; Robins, 1966; Rogler & Hollingshead, 1965).

Related to the paucity of appropriate data is the lack of a conceptual framework that encompasses early and late development or that deals satisfactorily with the life cycle as a whole. The recent book edited by Goulet and Baltes (1970) is a significant contribution toward a life-span developmental psychology, but in its focus on methods and models and on cognitive and intellectual functions, it makes little mention of personality processes.

Overall, we have only the beginnings of a developmental psychology of adulthood defined as an area of inquiry in which investigators are concerned with questions of orderly and sequential changes occurring with the passage of time, with issues of consistency and change in personality over relatively long intervals, and with issues of antecedent–consequent relationships.

CONCEPTUAL FRAMEWORKS

Psychologists agree that there are observable changes as well as observable consistencies in adult personality. The problems are how to delineate those personality processes that are the most salient at successive periods in adulthood, how to describe those processes in terms that are appropriate, and how to isolate those changes that are developmental from those that are not. Only after solving these problems can we assess the utility of various conceptual frameworks for explanation and prediction.

The Concept of Development

The term developmental refers here not only to those processes that are biologically programmed and inherent in the organism, but also to those in which the organism is irreversibly changed or transformed by interaction with the environment. As the result of one's life history with its accumulating record of adaptations to both biological and social events, there is a continually *changing basis within the individual* for perceiving and responding to new events.

The term developmental has been used with a wide variety of philosophical and scientific meanings (e.g., see Goulet & Baltes, 1970; Harris, 1957; Langer, 1969). It often implies movement toward a higher, more differentiated, or more desirable state or end point; and while for that reason the term is often an awkward one when used in conjunction with aging, some psychologists have written of developmental change in adulthood in terms of growth or expansion or actualization (Bühler, 1935, 1959, 1968; Jung, 1933; Kuhlen, 1964; Maslow, 1954; Rogers, 1963). Such writing is usually directed to the conditions that promote the development of human potential or mental health, with implications for psychotherapy. Others conceive of adult change as decline, adopting a biological model of decrement for conceptualizing psychological change. Still others adopt a model of stability of adult personality, accounting for change as the result of idiosyncratic sequences of biological and social events or as the effects of social-cultural influences.

Unlike the situation with regard to child development where directionality of change is clear, none of these views of directionality in adulthood rests on a compelling rationale. Is the organism biologically programmed only toward maturity, with postmaturity changes to be regarded as haphazard? Or is it programmed toward decline and death?

For the present, the student of adult personality will find it strategic to accept age relatedness alone as the criterion, that is, to call developmental those processes that can be demonstrated to vary in an orderly way with age regardless of the direction of change. This does not imply that age is a meaningful variable (Wohlwill, 1970). The psychologist is eventually concerned not with the passage of time itself, but with the biological, social, and psychological events that give substance and meaning to time. In exploring an uncharted field, however, it is a justifiable first step to use age as a preliminary index and to determine which, if any, personality phenomena are more associated with age than with other gross variables such as sex, health, ethnicity, level of education, or social class.

In determining age relatedness it is difficult to pinpoint which of the differences between younger and older persons are to be attributed to the effects of aging and which, to the differences between cohorts (i.e., groups of persons born at different points in history). Successive cohorts have presumably been influenced by different social and cultural conditions and as a consequence will presumably perform differently on personality measures. Neither cross-sectional nor longitudinal methods are free from the difficulty of disentangling aging from cohort effects. Schaie and his colleagues have developed sophisticated research designs for dealing with this problem (Baltes, 1968; Schaie, 1965, 1970, 1971), but thus far their methods have been applied only to narrow sets of empirical data (Baltes & Reinert,

1969; Schaie, 1971). Once identified, a cohort difference, like an age difference, will need to be investigated further, perhaps by methods that lie outside of the psychologist's area of expertise, to discover which social and historical events can be said to be reflected in the observed personality differences. To put this point differently, we are making progress in differentiating cohort differences from age differences, but neither cohort nor age is itself an explanatory variable. If we can succeed, nevertheless, in demonstrating regularities of age change among adults who vary in social and biological characteristics and in life experiences, we shall have taken an important step in weighing the relative merit of a developmental as compared with another conceptual approach to adult personality.

Theories of Personality Change

The issues regarding continuities and discontinuities in personality and how they are to be conceptualized are persistent and thorny problems in psychology. (Some of the issues have recently been restated by Bortner, 1967; Emmerich, 1969; Kagan, 1969; Mischel, 1969; and Neugarten, 1969.) While the problems are by no means new, they have probably been exacerbated as developmental psychologists have begun to shift attention from the first to the last part of the life cycle.

This is not the occasion for a full discussion of various theories as they bear upon changes in personality in adulthood and old age. (A recent paper by Looft, 1972, is relevant in this connection, for he compares various psychological approaches as they bear upon socialization and personality throughout the life-span.) It may be useful, however, to point briefly to the differing perspectives of psychoanalysis and ego psychology, on the one hand, and social psychology and symbolic interactionist theory, on the other, since these two bodies of theory have been of major influence and both have had the effect of deflecting attention from questions of developmental aspects of adult personality.

Ego Psychology

As a general psychological theory (as contrasted with a method of treatment) psychoanalysis is, of course, a developmental theory; but with its emphasis on a biologically determined sequence in the maturation of drives, it has provided few concepts to deal with normal change after adolescence. The psychoanalytic view is essentially that the sense of identity established in adolescence produces consistency in behavior thereafter; that the character structure becomes fixed in early adulthood; and that while the ego becomes an increasingly important and autonomous agent of change, the essential nature of the personality remains stable. (Luborsky and Schimek, 1964, have written a brief but useful description of psychoanalytic theory as it relates to developmental change throughout the life cycle.)

One major exception among psychoanalysts was Jung (1933), who described stages of development in adulthood, commenting in particular on an increase in introversion in middle and later life and on the reorganization of value systems that characterizes adult change.

A second major exception is Erikson (1959, 1963), who extended his view of developmental sequences to the whole life cycle in speculating on personality change and who delineated eight stages, each representing a choice or a crisis for the expanding ego. Following the crisis of ego identity in adolescence, the last three stages relate to the development of intimacy in early adulthood (the ability to merge one's self with the self of another); then the crisis of generativity (investment in the products of one's own creation and identification with the future); and in late adulthood, the crisis of ego integrity (the view that one's life has been meaningful and inevitable and has been the product of one's own making).

In building a psychology of the life cycle, the influence of Bühler (1935, 1959, 1968) has also been major, for she was among the first to undertake empirical studies to determine what general principles hold for change over the life-span and what shifts in motivations and needs are to be regarded as typical of various phases of adulthood. In her later work, Bühler has given a central place to concepts of the self, intentionality in behavior, goal seeking, and goal reformulation—all important concepts in ego psychology. Fromm (1941), Maslow (1954), Peck (1956), and White (1960, 1963) have also made important contributions. By and large, formulations of this group of theorists have stemmed from their clinical insights; and while they represent enormously useful analytic and interpretive descriptions, they have seldom led to systematic studies or to systematic theory regarding adult personality. This is primarily due to the fact that the formulations have neither focused on the processes of personality per se nor on the events that produce change, but have instead described the *tasks* for the ego or the changing preoccupations and value systems of the adult, or the characteristics of the healthy or actualized personality. Without more exposition of the processes that underlie adult change and without operational definitions of concepts, other investigators are unable to follow up in confirming and elaborating these conceptual frameworks, nor can they make progress in relating descriptive data to theory building.

There have also been the contributions of psychoanalysts who have focused on particular psychosexual events as the precipitants of developmental personality changes in adulthood. Bibring (1959) described changes in women's personalities associated with pregnancy; Benedek (1950, 1959, 1970) described changes associated with parenthood in both men and women and with the climacterium in women; and Deutsch (1944, 1945) elaborated the changes that accompany successive psychosexual events in women. These explications are exceedingly valuable, but because the major events of adult life are by no means limited to the psychosexual or to the biological, these explications offer too narrow a view for constructing a "sufficient" theory of adult personality.

Sociopsychological Perspectives

A contrasting body of theory has emerged from the social psychologists and role theorists (e.g., see Brim & Wheeler, 1966; Clausen, 1968; Sarbin, 1964). Brim (1960), for one, argued that there are no personality dispositions that are persistent across situations and that the personality can be defined as the sum (or the residues) of social experiences and social roles. Becker (1964) suggested that the effects of social structure on experience are primary in understanding stability and change in personality. He proposed that the process of adjustment to new situations is the sufficient explanation of change, while the process of personal commitment is the explanation of stability. Secord and Backman (1961) accounted for stability and change in terms of the relationships among the individual's behavior, his self-concept, and the behavior of others. Stability of personality arises from relative consistency and congruency among the three. Mischel's (1969) is a related point of view insofar as it emphasizes the external versus the internal consistencies. In arguing that the individual is not to be perceived as the carrier of a stable reservoir of motives and traits and that the genotypic–phenotypic explanation of stability is a conceptual trap (namely, that it is erroneous to postuate the same underlying trait or need taking various forms at various times), he urged that diverse behaviors be categorized in terms of the conditions that evoke and maintain them and that change be viewed as discrimination learning. Finally, those investigators who are concerned with cohort differences (e.g., Schaie, 1971) imply that we should look to social and historical contexts more than to developmental processes for explaining differences between age groups.

Advocates of the "social" and the "learning" perspectives have carried out a large number of empirical and experimental studies demonstrating the effects of social situations on behavior change, and those perspectives are important in suggesting interpretations of change over the life cycle that are alternatives to developmental interpretations. At the same time, such concepts as commitment or sense of continuity and consistency of self are left unexplored—concepts that become particularly important if we are to understand aspects of personality such as goal setting, self-regulation, and self-induced change. In short, the attention of this second group of theorists is on transactional aspects of personality, but not upon the selective, initiating, and executive aspects. Furthermore, because these studies have concentrated on short-term change in experimental and laboratory settings, their value for understanding long-term personality change as it occurs in everyday life remains unknown. This is the familiar problem that the personality phenomena that preoccupy the experimentalist are seldom those that preoccupy the psychologist concerned with the study of lives.

In this connection, the principles and methods of psychological ecology elaborated by Barker (1968; Barker & Barker, 1961) provide an empirical as well as a conceptual bridge for studying the individual's behavior and measurable aspects of the natural social setting. While the methods are laborious, they have been used with great effectiveness in studying consistencies among individuals in the same behavior setting and differences elicited by different settings. Barker's approach, while it has not yet been used for this purpose, has enormous potential for studying stability and change in the individual over long periods of time and for elucidating the relative weight of situational and developmental factors.

A Developmental Perspective

The first task for the developmental psychologist interested in adult personality is not to muster evidence against the importance of situational factors or of cohort differences, nor for that matter is it to muster evidence for the underlying stability of behavioral dis-

rewarding boldness and risk taking and saw themselves as possessing energy congruent with the opportunities presented in the outer world. Sixty-year-olds saw the environment as complex and dangerous and the self as conforming and accommodating to outer-world demands. This change was described as a movement from active to passive mastery.

Different modes of dealing with impulse life became salient with increasing age. Preoccupation with the inner life became greater; emotional cathexes toward persons and objects in the outer world seemed to decrease; the readiness to attribute activity and affect to persons in the environment was reduced; there was a movement away from outer-world to inner-world orientation. This change was described as increased *interiority*. There was also a constriction in the ability to integrate wide ranges of stimuli and in the willingness to deal with complicated and challenging situations. Differences with age appeared not only in projective test responses, but also in interview data when the investigator's attention was on latent rather than manifest content and when feeling states and modes of thought were inferred from indirect evidence. Thus, older men and women in verbalizing opinions in dogmatic terms, in failing to clarify past–present or cause–effect relationships, and in using idiosyncratic and eccentric methods of communication gave evidence of lessened sensitivity to the reactions of others and a lessened sense of relatedness to others.

Differences between the sexes appeared with age. Older men seemed more receptive than younger men of their affiliative, nurturant, and sensual promptings; older women, more receptive than younger women of aggressive and egocentric impulses. Men appeared to cope with the environment in increasingly abstract and cognitive terms; women, in increasingly affective and expressive terms. (Chiriboga and Lowenthal, 1971, reported findings that confirm these sex differences.) In both sexes, however, older people seemed to move toward more eccentric, self-preoccupied positions and to attend increasingly to the control and satisfaction of personal needs.

These findings are supported by those of other investigators who have studied samples of middle-aged and older men, among them Clark (1967), Gray (1947), Hays (1952), Schaw and Henry (1956), Lakin and Eisdorfer (1962), and Willoughby (1937–38); and by the observations of psychiatrists, among them Berezin (1963), Butler (1963), Meerloo (1955), and Zinberg and Kaufman (1963), all indicating that aging men seem to move from active involvement with the world to more introversive, passive, and self-centered positions. Shanan and Sharon (1965), in particular, in a study of Israeli men of European origin, used similar methods and reported findings strikingly parallel to the Kansas City findings with regard to the shift in saliency from outer to inner orientation beginning as early as the 40s.

We concluded from our series of studies that chronological age provides order in data that tap intrapsychic processes, processes that are not readily available to awareness or conscious control, and processes that do not have direct expression in overt patterns of social behavior. These studies were based upon cross-sectional samples and must therefore be interpreted with caution. Nevertheless, the findings indicated developmental rather than responsive processes, largely because age differences appeared well before the social losses of aging occurred and well before decrease in social interaction, decrease that is often presumed to precede psychological withdrawal. That is, we found neither a general decrease in competency of performance in adult social roles, nor a thinning of social interaction until the mid-60s or early 70s, yet there were measurable increases in inward orientation and measurable decreases in cathexes for outer-world events beginning in the late 40s and 50s.

Studies in Other Cultures

The indication that intrapsychic change in the second half of life has a developmental basis has received its major support from the work of Gutmann, who has been carrying out a unique set of studies of aging men in other, mainly preliterate, societies. As an earlier member of the Chicago group, Gutmann studied American urban men aged 40 to 70 and on the basis of Thematic Apperception Test (TAT) data, analyzed blind for age of respondent, suggested an age-related movement through successive ego-mastery styles. The instrumental-productive style (active mastery) was found mainly among younger men, those aged 40 to 55. This style seemed to be superseded by a more passive-receptive orientation (passive mastery) in which the self, rather than the world, is revised to meet the requirements of social situations and of external authorities. After age 65 this conformist mode seemed to be replaced to some degree by magical mastery, which involves projective rather than instrumental revisions of the world and the self. In this latter stage, primitive defensive operations, projection and denial, seemed to substitute for realistic activity (Gutmann, 1964; Neugarten & Gutmann, 1958).

To see if this continuum from active to passive to magical ego styles is not specific to a single sample, or even to a single culture,

Gutmann moved to different cultures and to those in which older men are honored and are assigned political, ceremonial, or magical power. Thus far Gutmann has carried out field studies in four different societies: the Lowland Maya (Mexico), the Highland Maya (Mexico), the Navajo (Arizona), and the Druze (Israel, Galilean highlands). While all four groups represent traditional cultures in which social change has been slow, they differ from each other in major economic, cultural, and ecological aspects. The traditional Navajo are migratory herdsmen, whose small bands, based largely upon kinship, are scattered across the high desert plateau of northeastern Arizona. Both the Lowland and Highland Maya are subsistence-level, village-dwelling corn farmers, but the Lowland Maya place high value on thrift, industry, and moderation, while the Highland Maya are described as a more unruly people who rely on external authorities to control rage and envy among themselves. The Galilean Druze are village-dwelling herdsmen and agriculturalists, who, although similar to other Arabic-speaking agriculturalists of the Levant in many of their values and social forms, are regarded as heretics in Islam because of their religious differences. They have survived 800 years of persecution.

In each instance, the investigator has gone to great lengths to establish rapport with respondents, then to interview them concerning their life histories, their present conditions of life, their definitions of pleasure, pain and remedy, their dreams, and their responses to TAT pictures. The results from these various studies support the earlier findings from studies of American men: the active-productive, passive-receptive, and magical orientations are distributed more by age than by culture. Just as in the United States samples, in the Navajo, the Maya, and the Druze, the younger men rely on and relish their own instrumentality and the products of their industry. Older men seem to rely on accommodation techniques whereby they influence external providers. The oldest men attempt to deal with reality projectively (i.e., by distorting reality or by denial) and rely on nonadaptive illusions of security and comfort (Gutmann, 1969).

It is regrettable that we do not yet have longitudinal data from our own or from other cultures that would serve to support or deny the developmental hypothesis. (Even more regrettable is the fact that in those research centers where longitudinal studies of aging are now in progress, there has been little attention given at all to intra-psychic personality processes.) Gutmann made a second field trip to the Navajo reservation four years after the first and reinterviewed and readministered the TAT to 75 men. While those data have not yet been fully analyzed, they indicate the same shift from Time 1 to

Time 2 that appeared in the cross-sectional analysis at Time 1, namely, in the direction of passive and/or magical mastery styles (Gutmann, personal communication, 1971).

A developmental view of intrapsychic change in old age is supported also by the work of Lieberman (1965; Lieberman & Coplan, 1969), who found systematic changes occurring in both cognitive and affective processes in persons over 70 as they near death. Because these differences are not the simple result of physical illness and because they are related to distance from death rather than to chronological age, Lieberman suggested that in the age range over 70, distance from death may be a more critical dimension of time than chronological age. While this suggestion has important implications for a possible reconceptualization of time and aging, it would nevertheless be consistent with a developmental perspective.

Socioadaptational Processes

Contrary to the findings regarding intrapsychic processes, age did not emerge in the Kansas City studies as a significant source of variation when the investigator's attention was primarily on socio-adaptational patterns. Thus, when attempts were made to operationalize Erikson's concepts of ego development or Peck's concepts of psychological crises or when the focus was on a multivariate approach to personality structure (as in the delineation of personality types based upon a broad set of ego functions), differences were not age related (Neugarten et al., 1964).

The inconsistency between intrapsychic and socioadaptational aspects of personality reflects to some degree the difference in type of data, for the first findings rested on projective tests; the second, on interviews. Not only are respondents less able to distort their responses on projective tests in the direction of social desirability, but the investigator's biases regarding age-appropriate behavior can be controlled better with projective data (which can be blinded for age) than with interview data. Nevertheless, the more essential difference lies not in method but in the areas of personality under scrutiny. With regard to the adaptive, goal-directed, and purposive area, processes more readily available to conscious control, differences were relatively independent of age in persons aged 50 to 80.

Nor did measures of psychological well-being prove to be age related. A multidimensional rating scale called Life Satisfaction was based upon five components: the extent to which the individual (a) takes pleasure from whatever the round of activities that constitutes his everyday life; (b) regards his life as meaningful and accepts resolutely that which life has been; (c) feels he has succeeded in achieving his major goals; (d) holds a positive image of self; and (e) maintains happy and optimistic attitudes and moods. Life satisfaction ratings, validated against a clinician's independent assessments, showed no overall age trends (Neugarten, Havighurst, & Tobin, 1961).

Although research on psychological well-being done by other investigators using a large variety of methods has resulted in inconsistent findings, the Kansas City finding is corroborated by certain other investigators (e.g., Birren, Butler, Greenhouse, Sokoloff, & Yarrow, 1963; Reichard, Livson, & Peterson, 1962). The implication from the literature as a whole is that such factors as work status, health, financial resources, and marital status are more decisive than chronological age in influencing degrees of adjustment in people who are age 50 and over. Although changes along these dimensions are themselves age associated, it appears that older people, like younger people, have differing capacities to cope with life stresses and to come to terms with their life situations and that chronological age is not the decisive factor.

Social Interaction

A third level of personality functioning is represented by the nature and extent of the individual's interactions with others. In this area our studies showed a gradual decrease with age on several different measures: first, on an index based upon the amount of each day the person spends in interaction with others; second, on measures related to performance in various life roles (worker, spouse, parent, grandparent, kin-group member, homemaker, friend, neighbor, citizen, club member, and church member). On the average, level of role activity was lower in successive age groups from 55 to 85; the degree of ego investment in present roles was lower; and individuals throughout the age range reported that their present levels of role activity were lower than they had been 10 years earlier. The general picture was one, however, of no sharp discontinuities at least through the 60s for the group as a whole and for most persons a relatively adequate level of role performance until late in life (Havighurst, 1957; Havighurst, Neugarten, & Tobin, 1968). In this sample of relatively healthy individuals of reasonably adequate financial means, the major change occurred after age 70. In a more representative group, it probably occurs somewhat sooner, when most men retire from work.

Not all studies by other investigators support the finding that levels of social interaction are age related (e.g., Lowenthal, 1964; Maddox & Eisdorfer, 1962; Scotch & Richardson, 1966; Tallmer & Kutner, 1969). Maddox (1966), for one, found that those persons aged 60 and over whose activity levels initially were higher or lower than the average for the group maintained their ranks over a seven-year period; and there is other evidence that a person develops a level of role activity over his lifetime that tends to persist into old age. Yet over the longer time period from middle age to advanced old age, the evidence is clear that there is a shrinkage in the social life space, whether it comes relatively early or relatively late after middle age.

Whether or not this general decrease in social interaction is to be interpreted as developmental is quite another question. First, interaction patterns are obviously not a function of personality alone, for no matter what the individual's makeup, he cannot achieve levels of social activity independent of the opportunities provided in the environment. On the other hand, interaction levels are partly a function of personality differences (some older people resist the shrinkage of their social worlds by substituting new activities for those they may have been forced to relinquish; others retreat to a low level of role activity because they prefer it; and so on). For the latter reason, social interaction patterns have always been an area for investigation by the personality psychologist. Second, whether the shrinkage of the social life space has developmental or inherent elements, or whether it is to be interpreted as a responsive process, remains a moot question. That is, the declining levels of social interaction may be paced by the withdrawal of other persons rather than by the inner psychological withdrawal described here.

To sum up, in studying the same individuals, we found inconsistent patterns in three different areas of personality functioning. In the intrapsychic area, increased interiority and other changes that we interpret as developmental occurred as early as the 50s. In the adaptational area, no age-related changes were found. In the social interaction area, changes in the direction of decline occurring by the late 60s and 70s may or may not have developmental components. The implication is not that intrapsychic aspects of personality are independent of social interaction, for in the broad sense personality is developed and maintained by transactions with other people. Rather, the issue deals with the relationships between the variables we have used. Investigators still lack refined measures of social interaction. It is also not known how much inner change (on measures of the type used here) may occur before it is manifested in social behavior (on measures of the type used here). Perhaps in the relatively advantaged group who constituted the Kansas City samples, the degrees of inner psychological change were all below the threshold in this regard. At the same time, we conclude, given the limitations of our methods and our variables, that intrapsychic changes in middle and later life proceed in ways that are not necessarily parallel to changes in social interaction or to levels of psychological well-being.

Such a conclusion is not incongruent with what we already know as students of personality. Many psychologists have commented on the difference between the inner and the outer lives, the private and the public; and the inner life is not always translated directly into the life of action. We have evidence from the Kansas City studies that *some* changes in adult personality are to be interpreted as developmental, but others are to be interpreted as the results of situational influences. This should not lead us to abandon the area of personality and aging because of its inconsistencies and obscurities, but instead to acknowledge that the area is as complex as any other within the broad field of personality and as rich in problems that need pursuing.

In speculating on the relationships between the intrapsychic and the socioadaptational, perhaps the former lie closer to biological determinants of behavior than do the latter, but the question could not be followed up for lack of appropriate data, that is, data that are longitudinal and that include measures of biological change.

The question may also be raised, "How is it that individuals continue to function effectively in their social environments despite increased interiority and, although there has not been space to discuss it here, despite certain losses in cognitive processes? The implication is that there are coping processes that mediate between different orders of personality, processes that relate particularly to the ability to synthesize, to rationalize, to reorganize experience, and to carry out patterns of action in line with one's goals. The next set of studies in this field might be most fruitful if they focus on such executive qualities of personality and on relatively discrete areas of social behavior rather than on global measures of social interaction or adaptation. Especially needed are investigations in which small samples of adults are studied in detail and in which attention is centered on intimate social networks and subtle aspects of interaction. Given the fact, furthermore, that those of our studies in which age differences were clearest were those in which the dimensions of personality were inductively derived, perhaps the most useful studies in the immediate future will also be those that depend upon inductive approaches and methods of naturalistic observation rather than upon deductive and experimental approaches. Studies that would be particularly valuable are those in which respondents are taught to give introspective accounts of the cognitive strategies they employ in dealing with inner- and outer-life events, studies in which investigators could move toward operationalizing variables based upon introspection and reminiscence.

Disengagement Theory

For psychologists unfamiliar with the literature in gerontology, it would be inappropriate to describe the Kansas City Studies of Adult Life without at least a brief discussion of the disengagement theory and its modifications, for the findings just reported (along with later findings to be summarized below) have usually been discussed within the framework of that theory. Furthermore, the disengagement theory set off a lively controversy among both American and European investigators that is only now abating.

To understand something of the controversy, it should be noted that in the social-psychological literature of gerontology, the disengagement theory represented a departure from the prevailing earlier view. Both views are based upon the observation that as people grow older the activities that characterized them in middle age become curtailed. The earlier view, which we labeled the "activity theory," implies that, except for changes in biology and health, older people are the same as middle-aged people, with essentially the same psychological and social needs. The decreased social interaction of old age results from the withdrawal of society from the aging person, and the decreased interaction proceeds against the desire of most older people. The person who ages optimally is the person who stays active and who manages to resist the shrinkage of his social world.

In the disengagement theory as first set forth by Cumming and Henry in the book *Growing Old* (1961), the decreased social interaction is characterized by mutuality; both society and the aging person withdraw, with the individual's withdrawal accompanied by decreased emotional involvement in the activities and relationships of his middle age. (This formulation was based upon a recognition of the significance of our findings regarding intrapsychic psychological changes, especially the fact that these changes seem to precede changes in social behavior.) As a second part of the theory, it was proposed that in old age the individual who has disengaged is the person who has a sense of psychological well-being and will be high in life satisfaction.

Some of the Chicago team were uncomfortable with the second part of the theory. As we studied the lives of the people in our sample, we did not find the consistent patterns that were predicted from our first formulations. Therefore, once all the data were in, we devised new and more carefully validated measures of social interaction and of psychological well-being and found that high life satisfaction was more often present in persons who were socially active and involved than in persons who were inactive and uninvolved. More important, we found diversity. At the same time that there was a positive relationship overall between *engagement* and life satisfaction, the relationship was not consistent and all four combinations of activity and satisfaction existed: high–high and low–low were most frequent, but there were also high–low and low–high (Havighurst, et al., 1968).

Given these findings, the team then moved back to studying differences in personality. Earlier we had worked out a set of empirically derived personality types (Neugarten et al., 1964, ch. 8), and now, in assessing all three kinds of data on each person—extent of his social interaction, degree of life satisfaction, and personality type—we found a high degree of order in the data. Certain personality types, as they age, slough off various role responsibilities with relative comfort and remain highly content with life. Other personalities show a drop in social interaction and a drop in life satisfaction. Still others have long had low levels of activity accompanied by high satisfaction, and these persons show relatively little change as they age. For instance, in one group of 70–79 year olds, persons who were living in the community and carrying out their usual daily rounds of activities, we empirically derived eight different patterns of aging. We attached the names Reorganizers, Focused, Disengaged, Holding-On, Constricted, Succorance Seeking, Apathetic, and Disorganized, each name conveying something of the style of aging common to each of the subgroups (Neugarten et al., 1968).

We have concluded from this line of studies that personality organization or personality type is the pivotal factor in predicting which individuals will age successfully and that adaptation is the key concept. Furthermore, although we lack systematic longitudinal data to confirm this view, it has appeared from the life history information available on the people we studied that the patterns reflect long-standing life-styles and that consistencies rather than inconsistencies in coping styles predominate as an individual moves from middle age through old age. Within broad limits, given no major biological accidents or major social upheavals, patterns of aging are predictable from knowing the individuals in middle age.

In demonstrating that there is no single social-psychological pattern by which people grow old and in suggesting that persons age in ways that are consistent with their earlier life histories, it is our view that given a relatively supportive social environment, older persons like younger ones will choose the combinations of activities that offer them the most ego involvement and that are most consonant with their long-established value patterns and self-concepts. Aging is not a leveler of individual differences except, perhaps, at the very end of life. In adapting to both biological and social changes, the aging person continues to draw upon that which he has been, as well as that which he is.

In the last of these studies, members of the Chicago group collaborated with a group of European investigators in collecting a set of pilot data pursuant to planning a large-scale cross-national study of patterns of retirement. The cross-national team adapted the methods used in the Kansas City Studies of Adult Life and gathered data on patterns of role activity and life satisfaction for 50 men aged 70–75 in each of six cities: Bonn, Chicago, Milan, Nijmegen, Vienna, and Warsaw. The data were gathered only for pilot purposes and the findings must be interpreted with great caution, but they indicated that over and above individual differences, patterns of role behavior varied systematically by city of residence and by former occupation (half the men in each city were retired school teachers; half, retired steelworkers). These data suggested, to a higher degree than anticipated, that even in industrialized centers in modern Western societies, differences in cultural traditions and in value systems produce systematic variations in patterns of social interaction in the aged. The data also suggested the same general level of positive relationship between level of activity and life satisfaction that was found in the Kansas City sample (Havighurst, Munnichs, Neugarten, & Thomae, 1969).

In limiting this description of the disengagement theory and its modifications to the work of the Chicago group, the intent is not to underestimate the work of other investigators, but only to give focus to the discussion. A very large number of studies have appeared in the past decade which bear directly or indirectly upon the disengagement theory, and modifications have been proposed not only by the Chicago group (Cumming, 1963; Havighurst et al., 1968; Henry, 1964; Neugarten et al., 1968) but by many others (e.g., Carp, 1968; Lowenthal & Boler, 1965; Maddox, 1966; Palmore,

1965; Rose, 1964; Tallmer & Kutner, 1969). The theory has been widely quoted, sometimes misinterpreted, often supported, and often refuted.

In the literature as a whole the argument has focused on social disengagement and, in particular, on the relationship of social disengagement to psychological well-being. With the exception of Gutmann's and Shanan's work mentioned previously, other researchers have not pursued the question of intrapsychic components. The issues have been whether or not steady decline in social engagement is indeed characteristic of aging; whether or not it is inevitable; what the patterns of social interaction may be in different samples of older people; whether rates of change are generally the same; and what the limits of sociocultural and historical factors may be. There has been controversy over whether it is the relatively engaged or the relatively disengaged older person who is generally best off.

How then do we stand today with regard to disengagement? First, as a description of social and psychological processes, it appears to be accurate. Psychological disengagement seems to precede social disengagement and seems to have developmental properties. Second, as a description of optimal or successful aging, it appears to be inadequate. There is a positive relationship overall between *social engagement* and life satisfaction. Personality types, when based upon a wide range of ego variables, play a central role in affecting this relationship and in producing diverse patterns of aging. Patterns of aging vary also in direct relation to the social setting, in particular, the extent to which the setting is one that provides a wide range of choices for the individual. In short, disengagement proceeds at different rates and different patterns in different people in different places and has different outcomes with regard to psychological well-being.

One final comment: The studies carried out by the Chicago group in pointing out, on the one hand, the importance of personality factors and, on the other hand, the importance of sociocultural settings in producing variations have had the net effect of putting the questions about aging back again within the complex of biological, social, and psychological factors that must be taken into account in attempting to explain any human behavior. As the individual ages, the factors that influence his behavior do not become fewer; and the investigator who enters the field of aging will not find the research problems simpler. If anything, the research problems are made more complex because of the necessity of dealing with each variable in terms of its past as well as its present influence on the individual.

As the past lengthens, its influence on the present (and future) becomes more difficult to assess.

In essence, this is the perspective of the developmentalist: the present behavior of the individual can be understood only in terms of his past; and a long life will therefore be harder to understand than a short one.

REFERENCES

Baller, W. R., Charles, D. C., & Miller, E. L. Mid-life attainment of the mentally retarded: A longitudinal study. *Genetic Psychology Monographs,* 1967, **75**, 235–329.

Baltes, P. B. Longitudinal and cross-sectional sequences in the study of age and generation effects. *Human Development,* 1968, **11**, 145–171.

Baltes, P. B., & Reinert, G. Cohort effects in cognitive development of children as revealed by cross-sectional sequences. *Developmental Psychology,* 1969, **1**, 169–177.

Barker, R. M. *Ecological psychology: Concepts and methods for studying the environment of human behavior.* Stanford: Stanford University Press, 1968.

Barker, R. G., & Barker, L. S. The psychological ecology of old people in Midwest, Kansas, and Yoredale, Yorkshire. *Journal of Gerontology,* 1961, **16**, 144–149.

Becker, H. Personal change in adult life. *Sociometry,* 1964, **27**, 40–53.

Benedek, T. Climacterium: A developmental phase. *Psychoanalytical Quarterly,* 1950, **19**, 1–27.

Benedek, T. Parenthood as a developmental phase. *Journal of the American Psychoanalytical Association,* 1959, **7**, 389–417.

Benedek, T. (Chapters 4, 5, 6, 7) In E. J. Anthony & T. Benedek (Eds.), *Parenthood.* Boston: Little, Brown, 1970.

Berezin, M. A. Some intra-psychic aspects of aging. In N. Zinberg (Ed.), *The normal psychology of the aging process.* New York: International Universities Press, 1963.

Bibring, G. L. Some considerations of the psychological processes of pregnancy. *Psychoanalytic Study of the Child,* 1959, **14**, 113–121.

Birren, J. E., Butler, R. N., Greenhouse, S. W., Sokoloff, L., & Yarrow, M. R. *Human aging.* (USPHS Publ. No. 986) Washington, D.C.: United States Government Printing Office, 1963.

Block, J. *Lives through time.* Berkeley, Calif.: Bancroft Books, 1971.

Bortner, R. W. Personality and social psychology in the study of aging. *Gerontologist,* 1967, **7**(2, Pt. 2), 23–36.

Brim, O. G., Jr. Personality as role-learning. In I. Iscoe & H. Stevenson (Eds.), *Personality development in children.* Austin: University of Texas Press, 1960.

Brim, O. G., & Wheller, S. *Socialization after childhood.* New York: Wiley, 1966.

Bühler, C. The curve of life as studied in biographies. *Journal of Applied Psychology,* 1935, **19**, 405–409.

Bühler, C. *Der menschliche Lebenslauf als psychologisches Problem*. (2nd ed.) Gottingen, W. Germany: Hogrefe, 1959.

Bühler, C., & Massarik, F. (Eds.) *The course of human life*. New York: Springer, 1968.

Butler, R. N. The life review: An interpretation of reminiscence in the aged. *Psychiatry*, 1963, **26**, 65–76.

Carp, F. M. Some components of disengagement. *Journal of Gerontology*, 1968, **23**, 382–386.

Chiriboga, D., & Lowenthal, M. F. Psychological correlates of perceived well-being. *Proceedings of the 79th Annual Convention of the American Psychological Association*, 1971, **6**, 603–604.

Chown, S. M. Personality and aging. In K. W. Shaie (Ed.), *Theory and methods of research on aging*. Morgantown: West Virginia University Library, 1968.

Clark, M. *Culture and aging*. Springfield, Ill.: Charles C Thomas, 1967.

Clausen, J. A. (Ed.) *Socialization and society*. Boston: Little, Brown, 1968.

Cumming, E. Further thoughts on the theory of disengagement. *International Social Science Journal*, 1963, **15**, 337–393.

Cumming, E., & Henry, W. E. *Growing old*. New York: Basic Books, 1961.

Deutsch, H. *The psychology of women*. Vol. 1 & 2. New York: Grune & Stratton, 1944, 1945.

Emmerich, W. Models of continuity and change. Paper presented at the meeting of the Society for Research in Child Development, Santa Monica, Calif., March 1969.

Erickson, E. H. Identity and the life cycle. *Psychological Issues*. 1959, No. 1.

Erikson, E. H. *Childhood and society*. (2nd ed.) New York: Norton, 1963.

Fromm, E. *Escape from freedom*. New York: Holt, Rinehart & Winston, 1941.

Glaser, B. G., & Strauss, A. *The discovery of grounded theory*. Chicago: Aldine, 1967.

Goulet, L. R., & Baltes, P. B. *Life-span developmental psychology*. New York: Academic Press, 1970.

Gray, H. Psychological types and changes with age. *Journal of Clinical Psychology*, 1947, **3**, 273–277.

Gutmann, D. An exploration of ego configurations in middle and later life. In B. L. Neugarten (Ed.), *Personality in middle and late life*. New York: Atherton, 1964.

Gutmann, D. *The country of old men; Cross-cultural studies in the psychology of later life*. (Occasional Papers in Gerontology, No. 5) Ann Arbor: Institute of Gerontology, University of Michigan-Wayne State, 1969.

Harris, D. B. (Ed.) *The concept of development*. Minneapolis: University of Minnesota Press, 1957.

Havighurst, R. J. The social competence of middle-aged people. *Genetic Psychology Monographs*, 1957, **56**, 297–395.

Havighurst, R. J., Bowman, P. H., Liddle, G. P., Matthews, C. V., & Pierce, J. V. *Growing up in River City*. New York: Wiley, 1962.

Havighurst, R. J., Munnichs, J. M. A., Neugarten, B. L., & Thomae, H. *Adjustment to retirement*. Assen, Netherlands: van Gorcum, 1969.

Havighurst, R. J., Neugarten, B. L., & Tobin, S. S. Disengagement and patterns of aging. In B. L. Neugarten (Ed.), *Middle age and aging: A reader in social psychology.* Chicago: University of Chicago Press, 1968.

Hays, W. Age and sex differences in the Rorschach experience balance. *Journal of Abnormal and Social Psychology,* 1952, **47,** 390–393.

Henry, W. E. The theory of intrinsic disengagement. In P. F. Hansen (Ed.), *Age with a future.* (Proceedings of the 6th International Congress of Gerontology, 1963) Copenhagen: Munksgaard, 1964.

Hess, R. D. High school antecedents of young adult performance. Paper presented at the meeting of the American Education Research Association, Atlantic City, February 1962.

Honzik, M. A 30-year study of personality consistency and change. Paper presented at the annual meeting of the American Psychological Association, New York, September 1966.

Jung, C. G. *Modern man in search of a soul.* New York: Harcourt, Brace & World, 1933.

Kagan, J. Continuity in development. Paper presented at the meeting of the Society for Research in Child Development, Santa Monica, Calif., March 1969.

Kagan, J., & Moss, H. A. *Birth to maturity.* New York: Wiley, 1962.

Kelly, E. L. Consistency of the adult personality. *American Psychologist,* 1955, **10,** 659–681.

Kuhlen, R. G. Developmental changes in motivation during the adult years. In J. E. Birren (Ed.), *Relations of development and aging.* Springfield, Ill.: Charles C Thomas, 1964.

Lakin, M., & Eisdorfer, C. A study of affective expression among the aged. In C. Tibbitts & W. Donahue (Eds.), *Social and psychological aspects of aging.* New York: Columbia University Press, 1962.

Langer, J. *Theories of development.* New York: Holt, Rinehart & Winston, 1969.

Lidz, T. *The person.* New York: Basic Books, 1968.

Lieberman, M. A. Psychological correlates of impending death: Some preliminary observations. *Journal of Gerontology,* 1965, **20,** 181–190.

Lieberman, M. A., & Coplan, A. S. Distance from death as a variable in the study of aging. *Developmental Psychology,* 1960, **2,** 71–84.

Looft, W. R. Socialization and personality throughout the life span: An examination of contemporary psychological approaches. Paper presented at the Third West Virginia Conference of Life-Span Developmental Psychology: Personality and socialization, Morgantown, May 1972.

Lowenthal, M. F. Social isolation and mental illness in old age. *American Sociological Review,* 1964, **29,** 54–70.

Lowenthal, M. F., & Boler, D. Voluntary versus involuntary social withdrawal. *Journal of Gerontology,* 1965, **20,** 363–375.

Luborsky, L., & Schimek, J. Psychoanalytic theories of therapeutic and developmental change: Implications for assessment. In P. Worchel & D. Byrne (Eds.), *Personality change.* New York: Wiley, 1964.

Maddox, G. L. Persistence of life style among the elderly: A longitudinal study of patterns of social activity in relation to life satisfaction. *Proceedings of the 7th International Congress of Gerontology* (Vienna), 1966, **6,** 309–311.

Maddox, G., & Eisdorfer, C. Some correlates of activity and morale among the elderly. *Social Processes,* 1962, **40,** 228–238.

Maslow, A. *Motivation and personality.* New York: Harper & Row, 1954.

Meerloo, J. Transference and resistance in geriatric psychotherapy. *Psychoanalytic Review,* 1955, **42,** 72–82.

Mischel, W. Continuity and change in personality. *American Psychologist,* 1969, **24,** 1012–1018.

Neugarten, B. L. Adult personality: Toward a psychology of the life cycle. In B. L. Neugarten (Ed.), *Middle age and aging: A reader in social psychology.* Chicago: University of Chicago Press, 1968.

Neugarten, B. L. Continuities and discontinuities of psychological issues into adult life. *Human Development,* 1969, **12,** 121–130.

Neugarten, B. L. Adaptation and the life cycle. *Journal of Geriatric Psychiatry,* 1970, **4,** 71–87.

Neugarten, B. L. Personality and the aging process. *Gerontologist,* 1972, **12**(1), 9–15.

Neugarten, B. L., & Gutmann, D. Age-sex roles and personality in middle age: A thematic apperception study. *Psychological Monographs.* 1958, **72**(17, Whole No. 470).

Neugarten, B. L., Havighurst, R. J., & Tobin, S. S. The measurement of life satisfaction. *Journal of Gerontology,* 1961, **16,** 144–149.

Neugarten, B. L., & Associates. *Personality in middle and late life.* New York: Atherton, 1964.

Neugarten, B. L., Havighurst, R. J., & Tobin, S. S. Personality and patterns of aging. In B. L. Neugarten (Ed.), *Middle age and aging: A reader in social psychology.* Chicago: University of Chicago Press, 1968.

Palmore, E. B. The effects of aging on activities and attitudes. *Gerontologist,* 1968, **8,** 259–263.

Peck, R. Psychological developments in the second half of life. In J. E. Anderson (Ed.), *Psychological aspects of aging.* Washington, D.C.: American Psychological Association, 1956.

Perlman, H. H. *Persona.* Chicago: University of Chicago Press, 1968.

Pressey, S. L., & Kuhlen, R. G. *Psychological development through the life span.* New York: Harper, 1957.

Reichard, S., Livson, F., & Peterson, P. G. *Aging and personality.* New York: Wiley, 1962.

Riley, M., & Foner, A. *Aging and society.* Vol. 1. New York: Russell Sage Foundation, 1968.

Rogers, C. R. Actualizing tendency in relation to "motives" and to consciousness. In M. R. Jones (Ed.), *Nebraska symposium on motivation: 1963.* Lincoln: University of Nebraska Press, 1963.

Rogler, L. H., & Hollingshead, A. B. *Trapped: Families and schizophrenia.* New York: Wiley, 1965.

Rose, A. A current theoretical issue in social geronotology. *Gerontologist,* 1964, **4**(1), 46–50.

Sarbin, T. R. Role theoretical interpretation of psychological change. In P. Worchel & D. Byrne (Eds.), *Personality change.* New York: Wiley, 1964.

Schaie K. W. A general model for the study of developmental problems. *Psychological Bulletin,* 1965, **64,** 92–107.

Schaie, K. W. A reinterpretation of age related changes in cognitive structure and functioning. In L. R. Goulet & P. B. Baltes (Eds.), *Life-span developmental psychology.* New York: Academic Press, 1970.

Schaie, K. W. Cultural change and repeated assessment in the study of adult personality. Paper presented at the annual meeting of the American Psychological Association, Washington, D.C., September 1971.

Schaie, K. W., & Marquette, B. W. Personality in maturity and old age. In R. M. Dreger (Ed.), *Multivariate personality research: Contributions to the understanding of personality in honor of Raymond B. Cattell.* Baton Rouge, La.: Claitor's Publishing Division, 1971.

Schaw, L., & Henry, W. E. A method for the comparison of groups: A study in thematic apperception. *Genetic Psychology Monographs,* 1956, **50,** 207–253.

Scotch, N. A., & Richardson, A. H. Characteristics of the self-sufficient among the very aged. *Proceedings of the 7th International Congress of Gerontology* (Vienna), 1966, **8,** 489–493.

Secord, P. F., & Backman, C. B. Personality theory and the problems of stability and change in individual behavior: An interpersonal approach. *Psychological Review,* 1961, **68,** 21–32.

Shanan, J., & Sharon, M. Personality and cognitive functioning of Israeli males during the middle years. *Human Development,* 1965, **8,** 2–15.

Tallmer, M., & Kutner, B. Disengagement and the stresses of aging. *Journal of Gerontology,* 1969, **24,** 70–75.

Terman, L. M., & Oden, M. H. *The gifted group at mid-life.* Stanford: Stanford University Press, 1959.

Tuddenham, R. D. Constancy of personality ratings over two decades. *Genetic Psychology Monographs,* 1959, **60,** 3–29.

White, R. W. Competence and the psychosexual stages of development. In M. R. Jones (Ed.), *Nebraska symposium on motivation: 1960.* Lincoln: University of Nebraska Press, 1960.

White, R. W. Ego and reality in psychoanalytic theory. *Psychological Issues,* 1963, **3**(3), 1–210.

Willoughby, R. R. The relationship to emotionality of age, sex, and conjugal condition. *American Journal of Sociology,* 1937–38, **43,** 920–931.

Wohlwill, J. F. Methodology and research strategy in the study of developmental change. In L. R. Goulet & P. B. Baltes (Eds.), *Life-span developmental psychology.* New York: Academic Press, 1970.

Zinberg, N., & Kaufman, I. Cultural and personality factors associated with aging: An introduction. In N. Zinberg (Ed.), *The normal psychology of the aging process.* New York: International Universities Press, 1963.

The Clinical Psychology
of Old Age

Clinical Psychology?

The four chapters in this section are grouped under the title "Clinical Psychology of Old Age"—not, perhaps, an accurate title, but hopefully a direction-setting one. The fact is that there is no clinical psychology of old age. The psychologist carrying his tool kit of the Wechsler, Rorschach, and Thematic Apperception Tests never got to the over-65s, and now that period in psychological history seems to have passed. Nor did the psychologist concern himself with the psychotherapy of older people. Thus, the development of personality theory in gerontology was never stimulated by the demands of practicing clinicians in the same way that it was stimulated in the case of children and younger adults. Freud himself rejected the elderly as a class, leading to an unfortunate neglect of the psychodynamic processes of later life by practicing analysts. Whatever else one may say about classical psychoanalysis, it has clearly been a major impetus toward the conceptualization of personality as a dynamic process. Dynamic psychology has in general bypassed the aging personality. This may account for the relative neglect of the interior of the aging person in this volume, no less than in the gerontological literature generally. In the Epilogue, Kastenbaum writes in compelling fashion of this neglect, so I shall not belabor the point here.

Psychology and its army of clinicians have increasingly concerned themselves with mental health on a community, as contrasted with an individual, level. Part of the impetus of the community mental health movement derived from dissatisfaction with the dis-

M. Powell Lawton received his PhD in clinical psychology from Columbia University in 1952. He has worked in clinical practice and clinical research for the Veterans Administration and the Commonwealth of Pennsylvania. He is presently the Director of Behavioral Research at the Philadelphia Geriatric Center. His major research interests are in the fields of social gerontology and ecological psychology.

hearteningly small numbers of people who could be helped under the one-to-one therapeutic model.

Another important rationale for the movement was psychologists' realization that they had greatly neglected social factors in maladjustment. New orientations followed, such as an awareness that calling a behavior pathological could be one way of maintaining a society's status quo. This larger-group-oriented approach to treatment is implicit in much recent history of gerontology, perhaps because of neglect of the interior by clinicians. The major issues in applied gerontology today concern income, health, housing, retirement, and leisure-time activity—all directions that seek to foster the good life through programs at a societal level.

A third, related, reason for a community, as opposed to an individual, approach to the mental health problems of the elderly is our recent heightened awareness of environment as an essential element in the behavioral system.

Thus, active forces have both turned gerontologists away from the individual and focused their attention on mental health in the aggregate. Each chapter in the section that started out as "Clinical Psychology" shows this emphasis to some degree. Kramer, Taube, and Redick provide figures that eloquently portray how great our problems are in delivering appropriate treatment to the elderly. They show clearly that mass segregation, that is, "treatment" in mental hospitals and nursing homes, has been virtually the only alternative for most psychologically disturbed older people. No single sentence could so compellingly demonstrate society's decision about the treatability of the aged as the one in Task Force Recommendation No. 3, drawn from Kramer et al.'s chapter: "Though people 65 and over constitute 10% of the United States population, they comprise only 2% of patients given outpatient mental health services, but 22% of annual mental hospital admissions." While Kramer and his colleagues do not explicitly state a position on the relative desirability of individual, community-oriented, or institutional care, they do suggest that socially oriented programs in the community, such as halfway houses, day care centers, homemaker programs, and so on, constitute the major viable alternatives to institutionalization. Their projected manpower requirements for giving barely minimal mental health treatment to the lowest-estimated proportion of those in need are so high as to discourage any prospect of individual treatment as a model. To give each needy person just six hours of individual professional time per year would require almost three times the professional manpower now expected in most disciplines three years hence. Thus, facts clearly support adoption of a model that applies treatment to the social factors that cause maladjustment.

Mensh's chapter deals explicitly with community-oriented approaches in treating psychological disturbances of the elderly. His extended historical and contemporary survey admirably reinforces the all-important fact that physical, social, and mental health are highly interrelated aspects of the same thing. He points out particularly how policy and the organization of services interact with the content of service given. He repeatedly demonstrates in the studies he quotes that no social program, however creative, can accomplish anything until means are found to connect the individual with the service. While this task, of course, has both social and individual components, Mensh argues strongly for mobilizing federal and private resources to help the individual know that a service exists, to match his need with what is offered, and to serve the largest number of individuals. Although Mensh was not asked to deal with individual treatment, or to contrast it with community treatment, he reminds us of the multiplicity of means for providing treatment in the community, and by implication reinforces the idea that we have only begun to explore ways of providing treatment to large numbers of people.

In their chapter "Psychosocial Treatment of the Aged," Gottesman, Quarterman, and Cohn cover most thoroughly the several areas of concern to the clinical psychologist. At this point, when the lack of a clinical psychology of old age is so obvious, we particularly need a theoretical model such as they give us, locating the determinants of behavior both internally and externally to the individual. They indicate how such a model can lead to new thoughts about treatment (i.e., "self-treatment") and to integration of disparate knowledge into a coherent recipe for practice. The institution, the community (both in large-group and small-group settings), and the one-to-one therapeutic relationship are considered, with more or less equal time being given to each. They examine closely a number of approaches to therapy, communicating clearly that no model of therapy is inapplicable solely because of the patient's age.

Of all chapters in this section, Gurland's is the only one that focuses totally on the individual. He discusses criteria by which we judge psychopathology, rightly calling into question some value-laden uses of diagnostic labels. Amid the dearth of material in recent literature on clinical aspects of aging, it is useful to have Gurland's discussions of pathological symptoms in old age, psychiatric and psychological diagnostic methods, and his review of the very careful work in progress on the structured interview. Gurland discusses briefly the importance of diagnosis, since physical and central nervous system disorders must frequently be distinguished from the more clearly psychological and social disorders or, more likely, the relative contributions of these several etiological factors sorted out.

Gurland focuses on behavioral or objective signs as the basis for diagnosis, and in this behaviorist context, it is understandable that he devotes less than a page to discussion of psychodynamics. However, once again, by implication the older person's interior is overlooked. Can there not be a psychodiagnostic based partly upon feelings, attitudes, self-perceptions, *Weltanschauung*? Unless we ask the older person how he feels, we shall not really know how best to administer treatment, whether through reassurance, behavior therapy, occupational therapy, or group activity.

These four chapters offer much that will advance the psychologist's concern for the mental health of the elderly. At some later date, however, someone else must introduce or resuscitate questions such as the following:

1. Can we increase the effectiveness of psychologically oriented treatment of the elderly patient through diagnostic methods, whether through interviews or a specially tailored version of the psychological test battery?

2. What kinds of treatment or placement decisions can be aided by formal asessment?

3. What behaviors, in which older people, can be modified by behavior-therapeutic methods? Very little has been reported on the use of these techniques with the elderly.

4. Are group-oriented methods such as encounter or confrontation adaptable to the elderly participant?

In short, while this volume reminds us of the potential effectiveness of socially oriented approaches to treatment, we need concurrent attention to the individual and his unique problems.

A Broad Clinical Assessment of Psychopathology in the Aged

BARRY J. GURLAND

The perspective of this chapter is one of breadth rather than depth. Any one of the topics touched upon is better treated by other authors. If this chapter has any merit it is to highlight the broadening front of advances in techniques for the assessment of psychopathology in the elderly. The wide range of available techniques presents special advantages and problems. Special effort is needed to keep in mind the contributions and limitations of techniques outside one's own discipline and to integrate the information from these many sources. In the elderly, perhaps even more than in young age groups, a complex assessment is required that cuts across conventional disciplinary boundaries.

Although the term psychopathology strictly refers to the *study* of the symptoms of mental disorder, in this chapter and in accordance with popular usage, we will use psychopathology to mean morbid psychological symptoms. The task of assessing psychopathology requires that the latter be defined, detected, quantified, and classified, and further, that consideration be given to natural history (prognosis), response to therapy, and etiology. A full assessment of psychopathology in the aged will cover all these steps.

Barry J. Gurland trained in psychiatry at the Maudsley Hospital in London. He is currently Head of the Section on Diagnosis and Psychopathology in Biometrics Research at the New York State Psychiatric Institute, where he also serves as United States Director of the United States–United Kingdom Diagnostic Project. His research interests center around the classification of psychological symptoms and social maladjustment.

The author wishes to thank Roni Gurland for her assistance in surveying the literature, and J. Zubin and L. Sharpe for their helpful comments.

Definition of Psychopathology

"It often seems to be assumed that mental health and illness are objective phenomena rather than convenient constructs . . . [Clausen, 1969]." Not only are they constructs but opinions differ as to their definitions. The characteristics of aged subjects may be arranged along a continuum of consensus on whether or not these characteristics represent psychopathology. At one extreme are characteristics that all experts agree to be pathological. At the other extreme are characteristics viewed as pathological only by a small minority. By attempting to clarify the issues that could influence the placement of a characteristic on this continuum, it may be possible to arrive at an operational definition of psychopathology, which will serve for the remainder of the chapter.

Combinations of Criteria of Psychopathology

There is a high consensus of opinion that psychopathology is being manifested when an old person contemporaneously expresses distress, disturbs others, is incompetent, and shows a change from his previous state (especially when this change is rapid and marked); when this constellation of events is not commonly seen in subjects of that age; when the causes of these events are seen to originate in the subject rather than in his circumstances; when the events are judged to be maladaptive; and when a treatment is available to slow down, or reverse, the progress of these events.

Consensus is enhanced by a combination of the above events, partly because the combination will include various criteria of psychopathology, each with its own band of adherents. More important, however, is the fact that combinations of these criteria summate. Thus, a combination of unusual behavior and personal distress is much more likely to be deemed psychopathological than either criterion alone.

Single Criteria of Psychopathology

Taken singly, each criterion of psychopathology can be found wanting. Personal distress could be a perfectly reasonable transient response to bereavement. Discomfort caused to others could be a reflection of the latter's hypersensitivity. Incompetence might result from the abnormal demands of a task. Change from a previous state might be for the better rather than for the worse. Perlin and Butler (1963) pointed out that in their sample of healthy male volunteers, "positive and constructive changes were reported as developing in the geriatric period. Changes were not uniformly viewed as deficiencies or losses, as it is frequently implied or described in the literature pertaining to old age."

The above list of exceptions to the single criteria of psychopathology could be much longer. However, difficulties in applying a single criterion such as (a) prevalence, (b) etiology, (c) maladaptation, or (d) treatment, particularly need further explanation.

Prevalence. The more uncommon a behavior, the more likely it is to be viewed as psychopathological. Some authors have defined the effects of normal aging as those occurring sooner or later in nearly every member of the species, so that they are "unavoidable, constant and present in every species and every individual [Korenchevsky, 1961]." Pathological effects are those occurring in only some elderly and also some younger subjects (Libow, 1963). Common behaviors, even if distressing, may well be regarded as normal accompaniments of aging. This view may spring from a statistical concept of normality and also perhaps from a reluctance to accept too many problems as the concern of the mental health profession. Yet, several community studies of the elderly have shown that the prevalence of definite psychopathology in the elderly population is substantial (Bremer, 1951; Essen-Moller, Larsson, Uddenberg & White, 1956; Kay, Beamish, & Roth, 1964; Leighton, Harding, Macklin, Hughes, & Leighton, 1963; Leighton, Harding, Macklin, Macmillan, & Leighton, 1963; Lowenthal, Berkman, & Associates, 1967; New York State Department of Mental Hygiene, Mental Health Research Unit, 1960, 1961; Nielsen, 1962; Primrose, 1962; Sheldon, 1948). Furthermore, when Perlin and Butler (1963) evaluated 47 "normal" male volunteers over the age of 65, they found that 29 subjects presented diagnosable functional "psychopathology." Depression was the most common symptom. Also common were nightmares, obsessions, hypochondriacal ideas, suspiciousness, psychosomatic symptoms, and anxiety. Thus, the high frequency of a symptom in the elderly does not seem properly to disqualify it from being psychopathological. It could even be that the rare, extremely well preserved old person is the standard of normality and that elderly people commonly show psychopathology (Birren, 1964; Korenchevsky, 1961).

Although mere prevalence may be a poor criterion of psychopathology, statistical analysis of the distribution of characteristics in a population may be of greater importance for a definition of psychopathology. The classic illustration of such an analysis is the observation of the "bump" on the lower end of the distribution curve for IQ scores in the general population. Such a departure from a smooth distribution indicates that the polygenic determinants of IQ are not shared in random combinations by the entire population. There is an added cause associated with very low IQ. Since the "bump" is small, the added cause is uncommon. Both the uniqueness of the cause and its uncommonness mark the resultant characteristic as possibly psychopathological, which possibility is reinforced by the incompetence and maladaptiveness associated with a low IQ. However, this kind of evidence has not yet been presented for defining psychopathology in the aged.

Etiology. The assumed cause of a given behavior appears to influence whether or not that behavior is defined as psychopathological. Undesirable behaviors held to be caused by a process within the subject are more likely to be called psychopathological than those regarded as imposed on the subject by others around him (unless the imposed changes became autonomous). This is especially true when the process is regarded as inborn, or is evidenced by gross changes in tissue or metabolism. Thus, many researchers attempt to compare the behavior of elderly subjects diagnosed as having organic changes with those not having such changes, in the hope of thereby isolating and identifying pathological or demented behavior. Yet, the causes of certain behaviors could be explained plausibly by more than one scientific model (Zubin, 1967), and it may be the discipline to which one belongs that determines which model is chosen. For example, an elderly subject with almost no friendly contacts may be seen as being rejected by his community, withdrawn because of a depressive or paranoid process, or disengaged for the purpose of adapting to the terminal phases of his life. Therefore, causal hypotheses are an uncertain guide to the presence or absence of psychopathology.

Maladaptation. A commonly used criterion for psychopathology is maladaptiveness. However, behavior may be adaptive for one purpose and yet maladaptive for another. Perlin and Butler (1963) found that lifelong psychopathology could be adaptive in the elderly. For example, obsessive-compulsive mechanisms were helpful in an enforced retirement vacuum, and schizoid detachment appeared to protect individuals from the inevitable losses of this period in life. Similarly, depressive disorders which might have been adaptive when early man spent long winters in caves (Price, 1968) are handicaps in modern society. In certain cultures and at certain times, hallucinating individuals (e.g., certain shamans) may be able to capitalize on their symptoms to improve their adaptation within their group.

Treatment. It may seem paradoxical to suggest that a behavior is more likely to be called psychopathological when there is an appropriate treatment available. It is reminiscent of a scientist who discovers the cure before he finds the disease. Yet, the introduction of antidepressants was followed by the acceptance of many minor complaints as being caused by depression. Conversely, the ignorance or lack of potent remedies may lead to the dismissal of many minor problems of aging as being "normal." Goldfarb (1962) warned that a lack of clinical orientation may lead to the unwarranted dismissal of signs of depression such as constipation and early morning waking as "natural for old age."

Applying the Criteria to Certain Characteristics of the Aged

Some illustrative instances of the characteristics that increase with age are (a) cognitive impairment, (b) some forms of depression, (c) social isolation, (d) admission to an institution, and (e) diminished energy. A question is raised about which of such characteristics are part of the normal aging process and which should be attributed to pathology. This question further exposes the difficulties of applying the concepts of normality and psychopathology.

Cognitive impairment. Complicating still further the problem of determining whether a given level of cognitive impairment is pathological is that it is necessary to examine not only the quantity but also the quality of cognitive impairment. There is some evidence that at least two kinds of memory dysfunction may occur in the elderly: a benign, inconsistent failure of recall of information once learned, or a malignant loss of ability to store new information (Kral, 1965, 1966). Inglis (1970) suggested that in pathological memory disorder of the elderly it is the S-system (short-term storage system of Broadbent, 1957) that is disordered, while the effect of age itself is on the retrieval phases of memory. Lauter and Meyer (1968) concluded that while senile dementia appears psychologically to have a different structure from the effects of normal aging, in the light of studies they have reviewed, the idea of a permanent decrease of the intellectual capacity should be replaced by a concept of change in the structure of intelligence with age.

Another difficulty is that self-reports of memory difficulties may partly reflect stereotypes. Lowenthal et al. (1967) pointed out that at first sight a decline in memory appeared to be a normal function of aging since it was reported by nearly half of the elderly community residents they studied. However, this decline was not borne out by objective testing using the Kent E-G-Y.

Even the criterion of pathology provided by evidence of gross brain pathology (i.e., diffuse or arteriosclerotic) is not without its difficulties. Possible histological substrates to memory impairment in the elderly have been postulated in the form of lipofuscin accumulation (Constantinidis, 1968), or an increase in hypodiploid cells (Hamerton, Taylor, Angell, & McGuire, 1965; Jacobs, Brunton, & Court-Brown, 1964; Jacobs, Brunton, Court-Brown, Doll, & Goldstein, 1963; Jacobs, Court-Brown, & Doll, 1961). Nielsen (1968) found a statistically higher percentage of hypodiploid cells in patients with senile dementia compared with a control group of the same age. Roth, Tomlinson, and Blessed (1967) related clinical assessment and argentophile plaques in the brain at postmortem in 90 elderly psychiatric and medical patients and found cognitive impairment to be significantly correlated with the number of plaques. Nevertheless, this correlation was less for patients with a diagnosis of definite senile dementia, and the authors suggest that senile dementia may therefore have some other, as yet undiscovered, pathological process.

Fortunately, the clinician is usually spared the difficulty of assessing minor states of cognitive impairment since subjects with cognitive impairment are often only brought for treatment when their financial affairs become muddled (Busse, 1959) or when their decline becomes so rapid that there is visible change in less than two years (Post, 1971). The speed of a decline in intellectual functions with age may represent a watershed of the practical and the theoretical criteria of abnormality. A gradual decline in intellectual functions with age is, in practice, accepted by society and health professionals as normal, while a precipitate decline is viewed as abnormal. Similarly, the processes theorized for normal aging tend to be described as gradual (e.g., lipofuscin accumulation), while rapid processes are almost invariably theorized as pathological (e.g., cerebral thrombosis).

Depression. As expected, ambiguities emerged when an attempt was made to apply some of the criteria of psychopathology to the presence of cognitive impairment in the aged. The same uncertainty results from an examination of depressive symptoms. Depression in old age is associated with, and possibly caused by, an increase of psychologically stressful losses (Busse, 1959; Kay, 1959; Post, 1965). The losses may be those of close relatives or friends, job and status, or abilities. Sometimes they are reactions to a decline in cognitive ability or in general physical health. Thus, the depressions are partly a reaction to the changing circumstances that *normally* accompany old age. Furthermore, depression of a mild and transient nature is very common in the elderly (Busse, Barnes, Silverman, Thaler, & Frost, 1955) and have been hypothesized as related to the normal aging changes in the neurophysiology of the brain (Post, 1968).

Social isolation. Similarly, social isolation in old age may be ascribed to various causes, some of which may be seen as normal accompaniments of aging and some of which are clearly pathological processes (Connolly, 1962; Gruenberg, 1954; Kay & Roth, 1961). Lowenthal et al. (1967) suggested that isolation in the elderly can result either from role loss or as a consequence of mental disorder. Advancing age brings with it death of companions, decreased mobility, and loss of social attractiveness. In some cases, however, the pattern of isolation seems a lifelong characteristic. In still other cases, the development of withdrawal of social interests, suspiciousness, and antipathy toward others can be seen as a paranoid process arising as a late manifestation of schizophrenia with varying degrees of completeness (Post, 1966; Roth & Kay, 1962), sometimes precipitated by the effects of aging. Whatever the assumed cause, moderate degrees of isolation may be well tolerated by the elderly subject, although in the absence of even one intimate relationship the isolation is often accompanied by feelings of loneliness (Lowenthal et al., 1967).

Institutionalization. Admission to an institution is equally difficult to clearly assign to either the domain of normal or abnormal events of aging. It is only too well known that admission to an institution increases rapidly with age. Yet, surveys show that many old people living in the community have the same symptoms as those living in institutions. Supportive families, a spouse, good community facilities, and a certain amount of social invisibility (Lowenthal et al., 1967) may operate in favor of the elderly remaining in the community. However, the reasons for admission cannot be ascribed entirely to deficiencies in the community. Some old people cannot be maintained without being an overwhelming burden on others even in the best of communities, and these subjects tend to suffer from extreme physical or cerebral organic disease rather than advanced age.

Diminished energy. Diminished energy and reduction in psychomotor speed may result of course from overt physical illness but also possibly from more subtle effects of normal aging. However, Lowenthal et al. (1967) suspected that with advances in treating physical disorders in the elderly, failing energy may become accepted as normal only in the very old. Here again, it is hard to make the distinction between normal and pathological effects of aging.

Applying the Criteria to the Whole Man

The discussion so far has been limited to considering criteria of psychopathology and their application to the component character-istics of the aged person. However, when considering the issue of normality or abnormality, the whole man must be taken into ac-count. This requires an assessment also of the positive mental assets and strengths that may protect the individual against the impairment of function that otherwise would result from psychopathological symptoms (Jahoda, 1958). Clausen (1969) emphasized that it is important to evaluate the elderly subject's positive mental health in the areas of interpersonal relations, personal resourcefulness, control over life activities, and accuracy of self-perception. However, the subject whose only defect is that he lacks positive mental health has a defect that, as yet, relatively few would call psychopathological.

A Relativistic, Problem-Oriented Definition of Psychopathology

As Clausen (1968) stated, "mental health is a state devoutly to be wished but desperately difficult to define." In light of the uncertainty prevailing about the definition of psychopathology, there must be doubt about the scientific value of this term. Psychology is concerned with the whole range of human behaviors. The term psychopathology, distinguishing a part of this range, perhaps has greater value for administrative than for scientific issues. By assign-ing certain behaviors to the domain of psychopathology, a value and a priority are accorded to the need to change (or find a way to change) those behaviors. Busse (1959) emphasized that "society plays a large role in determining when and if a person is suffering from a mental disorder. At the point when his behavior or depressed thoughts are no longer acceptable to them, he will be considered sick and will be treated accordingly. This reaction of society to the indi-vidual is extremely important in elderly patients [p. 365]." Further-more, the methods whereby change in behavior can be attained are largely circumscribed by bestowing upon a behavior the designation of psychopathology. For instance, punishment is prohibited in its naked form. More positively, certain public resources are devoted to the modification of psychopathological behaviors. However, as with other administrative policies, differences of opinion will abound regarding the definition of psychopathology, fashions will come and go, and standards will vary among cultures.

Despite the administrative rather than scientific nature of the term psychopathology, it serves a useful function in this chapter. The degree of consensus on psychopathology acts as a guide as to which behaviors are definitely, and which are probably, the proper concerns of the mental health professions. An appropriately broad approach may be taken and psychopathology by all shades of opinion may be discussed, but the most serious discussion may be reserved for psychopathology on which there is a high consensus. Furthermore, making explicit the disagreement on definition that inevitably prevails in a discussion of assessing psychopathology may remove some of the sting of this dissension.

While it is useful to take consensus on the nature of psychopathology as a guide to priorities for research and clinical attention, it does not seem useful to invest much energy in defining exact boundaries between pathological and normal characteristics of aging. The latter task is inherently difficult and even futile. In fact, there might even be heuristic value in dropping the concept of psychopathology and turning rather to a consideration of which characteristics of aging are undesirable and which can be controlled. The word "problem" could be usefully substituted for the word "psychopathology." The goal of this chapter would then be to discuss the broad assessment of problems in the aged. However, a merit of the concept of psychopathology is that it focuses on problems that are within the competence and responsibility of the mental health professions. For this reason the term psychopathology will continue to serve as the focal point of this chapter, but with full recognition of its relative nature— relative, that is, to the state of current knowledge, to disciplinary viewpoints, to the social and administrative context, and to the strengths or positive qualities of the individual.

THE STATE OF THE ARTS OF ASSESSMENT OF PSYCHOPATHOLOGY

General Comparison of Psychiatric and Psychological Techniques

The relative status of psychiatric and psychological techniques requires clarification. This may be achieved by describing the strengths and weaknesses of the two approaches. Hopefully, this will show that, as in the treatment of neurosis (Sloane, 1969), the paths of psychology and psychiatry are converging.

At its best, the psychiatric approach to assessing psychopathology is quick and flexible, takes a rich variety of clinically relevant information into account, including data not easily objectified, and weighs and sifts these data in a logical manner. At worst, this approach is unreliable, subject to bias, and narrowed by adherence to a medical model.

In contrast, the psychological approach, at its best, is reliable, with all the attendant virtues of making possible meaningful comparisons between patients, or groups of patients, and over time; is quantifiable; is based upon experimentally derived theory; and is subject to refined statistical analyses. At worst it is time consuming, remote from the dysfunction that is a problem for the patient, and vulnerable to distortion by response set and other irrelevant variables.

Fortunately for the patient there is an established tradition of interaction between the psychiatric and psychological approaches, a theme which recurs in several of Zubin's papers (Zubin, 1967, 1968, 1970; Zubin & Sutton, 1970). In particular, there is a recent, strong movement for psychiatry to apply more of the methods of psychology. This trend emerged with a gathering of interest in the degree and nature of unreliability of psychiatric diagnosis and the clinical interview (Krietman, Sainsbury, Morrissey, Towers, & Scrivener, 1961; Ward, Beck, Mendelson, Mock, & Erbaugh, 1962). Such unreliability arises because judgments on the patient's behavior are often highly subjective and because clinicians differ in the scope and style of their interviewing, in their definitions of psychopathological terms, and in their diagnostic criteria (Hemsi, Whitehead, & Post, 1968). Partially associated with this unreliability is the heterogeneity and overlap of symptoms shown by patients in different diagnostic groups (Zigler & Phillips, 1961).

In an effort to make diagnosis more reliable, the World Health Organization has sponsored an international glossary describing each diagnostic category of the psychiatric section of the International Classification of Diseases in widely acceptable terms. Of equal importance is the introduction of structured interview techniques that bear many of the virtues commonly associated with psychological tests.

Structured interviews to assess the mental state of patients (e.g., Spitzer, Fleiss, Burdock, & Hardesty, 1964; Wing, Birley, Cooper, Graham, & Isaac, 1967) provide for consistency in interview style, uniform coverage of a wide range of symptoms, definitions of psychopathological terms, and reliable data on small units of behavior (including expressed feelings, speech patterns, appearance, and motility). Diagnosis can be reliable when made by psychiatrists who are trained to use a structured interview (Wing et al., 1967). Furthermore, rigorously consistent computer diagnoses can be derived from the ratings of discrete items (Spitzer & Endicott, 1969).

A major advantage of structured interviewing is that it shifts the effort of the psychiatrist from making a diagnosis, which often requires no more than three minutes of interview time (Sandifer, Horden, & Green, 1969), to the meticulous detailing of the patient's psychopathology. The clinical usefulness of individual symptoms or syndromes for classification, choice of therapy, prognosis, and evaluation of outcome may then be examined. The symptoms recorded in a structured interview may be used for classifying the patient in terms of a computer diagnosis, clinically defined syndromes, or factorially derived dimensions; or for locating him on a continuum of depression, for example; or for placing him in an empirically derived typology. Conventional classification may even be essentially bypassed when symptoms are subjected to discriminant function analysis for the purpose of predicting treatment response or outcome. Syndromes of psychopathology can also be expressed in terms of the probability of a certain disorder being present in a given individual, and a whole array of probabilities for a variety of disorders can be obtained. The use of syndromes or symptoms (instead of diagnosis) for treatment selection, outcome prediction, and epidemiological investigation avoids many of the contentious issues associated with diagnosis.

There are other ways in which the introduction of the structured clinical interview has brought psychiatry and psychology closer together. For example, the style and spirit of the structured interview seem acceptable to both psychiatrists and psychologists, and interviewers can be drawn from either discipline. Another way is that certain tests which were developed by psychologists (sometimes from rudiments in clinical psychiatry) can be incorporated bodily in the structured interview, as will be described below.

The current work of the Cross-National Study of Diagnosis of the Mental Disorders in the United States and the United Kingdom can serve as an illustration of the application of a structured interview to the geriatric age group. This project has completed studies directed at psychiatric disorders in the 20–59 year age group (Cooper, Kendell, Gurland, Sartorius, & Farkas, 1969; Gurland, Fleiss, Cooper, Sharpe, Kendell, & Roberts, 1970; Kendell, Cooper, Gourlay, Copeland, Sharpe, & Gurland, 1971) and is now concerned with psychiatric disorders in older age groups. About 900 hospitalized psychiatric patients in the younger age group in

New York and London have been interviewed by project psychiatrists using structured interviews. The resulting data have been factor analyzed (Fleiss, Gurland, & Cooper, 1971), and those items that fell clearly into one or another of the factors became the backbone of a shortened mental state schedule with about half the number of the items contained in the original schedule. Items of diagnostic importance not appearing in the factors (either for reasons of infrequency or because they loaded equally on two factors) were added to the shortened schedule. A psychological test, the Mental Status Questionnaire (Kahn, Goldfarb, Pollack, & Peck, 1960), was imbedded in the interview. Other items were also added to expand those areas of psychopathology considered of particular importance in the elderly such as memory disturbance, disorientation, nihilistic delusions, and hypochondriasis. Raters were instructed not to make allowances for the patient's age or physical illness. Where it was anticipated that behaviors might change as a result of normal aging, a distinction was made in the ratings between gradual and rapid changes. A separate interview was introduced to assess the patient's physical state. Pilot work on a series of 100 newly admitted patients over the age of 65 to public mental hospitals in New York and London indicates that the interview can be rated reliably and that most elderly patients who can participate adequately in a short, unstructured interview can also tolerate the structured mental state interview described above.

With the emphasis of clinical assessment shifted to a detailed record of symptomatology, one becomes more aware of the nature of the difficulty in assessing elderly psychiatric patients. Some of these difficulties are shared by psychological testing. The older the patient, the more inclined he is to become fatigued during the interview and to have difficulty in grasping complex questions. Thus, interviews must be kept brief and questions straightforward. Since the elderly patient may become anxious and unable to cooperate when put under stress by questions directed at his cognitive abilities, such questioning must be tactful and must not be massed in one portion of the interview.

Some difficulties are peculiar to the psychiatric approach in that judgments are required "on-line" during an interview which in psychological tests are left to subsequent analysis. In this respect a major problem is that most interviewers are much younger than the elderly interviewee and thus do not possess the apperceptual mass for distinguishing between normality and abnormality. Generally, the interviewer has more experience with patients less than 60 years of age and can also apply the norms he has learned from observation of himself and his peers to younger patients. Whereas symptoms from physical illness are infrequently encountered in patients under 60 years of age, such symptoms are common in the elderly. Thus, a decision has to be made as to whether to assign ambiguous symptoms, for example, tiredness, to the realm of psychopathology, physical pathology, or normal aging. We have already indicated that we have tried to limit such arbitrary judgments in our structured interview.

Both psychiatric and psychological tests have sometimes to contend with limited information obtained only from the patient at a single interview. Clausen (1969) pointed out that some of the changes of age may not show up on a short interview, but will appear in social role functioning when observed over time. Multiple interviews, with the patient over time and with other informants, are finding a place in the techniques of both disciplines.

Specific Consideration of the Range of Assessment Techniques

Psychiatric. In the light of the unreliability of diagnosis as generally practiced, it is small wonder that clinical diagnosis has fallen into disrepute and that clinicians pay more attention to the patient's symptoms than to his diagnosis in prescribing treatment. Diagnosis is often used merely as an administrative tool to qualify the patient for insurance benefits or for admission to an institution. Added to this is the clinician's reluctance to apply diagnoses such as schizophrenia, which might carry a stigma for the patient, or to submerge the "whole man" under a label. Furthermore, there is still the frequent belief that diagnosis in the elderly is likely to be an untreatable organic brain syndrome no matter what his symptoms are. Clinicians who have a special interest in careful diagnosis have found that the public hospital diagnosis of organic disorder is frequently applied to cases that they would call functional (Butler, Dastur, & Perlin, 1965; Larsson, Sjögren, & Jacobson, 1963). Finally, there are connotations attached to diagnostic labels of the International Classification of Diseases that are unacceptable to many clinicians, namely, that a Kraeplinian medical model is implied.

Diagnosis that is poorly regarded is probably also badly practiced, and thus a vicious circle is established. Conversely, the renaissance of clinical diagnosis in the elderly began in hospitals with a tradition of careful clinical assessment. Roth, Busse, Kay, Post, Simon, Neal, and many others have shown that such diagnostic groups as senile, arteriosclerotic, affective, schizophrenic, and confusional psychoses all differ from each other in symptomatology and pattern of outcome (i.e., death and discharge rates). For instance, Roth and Kay (1962) reported in their series of elderly psychiatric admissions that two years after admission the majority of those patients diagnosed as having affective psychoses were discharged, the majority with senile and arteriosclerotic organic disorders were dead, and those diagnosed as paraphrenic remained hospitalized; while the acute confusional cases showed an even balance between the discharged and the dead. Corsellis (1962a, 1962b) added evidence that, contrary to the emphasis that Rothschild (1937, 1942) placed on his own negative findings, pathology in the brain was strongly related to both the clinical diagnosis and the outcome of mental disease in the elderly. Corsellis found in an unselected series of 300 necropsies that wherever a given type of brain pathology (e.g., vascular change, or atrophy, or senile plaque formation and neurofibrillary changes) was postulated as occurring in a particular diagnostic group (e.g., functional, senile, cerebrovascular, or mixed), the pathology was found to a moderate to severe degree in about 75% of the appropriate cases. Conversely, when its absence had been postulated, the pathology was found in only 25% of cases. With the development of diagnostic sensitivity, it became evident that a high proportion of elderly psychiatric admissions had functional syndromes that were treatable. Also, the high prevalence of such symptoms among the elderly in the community became apparent.

Drawing on the writings of others, especially Post (1962, 1965, 1966, 1968), Roth and Kay (Kay, 1959; Roth, 1955; Roth & Kay, 1956, 1962), and Busse (1959, 1960, 1970; Busse & Pfeiffer, 1969), one can attempt a description of the current state of the art of psychiatric diagnosis in the elderly patient. The experienced clinician can usually distinguish confidently between an affective disorder (including neurotic depression), a neurosis other than neurotic depression, schizophrenia of late onset (paraphrenia), a confusional state and a chronic brain syndrome. Such distinctions can generally be made on the basis of a clinical assessment that includes an evaluation of the mental status and physical condition of the patient, an adequate psychiatric and medical history from the patient and an informant, and a routine examination of blood and urine. Prolonged observation in a hospital is not usually necessary for diagnosis; it is also rarely necessary to invoke specialized psychological or neurological procedures for this purpose.

The characteristic features of the diagnostic syndromes may not be so readily evident in conditions of acute onset. An incorrect diagnosis of chronic and progressive dementia may easily be made in these acute conditions. In the first place, the patient with a functional disorder may not be able to report his functional symptoms and may be so distressed or preoccupied that he temporarily shows features of cognitive impairment such as disorientation or faulty memory. In this respect, the signs of senile decrepitude, peripheral arteriosclerosis, or the presence of neurological signs do not help in the individual case to decide between a diagnosis of affective or organic disorder. However, a fluctuation in cognitive impairment and the presence of visual hallucinosis weigh the diagnosis in favor of an organic rather than an affective condition. In the second place, the major clue to the existence of an acute confusional state rather than a chronic organic condition may be a minor infection which is easily overlooked, or some medication which escapes suspicion because it has been prescribed by a doctor (e.g., digitalis). Important features for indicating the likelihood of an acute rather than a chronic organic condition are a fluctuation in consciousness, fearfulness rather than apathy, the presence of visual hallucinations, and elaborations of misperceptions. Acute cases, whether affective or organic, will probably require hospitalization, but the choice between a medical or a psychiatric ward may hinge on whether the diagnosis is that of an affective or an organic state. The placement of the patient in the wrong kind of ward may have serious consequences for him (Kidd, 1962, 1963).

The distinction between chronic organic syndromes and functional disorders is usually less difficult, because the evolution of the symptoms is easier to perceive. Where cognitive defects precede functional symptoms the diagnosis is probably organic, and vice versa. Occasionally, functional symptoms may be the first sign of an underlying organic disorder, but this possibility can be postponed from consideration in the absence of definite neurological signs or evidence of a physical condition.

Other diagnostic decisions that are difficult, yet important for treatment, involve the recognition of mild affective disorders not accompanied by a complaint of altered mood (McDonald, 1967) and of severe affective disorders (depressive or manic) resembling paraphrenia because of accompanying paranoid delusions and even hallucinations. An affective condition is the more likely diagnosis if the content of the delusions or hallucinations is in keeping with the altered mood.

Early symptoms in organic disorder such as depression, anxiety, importuning, obsessionality, jealousy, and hoarding behavior may easily be confounded with neurotic behavior. However, depressive syndromes in progressive cerebral disease tend to be intermingled with periods of confusion or euphoria in a "fragmented" fashion (Roth & Kay, 1962), while obsessional symptoms that are provoked by organic disorders tend to be atypical in that they are often stereo-typed and not resisted (Post, 1962).

In depressive states the risk of suicide must be assessed, bearing in mind that it is particularly high in the elderly. Sinister features include marked pessimism and hopelessness and delusions of worth-lessness and of incurable disease (Sainsbury, 1962). Also important to prognosis, if not to treatment, is the separation of the presenile dementias from senile dementia and the separation of either from arteriosclerotic dementia. Favoring a diagnosis of arteriosclerosis rather than senile dementia are the presence of focal neurological signs, a fluctuating course, epileptiform convulsions, emotional incon-tinence, and the preservation of insight. Nevertheless, the clinical distinction among senile, arteriosclerotic, and other dementias is often impossible. Furthermore, the separation of senile dementia and Alzheimer's disease may be of only academic importance since Lauter and Meyer (1968) hypothesized that these are simply different age manifestations of one disease entity.

The neuroses are also difficult to classify, but in any case they are usually seen with an accompanying depression. Neuroses other than neurotic depression appear to decrease in frequency with ad-vancing age (Kessel & Shepherd, 1962), possibly because elderly patients with neurotic symptoms usually come for treatment only when a depression is superimposed.

Clausen (1969) pointed out that "if one merely deals with symptoms, there is no need to conceptualize personality. If, however, one is concerned with a broader conception of mental health, it becomes necessary to consider the enduring organization of tend-encies to behavior [p. 117]." However, the presence of a personality disorder is often difficult to assess and even more difficult to classify.

The diagnostic problems mentioned above for the most part concerned difficult distinctions between different psychopathological syndromes. Difficulty may also arise in distinguishing between symptoms that are, or are not, due to mental disorder. Some remarks on this topic were made earlier in this chapter, when discussing criteria for judging whether a degree of cognitive impairment is psychopathological. In addition, Lowenthal et al. (1967) discussed the distinction between symptoms associated with mental disorder and with low morale. The former may occur when the subject feels a personal failure to achieve goals in life; the latter, when the failure is in gaining approval from others. Thus, symptoms that precede mental disorder may refer to the "inner world" (e.g., free-floating worry), while those associated with low morale may refer to the external world (e.g., irritability). Perlin and Butler (1963), in their evaluation of apparently normal volunteers, distinguished patients with a "senile quality" characterized by diminished involvement with their environment; mild impairment in comprehension; decreased affective interaction; uncomplicated style of communication; and a tendency to cry or become confused under stress.

Some of these diagnostic dilemmas must be solved by repeated examination of the patient over time and perhaps after a trial of treatment. The course of the condition, whether fluctuating, improving, or steadily deteriorating, may determine the diagnosis. Confusional states may clear up after treatment of the underlying physical condition. Acutely disturbed patients with functional disorders may become sufficiently calm to reveal their diagnostic features. It remains an open question whether the response of symptoms to, for example, antidepressants, phenothiazines, or lithium, can be used as a diagnostic test. Other advantages may also accrue from repeated examinations. Epstein and Simon (1969) stated that the chance of mortality can be predicted better if the psychiatric diagnosis and physical condition of the patient are known, together with his progress in the few days following initial evaluation.

Psychodynamic. This section draws heavily on the work of Goldfarb (1953, 1956; Goldfarb & Sheps, 1954; Goldfarb & Turner, 1953), who stressed the importance of assessing the intrapsychic processes of the elderly patient. This applies to all patients, whether or not they have environmental and physical factors also affecting their psychopathology. Aging often leads to a failure of mastery over life circumstances. Different strategies must be adopted by the elderly for problems when previous approaches are no longer available or effective. One reaction may be a loss of confidence and a withdrawal of interest from goals that are unlikely to be attained (Welford, 1963). Werner, Perlin, Butler, and Pollin (1961) categorized the reactions to deteriorative processes in oneself as compensation (e.g., obtaining a hearing aid), acceptance, limitation (of activities), complaint, and qualification (minimization of loss). However, the loss of customary gratifications without compensation may lead to feelings of fear that follow from a sense of helpless vulnerability and also to resentful anger. There may develop an expectation of further deprivations or punishment. This expectation may derive from guilt about being angry, or from a belief that the anger will be visible to others and met with retaliation. Either way, there is a growing fear and despair, and the patient seeks help (or dependency). The dependency seeking may be overt or may be disguised as symptoms.

Thus, the clinician must in all cases carefully assess the losses that the patient has suffered, either as a result of normal aging processes, or of pathology, or of both. Helping to restore these losses is important, as are the acceptance and understanding of the patient's interim need for dependency and his eventual need to regain a sense of mastery. Goldfarb emphasized that emotional factors may play a large part in the disability of even seemingly gross brain damage. He advised a therapeutic trial of psychodynamically oriented care before a final decision is made to place the patient permanently in an institution.

Psychological. An important thrust of psychological testing in the elderly has been toward separating patients with progressive cognitive impairment from patients with other dysfunctions, especially depressive states. This separation is made difficult by the cognitive impairment that may occur in normal aging or as a temporary result of depression. Other difficulties in testing arise from the easy fatigability, sensory impairments, preoccupation, and anxiety of elderly patients and from the effects of electroshock therapy on memory.

Despite the difficulties, psychological tests are valuable for weighing diagnostic decisions and for alerting the clinician to the possibility of a misdiagnosis of cognitive impairment. Roth and Kay (1962) found that their five diagnostic groups differed widely in psychological test scores. They stated that "these differences are valuable adjuncts in diagnosis, particularly in difficult cases . . . [p. 80]."

Verbal-learning tasks are perhaps the most satisfactory for separating organic and functional states. Inglis (1970) regarded the New Word Learning and Retention Test as being well standardized in the geriatric field. Successful results in differentiating organics, functionals, and normals have also been reported with the Paired Associate Learning Test (Caird, Sanderson, & Inglis, 1962; Inglis, 1959b; Irving, Robinson, & McAdam, 1970), and the Modified Word Learning Test (MWLT; Bolton, Savage, & Roth, 1967; Walton & Black, 1957). The MWLT has been shown to separate organics and other patients with very little overlap (Walton & Black, 1957, 1959) and to correlate with objective signs of brain damage (Walton & Black, 1957) and with the electroencephalogram (EEG; White & Knox, 1965). The Synonym Learning Test (Kendrick, Parboosingh, & Post, 1965) also has a very high correlation with psychiatric diagnosis (Hemsi et al., 1968; Irving et al., 1970).

Time limitations have an important effect on performance of the elderly (Lorge, 1936), and this effect is exaggerated in the presence of dementing processes. The Digit Copying Test (Clément,

1963), measuring psychomotor speed, has been shown to discriminate between organic and depressive states (Hemsi et al., 1968).

Perceptual tasks are as yet of uncertain value for diagnosis. Davies (1968) questioned the discriminating power of several of the perceptual tests, including the Memory for Designs Test (Graham & Kendall, 1960), the Trail Making Test (Reitan, 1955), the Perceptual Mazes (Elithorn, 1955), and the Spiral Aftereffect (Price & Deabler, 1955). However, the Bender Gestalt Test (Bender, 1938) seems more promising (Shapiro, Field, & Post, 1957). Zubin suggested that

> much of the difficulty in interpreting the results of perceptual tests stems from the fact that traditional perceptual experiments do not allow for the separation of sensitivity to the stimulus from the criterion of decision making in the response. In other words, we are not able to tell whether the sensitivity of the aged person is lower, or whether he requires more information before responding yes or no to the presence or absence of a stimulus. Signal Detection Theory, which permits the differentiation of sensitivity (d') from criterion (Lx) can help in this connection [J. Zubin, personal communication, 1972].

Contrasts between subtest scores (e.g., verbal "hold" versus performance "don't hold" scores) of the WAIS or other test batteries have been widely used in clinical testing, although with variable success in discriminating organic and functional states (Savage & Bolton, 1968). Davies (1968) used a battery of tests of brain damage, for example, the perceptual tasks mentioned above as well as the Digit Code Test (Clément, 1963), Progressive Matrices (Raven, 1938), Mill Hill Vocabulary Test, (Raven, 1943), and the Synonym Test, on a sample of 540 volunteers between 20 and 80 years of age. There were differential declines with age and differential sensitivity to brain damage. He concluded that the Mill Hill Vocabulary Test is an index of the best intellectual level attained, since age does not lower it much, but that brain damage did lower it. Orme (1957) also found the Mill Hill Vocabulary Test to discriminate organic cases from elderly normals and depressives. In Birren's (Birren, Butler, Greenhouse, Sokoloff, & Yarrow, 1963) studies, reaction time, progressive matrices, and digit symbol tasks have been shown to decline with age, while comprehension subtests and dichotic digit span decline with subclinical (and, presumably, clinical) ill health.

De Ajuriaguerra and Tissot (1968) observed that in senile dementia cognitive disintegration proceeds in stages that are similar, but in inverse order, to those that evolve in infancy. They suggested that these levels can be used to measure the progress of deterioration in an individual. However, there is as yet relatively little spill-over from this recent work into the assessment of the disordered dement and presumably the levels they describe are more appropriate to advanced cases.

The use of serial testing over time appears to improve the discriminating power of psychological tests (Kendrick, 1965, 1967), although this is not a simple solution since even patients with chronic cognitive impairment may have superimposed fluctuations in their condition.

It frequently happens that, when the clinician is in doubt, the results of the psychological tests are also in doubt (Post, 1965). Inglis (1966) pointed out that although organic and functional patients could be differentiated on the basis of tests of acquisition (Isaacs, 1962; Isaacs & Walkley, 1964; Newcombe & Steinberg, 1964; Riddell, 1962), "even relatively high correlations between test scores and diagnostic criteria can result in very great errors in classification."

The prognostic power of a psychological test must also be very high to be clinically useful. Epstein and Simon (1969) found that for the patients in their study, the prediction of death or discharge could be made as well by a simple clinical test of orientation as by the score obtained on the four verbal subtests of the WAIS that were used. However, Sanderson and Inglis (1961) showed "a closer association between test scores and mortality than between mortality and initial diagnosis." Impaired learning ability related to mortality over the next two years. Kral and his colleagues, Mueller and Cahn, found that low scores on a modified Wechsler Memory scale predicted mortality over a four-year period (Kral, 1962; Kral, Cahn, & Mueller, 1964; Kral & Mueller, 1966).

Much of the work mentioned above has been aimed at discriminating patient groups as defined by the criterion of a skilled diagnostician. Some of this work is extremely sophisticated. Kendrick and Post (1967) used a Bayesian statistical approach to establish appropriate cutoff points for identifying patients with diffuse brain damage. However, equally important work has been focused on the nature and outcome of the memory disorders in the elderly without regard to diagnosis. Inglis (1970) favored such analytic description of behavior itself, since it may lead to "discovery of relevant independent variables that can give us power to secure prophylaxis and change." He added, "there is little to be gained, and much to be lost, by the creation of further psychological tests founded on diagnostic guesswork." Emphasis is placed on determining the steps in the learning–memory processes which are disturbed in the aging individual. The program organized by Inglis (1970) led him to select objective measures of the main phases of learning by different modalities and by different modes of reproduction. He found (Inglis, 1957) that elderly patients with memory disorders have marked disability in acquisition, although there were also defects in retention (Inglis, 1959a). In line with the above principles, dichotic listening performance has been used (Caird & Hannah, 1964; Caird & Inglis, 1961; Inglis & Sanderson, 1961), to examine to what extent memory disorder in elderly psychiatric patients is based upon a breakdown of the short-term storage S-system.

Psychological assessment techniques are perhaps most powerful when they isolate the components of a disorder in a way that lends itself to rational treatment. Eisdorfer's (Eisdorfer, Nowlin, & Wilkie, 1970) concept of high arousal leading to response suppression in the elderly induced him to attempt to improve the performance of the elderly by administering an autonomic blocking agent. Whether or not this approach will prove useful in clinical work remains to be seen, but it is an excellent paradigm. Similarly, the technique of behavioral analysis as described by Kanfer and Saslow (1967) assesses in a comprehensive way the factors maintaining the patient's disabilities and provides information required to plan the patient's treatment.

Laboratory methods. The appeal of laboratory methods is their potential for precision and consistency, their requirement of only passive cooperation on the part of the subject, and their relative freedom from cultural influences.

Biopsy is the most direct method for the detection of brain pathology. However, it has the obvious drawbacks of an operative procedure, and, in addition, it is limited by the imperfect relationship between anatomical changes in the brain and cognitive impairment. Nevertheless, biopsy may return to favor if specific anatomical changes in the brain are found to be remedial.

The EEG has been found to show abnormalities (mostly showing of the dominant rhythm) that increase with age and especially in the presence of a dementing process. Roth and Kay (1962) stated that EEGs are of some value in distinguishing between acute and chronic organic disorders. High-voltage, frontally predominant paroxysmal slow waves are characteristic of the acute condition, while chronic states may show slow alpha rhythm. However, Wang (1969) stated that EEG abnormalities of diffuse slow activity in the theta or delta range, although more common in organic than functional states, are not specific for the type of brain disorder. "Dynamic" EEGs (Busse & Wang, 1965) with photic and pharmacological stimulation, or serial EEGs (Wang, 1969), may have more promise; Obrist (Obrist, Kleemeier, Justiss, & Henry, 1963) noted that a decrease in the evoked cortical response to a stimulus may predict death.

Skull X rays and air encephalograms have not proved helpful in the detection of cortical atrophy in early stages of a dementing process (McCormick, 1962), although clearly there are times when they may localize a tumor.

Cerebral blood flow is only rarely directly assessed, unless an aneurysm or carotid stenosis is suspected and an arteriogram requested. Catheterization for direct measures of blood flow and cerebral metabolism is mainly a research tool. Recent development of a nonintrusive safe means of measuring blood flow by inhalation of a radioactive isotope (Obrist, Chivian, Cronqvist, & Ingvar, 1970; Obrist, Thompson, King, & Wang, 1967) offers more promise for clinical applications.

The probable relationship between hypodiploid chromosome changes in elements of the peripheral blood stream, similar chromosome changes in the brain cells, and some dementing processes (Jarvik, 1963; Nielsen, 1968) may also eventually provide a clinical assessment procedure.

Certain general physical disorders, detectable in the laboratory, may give rise to an array of functional or organic psychological symptoms, but especially to confusional states. The relevant laboratory tests are those for levels of serum electrolytes (especially sodium and potassium), macrocytic anemias, folate, vitamin B_{12}, and ascorbic acid levels, and tests of hypothyroid functioning including serum iodide levels. More recently, the erythrocyte sedimentation rate has been shown to be of possible importance for the identification of a dementia due to an immune reaction and which may respond to steroid treatment (Chynoweth & Foley, 1969).

The detection of elevated levels of ribonuclease in the elderly was once thought to indicate that some elderly organics suffered from a deficiency in brain RNA. Treatments designed to raise brain RNA enjoyed a vogue (Cameron, Solyom, Sved, & Wainrib, 1963; Cameron, Sved, Solyom, Wainrib, & Barik, 1963). Although the results were disappointing, the close link between theory, laboratory tests, and treatment remains an ideal model to emulate.

Occupying a borderland between laboratory and clinical testing are such techniques as pharmacological load responses (Lehmann & Ban, 1968). The immediate clinical response of a patient's cognitive functions to the administration of a pharmacological agent such as carbon dioxide (or hyperbaric oxygen or barbiturates) may be a predictor of his long-term prognosis and response to therapy.

Social background and attitudes. Problematic behavior in an elderly person may not be susceptible to assessment until information is forthcoming about the patient's social background, his attitudes, and the attitudes of those around him. Recent environmental losses (of close companions, income, home, or status) may lead to impaired functioning in daily activities, possibly because of an intervening depressed mood (Birren et al., 1963). Chronic isolation may also have a deleterious effect. Weinstock and Bennett (1968) found that certain social isolates showed cognitive impairment that improved on admission to an institution, probably as a result of resocialization. Relocation in an unfamiliar environment may also lead to deterioration in certain sensitive subjects. Bloom, Blenkner, and Markus (1969) worked with the Modified Embedded Figures Test in attempting to identify "field dependent" elderly subjects likely to have difficulty in coping with relocation in an institutional environment.

Lowenthal et al. (1967) noted that in indicator of morale, although highly correlated with psychiatric impairment, was quite distinct in kind. Lowered self-esteem may be provoked by the denigrating attitudes of others, to which the aged are particularly vulnerable. Even a self-report of diminished or impaired cognitive functions may merely reflect a stereotype the elderly person has adopted from his social group. Nash and Zimring (1969) showed that improvement in short-term memory in the elderly may be partly a function of the subject's expectation. Furthermore, an apparent deterioration in the patient may turn out to be a change in the tolerance level of those around him.

Physical health. There is an intimate link between physical and psychiatric ill health for both hospitalized and nonhospitalized elderly subjects (Lowenthal et al., 1967). This link strengthens with advancing age. Weiss and Schaie (1962) found that in older patients attending a municipal psychiatric clinic, many of the complaints manifested were related to the area of physical health. Simon and Neal (1963), in their study of psychiatric admissions (who had become inpatients only after the age of 60) to a receiving hospital, noted that over 40% of the disorders were considered acute psychological responses to some type of acute physiological discomfort.

In acute confusional states a special search must be made for cardiac failure, respiratory disease (which may easily be overlooked), myocardial infarction (which may be painless), electrolyte disturbance, malignant disease, or nutritional deficiences, as well as a history of ingesting alcohol or drugs, or of head trauma. Albert (1968) noted that cardiac insufficiency may produce only temporary cognitive impairment if the insufficiency is quickly treated, but permanent impairment if it is not treated soon enough.

Even where the diagnosis is undoubtedly that of a chronic organic disorder, the assessment should still take into account the possibility of remedial conditions such as aggravating infection or toxemia, cerebral tumor, syphilis, myxoedema, malnutrition, macrocytic anemia, and other conditions. Among the rarer remedial conditions are B_{12} deficiencies in the presence of a normal blood picture (Murphy, Srivastava, Varadi, & Elwis, 1969; Strachan & Henderson, 1965) and dementias with a raised erythrocyte sedimentation rate that may respond to steroid administration (Chynoweth & Foley, 1969).

Disability. In the individual patient there may be a surprising contrast between the number of psychopathological symptoms he manifests and the degree of his physical or social disability (Perlin & Butler, 1963). Therefore, as Gruenberg (1968) stressed, disability must be measured in its own right. Level of disability is not only of value for assessment of the subject's current status but also may be a crucial variable in prognosis. Lowenthal (1964) found that scores on a Social Self-Maintenance Scale (need for safety supervision, ability to relate experiences, quality of social activities, and responsibility for care of own health) and on a Physical Self-Maintenance Scale (toilet activities, feeding, etc.) were predictive of mortality and length of hospitalization.

CONDENSING AND INTEGRATING THE DATA

The assessment of psychopathology in the elderly psychiatric patient requires that he be thoroughly examined with a mental state interview, a proper psychiatric history be taken, his physical condition assessed, and his psychological and other special tests reviewed. Information obtained from an informant who knows the patient is often vital in determining the patient's condition. The clinician must also take into account the capacity of the patient to look after himself at home; the support (financial and personal) he receives from family or friends; the nature of the burdens he imposes on those who must look after him and the psychological effect of this stress on them; the medical, psychiatric, or social services he requires and can receive in the community; the physical layout of his home; and his personality assets and other evidence of positive mental health.

The amount of information required for assessment purposes, the number of sources to be contacted, and the variety of disciplinary skills at play, all point to the importance of interdisciplinary team-work in the clinical assessment of the elderly subject. Goldfarb (1969), in his seven-year follow-up study of elderly subjects in institutions, demonstrated the value of integrating data from the several disciplines represented in his team. He found that mortality was best predicted by the diagnosis of severe chronic brain syndrome, the score on a psychological test (the Mental Status Questionnaire), impairment of the subject's ability to look after himself, and physical incontinence.

The role of the clinician in the assessment team is in flux. One possibility is that his role be restricted to integrating assessment data and translating it into a treatment program. Perhaps even the task of conducting the mental state interview could be taken over by a less broadly trained paraprofessional. There is no firm evidence as yet that paraprofessionals can be taught to elicit and judge psycho-pathology as well as a psychiatrist or psychologist. What is striking is that the notion has some credence. This is a tribute to the power of the structured interview as a means of conveying to the interviewer much of the skills and experience of seasoned psychopathologists. In this sense, the structured interview is a channel of communication between one interviewer and another, as well as between the inter-viewer and the patient.

If the clinician is to integrate and utilize this extensive data properly, he will need the benefit of condensed and easily assimi-lable information. In this respect, there appears to be a gap in the skills presently available in an assessment team, namely, skills in the concise presentation of comprehensive data on a patient. Tradition-ally, the functions of condensing and presenting data are carried out in narrative fashion by a member of each discipline in the team, or by a junior psychiatrist or psychologist. However, with the mounting information required to plan and evaluate the management of geriat-ric patients, a more concerted effort must be made to communicate this information in the most efficient form possible. There is a need for a team member with special skills in this area. These skills would include a knowledge of structured interview techniques in all the relevant spheres, of mathematical and computer-assisted methods for reducing data, and of the art of communicating graphically as well as verbally. This communication expert would be responsible for selecting, supervising, and processing the structured interviews administered by the various team members. None of this would preclude team members from using unstructured methods and narra-tive accounts as well, but it would foster the most economic use of the time devoted to the clinical assessment of the elderly patient.

This procedure need not be more expensive in time and personnel than that in current practice in hospitals. The possibility of providing such services in office practice also needs careful consideration, although there are obvious inherent difficulties.

SUMMARY AND CONCLUSION

This chapter discussed the need for the clinical assessment of psychopathology in the elderly to transcend traditional boundaries within the field of mental health. For research purposes the elderly subject may be parceled out among several different disciplines, separated into Zubin's six scientific models, and divided into normal and abnormal compartments. Consequently, the contributions of research to the clinical field may appear in a fragmentary fashion. It is the job of the clinician to put it all together, and in this process he will find it necessary to forgo rigid distinctions between normality and abnormality, the techniques of psychiatry and psychology, and the conditions arising from physical, psychological, and sociological determinants.

The line between normality and abnormality is exquisitely difficult to draw in the elderly. A survey of the criteria for abnormality finds them all to be debatable. It is not surprising that clinicians differ about where to draw this line. Those clinicians mainly in institutional practice probably have a narrower concept of abnormality than those who treat community residents with the whole range of problems for which people seek help. Such differences of opinion flow over into disagreements about methods of assessment, about who should be treated, and about the appropriate targets for preventative efforts. Perhaps the issues could be made clearer by abandoning the term abnormal or its synonyms such as psychopathology, mental disorder, and the like. Those terms were more useful when the recognized patient population included only those with severe symptoms, and when the less dramatic discomforts of aging were regarded as inevitable and not meriting treatment. Decisions about treatment and prevention could now more fruitfully depend upon pragmatic considerations such as the natural history of a given behavior, whether it is distressing or disabling to the patient or to others, and whether there is an effective way to modify it.

A further advantage arising from dropping rigid distinctions between normality and abnormality is that one might perceive more clearly the necessity for drawing upon the whole body of knowledge about aging when assessing the clinical status of the elderly patient.

Similarly, although physical, social, and psychological spheres are convenient constructs for examining causes and effects in the elderly patient, they are so highly interrelated in this age group that one sphere cannot be assessed and understood except in relation to the other two. All these relevant spheres were discussed in an attempt to illustrate the breadth of the approach required in assessing the elderly patient with mental health problems.

The broad and comprehensive approach to clinical assessment avoids the distortion of the specialized and selected viewpoint but raises new problems. In the first place, the techniques of the various disciplines must be amalgamated. In this chapter, a new structured clinical interview specifically developed for geriatric use was described in detail as an example of the merging of the techniques of psychiatry and psychology.

Also, there is the problem of collecting and integrating information from a wide number of sources. The abundance of data which are gathered must be reduced to manageable proportions and presented in digestible form. A team approach seems to be essential, with members of the relevant disciplines being represented in the collection and reporting of the data. However, this procedure is vulnerable to inconsistency and bias on the part of the various interviewers, to inefficient summarization of data, and to selective listening on the part of the clinician who translates the data into a decision on the management of the patient. Therefore, it was suggested in this chapter that there is a need for a staff member with the skills required to collate and present the data relevant to the management of the patient.

The major theme of this chapter was that the assessment of mental health problems in the elderly subject is facilitated by an erosion of the customary interdisciplinary boundaries in the clinical field. A new role should be created for a professional who is skilled in the science of accurate and efficient interdisciplinary communication.

REFERENCES

Albert, E. Discussion contribution to Epidemiology and genetics of senile dementia. In C. Muller & L. Ciompi (Eds.), *Senile dementia*. Bern, Switzerland: Hans Huber, 1968.

Bender, L. A visual motor gestalt test and its clinical use. (Res. Monograph No. 3) New York: American Orthopsychiatric Association, 1938.

Birren, J. E. Neural basis of personal adjustment in aging. In P. F. Hansen (Ed.), *Age with a future*. Copenhagen: Munksgaard, 1964.

Birren, J. E., Butler, R. N., Greenhouse, S. W., Sokoloff, L., & Yarrow, M. Summary and interpretations. In J. E. Birren, R. N. Butler, S. W. Greenhouse, L. Sokoloff, & M. R. Yarrow (Eds.), *Human aging: A biological and behavioral study.* (USPHS Publ. No. 986) Washington, D.C.: United States Government Printing Office, 1963.

Bloom, M., Blenkner, M., & Markus, E. Exploring predictions of differential impact of relocation on infirm aged. *Proceedings of the 77th Annual Convention of the American Psychological Association,* 1969, **4,** 731–732. (Summary)

Bolton, N., Savage, R. D., & Roth, M. The Modified Word Learning Test and the aged psychiatric patient. *British Journal of Psychiatry,* 1967, **113,** 1139–1140. (Abstract)

Bremer, J. A social psychiatric investigation of a small community in northern Norway. *Acta Psychiatrica et Neurologica Scandinavica,* 1951. (Supplement No. 62).

Broadbent, D. E. Immediate memory and simultaneous stimuli. *Quarterly Journal of Experimental Psychology,* 1957, **9,** 1–11.

Busse, E. W. Psychopathology. In J. E. Birren (Ed.), *Handbook of aging and the individual.* Chicago: University of Chicago Press, 1959.

Busse, E. W. Mental disorders of the aging. In W. Johnson (Ed.), *The older patient.* New York: Hoeber, 1960.

Busse, E. W. Psychoneurotic reactions and defense mechanisms in the aged. In E. Palmore (Ed.), *Normal aging.* Durham: Duke University Press, 1970.

Busse, E. W., Barnes, R. H., Silverman, A. J., Thaler, M., & Frost, L. L. Studies of the process of aging. X: The strength and weakness of psychic functioning in the aged. *American Journal of Psychiatry,* 1955, **111,** 896–903.

Busse, E. W., & Pfeiffer, E. Functional psychiatric disorders in old age. In E. W. Busse & E. Pfeiffer (Eds.), *Behavior and adaptation in late life.* Boston: Little, Brown, 1969.

Busse, E. W., & Wang, H.-S. The value of electroencephalography in geriatrics. *Geriatrics,* 1965, **20,** 906–924.

Butler, R. N., Dastur, D. K., & Perlin, S. Relationship of senile manifestations and chronic brain syndromes to cerebral circulation and metabolism. *Journal of Psychiatric Research,* 1965, **3,** 229–238.

Caird, W. K., & Hannah, F. Short-term memory disorder in elderly psychiatric patients. *Diseases of the Nervous System,* 1964, **25,** 564–568.

Caird, W. K., & Inglis, J. The short-term storage of auditory and visual two-channel digits by elderly patients with memory disorder. *Journal of Mental Science,* 1961, **107,** 1062–1069.

Caird, W. K., Sanderson, R. E., & Inglis, J. Cross-validation of a learning test for use with elderly psychiatric patients. *Journal of Mental Science,* 1962, **108,** 368–370.

Cameron, D. E., Solyom, L., Sved, S., & Wainrib, B. Effects of intravenous administration of ribonucleic acid upon failure of memory for recent events in pre-senile and aged individuals. In J. Wortis (Ed.), *Recent advances in biological psychiatry.* New York: Plenum Press, 1963.

Cameron, D. E., Sved, S., Solyom, L., Wainrib, B., & Barik, H. Effects of ribonucleic acid on memory defect in the aged. *American Journal of Psychiatry,* 1963, **120,** 320–325.

Chynoweth, R., & Foley, J. Presentile dementia responding to steroid therapy. *British Journal of Psychiatry*, 1969, **115**, 703–708.

Clausen, J. A. Conceptual and methodologic issues in the assessment of mental health in the aged. In A. Simon & L. J. Epstein (Eds.), *Aging in modern society*. Washington, D.C.: American Psychiatric Association, 1968.

Clausen, J. A. Methodological issues in the measurement of mental health of the aged. In M. F. Lowenthal & A. Zilli (Eds.), *Interdisciplinary topics in gerontology: Colloquium on health and aging of the population*. New York: Karger, 1969.

Clément, F. Une épreuve rapide de mesure de l'efficience intellectuelle. *Revue de Psychologie appliquée*, 1963, **13**, 1215.

Connolly, J. The social and medical circumstances of old people admitted to a psychiatric hospital. *Medical Officer*, August 1962.

Constantinidis, J. Discussion of the role of intraneuronal lipofuscin in senile dementia. In C. Muller & L. Ciompi (Eds.), *Senile dementia*. Bern, Switzerland: Hans Huber, 1968.

Cooper, J. E., Kendell, R. E., Gurland, B. J., Sartorius, N., & Farkas, T. Cross-national study of diagnosis of the mental disorders: Some results from the first comparative investigation. *American Journal of Psychiatry*, 1969, **125**, 21–29. (Supplement)

Corsellis, J. Distribution of neuropathological changes in mental hospital patients with particular reference to age at death. In H. Blumenthal (Ed.), *Aging around the world: Medical and clinical aspects of aging*. New York: Columbia University Press, 1962. (a)

Corsellis, J. *Mental illness and the aging brain*. (Maudsley Monograph No. 9) London: Oxford University Press, 1962. (b)

Davies, A. D. M. Measures of mental deterioration in aging and brain damage. In S. S. Chown & K. F. Riegel (Eds.), *Interdisciplinary topics in gerontology*. Vol. 1. *Psychological functioning in the normal aging and senile aged*. New York: Karger, 1968.

de Ajuriaguerra, J., & Tissot, R. Some aspects of psychoneurologic disintegration in senile dementia. In C. Muller & L. Ciompi (Eds.), *Senile dementia*. Bern, Switzerland: Hans Huber, 1968.

Eisdorfer, C., Nowlin, J., & Wilkie, F. Improvement of learning in the aged by modification of autonomic nervous system activity. *Science*, 1970, **170**, 1327–1329.

Elithorn, A. A preliminary report on a perceptual maze test sensitive to brain damage. *Journal of Neurology, Neurosurgery, and Psychiatry*, 1955, **18**, 287.

Epstein, L. J., & Simon, A. Prediction of outcome in geriatric mental illness. In M. F. Lowenthal & A. Zilli (Eds.), *Interdisciplinary topics in gerontology: Colloquium on health and aging of the population*. New York: Karger, 1969.

Essen-Moller, E., Larsson, H., Uddenberg, C. E., & White, G. Individual traits and morbidity in a Swedish rural population. *Acta Psychiatrica et Neurologica Scandinavica*, 1956. (Supplement 100)

Fleiss, J. L., Gurland, B. J., & Cooper, J. E. Some contributions to the measurement of psychopathology. *British Journal of Psychiatry*, 1971, **119**, 647–658.

Goldfarb, A. I. Psychotherapy of aged persons: I. The orientation of staff in a home for the aged. *Mental Hygiene*, 1953, **37**, 76–83.

Goldfarb, A. I. The rationale for psychotherapy with older persons. *American Journal of Mental Science*, 1956, **232**, 181–185.

Goldfarb, A. I. The psychotherapy of elderly patients. In H. Blumenthal (Ed.), *Aging around the world: Medical and clinical aspects of aging*. New York: Columbia University Press, 1962.

Goldfarb, A. I. Predicting mortality in the institutionalized aged. *Archives of General Psychiatry*, 1969, **21**, 172–176.

Goldfarb, A. I., & Sheps, J. Psychotherapy of the aged: III. Brief therapy of interrelated psychological and somatic disorders. *Psychosomatic Medicine*, 1954, **16**, 209–219.

Goldfarb, A. I., & Turner, H. Psychotherapy of aged persons: II. Utilization and effectiveness of "brief" therapy. *American Journal of Psychiatry*, 1953, **109**, 916–921.

Graham, F. K., & Kendall, B. S. Memory for Designs Test: Revised general manual. *Perceptual and Motor Skills*, 1960, **11**, 147–188.

Gruenberg, E. M. Community conditions and psychoses of the elderly. *American Journal of Psychiatry*, 1954, **110**, 888–896.

Gruenberg, E. On measuring mental morbidity. In S. B. Sells (Ed.), *The definition and measurement of mental health*. Washington, D.C.: United States Department of Health, Education, and Welfare, 1968.

Gurland, B. J., Fleiss, J. L., Cooper, J. E., Sharpe, L., Kendell, R. E., & Roberts, P. Cross-national study of diagnosis of mental disorders: Hospital diagnoses and hospital patients in New York and London. *Comprehensive Psychiatry*, 1970, **11**(1), 18–25.

Hamerton, J. L., Taylor, A. I., Angell, R., & McGuire, V. M. Chromosome investigations of a small isolated human population: Chromosome abnormalities and distribution of chromosome counts according to age and sex among the population of Tristan da Cunha. *Nature*, 1965, **206**, 1232–1234.

Hemsi, L. K., Whitehead, A., & Post, F. Cognitive functioning and cerebral arousal in elderly depressives and dements. *Journal of Psychosomatic Research*, 1968, **12**, 145–156.

Inglis, J. An experimental study of learning and "memory function" in elderly psychiatric patients. *Journal of Mental Science*, 1957, **103**, 796–803.

Inglis, J. Learning, retention and conceptual usage in elderly patients with memory disorder. *Journal of Abnormal and Social Psychology*, 1959, **59**, 210–215. (a)

Inglis, J. A paired-associated learning test for use with elderly psychiatric patients. *Journal of Mental Science*, 1959, **105**, 440. (b)

Inglis, J. *The scientific study of abnormal behavior: Experimental and clinical research*. Chicago: Aldine, 1966.

Inglis, J. Memory disorder. In C. G. Costello (Ed.), *Symptoms of psychopathology*. New York: Wiley, 1970.

Inglis, J., & Sanderson, R. E. Successive responses to simultaneous stimulation in elderly patients with memory disorder. *Journal of Abnormal and Social Psychology*, 1961, **62**, 709–712.

Irving, G., Robinson, R. A., & McAdam, W. The validity of some cognitive tests in the diagnosis of dementia. *British Journal of Psychiatry,* 1970, **117,** 149.

Isaacs, B. A preliminary evaluation of a paired-associate verbal learning test in geriatric practice. *Gerontologia Clinica,* 1962, **4,** 43–55.

Isaacs, B., & Walkley, F. A. A simplified paired-associate test for elderly hospital patients. *British Journal of Psychiatry,* 1964, **110,** 80–83.

Jacobs, P. A., Brunton, M., & Court-Brown, W. M. Cytogenetic studies in leucocytes on the general population: Subjects of ages 65 years and more. *Annals of Human Genetics,* 1964, **27,** 353–365.

Jacobs, P. A., Brunton, M., Court-Brown, W. M., Doll, R., & Goldstein, H. The change of human chromosome count distributions with age, evidence for a sex difference. *Nature,* 1963, **197,** 1080–1081.

Jacobs, P. A., Court-Brown, W. M., & Doll, R. Distribution of human chromosome counts in relation to age. *Nature,* 1961, **191,** 1178–1180.

Jahoda, M. *Current concepts of positive mental health.* New York: Basic Books, 1958.

Jarvik, L. F. Senescence and chromosomal changes. *Lancet,* 1963, **1,** 114–115.

Kahn, R. L., Goldfarb, A. I., Pollack, M., & Peck, A. Brief objective measures for the determination of mental status in the aged. *American Journal of Psychiatry,* 1960, **117,** 326–328.

Kanfer, F. H., & Saslow, G. Behavioral analysis: An alternative to diagnostic classification. In T. Millon (Ed.), *Theories of psychopathology.* Philadelphia: Saunders, 1967.

Kay, D. W. K. Observations on the natural history and genetics of old age psychoses. A Stockholm survey, 1931–1937. *Proceedings of the Royal Society of Medicine,* 1959, **52,** 791–794. (Abridged)

Kay, D. W. K., Beamish, P., & Roth, M. Old age mental disorders in New-castle-upon-Tyne. Part I: A study of prevalence. *British Journal of Psychiatry,* 1964, **110,** 146–158.

Kay, D. W. K., & Roth, M. Environmental and hereditary factors in the schizophrenias of old age (late paraphrenia) and their bearing on the general problem of causation in schizophrenia. *Journal of Mental Science,* 1961, **107,** 649–686.

Kendell, R. E., Cooper, J. E., Gourlay, J., Copeland, J. R. M., Sharpe, L., & Gurland, B. J. Diagnostic criteria of American and British psychiatrists. *Archives of General Psychiatry,* 1971, **25**(2), 123–130.

Kendrick, D. C. Speed and learning in the diagnosis of diffuse brain damage in elderly subjects: A Bayesian statistical approach. *British Journal of Social and Clinical Psychology,* 1965, **4,** 141–148.

Kendrick, D. C. A cross-validation study of the use of the SLT and DCT in screening for diffuse brain pathology in elderly subjects. *British Journal of Medical Psychology,* 1967, **40,** 173–177.

Kendrick, D. C., Parboosingh, R. C., & Post, F. A synonym learning test for use with elderly psychiatric subjects: A validation study. *British Journal of Social and Clinical Psychology,* 1965, **4,** 63–71.

Kendrick, D. C., & Post, F. Differences in cognitive status between healthy, psychiatrically ill, and diffusely brain-damaged elderly subjects. *British Journal of Psychiatry,* 1967, **113,** 75–81.

Kessel, N., & Shepherd, M. Neurosis in hospital and general practice. *Journal of Mental Science,* 1962, **108,** 159–165.

Kidd, C. B. Misplacement of the elderly in hospital. A study of patients admitted to geriatric and mental hospitals. *British Medical Journal,* 1962, Dec. 8, 1491–1494.

Kidd, C. B. Some epidemiological aspects of mental illness occurring in old age. Paper presented at the 6th International Congress of Gerontologists, Copenhagen, 1963.

Korenchevsky, V. *Physiological and pathological aging.* New York: Karger, 1961.

Kral, V. A. Senescent forgetfulness: Benign and malignant. *Canadian Medical Association Journal,* 1962, **86,** 257–260.

Kral, V. A. Recent research in geriatric psychiatry. *Medical Services Journal of Canada,* 1965, **21,** 553–562.

Kral, V. A. Memory loss in the aged. *Diseases of the Nervous System,* 1966, **27,** 51–54.

Kral, V. A., Cahn, C., & Mueller, H. Senescent memory impairment and its relation to the general health of the aging individual. *Journal of the American Geriatrics Society,* 1964, **12,** 101–113.

Kral, V. A., & Mueller, H. Memory dysfunction: A prognostic indicator in geriatric patients. *Canadian Psychiatric Association Journal,* 1966, **11,** 343–349.

Kreitman, N., Sainsbury, P., Morrissey, J., Towers, J., & Scrivener, J. The reliability of psychiatric assessment: An analysis. *Journal of Mental Science,* 1961, **107,** 887–908.

Larsson, T., Sjögren, T., & Jacobson, G. Senile dementia. *Acta Psychiatrica et Neurologica Scandinavica,* 1963. (Supplement 167).

Lauter, H., & Meyer, J. E. Clinical and nosological concepts of senile dementia. In C. Muller & L. Ciompi (Eds.), *Senile dementia.* Bern, Switzerland: Hans Huber, 1968.

Lehmann, H. E., & Ban, P. A. Pharmacological load tests as predictors of pharmacotherapeutic response in geriatric patients. Paper presented at the 7th Annual Meeting of the American College of Neuropsychopharmacology, Puerto Rico, December 1968.

Leighton, D. C., Harding, J. S., Macklin, D. B., Hughes, C. C., & Leighton, A. H. Psychiatric findings of the Stirling County study. *American Journal of Psychiatry,* 1963, **119,** 1021–1026.

Leighton, D. C., Harding, J. S., Macklin, D. B., Macmillan, A. M., & Leighton, A. H. *The character of danger: Psychiatric symptoms in selected communities.* New York: Basic Books, 1963.

Libow, L. Medical investigation of the processes of aging. In J. E. Birren, R. N. Butler, S. W. Greenhouse, L. Sokoloff, & M. R. Yarrow (Eds.), *Human aging: A biological and behavioral study.* (USPHS Publ. No. 986) Washington, D.C.: United States Government Printing Office, 1963.

Lorge, I. The influence of the test upon the nature of mental decline as a function of age. *Journal of Educational Psychology,* 1936, **27,** 100–110.

Lowenthal, M. F. *Lives in distress.* New York: Basic Books, 1964.

Lowenthal, M. F., Berkman, P. L., & Associates. *Aging and mental disorder in San Francisco: A social psychiatric study.* San Francisco: Jossey-Bass, 1967.

McCormick, W. O. A study of the relationship between dementia and radiologically diagnosed cerebral atrophy in elderly patients. Unpublished doctoral dissertation for the Academic Postgraduate Diploma in Psychological Medicine at the Institute of Psychiatry, London, 1962.

McDonald, C. The pattern of neurotic illness in the elderly. *Australian and New Zealand Journal of Psychiatry,* 1967, **1,** 203–210.

Murphy, F., Srivastava, P. C., Varadi, S., & Elwis, A. Screening of psychiatric patients for hypovitaminosis B. *British Medical Journal,* 1969, **3,** 559–560.

Nash, M. M., & Zimring, F. M. Prediction of reaction to placebo. *Journal of Abnormal Psychology,* 1969, **74,** 568–573.

Newcombe, F., & Steinberg, B. Some aspects of learning and memory function in older psychiatric patients. *Journal of Gerontology,* 1964, **19,** 490–493.

New York State Department of Mental Hygiene, Mental Health Research Unit. *A mental health survey of older people.* Utica, N.Y.: State Hospital Press, 1960, 1961.

Nielsen, J. Geronto-psychiatric period-prevalence investigation in a geographically delimited population. *Acta Psychiatrica et Neurologica Scandinavica,* 1962, **38,** 307–330.

Nielsen, J. Chromosomes in senile dementia. In C. Muller & L. Ciompi (Eds.), *Senile dementia.* Bern, Switzerland: Hans Huber, 1968.

Obrist, W. D., Chivian, E., Cronqvist, S., & Ingvar, D. H. Regional cerebral blood flow in senile and pre-senile dementia. *Neurology,* 1970, **20,** 315–322.

Obrist, W. D., Kleemeier, R. W., Justiss, W. A., & Henry, C. E. A longitudinal study of EEG-intelligence test correlations in old age. Paper presented at the 6th International Congress of Gerontologists, Copenhagen, 1963.

Obrist, W. D., Thompson, H. K., Jr., King, C. H., & Wang, H.-S. Determination of regional cerebral blood flow by inhalation by 133-xenon. *Circulatory Research,* 1967, **20,** 124–135.

Orme, J. E. Non-verbal and verbal performance in normal old age, senile dementia and elderly depression. *Journal of Gerontology,* 1957, **12,** 408–413.

Perlin, S., & Butler, R. N. Psychiatric aspects of adaptation to the aging experience. In J. E. Birren, R. N. Butler, S. W. Greenhouse, L. Sokoloff, & M. R. Yarrow (Eds.), *Human aging: A biological and behavioral study.* (USPHS Publ. No. 986) Washington, D.C.: United States Government Printing Office, 1963.

Post, F. *The significance of affective symptoms in old age.* (Maudsley Monograph No. 10) London: Oxford University Press, 1962.

Post, F. *The clinical psychiatry of late life.* New York: Pergamon Press, 1965.

Post, F. *Persistent persecutory states of the elderly.* New York: Pergamon Press, 1966.

Post, F. The factor of aging in affective illness. In A. Coppen & A. Walk (Eds.), *Recent developments in affective disorders: A symposium. (British Journal of Psychiatry,* Spec. Pub., No. 2) Kent: Headley, 1968.

Post, F. The diagnostic process. In D. W. K. Kay & A. Walk (Eds.), *Recent developments in psychogeriatrics. (British Journal of Psychiatry,* Spec. Pub., No. 6) Kent: Headley, 1971.

Price, A. C., & Deabler, H. L. Diagnosis of organicity by means of spiral aftereffect. *Journal of Consulting Psychology,* 1955, **19,** 299–302.

Price, J. The genetics of depressive behavior. In A. Coppen & A. Walk (Eds.), *Recent developments in affective disorders. (British Journal of Psychiatry*, Spec. Pub., No. 2) Kent: Headley, 1968.

Primrose, E. J. R. *Psychological illness: A community study.* Springfield, Ill.: Charles C Thomas, 1962.

Raven, J. C. *Progressive matrices.* London: Lewis, 1938.

Raven, J. C. *The Mill Hill Vocabulary Scale.* London: Lewis, 1943.

Reitan, R. M. The relation of the Trail Making Test to organic brain damage. *Journal of Consulting Psychology*, 1955, **19**, 393–394.

Riddell, S. A. The relationships between tests of organic involvement, memory impairment and diagnosis in elderly psychiatric patients. *British Journal of Social and Clinical Psychology*, 1962, **11**, 228–231.

Roth, M. The natural history of mental disorders in old age. *Journal of Mental Science*, 1955, **101**, 281–301.

Roth, M., & Kay, D. W. K. Affective disorders arising in the senium. II. Physical disability as an aetiological factor. *Journal of Mental Science*, 1956, **102**, 141–150.

Roth, M., & Kay, D. W. K. Psychoses among the aged. In H. Blumenthal (Ed.), *Aging around the world: Medical and clinical aspects of aging.* New York: Columbia University Press, 1962.

Roth, M., Tomlinson, B. E., & Blessed, G. The relationship between quantitative measures of dementia and of degenerative changes in cerebral grey matter of elderly subjects. *Proceedings of the Royal Society of Medicine*, 1967, **60**, 254.

Rothschild, D. Pathological changes in senile psychosis and their psychiatric significance. *American Journal of Psychiatry*, 1937, **93**, 757–788.

Rothschild, D. Neuropathological changes in arteriosclerotic psychosis and their psychological significance. *Archives of Neurology and Psychiatry*, 1942, **48**, 417–436.

Sainsbury, P. Suicide in the middle and later years. In H. Blumenthal (Ed.), *Aging around the world: Medical and clinical aspects of aging.* New York: Columbia University Press, 1962.

Sanderson, R. E., & Inglis, J. Learning and mortality in elderly psychiatric patients. *Journal of Gerontology*, 1961, **16**, 375–376.

Sandifer, M. G., Horden, A., & Green, L. M. The interview impact of the first three minutes. Paper presented at the 122nd Annual Meeting of the American Psychiatric Association, Florida, May 1969.

Savage, R. D., & Bolton, N. Factor analysis of learning impairment and intellectual deterioration in the elderly. *Journal of Genetic Psychology*, 1968, **113**, 177–182.

Shapiro, M. B., Field, J., & Post, F. An enquiry into the determinants of a differentiation between elderly "organic" and "non-organic" psychiatric patients on the Bender Gestalt Test. *Journal of Mental Science*, 1957, **103**, 364–374.

Sheldon, J. H. *The social medicine of old age: Report of an inquiry in Wolverhampton.* London: Oxford University Press, 1948.

Simon, A., & Neal, M. W. Patterns of geriatric mental illness. In R. H. Williams, C. Tibbitts, & W. Donahue (Eds.), *Processes of aging.* New York: Atherton Press, 1963.

Sloane, B. The converging paths of behavior therapy and psychotherapy. *International Journal of Psychiatry*, 1969, **7**, 493–503.

Spitzer, R. L., & Endicott, J. DIAGNO: A computer program for psychiatric diagnosis utilizing the differential diagnostic procedure. *Archives of General Psychiatry*, 1968, **18**, 746–756.

Spitzer, R. L., Fleiss, J. L., Burdock, E. I., & Hardesty, A. S. The mental status schedule: Rationale, reliability and validity. *Comprehensive Psychiatry*, 1964, **5**, 384–395.

Strachan, R. W., & Henderson, J. G. Psychiatric syndromes due to avitaminosis B with normal blood and marrow. *Quarterly Journal of Medicine and Neural Surgery*, 1965, **34**, 303–317.

Walton, D., & Black, D. A. The validity of a psychological test of brain damage. *British Journal of Medical Psychology*, 1957, **30**, 270–279.

Walton, D., & Black, D. A. The predictive validity of a psychological test of brain damage. *Journal of Mental Science*, 1959, **105**, 807–810.

Wang, H.-S. Organic brain syndromes. In E. W. Busse & E. Pfeiffer (Eds.), *Behavior and adaptation in late life*. Boston: Little, Brown, 1969.

Ward, C. H., Beck, A. T., Mendelson, M., Mock, J. E., & Erbaugh, J. K. The psychiatric nomenclature: Reasons for diagnostic disagreement. *Archives of General Psychiatry*, 1962, **7**, 198–205.

Weinstock, C., & Bennett, R. The relations between social cognition and related cognitive skills in residents of a home for the aged and their waiting list counterparts. Paper presented at the annual meeting of the Gerontology Society, Denver, November 1968.

Weiss, J. M. A., & Schaie, K. W. Symptom formation among older patients in a psychiatric clinic population. In H. Blumenthal (Ed.), *Aging around the world: Medical and clinical aspects of aging*. New York: Columbia University Press, 1962.

Welford, A. T. Social psychological and physiological gerontology. In R. H. Williams et al. (Eds.), *Processes of aging: Social and psychological perspectives*. New York: Atherton Press, 1963.

Werner, M., Perlin, S., Butler, R. M., & Pollin, W. Self-perceived changes in community-resident aged: "Aging image" and adaptation. *Archives of General Psychiatry*, 1961, **4**, 501–508.

White, J. G., & Knox, S. J. Some psychological correlates of age and dementia. *British Journal of Social and Clinical Psychology*, 1965, **4**, 259–265.

Wing, J. K., Birley, J. L., Cooper, J. E., Graham, P., & Isaac, A. D. Reliability of a procedure for measuring and classifying "present psychiatric state." *British Journal of Psychiatry*, 1967, **113**, 499–515.

Zigler, E., & Phillips, L. Psychiatric diagnosis and symptomatology. *Journal of Abnormal and Social Psychology*, 1961, **63**, 69–75.

Zubin, J. Classification of the behavior disorders. *Annual Review of Psychology*, 1967, **18**, 373–406.

Zubin, J. Classification of human behavior. Paper presented at the meeting of the Canadian Psychological Association, Alberta, Canada, June 1968.

Zubin, J. Position paper on descriptive psychopathology and cross-cultural studies. Conference on schizophrenia—The implications of research findings for treatment and teaching. Washington, D.C.: National Institute of Mental Health, May 1970.

Zubin, J., & Sutton, S. Assessment of physiological, sensory, perceptual, psychomotor and conceptual functioning in schizophrenic patients. *Acta Psychiatrica et Neurologica Scandinavica*, 1970, **46**, 247–263. (Supplement)

Psychosocial Treatment of the Aged

LEONARD E. GOTTESMAN, CAROLE E. QUARTERMAN,
AND GORDON M. COHN

Many older persons have complaints or engage in behaviors that may be symptomatic of breakdown either in the individual or in his social system or in both. Such indices of dysfunction occur in many who never break down, and, in fact, this group of older people far exceeds the few who experience severe mental and behavioral disturbances. The problems of these individuals are real and as appropriate a treatment target as those of people who are severely upset. For example, the usual social cry is to eliminate poverty because it leads to stress, which in turn leads to mental breakdown. A more valid argument is to eliminate poverty because it leads to problems *whether or not* breakdown follows.

In dealing with behavior, traditional psychology and psychological treatments have addressed themselves either to a person's biological capabilities or to his attitudes. Even where some psychologists have emphasized the multiple causation of behavior, they have treated the individual rather than his world and have viewed problems as either situationally or historically determined, rather than from a developmental perspective.

Psychology must now begin to go beyond man into his world. The new necessity of treating the aged has added a developmental dimension to intervention techniques. In this chapter, we will discuss

    Leonard E. Gottesman received his PhD in personality and psychopathology from the University of Chicago in 1959. He is currently a senior research psychologist at the Philadelphia Geriatric Center, and also serves as President of the Division of Adult Development and Aging of the American Psychological Association. His major research interest centers on the social/psychological treatment of the aged.

    Carole E. Quarterman is currently enrolled in the PhD program in clinical psychology at the University of Michigan.

    Gordon M. Cohn is currently enrolled in the PhD program in industrial and organizational development at Case Western Reserve University.

the implications of such an increased awareness of the social and developmental dimensions of human functioning for treatment techniques of the aged. First, we will present *a treatment model* which attempts to account for the significance of these added dimensions. Second, we will illustrate briefly how these dimensions present special considerations regarding the treatment of certain *special populations*. The third and major part of the chapter will review and evaluate *literature regarding treatment* by organizing it according to the treatment model.

TREATMENT MODEL

While much of psychology has devoted itself to describing the variation in behavior or feelings which occurs among individuals, the focus of a discussion of treatment must be the multiple causation of behavior and the changes in the relationship of determining elements over time.

In these terms, the treatment process involves a person (or persons) who sets out to influence and change another person's feelings or behavior. The treater may direct influence at any of several elements which together determine how one acts of feels. These elements include: (a) the person's capacities, (b) societal demands, (c) the expectations of the people who are most significant in his life, and (d) self-expectations. These four variables interact over the life-span. Generally, experiences of comfort or growth occur when the elements are approximately congruent with one another. Conversely, discomfort and behavioral disturbance increase when there is considerable incongruence among the elements.

The treater, who must always become a part of his subject's world, attempts to change one of the interacting elements or their relationship to one another.

Any single behavior (sight, hearing, etc.) or any complex behavior (productivity, criminality, etc.) may be charted. Figure 1 shows, for example, the amount of walking done by a hypothetical person at any point in his lifetime.

Actually, the amount of walking is the outcome of interaction among biological capacities, social elements, expectations of significant others, and self-expectation. Each of these elements also varies over time. A more correct depiction of behavior and its determinants would therefore look like Figure 2.

The thesis of this chapter is that therapy may influence individual behavior by changing any one or any combination of a be-

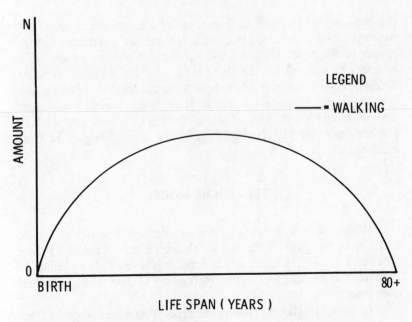

Fig. 1. Walking during a life-span.

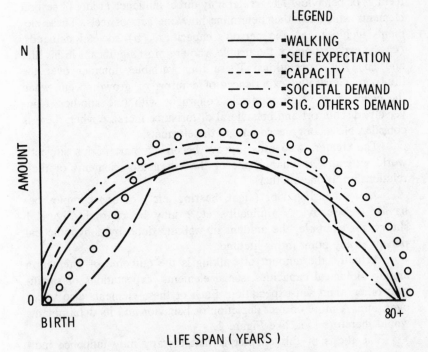

Fig. 2. Walking and its determinants during a life-span.

havior's causal elements. Today emphasis in treatment has shifted from the self (e.g., psychoanalysis) to significant others (e.g., family therapy) and to society (e.g., community psychology). In order to understand the potential value of therapeutic interventions aimed at each of the determinants of behavior and to help in selecting the one that is the best target for intervention at a given moment we shall briefly discuss some of the more salient characteristics of each.

Biological Capacities

Variation in the amount of walking a hypothetical person is capable of at each point in his life is shown by the broken line in Figure 3.

Notice that throughout life one is generally capable of more of any behavior than he actually engages in. Aging tends to bring behavior closer to capacity, but Birren (1964) has shown that most people continue to operate below their own capacity well into the end of their lives. Severe limits on behavior caused by declines in perceptual, cognitive, and motor limits generally do not appear until

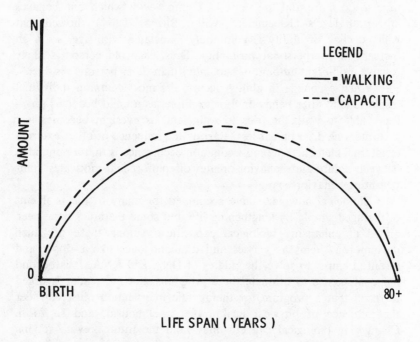

Fig. 3. Walking and capacity to walk during a life-span.

age 70 or later. Since not all biological capacities are equally affected by age, even in the case of organically impaired persons many behavioral capacities remain (e.g., Malamud, 1965).

Therefore, it would appear that extreme personal discomfort and behavior disruption for the aged seldom comes solely from the discrepancy between capacity and behavior. Allport (1961) and Maslow (1951) both suggested that if there are no personal or interpersonal constraints, such a discrepency can motivate personal change and growth, and that in such cases, satisfaction and pleasure are likely to ensue. In contrast to this possibility, studies of geriatric patients in institutions have shown that physical damage can result if one consistently does less than he is capable of doing (e.g., muscle atrophy after a stroke). Obviously, when the behavior damaged is one that is important to the person, then psychological damage may also occur.

Since during most of life, individual capacity exceeds actual behavior, there is always some reserve that can be experienced both as a comfortable base (a feeling of "I can do that") and as a motivating force to do more. For some people, severe illness, changes in perceptual abilities, or body changes may reduce the comfort zone between ability and behavior and simultaneously reduce both the urge to do more and the sense of comfort with which one behaves at certain levels (Kleemeier, 1959). Birren (1964) showed that while decline of ability is commonly associated with age, so is an increase in interpersonal variability. Thus, each old person is likely to have a different amount of capability than other persons his age.

When a change in ability occurs, the most common individual response is to alter behavior. For example, as a child becomes physically able to walk, he tries to walk, and as eyesight becomes less accurate, one drives a car less. Barring the influence of other external or internal elements, the most common occurrence is that a nonmatch between ability and behavior creates discomfort and motivates compensating behavior change.

Biological advances have accounted for many of the problems of the aged simply by lengthening life, but some therapies have been aimed at enhancing biological capacities. Among these are such unglamorous items as glasses and dramatic ones like L-dopa, and recent attempts to solve the riddles of DNA and RNA. It is beyond our competence to evaluate these programs, but the reader is urged to recall that a program for therapeutic intervention must consider the influence of physical health, diet, metabolism, and so forth. Changes in biological capacity may hold the future key to solving many of the problems of the aged. Currently, however, according to

Birren (1969), the therapeutic areas with the best potential payoff are in the personal and social realms.

Societal Demands

The discussion can be expanded by considering the effect on behavior of societal demands and/or opportunities. In Figure 4, the "-.-" line stands for the demand and/or permission to walk afforded by the larger societal system.

This demand is extremely important in understanding what a person does or how he feels. In an institution, for example, a patient may be prevented from dressing himself even though he is capable of doing so. Similar underdemands or limitations may be described at other times in life such as where a child in school is prevented from reading by lack of books or rules against use of the library during certain hours. In the case of the aged, nonfits between behavioral capability and the economic (money and work), political (voting power), educational, communication, and familial aspects of the social system are often central to understanding why behavior falls

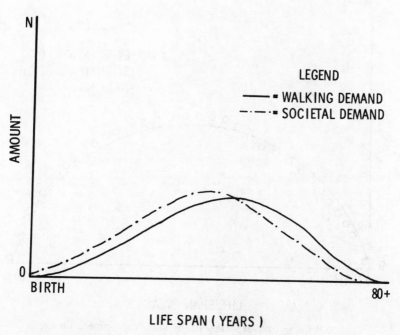

Fig. 4. Walking and societal demands during a life-span.

below behavioral capability. Notice that the social system may require either more or less of a certain behavior than a person's capability. Societal demands are not static. They differ from one society to another, from one era to another, and at different points in the life-span. Their great variability suggests that they are alterable under certain conditions. It is important that they be alterable because it is assumed that a nonmatch between capability and societal limits may become either uncomfortable to the person or upsetting to the system. When such a system–capability disjunction exists, the *treatment* called for may be to change the society. Treatments that are focused at the societal level are discussed in detail below.

Expectations of Significant Others

But nonfit between capability and the societal limits also does not necessarily lead to personal discomfort or behavioral breakdown. Such a mismatch coexists with expectations of the significant others in the person's life—his family, close friends, or associates. These significant others are a third element in the treatment model. (See Figure 5.)

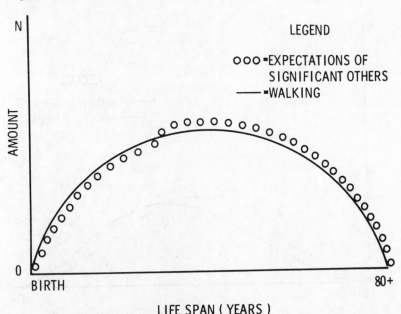

Fig. 5. Walking and expectations of significant others during a life-span.

For the model of treatment the important points are (a) that the numbers, identity, and importance of significant others change throughout life, and (b) that the nature of their expectations changes at different ages of the subject. Rogers (1961), more than any other theorist, explicated the importance of significant others in the formation of "conditions of worth." Expectations of others are internalized to some extent, and even those that are not internalized continue to be important external motivators. If an aged widower, for example, wishes to marry again and finds that his children object, stress will ensue and disturbed behavior may appear. The most appropriate therapeutic intervention needed to change his behavior may be to alter the attitude of his children. In the section on therapeutic techniques that follows, we shall also discuss attempts to create new social groupings (e.g., retirement villages) or a close relationship between an older person and a counselor or therapist as other examples of possible therapies aimed at effecting behavior by changing significant other relationships.

Self-Expectations

There is one final element in the treatment model. In any behavioral situation, one has a set of expectations of himself that interact with the other behavioral determinants. These expectations are partially determined by biological imbalances, partially by perceptions of external realities, and partially by a set of psychological sets that one has internalized from experiences with people and things during one's life. Figure 6 illustrates self-expectations in relationship to walking.

When the self-demand is different from capability, it may call forth discomfort, physical illness (Gurin, Veroff, & Feld, 1960), withdrawal (Cumming & Henry, 1961), self-doubt, acting out, or suicide. However, cases of individual disturbance caused by mismatches between self-expectations and capability are rare, and it must be reemphasized that the empirical evidence shows that when capability changes, so usually does behavior. Disturbances may come also from dysfunction of self-expectations with either societal opportunity or the attitudes of significant others. Perhaps the most vivid example of such disturbance is the self-blaming anxiety many older people feel about not being able to live on the below-poverty-level income that their social security check affords them. We feel that too often the goal of therapeutic interventions is to change self-expectations through counseling or psychotherapy when changes in society

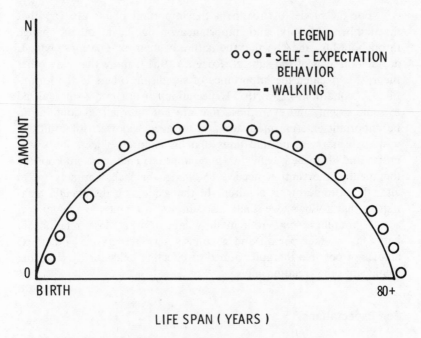

Fig. 6. Walking and self-expectations during a life-span.

or in the expectations of significant others would be more appropriate. The individual's ability to cope with a less-than-perfect world is nevertheless often the most reasonable tool for correcting an imbalance among behavior determining elements. Individual disturbance in the absence of apparent extrapersonal causes must also not be overlooked. These therapeutic considerations are all discussed below.

SPECIAL POPULATIONS

The bulk of the population, by definition normal, was the primary focus in developing this model because the principles of treatment are relevant to everyone. In this section, we will show the way these principles may be used to suggest treatment approaches to three specialized aged populations: neurotic persons, marginal persons, and minority group members.

Neurotic persons. These persons have self-expectations that lead them to have distorted ways of dealing with stress. For example, some people when they experience difficulty in meeting the usual demands of life or when they face unusual demands will dig in their heels and become involved with minutia. Evidence derived from retrospective studies suggests that these coping patterns are consistent for a person throughout his life (Reichard, Livson, & Petersen, 1962), and that the number of persons with neurotic patterns of adjustment do not increase with age (Leighton, 1963; Pasamanick, 1962). "Old people don't get crotchety—crotchety people get old." For the neurotic person, the increased stress of biological aging and of changed expectations of society or significant others may bring out exacerbated expression of characteristic coping patterns. If, for example, a cataract were the cause of additional stress, then an operation to remove the cataract might have marked influence on behavior. The theory suggests, however, that similar improvement of behavior might come from changed family attitudes or social demands. Rather than limiting us to one approach, the treatment tactic would be to alter the relationship among all four causes of behavior.

Marginal persons. These persons are by definition at the edge of social acceptability during most of their lives and are likely to have established patterns of behavior that are protected against general social expectations. Often these people's way through life depends upon the help given by a significant other or on the income from menial employment. Because their existence is so tenuous, marginal people may be more disrupted than people in general by the loss of a friend or of a job. Some evidence now exists (Gottesman, Bourestom, Donahue, & Coons, 1971; Lieberman, 1969) that a large proportion of the elderly in institutions are lifelong marginal persons who have lost supports in old age.

Institutionalization entails an alteration of societal demands and may be therapeutic for some persons. Because institutions give greater support and less freedom than the open society, they may simulate the world of the marginal person earlier in life. That which we decry as institutionalism may result because the institution is too controlling.

In addition to those who may require institutionalization, many marginal persons will have established specialized coping patterns (e.g., the hobo) that are insulated from the central tendencies of society so that they may experience less disturbance as they age. A common but often overlooked example is suggested in the research of Reichard et al. (1962) and Perlin and Butler (1963). Both these groups of investigators have shown that persons who have been marginally employed may improve in their self-concepts when the social demand for a productive work-life is removed.

Minority aged. Several authors (Benedict, 1971; Havighurst, 1971; Taft & Sweda, 1971) have emphasized the lack of information about minority aged persons and have cautioned against viewing any minority as monolithic (Jackson, 1971; Taft & Sweda, 1971). These surveys have also reported that the aging minority group may be subject to the additional pressures of a quick anglicizing of his ethnic group.

From preliminary data, it seems that the members of some minority groups may have established specialized coping methods, different sets of standards, and different ways of behaving normally than the main body of society. In many instances, the ghettoization of minority groups may have strengthened the internal ties among group members and insulated them from some societal pressures.

There has been a shortage of institutional beds for minority group members, but their low rates of institutionalization (Gottesman, Donahue, Coons, & Cearlo, 1969) have also come partly from cohesive family ties. Emotional strength among some minorities may be interpreted from their low rates of neurotic disturbance and suicide (Riley & Foner, 1968).

Recent experience has shown that greater involvement in the common culture has increased rates of institutionalization, suicide, and neurosis. Our treatment model suggests that these trends might be averted by programs that strengthen ethnic identification. Such ties as the mutual benefit societies of many European immigrant groups earlier in this century would maximize the congruence among individual abilities, significant others, and societal demands.

To summarize, our treatment model postulated that the behavior of an individual at any point in time is the complex function of his abilities, his self-expectations, and the expectations of his significant others and society at large. Furthermore, the model emphasized that each of the four elements varies over time. It was shown that non-alignment (incongruence) among elements creates tension that in turn triggers personal adjustive behaviors, some of which may be considered as normal and others as abnormal. Such a consideration of adjustive behaviors as normal or abnormal must include an awareness of the individual's unique lifelong coping patterns in relation to his membership in special groups, such as his ethnic background. The issue of successful adjustive behaviors is a primary one with which treatment techniques must deal, and it is around just this issue that our treatment model provides the direction for deriving treatment techniques for the aged.

TREATMENT TECHNIQUES

The above model asserts that behavior results from the interactions of the individual's capacities with the expectations of self, of significant others, and of the larger society and that these interactions can create stress that distorts behavior. The model shows that therapy can be aimed at one or more of several sites, though its interactive relationship at one site may affect a disorder at another.

Within our model, the four determinants of behavior can each be the site of disorder. This is shown along the top of Table 1. If an older person is unable to drive a car, the categories from left to right suggest that his disability may have resulted from physical incapacity (poor eyesight or coordination), disturbed self-expectations (fear about driving), troubles with significant others (neighborhood or family attitudes about elderly people driving), or problems in society (laws that deny insurance or driving permits to old people). In the table, two additional sites of possible disorder are added: the therapist, a special form of the significant other, and treatment institutions, a miniature replication of society.

Five classes of treaters are shown on the left in Table 1. As illustrated on the first line, a form of treatment is self-treatment. The person himself can also have an effect on his family, the therapist, institutions, or society. Line 2 illustrates several ways that family and friends can treat a disordered person, themselves, a therapist, and so on. In a similar manner, lines 3, 4, and 5 show how therapists, institutions, and society can each have an influence on every other element illustrated in the table.

Some possible therapeutic actions available to each treater are entered in the cells. An individual can adapt his own behavior, change his expectations, support or help out his family and initiate change, or agitate for change in society. The family or therapist can support a troubled person, serve as a model for him, and offer him understanding, psychotherapy, or medication.

Notice in the table that each potentially therapeutic element in the model has a great many actions open to it. Thus, if an older person becomes unable to drive a car, his treatment can be applied to any one or to several of the four determinants. It would be differentially effective at each level. Unless laws were changed, improved eyesight attitudes or neighborhood opinion would not permit driving. On the other hand, if a way were found for all old people to have improved eyesight (or coordination), attitudes, public opinion, and laws might change over time.

TABLE 1

Some Possible Therapies

Treater	Site of the disorder					
	Self		Significant other		Society	
	Physical capacity	Expectation	Family/friend	Therapist	Institution	Real world
Self	Adapt, medicate, use appliances	Adapt	Support, help	Teach	Reform	Initiate, support, agitate change
Family/friend	Medicate, understand, ignore	Support, model, punish, understand	Model, advise, communicate	React, complain, compliment	Compliment, complain, investigate	Initiate, agitate, support change
Therapist	Medicate, use prostheses	Medicate, understand, therapy	Group therapy	Schooling, introspection	Organizational development	Initiate, agitate, support change
Institution	Contain, care for, medicate	Support, punish, understand	Inform; share care, help	Hire; train, assign	Administer, plan change	Lobby, meet, lead
Real world	Laws, social support, assistance programs	Norms	Support, limit	Support, limit	Laws; assistance programs	Legislation, evolution, revolution

In some cases, ill health limits the behavior of older people so that societal encouragement to do more can only be stressful. In other cases, support from friends, strong personal desire, or societal pressure may facilitate behavior.

The task of therapy is not only locating the site of disorder but also planning the level at which intervention is most feasible or potentially effective. In the sections that follow, we shall discuss four levels of treatment: (a) *Self-treatment* or adaptation and adjustment, which focuses both on self and environment within the context of natural life space; (b) *Individual psychological treatments*—medical, relational or behavioral—which focus on physical disabilities or self-imposed stress and usually are done in an office, agency, or institution (c) *Small group therapy,* which focuses on stress imposed by significant others, usually done in an office, institution, or community agency; and (d) *Societal treatment,* which focuses on stress imposed by the larger society and is done in an institutional setting or in the natural societal setting.

Self-Treatment

The majority of older people handle numerous psychologically stressful situations and go on about the business of living, free from externally imposed psychological treatment programs. As we ponder treatment technique for the aged, we must certainly include the self-treatment process. How does self-treatment occur, and on what does its success or failure depend—personality, health, intelligence? When considered as a legitimate form of treatment, self-treatment raises such issues as criteria for success, the individual's accountability to society, and age-related changes in ability to treat oneself.

For self-treatment, adaptation is the key concept. Havighurst (1968) distinguished between adaptation and adjustment. Growing older means an adaptation to changes in the structure and functions of the human body and to changes in the social environment. Examples of situations to which people over the age of 60 have to adapt are losses of spouse, worker role and status roles, the changing expectations of others with regard to their energy, autonomy, or creativity, as well as managing with less money in a less supportive environment.

The continuous process of adaptation is seen as being ruled "more or less actively and autonomously by the ego or personality." This is consistent with our treatment model, which views the self as the site of internal interactions such as unconscious processes, conscious interpretation, integration and change, as well as the initiator of interactions with others in the environment.

Accordingly, adjustment is seen by Havighurst as the product of adaptation on this self-treatment process. He concluded that personality organization and coping style are the major factors in the life adjustment of an individual as he grows older. Reichard et al. (1962) reported a study of 82 older men in which five strategies of adjustment were revealed. These included: (a) constructive (active, well-integrated, optimistic, self-sufficient, future-oriented), (b) dependent (passive and dependent, rather than active and self-sufficient, but fairly well integrated), (c) defensive (armored, minor neurotic traits, overcontrolled, habit-bound, conventional, compulsively active), (d) angry (blamed circumstances or other people for own failures, aggressive, complaining, suspicious), and (e) self-hating (critical and contemptuous of themselves, passive, depressed). The less well adjusted appear to have been less well adjusted throughout their lives.

To understand the adaptation process, Havighurst (1968) designated seven variables that should be systematically described for an individual. These include personality, social interaction, norms and expectations of the subculture in which the person lives, economic security, health and vigor, and societal provisions to assist adaptation. Each of these variables, of course, can affect the individual's potential for treating himself. Of special interest here might be how the members of the special groups mentioned above engage in the self-treatment process. It is obvious that when there is a close "fit" between the personality, the social environment, and the physical organism, adaptation is seen as relatively easy.

There are several roles that others, particularly professionals, can play in relation to self-treatment. The first step should be increased recognition of self-treatment as a valid treatment technique with the greatest preventive potential. The second step is to actively strive to maximize the opportunity for successful self-treatment by attempting to thoroughly understand the processes involved and then educating individuals about the attainment of mental health. All too often we teach people how to be sick but not how to be well. An important way to maximize the individual's potential for self-treatment is to focus all other treatment techniques toward this goal.

Noninstitutional Social Treatment

Havighurst (1968) viewed the social setting as providing a set of possibilities from which the ego can work out a pattern of aging that, depending on the individual's life history, is comfortable to the person and is approved or at least tolerated by the society. He further stated that with increasing age (60+), this adaptation takes place within a negative framework for the first time in the life-span.

Traditionally, treatment by psychologists, psychiatrists, and others has focused on the internal causes of stress for individuals while neglecting the possibility of focusing on the interaction between internal sources of stress and external ones. Several authors (Briggs, 1968; Havighurst, 1968; Lawton & Simon, 1968; Rich, 1968; Schwartz & Proppe, 1970) have indicated that the former approach leads to a view of the aged as "devalued," that is, functioning with internal deficits due to age.

Halleck (1971) felt that when in traditional framework the therapist is viewed as healer, he has the often unattainable goal of encouraging the client to be himself while at the same time staying within a set of values imposed from the outside. If the client fails to reach his goals, he can have no one to blame but himself.

A newer approach, called ecological by some (Briggs, 1968; Duncan, 1968; Lawton & Simon, 1968; Rich, 1968) and transactional by others (Kelly, 1966; Schwartz & Proppe, 1970), through an analysis of the interactive process, has the built-in potential for identifying realistic points of attack to maximize the functioning of the individual. In fact, Rich (1968) argued that it is "not possible to assess potential for psychological functioning without fully understanding the complex environmental stimulus patterns to which an individual is exposed [p. 117]."

Social treatment as an alternative technique is especially viable when dealing with an aged individual or population, many of whose problems are clearly caused by external system-based stress. The question of the impact of the environment on the mature individual has not been dealt with extensively in the gerontological literature; we need to consider questions of how systems impose psychological stress on individuals and to identify age-related differences.

The amount of system-generated stress depends upon the relationship of the impinging system to the individual's needs, that is, how directly a system operates to hinder or deprive a person of fulfilling a particular need, plus how basic that need is. Maslow's (1951) theory places basic human needs in the following hierarchy: physiological satisfaction, safety, love, esteem, knowledge, and self-actualization. Halleck (1971) saw few natural environmental stresses, but rather man-created sources of stress, such as oppressive social institutions. The individual's stress tolerance level is, then, a result of his biological strengths as well as the degree of opportunity to change his environment. Age adds a developmental dimension to this analysis.

As people age, environmental factors seem to exert greater influence, thereby increasing the potential impact of socially imposed stress. Stress tolerance is proportional to weaknesses in personality and health (Butler, 1968; Havighurst, 1968; Lawton & Simon 1968). Rational adjustment such as buying less food if one is poor are a first reaction. These are followed by feelings of powerlessness, loss of dignity, low self-esteem, and insecurity. In extreme cases, more deteriorative behaviors like depression, withdrawal, or acting out may ensue.

Kuhlen (1968) identified five areas of age-related need frustration, all of which are influenced by social systems. They are (a) degree of status accorded people of different ages, (b) limitations and pressures of time and money, (c) physical change and decline, (d) skills deficit for older people generated by rapid technological advances, and (e) inability to do anything about some of the disturbing circumstances and sources of unhappiness.

The argument can be advanced that all the systems within present-day American society that emphasize youth, money, and power are sources of stress for our older people. Kastenbaum (1971) suggested that the social expectation that it is natural to die when one is old withdraws supports from the aged in ways that increase the likelihood of death. Glaser and Strauss (1968) called the phenomenon "social death."

Neugarten and Moore (1968) discussed the changing age-status system in America by documenting changes in four systems: family, economic, political, and legal. They found the "quickening of the family cycle to be socially, not biologically, regulated." Marriage, parenthood, empty nest, and grandparenthood all occur earlier now than in 1900. This fact, coupled with increasing longevity, has resulted in an increasing number of three-, four-, and five-generation families. It becomes clear that it might be stressful for an older person to exist within a system that values youthfulness and economic contribution and assigns no particularly positive expectation, guidelines, or status to the new role of grandparenthood.

In analyzing the economic system, Neugarten and Moore (1968) showed that old age actually has become synonymous with age of retirement. Such forced and arbitrary retirement from the labor force leaves many older people unable to earn sufficient money to maintain a decent standard of living in which they can secure necessary goods and services. There is no doubt that financial insecurity is stressful in a society that values highly economic production. This is one reason that Tibbetts (1968) suggested that society alter its traditional values in order to define new ones based upon some value other than economics.

Other systems (political, legal, educational, and the mass media) function in similarly stressful ways for older people. Thus, we see a political system that has long emphasized youth-oriented platforms and legislation (Neugarten & Moore, 1968) persisting despite more (since the 1930s) adequate recognition of the needs of the aged.

Our educational system also produces stress by failing to offer opportunity for contemporary, functional education that the aged might choose to take part in. The mass media seem able to deal only with stereotypes of old age. Among the most prominent are the "cute" old person who leaves us in wonder of his ability to continue everyday activities and "the dependent, helpless, useless" old person. If he is not portrayed in one of these ways, the older person is often not even noticed at all.

Furthermore, a social system analysis shows that blacks, chicanos, or other minority group members who are also old and poor have a triple plight in which environmental oppression and "benign neglect" are the origin of many of their problems.

Schwartz and Proppe (1970) claimed that it is appropriate to abandon the traditional psychological bias in favor of a social transactional one, since the latter interpretation is more closely tied to designing compensatory environments for the aged.

Beattie and Bullock (1963) pointed out that such a perspective must include an awareness of the dynamic and ever-changing nature of both individual needs, resources available (i.e., demographic, political, ecological, familial, technologic), and the framework or contexts in which they appear. It is here that the issue is raised of who and what needs should be treated.

In an attempt to answer this question by just looking at statistics, Cottrell (1966) found the most needy of the aged to be old, poorly housed, mentally ill, poverty stricken, illiterate Negro women. Such a composite profile immediately raises the question, "What about the other elderly and their individual needs?" The process of aging increases differences among people. Social treatment must provide a variety of integrated, complimentary, and comprehensive services rather than any single plan intended for all older people.

The view of aging, age-related behavior, and so-called pathological behavior as transactional, that is, as a reciprocal interaction of a specific social situation and the individual's adaptive behavior (Kelly, 1966; Rich, 1968) favors Beattie and Bullock's (1963) goal of a supportive environment for social treatment. They defined such an environment as one in which the physical, psychological, and social aspects impinging on the individual promote the maximum realization of potential self-determination throughout the life-span. As Halleck (1971) pointed out, no aspect of psychiatric therapy is politically neutral, since for treatment to occur, the patient must often examine or confront the social system that at least partially caused his problems.

One need of older people in America is for militant allies to help them achieve their self-determined goals by changing social systems if necessary. Such social treatment can include educating old people about the reality of the way social systems function, especially in relation to their needs, and about the options open to them for change. The treatment can also aim at organizing older people and helping them form alliances in an attempt to bring about changes in external constraints (e.g., National Council for Senior Citizens, Ralph Nader's group, etc.).

Ideally, social treatment would be primarily preventative in nature. However, the start must be made now to meet the present needs of older people. The most potent societal intervention today is providing economic supports. Barfield and Morgan (1968), reporting the results of a national sample of retirees studied longitudinally, showed that an adequate income is the strongest determinant of postretirement satisfaction. Medical programs have already added considerably to the number of people who grow old with physical independence, but much revision is needed to make health service delivery more effective. The health maintenance organizations have advantages both because they emphasize prevention rather than more expensive curative procedures and because they do not segregate the old as a disadvantaged minority group.

Except for Old Age and Survivors Disability Insurance (OASDI), most programs for older people have been sold by emphasizing old people's disadvantaged status. These appeals have created stress on older people by inadvertently adding to the negative image of the old (Calhoun & Gottesman, 1963). Recently, others have noted a similar, unanticipated negative effect of the juvenile court movement and of laws protecting women. The antidote appears to be that social treatment programs follow the OASDI by being universally applicable to all age groups.

Societal programs especially must be evaluated for the extent to which they are naturalistic or contrived to meet the needs of their subjects. They must also be evaluated by the extent to which they segregate their subjects from the rest of society.

Our position is that programs are more desirable if they are naturalistic and if they require little segregation or surrender of autonomy. Such programs are likely to come closest to meeting people's needs because they are ultimately designed by their own clientele. From a psychological point of view, they foster the highest level of personal maturity.

The Miami Beach retirement strip (see pp. 405–406) is a "program" that, as far as we know, evolved naturally and is maximally open in allowing its residents free entrance, exit, and use of facilities, as long as they have money. It is markedly segregated by age, except for a few young "hippies" who have moved into some of the hotels.

The various planned communities for the old are not naturalistic, often not integrated socially, but generally have completely permeable boundaries going both in and out. There is considerable evidence that such communities are preferred by the old as long as they do not have "too many old people!" The preference of many older people for their own kind of people is a laudable behavioral defense against society's status punishments as well as a search for soulmates with whom to form relationships. It is probably much harder for an older person to find a pinochle match in a young suburb than in Sun City.

The spectre of extreme old age (sans teeth, etc.) is more literary than true for most old people, and even the threat of a "one-person nursing home" maintained by each family is not as psychologically unsound as it is fiscally fearsome. We literally do not know the social costs of a preventative program that would foster maximum use of intra- and intergenerational relationships and community funds, which would be expended to support and prolong them.

Social programs could foster the interaction on more equal footing of the old with people of other ages, if they were planned for all older people and not just the disabled. To the extent that money, medical needs, and transportation were not problems, people could pick relationships on the basis of social needs that, while age related, could be tied to an individual's biological age and not to his chronological calendar.

Social "treatment" programs have largely stemmed from the Federal government. Cottrell (1966) analyzed the 10 objectives in the preamble to the Older Americans Act. These include adequate income, physical and mental health, suitable housing, restorative services for those in institutions, opportunity for employment, retirement in health, honor, and dignity, pursuit of meaningful activity, efficient community services, immediate benefit from proven research, and the opportunity to exercise individual initiative. This statement recognizes the needs and rights of the aged. However, Cottrell concluded that much of it was "pious rhetoric," without effective means of translating it into reality.

In recent years, several governmental agencies have championed programs to meet the needs of older people. However, Jackson (1971) pointed out that these needs are still at a crisis level and that a massive coalition of those committed to maximizing the human functioning possible for older people is necessary to more rapidly bring about positive social change and the accompanying psychological and medical improvements.

This will require a philosophy, value system, and commitment on the part of all the possible initiators of treatment—self through society—to address themselves to the task of identifying individual potentialities and appropriate methods of intervention to maximize them. Our individual responsibility is to make ourselves knowledgeable in social system analysis techniques, to present points of possible modification, and to create methods of effecting social change that will allow the individual to cope with his own problems.

Individual Psychological Therapies

Therapeutic interventions aimed at altering personality organization and coping style might be of considerable value in aiding adaptation, especially when external conditions are, as in the case of most older people, not ideal. But most psychotherapists have been pessimistic about their ability to work with the aged. They see older patients as having less psychic energy and being, therefore, passive, anergic, and unchangeable. Furthermore, they see older people as slow in solving problems and learning new skills. Most therapists assume older people cannot hope for a better tomorrow for themselves since they must anticipate inevitable poorer health, lower income, deteriorating appearance, and death (Riley & Foner, 1968; Weinberg, 1969).

Contrary to the above description, it can be argued that older people are the victims of a class stereotype. Most older people do, in fact, adapt successfully to physical changes, the loss of a spouse, retirement, and the other stresses of the old. There has been no demonstrable increase in either neuroses (Pasamanick, 1962), or functional psychoses (Simon, Lowenthal, & Epstein, 1970) attributable to age. Increased hospitalization rates among the aged are most often attributable to the loss of social supports among those who have been marginal since earlier in their lives.

The pessimism of therapists may therefore more appropriately be attributed to the fact that most practitioners' views of the aged are based on observation of the experiences of an atypical sample of older people. While 25–33% of all institutionalized persons are old, only 5% of all people over the age of 65 reside in any institution. Yet it appears from most published literature that institutionalized old people form the reference group of most therapists. Associated, too, is the fact that therapists are generally asked to modify behavior that is bothersome to those who are not themselves aged.

Nonresidential treatment centers do not now serve the aged. The aged are 10% of the national population and in 1968 were 30% of the patients resident in state and county mental hospitals. Yet, Kramer reports in this volume (pp. 428–528) that in 1968 persons over the age of 65 represented only 2% of the cases in outpatient psychiatric clinics, 2.6% in day care centers, and 4% in community mental health centers.

Increasing these numbers would require salesmanship directed toward both professionals and their potential clients. Older people, when they feel they need help, typically seek ministers, physicians, and members of their families, rather than therapists. Whether or not they would accept psychotherapy if available is at least open to question (Gurin et al., 1960).

Given a questionable market, those who might wish to develop improved psychotherapeutic treatment techniques for the elderly face several problems. It is difficult to find discussions of principles of psychotherapy with the aged. There are few published studies or clinical reports of work with older people. Published descriptions that do exist are generally quite vague. Finally, almost no material comparing techniques is available. If individual psychotherapy is to be developed for the aged—and the trend is away from it for people of all ages—then much more theorizing and research must be done. Here we shall briefly summarize the major directions individual psychotherapeutic interventions have taken till now.

The major positions regarding *relational psychotherapy* for the aged were summarized by Rechtschaffen (1959). More recently, Busse and Pfeiffer (1969) summarized more *medically oriented* treatment. Gendlin and Rychlak (1970) and Krasner (1971) summarized *behavior therapy* and other recent developments. Although little attention is paid to the aged in the last two works, they are summarized briefly here because they are, in the present authors' view, relevant to the aged.

Relational therapies. Freud's view that most older people are not suitable for psychotherapy is still widely accepted. He felt that older people were too rigid to learn, that their problems were too old to be economically retraced, and that even if successful, an old person would not live long enough to warrant investment in psychoanalysis. However, Abraham (1949) suggested that the age of the neurosis, not the age of the patient, was at issue and reported several successful cases of treatment of older people who had developed neuroses late in life.

Alexander (1944) suggested that even where the attainment of insight is not economical or feasible, the therapist may use a modified psychoanalytic approach to help the patient regain tranquility and maintain independence. Goldfarb (1955, 1969) suggested a similar view by encouraging the therapist to accept (or foster) the realistic dependency of the aged as a way of helping them deal with the difficulties they are experiencing. He reported that by using this approach only relatively brief contacts between patient and therapist are needed and that even organically impaired persons can be treated.

A second theme is that the therapist becomes in reality a significant person in the patient's life. Grotjahn (1955) suggested that in order for the patient to work out his reversed oedipal complex, it is important for the therapist to allow the patient to view him as a child. This view indicates that older people do have to overcome their children. Meerloo (1953), on the other hand, while not suggesting any attempt to dissolve transferences, and encouraging the therapist to form real relationships with his patients, urged that attempts be made to see the patient's ability to review his life more easily as death approaches as a way of helping him discover hidden resources and conquer life more easily.

Kubler-Ross (1969) went one step further when dealing with patients' feelings about their impending death by providing a context in which patients can deal with their feelings just as they might any other trauma in their lives. Her therapy is essentially relational or supportive, although it does not reject the search for insights.

Medical therapies. Busse and Pfeiffer (1969) reviewed specific therapies for aged persons with complaints of possible psychological origin. They suggested that sleep disturbances, hypochondriasis, depression, mania, and paranoid reactions all tend to use relatively primitive, simple, poorly focused defense mechanisms, partly as a result of reduced overall capacity for adaptation in the older person, partly because of some cerebral deterioration, and partly because of loss of self-esteem. They recognize the importance of adequate sleep, but also the value of sleep as a psychological escape and of insomnia as an expression of anxiety stemming from feelings of hostility and guilt. They recommend symptomatic treatment with drugs after consideration of the specific meaning of insomnia in a specific individual. Hypochondriasis is also seen as a psychological escape and is encouraged as an acceptable way to express problems in our society. The treatment that is recommended is to give the patient placebos, encourage his relatives to accept him as sick, and for the physician, too, to "accept" the patient's sickness. They emphasize the fact that in many settings sickness is a valuable "social crutch" and should not be taken away.

Depression in old age is common and is generally based upon the loss of positive reinforcements rather than on guilt as is more common in younger people. In mild cases, Busse and Pfeiffer (1969) recommended encouraging the older person to form interpersonal ties through continued activity. In more severe or psychotic depression, they recommended the limited use of psychotherapy coupled with drugs and, in certain cases, electroconvulsive therapy. Paranoid reactions are seen by Busse and Pfeiffer as among the most common reactions in old age. Treatment is based on (a) the use of psychotherapy to restore self-esteem, (b) the reduction of threatening circumstances in the extended environment, and (c) the use of psychotropic drugs to alleviate anxiety.

Wang (1969), discussing therapies for organic states among the aged, offered no new techniques. After admitting the difficulty of differential diagnosis between organic and functional disorder, he concluded:

> All too frequently aggressive therapeutic approaches are reserved for patients with [functional] disorders . . . even if it were possible to differentiate clinically between these two groups, the belief that organic disorders have a poor prognosis is true only when viewed as a group and when compared to psychogenic disorders as a group. There are considerable individual variations with each [group] and hence overlapping between them [p. 285].

For this reason, he recommended that the same therapeutic interventions be used for organic individuals as for the functionally disturbed.

Behavior therapy. Gendlin and Rychlak (1970) published an excellent recent review of developments in psychotherapeutic processes and Krasner (1971), a more detailed consideration of behavior therapy. Both pieces make clear that, as in the past, age has been given little consideration as a variable related to psychotherapy. Both agree that in recent years the focus of psychotherapy has moved away from emphasis on the intrapsychic to behavior therapy and interactional concepts like roles, games, social attitudes, and interactions of small and large social systems. Since these developments are parallel to the point of view of this chapter, we will summarize them briefly here.

Gendlin and Rychlak (1970) reported that systems of treatment are proliferating in great number but that together they seem to share three themes. First, they are moving away from elaborate internal conceptual nets and toward a more general "spirit" of therapy to which myriad techniques can be attached. Second, they are emphasizing briefer interventions aimed at specific problems, rather than deep therapy aimed at redoing a life. Finally, the new therapies take patients through small, specific steps of treatment or even package the treatment into a game or formula which the patient can carry out himself. These emphases on the present life of the person challenge the relevance of Freud's concern about deeply entrenched neuroses.

Krasner (1971) reported the expansion of behavior therapy from one narrowly tied to learning theory to one which bases its work on general psychological principles rather than the medical model on which older views of therapy were predicated. In Wolpe's (1969) narrower view, behavior therapy was defined as "the use of experimentally established principles of learning for the purpose of changing unadaptive behavior. Unadaptive behaviors are weakened and eliminated, adaptive habits are initiated and strengthened [p. vii]."

Ullman and Krasner's (1969) more recent view, in contrast, was that "treatment is deducible from the socio-psychological model that aims to alter a person's behavior directly through the application of psychological principles [p. 244]." Krasner contrasted this to evocative therapy which is "treatment deducible from a medical and psychoanalytic model that aims to alter a person's behavior indirectly by first altering intrapsychic organizations [p. 485]." By broadening the definition of behavior therapy, Krasner in effect included much of the ground to which psychoanalytic therapy has moved. Gendlin and Rychlak (1970) concluded a year earlier, in fact, that by recognizing the role of interpersonal interaction, behavior therapy was accepting much of what it had originally rejected in its more mechanistic formulations. Recent developments in behavior therapy seem to have added three elements: first, that therapy is appropriately susceptible to testing and research; second, that explicit strategies may be laid down; and third, that specific goals of therapy may be set.

Krasner (1971) divided the techniques of behavior therapy into four major techniques, as follows:

1. *Positive reinforcement* developed from Skinner's concepts of operant conditioning, in which desirable behaviors are systematically rewarded. These techniques were originally developed in institutional settings and were highly successful in training adult schizophrenic

patients to engage in either instrumental or social behaviors. These techniques have now become very sophisticated as they have trained increasingly more complex responses, and their proponents have taught people other than professional to provide the reinforcements. Systematic reinforcement has also been used to influence verbal behavior in the psychotherapy situation and in token economies in institutions, classrooms, and even open nonhospital communities.

Since many of the original programs were developed using aged subjects, there is no doubt about the success of these programs or their applicability to the aged. Evidence regarding their use is summarized among other institution-based programs below.

2. *Desensitization* is a technique which generally substitutes relaxation (or some other favorable response) for anxiety (or some other undesired response). A subject is taught to approach a feared behavior more and more closely, each time overcoming his anxiety by relaxation, until he can do the feared thing. Most studies of desensitization have been uncontrolled and most do not consider the role of the therapist in supporting the anxious person. Where tested, however, the technique has been effective. Age has not been a variable considered in desensitization research. Perhaps it is just here that the old person who has not relaxed "all his life" is relevant. If relaxation, without guilt, were a desired goal, then experiments with the aged would be a good test of theories regarding age of habit.

3. *Aversive procedures* either prevent an undesirable response from occurring, or punish the subject when he behaves in certain undesired ways. Many of these procedures have used chemical or electrical shock punishments with some success, while others have used the "relative noxiousness of control that family partners exert on each other." A few studies have "fined" subjects for each performance of some undesired behavior. Studies of aversive procedures have reported some degree of success but have been criticized for overlooking the influence of the person who does the punishing and the possibility of the subject's learning to avoid punishment.

4. *Modeling* is based upon the assumption that one acquires intricate response patterns by observing the performance of appropriate models. This procedure closely replicates many explanations of how socialization occurs for everyone. It also can be an explanation for the influence of the psychotherapist on his patient and for significant people on each other. No specific age gradient has been considered in this research either.

Many psychologists have criticized behavioral approaches to therapy for reasons ranging from their being too mechanistic and naive to their being simply a warming-over of very old ideas. The opinion of these authors is that behavior therapies should be applauded for trying to specify and sort out the variables on which behavior modification occurs. We are distressed that age has not been considered a variable but at the same time pleased that at least explicitly the older person has not been excluded as an appropriate subject.

Other recent developments. Gendlin and Rychlak (1970), in their review, remind us that our old problems are still around. They reported, for example, when subjects of psychoanalystic therapy were described demographically, of 144 subjects treated by 30 analysts on the East Coast only 3% were 50 or over (Weintraub & Aronson, 1968). Likewise, when Friedman and Simon (1968) surveyed 200 new admissions to a state hospital, only a small number were found unsuitable for psychotherapy. Age (over 60), however, was a major criterion accounting for the investigators' decision of unsuitability! From evidence summarized in our theoretical model and by Birren (1964) and Botwinick (1967) we may conclude that age per se will not limit the effectiveness of positive reinforcement, desensitization, aversive stimuli, and modeling.

A major new development favoring our model is the recent trend away from the professional therapist as the only possible intervener. Gendlin and Rychlak (1970) reported on the basis of studies of lay counselors that the subprofessional, the parent, the teacher, and others significant in the subject's life are at least as good judges of his behavior as are professionals, and with some training (and sometimes without special training) are often as effective change agents as a trained professional. For our model these developments in the understanding of the therapeutic process both clarify the possible roles of professionals as treaters and underscore the usual case where they are literally not needed.

One study in fact employed the old person as therapist to the young. Cowen, Liebowitz, and Liebowitz (1968) reported an experimental therapy in which six elderly men and women recruited from a "golden age club" served as mental health aides to work with primary grade children. Twenty-five children were seen for 4 to 15 hours each. Although there were no controls, the teachers rated the children as improved.

Viewed together, individual therapeutic interventions rely on four techniques: the use of drugs, the use of positive and negative reinforcers, the formation of relationships, and the changing of environmental circumstances, In our model, a psychotherapist is only one example of a significant other, and a change in environmental circumstances means a change in the social opportunities and demands upon which behavior partly depends. A proper consideration of treatment must go more deeply into each of these.

Group Treatment

While the expectations of an individual for himself ultimately mediate his reactions to the fit between his behavior and his abilities, the significant people in his life contribute to his expectations in both historical and contemporary ways. If an old person is not working, he may accept his unemployment with equanimity. Or he may, even if he knows the odds are poor of finding one, seek a job frantically, either because of internalized values (Reichard et al., 1962) or because the important people around him tell him that he ought to be working.

One of the principle problems among the elderly is the failure or loss of support of close others. Another source of problems is that an older person becomes extremely dependent. Dependency may be forced upon them as the significant people in their lives ask for and accept less from them because doing so defines the younger person as mature. Dependency may also be forced upon the old because equality cannot be tolerated in a relationship, or because of reversal of the Oedipal situation (Grotjahn, 1955). More realistic reasons for dependency in older people may stem from needs that can in fact be most easily met by turning to more energetic, achievement-oriented youth.

On the other hand, dependency on others can be used therapeutically. Linden (1953) and Liederman, Green, and Liederman (1967) advocated group therapy for older persons. In view of the Shanas, Townsend, Wedderburn, Friis, Milhoj, and Stehouwer (1968) finding of the continued strength of parent–child–grandchild ties throughout life, the family treatment model developed in working with children may have been greatly underused. Recently, students at the University of Michigan brought three generations of unrelated persons together for a weekend. All participants found the experience rewarding, and one person even began to organize an intergenerational commune (Higgin, 1971). For more than a year, Syracuse University has been operating a multigenerational dormitory successfully. From it, new groups of significant others and changed attitudes of young and old residents have been reported (Sanderson, 1971).

In Miami Beach, a community of old people who are becoming significant to one another exists spontaneously. In a 20- or 30-block area along lower Collins Avenue, many thousands of old people have chosen to live side by side in retirement hotels. The impression one gains observing life on that geriatric strip is one of considerable positive mental health based upon residents' relationships with one another.

The Foster Grandparent Program is another excellent example of how therapeutic it is to provide an older person the opportunity to form a relationship in which someone new, an institutionalized child, for example, becomes significant to him, and he himself becomes significant to someone else.

For conceptual purposes it is possible to arrange these group treatment techniques into three categories: family groups, groups bringing unrelated strangers together for temporary relationships only, and new (or old) environments which foster the formation or maintenance of significant relationships. Such group treatment techniques are being increasingly employed when working with the aged.

There are several examples which have been used with persons with more severe psychological disturbances. The city psychiatric service in Amsterdam, recognizing the important effect of significant others, long ago established the practice of working actively with neighbors, friends, and family in every instance of disturbance in a community residence. By reassuring these people and enlisting their efforts in dealing with psychologically disturbed people close to them, the program has been highly successful in substantially reducing the need for hospital beds.

Sainsbury (1969) reported the results of several year's experience in Chichester, England, where families were offered supportive services instead of an institutional placement of a relative. His program (Sainsbury & Grad, 1962) offers counseling, home medical care, home aides, partial hospitalization, legal counseling, and guardianship, but also nursing home and psychiatric hospitalization. In his study, avoiding institutionalization is reported as a hardship but preferred by many families.

Blenkner (1968) reported the experience of a study in the United States which provided all needed services to a group of community-based aged persons. She reported that the persons who received the most services had the highest rates of both institutionalization and death. She attributed this finding to the damage done to people by professional interference in their lives.

A three-year experience in England (Lear, Corrigan, Bhattacharyya, Elliot, Gordon, & Pitt-Aitkens, 1969) in sharing the care of 73 elderly patients between their families or community services and psychogeriatric wards of a mental hospital was found to have advantages for the patients, the family, and the institution.

The patient spent approximately one month at the hospital and one month at home. The treatment team consisted of both hospital and community personnel, with the social worker providing the vital link between home and hospital. All team members were involved to some extent on a continuing basis with the patient, and the family had opportunities to hold discussions with the ward staff. Where needed, the hospital provided help at home, such as laundry service for incontinent patients and home helps.

Though the idea of sharing was sometimes resisted by families, and more often by general practitioners, it was advantageous to all parties. With a greater emphasis placed on personal needs than on symptoms the patients were seen more as persons and less as cases, and even on the hospital wards the atmosphere of depression and stagnation was reduced. In addition, the patients were able to retain their places in the family and community. Families, knowing that they could count on help and periodic relief from the very real burdens imposed by the care of a helpless person, were better able to mobilize their resources and were freed from the guilt that usually accompanies the permanent institutionalization of an aged parent. Professional staff members were provided a valuable learning experience in their contact with families and insights into family relationships. Finally, the plan has clear economic advantages, for each hospital bed can be used by two families instead of one.

The most serious problem with programs that support family care is that many older people do not have families. Kramer (1970) pointed out that most admissions to mental hospitals are from never married, separated, divorced, or widowed persons or from persons in single-parent or other atypical living situations. Among those over 65, the never-married are nearly twice as likely to be hospitalized, less likely to be released, and, if released, more likely to be readmitted than either the married or the divorced.

There are community programs even for persons who lack families. For example, Fairweather, Sanders, Kressler, and Maynard (1969) suggested that it may be possible to create new networks of significant others for ex-mental patients and other marginal persons.

In his study, a group of patients from a mental hospital organized an independent living arrangement and business (janitorial and gardening service) in the community that was totally separate from the hospital. After the study was completed and funds for maintaining the arrangement were unavailable, several members of the original group decided to maintain the arrangement in smaller quarters on a self-supporting basis.

Providing community supports for marginal people without families is neither easy nor inexpensive. Furthermore, Kay, Bergmann, and Foster (1970) found that even with extensive home supports, institutional care was still necessary for some persons. These investigators followed two probability samples totaling 758 persons in Newcastle on Tyne for three years. When samples of neurotics and chronic brain syndrome persons matched for age and sex were compared, the chronic brain syndrome patients died or used hospitals and nursing homes at a far greater rate than neurotic persons, even though intensive home helps were available.

Kay et al.'s (1970) study is an extremely important one because it confirms the persistent feelings among many clinicians that even with the most sophisticated "home helps" one group of patients, those with chronic brain syndrome, will still contain a small group of persons for whom a special care setting is necessary. The work of Kay and his colleagues suggests that these patients are those whose problems have gone beyond the help of social supports. This group, like the organic patient in Simon et al.'s study (1970), also had considerable need for physical care. Although the death rate was high, even in these groups, many patients were still alive after follow-up for two (Simon et al.) or three (Kay et al.) years.

The more community programs we have, the more "sifted" the institutional patient. Nevertheless, since neither Kay et al. nor Simon et al. presented data with regard to the patients' functional abilities, one can conjecture that even in much-sifted groups with significant impairment, many capabilities to carry on some aspects of life remain.

Institutional Treatment

Of course, it would be quite unrealistic to assume that community-based treatment is available to a large number of older people. Discussion of the institution is included here partly because it is the treatment received by most older people receiving any formal treatment at all.

In our model, institutionalization is the most extreme form of treatment because it alters opportunities and expectations by removing the person into an encapsulated portion of the world. In doing so, it generally removes almost all autonomy and sets up a treatment circumstance that is in diametric opposition to the self-treatment value that underlies this chapter.

On the other hand, because of its radical nature (cut off from the rest of the world) the institution replicates many of the interventions already described. A major question is whether other forms of treatment aimed at enhancing the individual's capacity for self-care are helped or hindered by the institutional setting. In general, the conclusion of most authors is that the institutional setting is necessary because of the lack of community supports for the patient. While institutional programs do change behavior successfully while people are in them, there is little evidence that the institution is a place to send a patient for cure.

It is not surprising that considerable attention has been paid to old people in institutions. In 1970, the aged in institutions totaled 814,000 persons, about 5% of all older people (see Kramer, pp. 428–528, this volume). About one in seven of these were in a psychiatric facility and most of the rest were in a nursing home.[1] Conservatively estimated, about one nursing home patient in four is diagnosed as mentally ill and an additional one in four has some reported mental disturbance. After reviewing all available data, Kramer concluded that the number of mentally ill in nursing homes now exceeds those in mental hospitals.

The institutionalized aged person is almost always a public charge. Although younger mentally ill persons have been using private facilities more in the last decade, the aged have only moved from one form of public payment to another. In fact, the Medicare legislation of the last five years has added many previously privately supported residents of homes for the aged to the federal rolls.

Characteristics of institutionalized persons. Viewed from inside institutions, the aged are a considerable challenge. Eighty-eight percent of nursing home residents and all residents of homes for the aged are over 65. One-third of mental hospital residents and about one-quarter of admissions to mental hospitals are old. Because they use public monies and are close to professionals, the old people, captive in institutions, have been the object of study far in excess of their numbers among the aged.

Gottesman et al. (1969) suggested that a major characteristic of the institutionalized aged is social marginality. They compared a selected sample of 139 long-term and 109 recent patients in a large

---

[1] Independently derived calculations put the number of residents over the age of 65 in psychiatric facilities in 1968 at about 120,000 (see pp. 428–528 by Kramer, Taub, & Redick in this volume) and the number of nursing home residents that same year at about 743,000 (National Center for Health Statistics, 1971).

state mental hospital with the 1960 urban Michigan census.[2] Both hospital groups were more poorly educated; more were never married; and more were living alone or with a nonrelative when admitted. Aged long-hospitalized patients had, in many cases, never left their parents' home before becoming mental patients.

Simon et al. (1970) reported that 600 persons over 60 first admitted to a psychiatric screening ward in San Francisco differed from a community sample mainly in being economically poorer, alone, and not having worked in many years. Rather than suffering from new social trauma of old age the admitted group had been massively impaired for some time. The precipitating condition in 53% of their cases was acute brain syndrome traceable to physical causes, like alcoholism, malnutrition, or congestive heart failure. Further, at admission, four-fifths of those admitted were found to need at least moderate amounts of supervision for physical ailments. The elderly marginal persons had failed the major social test of their age—they had become unable to manage for themselves.

There are data that the institutionalized aged have an atypically high expectation of death. Kramer, Taube, and Starr (1968) reported that the institutionalized aged group over 65 has a death rate of 235 per 1,000 residents or four times that of persons their age in the general population. He also reported data from New York State showing that the death rate among aged mental patients increased from 1930 to 1962, while it decreased among noninstitutionalized persons of the same age. Goldfarb (1969) reported that even after excluding the acutely ill, more than half of the elderly persons admitted to psychiatric hospitals and nursing homes will be dead within three years. Although first- and second-year mortality rates are considerably lower in homes for the aged, by the third year 48% of that group will also be dead.

Most of these studies have asked how the institutionalized in different settings differed from those outside. But several epidemiologic studies have shown that for every person inside, there are two or three noninstitutionalized persons over 65 with diagnosable mental disturbance. These people in normal communities are similar to those in institutions, but, have found a way to make it in a normal world.

---

[2] For purposes of the major study, these samples were controlled to be 50% of each sex and are therefore not completely representative of the general population of the aged, which is disproportionately female.

The key to treatment of the institutionalized aged might be found not in how they differ from aged persons in general, but rather in how the institutionalized and similar noninstitutionalized manage in a variety of settings.

Types of institutional settings. Traditionally, we have thought of settings for the aged as the home for the aged, the nursing home, and the mental hospital. As stereotypes, the characteristics of each of these settings are well known and they have been summarized by Goldfarb (1969).

There is a pecking order. The home for the aged is on top, with the younger, most functional residents with least severe mental disorder; the mental hospital is next; and the nursing home lowest, having the least intact patients in physical, mental, and *social* status! Since we will argue that the social setting is a primary determinant of behavior, for purposes of the discussion of treatment it is important to know the variety of settings that are available and how residents are selected to live in each type.

Gottesman et al. (1971) found a number of settings available to their geriatric ex-mental patients. Some ex-patients went to rooming houses, some to a room in a single-family home, some to nursing homes, and a few to their own families or to independent apartments. The study, which followed each released patient for up to two years, found diversity among the types of settings. Large rooming houses offered considerable freedom and encouraged normally responsible behavior; small room and boards were intimate, demanding, and often intolerant of deviant behavior. Family placements were rare (in a geriatric group), moderately tolerant of deviance, and highly conducive to normal behavior. Private apartments, also rare, encouraged maximum ex-patient independence and contact with the normal world. Nursing homes restricted patients most, and permitted little normal behavior within them or with the outside world.

Bok (1971), reporting on the same study, showed that placement into one type of setting rather than another was often as dependent on availability of place and of funds as on the staff's view of patient needs.

Blenkner (1968) wrote that "the flow of care of the aged follows the public dollar," and in 1964 Gottesman warned that changes in federal regulations would move the elderly mentally ill from mental hospitals into nursing homes. This has happened. During the period from 1950 to 1960, residents of nursing homes increased 31.5%, while elderly residents of mental hospitals decreased 12%, and first admission of old people to mental hospitals also decreased. The reasons have not been either a marked increase in deaths among the institutionalized elderly nor a marked increase in success of therapeutic programs. What has happened is that several changes in federal regulations, culminating in Titles XVIII and XIX of the Social Security Act, have moved the locus of care of the aged. A different administrative decision could move care back to the mental hospital, to the poor house, or to the community. These moves cannot be called successful treatments which return patients to the community, for in actuality it is only an administrative transfer.

It is possible that the usual goal of movement from a "therapeutic environment" back to "normal life" is unrealistic. Data summarized above have shown that most residents in all three major types of old age institutions have been living in more or less marginal circumstances during much of their lives. Their entry into an institution is generally viewed by everyone as a step downward and is brought about by a failure in a tenuous support system. Generally, though the settings they enter are called therapeutic, both experience and expectation are that the placement is a permanent one unless the resident's situation worsens markedly. In the mental hospital and the nursing home even a worsened condition is of little consequence. The institutions are expected to take and keep even the most disturbed residents (Glaser & Strauss, 1968).

Therapeutic programs. Many institutionalized persons do live for many years. A number of programs have attempted to develop treatments for them within the hospital framework. Most have been in mental hospitals, but they are also relevant to other settings. Most of these programs have been successful in changing patients behavior while they are being treated. Few patients have been cured.

Historically, Jones' (1953) early study of a therapeutic community for the treatment of returned war veterans was quickly followed by Stanton and Schwartz's (1954) description of a therapeutic milieu in a small private mental hospital. These studies were followed by treatment programs for the elderly in several places in the United States and abroad (Cosin, Mort, Post, Westropp, & Williams, 1958; Linden, 1953; Rechtschaffen, Atkinson, & Freedman, 1958; Wolff, 1956, 1957a, 1957b, 1958, 1959).

Responding to several facets of the problem presented by the mental hospital, the major studies made various attempts to develop therapeutic programs which emphasized one or a combination of three major approaches (Krasner, 1971; Schwartz, Schwartz, & Field, 1964).

A number of hospitals had responded to serious overcrowding and staff shortages by developing massive institutionally monolithic programs in which all patients were treated alike, almost as members of herds, being given identical food, identical clothing, identical scheduling of their days, and identical inadequate treatment. In trying to improve services, these hospitals searched for ways of increasing the *individualization* of patient care by attempting to reduce the size of hospitals, to break down homogeneous wards and services, to establish programs for direct contact between the patient and his physician, or to broaden the range of relationships between the patient and hospital personnel.

Other hospitals, sensitive to the virtual ostracism of the mental hospital and its patients from normal society, attempted to find ways of *breaking down the barriers between hospital and community.* Some tried to change public attitudes toward mental hospitals by establishing a more open hospital policy permitting closer contact between patients and members of the nonhospital community. Others attempted to establish psychiatric treatment units as part of general hospitals within the community itself. Still others instituted changes that would decrease the social distance between the hospital and the community and established volunteer programs to foster interaction between members of the normal community and mental hospital patients.

A third group of programs was designed to develop milieux within the hospital that would be conducive *to cure.* This group of programs was given impetus by an increasing volume of evidence that mental illness was at least in part influenced by the social and psychological environment of the patient both before and during his hospitalization. Theorists and practitioners working within the mental hospital context were suggesting that mental illness—particularly schizophrenia, the most prevalent psychosis among younger patients —was a manifestation of withdrawal by the patient from social participation in the normal world and an escape into a highly personalized and infantile world of his own. These theorists noted further that rather than counteracting this tendency of patients to withdraw, the prevalent pattern in most mental hospitals took the patient further into a world apart and forced him frequently into a totally dependent role in which all individuality, assertiveness, and sociability were discouraged.

A group of behaviorally oriented investigators also intent on a cure began developing programs only a few years after the socially oriented milieu theorists. They reasoned that the socially undersirable behavior of mental patients could be molded by arranging a set of rewards that would make desired behaviors "pay." This technique, variously called behavior therapy, behavior modification, reinforcement therapy, reward and punishment treatment, and behavior management, has become very popular. New York State, for example, has recently introduced it into all its state mental hospitals (*New York Times,* 1971).

While programs were being developed, theorists looking at the problems of the aged were independently suggesting that a basic problem in the aged was also social withdrawal, occasioned not by a psychotic process but by the combination of two diverse factors. The first factor was decreased physical capabilities which inhibited mobility and decreased perceptual and motor skills which reduced active participation in society. The second, and probably the more important, factor was the relegation of the older person by society to a role that forced him into a passive, dependent, noninstrumental relationship with the world.

On the basis of a growing conviction of the importance of social causation in geriatric withdrawal and of the exacerbation of this withdrawal by institutional conditions in homes for the aged and nursing homes, a number of investigators initiated programs to provide opportunities for activities that would stimulate patients' mental and social abilities (Donahue, 1950; Donahue, Hunter, & Coons, 1953). Rechtschaffen et al. (1958), working in a mental hospital, instituted a program for geriatric patients including work in hospital industries or at routine chores, occupational therapy, psychotherapy and shock treatment, and social planning for discharge. Other studies used many of the therapeutic interventions described by Schwartz et al. (1964) as characterizing the "milieu approach." These included attempts to make the hospital "atmosphere" more therapeutic by changing patient or staff attitudes, attempts to use aspects of the hospital's environment therapeutically; increasing patients' participation in their own treatment, the operation of the institution, or the treatment of other patients; and manipulation of ward characteristics such as location, size, and layout.

Gottesman et al. (1969, 1971) used four hospital milieux to compare a therapy emphasizing paid work and planned activities with traditional treatment. Their subjects were 320 patients over age 55. Most were diagnosed schizophrenic, and the group averaged 16 years of hospitalization. They found that a sheltered workshop and planned ward activity programs were able to involve between 87 and 94% of several types of patients for 5 to 10 hours per day. In contrast, on a typical mental hospital ward with a comparable group of patients, only a few star patients did most things while most were inactive. Patient performance on all wards was unrelated to sex, age, marital status, living arrangements prior to hospitalization, education, or job history.

Performance was related to the patient's prior history as a hospital worker and to his centrality in the social fabric of his ward. The least active patients were those with the most severe disturbance in their orientation for time, place, and person, but even severely disoriented persons were usually active when opportunities were available.

There were positive effects that went beyond patient activity. Patients viewed active wards as more complex, orderly, and less distorted with personal meanings (Gutmann, Gottesman, & Tessler, 1968). They viewed their problems in psychic and interpersonal terms and anticipated dealing actively with them. In a milieu that more closely approximated a nonhospital round of life, since it had work, pay, and play as well as inactivity, patients knew each other better and were happier than in traditional wards.

Gottesman found that when no program activities were available on the wards, patient activities stopped. Patients, like people outside of hospitals, did not make their own opportunities. Despite marked behavioral effects, the programs did not affect hospital release rates. Neither did they markedly ameliorate psychotic symptoms or confusion. What they did was provide a human environment that maximized opportunities for patients to use the abilities that they had before they entered the research wards.

In 18 months, only 4% of their patients died. Twelve percent of the patients were released from the hospital in less than 6 months, and 29% more after periods of up to 18 months. Release was not associated with type of treatment, but with patients' personal and social characteristics and with placement opportunities outside. Women had a much greater likelihood of release both early and later in the study. Patients ages 65–69 were more likely to be released than either younger patients, for whom fewer governmental support programs were available, or older patients, who were more likely to have deteriorated physically and mentally. Of those who stayed in the hospital, younger patients were more likely to be retained in the experimental treatment and older patients to be returned to regular hospital wards. Widows were more likely to leave the hospital than patients of any other marital status.

The most active patients were, depending upon available community programs, either released or retained for further treatment until a placement was found. The least active were transferred to custodial wards. The moderately active were released to nursing homes. But active patients were likely to have been active as hospital workers prior to entering the study. Patients who worked off their wards and were "out of sight" were not likely to be released (Bok,

1971). Finally, patients were more likely to be released if they had shorter hospitalizations and if they had a family member who had shown even slight interest in them.

Results of other programs have been fairly consistent. Rapoport (1960) evaluated Jones' (1953) prototypic program. Of 100 young neurotic ex-service men treated in a milieu which served as a model in many ways for Fairweather's (1964) study, 61% were rated improved after treatment for periods of three months to one year. Six months after discharge, however, only 31% of these patients were still rated improved.

Fairweather (1964) demonstrated that with patients averaging 37 years of age the use of a small-group task-oriented approach as opposed to a traditional hospital program can increase the amount of social interaction at all levels of social intimacy. Such treatment can also shift patient orientation from the hospital staff to other patients and give them more optimistic views about their future. Experimental patients in Fairweather's study when discharged showed better adjustment in employment, verbal communication, and friendships. He and his co-workers found, however, that these changes did not persist outside the hospital and that the likelihood of a patient's returning was related more to his chronicity than to his treatment experience.

Fairweather suggested, and in fact predicted, that patients in his program, once discharged would not maintain improvements demonstrated in the hospital because of the lack of support available to them in the community. He is now conducting a study of this hypothesis, and the results are encouraging when patient groups are continued in a protected community setting after discharge (Fairweather et al., 1969).

A study reported by Burdock, Elliott, Hardesty, O'Neill, and Sklar (1960) and Sklar and O'Neill (1961) presented similar results with older patients. Their carefully controlled study concerned 111 experimental and 105 control first-admission women over 65 years of age and diagnosed senile psychosis, psychosis with cerebral arteriosclerosis, or psychosis with cardiovascular renal disease. The experimental intervention included a variety of changes: increased staff, more space per patient, group meetings, and the use of occupational, physical, and recreational therapies. Using a "simple manifest behavior" rating scale they reported no difference between experimental and control patients at five days; significantly more experimental than control patients improved by four weeks; but by six months so many experimental patients had been discharged that statistical comparisons of behavior ratings were impossible. The rate of discharge did not remain constant, however. At four weeks it was 5%; by the fourth month it had risen to 10%; but by the end of the first year had dropped again to 1%.

Another effort has been recently described by Sanders, Smith, and Weinman in their book entitled *Chronic Psychoses and Recovery* (1967). Bourestom (1970) summarized that study as follows:

> Working with patients at the Philadelphia State Hospital who ranged in age from 19 to 72 and who had been hospitalized on the average of nine years, these investigators compared three socio-environmental programs which differed primarily in the amount of structured activity, demands for patient participation and assumption of patient responsibility. The basic experimental design in this study also included a control condition in which no environmental structure was imposed and the demand characteristics of the environment were generally nonexistent. Patients were studied for three years altogether, two of which involved follow-up in the community after the completion of treatment.
>
> The investigators assessed the outcomes of the programs in a number of ways including changes in social behavior, psychiatric status, release rates, status of the patient in the community and rehospitalization rates. In these terms all three socio-environmental programs were superior to the control condition, but only when—and this is exceedingly important—only when age and length of hospitalization were considered. The results showed that all three programs had the greatest impact on older patients and those who had been hospitalized the longest periods of time. These patients were more likely to show improvement under the treatment programs while they were in the hospital, they were likely to adapt better to community situations, and they were less likely to return to the hospital than were their more acutely ill counterparts. In attempting to explain these results the authors link age and institutionalization conceptually to the amount of drive interference in acquiring new responses, but as Appleby (1969) pointed out in his review of this work, they have equal plausibility as indices of acquiescence essentially reflecting the degree to which one permits himself to be shaped by environmental stimuli. Whatever the conceptual linkage, the effects of these programs relative to age and length of hospitalization are of considerable interest and, it seems to me, of practical value for programming in mental hospitals [p. 190].

Brody, Kleban, Lawton, and Silverman (1971) reported a study that sought specific individualized treatment results rather than general improvement of behavior. They used a four-step process which included for each individual (a) a base-line evaluation, (b) a plan for a specific goal which the staff felt could be achieved (these improvable areas were called "excess disabilities"), (c) individualized multidisciplinary treatment, and (d) final evaluation. From an original group of 32 pairs of women matched on age, mental function, and functional health, they reported data for the surviving 22 experimental and 26 control subjects. The results showed that many areas for possible improvement (i.e., excess disabilities) existed among the patients. When rated by project staff and by independent outside observers, experimental patients improved more than controls. In support of the specificity of their treatment, the investigators pointed out that no general improvement was noted even though there was improvement of individual excess-disabilities.

In another unusual study, Simon et al. (1970) compared patient characteristics to treatment outcomes in naturalistic treatment settings. Persons over 65 years of age, who had had no previous admissions, entered a psychiatric screening ward, and then were observed for two years. They were classified into four groups. In each case, outcome had more to do with the patient's physical, mental, and social condition at intake than with what was done to him. After screening, the first group, composed of 125 patients who were sent to and stayed in a state hospital, remained in poor mental condition, improved somewhat physically, but deteriorated in self-care ability, "probably reflecting the limited range of opportunities available in state hospitals."

The second group of 35 patients went to "other facilities" than the state hospital, and, although in equally bad condition initially, improved in both physical and mental condition. These patients were generally diagnosed as having acute brain syndrome and had an illness with a primary physical rather than mental basis.

A third group of 37 patients discharged from general hospital psychiatric wards and the final group of 52 patients discharged from the screening wards all improved after discharge. Those who had spent some time in the mental hospital were less socially active but had fewer physical symptoms and a higher functional status than those released from the screening wards directly into the community.

Behavior therapies were originally developed in mental hospitals where they used the typical chronic aged schizophrenic patient as a subject. At first they set very limited and often artificial goals like teaching patients to play pinball machines, or to pull a lever (e.g., Ayllon & Haughton, 1962; Coleman, 1963; Lindsley, 1962; Mackay, 1965), and focused their attention on developing an understanding of the most effective ways to use reinforcements.

In a more recent study, Atthowe and Krasner (1968) used a token economy to shape a broad range of desirable behavior. They worked with a group of patients of 57 years median age with a median of 22 years of hospitalization. They reported an increase in attendance at group activities, more patients going on passes, drawing cash, and using the ward canteen among 32 experimental patients.

The entire ward also showed improved behavior and there was improved continence, cooperativeness, and social interaction.

Folsom (1966) and his co-workers (Anon, 1969; Taulbee & Folsom, 1966) described a program that combined "reality orientation" and "attitude therapy." Reality orientation systematically trains the patient to orient himself in space and time by frequent classes and the making of physical space. Attitude therapy trains staff to behave in planned and consistent ways (i.e., attitudes) toward patients. In both cases treatment is individualized. While these programs have not been evaluated experimentally their proponents claim that they are highly successful in treating severely regressed geriatric patients.

Krasner (1971), in his recent summary of behavioral approaches to treatment, suggested that their success is not only in shaping the behavior of disturbed patients. The key, he observed, is their success in training staff members to attend more closely to patient behavior and to use their own social behaviors to reinforce desirable behavior of others.

When viewed in this light, all of the therapies described in this section can be characterized as ways of reorganizing the social life space of elderly institutionalized persons so that they are encouraged and allowed to behave in more normal ways. The programs do not cause either release or cure. They are highly successful in making the overt behavior of the patient more socially acceptable.

The nursing home. Overcrowding of mental hospitals with chronically ill patients and high costs of maintaining them were the pressures that made possible most of the research cited above. The same factors led to considerable pressure to release into the community the chronic elderly mental patient no longer in need of active care. Federal programs providing medical assistance have made the nursing home the recipient of these patients. There is a danger that many of the same problems which mental hospitals have spent years trying to overcome will be repeated in nursing homes.

In order to try to forestall a repetition of problems, Gottesman and Bourestom (1969) are now engaged in a study which will describe the total patient experience in a nursing home, measure the multiple factors which contribute to it, and suggest ways in which nursing homes may be changed, if such change is desirable.

Several facts are already evident. It is already clear that while mental hospitals are moving toward smaller units, nursing homes are *increasing in size.* In Michigan, between 1950 and 1954 only 20% of new homes licensed had over 100 beds; between 1965 and 1969, 46% were large homes. While mental hospitals have been moving toward decreased centralized control, nursing homes have been moving toward *increased control* by a few corporations. In the Detroit area, six corporations control 18% of 169 homes and 30% of the beds. While mental hospitals have been trying to have more contacts with the noninstitutional community, nursing homes are becoming more *cut off*. Current legislation forces nursing homes to create distinctly separated parts with narrowly defined patient populations and rigid staffing patterns. Homes must be either skilled, intermediate, or basic care specialists, or they cannot qualify for the federal monies that support the 87% of all nursing home patients' care.

Some mental hospitals have begun to provide milieux that maximize a resident's opportunity for independence. On the other hand, nursing homes are rewarded for keeping people sick; if a patient were able to make her own bed, the home would either have to send her away (recall that nursing home patients are generally there because they have no home) or lose payment for her.

Nursing homes are also caught in struggles among public, private, and voluntary services. Perhaps because they were caring for persons who were even less socially desirable than the mental patient, most nursing homes developed as small, marginal, private enterprises, rather than as either government or voluntary agencies. In the 1950s Medicare legislation and other favorable governmental policies fostered a fast growth of an industry controlled by persons expert in the *construction of facilities* and the management of business. Today, these persons, who were never experienced in providing for people's psychosocial/medical needs, have a problem which the government did not want and voluntary organizations could not afford. Because of their past financial success, because of a long-standing distrust of government and the voluntary sector for business, and because of an implicit social value that "people care" does not belong in the private sector, there is an atmosphere of great friction and distrust between the government, which pays most of the bills, and the suppliers of a service, which no one is able to define.

Part of the difficulty in defining service is that nursing homes are paid to meet goals that may be unattainable. Fees are paid for curative and restorative services. Unfortunately, the three conditions that occur with greater frequency among nursing home patients than in noninstitutionalized disabled aged persons are not really responsive to either cure or rehabilitation. The 1964 National Health Survey found that the only conditions that occur more often among nursing home patients are mental conditions (43.9% versus 14.0%), vascular conditions affecting the central nervous system (36.0% versus 7.0%), and paralysis due to stroke (15.7% versus 5.2%). In all other conditions the rate for physically limited but noninstitutionalized old people equals and exceeds the institutionalized. The important difference between those in nursing homes and many outside is that they have no families to care for them and must spend long years in a special setting.

Sixty-five percent of patients in nursing homes stay in them over one year, and 17% five years or more. If one estimates even grossly, all of the services any patient receives require only a very small part of a day to give. Almost no nursing home patients make their own beds, cook, wash, iron, clean, shop, go for walks, or engage in any other significant activity of life. Most sit from arising to bedtime with only meals to punctuate their day.

There is no doubt that the tragedy which mental hospitals have been trying to overcome—the tragedy of people with years filled with nothing to do—is now being replayed. Nursing homes, like mental hospitals, have no cures to give and nursing care fills only small parts of each day. Nursing homes must be recompensed for bringing life back to their residents. Dull as it seems, life for most of us is cleaning, cooking, dressing, working, socializing, and helping others. Of these activities, many are within the capability of many nursing home patients. There is no reason to suppose a priori that the nursing care needed could not be so distributed in the day as to leave room for other activities. Recalling that the goal is not cure but a meaningful life, the success of mental hospitals in providing a sheltered workshop and opportunities for geriatric mental patients to take part in individual and group activities could be replicated. At least it must be tried.

SUMMARY

We see a need to develop opportunity systems sufficient in variety to deal with experienced stress from the perspective of the reality of aging within a dynamic psychological, biological, and social context.

We presented a general treatment model which attempts to legitimate as a target of treatment the psychological discomfort of individuals regardless of whether or not it is diagnostically labeled or intrapsychically caused. When the emphasis is placed on the maximization of the individual's potential and self-determined goals within his world, several treatment techniques become apparent depending upon the loci of the sources of stress for the individual, that is, biological, intrapsychic, interpersonal, or societal, plus any combination of these. The treatment models so identified were self-treatment, societal treatment, individual psychological treatment, small-group treatment, and institutional treatment.

Self-treatment or adaptation is described as the most frequent and most desirable means people use to deal with incongruence among the several behavior-causing elements.

Societal treatment is described as an attempt to arrange societal opportunities and demands so as to maximize the individual's choices in adapting to aging. At times this treatment is one of removing unrealistic impediments to individual freedom, at other times it is providing new opportunities or societal supports, training them to assert themselves, or advocating their needs. Societal treatment is described as the most promising new area today.

Individual psychological treatment has included approaches relying on personal relationships between a therapist and his patient, medically oriented treatments often adding drugs or using them instead of relationships, and behavioral therapies which have used principles derived from psychological theory of learning to change behavior. The chapter finds fault with an overemphasis on personal responsibility or personal change when the problem is in society or in others. Nevertheless there is evidence that individual therapy has been helpful. It is likely to be useful to older persons if professionals are willing to treat them and if old people are willing to seek professional help. Medical therapies have been highly successful when they have used drugs and have more than other approaches recognized the contribution of physical factors to behavior. Behavior therapy has been very successful, but only recently used outside of the institutional settings.

Small-group treatment can be used in both contrived settings like psychotherapy and in naturalistic ones like families or communities of aged persons. This technique is valuable because it can be more naturalistic and more long lasting than individual therapy.

Institutional treatment is the most common treatment used for people who receive outside help. This is viewed as bad because other more naturalistic approaches leave the person more freedom to use his strengths maximally. On the other hand, there is considerable evidence that most institutionalized old persons are selected from people who have been chronically marginal all their lives. Institutional treatment may be the best way of providing social supports for persons without other alternatives. Institutional treatment has been highly successful in changing or molding behavior. Both milieu approaches which rely on general restructuring of environment and behavioral approaches with more specific goals have been successful.

The nursing home is discussed separately because it has now become the major site for the institutionalized elderly. The chapter reviews evidence that this is a negative development because the homes do not now have social therapeutic programs and do not get reimbursed for offering them.

The thrust of the chapter is a wish for major priority to be given to self-care and small-group treatment. Social changes are urged to create these emphases. Individual therapy should be a less central intervention than usual among psychologists. Institutional treatment is seen as necessary for some persons but needs to emphasize the creation of a way of life for them.

REFERENCES

Abraham, J. The applicability of psycho-analytic treatment to patients at an advanced age. In E. Glover (Ed.), *Selected papers of psychoanalysis.* London: Hogarth Press, 1949.

Alexander, F. G. The indications for psychoanalytic therapy. *Bulletin of the New York Academy of Medicine,* 1944, **20,** 319–334.

Allport, G. *Pattern and growth in personality.* New York: Holt, Rinehart & Winston, 1961.

Anon, 1969. *Reality orientation.* Washington, D.C.: American Psychiatric Association, 1969.

Atthowe, J. M., & Krasner, L. Preliminary report on the application of contingent reinforcement procedures (token economy) on a "chronic" psychiatric ward. *Journal of Abnormal Psychology,* 1968, **73,** 37–43.

Ayllon, I., & Haughton, E. Control of the behavior of schizophrenic patients by food. *Journal of the Experimental Analysis of Behavior,* 1962, **5,** 343–352.

Barfield, R., & Morgan, J. *Early retirement.* Ann Arbor, Mich.: Survey Research Center, 1968.

Beattie, W. M., & Bullock, J. *Preface for a counseling service: A study of 1,085 residents of nursing homes and homes for the aged.* St. Louis: Health & Welfare Council of Metropolitan St. Louis, 1963.

Benedict, R. E. Triple jeopardy: Report of a conference on the minority aged. Ann Arbor, Mich.: Institute of Gerontology, 1971.

Birren, J. E. *The psychology of aging.* Englewood Cliffs, N.J.: Prentice-Hall, 1964.

Birren, J. E. Prospects of gerontology. Closing address at the 8th International Congress of Gerontology, Washington, D.C., August 1969.

Blenkner, M. The place of the nursing home among community resources. *Journal of Geriatric Psychiatry,* 1968, **1**(2), 135–144.

Bok, M. Some problems in milieu treatment of the chronic older mental patient. *Gerontologist,* 1971, **2**(1), 141–147.

Botwinick, J. *Cognitive processes in maturity and old age.* New York: Springer, 1967.

Bourestom, N. C. Evaluation of mental health programs for the aged. *Aging and Human Development,* 1970, **1**(3), 187–198.

Briggs, J. C. Ecology as gerontology. *Gerontologist,* 1968, **8**(2), 78–89.

Brody, E. M., Kleban, M. H., Lawton, M. P., & Silverman, H. A. Excess disabilities of mentally impaired aged: Impact of individualized treatment. *Gerontologist,* 1971, **2**(2), 124–133.

Burdock, E. I., Elliott, H. E., Hardesty, A. S., O'Neil, F. J., & Sklar, J. Biometric evaluation of an intensive treatment program in a state mental hospital. *Journal of Nervous and Mental Diseases,* 1960, **130**, 271–277.

Busse, E., & Pfeiffer, E. Functional psychiatric disorders in old age. In E. Busse & E. Pfeiffer (Eds.), *Behavior and adaptation in late life.* Boston: Little, Brown, 1969.

Butler, R. N. The facade of chronological age: An interpretive summary. In B. Neugarten (Ed), *Middle age and aging.* Chicago: University of Chicago Press, 1968.

Calhoun, M., & Gottesman, L. E. Stereotypes of old age in two samples. Paper presented at the meeting of the Midwest Psychological Association, Chicago, April 1963.

Coleman, K. K. The modification of rigidity in geriatric patients through operant conditioning. Unpublished doctoral dissertation, Louisiana State University, 1963.

Cosin, L. E., Mort, M., Post, F., Westropp, C., & Williams, M. Experimental treatment of persistent senile confusion. *International Journal of Social Psychiatry,* 1958, **4**, 24–42.

Cottrell, F. Politics of aging. Paper presented at the meeting of the Institute for State Executives in Aging, University of Southern California, Idyllwild Campus, February 1966.

Cowen, E. L., Liebowitz, E., & Liebowitz, G. Utilization of retired people as mental health aides with children. *American Journal of Orthopsychiatry,* 1968, **38**, 900–909.

Cumming, E., & Henry, W. H. *Growing old: The process of disengagement.* New York: Basic Books, 1961.

Donahue, W. An experiment in the restoration and preservation of personality in the aged. In W. Donahue & C. Tibbetts (Eds.), *Planning the older years.* Ann Arbor: University of Michigan Press, 1950.

Donahue, W., Hunter, W. W., & Coons, D. A study of the socialization of old people. *Geriatrics,* 1953, **8**, 656–666.

Duncan, L. E. Ecology and aging. *Gerontologist,* 1968, **8**(2), 80–83.

Fairweather, G. W. *Social psychology in treating mental illness: An experimental approach.* New York: Wiley, 1964.

Fairweather, G. W., Sanders, D., Kressler, D., & Maynard, H. *Community life for the mentally ill.* Chicago: Aldine, 1969.

Folsom, J. C. Reality orientation for the elderly mental patient. A paper presented at the meeting of the American Psychiatric Association, May 1966. (Mimeo)

Friedman, M., & Simon, W. B. How many public mental patients can benefit from psychotherapy? *Psychotherapy,* 1968, **5**, 142–145.

Gendlin, E., & Rychlak, S. Psychotherapeutic processes. *Annual Review of Psychology,* 1970, **21**.

Glaser, B., & Strauss, H. *Time for dying*. Glencoe, Ill.: Free Press, 1968.

Goldfarb, A. I. Psychotherapy of aged persons. IV. One aspect of the psychodynamics of the therapeutic situation with aged patients. *Psychoanalytic Review*, 1955, 180–187.

Goldfarb, A. I. Institutional care of the aged. In E. Busse & E. Pfeiffer (Eds.), *Behavior and adaptation in late life*. Boston: Little, Brown, 1969.

Gottesman, L., & Bourestom, N. A. multifaceted study of nursing homes. Proposal submitted to the National Institute of Mental Health. Ann Arbor, Mich.: Institute of Gerontology, 1969.

Gottesman, L. E., Bourestom, N. Donahue, W., & Coons, D. The technology of milieu treatment of the aged mental patient. Ann Arbor, Mich.: Institute of Gerontology Library, 1971.

Gottesman, L. E., Donahue, W., Coons, D., & Ciarlo, J. Extended care of the aged: Psychosocial aspects. *Journal of Geriatric Psychiatry*, 1969, **2**(2), 220–237.

Grotjahn, M. Analytic psychotherapy with the elderly. *Psychoanalytic Review*, 1955, **42**, 419–427.

Gurin, G., Veroff, J., & Feld, S. *Americans view their mental health*. New York: Basic Books, 1960.

Gutmann, D., Gottesman, L. E., & Tessler, S. A comparative study of ego functioning in geriatric patients. Paper presented at the meeting of the Gerontological Society, Denver, October 1968.

Halleck, S. *The politics of therapy*. New York: Science Press, 1971.

Havighurst, R. J. A social–psychological perspective on aging. *Gerontologist*, 1968, **8**(2), 67–71.

Havighurst, R. J. (Ed.) Research proposals in applied social gerontology: Second report. *Gerontologist*, 1971, **11**(1), 1–98.

Higgin, J. An intergenerational workshop. Ann Arbor, Mich.: Institute of Gerontology Library, 1971.

Jackson, J. Negro aged: Toward needed research in social gerontology. *Gerontologist*, 1971, **11**(2), 52–57.

Jones, M. *The therapeutic community*. New York: Basic Books, 1953.

Kastenbaum, R. While the old man dies. In A. H. Kutscher (Ed.), *Psychosocial aspects of terminal care*. New York: Columbia University Press, 1971.

Kay, D. W., Bergmann, K., & Foster, E. M. Mental illness and hospital usage in the elderly: A random sample followed up. *Comprehensive Psychiatry*, 1970, **11**, 26–35.

Kelly, J. Ecological constraints on mental health services. *American Psychologist*, 1966, **21**, 535–539.

Kleemeier, R. W. Behavior and the organization of the bodily and external environment. In J. E. Birren (Ed.), *Handbook of aging and the individual*. Chicago: University of Chicago Press, 1959.

Kramer, M. Problems in psychiatric epidemiology. *Proceedings of the Royal Society of Medicine*, 1970, **63**, 553–562. (Summary)

Kramer, M., Taube, C., & Starr, S. Patterns of use of psychiatric facilities by the aged: Current status, trends, and implication. *Psychiatric Research Report*, 1968, **23**, 89–150.

Krasner, L. Behavior therapy. *Annual Review of Psychology*, 1971, **22**, 483–532.

Kubler-Ross, E. *On death and dying*. London: Macmillan, 1969.

Kuhlen, R. G. Developmental changes in motivation during the adult years. In B. Neugarten (Ed.), *Middle age and aging*. Chicago: University of Chicago Press, 1968.

Lawton, M. P., & Simon, B. The ecology of social relationships in housing for the elderly. *Gerontologist*, 1968, **8**(2), 108–115.

Lear, T. E., Corrigan, G., Bhattacharyya, A., Elliott, J., Gordon, J., & Pitt-Aitkens, T. Sharing the care of the elderly between community and hospital. *Lancet*, 1969, **2**, 1349–1353.

Leighton, D. C. *The character of danger*. New York: Basic Books, 1963.

Lieberman, M. A. Institutionalization of the aged: Effects on behavior. *Journal of Gerontology*, 1969, **24**(3), 330–340.

Liederman, P., Green, R., & Liederman, V. Outpatient group therapy with geriatric patients. *Geriatrics*, 1967, **22**, 148–153.

Linden, M. Group psychotherapy with institutionalized senile women: Study in gerontologic human relations. *International Journal of Group Psychotherapy*, 1953, **3**, 150–170.

Lindsley, O. R. Operant conditioning mentods in diagnosis. In, *Sixth Hahnemann symposium on psychosomatic medicine*. Philadelphia: Lea & Febiger, 1962.

Mackay, H. A. Operant techniques applied to disorders of the senium. Unpublished doctoral dissertation, Queen's University, Ontario, 1965.

Malamud, N. A comparative study of the neuropathologic findings in senile psychoses and "normal" senility. *Journal of the American Geriatric Society*, 1965, **13**, 113–117.

Maslow, A. H. Deficiency motivation and growth motivation. In M. A. Jones (Ed.), *Nebraska symposium on motivation*. Lincoln: University of Nebraska Press, 1951.

Meerloo, J. A. M. Contribution of psychoanalysis to the problem of the aged. In M. Heiman (Ed.), *Psychoanalysis and social work*. New York: International Universities Press, 1953,

National Center for Health Statistics. Comparison of selected characteristics of institutions for the aged: United States, 1963 and 1968. *Monthly Vital Statistics Report*, 1971, **20**(1, Supplement 15).

Neugarten, B., & Moore, J. The changing age-status system. In B. Neugarten (Ed.), *Middle age and aging*. Chicago: University of Chicago Press, 1968.

Pasamanick, B. A survey of mental disease in an urban population. VI. An approach to total prevalence by age. *Mental Hygiene*, 1962, **46**, 567–572.

Perlin, S., & Butler, R. N. Psychiatric aspects of adaptation to the aging experience. In J. ..... Birren (Ed.), *Human aging* (USPHS Publ. No. 986) Washington, D.C.: United States Government Printing Office, 1963.

Rapoport, R. N. *Community as doctor*. Springfield, Ill.: Charles C Thomas, 1960.

Rechtschaffen, A. Psychotherapy with geriatric patients: A review of the literature. *Gerontology*, 1959, **14**, 73–84.

Rechtschaffen, A., Atkinson, S., & Freedman, J. G. An intensive treatment program for state hospital geriatric patients. *Geriatrics*, 1958, **9**, 28–34.

Reichard, S., Livson, F., & Petersen, P. *Aging and personality*. New York: Wiley, 1962.

Rich, T. Ecological psychology and aging. *Gerontologist*, 1968, **8**(2), 116–119, 134.

Riley, M., & Foner, A. (Eds.) *Aging and society*. Vol. 1. *An inventory of research findings*. New York: Russell Sage Foundation, 1968.

Rogers, C. R. *On becoming a person*. Boston: Houghton Mifflin, 1961.

Sainsbury, P. Community psychiatric services and the general practitioner. *Journal of the Royal College of General Practitioners*, 1969, **17**(3), 17–29.

Sainsbury, P., & Grad, J. The burden on the community. In, *The epidemiology of mental illness: A symposium*. London: Oxford University Press, 1962.

Sanders, R., Smith, R. S., & Weinman, B. *Chronic psychoses and recovery*. San Francisco: Jossey-Bass, 1967.

Sanderson, C. A. The week after next. *Gerontologist*, 1971, **11**(2), 1–58.

Schwartz, A., & Proppe, H. Toward person/environment transactional research in aging. *Gerontologist*, 1970, **10**(3), 228–232.

Schwartz, M. S., Schwartz, C., & Field, M. *Social approaches to mental patient care*. New York: Columbia University Press, 1964.

Shanas, E., Townsend, P., Wedderburn, D., Friis, H., Milhoj, P., & Stehouwer, J. *Old people in three industrial societies*. New York: Atherton, 1968.

Simon, A., Lowenthal, M., & Epstein, L. *Crisis and intervention*. San Francisco: Jossey-Bass, 1970.

Sklar, J., & O'Neill, F. J. Experiments with intensive treatment in a geriatric ward. In P. H. Hoch & J. Zubin (Eds.), *Psychotherapy of aging*. New York: Grune & Stratton, 1961.

Stanton, A. H., & Schwartz, M. S. *The mental hospital*. New York: Basic Books, 1954.

Taft, T., & Sweda, G. *Southwest Detroit: Drug abuse treatment and rehabilitation program*. Detroit: City of Detroit Health Department, 1971.

Taulbee, L. R., & Folsom J. C. Reality orientation for geriatric patients. *Hospital & Community Psychiatry*, 1966, May, 22–25.

Tibbetts, C. Some social aspects of gerontology. *Gerontologist*, 1968, **8**(2), 131–133.

Ullman, L. P., & Krasner, L. *A psychological approach to abnormal behavior*. Englewood Cliffs, N.J.: Prentice-Hall, 1969.

Wang, H. S. Organic brain syndromes. In E. Busse & E. Pfeiffer (Eds.), *Behavior and adaptation in late life*. Boston: Little, Brown, 1969.

Weinberg, J. Rehabilitation of geriatric patients. *Illinois Medical Journal*, 1969, **136**, 63–66.

Weintraub, W., & Aranson, H. A survey of patients in classical psychoanalysis: Some vital statistics. *Journal of Nervous and Mental Diseases*, 1968, **146**, 98–102.

Wolff, K. Treatment of the geriatric patient in a mental hospital. *Journal of the American Geriatric Society*, 1956, **14**, 472–476.

Wolff, K. Group psychopathology with geriatric patients in a mental hospital. *Journal of the American Geriatric Society*, 1957, **5**, 13–19. (a)

Wolff, K. Occupational therapy for geriatric patients in a mental hospital: Therapeutic possibilities and limitation. *Journal of the American Geriatric Society*, 1957, **5**, 1019–1024. (b)

Wolff, K. Active therapy replaces custodial care for geriatric patients in mental hospitals. *Geriatrics*, 1958, **13**, 174–175.

Wolff, K. Group psychotherapy with geriatric patients in a state hospital setting: Results of a three-year study. *Group Psychotherapy*, 1959, **12**, 218–222.

Wolpe, J. *The practice of behavior therapy*. New York: Pergamon, 1969.

Patterns of Use of Psychiatric Facilities by the Aged: Past, Present, and Future

MORTON KRAMER, CARL A. TAUBE, and RICHARD W. REDICK

CONTENT GUIDE

Morton Kramer received his ScD in hygiene (biostatistics) from Johns Hopkins University in 1934. He is currently Chief of the Biometry Branch of the National Institute of Mental Health. He formerly served as statistician in the New York State Department of Health, in the Department of Health of Puerto Rico, and in the Office of the Controller of Tuberculosis of Cuyahoga County, Ohio, and as Chief of Research of the Office of International Health Relations of the Public Health Service. He has written extensively in his main field of interest, the application of biostatistical and epidemiological methods to research on the prevention and control of mental disorders.

Carl A. Taube received his BA in sociology from Princeton University. He is currently Chief, Survey and Report Section, Biometry Branch, Office of Program Planning and Evaluation, National Institute of Mental Health.

Richard W. Redick received his PhD in sociology with specialization in demography and ecology from the University of Chicago. He is currently

Trends in Patient Care Episodes 1955–68
  Major trends
  Patterns of use in 1966
  All ages by type of facility
  Sex
  Age
  Age and sex
  Diagnosis

Predictions of future needs for and extent of use of mental health services by the aged
  Number of aged in 1975 and 1980
  Number of persons in need of services
  Selection of rates of need
  Estimated number of persons in need
  Types of services needed
  Extent of use of psychiatric facilities and professional personnel by the aged with psychiatric disorders
  Psychiatric facilities
  Use of psychiatrists
  Use of other physicians and other types of professionals
  Use of short-stay hospitals by the aged

Types and numbers of personnel needed to deliver psychiatric and other services required by the aged

Effects of various programs initiated by state and/or local agencies to modify patterns of use of state hospitals by the aged

Relationship of living arrangements of the aged to patterns of use of psychiatric and other facilities

Impact of major social problems on needs for mental health services
  Crime and violence
  Alcoholism
  Poverty
  Suicide

Supervisory Survey Statistician, Survey and Reports Section, Biometry Branch, Office of Program Planning and Evaluation, National Institute of Mental Health. His major interests currently focus on the study of the patterns and trends in the utilization of psychiatric facilities and projected future needs for psychiatric care facilities, application of demographic techniques to studies of mentally ill populations, and utilization of United States census and vital statistics data to ascertain the possible mental health needs of a community.

Impact of future congressional actions on mental health centers, Medicare, Medicaid, delivery of health services, and national health insurance
  Community mental health centers
  Medicare and Medicaid
  National health insurance legislation

Concluding comments

Presented in this chapter is a discussion of trends in patterns of use of various types of psychiatric facilities by the aged; predictions of future needs of mental health services for the aged; estimates of numbers of psychiatrists, psychologists, psychiatric nurses, and psychiatric social workers needed to care for persons with mental disorders relative to estimates of the available supply of such professionals in 1970, 1975, and 1980; and other areas of concern for planning of mental health, general health, and related services for the aged, such as community care of the aged with disabling conditions, hospitalization of the aged for all diseases and disabling conditions, and living arrangements of the aged.

It is hoped that a consideration of these topics and of the questions they may suggest will help to define more clearly the role of psychology and psychologists not only in the actual delivery of medical, psychiatric, psychological, and related human services required to maintain and to improve the mental, physical, and social well-being of the aged, but also in the many activities on which the delivery of such services depends, such as the following:

1. *Planning* of mental health and related medical, social, welfare, recreational, educational, and other human service programs;

2. *Coordination* of such activities (governmental and nongovernmental) at the community, city, county, state, regional, and national levels;

3. *Delivery* of direct psychologic services to patients in various treatment settings;

4. *Research* on (a) diagnosis, treatment, and rehabilitation of persons with mental disorders and other illnesses; (b) epidemiology of mental disorders and various psychological states; (c) evaluation of programs designed to prevent and control mental disorders and to improve the mental, physical, and social health of the population; and (d) the role of psychologists and the needs for psychological services in health delivery systems;

5. *Recruitment and training* of manpower required to provide the various psychologist services required to improve the health of the nation.

STATE AND COUNTY MENTAL HOSPITALS 1946–66

The trends observed in patterns of use of psychiatric facilities are in large part a reflection of changes that have taken place in society's attitude toward the care and treatment of the mentally ill during the past quarter of a century. To provide some background against which to view these happenings, a brief review will be given of significant events that facilitated and catalyzed the changes.

Historical Background

For a long period of time the state and county mental hospitals were the primary resource for the care and treatment of the mentally ill. In 1946, 42% (586,333 beds) of all hospital beds were located in public and private psychiatric hospitals. About 80% of these mental hospital beds were located in the state and county mental hospitals. At that time there were only 500 outpatient psychiatric clinics and 109 general hospitals providing psychiatric services. In 1969, although beds in public and private psychiatric hospitals still accounted for 31% of all hospital beds and 80% of the mental hospital beds were still in state and county hospitals, there were 1,400 general hospitals routinely admitting psychiatric patients for diagnosis and treatment, and 2,088 outpatient psychiatric clinics were in operation.

The care of the mentally ill in state and county mental hospitals has been documented extensively over the years, and the records of patients admitted to these hospitals have been a primary source of statistical data on mental disorders. Statistics derived from these records have provided a first approximation to a descriptive epidemiology of the mental disorders. Studies of first admission rates to public hospitals by age, sex, migration factors, marital status, and other socioeconomic variables have demonstrated the high toll mental disorders take in every age group, in the lower socioeconomic groups, in nonwhites versus whites, in the highly urbanized versus the more rural areas, in migrant versus nonmigrant population groups, and in the never married, separated, divorced, and widowed versus the married groups.[1] Other studies provided extensive documentation of the age, sex, marital status, length of stay, and diagnostic characteristics of the populations resident in these institutions and of the manner in which an increasing number of patients accumulated in these hospitals (Kramer, 1967; United States Department of Health, Education, and Welfare, 1964a). Despite the fact that the proportion of first admissions being returned to their communities during the first 12 months following hospitalization increased from 50% in 1946 to about 63% in 1955, the chances of return to the community for those patients not released in the first year diminished rapidly with increasing length of hospitalization (Kramer, Goldstein, Israel, & Johnson, 1955; Pollack, Person, Kramer, & Goldstein, 1959).

These patients became the hard-core chronic population and grew old in the hospital. The accumulation of these patients, particularly the schizophrenics, was due not only to the severity of their illness, but also to such factors as lack of adequate treatment and rehabilitation programs, insufficient staff, depersonalizing problems related to organizational structure and size of hospital, insufficient community resources to bridge the gap between hospital and community, and decreased interest in patients on the part of relatives, friends, and the community at large.

The problems of providing medical and psychiatric care to the large numbers of aged with diseases of the senium (brain syndromes associated with the senile brain disease and cerebral arteriosclerosis) also had their impact on the public mental hospitals as evidenced by studies highlighting the increased rates of admission of patients 65 years of age and over (Kramer et al., 1961; Locke et al., 1960; Pollack et al., 1961).

Although their stay was relatively short, largely because of high mortality rates resulting from their generally poor physical condition at time of admission, the large number of admissions of aged patients contributed substantially to the growth of the public hospital population (Kramer et al., 1955; Pollack et al., 1959).

---

[1]A partial listing of studies of demographic and socioeconomic characteristics of first admissions to public mental hospitals follows: American Psychopathological Association (1945); Dayton (1940); Faris and Dunham (1939); Fowler, Greenberg, McCaffrey, and Rogott (1955); Group for the Advancement of Psychiatry (1961); Jaco (1960); Kramer, Pollack and Redick (1961); Locke, Kramer, and Pasamanick (1960); McCaffrey (1955); Malzberg (1955, 1958); Malzberg and Lee (1956); Pollack, Locke, and Kramer (1961); Pollock (1941); Pugh and MacMahon (1962).

Another factor that contributed to the increase in number of long-term patients was the reduction in mortality in the patient population that occurred as the result of programs that provided better health care for patients and improved their living conditions within the hospital setting (Kramer, Taube, & Starr, 1968). The application of effective techniques from public health practice resulted in better levels of environmental sanitation, control of tuberculosis and other infectious diseases, and improved nutritional standards. The application of advances in clinical medicine, such as the use of sulfonamides and antibiotics, resulted in more effective treatment for pneumonia and other infections. All of these efforts resulted in a considerable saving of lives and led to an aging phenomenon among hospital patients similar to that occurring for persons in the general population.

The increasing size of the mental hospital population was a matter of much concern to public health officials, hospital administrators, other professionals, lawmakers, and the laity which precipitated considerable action dedicated to changing the situation.

During the 10-year period following the passage of the National Mental Health Act in 1946 (Public Law 79-487) many innovations were introduced to provide more effective and adequate psychiatric services to the nation and additional facilities required to meet the rapidly increasing need and demand for such services. Increasing numbers of outpatient clinics were opened (Bahn, 1961). Psychiatric services were established in general hospitals at an accelerated rate. Additional nursing homes were opened and served to take some of the pressure off of the mental hospitals for beds for the aged. Many new approaches to the treatment and rehabilitation of the mentally ill appeared: intensive treatment for the acutely ill, total push for the chronically hospitalized, group psychotherapy, the open hospital, and various programs for counteracting the dehumanizing effect of long-term institutionalization in the impersonal environment of the large state institutions. The introduction of tranquilizers in the early 1950s was the event of signal importance that foreshadowed the development of further possibilities for improved treatment of the mentally ill. The fact that these drugs controlled agitated and excited behavior provided increased opportunities for using additional treatment and rehabilitation procedures for returning many hospitalized patients to the community, for developing community programs to prevent hospitalization, as well as for treating and maintaining the mentally ill in communities. Such prospects engendered favorable changes in attitudes of staff, patients, their families, and community toward one another.

Changes in the Total Resident Patient Population

During the period 1946–54, the numbers of patients in the state and county mental hospitals increased at an average annual rate of 2.1% (see Figure 1). Despite changed attitudes toward the treatment of the mentally ill, which resulted in more and more patients being returned to the community, the rates of net release were still not sufficiently high to counterbalance an increasing number of admissions. Consequently, the mental hospital population continued to grow. A major turning point occurred between 1955 and 1956 when the first drop occurred in this patient population. This was the year that the use of tranquilizers had become widespread in these hospitals. The decrease in inpatient population has continued over the years at an increasing rate, so that by the end of 1970 the resident population was 338,592 or 40% less than its peak of 558,922 in 1955.

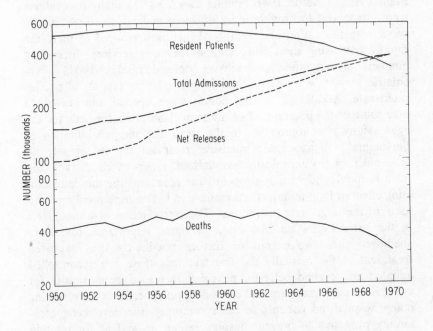

Fig. 1. Number of resident patients, total admissions, net releases, and deaths, in state and county mental hospitals, United States, 1950–70.

Since changes in number of resident patients during a year are determined by the annual additions to and subtractions from the patients in residence at the beginning of the year, the total resident patient count is affected by any community or intrahospital program that increases or decreases (a) the number of additions, (b) placements on leave, (c) returns from leave, and (d) deaths (Kramer, 1969). Indeed, the major changes to be noted below have been due to the success or failure of programs designed to modify any of these components of patient movement within various age and diagnostic groups.

Changes Specific for Age and Diagnosis

Table 1 shows the numbers of resident patients in state and county mental hospitals and the corresponding resident patient rates for 1955 and 1968 specific for age and broad diagnostic groups, and Table 2 shows the corresponding percentage of changes between 1955 and 1968. Striking decreases have occurred in each of the 25 and over age groups, while equally striking increases have occurred in the under 25 age groups. The percentage of decreases varied widely, being largest in the 35–44 age group (45%) and smallest in the 75 and over age group (18%). The percentage of increase also varied widely from 176% in the under 15 age group to 47% in the 15–24 age group.

The changes in the resident population also varied by diagnosis. Among the schizophrenic patients there was an overall decrease of 27%. Decreases occurred in five age groups ranging from a high of 50% in the 35–44 age group to 12% in the 65–74 age group. Three age groups—under 15, 15–24, and 75 and over—had increases of 374, 34, and 14%, respectively. Marked decreases also occurred among patients with mental disorders of the senium in each of the 55 and over age groups: 55–64, 43%; 65–74, 39%; and 75 and over, 27.5%. For all other diagnoses, decreases occurred in each of the 25 and over age groups, ranging from 43% for patients 45–54 to 19% for those 75 and over. Marked increases occurred in the age groups under 15 (138%) and 15–24 (58%).

Tables 1 and 2 also show changes in the resident patient rates; that is, the number of residents in the state and county mental hospitals, at the end of the year per 100,000 of the general population. Relative changes in resident patient rates are a function not only of the relative changes in the number of resident patients (i.e.,

TABLE 1

Number of Resident Patients and Resident Patient Rates, State and County Mental Hospitals, United States, 1955 and 1968

Age in years	All mental disorders		Schizophrenia		Senium		All other mental disorders	
	1955	1968	1955	1968	1955	1968	1955	1968
	Number							
All ages	558,922	399,152	267,995	194,922	73,772	49,158	217,155	155,072
under 15	2,301	6,365	374	1,774	—	—	1,927	4,591
15-24	17,276	25,315	8,156	10,887	—	—	9,120	14,428
25-34	57,634	36,546	36,819	21,531	—	—	20,815	15,015
35-44	96,304	52,623	63,269	31,314	—	—	33,035	21,309
45-54	117,500	71,166	65,895	41,815	—	—	51,605	29,351
55-64	109,622	86,997	50,302	46,689	8,672	4,924	50,648	35,384
65+	158,285	120,140	43,180	40,912	65,100	44,234	50,005	34,994
65-74	92,223	66,177	31,396	27,450	24,842	15,067	35,985	23,660
75+	66,062	53,963	11,784	13,462	40,258	29,167	14,020	11,334
	Rate per 100,000 population							
All ages	344.4	202.0	165.1	98.7	45.5	24.9	133.8	78.4
under 15	4.7	10.7	.8	3.0	—	—	3.9	7.7
15-24	86.1	79.9	40.7	34.3	—	—	45.4	45.6
25-34	246.0	157.8	157.1	92.9	—	—	88.9	64.9
35-44	427.2	226.4	280.6	134.7	—	—	146.6	91.7
45-54	622.8	312.2	349.3	183.5	—	—	273.5	128.7
55-64	753.7	486.7	345.8	261.2	59.6	27.5	348.3	198.0
65+	1,125.1	627.9	306.9	213.9	462.7	231.2	355.4	182.9
65-74	979.4	561.5	333.4	232.9	263.8	127.8	382.2	200.7
75+	1,419.8	734.9	253.3	183.3	865.2	397.2	301.3	154.4

TABLE 2

Percentage Change in Number of Resident Patients and Resident Patient Rates,
State and County Mental Hospitals, United States, 1955-68

Age in years	Diagnostic group			
	All mental disorders	Schizophrenia	Senium	All other mental disorders
Percentage change in number				
All ages	− 28.6	− 27.3	−33.4	− 28.6
under 15	176.6	374.3	−	138.2
15-24	46.5	33.5	−	58.2
25-34	− 36.6	− 41.5	−	− 27.9
35-44	− 45.4	− 50.5	−	− 35.5
45-54	− 39.4	− 36.5	−	− 43.1
55-64	− 20.6	− 7.2	−43.2	− 30.1
65+	− 24.1	− 5.3	−32.1	− 30.0
65-74	− 28.2	− 12.6	−39.3	− 34.3
75+	− 18.3	14.2	−27.5	− 19.2
Percentage change in rates per 100,000 population				
All ages	− 41.3	− 40.2	−45.3	− 41.4
under 15	127.7	275.0	−	97.4
15-24	− 7.2	− 15.7	−	.0
25-34	− 35.9	− 40.9	−	− 27.0
35-44	− 47.0	− 52.0	−	− 37.4
45-54	− 49.9	− 47.5	−	− 52.9
55-64	− 35.4	− 24.5	−53.1	− 43.2
65+	− 44.2	− 30.3	−50.0	− 48.5
65-74	− 42.7	− 30.2	−51.6	− 47.5
75+	− 48.2	− 27.6	−54.1	− 48.8

the numerator of the rate) but also the relative changes in the general population (denominator of the rate).[2]

The decrease in number of patients in state and county mental hospitals in the 65 and over age group—particularly those with

---

[2]When the percentage of change between two points in time in the number of resident patients is equal to that of the general population in the same age group during the same time interval, the ratio of the rates is unity. However, when the relative increases in the numerator and denominator are not equal, the ratios of the number of patients can differ considerably from that of the rates, depending on the magnitudes and directions of the respective changes.

TABLE 3

Number of First Admissions (Admissions with No Prior Inpatient Care) and First Admission Rates per 100,000 Population and Percentage Change in Numbers and Rates, State and County Mental Hospitals, 1962, 1965, 1969

Age at admission and sex	Number of first admissions			Rate per 100,000 population			Percentage change in numbers		Percentage change in rates	
	1962	1965	1969	1962	1965	1969	1962-65	1965-69	1962-65	1965-69
Both sexes, all ages	129,698	144,090	163,983	70.6	75.1	82.1	11.1	13.8	6.4	9.3
Under 15	3,460	4,510	6,553	6.0	7.5	11.0	30.3	45.3	25.0	46.7
15-24	19,473	25,878	37,501	76.9	88.6	114.4	32.9	44.9	15.2	29.1
25-34	22,761	25,625	26,614	105.1	118.5	111.4	12.6	3.9	12.7	- 6.0
34-44	23,146	25,669	30,779	96.0	106.6	134.3	10.9	19.9	11.0	26.0
45-54	19,243	21,205	24,676	91.2	96.6	106.8	10.2	16.4	5.9	10.6
55-64	13,280	14,597	18,264	82.4	86.1	100.3	9.9	25.1	4.5	16.5
65+	28,335	26,606	19,591	163.7	146.5	100.6	- 6.1	-26.4	-10.5	-31.3
Males, all ages	72,663	82,536	98,885	81.4	88.5	102.7	13.6	19.8	8.7	16.0
Under 15	2,339	2,971	4,036	7.9	9.7	13.4	27.0	35.8	22.8	38.1
15-24	11,330	15,352	22,548	94.4	109.3	145.5	35.5	46.9	15.8	33.1
25-34	12,301	14,361	16,389	119.1	138.7	142.7	16.7	14.1	16.5	2.9
35-44	12,938	14,774	17,292	111.6	127.3	156.6	14.2	17.0	14.1	23.0
45-54	11,442	12,771	16,805	111.0	119.3	151.2	11.6	31.6	7.5	26.7
55-64	7,731	8,749	10,229	99.5	107.7	118.6	13.2	16.9	8.2	10.1
65+	14,582	13,618	11,582	188.8	171.7	139.6	- 6.6	-15.0	- 9.1	-18.7
Females, all ages	57,035	61,554	65,099	60.4	62.4	63.0	7.9	5.8	3.3	1.0
Under 15	1,121	1,539	2,517	3.9	5.2	8.7	37.3	63.5	33.3	67.3
15-24	8,143	10,526	14,953	61.2	69.4	86.5	29.3	42.1	13.4	24.6
25-34	10,460	11,264	10,225	92.3	100.0	82.4	7.7	- 9.2	8.3	-17.4
35-44	10,208	10,895	13,487	81.5	87.4	113.5	6.7	23.8	7.2	29.9
45-54	7,801	8,494	7,871	72.2	75.2	65.7	8.9	- 7.3	4.2	-12.6
55-64	5,549	5,848	8,035	66.5	66.2	83.8	5.4	37.4	- .5	26.6
65+	13,753	12,988	8,009	143.5	127.0	71.7	- 5.6	-38.3	-11.5	-43.5

mental disorders of the senium—has, for the most part, been the result of sharp reductions in first admissions for patients 65 years and over (Table 3). Many state hospital systems adopted policies that resulted in these reductions which, in turn, led to increased use of nursing homes and related facilities for aged patients. Consequently, between 1962 and 1965, the first admission rate for the 65 and over age group dropped by 9% for males, 12% for females, and 11% for both sexes combined. Between 1965 and 1969, the corresponding decreases were 19% for males, 43% for females, and 31% for both sexes combined.

The total percentage change in resident patients that occurred between 1955 and 1968 masked the striking changes observed in the average annual rates of change during this period. In Table 4, which shows the annual rates of change for two 7-year periods, 1955–61 and 1962–68, the rate of decrease was more rapid during the later than the earlier period. For example, the annual relative rate of decrease in number of patients for all ages and all diagnoses was 1.87% during 1955–61, but 4.15% during 1962–68, and, for patients 65 and over, the corresponding decreases were .06 and 3.83%.

Differences in the annual relative rates of change by diagnostic group were as follows:

	1955–61	1962–68
Schizophrenics	− .01	−4.74
Senium	−1.00	−4.66
All others	−1.92	−3.20

Striking changes occurred among schizophrenics 15–24, 55–64, and 65 years and over wherein the trends in the annual relative rates of changes between the two time periods were reversed from an increasing to a decreasing trend.

Thus, even though both numerator and denominator increase, the relative increase in the denominator can be great enough to produce a decrease in the rate. To illustrate with data presented in Table A, Appendix D, in the 15–24 age group, the number of patients *increased* by 46.5% and the general population *increased* by 58.1%. Thus, the rate *decreased* by 7.2%. Also the increase in rates can be much less marked than the increase in numbers. Thus, in the under 15 age group, the number of patients *increased* by 177%, while the general population *increased* by only 22%. Thus, the rates *increased* by 127%. Similarly, the rates can decrease more rapidly than the number of patients. This results when the general population group is *increasing* while the number of patients is *decreasing*. This explains why the number of resi-

TABLE 4

Average Annual Relative Rates of Change in the Year End Resident Populations of State and County Mental Hospitals for All Diagnoses and Selected Diagnostic Groups, Both Sexes: For the Periods 1955-68; 1955-61; 1962-68

Ages and years	All diagnoses	Schizophrenia	Senium	All other
All ages				
1955-68	− 1.16	− 1.11	−1.58	− 1.08
1955-61	− .87	− .01	−1.00	− 1.92
1962-68	− 4.15	− 4.74	−4.66	− 3.20
<15				
1955-68	3.86	5.27	−	3.46
1955-61	13.24	24.79	−	10.04
1962-68	5.36	3.27	−	6.23
15-24				
1955-68	1.99	1.65	−	2.28
1955-61	5.27	6.57	−	4.07
1962-68	1.15	− 1.19	−	3.21
25-34				
1955-68	− 1.49	− 1.83	−	− .94
1955-61	− 2.88	− 2.82	−	− 2.98
1962-68	− 3.58	− 4.64	−	− 1.92
35-44				
1955-68	− 2.06	− 2.46	−	− 1.37
1955-61	− 3.51	− 3.80	−	− 2.95
1962-68	− 5.72	− 6.97	−	− 3.66
45-54				
1955-68	− 1.81	− 1.69	−	− 1.97
1955-61	− 1.44	.02	−	− 3.47
1962-68	− 6.08	− 6.90	−	− 4.83
55-64				
1955-68	− .76	− .21	−2.07	− 1.20
1955-61	.13	2.01	−3.42	− 1.30
1962-68	− 3.92	− 3.36	−4.59	− 4.54
65+				
1955-68	− 1.06	− .26	−1.52	− 1.26
1955-61	− .06	2.66	− .69	− 1.82
1962-68	− 3.83	− 3.04	−4.67	− 3.62
65-74				
1955-68	−	−	−2.00	−
1955-61	−	−	−1.84	−
1962-68	−	−	−5.19	−
75+				
1955-68	−	−	−1.25	−
1955-61	−	−	− .02	−
1962-68	−	−	−4.40	−

UTILIZATION OF OTHER FACILITIES 1955–68

Although the period 1955–68 was one of marked decline in the resident population of state mental hospitals, it was, as already indicated, one of marked increase in the establishment and use of a variety of community-based facilities, such as outpatient clinics, day care facilities, community mental health centers, halfway houses, and psychiatric services in general hospitals. In addition, nursing homes appeared in increasing numbers. Indeed, the downward trend in the resident mental hospital population is related closely to the upward trend in the availability and use of these other facilities. For example, the outpatient clinic or general hospital service served as alternatives for treatment which either prevented, or at least, delayed the admission of certain types of patients to mental hospitals; outpatient clinics also provided a resource for follow-up care, and thus facilitated the earlier discharge of some types of patients from the mental hospital; and nursing homes not only provided facilities for the care of the aged mentally ill, thus precluding admission to a mental hospital, but also provided a place to which many aged long-term mental hospital patients whose needs were primarily custodial could be transferred.

The above changes were encouraged and catalyzed by several major developments in legislation and insurance coverage that affected the delivery and patterns of use of psychiatric services during the years 1955–68. For example, community mental health centers were established by an Act of Congress in 1963. In addition, many private insurance carriers expanded their coverage to include payment for mental health services so that increased numbers of persons could afford such care. This accelerated the growth of psychiatric services in general hospitals and increased the numbers of admissions for these services (Giesler, Hurley, & Person, 1966). The Social Security Amendments of 1965 also provided insurance benefits for the care of the aged mentally ill (Public Law 89–97, 1965). The

---

dent patients for persons 65 years and over decreased by 24% while the rate decreased by 44%. The general population for persons 65 years and over increased by 36% during this time interval. The extraordinary rate of increase in the number of patients in the under 15 age group (176%) is due only in part to the increase in the number of children in this age group in the general population. It is also a result of an increasing demand for services for seriously emotionally disturbed children and adolescents and inadequate and insufficient services for them in other community resources.

benefits under Section A of Title XVIII encourage the use of general hospitals, extended care facilities, and services provided by home health agencies.

The supplementary medical insurance benefits of Section B provide additional coverage for outpatient psychiatric services and for home health services. These benefits undoubtedly increased the number of aged mentally ill admitted to general hospitals and to nursing homes. Title XIX also provides grants to states for medical assistance for aged persons in mental institutions. To participate, a state must meet certain standards and provide evidence that it is making satisfactory progress toward developing and implementing a comprehensive mental health program.

Against this background, some of the major trends in the use of the facilities mentioned above will now be discussed.

Outpatient Clinics

The period 1946–68 was one of rapid growth of outpatient psychiatric clinics. The number of clinics increased from 500 in 1946 to 1,985 in 1968. However, these facilities have been heavily weighted with children under 18 years who account for about 33% of the patient load and adults in the 18–44 age groups who account for another 51% (Table 5). Patients 45–54 years account for 10%; 55–64, 4%; and 65 years and over, only 2%. Table 5 indicates that although the number of terminations in the 65 and over age group has increased during the 5-year interval 1963–68 from 10,000 to 17,000, they accounted for only 2% of the total terminations. Also the age-specific termination rate for this age group was only 89 per 100,000 in 1968 as compared to a resident patient rate of 627 per 100,000 and first admission rate of 155 per 100,000 for state and county mental hospitals.

Day Care Services

Day care services likewise seem to be playing a relatively minor role in the care of aged patients. These services have been slow to catch on not only for the elderly but for all ages. Despite a 300% increase in the number of partial hospitalization programs between 1963 and 1967, less than 1% of the total admissions to all mental health facilities in 1967 occurred in these programs (National Institute of Mental Health, 1969). Between 1967 and 1969, the number

TABLE 5

Estimated Number, Rate per 100,000 Population, and Percentage of Distribution
of Terminations by Age, Outpatient Psychiatric Services,
United States, 1963-68

Year	Age at admission							
	All ages	Under 18	18-24	25-34	35-44	45-54	55-64	65 and over
Number of terminations[a]								
1963	446,601	159,648	56,166	82,441	77,863	42,191	17,896	10,396
1964	516,388	177,483	70,714	95,219	88,501	50,632	21,968	11,871
1965	536,845	205,374	72,537	92,817	84,389	48,785	21,607	11,336
1966	612,562	242,102	83,529	103,315	91,572	54,406	24,949	12,689
1967	703,054	255,452	101,532	125,339	107,789	67,194	30,771	14,977
1968	815,169	268,445	131,759	155,334	125,742	80,191	36,683	17,015
Rate per 100,000 population								
1963	241.1	234.4	342.5	381.6	322.0	198.6	110.1	59.6
1964	274.6	255.3	416.7	441.7	365.6	235.2	132.9	67.0
1965	281.6	292.1	403.5	430.0	349.7	223.7	128.5	63.0
1966	317.6	343.4	436.5	475.4	380.4	246.5	146.2	69.5
1967	361.0	361.4	512.0	567.0	458.0	306.2	167.1	82.1
1968	412.6	379.2	640.1	670.6	541.1	351.8	205.2	89.0
Percentage of distribution								
1963	100.0	35.8	12.6	18.5	17.4	9.4	4.0	2.3
1964	100.0	34.4	13.7	18.4	17.1	9.8	4.3	2.3
1965	100.0	38.3	13.5	17.3	15.7	9.1	4.0	2.1
1966	100.0	39.5	13.6	16.9	14.9	8.9	4.1	2.1
1967	100.0	36.3	14.5	17.8	15.3	9.6	4.4	2.1
1968	100.0	32.9	16.2	19.1	15.4	9.8	4.5	2.1

[a]Includes Veterans Administration clinics, but excludes those in Puerto Rico
and the Virgin Islands.

of day care programs increased in number from 500 to 757, an
increase of almost 50%. There was a corresponding increase in the
estimated number of admissions from 27,000 to 50,400, an increase
of almost 100%. Most of this increase, however, is accounted for by
federally funded community mental health centers which began
operation during this interval. Of the estimated 11,000 admissions
to day care programs in community mental health centers during
1969, only 2.6% or only 260 persons were 65 years or older (Na-

tional Institute of Mental Health, unpublished data). Day care programs of other facilities are probably not serving a much more significant proportion of the aged.

Community Mental Health Centers

The community mental health centers were established by an Act of Congress in 1963 (Public Law 88-164, 1963) as the basis of an intensified national effort to improve the delivery of mental health services to all members of the population regardless of race, creed, color, residence, and economic status.[3] This program has as its objective the establishment of a network of community mental health centers throughout the nation. These centers will provide a comprehensive program of mental health services at the local catchment area level by initiating services not already available and integrating and coordinating them with existing services. The purpose of such services is to maintain patients close to their own environment and to protect their links with family and community. Each center must provide five essential elements of service to residents of a catchment area which may vary in size from 75,000 to 200,000 population: (a) 24-hour inpatient services; (b) outpatient services; (c) partial hospitalization services such as day care, night care, weekend care; (d) emergency services 24 hours per day; and (e) consultation and education services available to community agencies and professional personnel. To reach the goal of fully comprehensive services, four additional services are needed: (f) rehabilitative, including vocational and educational programs; (g) training; (h) research and evaluation; and (i) central administrative services.

Since community mental health centers have been in operation a relatively short time, only limited data are available on character-

---

[3]The Community Mental Health Centers Act of 1963 (Public Law 88-164, 1963) authorized funds for constructing comprehensive community mental health centers throughout the nation. The 1965 Amendments to the Act (Public Law 89-97, 1965) authorized funds to assist in the initial cost of staffing these new centers. Subsequent amendments in 1968 (Public Law 90-574) and 1970 (Public Law 91-211) authorized special grant programs for construction and staffing of alcoholic and narcotic addiction treatment and rehabilitation facilities, and also specialized grants for children's services and consultation services. These amendments also provided authority for the awarding of Initation and Development grants and authorized higher preferential rates of support for poverty designated areas.

istics of patients using these centers. As of the end of June 1971, 450 centers were funded of which 274 were in operation. In 1969, persons 65 years and over accounted for only 10,000, or 4% of the 250,000 admissions to these services (National Institute of Mental Health, unpublished data). Because of difficulties in determining the extent of future federal support for constructing and staffing these centers, it is not possible to make an adequate prediction of the extent of their future role in providing direct mental health services to the aged. If these centers are to play a major role in providing such services, considerable effort will be needed to define what this role shall be and how centers should relate to other psychiatric facilities, nursing homes, and other social and welfare services that are so essential in providing mental health and related services to the aged.

Halfway Houses

Data on trends in services provided by halfway houses are not available, however, in 1969 there were 13,322 halfway house beds in the United States (Cannon, 1971).

The need for growth in such services is obvious. Current resources of this type meet at most one- to two-fifths of the potential demand. To illustrate, consider the population of persons discharged or placed on leave annually from state and county mental hospitals (492,000 persons) and assume that halfway houses would be appropriate for one-fourth of these persons. Then 38,000 halfway house beds or two and one-half times the number currently available would be needed. Table 6 illustrates the variation by region in the number of halfway house beds per 1,000 discontinuations from state and county mental hospitals. For the United States as a whole, the ratio was 27 per 1,000 varying from a low of 13 per 1,000 in the East South Central states to 80 per 1,000 in the Mountain states.

Psychiatric Services in General Hospitals

The National Institute of Mental Health has annually gathered data on characteristics of patients discharged from psychiatric services of general hospitals by sex and diagnosis. However, the universe of respondents was quite incomplete until about 1968 when improved reporting techniques produced satisfactory age, sex, and diagnosis data. About 13% of the 486,000 discharges from these services

TABLE 6

Number of Halfway House Beds and Beds per 1,000 Discontinuations
from State and County Mental Hospitals by Geographic Region,
United States, 1969

Geographic division	Total halfway house beds	Discontinuations[a] from state and county mental hospitals	Halfway house beds per 1,000 discontinuations
United States	13,322	491,952	27
New England	1,078	48,661	22
Middle Atlantic	1,363	75,535	18
South Atlantic	2,461	82,182	30
East North Central	2,034	97,455	21
East South Central	381	30,076	13
West North Central	955	42,210	23
West South Central	1,155	42,888	27
Mountain	1,035	12,868	80
Pacific	2,860	60,077	48

Note. The source for these data was Cannon (1971).

[a]Includes all persons who were discharged, placed on extended leave, escaped, or otherwise discontinued receiving inpatient service during the year.

consisted of patients 65 years and older, representing a discharge rate of 334 per 100,000 population 65 years and over. Trend data are not available on a national basis to demonstrate the impact of Medicare in the use of general hospitals by the aged mentally ill. However, a special study carried out by the Social Security Administration has shown that since the passage of Medicare, general hospitals are being used more extensively by such patients (Social Security Administration, 1969). This study, carried out in 327 general hospitals, indicated a 29% increase in the number of discharges 65 years and over with a primary diagnosis of mental disorder between January 1965 to June 1966 and July 1966 to December 1967; that is, between periods which were of 18-months duration before and after the start of Medicare (Table 7).

In addition to the increase in the number of admissions, it was also noted that total days of care increased 49% and average length of stay per discharge increased from 16.2 to 18.7 days, or 15%, for aged psychiatric patients between these two periods. Additional data showed that the average stay and the change in this average varied considerably by diagnosis and by whether or not the hospital had a separate psychiatric unit (Table 8).

TABLE 7

**Psychiatric Discharges: Comparison of Utilization in PAS Hospitals
18 months Before and After Initiation of Medicare by Age**

Age	January 1965-June 1966	July 1966-December 1967	Percentage of change
Discharges			
Total[a]	85,259	88,606	3.9
Under 65	76,795	77,706	1.2
Under 15	2,849	2,710	−4.9
15-44	46,048	47,131	2.4
45-64	27,898	27,865	−.1
65 and over	8,457	10,897	28.9
65-74	5,632	7,001	24.3
75 and over	2,825	3,896	37.9
Days of care			
Total[a]	1,015,123	1,125,022	10.8
Under 65	878,158	920,973	4.9
Under 15	21,580	22,031	2.1
15-44	516,220	544,306	5.4
45-64	340,358	354,636	4.2
65 and over	136,921	204,019	49.0
65-74	83,263	129,391	55.4
75 and over	53,658	74,628	39.1
Average length of stay (in days)			
Total[a]	11.9	12.7	6.7
Under 65	11.4	11.9	4.4
Under 15	7.6	8.1	6.6
15-44	11.2	11.5	2.7
45-64	12.2	12.7	4.1
65 and over	16.2	18.7	15.4
65-74	14.8	18.5	24.3
75 and over	19.0	19.2	1.1

Note. The source for these data was the Social Security Administration (1969). PAS hospitals are those hospitals participating in the Professional Activity Study of the Commission on Professional and Hospital Activities.
[a]Includes data for persons whose ages are not recorded

TABLE 8

Psychiatric Discharges Aged 65 and Over: Comparison of Utilization in PAS Hospitals 18 months Before and After Initiation of Medicare by Diagnosis and Presence of Psychiatric Unit in Hospital

Primary discharge diagnosis	International classification of diseases code	Discharges			Days of care			Average length of stay (in days)		
		January 1965-June 1966	July 1966-December 1967	Percentage change	January 1965-June 1966	July 1966-December 1967	Percentage change	January 1965-June 1966	July 1966-December 1967	Percentage change
All hospitals										
Total[a]	300-329	8,457	10,897	28.9	136,921	204,019	49.0	16.2	18.7	15.4
Acute brain disorders	300-307	693	795	14.7	8,378	10,060	20.1	12.1	12.7	5.0
Chronic brain disorders	308-317	2,691	3,767	40.0	55,994	88,053	57.3	20.8	23.4	12.5
Psychotic disorders	318-322	1,041	1,402	34.7	21,036	31,668	50.5	20.2	22.6	11.9
Psychophysiologic autonomic and visceral disorders	323	357	395	10.6	2,757	3,291	19.4	7.7	8.3	7.8
Psychoneurotic disorders	324	3,163	3,968	25.4	43,358	64,040	47.7	13.7	16.1	17.5
Personality disorders	325-328	503	554	10.1	5,145	6,677	29.8	10.2	12.1	18.6
Mental deficiency	329	9	16	77.8	253	230	−9.1	28.1	14.4	−48.8
Hospitals with psychiatric units										
Total[a]	300-329	4,922	6,207	26.1	83,552	120,359	44.1	17.0	19.4	14.1
Acute brain disorders	300-307	339	363	7.1	4,362	5,087	16.6	12.9	14.0	8.5
Chronic brain disorders	308-317	1,466	1,912	30.4	25,542	36,710	43.7	17.4	19.2	10.3
Psychotic disorders	318-322	823	1,102	33.9	18,017	26,547	47.3	21.9	24.1	10.0

TABLE 8

Psychiatric Discharges Aged 65 and Over: Comparison of Utilization in PAS Hospitals 18 months Before and After Initiation of Medicare by Diagnosis and Presence of Psychiatric Unit in Hospital (Continued)

Primary discharge diagnosis	International classification of diseases code	Discharges			Days of care			Average length of stay (in days)		
		January 1965-June 1966	July 1966-December 1967	Percentage change	January 1965-June 1966	July 1966-December 1967	Percentage change	January 1965-June 1966	July 1966-December 1967	Percentage change
Psychophysiologic autonomic and visceral disorders	323	144	146	1.4	1,297	1,302	.4	9.0	8.9	− 1.1
Psychoneurotic disorders	324	1,926	2,435	26.4	31,973	47,396	48.2	16.6	19.5	17.5
Personality disorders	325-328	222	244	9.9	2,329	3,259	39.9	10.5	13.4	27.6
Mental deficiency	329	2	5	150.0	32	58	81.2	16.0	11.6	−27.5
Hospitals without psychiatric units										
Total[a]	300-329	3,535	4,690	32.7	53,369	83,660	56.8	15.1	17.8	17.9
Acute brain disorders	300-307	354	432	22.0	4,016	4,973	23.8	11.3	11.5	1.8
Chronic brain disorders	308-317	1,225	1,855	51.4	30,452	51,343	68.6	24.9	27.7	11.2
Psychotic disorders	318-322	218	300	37.6	3,019	5,121	69.6	13.8	17.1	23.9
Psychophysiologic autonomic and visceral disorders	323	213	249	16.9	1,460	1,989	36.2	6.9	8.0	15.9
Psychoneurotic disorders	324	1,237	1,533	23.9	11,385	16,644	46.2	9.2	10.9	18.5
Personality disorders	325-328	281	310	10.3	2,816	3,418	21.4	10.0	11.0	10.0
Mental deficiency	329	7	11	57.1	221	172	−22.2	31.6	15.6	−50.6

Note. The source for these data was the Social Security Administration (1969). PAS hospitals are those hospitals participating in the Professional Activity Study of the Commission on Professional and Hospital Activities.

[a] Discharges with a primary diagnosis of mental, psychoneurotic, and personality disorders.

Nursing Homes

Nursing homes have experienced a phenomenally rapid growth since 1939. In that year, the first national count of such facilities by the United States Bureau of the Census indicated that there were about 1,200 homes with approximately 25,000 beds. In 1967 the number of homes had increased to about 19,000—almost a twenty-fold increase—and the number of beds had increased to 836,000— over 30 times the number available in 1939. Much of the recent increase is due in part to the impact of Medicare and Medicaid. Between 1963 and 1967 the number of beds increased by almost 50% (National Center for Health Statistics, 1969).

In the middle 1950s, state hospital administrators recognized that many of the aged patients in their hospitals could be equally well cared for in alternate care facilities, and began systematically to place selected patients in nursing care homes and other related facilities. The intensity of this effort varied among the states due to such reasons as the uneven distribution of alternate facilities. For example, an unpublished survey of the resident patient population of the Texas State Mental hospitals in 1963 indicated that for 65% of the residents 65 years and over the most appropriate placement would have been a nursing care home, had they been available. A similar unpublished study in St. Elizabeths Hospital in 1961 also indicated that the most appropriate placement for 25% of its elderly patients would be a nursing care home; for another 13%, a chronic disease hopsital; and for an additional 15%, a foster care home.

By 1963, nursing homes had become a resource for the care of the aged mentally. ill second only to the state mental hospital. In mid-1963, about 292,000 persons with mental disorders were resident in either long-stay psychiatric inpatient facilities or in nursing homes, geriatric hospitals, homes for the aged, and related facilities in the United States. This represents a rate of 1,662 per 100,000 population 65 years old and older. Fifty-one percent of these patients were in state and county mental hospitals and 43% were in nursing homes and related facilities. An additional 5% were in Veterans Administration hospitals and 1% were in private mental hospitals (Kramer et al., 1968).

The number of mentally ill aged in nursing homes given above is probably a minimum estimate, since these data are based upon an interview survey (National Center for Health Statistics, 1967) in which diagnostic information was obtained from professional nurses rather than from an examination of the patient by a psychiatrist.

Table 9 summarizes the conditions reported in this study and illustrates the problems associated with collecting diagnostic data in institutions that generally do not have licensed physicians or psychiatrists on their regular staff. As of 1963, a total of about 404,194

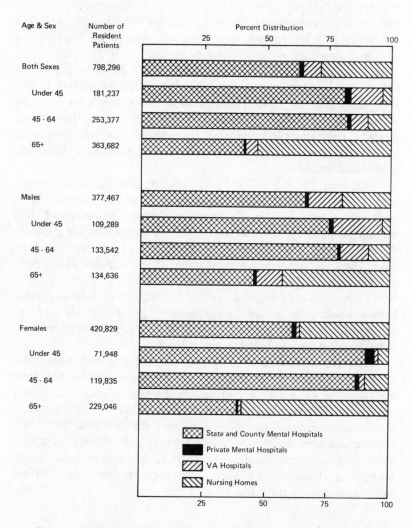

Fig. 2. Percentage distribution of patients with mental disorders resident in selected long-term institutions by age and sex, United States, 1963. (The sources for these data were the National Center for Health Statistics, 1967, and the United States Department of Health, Education, and Welfare, 1964b.)

persons 65 years of age and over were in nursing homes. Of these, more than 118,000 patients were reported to have senile psychosis and an additional 5,700 were reported to have a specified mental disorder other than senile psychosis. The sum of these two, 124,000 patients, may be considered a minimum estimate of the number of mentally ill aged in nursing homes. This corresponds to a rate of 694 per 100,000 population 65 years and over. An additional 26,500 patients were reported to be senile without mention of psychosis and another 63,700 patients were reported to have ill-defined mental or nervous trouble, without mention of senility. If these latter two groups are added to the former, then the resident patient rate for persons 65 years and over with mental disorders in nursing homes rises from 694 to 1,199 per 100,000. These data give a rough estimate of the number of mentally ill aged in nursing homes and related facilities in 1963 and point to the needs and problems associated with future collection of more precise data from these extended care facilities.

Between 1963 and 1967 the resident population of nursing care homes increased from 505,000 to 756,000, almost 50% (National Center for Health Statistics, 1969). While recent data are not available on the number of such residents who are mentally ill, it seems safe to assume that the percentage has not decreased since 1963. A minimum estimate then of the number of mentally ill aged in nursing homes in 1967 would be 186,000. Thus, by 1967, based upon this estimate, the number of mentally ill aged in nursing homes would have surpassed the number resident in all types of psychiatric inpatient facilities. Available evidence indicates that these trends have continued to the present.

A survey conducted in early 1968 showed that there were about 20,000 admissions to all nursing and personal care homes from mental hospitals in the year preceding the survey (National Center for Health Statistics, unpublished data). While this represents a sizable proportion of the total discharges 65 and over from psychiatric inpatient facilities, it represents only 3% of the total admissions to nursing care homes (Table 10). Admissions from mental hospitals to personal care homes, however, represent 15% of the total admissions to these homes.

TRENDS IN PATIENT CARE EPISODES 1955–68

Despite the developments discussed in the preceding section, major imbalances continue to exist in the provision of psychiatric

TABLE 9

Number of Residents with Mental Disorders and Senility in Nursing Homes and Related Facilities by Age and Sex, United States, May-June 1964

Sex and diagnosis	Number of residents						
	All ages	Under 45	45-64	Total 65+	65-74	75-84	85+
Both sexes							
Total, all disorders	249,159	8,669	26,287	214,203	44,960	98,798	70,445
Chronic brain syndrome (CBS) with senile brain disease							
CBS with psychosis (International classification of diseases—ICD—code 304)	120,974	978	1,737	118,259	15,150	55,665	47,444
Senility (ICD code 794)	27,438	257	653	26,528	4,311	12,703	9,514
Other specified mental disorders without mention of senility (ICD codes 300-303, 305-329)	10,128	611	3,777	5,740	2,551	2,415	774
Mental or nervous trouble ill defined (ICD codes 327, 780.7, 780.8)	90,619	6,823	20,120	63,676	22,948	28,015	12,713
Males							
Total, all disorders	83,630	4,500	13,567	65,563	17,656	30,184	17,723
CBS with senile brain disease							
CBS with psychosis (ICD code 304)	35,041	101	946	33,994	5,289	17,015	11,690
Senility (ICD code 794)	8,331	49	254	8,028	1,780	4,041	2,207
Other specified mental disorders without mention of senility (ICD codes 300-303, 305-329)	6,413	563	3,038	2,812	1,295	1,102	415
Mental or nervous trouble ill defined (ICD codes 327, 780.7, 780.8)	33,845	3,787	9,329	20,729	9,292	8,026	3,411

TABLE 9

Number of Residents with Mental Disorders and Senility in Nursing Homes and Related Facilities by Age and Sex, United States, May-June 1964 (Continued)

Sex and diagnosis	Number of residents						
	All ages	Under 45	45-64	Total 65+	65-74	75-84	85+
Females							
Total, all disorders	165,529	4,169	12,720	148,640	27,304	68,614	52,722
CBS with senile brain disease	85,933	877	791	84,265	9,861	38,650	35,754
CBS with psychosis (ICD code 304)	19,107	208	399	18,500	2,531	8,662	7,307
Senility (ICD code 794)							
Other specified mental disorders without mention of senility (ICD 300-303, 305-329)	3,715	48	739	2,928	1,256	1,313	359
Mental or nervous trouble ill defined (ICD codes 327, 780.7, 780.8)	56,774	3,036	10,791	42,947	13,656	19,989	9,302

Note. Includes geriatric hospitals. The source for these data was the National Center for Health Statistics (1967).

TABLE 10

Number of Nursing and Personal Care Homes, Total Admissions, and
Admissions from Mental Hospitals, United States, 1967

Type of home and bed size	Number of homes	Annual admissions	Admissions from mental hospitals	Mental hospital admissions as a percentage of total admissions
All homes	18,185	588,246	20,340	3
Under 25 beds	7,778	46,503	4,174	8
25-49 beds	4,719	98,689	3,915	3
50-99 beds	3,935	222,444	5,993	2
100+ beds	1,753	220,610	6,258	2
Nursing care homes	10,330	499,348	12,178	2
Under 25 beds	2,497	23,465	985	4
25-49 beds	3,397	82,155	2,300	2
50-99 beds	3,177	204,555	4,744	2
100+ beds	1,259	189,173	4,149	2
Personal care homes with nursing	3,712	64,809	4,327	6
Under 25 beds	1,762	8,779	896	10
25-49 beds	859	11,354	858	7
50-99 beds	633	14,974	776	5
100+ beds	458	29,702	1,797	6
Personal care homes	4,143	24,089	3,835	15
Under 25 beds	3,519	14,259	2,293	16
25-49 beds	463	5,180	757	14
50-99 beds	125	2,915	473	16
100+ beds	36	1,735	312	17

Note. The source for these data was provisional information from the National Center for Health Statistics.

services to the various age, sex, racial, and socioeconomic groups of the population. To illustrate the situation, an index, patient care episodes (see Footnote c, Table 11), will be used which measures the volume of psychiatric services provided in the United States by a universe of psychiatric facilities consisting of mental hospitals (state, county, and private), Veterans Administration hospitals, psychiatric services in general hospitals, outpatient clinics, and community mental health centers.

Major Trends

Table 11 shows the changes between 1955 and 1968 in the volume of services provided by each type of psychiatric facility.

TABLE 11

Estimated Patient Care Episodes, Number, Percentage Distribution, and Rate per 100,000 Population by Type of Facility. United States, 1955 and 1965-68

| Year | Total all facilities | Inpatient services[a] | | | | | Outpatient psychiatric services[a] | Community Mental health centers[b] |
		All inpatient services	State and County mental hospitals	Private Mental hospitals	General Hospitals with psychiatric services	Veterans Administration hospitals[d]		
				Patient care episodes[c]				
1968	3,380,818	1,602,238	791,819	118,126[e]	558,790[f,g]	133,503	1,507,000	271,590
1967	3,139,742	1,632,321	801,354	124,258[e]	578,513	128,196	1,383,000	124,421
1966	2,764,089	1,578,089	802,216	103,973[h]	548,921[g]	122,979	1,186,000	Not available
1965	2,636,525	1,565,525	804,926	125,428	519,328	115,843	1,071,000	Not available
1955	1,675,352	1,296,352	818,832	123,231	265,934	88,355	379,000	Not available
				Percentage distribution				
1968	100.0	47.3	23.4	3.5	16.5	3.9	44.7	8.0
1967	100.0	52.0	25.5	4.0	18.4	4.1	44.0	4.0
1966	100.0	57.1	29.0	3.8	19.9	4.4	42.9	Not available
1965	100.0	59.4	30.5	4.8	19.7	4.4	40.6	Not available
1955	100.0	77.4	48.9	7.3	15.9	5.3	22.6	Not available

Rate per 100,000 population

Year								
1968	1,711.3	811.0	400.8	59.8	282.8	67.6	762.8	137.5
1967	1,604.3	834.1	409.5	63.5	295.6	65.5	706.7	63.6
1966	1,427.0	814.8	414.2	53.7	283.4	63.5	612.3	Not available
1965	1,374.0	815.9	419.5	65.4	270.6	60.4	558.1	Not available
1955	1,032.2	798.6	504.5	75.9	163.8	54.4	233.5	Not available

[a] Excluding federally funded community mental health centers.

[b] Includes only federally funded community mental health centers. Includes inpatient and outpatient services of these centers.

[c] Patient care episodes are derived from the sum of the two numbers, that is, residents at the beginning of the year or on the active rolls of the outpatient clinics, plus admission during the year. The number of patients at the beginning of the year is an unduplicated count and is equal to the number of individual patients in this status. The number of admissions contains a certain amount of duplication. Since one person may be admitted to the same service more than one time per year, or to two or more different services per year, this index is not equal to the unduplicated number of individuals admitted to services and should not be interpreted as such. Special studies have indicated that of the patients admitted per year to a universe of psychiatric services, consisting of all inpatient and outpatient services in a state (excluding psychiatrists in private practice), 19% were admitted to more than one service.

[d] Includes both neuropsychiatric and general medical and surgical hospitals.

[e] Includes residential treatment centers for children which began reporting nationally in 1967.

[f] The drop in the number of patient care episodes for 1968 is due largely to the reclassification of about 50 general hospital inpatient units. These units are counted as part of a community mental health center for 1968.

[g] These estimates differ from previous National Institute of Mental Health published estimates in that they include an estimate for undercoverage in the known universe of hospitals surveyed.

[h] During 1965, the universe of known private mental hospitals was reviewed by the Biometry Branch, National Institute of Mental Health, in conjunction with the state mental health authorities and the National Association of Private Psychiatric Hospitals. In this review, it was found that of the 238 hospitals classified as private mental hospitals for 1965 and preceding years, 64 were in fact hospitals for alcoholics, geriatric hospitals, or nursing homes, or for some other reason should not be considered private mental hospitals. The apparent drop in the number of hospitals in operation and in patient care episodes in 1966 is due, therefore, to a more careful classification of facilities, rather than a change in the number of hospitals.

The following are the highlights of these trends:

1. The total number of patient care episodes for all facilities doubled, increasing from 1.7 million in 1955 to 3.4 million in 1968.

2. Patient care episodes for all inpatient services accounted for over three-fourths of the total episodes in 1955 but under one-half of the total episodes in 1968.

3. State and county mental hospitals accounted for one-half of the total patient care episodes in 1955, but for only about one-fourth in 1968.

4. The number of patient care episodes for outpatient services quadrupled so that in 1968 these services accounted for 45% of all episodes as compared to only 23% in 1955.

5. The number of patient care episodes in general hospital inpatient psychiatric units more than doubled.

6. During 1967, the first year for which reports on the volume of services provided by community mental health centers were included, 74 centers were operating and provided 124,421 episodes of care. By 1968, 165 centers were operating and provided more than twice as many episodes, 271,590, or 8%, of the total episodes provided by all facilities.

Patterns of Use in 1966

To illustrate variations in the patterns of use of the universe of psychiatric facilities by age and sex, certain data will be presented for the year 1966[4] for total patient care episodes and the components of this index—patients under care at the beginning of the year plus admissions during the year.

---

[4]The year 1966 was selected for two reasons. It was the first year that sufficiently complete data were available from which a satisfactory composite picture of the patterns of use of the universe of psychiatric facilities could be developed to illustrate the considerable differences in sex, age, and diagnostic composition of the patients under care of each facility. Second, it was the year *before* community mental health centers delivered any significant volume of direct patient services. Thus, the situation that existed in this year indicated some of the problems that centers plus the other providers of mental health services would have to solve if all these services were to be coordinated and integrated in a way that would provide comprehensive mental health services to the nation.

All ages by type of facility. In 1966, there were 2,764,000 patient care episodes (Table 11). These episodes were generated by approximately 2,461,000 separate individuals, or about 1.2% of the total population of the United States.[5] Of the total patient care episodes, 29% occurred in state and county hospitals, 5% in Veterans Administration hospitals, and 4% in private mental hospitals. Thus, mental hospitals accounted for about 37% of the total patient care episodes. The remaining episodes were accounted for by general hospitals with psychiatric services (20%) and out-patient psychiatric clinics (43%).

The rates of population movement for the different types of facilities varied widely. Thus, in the public mental hospitals there were 74 annual admissions per 100 patients in the hospital at the beginning of the year. The corresponding ratios for private mental hospitals were 640; for general hospitals with psychiatric services,

TABLE 12

Total Patient Care Episodes by Type of Facility and Sex,
United States, 1966

Type of facility	Patient care episodes (in thousands)		
	Both sexes	Males	Females
Total, all facilities	2,764	1,446	1,318
Mental hospitals	1,029	575	454
State and county	802	413	389
Veterans Administration	123	123	—
Private	104	39	65
Psychiatric inpatient services of general hospitals	549	220	329
Outpatient clinics	1,186	651	535

[5]Patient care episodes were converted to unduplicated numbers of persons by multiplying the episodes by a factor of .81. This is an approximate factor derived from studies of the Maryland Psychiatric Case Register which indicated that every case in the register had an average of 1.23 episodes of care per year in a universe of services that was similar in composition to the universe used in the determination of patient care episodes for the United States (Bahn, Gorwitz, Klee, Kramer, & Tuerk, 1965).

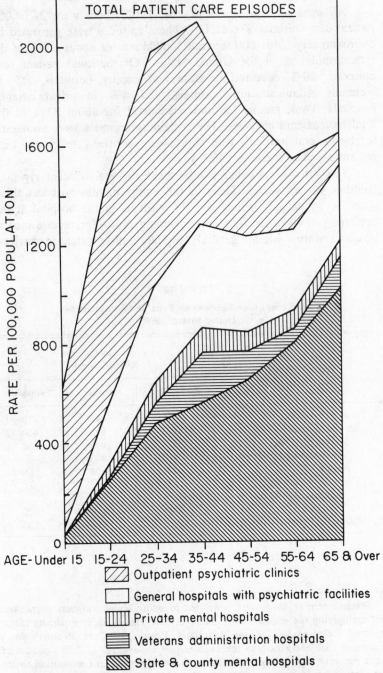

Fig. 3. Number of patient care episodes per 100,000 population in psychiatric facilities by type of facility and age, United States, 1966.

2,314; and for outpatient psychiatric clinics, about 113 annual admissions per 100 patients under care at the beginning of the year.

Sex. Of the total patient care episodes in 1966, 53% were accounted for by males and 47% by females. The corresponding rates were 1,427 per 100,000 for both sexes combined; 1,542 per 100,000 males and 1,319 per 100,000 females. The distribution of patient care episodes by sex and type of facility is shown in Table 12.

Age. The rates of patient care episodes by age and type of facility for 1966 are shown in Figure 3 and in Table B in Appendix D. For all services combined, the rate rises from 613 per 100,000 persons in the under 15 age group to a maximum of 2,172 per 100,000 persons in the 35–44 age group. From this peak, the rate decreases to 1,597 per 100,000 in the 55–64 age group, and then increases slightly to 1,686 per 100,000 for persons 65 years and over.

Figure 3 also demonstrates the striking differences in the volume of services each type of facility provides to the different age groups. The outpatient clinics provide services predominantly to persons under 35 years of age, and the mental hospitals to persons 35 years and over. The rate for mental hospitals increases with advancing age, while that for outpatient clinics and general hospitals decreases. The high rate of patient care episodes in mental hospitals for the 65 and over age group is accounted for by two factors mentioned earlier, namely, the large number of patients in the resident population who grew old in the hospital setting (particularly patients with the functional psychoses) and the high admission rate for patients with mental disorders of the senium. (See Figures 4 and 5 and Tables C and D in Appendix D.)

Age and sex. The rate of patient care episodes for all facilities combined was higher for males than for females in every age group except those 25–34 years. However, there were considerable differences in the age-specific rates by sex and type of facility (Figure 6).

The admision rates for 1966 specific for age, sex, and type of facility are shown in Figure 7. The male rates for the state, county, and Veterans Administration hospitals combined exceed those for females in every age group, while in the private mental hospitals and general hospitals the female rates are higher. In outpatient clinics, male admission rates are considerably higher than female rates in the under 15 and 15–24 age groups and slightly higher than female rates in all other age groups except 25–34 years where the female rate is higher.

Diagnosis. Brain syndromes, schizophrenia, depressive, alcoholic, personality, psychoneurotic, and transient situational personality

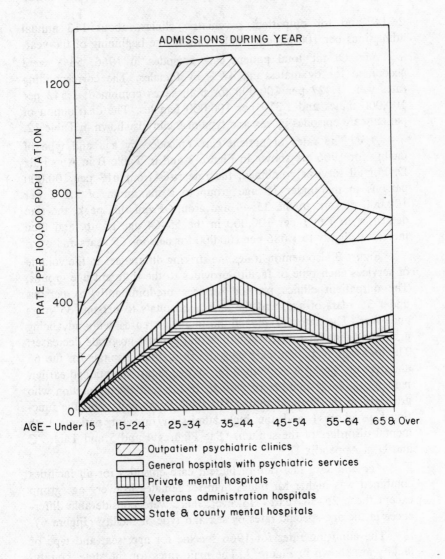

Fig. 4. Number of patients per 100,000 population admitted to psychiatric facilities by type of facility and age, United States, 1966.

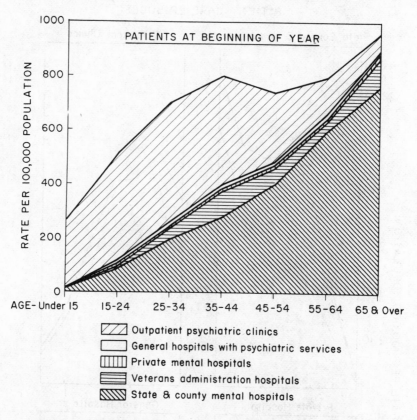

Fig. 5. Number of patients per 100,000 population resident in in-patient psychiatric facilities and on the rolls of outpatient psychiatric clinics at beginning of year by age, United States, 1966.

disorders are the major categories of mental disorders.[6] The relative importance of each category of disorder varied considerably among patient movement groups in each type of facility. This is summarized in Table 13, which presents the five leading diagnoses among first admissions to and resident patients in state, county, and private mental hospitals, discharges from general hospitals with psychiatric services and terminations from outpatient psychiatric clinics in the

[6]A more detailed description of each of the diagnostic categories can be found in the definitions in the *Diagnostic and Statistical Manual* (American Psychiatric Association, 1968) and in the Registrar General's Glossary of Mental Disorders (General Register Office, 1968).

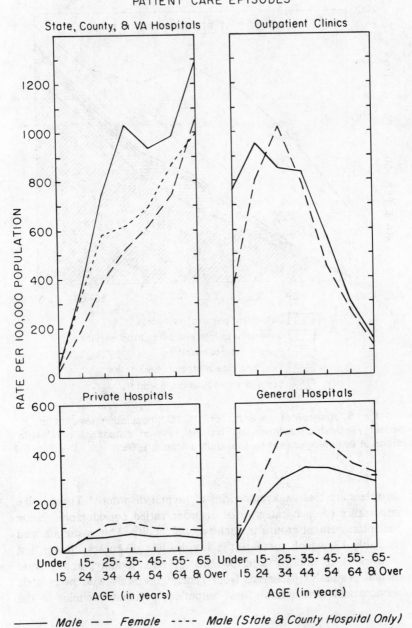

Fig. 6. Number of patient care episodes per 100,000 population for public and private mental hospitals, general hospitals with psychiatric services, and outpatient psychiatric clinics by age and sex, United States, 1966.

ADMISSIONS DURING YEAR

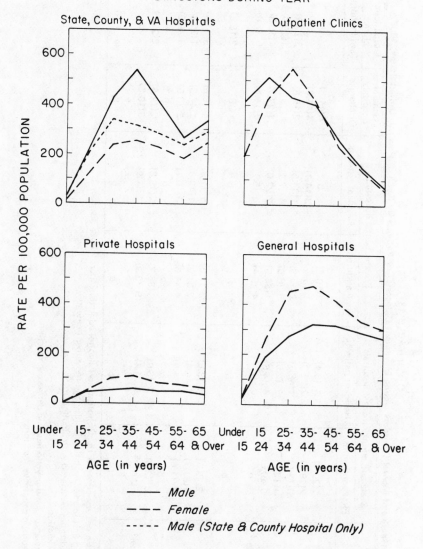

Fig. 7. Number of admissions during year per 100,000 population to public and private mental hospitals, general hospitals with psychiatric services, and outpatient psychiatric clinics by age and sex, United States, 1966.

TABLE 13
Ranking of Major Categories of Mental Disorders among Movement Categories of Patients by Type of Facility, United States, 1968

Mental disorder	State and county mental hospitals		Private mental hospitals		General hospitals	Outpatient clinics
	First admissions	Resident patients	Total additions	Resident patients	Discharges	Terminations
All ages						
Alcoholic disorders[a]	1(20.1)	3 (5.4)	3(10.4)	b	5(11.3)	b
Brain syndromes[c]	2(19.4)	2(22.3)	b	3(14.7)	4(11.8)	b
Schizophrenia	3(17.9)	1(48.7)	2(19.9)	1(34.5)	2(15.8)	3(12.3)
Personality disorder[d]	4(12.0)	5 (2.5)	5 (6.5)	4 (7.1)	b	1(19.0)
Depressive disorder[e]	5 (9.6)	4 (4.6)	1(34.5)	2(22.0)	1(27.7)	4(10.3)
Psychoneurotic disorder[f]	b	b	4 (9.4)	5 (5.1)	3(14.4)	5 (7.6)
Transient situational personality disorder		b	b	b	b	2(18.3)
65 years of age and over						
Alcoholic disorders[a]	2 (5.3)	4 (3.8)	3 (7.0)	5 (1.9)	4 (6.5)	5 (4.6)
Brain syndromes[c]	1(81.7)	1(44.4)	2(31.9)	1(49.3)	1(44.8)	1(30.8)
Schizophrenia	4 (1.6)	2(34.0)	4 (4.0)	3(16.1)	5 (3.3)	3 (8.6)
Personality disorder[d]	b	b	b	b	b	2(21.1)
Depressive disorder[e]	3 (2.5)	3 (5.9)	1(36.7)	2(18.8)	2(24.9)	b
Psychoneurotic disorder[f]	b	5 (.4)	5 (3.9)	4 (1.9)	3(10.3)	b
Transient situational personality disorder	5 (.7)	b	b	b	b	4 (6.3)

aIncludes brain syndromes associated with alcoholism and alcohol addiction (personality disorders).
bDisorder not among first five for specified facility and movement category.
cExcludes brain syndromes associated with alcoholism.
dExcludes alcohol addiction.
eIncludes affective reactions and psychoneurotic depressive reaction.
fExcludes psychoneurotic depressive reaction.

United States for persons 65 years and over for 1968.[7] The details are given in Table E, Appendix D.

The differences in length of stay and readmission rates for various groups of patients produced the diagnostic distribution of the resident populations in long-term mental hospitals, also shown in Table 13.

The differences in the age, sex, diagnostic, and other character-istics of the patients under care of different services result from the interaction of several factors which determine what types of patients are admitted to a specific facility and their length of stay. These include referral practices of case-finding agencies (namely, various health, educational, welfare, and correctional agencies, psychiatrists, and other physicians in private practice); the administrative, legal, fiscal, and clinical policies of each type of facility that determine criteria for admission and release; the availability and effectiveness of specific types of programs to meet the changing needs of patients; the extent to which alternate forms of care are available in a given area; the attitudes of patients and their families toward acceptability of treatment in a specific type of facility and whether a patient has health insurance that covers diagnosis and treatment of mental dis-orders in a general hospital, private mental hospital, or other type of facility.

PREDICTIONS OF FUTURE NEEDS FOR AND EXTENT OF USE OF MENTAL HEALTH SERVICES BY THE AGED

The preceding sections have provided background data on trends in patterns of use of various psychiatric facilities and nursing homes during the period 1946–68 and of patterns of use during 1966 for a universe of facilities, including the mental hospitals, out-patient clinics, and psychiatric services in general hospitals. The data revealed, in particular, that mental hospitals will continue to play a decreasing role in the care of the aged mentally ill while psychiatric services in general hospitals and nursing homes will continue to play an increasingly important one and that outpatient clinics, halfway houses, and community mental health centers will continue to provide services to only a relatively small proportion

---

[7]Data are presented for 1968 rather than 1966, since 1968 was the first year for which data on the age distribution of terminations from psychiatric services of general hospitals were available.

of the aged mentally ill unless a strong impetus is given to the development and expansion of these services.

However, it is almost impossible to predict with any degree of accuracy the numbers and types of mental health facilities that will be required by the aged in 1970 and 1980. This is because future trends will depend not only on the expected increases in the size of the aged population and their actual needs but also on a series of political, administrative, and clinical decisions that will determine how many facilities of various types will be available, how their construction and staffing will be financed, how much manpower will be trained to staff these facilities, who will be admitted to what services, and how persons using these services will pay for them. These factors can be further influenced by scientific discoveries that may lead to prevention of certain conditions and more effective treatment of others. Answers to the following questions could assist in making predictions of future needs for mental health services of the aged and the extent to which they might be met:

1. How many aged persons will there be at specified future dates, for example, 1975 and 1980?

2. How many aged persons will need services?

3. What services will they need?

4. To what extent will the universe of psychiatric services meet the needs for services?

5. What types of personnel and how many of each will be needed to deliver these services?

6. What effect will various programs instituted by state and/or local agencies (both governmental and nongovernmental) to modify patterns of use of mental hospitals for the aged have on the mental hospital per se and on other facilities and services?

7. Will the trends in patterns of use of mental health facilities which were set in motion by the community mental health centers, Medicare, and Medicaid legislation continue into the future?

8. What effect will legislation that may be enacted to establish a national health insurance plan and to provide more effective delivery of health services have on the delivery of mental health services and the use of psychiatric facilities?

9. What breakthroughs, if any, are likely in etiologic research that may reduce the incidence of mental disorders of the aged and, in therapeutic research, that may lead to more effective treatment of these disorders?

10. What effect will current life-styles and problems resulting from environmental pollution, social, racial, and political unrest have on the physical, mental, and social well-being of persons who

will enter the ranks of the aged, as well as on the aged who are growing older?

The discussion that follows will deal with several of the above questions for which data are available to make some predictions.

Number of Aged in 1975 and 1980

Traditionally the aged population is defined as being the population 65 years and over. However, this is an arbitrary definition determined in large part by the age generally used for retirement and at which many persons become eligible for certain social security benefits. There is no reason why a lower age limit could not be pegged at 55 years or even younger depending on the purpose of the estimates. Data to be presented later will use the lower limits of 45 years and 55 years, as well as the generally accepted one of 65 years.

The sine qua non for determining the number of aged in need are estimates of the size of the base population at high risk state and the proportion that develop the conditions requiring services. Estimates of the numbers of persons at the high-risk state will be presented in this section and of the proportion requiring services in the next.

The United States Bureau of the Census has made estimates of the future number of persons in the different age groups based on different assumptions of trends in fertility, mortality, and net immigration from abroad. The actual population for 1970 and estimates for 1975 and 1980 are presented in Table 14. It is expected that the population 65 years and over will increase from 20,050,000 to 21,502,000 or by 7.2% between 1970 and 1975, and from 21,502,000 to 23,491,000, an additional 9%, between 1975 and 1980. As a result, between 1970 and 1980 this population will have increased by 3,441,000 or by 17.2% of the 1970 number.

Number of Persons in Need of Services

This discussion will be limited to a consideration of needs for mental health services by persons who are known to be mentally ill or, more precisely, who suffer from a mental disorder listed in the *Diagnostic and Statistical Manual* (American Psychiatric Association, 1968). The number of mentally ill persons, so defined, who are in need of mental health services is dependent on the number of persons

TABLE 14
Projections of the Population of the United States by Age According to Four Different Series Projections

Age	1970	1975				1980				Percentage change[a]		
		Series B	Series C	Series D	Series E	Series B	Series C	Series D	Series E	1970-75	1975-80	1970-80
All ages	203,166	219,101	217,557	215,588	214,735	236,797	232,412	227,510	225,510	6.1	5.5	12.0
<5	17,167	21,414	19,968	18,187	17,432	26,092	23,245	20,305	19,156	5.9	11.6	18.3
5-9	19,955	17,949	17,851	17,662	17,565	21,536	20,096	18,322	17,569	-11.5	3.7	- 8.2
10-14	20,788	20,714	b	b	b	18,106	18,008	17,820	17,723	- .4	-14.0	-14.3
15-24	35,441	40,012	b	b	b	41,737	b	b	b	12.9	4.3	17.8
25-34	24,908	31,321	b	b	b	36,780	b	b	b	25.7	17.4	47.7
35-44	23,072	22,607	b	b	b	25,523	b	b	b	- 2.0	12.9	10.6
45-54	23,203	23,670	b	b	b	22,352	b	b	b	2.0	- 5.6	- 3.7
55-64	18,582	19,912	b	b	b	21,180	b	b	b	7.2	6.4	14.0
65-74	12,425	13,297	b	b	b	14,606	b	b	b	7.0	9.8	17.6
75-84	6,291	6,610	b	b	b	7,092	b	b	b	5.1	7.3	12.7
85+	1,334	1,595	b	b	b	1,793	b	b	b	19.6	12.4	34.4
65+	20,050	21,502	b	b	b	23,491	b	b	b	7.2	9.3	17.2

Note. The four series shown use identical assumptions of mortality and immigration differing only according to fertility assumptions involved. For Series B, C, D, and E it is assumed that, on the average, women will bear 3.10, 2.78, 2.45, and 2.11 children, respectively, during their lifetime. Series A, used in previous projections, was dropped because recent experience had shown it to be too high. All numbers are shown in thousands.

[a]Using Series D projection for 1975 and 1980. The source for these data was the United States Bureau of the Census (1970a).
[b]Population projections the same for all four series in these age groups.

in the population with mental disorders. Unfortunately, the development of systematic annual morbidity statistics on the mental disorders presents a problem that up to now has defied solution. The major impediments to the development of such statistics are the continued absence of the essential tools required to collect the basic data; namely, standardized case finding techniques for detecting persons in the general population with mental disorders, differential diagnostic techniques that make it possible to assign each case to a specific diagnostic group with a high degree of reliability, and reliable methods for establishing a date of onset of a disorder, and its date of termination. As Frost (1927) stated in his well-known paper on epidemiology:

> Since description of the distribution of any disease in a population obviously requires that the disease must be recognized when it occurs, the development of epidemiology must follow and be limited by that of clinical diagnosis and of the rather complex machinery required for the systematic collection of morbidity and mortality statistics [p. 173].

These problems are particularly difficult to resolve for the mental disorders of the aged population. As Stromgren (1963) has emphasized, diagnostic classification of geriatric disorders is extremely complex:

> The abnormalities under consideration very often have no clear-cut borderlines. In many cases the onset is so insidious that it is impossible to state the time at which a person is passing from the "health" group into the "ill" group. In addition, the nosological entities in many cases are not sharply defined, with the result that frequently it may, in principle, be impossible to say definitely whether the case under consideration should be included in the group. [pp. 135–136].

As a result of the above problems, annual morbidity statistics on the incidence and prevalence of the mental disorders as a group or of individual disorders within the group do not exist for the United States or for that matter, any other country. Occasionally, community surveys of mental disorders have been carried out in the United States and elsewhere which have provided estimates of the prevalence of mental disorders, including age groups relevant to this paper; namely, 45–54, 55–64, and 65 years and over (Table 15; Dohrenwend & Dohrenwend, 1969; Lin & Standley, 1962). The reported rates cannot be compared meaningfully since in each survey there were differences in the definitions of a case of mental disorder, the case finding techniques, the diagnostic procedures, and the classifications of mental disorders. In addition, different measures of prevalence were used. In some instances it was point prevalence, and in

TABLE 15

Prevalence Rates for Mental Illness among Noninstitutional Population in Older Age Groups Reported in Selected North American and European Surveys

Investigator	Date of investigation	Place	Oldest population groups studied	Number of persons in oldest age groups	Case-finding method[a]	Type of prevalence measure	Prevalence rate per 1,000 population	Category of mental illness studied
Srole, Langner, Michael, Opler, and Rennie (1962)	1954	Midtown New York, New York	50-59	440(sample)	1, 3	Point	308	Impaired (includes persons with marked and severe symptom formation and the incapacitated)
Hare and Shaw (1965)	November 1960-October 1961	Croydon, England	65+	185(sample)	1, 3	Interval	320	Nervous disturbance (severe, moderate, mild)
Essen-Moller (1956)	1947	Rural Sweden	60 and over 60-69, 70-79, 80+	443, 231, 157, 55	1	Point	172, 152, 197, 491	Evident pathology of mental illness
Pasamanick, Roberts, Lemkau, and Krueger (1959)	1952-55	Baltimore, Maryland	65+	Not indicated	1, 3	"Prevalence as of date of clinical evaluation"	99	Psychoses, psychoneuroses, and psychophysiologic, autonomic and visceral disorders
New York State Department of Mental Hygiene (1960)	1952	Syracuse, New York	65 and over 65-74, 75-84, 85+	1,805, 1,198 505, 97	1, 3	Period	45, 29 61, 165	Persons living at home with certifiable mental illness
Kay, Beamish, and Roth (1964)	1960	Newcastle, England	65+	309(sample)	1, 3	Point	246	All psychiatric disorders
Shepherd, Cooper, Brown, and Kalton (1966)	1962	London, England	45-64 65+	4,797 2,229	2, 3	Period	162 135	Formal psychiatric illness, psychosomatic conditions, organic illness with psychiatric overlay, and psychosocial problems

[a]Case-finding methods were 1, population survey through household interviews; 2, persons seen by a general practitioner; and 3, verification through review by a psychiatrist of all or a sample of suspected cases.

others, interval or period prevalence.[8] Despite their lack of comparability, these surveys emphasized that sizable proportions of the aged population suffer from mental disorders and their associated disabilities.

The question arises as to whether any of the rates reported in the above surveys should be used as a basis for estimating the number of aged mentally ill in the United States. It is felt that judicious use of the rates summarized in Table 15 in conjunction with other available data on patterns of use of psychiatric facilities in the United States will provide fairly reliable estimates. These estimates will reemphasize to Congress, state legislators, health and social planners, researchers, and training institutions the size and complexity of the problem this country will certainly face in the next 10 years in providing mental health services to the aged.

Selection of rates of need. For purposes of these estimates, it is assumed that the number of persons in need of services is identical to the number of persons with mental disorders. So, to obviate the problem of selecting a single rate for determining the number of persons with mental disorders, several levels of rates have been used, namely, 2, 10, and 20% of the population.

With the exception of the minimum rate (2%), each of these rates was suggested by the data in Table 15. Rates of 10–20% were suggested by the studies of Shepherd, Cooper, Brown, and Kalton (1966) on the prevalence of psychiatric morbidity among patients on the lists of a group of general practitioners in London and by the surveys of Pasamanick, Roberts, Lemkau, and Krueger (1959) in which a random sample of the population in Baltimore was evaluated clinically by internists and psychiatrists. Rates higher than 20% could have been used, but it was decided that the order of magnitude of those selected were sufficient to illustrate the size of the problem.

The minimum rate was suggested by the data on patient care episodes for 1966, reported in Table B in Appendix D, which indicated that at least 1% of the total United States population was under the care of an inpatient or outpatient psychiatric service. In

---

[8]Point prevalence is the proportion of persons in a defined population who were active cases of mental disorders as of a specified date (i.e., point in time. Interval or period prevalence is the proportion of persons in a defined population who were active cases of mental disorder during a defined interval period of time, including those who were active at the beginning plus those who became active during the interval.

several age groups 1.5–2% of the population were under care; thus, 2% seemed reasonable as a minimum estimate of need.

To simplify the computations further, the various rates of need were applied uniformly to each age group, such that estimates were obtained of the number of people needing services in each age group on the assumption that their respective needs were 2, 10, and 20%.

In order that the definition of need will be compatible with data in the next section on expected number of persons who receive services during a year in a psychiatric facility, it is further assumed that the need rates include persons under care of such facilities. It is estimated that the need rates for the noninstitutional population would be increased by 1–2% if patients under care in the universe of psychiatric facilities were added. If mentally ill patients in nursing homes on a given date were also added, then the rate would be increased by 3–4%. Accordingly, the number of persons in a given population group with mental disorders during a year will be defined as all members of the group known to have been mentally ill during the year, including those who spent some time in an institution as well as those who did not.

Estimated number of persons in need. Tables F and G in Appendix D present the estimated number of persons in need of services in 1975 and 1980, for all ages and those under 65 years and 65 years and over. This was obtained by applying the rates of 2, 10, and 20% to the population projections prepared by the United States Bureau of the Census.

The estimated numbers of persons in need are summarized in the following for persons of all ages, under 65 years, and 65 years and over:

	Estimated level of need: 1975			Estimated level of need: 1980		
	2%	10%	20%	2%	10%	20%
	(Numbers in thousands)					
All ages	4,312	21,559	43,118	4,550	22,751	45,502
Under 65	3,882	19,409	38,817	4,080	20,402	40,804
65 years +	430	2,150	4,300	470	2,349	4,698

In a subsequent section, these estimates of population in need of services will be related to numbers of persons expected to receive services in 1975 and 1980.

Types of Services Needed

The specific services a patient needs depends on his age, sex, physical and psychological status, symptoms, diagnoses, and the types of treatment and rehabilitation services required to assist him in achieving his maximum rehabilitation potential.

No attempt will be made to estimate the specific types of services patients may need. Specification of the optimum combination of services required to bring a patient to his maximum rehabilitation potential is a complicated procedure. Developing such estimates is a task for a group of properly qualified clinicians, psychologists, social workers, and other professionals involved in the treatment and rehabilitation process. A classification of various services patients may receive is provided in Appendix A as a guide to those who may be dealing with this problem.

The treatment and rehabilitation services a patient receives also depend on several factors which include the following: (a) his socioeconomic status and financial resources; (b) if in an institution, the type of institution and the availability and adequacy of the services it can provide; (c) if at home, the type of housing, its location and physical characteristics as well as the composition of the household and the availability, willingness, and capability of family, friends, and neighbors to assist the patient; (d) the availability of home care nursing, outpatient facilities, and social services; and (e) the theoretical orientation and experience of the patient's therapist and/or members of the therapeutic team and the objectives of the treatment and rehabilitation plan developed for him.

Since patients' needs change with time, their progress must be assessed periodically to determine not only the extent to which goals of treatment plans are being reached, but also their status at the time of evaluation, their continuing needs for specific services, and whether such services can best be provided in the community or in the inpatient services of a general hospital, a public or private mental hospital, a nursing home, a community mental health center, or another type of facility.

The extent to which different facilities are used is a function of several variables:

1. The events that lead an individual to seek medical, psychiatric, and social services and the factors that influence and determine his decision to select a specific physician or caretaker agency (Appendix B).

2. The characteristics of the patient, including the severity of his psychiatric disturbance, the presence or absence of associated problems of physical illness and disability and their severity; his ability to care for himself and provide for his basic requirements of daily living (Appendix C); the presence or absence of spouse, family, and friends to whom he can turn for assistance and guidance; his housing and living arrangements and financial status; and the attitudes of the patient and of significant others toward the use of medical and psychiatric care and the use of mental hospitals and nursing homes.

3. The characteristics of the patients' physicians, and/or other caretakers including their degree of sophistication and competency and their referral practices.

4. The characteristics and referral practices of various health and other social service agencies, or of family members or friends whom the patient may have contacted.

5. The availability and location of specific types of facilities, their criteria for admission, and their policies concerning length of stay.

As a result of the complexity of the phenomena involved, data are not available on patterns of use of specific types of caretakers and caretaker agencies for every possible permutation and combination of factors that may determine specific pathways into care for members of different subgroups of the population. However, patient data are available on the rates of use of selected types of facilities and caretakers by age, sex, and other demographic and socioeconomic variables that illustrate the end result of a complex set of interactions that determined patients' specific pathways into care.

Estimates will be presented in the following section on the expected number of persons who will be under care of at least one of the components of the universe of psychiatric facilities in 1975 and 1980 based on certain assumptions regarding current trends in the use of such facilities. Since these facilities are not the only set of resources used by the aged with mental disorders and other conditions associated with psychiatric problems, data will also be presented to provide some notion of the following:

1. The extent to which private psychiatrists, family physicians, medical specialists, other professionals, and general hospitals are used by the aged.

2. The reported occurrence of selected chronic conditions in which psychological mechanisms may play an important role either as possible etiological agents or as factors that complicate and prolong treatment and duration of hospitalization for these conditions.

Estimates will not be made of the future use of psychiatrists and other physicians in private practice by the aged mentally ill or of the occurrence of chronic conditions just mentioned. The reason for this is that unless proposed national health insurance legislation makes some fundamental changes in the medical care delivery system as well as in the system of paying for care (health insurance) or there is some unexpected breakthrough in prevention and/or treatment of the conditions, it is assumed that the rates of use of private physicians and the frequency of occurrence of these chronic conditions in 1975 and 1980 would be at least as high as the current estimates to be cited.

Extent of Use of Facilities and Professional Personnel by the Aged with Psychiatric Disorders

Psychiatric facilities. Estimates of the numbers of persons who will be under the care of at least one of the components of the universe of psychiatric facilities in 1975 and 1980 were made under two basic assumptions:

Procedure 1: The rates of patient care episodes for each facility observed in 1968 would not change over the period 1970–80; that is, the rate for 1968 would apply in 1975 and 1980 (Table F in Appendix D).

Procedure 2: The annual relative rates of change for each type of facility during the period 1970–80 would be the same as that which occurred during the period 1955–68 (Table G) with some exceptions.[9]

The methodology used to arrive at these projections involved the fitting of arith log lines by eye to the rates of patient care episodes for each type of facility and extrapolating to 1975 and 1980. The rates were converted to numbers and the total patient care episodes were obtained by summing the expected episodes for each facility type. The age distribution of the total patient care episodes in 1975 and 1980 were obtained by assuming that the age distribu-

---

[9]For outpatient clinics the maximum rate allowed was 1,000 per 100,000 (1%). The projected rate for 1980 went far beyond this, and seemed to be too unrealistic. For community mental health centers, sufficient data were not available to provide guidelines to the trend of these services during the 1970s, therefore, estimates for 1975 and 1980 were derived by assuming a 10% annual increase in the 1968 rate of 137 per 100,000 population.

tion of patient care episodes observed in 1966 for all facilities combined would still apply at the later dates. Another assumption had to be made concerning the relationship of patient care episodes to the unduplicated numbers of persons who accounted for the episodes. As indicated previously, studies from the Maryland Psychiatric Case Register showed that every case in the register had an average of 1.23 episodes of care per year in a universe of services that was similar in composition to the universe used in the determination of patient care episodes. Thus, patient care episodes should be multiplied by a factor of .81 to convert them to persons. For purposes of the computations used in Tables F and G in Appendix D a factor of .80 was used.

The estimated number of patient care episodes resulting from Procedure 1 are given in Table F in Appendix D and those from Procedure 2 in Table G in Appendix D. These tables show, respectively, the estimated numbers of persons needing care, estimated numbers of persons receiving care in the defined universe of facilities, and the percentage not receiving care.

Table 16 summarizes for each set of projections in Tables F and G in Appendix D the numbers needing, receiving, and not receiving services in 1975 and 1980 and the corresponding percentages for persons all ages and those 65 years and over, assuming 10% of the population need services. About 80–84% of those in need of services among persons of all ages as well as those 65 years and over would not be receiving services in the defined universe of facilities. If we assume further that, for persons 65 years and over, an additional number would receive services in nursing homes at least equal to the number receiving services in the other facilities, then in 1975 the percentage of persons receiving care in psychiatric facilities and nursing homes based on only the 1968 level of rates would be increased to 32% and that based on the 1955–68 trend would be increased to 40%.

Use of psychiatrists. Adequate data are not available for estimating the number of aged population in the United States who are under the care of private psychiatrists on an outpatient basis. Some relevant information suggests that the proportion may be small. For example, data available from the Monroe County (New York) psychiatric case register on the number of patients admitted to private psychiatric outpatient practice indicated that for the population 65 years and over, the admission rate for males was low (1.6 per 1,000 persons) and only slightly higher for females (1.8 per 1,000 persons). The maximum rate was reported in the 35–44 age group,

TABLE 16

Estimated Number and Percentage of Persons Needing, Receiving, and
Not Receiving Psychiatric Services (Assuming 10% of Population in Need of
Services) and Based on Two Assumptions Concerning Past Use Rates of Services,
All Ages and 65 Years and Over, United States, 1975 and 1980

Item	1975		1980	
	1955-68 use rate continues	1968 use rate prevails	1955-68 use rate continues	1968 use rate prevails
All ages				
Number				
Needing services	21,559	21,559	22,751	22,751
Receiving services	3,636	2,955	4,337	3,118
Not receiving services	17,923	18,604	18,414	19,633
Percentage				
Receiving services	16.9	13.7	19.1	13.7
Not receiving services	83.1	86.3	80.9	86.3
65 years of age and over				
Number				
Needing services	2,150	2,150	2,349	2,349
Receiving services	411	334	490	352
Not receiving services	1,739	1,816	1,859	1,997
Percentage				
Receiving services	19.1	15.5	20.9	15.0
Not receiving services	80.9	84.5	79.1	85.0

Note. All numbers are shown in thousands.

3.5 per 1,000 for males, and about 5.5 per 1,000 for females (Bahn, Gardner, Alltop, Knatterud, & Solomon, 1966).

A National Health Interview Survey conducted in the period July 1963–June 1964 reported the percentage of the noninstitutional population that visited a psychiatrist during the year. The number of persons 65 years and over in the interview sample who reported such visits was too few to permit an estimate to be made. The maximum rate was 9 per 1,000 for persons 17–24 and 25–44 years of age, and 6 per 1,000 for persons 45–64 years of age.

Use of other physicians and other types of professionals. The extent to which other physicians in private practice (e.g., family physicians) provide care for psychiatric conditions and emotional problems in the population 65 years and over in the United States is unknown. As stated earlier, Shepherd et al. (1966), from their studies in London, England, determined that the psychiatric morbidity rate among persons 65 years and over who consulted their general practitioner during a year was 11% for males and 15% for females. Diagnostic distributions were not presented by age groups of patients, but, overall, the following conditions were included: formal psychiatric illness (psychosis, psychoneurosis, and personality disorders), psychosomatic conditions, organic illness with a psychiatric overlay, and psychosocial problems.

Based on clinical examinations and psychiatric evaluations of a random sample of the noninstitutionalized population of Baltimore, Pasamanick et al. (1959) estimated that 10% of the population 65 years and over had a psychotic, psychoneurotic, or psychophysiological disorder that required attention. The prevalence of personality disorders was not reported because the investigators believed the judgments of both the examining physicians and psychiatrists were not very reliable for these conditions.

The National Health Interview Survey reported that during the period July 1963–June 1964, 68% of the population 65 years and over in the United States visited a physician at least once (National Center for Health Statistics, 1966a). About 83% of the persons in this age group reported one or more chronic conditions including 49% who had chronic limitations of activity caused by chronic illness. Selected conditions that represent major problem areas in the care of the aged and the percentage causing activity limitations are

Condition (International classification of diseases code number)	Number of conditions reported in thousands	Percentage causing activity limitation
Heart conditions (410–443, 782.1)	2,917	63.6
High blood pressure (444–447)	2,815	24.9
Arthritis and rheumatism (720–727)	5,629	31.9
Digestive conditions (530–553, 560–561, 570, 572–587, 784, 785)	3,591	20.8
Vascular lesions of central nervous system (330–334)	619	70.4
Visual impairments[10]	2,499	31.8
Orthopedic impairments (excluding paralysis or absence of limb)	3,199	33.8
Hearing impairments	3,712	5.9

---

[10]Impairments are classified by means of a special supplementary code which is used to group them according to the type of functional impairment and etiology. A report from the United States National Health Survey (*Health Statistics,* Series B, No. 35) presents a more complete explanation of the classification of impairments.

Many of the above conditions are those that various investigators have demonstrated to be associated with chronic psychiatric disturbance (National Center for Health Statistics, 1966b).

Persons 65 and over also experience a high injury rate. About 2,919,000 aged persons, or 170 per 1,000, reported accidents for which they received medical attention or that restricted their activities for at least one day.

Persons in the 65 and over age group consulted a variety of medical specialists and other types of ancillary professionals far more frequently than they did psychiatrists. Thus, the percentage of the population visiting such professionals at least once in the year prior to the survey interview were as follows:

Specialist or practitioner	Percentage of population 65 years and over with one or more visits
Ophthamologist	9.9
Optometrist	9.9
Podiatrist	4.5
Chiropractor	2.9
Dermatologist	1.4
Orthopedist	1.4

Since chronic psychiatric disturbances may be associated with other forms of chronic ill health, it is important to determine the manner in which nonpsychiatric physicians and other professionals who have frequent contact with the aged treat and manage patients who manifest such diturbances.

Use of short-stay hospitals by the aged. The aged also have a high admission rate to short-stay hospitals and a longer average length of stay in these hospitals. Hospital discharges from short-stay hospitals increased with advancing age from 115.2 per 1,000 persons under 45 years to 195.6 per 1,000 persons 75 years and over (Table 17). The average length of stay for discharges 65 years and over was 12.7 days compared to only 6.4 days for those under 45 years of age. Heart diseases were most responsible for hospitalization of the aged. About 11% of the discharged patients 65 years and older were diagnosed with this condition (Table 18).

TABLE 17

Number of Discharges from Short-Stay Hospitals, Rate per 1,000 Persons,
Number of Hospital Days and Average Length of Hospital Stay for Discharges,
and Number and Percentage of Surgically Treated by Age and Sex,
United States, July 1963-June 1965

Age and sex	Discharges		Hospital days		Surgically treated discharges	
	Number (in thousands)	Per 1,000 persons	Number (in thousands)	Average length of stay	Number (in thousands)	Percentage of total discharges
All ages						
Both sexes	24,012	128.3	198,539	8.3	13,012	54.2
Male	9,262	102.1	91,839	9.9	4,016	43.4
Female	14,750	153.0	106,700	7.2	8,996	61.0
Under 45 years						
Both sexes	15,210	115.2	96,698	6.4	9,366	61.6
Male	5,081	78.4	39,990	7.9	2,369	46.6
Female	10,129	150.7	56,708	5.6	6,997	69.1
45-64 years						
Both sexes	5,606	147.9	61,407	11.0	2,531	45.1
Male	2,738	149.8	33,206	12.1	1,106	40.4
Female	2,868	146.2	28,202	9.8	1,425	49.7
65 years and over						
Both sexes	3,196	186.3	40,434	12.7	1,115	34.9
Male	1,443	190.5	18,644	12.9	541	37.5
Female	1,753	183.0	21,790	12.4	574	32.7
65-74 years						
Both sexes	2,023	181.3	25,538	12.6	749	37.0
Male	918	182.4	12,067	13.1	367	40.0
Female	1,105	180.4	13,471	12.2	382	34.6
75 years and over						
Both sexes	1,174	195.6	14,896	12.7	366	31.2
Male	525	206.3	6,576	12.5	174	33.1
Female	649	187.7	8,319	12.8	192	29.6

Note. Data are based on household interviews of the civilian, noninstitutional population. The source for these data was the National Center for Health Statistics (1966a).

TABLE 18

Number and Percentage Distribution of Discharges from Short-Stay Hospitals by Condition for Which Hospitalized According to Age, United States, July 1963-June 1965[a]

Condition for which hospitalized	Number of discharges (in thousands)				Percentage distribution			
	All ages	Under 45 years	45-64 years	65+ years	All ages	Under 45 years	45-64 years	65+ years
All conditions	24,012	15,210	5,606	3,196	100.0	100.0	100.0	100.0
Infective and parasitic diseases	485	358	92	35	2.0	2.4	1.6	1.1
Malignant neoplasms	435	89	203	143	1.8	.6	3.6	4.5
Benign and unspecified neoplasms	1,184	703	373	107	4.9	4.6	6.7	3.3
Diabetes mellitus	233	82	71	80	1.0	.5	1.3	2.5
Other endocrine, allergic, and metabolic disorders	520	308	138	75	2.2	2.0	2.5	2.3
Mental, personality disorders, and deficiencies	527	308	163	57	2.2	2.0	2.9	1.8
Vascular lesions of the central nervous system	217	b	85	120	.9	b	1.5	3.8
Diseases of the eye and visual impairments	355	128	72	155	1.5	.8	1.3	4.8
Other diseases of nervous system and sense organs	466	280	122	64	1.9	1.8	2.2	2.0
Diseases of the heart, not elsewhere classified (NEC)	976	142	475	358	4.1	.9	8.5	11.2
Hypertension without heart involvement	236	50	109	78	1.0	.3	1.9	2.4

TABLE 18

Number and Percentage Distribution of Discharges from Short-Stay Hospitals by Condition for Which Hospitalized According to Age, United States, July 1963-June 1965[a](Continued)

Condition for which hospitalized	Number of discharges in (in thousands)				Percentage distribution			
	All ages	Under 45 years	45-64 years	65+ years	All ages	Under 45 years	45-64 years	65+ years
Varicose veins (excluding hemorrhoids)	150	80	63	b	.6	.5	1.1	b
Hemorrhoids	310	152	139	19	1.3	1.0	2.5	.3
Other circulatory diseases	360	136	124	100	1.5	.9	2.2	3.1
Upper respiratory conditions	1,474	1,373	71	31	6.1	9.0	1.3	1.0
Other respiratory conditions	1,418	819	361	238	5.9	5.4	6.4	7.4
Ulcer of stomach and duodenum	616	258	263	96	2.6	1.7	4.7	3.0
Appendicitis	395	342	42	b	1.6	2.2	.7	b
Hernia	633	291	232	109	2.6	1.9	4.1	3.4
Diseases of the gall bladder	507	161	211	135	2.1	1.1	3.8	4.2
Other digestive system conditions	1,238	614	393	231	5.2	4.0	7.0	7.2
Male genital disorders	269	61	75	133	1.1	.4	1.3	4.2
Female breast and genital disorders	850	550	258	42	3.5	3.6	4.6	1.3
Other genitourinary system conditions	958	540	277	141	4.0	3.6	4.9	4.4
Deliveries	3,727	3,722	b	—	15.5	24.5	b	—
Complications of pregnancy and the puerperium	606	601	b	b	2.5	4.0	b	b
Diseases of the skin	258	163	69	b	1.1	1.1	1.2	b
Arthritis, all forms	206	43	91	72	.9	.6	1.6	2.3
Conditions of bones and joints, NEC	415	232	149	33	1.7	1.5	2.7	1.0
Other conditions of the musculoskeletal system	417	272	108	37	1.7	1.8	1.9	1.2
Fractures and dislocations	909	509	223	177	3.8	3.3	4.0	5.5
Other current injuries	1,327	939	275	113	5.5	6.2	4.9	3.5
All other conditions and observations	1,334	893	270	172	5.6	5.9	4.8	5.4

Note. The source for these data was the National Center for Health Statistics (1966a).
[a]Data are based on household interviews of the civilian, noninstitutional population.
[b]Data, based on sample survey, do not meet standards of reliability or precision.

TYPES AND NUMBERS OF PERSONNEL NEEDED TO DELIVER PSYCHIATRIC AND OTHER SERVICES REQUIRED BY THE AGED

As may be seen by the estimates of expected use of psychiatric facilities, nursing homes, general hospitals, physicians, and ancillary medical professionals, the needs for personnel will be great. Estimates have been made of the number of psychiatrists, psychologists, psychiatric nurses, and social workers that will be needed to provide services to persons in need of psychiatric services. No attempt has been made to allocate numbers of these personnel to the different types of facilities nor has any attempt been made to estimate the needs for all types of personnel in all of the different community and institutional facilities where services may be provided.

As previously indicated, estimates of persons in need of psychiatric care were based on three levels of need: 2, 10, and 20%. The estimated numbers of personnel to be needed were based on assumptions concerning:

1. The average amount of time per year each professional discipline would spend with persons in need of services:[11] (a) psychiatrists and clinical psychologists: 3, 6, and 10 hours per patient per year; (b) social workers: 6, 12, and 20 hours per patient per year; and (c) psychiatric nurses: 6 and 10 hours per patient per year.

2. The number of weeks worked per year (50 weeks) and numbers of hours per week each professional would work (30 hours per week, or 1,500 hours per year).

The estimates of personnel derived for each level of need and assumed hours of service per patient per year are presented in Table H in Appendix D. They are summarized below for a 10% level of need for care for persons of all ages, assuming six hours per patient per year of selected professional disciplines, and are compared with the projected manpower pool for each of these professional disciplines in 1975 and 1980.

---

[11]The various assumed levels of time spent per patient per year were suggested by the Division of Manpower and Training Programs, National Institute of Mental Health.

| Discipline | 1975 | | 1980 | |
	Required	Expected[a]	Required	Expected[a]
Psychiatry[b]	86,235	30,300	91,004	38,700
Psychology[c]	86,235	30,000	91,004	44,800
Social work[d]	86,235	25,400	91,004	36,600
Nursing[e]	86,235	35,900	91,004	51,300

[a]The source for these data was the Division of Manpower and Training Programs, National Institute of Mental Health.
[b]One or more years of psychiatric training.
[c]MA or PhD with training in mental health field.
[d]MA with training in mental health field.
[e]Some training in psychiatric nursing.

Since the trend in providing mental health services seems to be away from setting up specialized facilities for categorical groups of persons such as the aged, it did not seem useful to try to predict manpower needs for elderly patients only. As the majority of these persons are treated in general purpose facilities, it seemed sufficient to highlight the overall shortages in manpower.

Following are some additional general observations with respect to the aged based on the series of projections given in Tables F, G, and H in Appendix D.

1. A 2% level of need for mental health services among the elderly seems to be an unrealistic assumption. Data for 1963 indicated that the rate per 100,000 population for persons 65 and over with mental disorders institutionalized in selected long-term institutions was of the order of 2,000–2,400 or 2–2.4% of the population. If the number of elderly persons using general hospital and outpatient psychiatric services were added, then the number of elderly persons with mental disorders using mental health services or nursing homes would approach 5% of the total population in this age group.

2. Projections of manpower needs as given in Table H do not take into account types of personnel employed in nursing homes currently caring for a sizable proportion of the institutionalized mentally ill. Available data indicate that professional staff other than nurses are relatively few in number and that only a small proportion of employees of any type in nursing homes have had any special training with respect to the problems of the mentally ill. Data from a 1964 nursing home survey indicated that the percentage of staff who had special training related to mental or social problems of the aged or chronically ill was as follows:

Type of personnel	Percentage who had attended a course on mental or social problems	
	Accredited course	Short course or workshop
Registered nurses	4.8	11.9
Licensed practical nurses	4.3	15.3
Nurses' aides	.7	4.2
Other professional staff	4.9	15.9

3. Mental health manpower planners realize that it will never be possible to train the necessary numbers of psychiatrists, psychologists, social workers, and psychiatric nurses to handle the expected increases in demand. The projected manpower needs in this chapter serve only to emphasize this fact. Concomitant with this realization has been an increased emphasis and interest in the development of new occupations in the mental health field at the subprofessional and nonprofessional level. A current National Institute of Mental Health supported project is training "geriatric outreach workers" whose primary function is "assisting older people to sustain their social, physical and emotional functioning enabling them to remain in their own home and community and postponing or averting the need for institutionalization." The introduction of such new categories of mental health workers could radically alter the current supply and demand for mental health manpower as well as changing the current utilization patterns of both health and mental health resources.

4. Projections of resource utilization as shown for 1975 and 1980 assume that although inappropriate utilization will continue to a certain extent, it will decrease at a rate similar to that in the past. For example, the decline in the geriatric population in state mental hospitals is due in part to more appropriate use of these facilities. Thus, projections based on these past trends assume that decreases due to more appropriate use will continue to occur at the same rate. New regulations relating to Medicaid, effective in May 1971, require at least an annual review of the health needs of Medicaid patients in mental institutions and skilled nursing homes. Assuming that the Medicaid program itself is not replaced by the Family Health Insurance Plan, this regulation may serve to accelerate the trend toward more appropriate use of such facilities.

EFFECTS OF VARIOUS PROGRAMS INITIATED BY STATE AND/OR LOCAL AGENCIES TO MODIFY PATTERNS OF USE OF STATE HOSPITALS BY THE AGED

The preceding projections of patterns of use of services and of needs for personnel have been based on the assumption that trends existing during the period 1955–68 will continue into the future. Many forces—federal, state, local—are working to change still further the patterns of use of various services. An example of a program introduced by a state mental health agency is one that has been underway in the New York State Hospital system since 1968 to prevent the inappropriate admission of elderly patients to their state hospitals.

The program is based on the premise that a highly individual approach is required in order to establish whether or not an elderly patient needs and may benefit from admission to a mental hospital. Such evaluations must take into account not only the patient's mental state but also his physical condition, his family, and socioeconomic and environmental factors. Kobrynski and Miller (1970) classified the aged mentally ill into four categories: (a) elderly persons afflicted with a major psychiatric illness which responds well to modern treatment; (b) elderly persons with mental disorders particularly associated with the aging process—organic brain syndrome, senile or arteriosclerotic dementia; (c) elderly persons with primarily physical illnesses; and (d) elderly persons who are in a satisfactory physical and mental state but who need financial assistance and shelter.

The purpose of the evaluation is to select from Categories a and b those patients who are most likely to benefit from the therapeutic services a mental hospital has to offer to induce clinical recovery or at least symptomatic improvement. For patients who are not admitted, the evaluation team makes recommendations for alternate patterns of care; for example, general hospitals for persons with primarily physical illness, and advice on community resources for those who are in a satisfactory physical and mental state but who need financial assistance and shelter.

This program has resulted in a dramatic change in the patterns of use of state hospitals by the aged. Admissions dropped sharply as did the death rate among patients in the hospitals. Certain major problem areas remain, however, as indicated by Kobrynski and Miller (1970):

Community placement of elderly patients who have improved sufficiently to resume life outside the mental hospitals has not been accelerated because of shortages in community facilities and services. Aware of these shortages, the New York State Department of Mental Hygiene has given high priority to the funding of geriatric programs in the community. Here belong the development and expansion of outpatient geriatric services, daycare centers and family care. Legislation was passed to allow the Department of Mental Hygiene and nonprofit agencies authorized by the Department to construct and operate hotels for appropriate groups. This program shows great promise for the geriatric group [p. 218].

While most mental health administrators would probably agree with the philosophy expressed by the New York State Department of Mental Hygiene, it is difficult to predict the rate of diffusion of such practices throughout all states. Such a policy assumes a certain level of community resources that may not be present in many areas. Even within New York State, the authors pointed out that

It is noteworthy that the reduction in the numbers of geriatric admissions has varied from hospital to hospital. The selective admission policy has been a flexible one and the mental hospital has taken into consideration the condition of geriatric services in its catchment area while observing the basic principles of the new admission policy [p. 218].

Even if the New York State program were widely adopted throughout the nation the effect of such an action on the expected number of aged persons in the state mental hospitals by 1975 and 1980 would be impossible to predict because of certain imponderables. One is the extent to which such a program can continue to achieve its goals in maintaining aged patients in the community. A large number of services would be required. For example, on the health side would be psychiatric, general health care, nursing, nutritional, dietary, and other services. On the social side are services to assist in homemaking; obtaining appropriate housing; providing transportation for visits to doctors, outpatient services, social agencies, and recreational activities; providing advice and assistance on financial matters; and developing educational, recreational, and social activities to provide increased opportunities for psychosocial stimulation. A second imponderable is whether the necessary facilities can be constructed and staffed, and services made available at a sufficiently rapid rate to meet both existing needs and those anticipated by 1980, as a result of an estimated 17% increase in the population 65 years and over by that time. A third imponderable is the extent to which federal, state, and local governments, as well as nongovernmental agencies, will make funds available to develop the facilities and services and to train staff. This is indeterminate at the present

time because of the financial crises currently facing these governmental branches.

RELATIONSHIP OF LIVING ARRANGEMENTS OF THE AGED TO THE PATTERNS OF USE OF PSYCHIATRIC AND RELATED FACILITIES

Community mental health programs place strong emphasis on
maintaining patients in their homes and community environments
and protecting their links with family and community. The extensive
benefits offered by Medicare for home care services and the requirements that state agencies must meet to participate in Medicaid reinforce efforts to accomplish this. For example, it becomes crucial to
determine the extent to which long-term hospitalization is due either
to the absence of a suitable living arrangement to which a patient
might be discharged, to lack of extra-hopsital-based services to
provide follow-up and rehabilitative services, or to other factors
related to the patient's need for services available only in a mental
hospital or nursing home. Consideration of such problems as these
underlines the need for systematic information about the composition of the households in which patients in the various marital status
categories are members and the relationship of household size and
composition not only to the rates at which its members become
mentally ill and enter into psychiatric treatment, but also to the
outcome of their treatment and adjustment to the community.

Central to the expectation that patients can be kept in their
homes without hardship to themselves or their families are certain
underlying assumptions. Among these are (a) patients have a home;
(b) patients have a family and/or another person(s) who are willing
to assume responsibility for them and are physically and financially
able to provide the necessary care; (c) patterns of organization and
interpersonal relations in the patient's household are such so as to
not impede or prevent recovery and rehabilitation; (d) the family
has sufficient understanding of the patient's illness and expected
behavior so as to develop attitudes which assist rather than retard
recovery and rehabilitation; (e) the patient's behavior and his needs
are such that his presence in the household does not produce undue
hardships for the other members of the household and does not
precipitate secondary attacks of disease and disability in the other
members; and (f) appropriate medical, psychiatric, nursing, social
work, and related services are readily accessible to meet the changing
needs of the patient and his family.

Several charts illustrate the distribution of the population of 1970 by type of living arrangement and size of family. Figure 8 shows the age variation in living arrangements of persons 14 years of age and over. In the 65 and over age group, 67% lived in families, 3% with nonrelatives, 25% lived alone, and 5% lived in group quarters. Figure 9 shows the age variations in distribution of persons

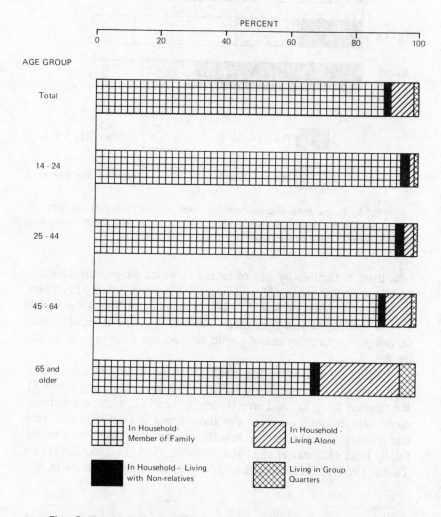

Fig. 8. Percentage distribution of persons 14 years of age and older by type of living arrangement and age, United States, March 1970. (The source for these data was the United States Bureau of the Census, 1971.)

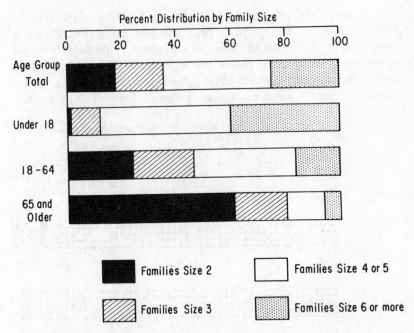

Fig. 9. Percentage distribution of members of families by size of family and age, United States, 1960. (The source for these data was United States Census of Population, 1960.)

who lived in families by size of family in which the persons reside.[12] In this same age group (65 and over), 61% lived in families of Size 2, 19% in families of Size 3, 13% in families of Size 4 or 5, and 6% in families of Size 6 or more. Persons living by themselves and in two-person families are of particular concern in programs for the aged.

Table 19 illustrates the effect of living arrangements in first admission rates to psychiatric facilities in Maryland during 1960–61 for persons 65 years and over living in families, with nonrelatives, alone, and in group quarters. For those living in families, rates were computed specifically for the relationship an individual bears to the family head (Kramer et al., 1968; Pollack, 1965; Pollack, Redick, & Taube, 1968). It is evident that there may be large variations in first

---

[12]Data on the number of persons in families by size of family are given for 1960. The corresponding data for 1970 were not yet available from the United States Bureau of the Census at the time this material was being prepared for publication.

TABLE 19

Number and Rate of First Admissions 65 Years and Over by Living Arrangements, Maryland, 1960-61

Living arrangements and relationship to head of household	Number of first admissions			Rate per 100,000 population		
	Total	Male	Female	Total	Male	Female
All persons 65 and older	584	230	354	266.1	244.9	281.9
Living in households	516	216	300	248.9	240.2	255.5
Members of families	387	176	211	231.6	228.4	234.2
In husband-wife families	293	130	163	230.4	195.0	269.5
Head	90	90	Not applicable	158.1	158.1	Not applicable
Wife	85	Not applicable	85	232.8	Not applicable	232.8
Child	—	—	—	.0	.0	.0
Other relative	118	40	78	351.6	411.2	327.3
In other male-head families	50	42	8	404.3	575.7	157.7
Head	16	16	Not applicable	268.4	268.4	Not applicable
Child	—	—	—	.0	.0	.0
Other relative	34	26	8	535.9	2,010.8	158.4
In female-head families	44	4	40	159.4	130.1	163.0
Head	16	Not applicable	16	103.1	Not applicable	103.1
Child	—	—	—	.0	.0	.0
Other relative	28	4	24	238.0	136.4	271.8
Living with nonrelatives	44	8	36	375.6	174.2	505.3
Living alone	85	32	53	298.7	386.8	262.5
Living in group quarters	68	14	54	557.9	349.5	659.9
Inmates of institutions	54	4	50	553.1	130.4	746.8
Persons in other group quarters	14	10	4	577.1	1,066.1	268.8

Note. The source for these data was unpublished data collected by the Biometry Branch, National Institute of Mental Health, and unpublished tabulations prepared by the United States Bureau of the Census.

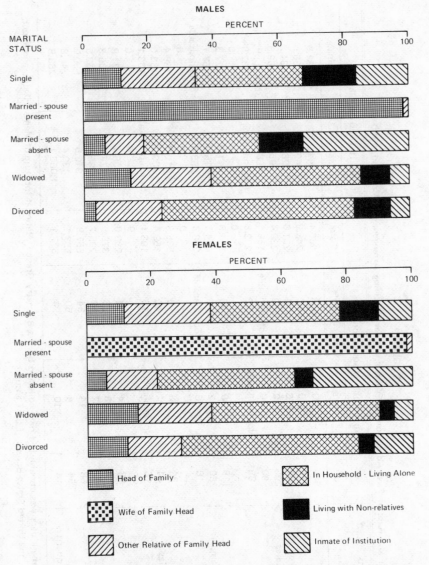

Fig. 10. Percentage distribution of persons 65 years old and over by type of living arrangement, sex, and marital status, United States, March 1970. (The source for these data was the United States Bureau of the Census, 1971.)

admission rates by living arrangements and sex. For example, the rate for males identified as other relatives of the head (e.g., brother of the head) in other male-head families is excessively high whereas the rate for females in the corresponding group is relatively low.

A demographic variable that is related closely to the interpersonal environment is marital status. The significant variations in admission, resident patient, release, and mortality rates for the never married, married, divorced, separated, and widowed in mental hospitals underscore the importance of this variable (Kramer, 1966, 1967, 1969). Knowledge about the living arrangements of persons in each marital status category is also of importance for planning community placement and home care. Figure 10 shows the living arrangements of persons 65 years and over by marital status and sex.

Of particular importance are the substantial proportions of divorced and widowed females who are heads of families and the large proportions of widowed, divorced, and separated (married, spouse absent) males and females who live alone. Among males, about 47% of the widowed and 59% of the divorced and 36% of the separated live alone (Kramer, 1967, 1969). Among females the corresponding figures are 53, 55, and 43%.

Estimates of the distribution of the United States population by household and family characteristics have not been made for 1975 and 1980. However, the data presented in Tables 20 and 21 give some clues as to the distributions that might be expected. Forthcoming data from the 1970 United States Census will make it possible to examine trends that have occurred in living arrangements of the population since 1960, thus providing a limited basis for projections.

IMPACT OF MAJOR SOCIAL PROBLEMS ON THE NEEDS FOR MENTAL HEALTH SERVICES

Major social problems may exert a marked effect on the aged's needs for mental health services and their use of psychiatric facilities. Several such problems will be discussed briefly: crime and violence, alcoholism, poverty, and suicide.

Crime and Violence

The increases in violence, crime, and civil disturbances occurring over the past few years have been a source of much concern and stress to many of the aged, particularly those who live in the inner cities and ghettos. Some are reluctant to leave their houses during the daytime as well as at night for fear of being robbed, attacked, or injured. Such fears prevent many from walking, taking buses or taxis, visiting friends and relatives, shopping for food and other

TABLE 20

Number and Percentage Distribution of Persons 14 Years of Age and Older by Type of Living Arrangement and Age, United States, March 1970

Type of living arrangement	Number (in thousands)[a]					Percentage				
	Total	14-24	25-44	45-64	65+	Total	14-24	25-44	45-64	65+
Total	147,472	38,162	47,886	41,712	19,713	100.0	100.0	100.0	100.0	100.0
In household, member of family	130,852	36,031	44,795	36,747	13,277	88.7	94.5	93.5	88.2	67.4
In household, living with nonrelatives	3,141	1,032	904	682	524	2.1	2.7	1.9	1.6	2.6
In household, living alone	10,692	550	1,585	3,598	4,958	7.3	1.4	3.3	8.6	25.2
Living in group quarters	2,787	546	601	686	953	1.9	1.4	1.3	1.6	4.8

Note. The source for these data was the United States Bureau of the Census (1971).
[a]Numbers do not always add exactly to totals due to rounding.

TABLE 21

Number and Percentage Distribution of Population 65 Years and Older by Marital Status, Type of Living Arrangement, and Sex, United States, March 1970

Type of living arrangement	Males						Females					
	Total	Single	Married (spouse present)	Married (spouse absent)[a]	Widowed	Divorced	Total	Single	Married (spouse present)	Married (spouse absent)[a]	Widowed	Divorced
Number[b]												
Total	8,364	653	5,721	281	1,510	199	11,349	871	3,824	200	6,196	259
Head of family	5,961	76	5,643	19	218	7	1,114	104	—	13	964	33
Wife of family head	—	—	—	—	—	—	3,762	—	3,762	—	—	—
Other relative of family head	674	149	79	33	372	41	1,765	230	62	30	1,401	42
In household, living alone[c]	1,129	217	—	100	695	116	3,829	348	—	85	3,256	141
Living with nonrelatives	297	105	—	36	131	22	367	101	—	11	242	12
Inmate of institution	302	105	—	91	93	12	512	88	—	61	333	31
Percentage												
Total	100.0	100.0	100.0	100.0	100.0	100.0	100.0	100.0	100.0	100.0	100.0	100.0
Head of family	71.2	11.7	98.6	6.8	14.4	3.5	9.8	11.9	—	6.5	15.6	12.7
Wife of family head	—	—	—	—	—	—	33.2	—	98.4	—	—	—
Other relative of family head	8.1	22.9	1.4	11.8	24.6	20.7	15.6	26.4	1.6	15.0	22.6	16.2
In household, living alone[c]	13.5	33.2	—	35.9	46.1	58.6	33.7	40.0	—	42.5	52.5	54.5
Living with nonrelatives	3.6	16.1	—	12.9	8.7	11.1	3.2	11.6	—	5.5	3.9	4.6
Inmate of institution	3.6	16.1	—	32.6	6.2	6.1	4.5	10.1	—	30.5	5.4	12.0

Note. The source of these data was the United States Bureau of the Census (1971). Numbers are shown in thousands.

[a] Includes those with legal separations or living apart because of marital discord, as well as married persons living apart due to (a) employment at considerable distance from home, (b) service in the armed forces, (c) residence in an institution, or (d) for any other reason than marital separation.

[b] Numbers do not always add exactly to totals due to rounding.

[c] Includes persons living in households and in group quarters other than institutions.

supplies, visiting physicians and outpatient services, or attending movies and social gatherings.

Measuring the resultant effect of these fears and anxieties on the incidence and prevalence of psychoneuroses, psychophysiological and behavioral disorders, and psychosocial problems, as well as on the delivery of health and social services, is difficult. However, there is no doubt that these problems exist and that community action is needed to minimize—hopefully to eliminate—the risks that make it difficult for the aged to engage in many of the pursuits of everyday life.

Alcoholism

Alcoholism is a major problem for persons age 45–64. During 1968, alcoholic disorders (brain syndromes with alcoholism and alcohol addiction) accounted for 38% of all male admissions in this age group to all types of inpatient psychiatric facilities, varying from 32% in the Veterans Administration hospitals to 47% in the state and county mental hospitals. In the state hopsitals, it is the leading admission diagnosis in this age group. By 1969 the proportion of male admissions with alcoholism in this age group increased to 57% in state mental hospitals. Many alcoholics in this age group suffer from associated mental, physical, and social problems for which they will require services for many years to come. Even in the 65 and over age group alcoholism accounted for 12% of all male admissions in 1968 and 11% in 1969. In 10 years the survivors of the population who are now 55–64 years of age will be 65–74 years old. The possible increase in needs for services among such survivors who have been or are still alcoholics can place additional stresses on the health delivery system.

Poverty

Persons living at or below the poverty level[13] constitute a very high risk group with respect to needs for health, mental health, and

---

[13]The poverty level is based on a poverty index developed by the Social Security Administration. This index provides a range of poverty income cutoffs adjusted by such factors as family size, sex of family head, number of children under 18 years of age, and farm-nonfarm residence. For example in

related social services. As of 1969, an estimated one-quarter of the 18.9 million persons 65 years of age and over and 13% of the 8.3 million persons 60–64 years of age were below the poverty level (United States Bureau of the Census, 1970b). Twenty-five percent of the females 60 years and over were below the poverty level compared to only 17% of the males in this age group. Studies of admissions to psychiatric facilities by age and family income indicate that admission rates among the aged are highest among those in the lower income levels. For example, a study of first admission rates to all psychiatric facilities in Louisiana and Maryland in 1960 showed that rates for mental disorders of the senium (the diagnostic category in which most of the aged admissions were concentrated) were generally highest in the two lowest family income levels, under $2,000 and $2,000–$4,000 (National Institute of Mental Health, unpublished data). Data on admissions to outpatient psychiatric services in the United States in 1969 indicated that among the aged those with family income levels below $3,000 had the highest utilization rate, with almost four-fifths of the admissions 65 years and over being in this income level category (National Institute of Mental Health, 1971a).

Data from the National Center for Health Statistics (1966a) 1963–65 survey on age patterns in medical care, illness, and disability indicated that persons 65 years of age and over in the lowest income levels (under $3,000 and $3,000–$4,000) had quite high rates of discharge from short-stay hospitals.

The survey also indicated that the highest proportion of persons in this age group with one or more chronic conditions and limited with respect to amount or kind of major activity in which they could engage, were in the lowest income level (under $3,000).

This evidence, along with the fact that more than one-half (55%) of the aged persons below the poverty level in the general population were identified as being unrelated individuals (i.e., living alone or with unrelated persons), would indicate that in planning for current and future psychiatric and other health and social services for the aged, the 4.8 million below the poverty level represent a particularly high risk group. Furthermore, the fact that many of them live alone or in nonfamily situations would further indicate that services other than home care or family care programs would be man-

---

1969, the poverty thresholds for nonfarm residents ranged from $1,757 for an unrelated individual 65 years old and over to $6,101 for a family with seven or more persons.

datory. Unless striking decreases occur during the decade in the number of poor persons and considerable improvement occurs in their health status, this group will continue to place heavy demands on health, mental health, social, and related human services.

Suicide

The aged population, particularly males, have very high suicide rates. Among males the suicide rates in the 55–64, 65–74, and 75 and over age groups are higher than those for any other age group. The maximum rate occurs in the 75–84 age group. Despite the fact that rates in these age groups have tended to decrease during the past 10 years, they still remain at a quite high level. Suicide rates among females in the 45 and over age group are considerably lower than the corresponding rates for males, however, female rates in the 45–54 and 55–64 age groups have tended to increase. Rates for females age 65–74 also showed increases for a period of several years, but are now tending to decrease. Although prevention of suicides in this age group is a difficult problem to solve, mental health and social agencies should collaborate with suicide prevention centers to do whatever is possible to provide services that may in some way reduce the risk of death through this means.

IMPACT OF FUTURE CONGRESSIONAL ACTION ON MENTAL HEALTH CENTERS, MEDICARE, MEDICAID, DELIVERY OF HEALTH SERVICES, AND NATIONAL HEALTH INSURANCE

The delivery of health and mental health services will undergo some important changes as a result of recent legislation either passed or proposed by Congress.

Community Mental Health Centers

The construction of new community mental health centers has been curtailed sharply due to the fact that no new funds were appropriated for their construction in fiscal year 1971. Funds were available for obligation during 1971 consisting of the carryover of unobligated balances from fiscal year 1970. The President's budget for fiscal year 1972 contained no request for construction funds.

However, Congress appropriated 15 million dollars for new construction.

In addition, Congress appropriated 135.1 million dollars for staffing grants for fiscal year 1972. Priority is being given to staffing applications from centers that have received prior construction support and are ready to begin operation. The funds requested for fiscal year 1972 provide for the continuation of existing centers funded through 1971 and the awarding of at least 42 new staffing grants.

While it is difficult to predict the extent to which additional community mental health centers will be constructed and staffed during this decade and the extent to which any increased level of services to the aged will be provided through these facilities, the Department of Health, Education, and Welfare has given priority to continuation and development of the program, and to development of services for the aged.

Medicare and Medicaid

The proposed 1971 Amendments to the Social Security Act provide that both Medicare beneficiaries and Medicaid recipients are eligible for enrollment in approved health maintenance organizations (HMOs). An HMO is an organized system of health care that provides comprehensive health maintenance and treatment services for an enrolled group of persons through a prepaid aggregate, fixed sum, or capitation arrangement. The basic purposes of an HMO are to seek improvements of the nation's health care system by working toward (a) an increased emphasis on the maintenance of health to prevent serious illness; (b) greater efficiency in the organization and use of scarce health services resources; (c) more equitable and predictable distribution of costs by risk sharing; (d) greater benefit for the system by more active and responsible participation of consumers, both in their own patient activity and in nonmedical decision making.

The proposed 1971 amendments to the Social Security Act would create incentives for individuals covered under Medicare and Medicaid to utilize HMOs or similar facilities for comprehensive care (Committee on Ways and Means, 1971). Potentially the HMOs can have a profound effect on delivery of health services. However, their impact on aged people needing mental health services will depend on the final form of the legislation not only with respect to financial incentives for HMOs but also the extent of coverage for mental health.

The proposed 1971 amendments would also provide disincentives to discourage prolonged stays in institutions. The proposed amendments would not only preserve all the limitations now in effect with respect to coverage for psychiatric care in both Medicare and Medicaid but would introduce additional restrictions in the Medicaid program. Of particular importance is the proposed imposition of a lifetime limit on number of days of inpatient care in a mental hospital for Medicaid beneficiaries where no such limit existed before. Other restrictions are proposed to discourage long stays in general hospitals and nursing homes such as reductions in the federal medical assistance percentages for care in general hospitals and for skilled nursing homes for which the state has established no effective utilization review programs. To encourage community care, a substantial increase is proposed in the federal Medicaid matching percentage to states under contract with HMOs or other comprehensive health care facilities.

As already indicated, 25% of the persons 65 years and over live alone, and 3% with nonrelated persons. These proportions are much higher for such persons in the low-income group where more than one-half of the aged below the poverty level in 1969 lived alone or with nonrelatives. Thus, all actions that would limit institutional stays and result in return of increased numbers of aged to live in the community would place increased demands on already overburdened community agencies for medical, psychiatric, nursing, homemaker, and other social services and for adequate housing.

National Health Insurance Legislation

National health insurance legislation is another unknown factor at this time. Although the passage of some form of such legislation seems likely within the next few years, the extent of the coverage to be provided is not yet clear. Currently there are more than half a dozen bills proposing various national health insurance plans. In some, fairly extensive coverage for psychiatric disorders is proposed; in others, little or no mention is made of such coverage. National health insurance would undoubtedly affect the demand for *covered* services and this in turn can exert a strong effect for services *not covered*. For example, if the number of persons using physicians and outpatient and general hospital services increases by a substantial amount, it is likely that more persons will be discovered who have emotional disorders requiring specialized mental health care. Referral of such persons to already overburdened mental health resources and agencies could place an additional load on such services which could not be met unless such resources are expanded to keep up with the increased demand. Until there is further specification of exactly what the national health insurance program will be, it is impossible to assess the expected impact of any such program on the delivery of health services, particularly to those persons in the 55–64 age group whose survivors will enter the ranks of those 65 years and over in the next 10 years.

CONCLUDING COMMENTS

This chapter has provided background data for the Task Force of the American Psychological Association to use in developing recommendations for the White House Conference on Aging on needs of the aged during the 1970s for mental health and related human services and on other matters related to this problem. Data have been presented on the magnitude of the problem of mental disorders and associated conditions and patterns of use of psychiatric facilities, general hospitals, psychiatrists and other physicians, and health professionals. Examples have been provided of the manner in which patterns of use of psychiatric facilities have changed over the past 25 years, the various factors that have produced these changes, and factors that may produce additional change in the next decade.

These data suggest many possible activities in which psychologists can become involved in meeting needs for mental health services for the aged such as program planning; coordination of activities at the federal, state, and local levels; delivery of direct services to patients in various treatment settings; basic, clinical, epidemiologic, social science, and behavioral research; and evaluation of the effectiveness of mental health services and recruitment and training of personnel.

This chapter underscores the fact that the basic, statistical, epidemiologic, evaluative, personnel, and administrative data needed to make various predictions is quite limited and in many instances quite crude and inadequate. For the most part, this is due to current limitations of the techniques available for collecting epidemiologic data on the incidence and prevalence of mental disorders and the complexity of collecting systematic annual data on the patterns of use of psychiatric and medical facilities and on the effectiveness of various therapeutic and rehabilitation programs.

The development of more refined and precise estimates of need and of rates of use and effectiveness of services requires an intensive research effort. This will result in the development of case-finding and diagnostic techniques for population surveys and in the design and implementation of randomized clinical trials and other types of evaluative studies to assess the effectiveness of particular procedures, programs, or staffing patterns. In addition, more basic knowledge is required on the causes of specific mental disorders so that primary preventive techniques may be developed to reduce the incidence of such disorders and their associated disabilities in every age group of the population.

The development of basic knowledge about causes of mental disorders in the aged presents many difficulties. Persons who reach advanced years are a highly selected population. Their current illnesses may have had their origin in many different ways and at different periods of their lives. Some may be traced to genetic factors. Others may have had their origins in single or multiple events associated with life experiences in different phases of an individual's physical, biological, psychological, emotional, educational, occupational, and social development. Others may have had their roots in the social, cultural, economic, and educational characteristics of the membership of various groups to which a person belonged over his lifetime, which have shaped his value system and determined his way of life. Others may be due to the aging process per se and the changes which degenerative diseases bring about in the biological, physical, and mental functions of an individual, which in turn, affect ways of life. Still others may be due to stresses resulting from loss of a spouse, other family members and friends; separation from children; lack of opportunity to participate in meaningful civic, cultural, or recreational activities, or lack of motivation to participate in such activities when they are available; and insufficient financial resources to maintain an adequate standard of living. Research to disentangle the multifactorial etiology of the mental diseases of the aged requires a variety of study designs, including long-term follow-up studies of specifically designated groups of persons. To quote Susser and Watson (1962):

An organism has stored within it a memory, so to speak, both of its genetic inheritance, and of its past experience. At any moment in time the individual organism, the phenotype, is a survivor of a process, through which its genetic inheritance, the genotype, is modified by experience. Populations, therefore, comprise the survivors of a process of selection working through the interaction of constitution and environment over time, and they are best studied by methods which allow for the time dimensions, for instance by analysing the experience of the component age groups, or by following each generation through its life cycle [p. 2].

Implementing longitudinal studies of the type suggested, however, presents many difficulties in the highly mobile population of the United States.

Strengthening of existing state and local statistical, epidemiologic, and related research programs and initiating such programs where they do not now exist are essential steps in developing the resources required for providing the mental health field with more information than is now available from national, state, and local sources. The design and implementation of studies that provide such facts require a sophisticated field team located in an area where it is possible to study the power structure, demography, and ecology of the community, to carry out epidemiologic investigations, and to study the effectiveness of treatment and rehabilitation techniques. Health departments, departments of mental health, and appropriate university groups will have to pool their skilled research manpower and other resources to plan and develop units where such research can be carried out. In addition, an intensified effort will have to be made to recruit and train the additional scientists required for biostatistical, epidemiological, social science, psychological, and related research. As a result of the expansion of action and research programs in mental health, child health and human development, chronic diseases, mental retardation, crime and delinquency, drug abuse and addiction, and delivery of health and related human services, an unprecedented demand now exists for scientists trained to carry out biostatistical, social science, and epidemiological research. This demand will require government and academic institutions to intensify their programs to recruit for training in these specialties the most promising and gifted of our high school and college graduates. Such action will be necessary in order to provide the many well-trained scientific and ancillary personnel required to solve the complex health, social, welfare, and economic problems that beset our Nation.

REFERENCES

American Psychiatric Association, Committee on Nomenclature and Statistics. *Diagnostic and statistical manual, mental disorders.* (DSM-II) Washington, D.C.: Author, 1968.

American Psychopathological Association. *Trends in mental disease.* New York: Columbia University Press, 1945.

Bahn, A. K. *Methodological study of population of outpatient psychiatric clinics, Maryland, 1958–59.* (USPHS Publ. No. 65) Washington, D.C.: United States Government Printing Office, 1961.

Bahn, A. K., Gardner, E. A., Alltop, L., Knatterud, G. L., & Solomon, M. Admission and prevalence rates for psychiatric facilities in four register areas. *American Journal of Public Health,* 1966, **56**, 2033-2051.

Bahn, A. K., Gorwitz, K., Klee, G. D., Kramer, M., & Tuerk, I. Services received by Maryland residents in facilities directed by a psychiatrist. *Public Health Reports,* 1965, **80**, 405–416.

Cannon, M. Halfway houses—A growing mental health resource. Paper presented at the 3rd Annual Community Psychiatry Conference on Planning and Organizing Halfway Houses, State University of New York at Buffalo, May 1971.

Committee on Ways and Means. *Report on H.R.1: Social Security Amendments of 1971.* Washington, D.C.: United States Government Printing Office, 1971.

Dayton, N. A. *New facts on mental disorders.* Baltimore: Thomas, 1940.

Dohrenwend, B. P., & Dohrenwend, B. S. *Social status and psychological disorder: A causal inquiry.* New York: Wiley Interscience, 1969.

Essen-Moller, E. Individual traits and morbidity in a Swedish rural population. *Acta Psychiatrica et Neurologica Scandinavica,* 1956. (Supplement 100)

Faris, R. E. L., & Dunham, H. W. *Mental disorders in urban areas: An ecological study of schizophrenia and other psychoses.* Chicago: University of Chicago Press, 1939.

Fowler, I. A., Gruenberg, E. M., McCaffrey, I., & Rogott, E. *The relationship of city-sized geographical location and proximity to mental hospitals with hospitalized incidence of psychosis of the aged* (Tech. Rep. of the Mental Health Research Unit, New York State Department of Mental Hygiene) Syracuse: Syracuse University Press, 1955.

Frost, W. H. Epidemiology in Nelson loose leaf system. In, *Public Health preventive medicine.* Vol. 2. New York: Thomas Nelson, 1927.

General Register Office. *Studies on medical and population subjects: No. 22. A glossary of mental disorders based on the international statistical classification of disorders, injuries and causes of death.* London: Her Majesty's Stationery Office, 1968.

Giesler, R., Hurley, P. L., & Person, P. H., Jr. *Survey of general hospitals admitting psychiatric patients.* (USPHS Publ. No. 1462) Washington, D.C.: United States Government Printing Office, 1966.

Group for the Advancement of Psychiatry, Committee on Preventive Psychiatry. *Problems of estimating changes in frequency of mental disorders.* New York: Author, 1961.

Hare, E. H., & Shaw, G. K. *Mental health on a new housing estate.* New York: Oxford University Press, 1965.

Jaco, E. G. *The social epidemiology of mental disorders.* New York: Russell Sage Foundation, 1960.

Kay, D. W. K., Beamish, P., & Roth, M. Old age mental disorders in Newcastle-upon-Tyne: Part I. A study of prevalence. *British Journal of Psychiatry,* 1964, **110**, 146–158.

Kobrynski, B., & Miller, A. D. The role of the state hospital in the care of the elderly. *Journal of the American Geriatric Society*, 1970, **18**, 210.

Kramer, M. *Some implications of trends in the usage of psychiatric facilities for community mental health programs and related research.* (USPHS Publ. No. 1434) Washington, D.C.: United States Government Printing Office, 1966.

Kramer, M. Epidemiology, biostatistics and mental health planning. *Psychiatric epidemiology and mental health planning.* (Psychiatric Research Rep. No. 23) Washington, D.C.: American Psychiatric Association, 1967.

Kramer, M. *Applications of mental health statistics.* Geneva, Switzerland: World Health Organization, 1969.

Kramer, M., Goldstein, H., Israel, R. H., & Johnson, N. A. *An historical study of the disposition of first admissions to a state mental hospital: Experience of the Warren State Hospital during the period 1916-1950.* (USPHS Publ. No. 45) Washington, D.C.: United States Government Printing Office, 1955.

Kramer, M., Pollack, E. S., & Redick, R. W. Studies of incidence and prevalence of hospitalized mental disorders in the U.S.: Current status and future goals. In P. H. Hoch & J. Zubin (Eds.), *Comparative epidemiology of mental disorders.* New York: Grune & Stratton, 1961.

Kramer, M., Taube, C., & Starr, S. Patterns of use of psychiatric facilities by the aged: Current status, trends and implications. In, *Aging in modern society.* Washington, D.C.: American Psychiatric Association, 1968.

Lin, T., & Standley, C. C. The scope of epidemiology in psychiatry. *Public Health Papers*, 1962, No. 16.

Locke, B. Z., Kramer, M., & Pasamanick, B. Mental diseases of the senium at mid-century. *American Journal of Public Health*, 1960, **59**, 998–1012.

Malzberg, B. *Statistical data for the study of mental disease in New York State, 1939–1941.* Albany: State Department of Mental Hygiene Report, 1955.

Malzberg, B. *Cohort studies of mental disease in New York State, 1943–1949.* New York: National Association for Mental Health, 1958.

Malzberg, B., & Lee, E. S. *Migration and mental disease: A study of first admissions to hospitals for mental disease, New York, 1939–1941.* New York: Social Science Research Council, 1956.

McCaffrey, I. *Socioeconomic environment and first admissions to mental hospitals of patients with cerebral arteriosclerosis and senile psychoses, Syracuse City, 1935–1941.* Syracuse: Mental Health Research Unit, New York State Department of Mental Hygiene, Syracuse University Press, 1955.

National Center for Health Statistics. *Age patterns in medical care, illness and disability: U.S. July 1963–June 1965.* (USPHS Publ. No. 1000, Ser. 10, No. 32) Washington, D.C.: United States Government Printing Office, 1966. (a)

National Center for Health Statistics. *Characteristics of patients of selected types of medical specialists and practitioners: U.S. July 1963–June 1964.* (USPHS Publ. No. 1000, Ser. 10, No. 28) Washington, D.C.: United States Government Printing Office, 1966. (b)

National Center for Health Statistics. *Prevalence of chronic conditions and impairments among residents of nursing and personal care homes.* (USPHS Publ. No. 1000, Ser. 12, No. 8) Washington, D.C.: United States Government Printing Office, 1967.

National Center for Health Statistics. *Health resources statistics.* (USPHS Publ. No. 1509) Washington, D.C.: United States Government Printing Office, 1969.

National Institute of Mental Health, Biometry Branch. *Mental health day/night treatment programs—1967.* (Statistical Note No. 6) Rockville, Md.: Author, 1969.

National Institute of Mental Health, Biometry Branch. *Admission rates by family income level—Outpatient psychiatric service 1969.* (Statistical Note No. 47) Rockville, Md.: Author, 1971 (a)

National Institute of Mental Health, Biometry Branch. *Diagnostic distribution of inpatient admissions to state and county menal hospitals, 1969.* (Statistical Note No. 49) Rockville, Md.: Author, 1971. (b)

New York State Department of Mental Hygiene, Mental Health Research Unit. A mental health survey of older people: Part III. *Psychiatric Quarterly Supplement,* 1960, **34,** 34–75.

Pasamanick, B., Roberts, D. W., Lemkau, P. W., & Krueger, D. B. A survey of mental disease in an urban population: Prevalence by race and income. In B. Pasamanick (Ed.), *Epidemiology of mental disorder.* Washington, D.C.: American Association for the Advancement of Science, 1959.

Pollack, E. S. Use of census matching for study of psychiatric admission rates. In, *Proceedings of the Social Statistics Section of the American Statistical Association.* Washington, D.C.: American Statistical Association, 1965.

Pollack, E. S., Locke, B. Z., & Kramer, M. Trends in hospitalization and patterns of care of the aged mentally ill. In P. H. Hoch & J. Zubin (Eds.), *Psychopathology of aging.* New York: Grune & Stratton, 1961.

Pollack, E. S., Person, P. H., Jr., Kramer, M., & Goldstein, H. *Patterns of retention, release and death of first admissions to state mental hospitals.* (USPHS Publ. No. 672) Washington, D.C.: United States Government Printing Office, 1959.

Pollack, E. S., Redick, R. W., & Taube, C. A. The application of census socioeconomic and familial data to the study of morbidity from mental disorders. *American Journal of Public Health,* 1968, **58,** 83–89.

Pollock, H. M. *Mental disease and social welfare.* Utica, N.Y.: State Hospitals Press, 1941.

Public Law 79–487—79th Congress, Chapter 538—2nd Session, July 3rd, 1946. *The National Mental Health Act.*

Public Law 88–164—88th Congress, S.1576, October 31, 1963. *Mental Retardation Facilities and Community Mental Health Centers Construction Act of 1963.*

Public Law 89–97—89th Congress, H. R. 6675, July 30th, 1965. *Social Security Amendments of 1965.*

Public Law 90–574—90th Congress—2nd Session, October 15, 1968. *Alcoholic and Narcotic Addict Rehabilitation Amendments of 1968.*

Public Law 91–211—91st Congress—2nd Session, March 13, 1970. *Community Mental Health Centers Amendments of 1970.*

Pugh, T. F., & MacMahon, B. *Epidemiologic findings in the United States mental hospital data.* Boston: Little, Brown, 1962.

Shepherd, M., Cooper, B., Brown, A. C., & Kalton, G. W. *Psychiatric illness in general practice.* London: Oxford University Press, 1966.

Social Security Administration. *A study of the use of general hospitals by aged psychiatric patients, January 1965–June 1966 and July 1966–December 1967.* (Health Insurance Statistics, HI-13) Washington, D.C.: Author, 1969.

Southern Regional Conference on Mental Health Statistics Definitions of terms in mental health, mental retardation and alcoholism programs. (2nd ed.) Rockville, Md.: Southern Regional Education Board and Biometry Branch, National Institute of Mental Health, 1970. (Mimeo)

Srole, L., Langner, T. S., Michael, S. T., Opler, M. K., & Rennie, T. A. C. *Mental health in the metropolis: The Midtown Study.* Vol. 1. New York: McGraw-Hill, 1962.

Stromgren, E. Epidemiology of old-age psychiatric disorders. In R. H. William, C. Tibbitts, & W. Donahue (Eds.), *Process of aging.* Vol. 2, New York: Atherton Press, 1963.

Susser, M. W., & Watson, W. *Sociology in medicine.* London: Oxford University Press, 1962.

Trussell, R. E., & Ellison, J. *Chronic illness in a rural area—The Hunterdon Study.* Cambridge: Harvard University Press, 1959.

United States Bureau of the Census. *Current population reports.* (Series P-25, No. 448) Washington, D.C.: United States Government Printing Office, 1970. (a)

United States Bureau of the Census. *Current population reports.* (Series P-60, No. 76) Washington, D.C.: United States Government Printing Office, 1970. (b)

United States Bureau of the Census. *Current population reports.* (Series P-20, No. 212) Washington, D.C.: United States Government Printing Office, 1971.

United States Census of Population. *Persons by family characteristics.* (Series PC-2, 4B) Washington, D.C.: United States Government Printing Office, 1960.

United States Department of Health, Education, and Welfare. *Patient movement data—State and county mental hospitals.* (USPHS Publ. No. 1282) Washington, D.C.: United States Government Printing Office, 1964. (a)

United States Department of Health, Education, and Welfare. *Patients in mental institutions, 1963.* (USPHS Publ. No. 1222) Washington, D.C.: United States Government Printing Office, 1964. (b)

APPENDIX A

Individual-Oriented Service[14]

A. *Contact Services.* The provision of information about the appropriateness or availability of services. Includes screening and referral services.

B. *Evaluation Services*

1. Psychiatric. A psychodiagnostic process including a medical history and a mental status examination.
2. Social. An evaluation to ascertain the social situation of the individual, including personal background, family background, family interactions, living arrangements, economic problems, and formulation of future goals and plans.
3. Psychological. An evaluation of cognitive processes and emotions and problems of adjustment in individuals through interpretation of tests of mental abilities, aptitudes, interests, attitudes, emotions, motivation, and personality characteristics.
4. Physical. An examination of the body by a physician.
   a. Neurological. An examination by a physician of the central, peripheral, and sympathetic nervous systems.
5. Educational-Vocational. An evaluation to determine an individual's academic or vocational interest, aptitudes, and achievements.
6. Speech. An evaluation to determine the cause and extent of speech disorders and need for corrective work.
7. Hearing. An evaluation to determine the cause and extent of hearing disorders and need for corrective work.

C. *Treatment Services*

1. Individual therapy. Treatment by individual interview and including supportive psychotherapy, relationship therapy, insight therapy, psychoanalysis, counseling, play therapy, hypnotherapy (with or without drugs), casework behavioral therapy, etc.
2. Group therapy. Treatment by the use of group dynamics or group interaction and including group psychotherapy, group play therapy, group psychoanalysis, psychodrama, therapy with groups of families or married couples, but excluding family therapy.
3. Family therapy. Therapy applied to a family as a unit. Significant members of the family are seen together and considered as patients. Excludes groups of families or married couples.

---

[14]The source of these data was the Southern Regional Conference on Mental Health Statistics, "Definitions of Terms in Mental Health, Mental Retardation and Alcoholism Programs." (2nd ed.) Rockville, Md.: Southern Regional Education Board and Biometry Branch, National Institute of Mental Health, 1970. (Mimeo)

4. Chemotherapy. Treatment by the use of medications including tranquilizers, antidepressants, anticonvulsants, sedatives, etc.

5. Detoxification. Treatment by use of medication, rest, fluids, and nursing care to restore physiological function after it is upset by toxic agents such as alcohol or barbiturates.

6. Somatic therapy. Treatment by the use of physical procedures other than chemotherapy or detoxification. Includes electroconvulsive therapy, CO_2 therapy, etc.

7. Collateral therapy. Treatment of the patient through interviews beyond the diagnostic level with collateral persons, such interviews centering around the patient's problems without the patient himself necessarily being seen. Includes treatment of a child by working with the parents or treatment of an oldster by working through family members.

8. Medical-surgical services. Other medical or surgical procedures.

D. *Rehabilitation-Restoration-Habilitation Services*

1. Vocational rehabilitation/counseling. A process to assist an individual in developing work skills, habits, and attitudes and to assist him in job placement.

2. Social rehabilitation services. The process of helping an individual in his psychosocial adjustment by· learning or relearning social skills, including occupational therapy, industrial therapy, recreational therapy, resocialization programs, music therapy, habit training, self-care training, etc.

3. Speech and hearing therapy. Corrective work for such disorders.

4. Special education service. Training and teaching of the mentally retarded and emotionally disturbed to increase their social, academic, and/or vocational skills.

5. Day training. Provides children and adolescents with training in self-help and motor skills, activities of daily living, and social development preliminary to special education or other placement.

6. Adult activity service. A service designed to involve patients and participants in pursuing hobbies, playing games, serving, cooking, etc. The distinction between this and vocational rehabilitation is that none of the skills acquired would qualify the patient for paid employment.

7. Sheltered workshop. A service in which the handicapped may receive work evaluation, social and personal adjustment training, vocational skill training, and extended employment either in transition to outside employment or as a terminal work adjustment (may be reported separately).

8. Behavioral modification. The modification of individual behavior through systematic application of learning theory and principles. Includes application of operant conditioning techniques—the Skinner-Lindsley principles of systematically strengthening certain responses and weakening others; and of behavior shaping through differential reinforcement.

9. Home service/visit. A service conducted in the temporary or permanent residence of the recipient to provide an objective assessment and help in meeting mental health problems, assist families in utilizing community resources, and provide direct services for patients or families.

E. *Care Services*

1. Personal care. Provides room and board, and assistance in activities of daily living.

APPENDIX B

Factors Related to an Individual's Decision to Visit His General Practitioner[15]

1. Events that may lead an individual to obtain the services of a general practitioner (GP).

  1.1 Crisis

    1.1.1 Accident

    1.1.2 Acute condition related to a disease or disabling condition

  1.2 Detection of a sign or symptom which the individual or a significant other decides needs the services of a physician.

    1.2.1 Bloody sputum

    1.2.2. Chest pain

    1.2.3 Back pain

    1.2.4 Fever

    1.2.5 Headache, etc.

    1.2.6 General feelings of ill health, etc.

  1.3 Periodic checkups in relation to:

    1.3.1 Patient's general program of medical care (e.g., annual physical checkup)

    1.3.2 Follow-up visits related to GP's treatment and rehabilitation program for a patient

  1.4 Requirements of organization in which person works:

    1.4.1 Preemployment examinations

    1.4.2 Disability insurance

    1.4.3 Retirement

    1.4.4 Individual health program, etc.

  1.5 Screening examinations carried out by health department, etc.

2. Factors that influence a person in arriving at a decision actually to obtain the services of his GP.

  2.1 Patient's degree of sophistication with respect to knowledge about health, disease, and disability (e.g., benefits of early detection of disease)

  2.2 Cultural factors

  2.3 Attitudes toward medical care in general and physicians in particular on part of:

    2.3.1 Patient

---

[15]The source of these data was an unpublished report by M. Kramer, Biometry Branch, National Institute of Mental Health.

2.3.2 His family
2.3.3 Significant others
2.4 Costs of medical care
2.5 Accessibility of medical care
2.6 An individual's value system concerning the importance of his state of health to:
    2.6.1 Himself
    2.6.2 Family
    2.6.3 Significant others
2.7 Patient's assessment of potential effects of illness on himself and significant others:
    2.7.1 Life of individual with disease
        2.7.1.1 His activities of daily living
        2.7.1.2 Occupational role
        2.7.1.3 Economic well-being
        2.7.1.4 Family role
        2.7.1.5 Community role
    2.7.2 Members of his immediate household
    2.7.3 The organization in which he works
    2.7.4 The community in which he lives

3. Manner in which the decision to visit GP was made.
3.1 By patient only (no discussion with members of family and/or significant others)
3.2 By patient following discussion with:
    3.2.1 Members of immediate family, no significant others
    3.2.2 Members of immediate family and significant others
    3.2.3 Significant others only
3.3 Attendance required as a result of certain mandatory requirements.

APPENDIX C

Examples of Classifications Developed by Chronic Disease Commission to Characterize Effects of Disabling Illnesses[16]

Classification of clinical evaluees according to ways in which they were restricted with respect to activities of daily living:

Disabled with respect to one or more activities of daily living as follows:
    Limited as to physical activity
    Limited as to diet

---

[16]This information was reprinted by permission of the publisher from R. E. Trussel and J. Ellison, *Chronic Illness in a Rural Area—The Hunterdon Study*. Cambridge, Mass.: Harvard University Press, 1959.

Limited with respect to one or more of the ways listed below:
Confined to bed all or part of the time.
Require assistance, mechanical or personal, in moving about, or unable to move about at all.
Require assistance in climbing stairs, or unable to climb stairs at all.
Restricted as to means of travel, or unable to travel at all.
Require services or assistance to insure personal safety.
Require personal assistance in feeding selves, or cannot feed selves at all.
Require mechanical and/or personal assistance in dressing selves at all.
Incontinent with respect to defecation, urination, or both.
Require personal assistance in performance of toilet functions.
Require personal assistance in performance of other bodily hygiene functions.
Have some speech defect, or cannot communicate vocally at all.
Have difficulty in writing, or cannot communicate in writing at all.
Not disabled with respect to one or more activities.

APPENDIX D

TABLE A

United States Population, Resident Patients and Resident Patient Rates per 100,000 Population for State and County Mental Hospitals, 1955 and 1968, and Percentage Change, 1955-68

Age group	United States population (in thousands)		Resident patient population state and county mental hospitals		Resident patient rate per 100,000 population		Percentage of change 1955-68		
	1955	1968	1955	1968	1955	1968	United States population	Resident patient population	Resident patient rate
Total	162,307	197,571	558,922	399,152	344.4	202.0	21.7	− 28.6	− 41.3
<15	48,798	59,670	2,301	6,365	4.7	10.7	22.3	176.6	127.7
15-24	20,054	31,700	17,276	25,315	86.1	79.9	58.1	46.5	− 7.2
25-34	23,430	23,165	57,634	36,546	246.0	157.8	− 1.1	− 36.6	− 35.9
35-44	22,544	23,240	96,304	52,623	427.2	226.4	3.1	− 45.4	− 53.0
45-54	18,866	22,792	117,500	71,166	622.8	312.2	20.8	− 39.4	− 49.9
55-64	14,545	17,875	109,622	86,997	753.7	486.7	22.9	− 20.6	− 35.4
65-74	9,416	11,786	92,223	66,177	979.4	561.5	25.2	− 28.3	− 42.7
75+	4,653	7,343	66,062	53,963	1,419.8	734.9	57.8	− 18.3	− 48.2
65+	14,069	19,129	158,285	120,140	1,125.1	628.1	36.0	− 24.1	− 44.2

TABLE B

Numbers and Rates per 100,000 Civilian Population of Patient Care Episodes in Psychiatric Facilities by Type of Facility, Age, and Sex, United States, 1966

Age (in years)	All facilities	Public and private mental hospitals				General hospitals with psychiatric services	Outpatient psychiatric clinics
		Total	State and county hospitals	Veterans Administration hospitals	Private hospitals		
				Number			
Both sexes							
Total	2,764,089	1,029,168	802,216	122,979	103,973	548,921	1,186,000
Under 15	368,382	15,822	13,840	65	1,917	16,475	336,085
15-24	443,944	96,377	76,866	2,480	17,031	84,314	263,253
25-34	444,719	140,487	104,511	17,452	18,524	98,898	205,334
35-44	517,165	205,684	134,363	48,484	22,837	117,681	193,800
45-54	403,171	188,478	145,299	25,627	17,552	100,678	114,015
55-64	275,594	160,113	138,486	8,693	12,934	66,431	49,050
65+	311,114	222,207	188,851	20,178	13,178	64,444	24,463
Males							
Total	1,446,091	574,855	412,900	122,979	38,976	220,117	651,119
Under 15	250,261	10,886	9,634	65	1,187	8,584	230,791
15-24	228,734	58,079	47,485	2,480	8,114	33,678	136,977
25-34	208,168	83,957	60,340	17,452	6,165	35,439	88,772
35-44	267,761	126,415	70,015	48,484	7,916	45,344	96,002
45-54	210,584	106,588	74,514	25,627	6,447	41,822	62,174
55-64	139,370	85,071	71,389	8,693	4,989	29,276	25,023
65+	141,213	103,859	79,523	20,178	4,158	25,974	11,380

Females

Total	1,317,998	454,313	389,316	a	64,997	328,804	534,881
Under 15	118,121	4,936	4,206	a	730	7,891	105,294
15-24	215,210	38,298	29,381	a	8,917	50,636	126,276
25-34	236,551	56,530	44,171	a	12,359	63,459	116,562
35-44	249,404	79,269	64,348	a	14,921	72,337	97,798
45-54	192,587	81,890	70,785	a	11,105	58,856	51,841
55-64	136,224	75,042	67,097	a	7,945	37,155	24,027
65+	169,901	118,348	109,328	a	9,020	38,470	13,083

Rate per 100,000 civilian population

Both sexes

Total	1,427.0	531.3	414.2	63.5	53.6	283.4	612.3
Under 15	613.3	26.3	23.0	.1	3.2	27.4	559.6
15-24	1,473.0	319.7	255.0	8.2	56.5	279.8	873.5
25-34	2,043.8	645.6	480.3	80.2	85.1	454.5	943.7
35-44	2,172.4	864.0	564.4	203.7	95.9	494.3	814.1
45-54	1,814.0	848.0	653.7	115.3	79.0	453.0	513.0
55-64	1,597.1	927.9	802.5	50.4	75.0	385.0	284.2
65+	1,685.6	1,203.9	1,023.2	109.3	71.4	349.2	132.5

Males

Total	1,541.6	612.7	440.2	131.1	41.4	234.7	694.2
Under 15	818.5	35.6	31.5	.2	3.9	28.1	754.8
15-24	1,592.0	404.3	330.5	17.3	56.5	234.4	953.3
25-34	2,001.8	807.3	580.2	167.8	59.3	340.8	853.7
35-44	2,338.1	1,103.9	611.4	423.4	69.1	395.9	838.3
45-54	1,958.6	991.3	693.0	238.3	60.0	389.0	578.3
55-64	1,690.9	1,032.1	866.1	105.5	60.5	355.2	303.6
65+	1,764.2	1,297.5	993.5	252.1	51.9	324.5	142.2

TABLE B

Numbers and Rates per 100,000 Civilian Population of Patient Care Episodes in Psychiatric Facilities
by Type of Facility, Age, and Sex, United States, 1966 (Continued)

Age (in years)	All facilities	Public and private mental hospitals				General hospitals with psychiatric services	Outpatient psychiatric clinics
		Total	State and county hospitals	Veterans Administration hospitals	Private hospitals		
		Rate per 100,000 civilian population					
Females							
Total	1,319.3	454.8	389.7	a	65.1	329.1	535.4
Under 15	400.7	16.8	14.3	a	2.5	26.8	357.1
15-24	1,364.6	242.8	186.3	a	56.5	321.1	800.7
25-34	2,082.6	497.7	388.9	a	108.8	558.7	1,026.2
35-44	2,018.8	641.7	520.9	a	120.8	585.5	791.6
45-54	1,678.5	713.7	616.9	a	96.8	513.0	451.8
55-64	1,511.4	832.6	744.4	a	88.2	412.2	266.6
65+	1,625.4	1,132.2	1,045.9	a	86.3	368.0	125.2

Note. Patient care episodes are derived from the sum of residents at the beginning of the year or on the active rolls of the outpatient clinics plus admissions during the year.

aFemale patients excluded because number is negligible.

TABLE C

Numbers and Rates per 100,000 Civilian Population of Total Admissions to Psychiatric Facilities by Type of Facility, Age, and Sex, United States, 1966

Age (in years)	All facilities	Public and private mental hospitals				General hospitals with psychiatric services	Outpatient psychiatric clinics
		Total	State and county hospitals	Veterans Administration hospitals	Private hospitals		
				Number			
Both sexes							
Total	1,637,432	481,954	327,014	65,025	89,915	526,186	629,292
Under 15	210,203	8,982	7,706	65	1,211	15,793	185,428
15-24	288,478	64,987	48,953	2,016	14,018	80,822	142,669
25-34	291,977	89,237	61,874	10,729	16,634	94,802	107,938
35-44	330,190	118,812	67,864	30,171	20,777	112,807	98,571
45-54	239,770	86,598	55,976	15,021	15,601	96,508	56,664
55-64	139,152	50,169	36,120	2,666	11,383	63,679	25,304
65+	137,662	63,169	48,521	4,357	10,291	61,775	12,718
Males							
Total	829,078	277,379	178,942	65,025	33,412	211,000	340,699
Under 15	141,606	5,956	5,189	65	702	8,229	127,421
15-24	144,891	38,336	29,704	2,016	6,616	32,283	74,272
25-34	130,532	51,248	35,073	10,729	5,446	33,971	45,313
35-44	163,515	73,713	36,325	30,171	7,217	43,466	46,336
45-54	119,845	50,796	30,062	15,021	5,713	40,090	28,959
55-64	67,396	26,727	19,684	2,666	4,377	28,063	12,606
65+	61,293	30,603	22,905	4,357	3,341	24,898	5,792

TABLE C

Numbers and Rates per 100,000 Civilian Population of Total Admissions to Psychiatric Facilities by Type of Facility, Age, and Sex, United States, 1966 (Continued)

All (in years)	All facilities	Public and private mental hospitals				General hospitals with psychiatric services	Outpatient psychiatric clinics
		Total	State and county hospitals	Veterans Administration hospitals	Private hospitals		
Females							
Total	808,354	204,575	148,072	a	56,503	315,186	288,593
Under 15	68,597	3,026	2,517	a	509	7,564	58,007
15-24	143,587	26,651	19,249	a	7,402	48,539	68,397
25-34	161,445	37,989	26,801	a	11,188	60,831	62,625
35-44	166,675	45,099	31,539	a	13,560	69,341	52,235
45-54	119,925	35,802	25,914	a	9,888	56,418	27,705
55-64	71,756	23,442	16,436	a	7,006	35,616	12,698
65+	76,369	32,566	25,616	a	6,950	36,877	6,926
Rate per 100,000 civilian poulation							
Both sexes							
Total	845.3	248.8	168.8	33.6	46.4	271.6	324.9
Under 15	349.9	14.9	12.8	.1	2.0	26.3	308.7
15-24	957.2	215.6	162.4	6.7	46.5	268.2	473.4
25-34	1,342.0	410.2	284.4	49.3	76.5	435.7	496.1
35-44	1,387.1	499.1	285.1	126.7	87.3	473.9	414.1
45-54	1,078.7	389.6	251.8	67.6	70.2	434.2	254.9
55-64	806.3	290.7	209.3	15.4	66.0	369.0	146.6
65+	745.9	342.3	262.9	23.6	55.8	334.7	68.9

Males							
Total	883.9	295.7	190.8	69.3	35.6	225.0	363.2
Under 15	463.1	19.5	17.0	.2	2.3	26.9	416.7
15-24	1,008.3	266.7	206.7	14.0	46.0	224.7	516.9
25-34	1,255.3	492.9	337.3	103.2	52.4	326.7	435.7
35-44	1,427.8	643.7	317.2	263.5	63.0	379.5	404.6
45-54	1,114.6	172.4	279.6	139.7	53.1	372.9	269.3
55-64	817.5	324.2	238.8	32.3	53.1	340.4	152.9
65+	765.8	382.3	286.2	54.4	41.7	311.1	72.4
Females							
Total	809.2	204.8	148.2	a	56.6	315.5	288.9
Under 15	232.6	10.2	8.5	a	1.7	25.7	196.7
15-24	910.5	169.0	122.1	a	46.9	307.8	433.7
25-34	1,421.2	334.4	235.9	a	98.5	535.5	551.3
35-44	1,349.2	365.1	255.3	a	109.8	561.3	422.8
45-54	1,045.2	312.0	225.8	a	86.2	491.7	241.5
55-64	769.2	260.1	182.4	a	77.7	395.2	140.9
65+	730.7	311.6	245.1	a	66.5	352.8	66.3

aFemale patients were excluded because numbers were negligible.

TABLE D

Numbers and Rates per 100,000 Civilian Population of Patients Resident in Psychiatric Facilities by Type of Facility, and on Rolls of Outpatient Psychiatric Clinics at Beginning of Year by Age and Sex, United States, 1966

Age (in years)	All facilities	Public and private mental hospitals				General hospitals with psychiatric services	Outpatient psychiatric clinics
		Total	State and county hospitals	Veterans Administration hospitals	Private hospitals		
				Number			
Both sexes							
Total	1,126,657	547,214	475,202	57,954	14,058	22,735	556,708
Under 15	158,179	6,840	6,134	–	706	682	150,657
15-24	155,466	31,390	27,913	464	3,013	3,492	120,584
25-34	152,742	51,250	42,637	6,723	1,890	4,096	97,396
35-44	186,975	86,872	66,499	18,313	2,060	4,874	95,229
45-54	163,401	101,880	89,323	10,606	1,951	4,170	57,351
55-64	136,442	109,944	102,366	6,027	1,551	2,752	23,746
65+	173,452	159,038	140,330	15,821	2,887	2,669	11,745
Males							
Total	617,013	297,476	233,958	57,954	5,564	9,117	310,420
Under 15	108,655	4,930	4,445	–	485	355	103,370
15-24	83,843	19,743	17,781	464	1,498	1,395	62,705
25-34	77,636	32,709	25,267	6,723	719	1,468	43,459
35-44	104,246	52,702	33,690	18,313	699	1,878	49,666
45-54	90,739	55,792	44,452	10,606	734	1,732	33,215
55-64	71,974	58,344	51,705	6,027	612	1,213	12,417
65+	79,920	73,256	56,618	15,821	817	1,076	5,588

Females							
Total	509,644	249,738	241,244	a	8,494	13,618	246,288
Under 15	49,524	1,910	1,689	a	221	327	47,287
15-24	71,623	11,647	10,132	a	1,515	2,097	57,879
25-34	75,106	18,541	17,370	a	1,171	2,628	53,937
35-44	82,729	34,170	32,809	a	1,361	2,996	45,563
45-54	72,662	46,088	44,871	a	1,217	2,438	24,136
55-64	64,468	51,600	50,661	a	939	1,539	11,329
65+	93,532	85,782	83,712	a	2,070	1,593	6,157

Rate per 100,000 civilian population

Both sexes							
Total	581.6	282.5	245.3	29.9	7.3	11.7	287.4
Under 15	263.3	11.4	10.2	—	1.2	1.1	250.8
15-24	515.8	104.1	92.6	1.5	10.0	11.6	400.1
25-34	702.0	235.6	196.0	30.9	8.7	18.8	447.6
35-44	785.4	364.9	279.3	76.9	8.7	20.5	400.0
45-54	735.2	458.4	401.9	47.7	8.8	18.8	258.0
55-65	790.6	637.1	593.2	34.9	9.0	15.9	137.6
65+	939.7	861.6	760.3	85.7	15.6	14.5	63.6
Males							
Total	657.8	317.1	249.4	61.8	5.9	9.7	331.0
Under 15	355.4	16.1	14.5	—	1.6	1.2	338.1
15-24	583.5	137.4	123.8	3.2	10.4	9.7	436.4
25-34	746.6	314.6	243.0	64.7	6.9	14.1	417.9
35-44	910.3	460.2	294.2	159.9	6.1	16.4	433.7
45-54	843.8	518.8	413.4	98.6	6.8	16.1	308.9
55-64	873.2	707.9	627.3	73.1	7.5	14.7	150.6
65+	998.5	915.3	707.4	197.7	10.2	13.4	69.8

TABLE D

Numbers and Rates per 100,000 Civilian Population of Patients Resident in Psychiatric Facilities by Type of Facility, and on Rolls of Outpatient Psychiatric Clinics at Beginning of Year by Age and Sex, United States, 1966 (Continued)

Age (in years)	All facilities	Public and private mental hospitals				General hospitals with psychiatric services	Outpatient psychiatric clinics
		Total	State and county hospitals	Veterans Administration hospitals	Private hospitals		
			Rate per 100,000 civilian population				
Females							
Total	480.1	250.0	241.5	a	8.5	13.6	216.5
Under 15	167.9	6.4	5.7	a	.7	1.1	160.4
15-24	454.1	73.8	64.2	a	9.6	13.3	367.0
25-34	661.1	163.2	152.9	a	10.3	23.1	474.8
35-44	669.7	276.6	265.6	a	11.0	24.3	368.8
45-54	632.2	401.6	391.0	a	10.6	21.2	210.4
55-64	715.3	572.5	562.1	a	10.4	17.1	125.7
65+	894.7	820.6	800.8	a	19.8	15.2	58.9

aFemale patients were excluded because numbers were negligible.

TABLE E

Percentage Distribution of Selected Diagnoses among Admissions and Resident Patients for State and County and Private Mental Hospitals, Discharges from General Hospitals with Psychiatric Services, and Terminations from Outpatient Psychiatric Clinics, All Ages and Age Group 65 and Over, United States, 1968

Mental disorder	All ages						65 years and over					
	State and county mental hospitals		Private mental hospitals		General hospitals with psychiatric services	Outpatient psychiatric clinics	State and county mental hospitals		Private mental hospitals		General hospitals with psychiatric services	Outpatient psychiatric clinics
	First admissions	Resident patients	Total additions	Resident patients	Discharges	Terminations	First admissions	Resident patients	Total additions	Resident patients	Discharges	Terminations
Total patients	175,637	399,152	89,138	10,454	485,896	796,683	29,350	120,140	10,697	2,485	63,924	16,448
All Diagnoses	100.0	100.0	100.0	100.0	100.0	100.0	100.0	100.0	100.0	100.0	100.0	100.0
Total brain syndromes[a]	19.4	22.3	6.1	14.7	11.8	3.5	81.7	44.4	31.9	49.3	44.8	30.8
Disorders of senium	14.1	12.5	3.1	10.3	4.4	.6	76.0	37.2	23.2	41.0	28.9	21.0
Other brain syndromes	5.3	9.8	3.0	4.4	7.4	2.9	5.7	7.2	8.7	8.3	15.9	9.8
Schizophrenic reactions	17.9	48.7	19.9	34.5	15.8	12.3	1.6	34.0	4.0	16.1	3.3	8.6
Depressive disorders	9.6	4.6	34.5	22.0	27.7	10.3	2.5	5.9	36.7	18.8	24.9	21.1
Affective reactions	2.0	3.5	7.9	7.7	5.4	1.3	.9	5.3	11.2	8.8	5.9	6.3
Psychoneurotic depressive reactions	7.6	1.1	26.6	14.3	22.3	9.0	1.6	.6	25.5	10.0	19.0	14.8
Alcoholic disorders[b]	20.1	5.4	10.4	4.3	11.3	3.3	5.3	3.8	7.0	1.9	6.5	4.6
Personality disorders[c]	12.0	2.5	6.5	7.1	7.1	19.0	.5	.4	1.1	.8	1.5	3.4
Psychoneurotic disorders[d]	3.3	.7	9.4	5.1	14.4	7.6	.4	.4	3.9	1.9	10.3	4.1
Transient situational personality disorders	4.4	1.1	3.3	3.8	3.5	18.3	.7	.2	.8	.8	.7	6.3
Mental deficiency	2.4	8.6	.3	.6	.9	3.1	.3	3.6	.0	.4	.2	.4
All other disorders	3.3	4.0	5.9	5.3	6.2	1.9	1.2	6.1	13.8	6.5	6.9	7.3
Undiagnosed	6.3	1.9	3.2	2.4	.9	19.1	5.3	1.1	3.8	3.2	.5	11.9
Without mental disorder	1.3	.2	.5	.2	.4	1.6	.5	.1	.6	.3	.4	1.5

[a] Excludes brain syndromes associated with alcoholism.
[b] Includes brain syndromes associated with alcoholism and alcohol addiction (personality disorders).
[c] Excludes alcohol addiction.
[d] Excludes psychoneurotic depressive reaction.

TABLE F

Extent to which Needs for Psychiatric Services would be Met in Relation to Various Assumptions of Need: Assuming 1968 Use Rates Only, by age, United States, 1975 and 1980

Age	Estimated general population (in thousands) (1)	Estimated patient care episodes (2)	Estimated number of persons receiving care (3)	Estimated number of persons needing care assuming:			Number in need not receiving care assuming:			Percent unmet need assuming:		
				2% in need (4)a	10% in need (5)b	20% in need (6)c	2% in need (7)d	10% in need (8)e	20% in need (9)f	2% in need (10)g	10% in need (11)h	20% in need (12)i
1975												
All ages	215,588	3,693,022	2,954,418	4,311,760	21,558,800	43,117,600	1,454,724	18,604,382	40,163,182	33.7	86.3	93.1
Under 15	56,564	502,251	401,801	1,131,280	5,656,400	11,312,800	729,479	5,254,599	10,910,999	64.5	92.9	96.4
15-24	40,012	594,577	475,662	800,240	4,001,200	8,002,400	324,578	3,525,538	7,526,738	40.6	88.1	94.1
25-34	31,320	590,884	472,707	626,400	3,132,000	6,264,000	153,693	2,669,293	5,791,293	24.5	84.9	92.5
35-44	22,607	686,902	549,522	452,140	2,260,700	4,521,400	0	1,711,178	3,971,878	.0	75.7	87.8
45-54	23,670	535,488	428,390	473,400	2,367,000	4,734,000	45,010	1,938,610	4,305,610	9.5	81.9	91.0
55-64	19,912	365,609	292,487	398,240	1,991,200	3,982,400	105,753	1,698,713	3,689,913	26.6	85.3	92.7
65+	21,503	417,311	333,849	430,060	2,150,300	4,300,600	96,211	1,816,451	3,966,751	22.4	84.5	92.2
1980												
All ages	227,510	3,897,246	3,117,797	4,550,200	22,751,000	45,502,000	1,506,894	19,633,203	42,384,203	33.1	86.3	93.1
Under 15	56,448	530,025	424,020	1,128,960	5,644,800	11,289,600	704,940	5,220,780	10,865,580	62.4	92.5	96.2
15-24	41,736	627,457	501,966	834,720	4,173,600	8,347,200	332,754	3,671,634	7,845,234	39.9	88.0	94.0
25-34	36,779	623,559	498,847	735,580	3,677,900	7,355,800	236,733	3,179,053	6,856,953	32.2	86.4	93.2
35-44	25,523	724,888	579,910	510,460	2,552,300	5,104,600	0	1,972,390	4,524,690	.0	77.3	88.6
45-54	22,352	565,101	452,081	447,040	2,235,200	4,470,400	0	1,783,119	4,018,319	.0	79.8	89.9
55-64	21,180	385,827	308,662	423,600	2,118,000	4,236,000	114,938	1,809,338	3,927,338	27.1	85.4	92.7
65+	23,492	440,389	352,311	469,840	2,349,200	4,698,400	117,529	1,996,889	4,346,089	25.0	85.0	92.5

Note. These data were revised using figures from the United States Bureau of the Census (1970a).

aColumn 4 = Column 1 X .02.
bColumn 5 = Column 1 X .10.
cColumn 6 = Column 1 X .20.
dColumn 7 = Column 4 − Column 3. (For this column, negative values were assumed to be zero, i.e., the need for services would be met.)
eColumn 8 = Column 5 − Column 3.
fColumn 9 = Column 6 − Column 3.
gColumn 10 = Column 7 ÷ Column 4.
hColumn 11 = Column 8 ÷ Column 5.
iColumn 12 = Column 9 ÷ Column 6.

TABLE G

Extent to which Needs for Psychiatric Services would be Met in Relation to Various Assumptions of Need: Assuming 1955-68 Trends in Use Rates of Services Continue, by Age, United States, 1975 and 1980

Age	Estimated general population (in thousands) (1)	Estimated patient care episodes (2)	Estimated number of persons receiving care (3)	Estimated number of persons needing care assuming:			Number in need not receiving care assuming:			Percentage of unmet need assuming:		
				2% in need (4)a	10% in need (5)b	20% in need (6)c	2% in need (7)d	10% in need (8)e	20% in need (9)f	2% in need (10)g	10% in need (11)h	20% in need (12)i
1975												
All ages	215,588	4,544,595	3,635,676	4,311,760	21,558,800	43,117,600	953,953	17,923,124	39,481,924	22.1	83.1	91.6
Under 15	56,564	618,065	494,452	1,131,280	5,656,400	11,312,800	636,828	5,161,948	10,818,348	56.3	91.3	95.6
15-24	40,012	731,680	585,344	800,240	4,001,200	8,002,400	214,896	3,415,856	7,417,056	26.9	85.4	92.7
25-34	31,320	727,135	581,708	626,400	3,132,000	6,264,000	44,692	2,550,292	5,682,292	7.1	81.4	90.7
35-44	22,607	845,295	676,236	452,140	2,260,700	4,521,400	0	1,584,464	3,845,164	.0	70.1	85.0
45-54	23,670	658,966	527,173	473,400	2,367,000	4,734,000	0	1,839,827	4,206,827	.0	77.7	88.9
55-64	19,912	449,915	359,932	398,240	1,991,200	3,982,400	38,308	1,631,268	3,622,468	9.6	81.9	91.0
65+	21,503	513,539	410,831	430,060	2,150,300	4,300,600	19,229	1,739,469	3,889,769	4.5	80.9	90.4
1980												
All ages	227,510	5,421,563	4,337,250	4,550,200	22,751,000	45,502,000	717,139	18,413,750	41,164,750	15.8	80.9	90.5
Under 15	56,448	737,332	589,865	1,128,960	5,644,800	11,289,600	539,095	5,054,935	10,699,735	47.8	89.6	94.8
15-24	41,736	872,871	698,296	834,720	4,173,600	8,347,200	136,424	3,475,304	7,648,904	16.3	83.3	91.6
25-34	36,779	867,450	693,960	735,580	3,677,900	7,355,800	41,620	2,983,940	6,661,840	5.7	81.1	90.6
35-44	25,523	1,008,411	806,729	510,460	2,552,300	5,104,600	0	1,745,571	4,297,871	.0	68.4	84.2
45-54	22,352	786,127	628,902	447,040	2,235,200	4,470,400	0	1,606,298	3,841,498	.0	71.9	85.9
55-64	21,180	536,735	429,388	423,600	2,118,000	4,236,000	0	1,688,612	3,806,612	.0	79.7	89.9
65+	23,492	612,637	490,110	469,840	2,349,200	4,698,400	0	1,859,090	4,208,290	.0	79.1	89.6

Note. These data were revised using figures from the United States Bureau of the Census (1970a).

aColumn 4 = Column 1 X .02.
bColumn 5 = Column 1 X .10.
cColumn 6 = Column 1 X .20.
dColumn 7 = Column 4 − Column 3. (For this column, negative values were assumed to be zero, i.e., the need for services would be met.)
eColumn 8 = Column 5 − Column 3.
fColumn 9 = Column 6 − Column 3.
gColumn 10 = Column 7 ÷ Column 4.
hColumn 11 = Column 8 ÷ Column 5.
iColumn 12 = Column 9 ÷ Column 6.

TABLE H

Estimated Number of Psychiatrists, Psychologists, Social Workers, and Nurses Needed to Care for all Persons in Need of Psychiatric Care Assuming Various Levels of Need for Care and Various Amounts of Time Spent per Patient per Year, United States, 1970, 1975, and 1980

Professional discipline and assumed hours per patient per year	Percentage of level of need for care in population								
	1970			1975			1980		
	2% in need	10% in need	20% in need	2% in need	10% in need	20% in need	2% in need	10% in need	20% in need
All ages									
Number of persons in need of care[a]	4,103,340	20,516,700	41,033,400	4,311,760	21,558,800	43,117,600	4,550,200	22,751,000	45,502,000
Clinical psychiatrists									
3	8,207	41,033	82,067	8,624	43,118	86,235	9,100	45,502	91,004
6	16,413	82,067	164,134	17,247	86,235	172,470	18,200	91,004	182,008
10	27,356	136,778	273,556	28,745	143,725	287,451	30,335	151,673	303,347
Psychologists									
3	8,207	41,033	82,067	8,624	43,118	86,235	9,100	45,502	91,004
6	16,413	82,067	164,134	17,247	86,235	172,470	18,200	91,004	182,008
10	27,356	136,778	273,556	28,745	143,725	287,451	30,335	151,673	303,347
Social workers									
6	16,413	82,066	164,134	17,247	86,235	172,470	18,200	91,004	182,008
12	32,827	164,134	328,267	34,494	172,470	344,941	36,402	182,008	364,016
20	54,711	273,556	547,112	57,490	287,451	574,901	60,669	303,347	606,693
Nurses									
6	16,413	82,066	164,134	17,247	86,235	172,470	18,200	91,004	182,008
10	27,356	136,778	273,556	28,745	143,725	287,451	30,335	151,673	303,347

Note. It was assumed that each profession would work 50 weeks during the year on an average of 30 hours per week or a total of 1,500 hours per year.

[a]Based on data from the United States Bureau of the Census (1970a).

Community Mental Health and Other Health Services for the Aged

IVAN N. MENSH

Anthropologists and historians have reconstructed the probable experiences of older members of prebiblical human groups, suggesting that these experiences were such that few members of the groups survived into the later years. Wars, famines, injuries, and diseases contributed to a relatively brief life-span even up to the twentieth century (life expectancy was 48 years in 1900). Since biblical days there has been a recorded history of community interest and efforts on behalf of the elders of community groups, a verbal history in folklore and tradition until the fifteenth century, and printed and written documents during the past several centuries. Gold and Kaufman (1970) traced the development of care of the elderly in terms of institutional facilities, recalling the earliest shelter for the aged in tents of the biblical era as one of the ideals of mankind expressed in the Talmud and another obligation "to provide for the support and comfort of the old (Ruth, IV, V5) . . . [p. 263]."

Care of the elderly is further traced by Gold and Kaufman through the Roman era in both Christian and pre-Christian times; in the Moslem world by the ninth century; in the eleventh century Jewish homes for the aged in the Near East, France, and Germany; in the Middle Ages and the formation of benevolent societies; and in the sixteenth century and later in England (e.g., the Elizabethan Poor Law of 1601 about which Clark, 1969, wrote: "The old Poor

Ivan N. Mensh received his PhD in psychology from Northwestern University in 1948. He was Professor and Head of Medical Psychology at Washington University School of Medicine between 1948–1958, and since 1958 has served in this capacity in the Department of Psychiatry at the University of California School of Medicine, Los Angeles. His major interests are in medical education, the selection of medical and other professional students, psychological changes with aging, and program evaluation.

Laws were not designed to abolish poverty but to prevent the poor from becoming a nuisance [p. 323]"), the British Empire, and in Europe. It is significant, however, that, except for the biblical and other traditions (in other religions and cultures as well as in Judaism and Christianity, e.g., the Orient's traditional veneration for the elderly, now unfortunately breaking down), the elderly received only "marginal attention," with the focus of community concern often primarily on "the public safety" rather than on the individual, that is, on the homeless poor, the criminal, and the mentally ill, with all of these unfortunates locked off indiscriminately and in miserable "shelters," if the institutions could be termed such.

In the United States, homes for the aged, the first visible community programs, began about a century ago. Even the word "geriatric" is only two generations old, coined in 1910 by I. L. Nascher, a German-born physician in New York City who was struck by the contrast between differences in care for the elderly and chronically ill patients which he saw in Germany and in "the New World," with contrast significantly in favor of the Old World. These early programs in the United States were supported by churches and religious groups, philanthropic groups, fraternal organizations, nationality groups, community organizations, federal or state governments, and trade unions. Well over half of the homes were the responsibility of religious and philanthropic organizations (Gold & Kaufman, 1970).

Anderson (1966) also pointed out the role of philanthropic individuals and groups in his review of public policy in the development of another community institution in the health field, the general hospital. As he described the era of "public policy without research," 1875–1920, he noted that in 1873 there were only 178 hospitals in the United States, mostly mental hospitals, but by 1910 there were 4,400 general hospitals. "The great majority of these hospitals . . . [were] financed by . . . private fortunes . . . from the rapid industrial expansion after the Civil War [p. 13]." An excellent review of social welfare programs across the centuries has been presented by Randall (1965).

Moving from this rapid overview of centuries of human interaction with, for, and against the elderly to the present day, we can define the current generation of community concern as that period since the 1930s and the passage of the Social Security Act, with its programs for assisting in financing and providing for the needs of the elderly, up to present day Medicare programs. Thus, in about 30 years, there have been acts and amendments including the disability benefits of the Social Security Act, old age security, aid to the totally disabled, aid to the needy blind, state plans for the indigent, the Older

Americans Act of 1965, the Old Age Assistance and Old Age Survivor's Disability and Health Insurance provisions, and the Administration on Aging's Title IV Research and Demonstration Grant Program. The latter, for example, has as its primary objectives the development of programs of comprehensive coordinated services for the aged, senior centers, retirement planning, voluntary and social employment, recreational and leisure-time activities, evaluation of living arrangements, and special services for the aged. In the field of mental health, in spite of the history of a century of mental hospitals, the community programs are very recent, with the comprehensive community mental health centers program barely 5 years old, a tender age for the too-few elderly served by the poorly nourished program.

Several events at different points in time mark our generation of mental health and other health programs and community concern for the elderly: the founding of the National Institute of Mental Health in 1947; the 1955 authorization by Public Law 182 of a Joint Commission on Mental Illness and Health and the report by the Joint Commission on Mental Illness and Health (1961); the 1961 Community Health Services and Facilities Act for the development of out-of-hospital health services particularly for the chronically ill and aged; the establishment in 1963 of the National Institute of Child Health and Human Development with one of its six areas of research and training devoted to the aging; and the Medicare Act of 1965. It should be noted here that the first White House Conference on Aging, in 1961 (authorization by Congress in 1958), recommended Medicare among other programs for the aged. Whether the Old Age and Survivor's Disability Insurance section of the Social Security Act or the Public Assistance Section should finance health services for the aged was a cause for a majority and minority split "along the familiar dichotomy of financing: through one or the other of these two sections [Anderson, 1966, p. 34]." Truman's President's Commission for the Health Needs of the Nation had as one of its significant outcomes Shanas' (1962) survey. President Kennedy's concern for health needs resulted in legislation for comprehensive community mental health, mental retardation, and other health programs.

THEORY IN HEALTH CARE AND ITS DELIVERY

Much of the literature on theory in health care and health care delivery has been based upon organizational, economic, and social theory concepts. For example, Glidewell (1966) stated:

The focus of attention in community mental health has been, and should continue to be, upon the psychosocial interaction between the individual and the small social organizations of which he is a member. The relevant dimensions of social organization are (1) emotional acceptance, (2) social power, (3) attributed competence, and (4) vulnerability to sanction. The relevant dimensions of individual behavior are psychosocial—(1) motivational, (2) emotional, (3) intellectual, (4) interpersonal. The biophysical and the socio-cultural, while often crucial, are nonetheless in the background for community mental health. . . . [p. 47].

Other theories relate to the effects of certain types of health care, that is, institutional, and there is vigorous interchange between those who argue that the data support the theory of institutionalization effects and those whose studies produce data that do not support the theory that "institutionalization may be conceived of as a condition which induces and/or is symptomatic of formal developmental regression in cognitive processes [Comalli, Krus, & Wapner, 1965, p. 12]." Even in community-living elderly males, at least in 80–90 year olds, Comalli (1965) concluded that "senescence is progressively marked by a developmental regression in perceptual-cognitive processes [p. 17]," suggesting that there is regression regardless of the effects of health. Further, the health state of an individual, as the individual perceives it (one of the criteria of the state of health), may only reflect that:

the number of symptoms reported by a patient [on the Cornell Medical Index, Brodman, Erdman, Lorger, & Wolff, 1949] is more a function of his habitual patterns of describing illness than of the presence of specific disease entities current or in the past. It is likely also that patients forget many symptoms of previous illnesses [Denney, Kole, & Matarazzo 1965, p. 53].

Anderson (1967) reviewed some of the studies pro and con the theory of institutional effects, indicating the methodological weaknesses in cross-sectional rather than longitudinal studies, the selection which operates in institutional sampling, and concluded that "institutionalization is too gross a contextual variable to explain any differences which might be found [p. 313]." The review summarized reports failing to show significant differences in self-esteem or adjustment due to institutionalization (Lepkowski, 1956; Pan, 1951; Scott, 1955; Tuckman, Lorge, & Zeman, 1961) and those studies reporting lower self-esteem and poorer adjustment among institutionalized than among community-living older individuals (Laverty, 1950; Mason, 1954; Pollack, Karp, Kahn, & Goldfarb, 1962).

Lieberman, Prock, and Tobin (1968) pointed out that, although there is "the general thrust of empirical evidence . . . suggesting that living in an institutional environment may have noxious physical and psychological effects upon the individual, whether young or old . . . [p. 343]," their study of institutionalized, community, and waiting-list (for a home) older individuals prompted them to conclude that "living in an institutional environment had both ameliorative effects . . . as well as adverse effects [p. 351]." (See also Prock, 1965.) This research group summarized more than a score of studies on effects of institutionalization other than those reviewed by Anderson. Lieberman (1969) again evaluated two decades of such studies, pointing out selection biases and discussing environmental change variables and measurement methods. It would seem, then, that the theory of institutional effects remains a significant theory to test but that evidence to date is not definitive, supporting or refuting the hypothesis, depending rather upon variations in samples, environments, and treatment or other institutional programs (see also Lawton & Nahemow, pp. 619–675, and Gottesman, Quartermans, & Cohn, pp. 378–427, this volume).

Among social role theories is that exemplified by Rosenblatt and Taviss' (1966) report with its emphasis on programs "to provide for re-engagement in a well-run, well-intentioned total institution." These writers reviewed the theories set forth by Goffman (1962), who categorized homes for the aged, blind, orphans, and indigent as one group among five residential institution classes, and by Cumming and Henry (1961) in their development of disengagement theory. Goffman was criticized for his depiction of "the central characteristics of total institutions which . . . does not conform to how well institutions for the aged are ordinarily run . . . [and for his point that] the inmates of total institutions are not permitted to disengage from the social system except as a form of withdrawal [p. 166]." Cumming and Henry's position was challenged by Rosenblatt and Taviss' observation that "it was not families that were relatively rejected by the aged but rather that these people have been rejected by whatever families exist [p. 168]." These counterarguments to disengagement rest on an empirical study in an experimental ward over a seven-month period. The study's value is primarily in its specifying the postulates of two theories and relating them to observations made systematically on a sample of 35 chronically ill patients in one ward of a home for the aged.

Lipman and Smith (1968) also evaluated disengagement theory, relating it to poor health and poverty and criticizing Cumming and Henry's samples for not including older individuals characterized by poor health and poverty:

These categories . . . are central to the life organization of many old people. We therefore included individuals with poor health and low income in our study of the aged. We dichotomized our study population of 765 respondents into high and low disengagement levels, eliminating those who did not measure consistently on all four operational criteria of disengagement: perceived life space, social life space, social participation and role count.

After finding that morale was positively related to engagement rather than disengagement (holding income level and health level constant) we attempted to assess the impact of combinations of economic insecurity, failing health, and disengagement from the social system upon the morale of our respondents. Holding age constant, it was found that high morale was positively associated with the possession of any two of the three variables: good health, adequate income, and engagement. Disengagement does not seem to represent an isolated variable; it appears to be intertwined with the total life organization of the aged individual [p. 26].

Cumming and Henry would have no quarrel with the concluding statement because of their theoretical position and its significance for understanding behavior. Carp (1969) warned, however, that "the variable inclusion of different aspects of criterion concepts into criterion measures contributes to the present state of confusion regarding adjustment and disengagement in later maturity [p. 341]."

Economic theories underlying community programs for the elderly cannot be divorced from the social context of our economic society. Therefore, it may be more appropriate to designate such theories as socioeconomic, trusting that we do disservice to neither social scientists nor economists. Fortunately, in many quarters one notes the inclusion of economics among the social sciences, reinforced by an increasing awareness of the complex interactions in society of the physical, psychological, and social environments with the economics of the many subcultures of our society. This complexity is emphasized in Bloom's (1969) study of more than 900 patients, aged 65 or older, in five public and three private general hospitals in Colorado, seen during 1959–61. All of these patients were experiencing their first significant psychiatric hospitalization.

An examination of the characteristics of the neighborhoods which furnish an overrepresentation of patients with acute or chronic brain syndromes (30 percent of all diagnoses, 22 percent both 65 or older and with brain syndromes) indicated that they have little socio-economic affluence, few young married families, and considerable social isolation and social disequilibrium when contrasted with those neighborhoods with lower admission rates [p. 54].

In his discussion, Bloom noted:

The etiological role of social factors in the development of disorders continues to be unclear. While Hollingshead and Redlich (1958) asserted that social class played an etiological role, the evidence is not clearly so unambiguous, as Miller and Mishler (1959) have pointed out. Furthermore, neither the data of Srole et al. [Srole, Langner, Michael, Opler, & Rennie] (1962) nor of Dunham (1965) support the etiology hypothesis advanced by Hollingshead and Redlich. . . . . The present data, focused on environmental rather than on individual characteristics, permit a particularly parsimonious hypothesis in support of the position developed by Dunham . . . namely, that psychiatric patients tend to congregate, probably in part by a process of social mobility, in particular sections of the community. . . . From the point of view of . . . community mental health philosophy, this type of hypothesis is most useful. It does not posit a simple cause–effect relationship but rather identifies neighborhoods where intervention programs can be undertaken. . . . Programs designed to decrease the degree of social isolation among older residents of certain urban areas can be undertaken, both by providing alternative life style opportunities as well as by modifying the physical living arrangement characteristics of the area. Suitable alternatives to hospitalization for geriatric patients can be explored. The usefulness of . . . services . . . commonly advanced in maintaining elderly people in the community, should be evaluated. . . . The strategy of epidemiology, as described by MacMahon, Pugh, and Ipsen (1960) has been to look for characteristics in life which, if changed, will yield a subsequent reduction in the incidence of some undesirable condition. Such pragmatic approaches are overdue . . . in particular regarding the disorders associated with aging [pp. 53–54].

Loeb, Pincus, and Mueller (1966) urged the necessity for a developmental perspective in aging, specifying

concepts of social life space, living space, role enactments, social interaction patterns, and disengagement . . . social development in aging includes organizational tasks concerning social space, living space, and time perspective. . . . [They hypothesized] that a congruence between organization of social space, living space, and time perspective leads to successful aging or high morale in old age . . . [an] individual's organization of time and space, both objectively and in terms of how it is experienced by him [p. 185].

Coe (1967) identified another social role hypothesis, stating that "a fundamental issue in the delivery and acceptance of medical care services [is] *the nature of the social encounter of the physician and his patient.*" In a series of tape-recorded discussions in small groups, "professional perspectives on the aged" were gathered from physicians, dentists, physical therapists, nurses, and social workers. As would be expected, these perspectives essentially represent the theories of aging and of health services of the responding professionals and their respective disciplines:

One of the generalizations . . . which stands out most clearly is that attitudes of health professionals toward aging are closely bound to professional ideology. Physicians tended to view older patients (and probably younger ones, too) in terms of the disease process. This, of course, is the typical approach taken with respect to the classical care model. Also "functionally" specific in their viewpoint were dentists. With physical therapists and nurses, particularly the latter, one observes the introduction of social-psychological variables as important, whereas social workers tended to ignore physical disease characteristics and focused on socio-emotional and socio-cultural components of aging [pp. 115–116].

Zampella (1966) suggested that a "medical team approach" by representatives of medical and surgical specialties, as well as general practitioners, could contribute to the "total care of the patient. . . . Maintenance of the elderly patient's integrity, independence and self-esteem is an important factor in his progress [p. 25]." This admirable suggestion should be examined in light of Coe's (1967) study and Freeman's (1970) report of a 1961 questionnaire study of 600 residents and interns about undergraduate instruction in geriatric medicine, and a review a decade later of the catalogues of 95 United States medical schools. Freeman concluded that "Medical training in the pathophysiology of aging has not kept progress with technical and social changes in the United States [p. 35]."

Lissitz (1970) wrote about the interrelations of institutional and of community care and theories underlying such care. These "reflect the attitudes and the values of society. Individual workers in gerontology also have viewpoints that determine and guide their work with the aged [p. 298]." Lissitz selected two sociological theories for review, "the Talcott Parsons [1951] theory of the social system and the George Simmel [1955] conflict school."

[In Parsons] the present social processes, norms, expectation, attitudes, and goals are seen and considered as functional and mainly effective in handling the challenges of longevity. The structure and function are supposedly aligned and synchronized. The social system is regarded as largely in equilibrium. All groups, including the aged within the social system, are supposedly in balance. Differences and conflicts exist, of course, but they are considered by this school and theory to be minor. They do not upset the "applecart" of the social system.

On the other hand, conflict theorists call the social system of Parsons and his followers an illusion. They believe society cannot be conceived in organismic terms. To them, dysfunction plays a more significant role and is intrinsic. Because they regard dysfunction as present within a society which is not a social system, they believe great needs are unmet. Social changes are regarded as necessary. In the conflict school theory, power is a major factor to be considered in the understanding of the aged [p. 298].

Lissitz also drew upon other theories in his review, for example, (a) Lewin's (1936) theory of life space; (b) Erikson's (1963) concept of "crises associated with developmental epochs in the life of man . . . when fields and life spaces change"; (c) Schutz' (1967) phenomenology, "how social facts are interpreted and become the basis of inter-subjective understanding"; and (d) Cumming and Cumming's (1962) and Cumming and Henry's (1961) theories. Lissitz developed his review in order to assist both practitioners and research workers in understanding "theoretical conceptions of institutional care [as these] are related to theoretical conceptions of community care of the aged. This interrelationship is vital and must be maintained in gerontology [p. 299]."

The economic role of the aged has been dramatically described by economist Chen (1966) who has written:

> When the aged are "poor" (that is not only income-poor, but also asset-poor), their predicament is perhaps of the harshest when compared with the income-poor and asset-poor younger persons, for many of the latter have the "prospect" of income and health and hope which are often denied to the aged [p. 45].

Wendel (1970) and Kershaw (1970) also wrote about the economic base of the aged. Wendel reported, for 1964, that families in the upper 20% of all incomes had 41% of the income, those in the lowest 20% had only 5% of all income dollars and, although there was a 14% decline in the number of poverty households from 1959 to 1965 (Kershaw reported a 35% drop in the number of the poor, 1959–68, from 38.7 million to 25.3 million), the decline among aged households, at the poverty level, was only 2.5%, about one-fifth of the drop of other households. Further, males over 65 had a median income 70% lower than men aged 35–44 ("the most productive years") and women past 65 had a median income only 46% of the median of men at their age range. With older persons spending 50% more for medical services than younger individuals, inflation, and low relative income, "the economic position of the aged is inferior to that of the population as a whole. It is also inferior in many ways to that of the aged of the past [Wendel, 1970, p. 74]."

Kershaw (1970) pointed out:

> Whatever definition of poverty is used, it is clear that the number of poor people in the United States has declined dramatically in recent years. . . . But economic growth (after the Second World War) was of less benefit to groups outside the labor market—husbandless mothers, the aged, the handicapped—and the number of families with no wage earners gradually increased as a proportion of the total. By the early 1960's it was clear that federal funds, distributed primarily through the welfare provisions of the Social Security Act, were not meeting the fundamental problem [pp. 2–3].

Although federal aid to the poor rose from 9.8 million in 1961 to $21.7 million in 1968, Kershaw's evaluation concluded that

> The problem of urban poverty is more difficult than had been thought and may be worsening in some neighborhoods. . . . Basic to all other problems is a lack of resources. All forms of public assistance now reach only 40 per cent of the poor, and in almost every case the recipients are not brought out of poverty [pp. 8–9].

Perhaps the most comprehensive and considered analyses and reports of studies of health services are those produced for two conferences held in October 1965 and May 1966, supported by the Health Services Research Section of the United States Public Health Service. The papers were published in the *Milbank Memorial Fund Quarterly*, 1966, **44**, No. 3 and 4, more than 530 pages in all.[1] They covered social, organizational, economic, political, and manpower theories and research in health services, together with analyses of both need and demand characteristics of health care and evaluation of community and other health care.

Among the reports published, Anderson's (1966) review of theory, policy, and practice in health services research and the delivery of health care divided the history of public policy on health services into two eras—public policy without research, 1875–1920, and public policy with research, since 1920. He cautioned, however, "The health field has such an aura of life saving, altruism and alleviation of pain and suffering that realistic thinking about money, resources and implementation is inhibited [p. 12]." It is of further interest, Anderson noted, that "During the last quarter of the 19th century apparently as many physicians were in practice in relation to the population as are currently practicing [p. 13]." (Hiestand, 1966, also noted the "remarkably stable" ratios over the past three decades: 131–135 physicians/100,000 population, 56–57 dentists/100,000, with nurses increasing each decade from 175 to 280/100,-000, population.) And this ratio has been maintained in spite of many other changes in the twentieth century: medical discoveries, licensure laws, hospital care expansion, population expansion, one-half of the 160 medical schools disappearing during the decade of 1910–20 following the Flexner Report, and the development and collapse of state and federal health insurance plans. By 1916, 16 states had state government-sponsored health insurance for their citizens; by 1920, the American Medical Association (AMA) and the insurance companies were successful in the collapse of the

---

[1]Listed by individual author in the reference list.

"agitation for government-sponsored health insurance." In 1933, the AMA and the American Hospital Association again were successful in opposing such plans.

In 1909, F. R. Brush, President of the American Hospital Association, evaluated the status of hospital health care; "[Once] the hospitals were for the poor. They are largely now for the rich. In time they may be for all [p. 182]." Anderson (1966) discussed another segment of health care, the outpatient department programs: "By the early 1920's . . . [such programs] for the indigent only. . . . never [were] . . . popular with the self-pay segment of the population [p. 16]." For the "self-pay segment" there emerged between 1935–52, the pattern of third-party payment. By the end of this period, voluntary health insurance was held by 60% of the population and one-half of the general hospital bill was covered by insurance. Unfortunately, there remains the need for evaluating "the benefit structure of voluntary health insurance, and . . . the operational and organizational problems of the system [p. 27]."

Rosenstock (1966) underlined the need to develop a model to explain health behavior. He urged that theory and model include the dimensions of personal perception—of susceptibility to illness, its seriousness, benefits, and "barriers" to taking action and internal and external cues to action—and of the variables operating in decisions on health care behaviors, influenced as they are by "personal, interpersonal and situational factors." Rosenstock also specified that there will remain a self-selected, poorly educated, low-income group who will not "expose themselves to scientific and health information transmitted through . . . mass media . . . ." He suggested that very personal, face-to-face contacts are needed to reduce the barriers existing with this latter group.

Feldstein (1966) sought a theoretical economic framework for explaining the variables associated with the supply and demand for health care services. He summarized the difficulties in (a) assessing the relative contributions of medical research and public health programs; (b) the definition of medical care; (c) defining measures, whether dollars, days, visits, or quality; and (d) in the choice of care, by patient or physician since this choice "depends on the knowledge and availability of substitutes." The community demand for medical care is affected by incidence of various illnesses, and by cultural, demographic, and economic variables. The physician's choice of various components of health and medical care varies with patient characteristics, institutional arrangements, the physician's own knowledge, and the "relative costs of alternate sets of care components" (hospitalization, primary physician's care, referral to specialists, nursing home, and so on). Importantly, "since most available research findings in the area of demand concern the private market, economic theory is called upon to develop models of demand for the governmental and philanthropic sectors as well [p. 165]."

In developing theories of community health programs, Revans (1966) stated that individuals external to the system are handicapped in understanding it.

> The problems of action . . . are but partially accessible to those who neither carry responsibility for the outcome of that action nor can be the victims of any misunderstanding which the action may create. . . . research interests are frequently so far from the necessities of practical operations as to seem, to the responsible administrator, positively harmful in the demands they may make upon managerial time [p. 207].

Revans further decried not only the lack of theory but also the lack of study of the general hospital as an organization, quoting Georgopoulous and Mann (1962): "The community general hospital could easily claim the dubious honor of being one of the least researched modern large-scale organizations in spite of its crucial function . . . ." Revans suggested that "so long as . . . [hospitals] were run by amateurs only for the deserving poor they made no demands upon official consciences and so called for no official examination. . . . one of the most obstinate of all hospital problems—the cult of individualism among the medical staff . . . [pp. 209–210]." The Georgopoulos and Mann study of 10 hospitals is one of the few organizational studies of the community hospital.

A different approach was suggested by Llewelyn-Davies (1966), combining not only organizational and clinical variables and theory but also incorporating economic, manpower, physical plant (bricks and mortar and equipment as capital expenditures and resources), social, and medical parameters. In this comprehensive approach, "the study of health systems as a whole" was urged:

> In all cases the object of research has been to consider the role of different elements in the system with a view to improve the service to the patients and reducing the cost to the community. Most of these studies have been principally concerned with clinical and organizational aspects of the problem. . . . A strong economic element . . . is directed toward making the best of scarce resources, particularly manpower. But the capital devoted to the health plant is also important. . . . [as are] social and medical parameters. . . . also the cost and distribution of the health plant [pp. 258–259].

> Cost–benefit analysis attempts to consider benefits and costs of a kind not directly measurable in normal accountancy. In doing so, it must, of course, make numerous, rather debatable assumptions. But these assumptions are explicit and can be considered and debated [p. 267].

Scott (1966) specifically selected organizational theory as the basis for an assessment of health care. Foci of study were organizational goals, tasks, control systems, and status systems; but Scott realistically observed that "organizational theory is not highly developed [p. 35]." Another reality is that the

one characteristic of medical organizations . . . [is] the plethora of specialty groups brought together under a single organizational canopy. Such skilled occupational groups have a "trained incapacity"—to use Veblen's happily descriptive phrase—to see situations in which they are involved from any perspective other than their own. They tend to exaggerate the importance of their own endeavors and see their own skills and standards as applicable to virtually every circumstance encountered . . . [p. 38].

That virtually every organization theorist insists on the importance of specific goals as a defining criterion of organizatoins is not surprising [p. 39].

The norms of physicians typically allow administrators little access to their medical performances, and, although colleague evaluations are supposed to substitute for such administrative control, contacts among physicians—even those working together in medical clinics—are often so limited or fragmented that no over-all impression of the quality of medical performance is gained (Freidson and Rhea, 1965). Such norms among physicians are intended to protect the right of each practitioner to make decisions for his own patients and to insure that non-medical criteria are not allowed to intrude into the decision-making process . . . [p. 45].

[To] protect individual practitioners from "inappropriate" control attempts by nonpractitioners . . . physicians have succeeded in achieving a considerable amount of autonomy for their activities . . . [p. 47].

Scott illustrated this power structure in organizational theory and practice by the study of Bates and White (1961), surveying 13 voluntary hospitals, and by Hamilton's (1957) study. Scott reported for the former study, for example, that

While the authority exercised by administrators and nurses was perceived in generally favorable terms by participants, perceptions of the physicians' use of authority tended to be generally unfavorable. This conflict . . . between "rules,". . . and "exceptions to the rules". . . makes the hospital . . . unique . . . [with] powerful groups . . . polarized around these foci. . . . The physician gains a tactical advantage . . . by his power to define virtually any problem as a medical emergency . . . [p. 50].

Fuchs (1966) pointed out that efforts to apply organizational and industrial theory to the health "industry," if industry it is, is extremely difficult because of the vast differences between the health system and a "typical" industry. In spite of the 6% of personal consumption expense which goes for health and medical care, there is "consumer ignorance [of the product he is buying] . . . . In the typical case he is even subject to the producer's recommendation concerning the quantity to be purchased [p. 67]." For example, the AMA report on medical care cost stated that "the 'quantity' of the hospital services consumed in 1962 was determined by physicians [American Medical Association, 1963–64, p. 19]." Recent studies do not suggest that 1962 was an atypical year.

Other differences identified by Fuchs and characterizing medical care are restricted competition, the distinction between need as opposed to demand and third-party payment, resulting in the consumer having less incentive to ascertain that value received is comparable to the cost. In addition,

> The health industry, with its curious mixture of philanthropy, government subsidies, imperfect labor markets and contributed labor time . . . [is unable to provide] the definition and measurement of levels of health, or at least changes in levels. . . . What portion of changes in health can be attributed to health services as distinct from the general and environmental factors that also affect health. . . . [In terms of validation] only a physician can provide judgments concerning a person's health status that will be widely accepted by third parties. . . . [Validation of the health system by mortality index change presents still another difficulty, Fuchs observed, in that] the failure of mortality indexes to decline with increasing expenditures for health services in recent years has led some people to conclude that mortality no longer measures health levels properly. But . . . the so-called "hotel" services of hospitals . . . [may account for the major increase in expenditures; p. 68 ff.].

Another criterion of medical care delivery is no less difficult to establish, Weinerman (1966) noted:

> The meager evidence to date suggests that independent and general practice is more familiar and acceptable from the patient's point of view, while specialty and group practice provide an objectively more rational and efficient standard of professional service. More convincing evidence must amait the development of relative standards for comparison . . . [p. 118].
> The paradox of modern medicine is undeniable: the single personal physician is both outmoded and indispensable . . . [p. 129].

Boulding (1966), another economist, also addressed himself to the application of economic and organizational theory to health and medical care, and specifically included aging because of the special consideration he deemed this period of life development merits.

> The very idea of autonomous choice implies first that the chooser knows the real alternatives which are open to him, and second that he makes the choice according to value criteria or a utility function which he will not later regret. . . . In the case of medical care . . .

the demander is usually a layman faced with professional suppliers who know very much more than he does. The demand for medical care, indeed, is primarily a demand for knowledge or at least the results of knowledge . . . an increasingly professionalized, socialized organized structure satisfies what the professional conceives of as needs . . . professions which set their own standards of what they ought to do . . . the activity originates from the professional rather than from the client, from the supplier rather from the demander [pp. 203–204].

Boulding then turned explicitly to aging and economic and physiological theory, with an infusion of social definition for value orientation, likening the human organism to the mechanism of an automobile but clearly differentiating the dissimilarities.

Homeostatic needs . . . [are] those which can be taken care of by the organism itself and those which require a professional decision . . . In the course of operation . . . wear and tear occur. . . . At this level need becomes professionalized. . . . The professional need is most apparent in breakdown. . . . Once . . . [the patient] puts himself into the hands of the professional, demand disappears and no substitute exists for trust in the professional's concept of need. . . . The difficulty with homeostasis . . . is that homeostasis is never really successful. No matter what occurs in the way of inputs, virtually all known organisms and organizations exhibit the phenomenon of aging, which is closely related to the phenomenon of growth. Aging . . . might almost be defined as that adverse change in state of the organism which no known input can remedy . . . [p. 205].

Aging introduces a very tricky problem into the concept of need for . . . maintenance . . . a problem of excruciating delicacy in the case of the human being . . . . In the case of the human being, the problem of the person himself becomes very acute, because persons cannot be regarded as purely instrumental (in fulfilling their economic functions). . . . Whereas the death of a machine is determined mainly by economic forces, this principle is quite inapplicable to persons . . . [p. 207].

[We should also consider] homeostasis of whole societies as well as individuals, as in population explosion. . . . [p. 209].

The conclusion cannot be avoided that, within limits which may be quite broad, health is a matter of social definition. . . . with mental health and human behavior in society, however, the limits seem to be broader, and the matter of social definition more important . . . [p. 213].

The ambiguity can be maintained between demand as defined by the consumer and need as defined by the professional. All fields of life seem to feel the necessity for working out an uneasy compromise between these two concepts. Undiluted consumer sovereignty . . . is ultimately intolerable . . . on the other hand, total professionalization . . . is likewise intolerable. . . . In the case of medical indigency . . . the temptation is to deny consumers sovereignty as the price of the relief of indigency. . . . If medical care is distributed according to demand, the rich will get most of it and the poor very little [p. 217].

If any research strategy emerges out of these considerations, it is that one should be extremely suspicious of research devoted specifically to finding out the need for medical care. Too much of such research has already been done, all of which has outlined "needs" which are absurdly inflated, and which if allowed to be fulfilled, would justify themselves with the greatest ease. A research program which concentrated solely on quantitative estimates of need would inevitably neglect the problem of demand and the problem of price structure. A great deal in research depends on how questions are framed. If the question is asked, how does one use a combination of the grants economy and the price structure in producing a system of medical care that compromises between needs and demands, a much richer and more satisfactory answer will likely result than if one simply asks, what is the need for medical care? Almost every-one who has raised children has heard the anguished cry, "But I need—" and soon learns to interpret this as meaning "I want something badly but I am not prepared to pay the price for it." This cautionary note seems a suitable place to end what is mainly an appeal to move gingerly into an inevitably uncertain future without forgetting that the movement must be made [p. 220].

ORGANIZATION, PROCESS, AND PRACTICE IN COMMUNITY MENTAL HEALTH AND COMMUNITY HEALTH PROGRAMS

This section will not describe hospitals, nursing homes, or retirement communities, for two reasons. First, these have been described and evaluated in a number of published studies and in many other reports in the professional, scientific, and lay literature. Therefore, they will be examined only when they appear as part of and integral to a more general community program for the older individuals in the area. The latter is important because of the in-creasing recognition of the need for multipurpose programming for individual and community needs. There is, for example, the coun-seling and consultation service of a foundation offering multiple services to the aged in two Ohio counties (Kaplan, Ford, & Wain, 1966). About 6% of the 170,000 population in these counties is past age 65, and, of these, 10% sought out or were referred for the services of the program over three years, averaging six to seven contacts per individual over this period. The services included (a) Meals-on-Wheels; (b) a small home for the ambulatory aged, supervised by resident staff and aides; and (c) a geriatric center for specialized treatment, both inpatient (60 beds) and outpatient, coordinated by a medical social worker. Two-thirds of the contacts with community physicians were initiated by the program and one-third by physicians, resulting in more than 150 aged persons being referred for the services. The latter included counseling in employ-ment, housing, personal relationships, parent–child relationships, and marital relationships, in addition to the three programs cited above. Physicians requested services for their older patients

when the patient's medical (130 instances) or family (25 cases) situation changed or when a new service was needed (11 cases) for an unchanged patient situation . . . [p. 28].

Services [were] primarily for a combination of health and social needs of the patient and family with a concentration of requests for . . . [two types of therapy: long term and rehabilitation; p. 30].

The potential range of community programs in the health area is extensive, as witness Graber's (1965) inventory of resources to meet health needs of the aging and aged. These resources included (a) single and multidisciplinary professional or supportive services in nine states where 23% of the United States population aged 65 or older live, in health maintenance clinics for periodic health appraisal, education, counseling, and referral; (b) health education in the areas of screening for disease, safety and accident prevention, nutrition, home care, mental health, regular health evaluations, and specific programs as with cancer, diabetes, and cardiac conditions; (c) medical screening for tuberculosis, diabetes, cancer, glaucoma, hypertension, and respiratory disease; (d) information and referral services; (e) preretirement counseling by other than health agencies; (f) Meals-on-Wheels; (g) homemakers; (h) home care by nurses, nutritionists, physical therapists, and health directors; (i) activity programs for nursing homes; (j) dental care; (k) loan closets; (l) volunteer services; and (m) comprehensive rehabilitation programs. These programs were reported by city, county, and district health departments and distributed so that there was "overdevelopment of facilities in one area as opposed to their non-existence or underdevelopment in another [p. 19]."

The impact of the community, specifically the neighborhood, on adjustment to the later years has been studied by Rosenberg (1968) among others. His study of nearly 1,600 45–80-year-old individuals (668 were 65 or older) from Philadelphia's white, working class (some were considered to be poor, others, solvent) inquired about the friendship patterns of the respondents: isolates, friends within the neighborhood, friends beyond the neighborhood. Rosenberg reported that

The poor old men seem to be less responsive to a neighborhood context related to socioeconomic status than the solvent old men . . . [p. 534].

For younger people . . . the neighborhood context in most cases exerts no effects on their isolation from friends or very weak effects at best. . . . In old age, the companionship of fellow employees, whether it was negligible or significant before, is absent. A man's time is spent at or near home, and he is exposed to neighbors more than before. . . . The role of neighbor becomes activated and replaces that of workers. [p. 537].

Bultena (1969) studied nearly 250 retired men in three planned retirement communities in Arizona, contrasting his findings with those of Laumann (1966), Vidich and Bensman (1958), and West (1945). Bultena reported that status differences continue, "contrary to the concept promoted in retirement communities that 'everyone's equal here' . . . ." The differential impacts of the neighborhood as a function of age heterogeneity and social class variables are illustrated by Bultena's summary.

Our analysis reveals that status, as measured by occupational rank, continues to be operative in the friendship interaction of retirees. However, a comparison of these data with the findings of an earlier study suggests that class considerations may be less pronounced in the structuring of close friendship ties in planned retirement communities than in other residential settings [p. 464].

Bultena and Wood (1969) further attributed morale and health differences among various older persons in community living patterns to the "differential characteristics of persons settling in these . . . types of communities . . . [p. 211]."

In another program, described by Robertson and Banks (1970), the Metropolitan YMCA of Chicago developed in 1966 a Senior Citizens Mobile Service. This provided, over a 65-block area, "transportation and group worker services to a neglected population of inner city aged [p. 267]." Since the program was designed to increase the extent of socialization among the older citizens living in this area, two simple surveys were conducted a year apart as part of the group worker's study of client needs for the service project. The respondent was asked "to name as many senior citizens as he knew in his vicinity." The four response classes identified were no one named, claimed to know other senior citizens although not by name, one other senior citizen named, and more than one senior citizen named. At least three respondents in each of 19 blocks gave responses at both time periods, of the 50 blocks sampled initially and 25 after a year of the project. The data "showed increasing acquaintanceship among aged citizens in the area. This measure was taken as a measure of the impact of the services in the area [p. 267]."

Matchar, Furstenberg, and Kalisch (1965) described an "Aging Center" coordinated program as part of Baltimore's Sinai Hospital, a community facility. "The purpose of the program has been to determine through on-going services the medical needs of the aged and the methods most suitable for keeping this group of patients (the aged and the chronically ill) functioning in the community at the highest possible level [p. 125]." To accomplish this, the center instituted an information and referral service to deal with all queries in relation to problems of the aged. The service's purpose is twofold, that is, to familiarize the staff with community needs and to help direct patients and families to appropriate programs.

The medical program was designed for continuous and comprehensive care of the over 250 medically indigent aged patients living in the hospital district, housed in an outpatient department with specialty clinics. Each patient has his own physician among the six part-time internists, with home visits and night calls as part of the service, as necessary.

The medical program and information and referral service were augmented by programs of group counseling and recreational therapy when, early in the history of the two initial programs, the prevalence of depression and loneliness became obvious to the staff. The groups are separate for men and women, each led by a social worker and physician. The recreational therapy program is directed by a volunteer graduate occupational therapist who recruited other volunteers, of both sexes and all ages, who had "empathy for older patients and some skill in arts and crafts [p. 125]." Social isolates were identified and were visited weekly by volunteers. "For some of these patients, it has been their only contact with the outside world [p. 126]."

The fifth program is the one designed for organized home care, for

non-ambulatory patients needing both medical and paramedical services but no longer requiring the more expensive facilities of an acute hospital. . . . The patients must live in the hospital district and are admitted largely from Sinai Hospital's service beds but also from the comprehensive ambulatory clinic, from the Emergency Service on occasion, by application from other hospitals. Sinai Hospital's Aging Center is somewhat unique in that the same physician is able to see the patient in the hospital, on Home Care, or on comprehensive ambulatory care as indicated. These patients, then, do not suffer from episodic or fragmented medical care [p. 126].

Matchar et al. indicated that they had difficulty in evaluating their study because of the small sample size and the lack of a control group. They reported that (a) among 367 patients (mean age 73) seen over the first three years of the programs, 6 were hospitalized for psychiatric conditions and 28 had died; (b) 246 home visits were made; (c) 77% of over 1,300 inquiries to the information and referral program related to medical problems; (d) there was an average of one office visit or consultation every other month for these patients; and (e) the "costs of comprehensive medical care, including hospitalization, are considerable. . . . But the cost is far less than compared with the cost to the family and community for custodial care in nursing homes and chronic hospitals, not to mention the emotional cost [p. 128]."

Booth (1965) also has described as one of the programs of a senior center the visits by a caseworker to the "hard-to-reach" aged isolate. The worker visited in order to motivate these individuals to try a group experience either "at the Center, in the nearest neighborhood group, or in their own residential setting . . . to determine his needs and wishes, and to help him deal with the problems—physical, emotional and environmental—keeping him from group participation [p. 25]."

Fraser's (1965) study illustrated that even information on resources in the community is lacking; for example, indicating the essential nature of information programs as part of the multipurpose and multiprogram efforts for older individuals, "lack of knowledge concerning appropriate and available community resources among older citizens and those responsible for their care and social needs of older people are far more complex and difficult to identify than those of younger citizens [p. 38]." Inadequate community resources for housing, medical, homemaker, protective care, and nursing home needs of the aging in Detroit were identified through a program which consisted of (a) meeting older persons "on [a] short-term individual basis in the office" or answering telephone inquiries about resources; (b) providing "minimum counseling"; (c) providing information and making referrals, but not intensive casework; (d) following of referrals "in certain difficult situations"; and (e) indicating gaps in services for the aging.

The San Francisco Senior Center (Vickery, 1965), in operation since 1948, functions 6 days a week, attracts 175 applicants from the senior citizen community each year, of whom about 100 join, and numbered well over 800 members in 1965. Multiservice, it also is multifunded, by the United Community Fund and three city departments—Adult Education, Recreation and Parks, and Public Health. The Center has as its goals the establishment or increase of feelings of belonging among older citizens, friendship, and enjoyment of activities. Six procedures are used to accomplish these goals. They are (a) an intake interview, (b) weekly staff intake review sessions, (c) quarterly review of individual participation patterns, (d) interstaff communication to provide immediate information sharing, (e) psychiatric consultation on atypical behavior, and (f) program planning geared to provide differential activities for the differential needs of individual members.

Frankel (1966) characterized the senior center (the San Francisco Center is among the pioneers of these programs) as "a new kind of environment to serve older people. . . ." By 1965 there were 700 centers (30 in New York City alone and 65 in California) providing social, recreational, and referral services. The National Council on Aging at that time reported 500 other programs developing into senior centers, facilitated by the Older Americans Act of 1965 (HR 3708), the Act which also established the Administration on Aging. The Act specified the

> establishment of new or expansion of existing programs to carry out such purposes, including establishment of new or expansion of existing centers providing recreational and other leisure time activities, and informational health, welfare, counseling, and referral services for older persons and assisting such persons in providing volunteer or community or civic services . . . [Title III, Section 301, 4].

Because of the social losses and isolation of older individuals, senior center multipurpose programs were developed to "facilitate, coordinate, and simplify the various essential services needed for the elderly." The services include, together with senior centers, Golden Age Centers, lounges, and day centers, in an

> attempt to provide a social environment, to coordinate services, and to develop new skills, interests, and social relationships through individual and group activity . . . in various . . . settings such as community centers, neighborhood centers, municipal centers, public and private housing developments, churches, synagogues, labor unions, and retirement villages. . . . [These centers are] sponsored by sectarian groups, private and public welfare agencies, municipal recreation departments, labor and organization groups, or combinations of the above [p. 25].

Frankel (1966), first chairman of the Senior Center Committee of the President's Council on Aging organized in 1963, further specified the characteristics of senior centers as

> a physical facility open to senior citizens at least five days a week and four hours a day, year-round, and operated by a public agency or a non-profit organization with community planning, which provides under the direction of paid professional leadership three or more . . . services . . . [p. 25].

These services include recreation, adult education, health services, counseling and other social services, information and referral services, community and voluntary services, and community leadership. Also included are self-government committees, leadership development, and local service organizations.

A very different program meets the needs of older people not only by providing additional income but also "a new sense of purpose" (Office of Economic Opportunity, 1966)—the Foster Grandparent Program. Participants are paid prevailing local wages for working 20 hours weekly, must be at least 60 years old, with incomes no greater than $3,000 for a couple or $1,800 for a single person. No educational skills are required, but there are requirements of "warm-heartedness, an interest in children, the willingness to serve, and the ability to read and to take supervision." These workers are expected to "supply attention, love, and understanding to youngsters —up to age 16—in hospitals, orphanages, charity wards, receiving homes, and institutions for the mentally retarded . . . in public and private non-profit institutions caring for children [p. 54]." Funded by the Office of Economic Opportunity and administered by the Administration on Aging, 22 of these projects began operation in 1965. In one program in Texas, 38 grandparents who were selected for

> this totally integrated program were public housing residents on city and county welfare rolls. . . . After an intenisve two-week training period, including on-the-job experience . . . the grandparents were assigned to work with children up to the age of four. These children, from low-income and minority group families, are hospitalized from periods of three weeks to one year [p. 54].

In another Foster Grandparent Program, 20 66–73-year-old participants work with 50 children; in still another city, participants are working with retarded, educable, trainable, emotionally disturbed children under 5 years of age; and still another group, with children under age 4 in a state hospital and two orphanages.

Another pattern of community care is that of the homemaker, often as part of a senior citizen center or other community program for the aged. An example is the three-year demonstration project in St. Louis (Safier, 1966) serving 167 families through six home-workers placed in three public and one voluntary agency, under the supervision of casework or nursing staff. The families "consisted primarily of either single elderly persons or two elderly persons, of whom at least one was chronically ill . . . often married couples, but many were elderly mothers and daughters living together or elderly siblings [p. 151]." Homemakers visited families on a part-time basis, without limitation on the duration of the service.

The agencies provided information on demographic characteristics, family relationships, social engagement or isolation, medical diagnosis, and physical and mental disabilities. Follow-up evaluation was done with families who continued the service for 3-, 9-, and

15-month periods. Although some agencies saw homemaker roles as practical housekeeping functions, it generally was recognized and encouraged that the roles of morale booster, socialization, and emotional support were significant. For these tasks and roles, careful selection (46 out of 144 applicants were recommended and 35 were placed, including the 6 in the demonstration project), orientation of agency staff, and constructive and stimulating supervision toward the homemakers' "own original and spontaneous judgment" developed as prerequisites for a satisfactory homemaker program. Safier reported both positive and negative qualities of the applicants to assist others in selection programs, as well as the dimensions of orientation for agency staff and supervisory relationships and content. She urged, through homemaker services, a program to promote what Tillich (1962) has called " 'the law of listening love' which . . . 'listens sensitively and reacts spontaneously' [p. 153]."

For community-living older individuals who can leave their homes but are infirm, MacDonell (1966) described a Canadian program utilizing two hospitals for day care, one a veterans hospital and the other a municipal hospital. A 20-bed ward in the 640-bed veterans hospital and 110-bed unit in the 440-bed municipal hospital are part of the "Functional Restitution Ward" units. These are designed "to provide a continuing activity program, to provide a means of continuous geriatric assessment, and to provide social relief [p. 25]."

Romney (1966) extended this day hospital concept to a broader base, for strengthened relationships between nursing homes, Golden Age Centers, and rehabilitation centers.

> The value system of a therapeutic milieu in rehabilitation medicine includes the reduction of boundaries between the hospital and the community. Housing, jobs, social life, negative attitudes to disabled, family overprotectiveness and architectural barriers present community problems for disabled people. The hospital is a closed system with therapy viewed as "complete" within its walls. The community represents an alien system to the hospital treatment team. Community problems are foreign to the therapists. Their solutions, however, are necessary for rehabilitation to be completed. . . . The method of the therapeutic community is extended to the outside community . . . . Emerging is the use of self-help methods toward community problem solution [p. 32].

An example of community cooperation, reported by Curtis and Miller (1966), appears between a city recreation and parks department and a private nursing home in their joint sponsorship of a senior citizens' club. The advantages of this cooperation are reflected in the ready availability of facilities without construction or rental costs, the reduction of "fears of the functionally well aged in the community of disability and nursing home placement [p. 33]," and the neighborhood aged's participation without the complication of transportation costs and schedules. In the division of responsibility, the home provides the physical facilities, supplies, and a small group of intact patients. The municipal department provides staff, program assistance, and administrative direction. The programs are planned by a committee of group members and staff advisors.

Blenker, Jahn, and Wasser (1964) and Blenker (1967) introduced one of the few controlled studies of community services for the aged by randomly assigning noninstitutionalized aged to one of three programs varying from a "minimal" service through information and referral to other health and welfare resources to an intensive, direct service by both social workers and public health nurses. Unfortunately, sample size negated a significant study of differential effects. At a six-month follow-up, the death rate was "considerably higher on the maximum service program" (24%), 12% on the "midway program," and 6% on the minimal program. In a second study (Blenkner, Bloom, & Nielsen, 1971), 164 noninstitutionalized aged protective services clients who were referred by 13 social and health agencies were divided between an experimental, "highly developed demonstration service" and control programs of "normally available services" as given by their referring agencies. The rate of institutionalization was higher among experimental subjects than among controls, as shown in Table 1. In addition, the death rate after one year

TABLE 1

Rates of Institutionalization and Mortality at Different
Follow-up Intervals

Subjects	Experimental	Control
Institutionalization		
One year	25	14
Five years	61	47
Mortality, institutionalized subjects		
One year	26	15
Four years	69	68
Mortality, noninstitutionalized subjects		
One year	23	20
Four years	56	43

Note. Data were taken by permission of the publisher, the Family Service Association of America, from M. Blenkner, M. Bloom, and M. Nielsen. "A Research and Demonstration Project of Protective Services." *Social Casework,* 1971, 52, 483-499.

for the experimental group that became institutionalized was greater than that for the institutionalized control group; after four years, the rates did not differ. For those who were not institutionalized, death rates did not differ after one year, but, after four years, the experimental service group's death rate departed significantly more from their expected death rate than did the control group's.

Ross (1968) explored another group of services for "the small, but growing minority (of older Americans) who are not able to take advantage of even the minimum level of services that society provides, and who have no one who can help them to do so [p. 50]." Ross estimated that 5% of the aged are in need of protective services, the aged who are incapable of caring for themselves and their interests and who have no resources in relatives or other individuals to provide support and supervision, yet remain in the community. When these older individuals come to the attention of the community, public mental hospitalization usually follows. However, this kind of protective service is inadequate in two respects: those who could function reasonably well in their own homes with the aid of supportive services would not benefit from involuntary hospitalization, and many state commitment laws assume that a family member will initiate the process. If there is no family member to assume this responsibility,

> in most communities the police force is the only public agency that will accept this function, and it does so only where the person's behavior is a clear danger to society, but is reluctant to act when the danger is to self . . . [p. 51]. At present, there is no community in this country which has an agency willing to accept primary responsibility for all protective service cases in the community [p. 52].

Ross further noted that

> protective service for adults is now widely recognized as a real need, just as protective service for children was recognized as a need in the first quarter of this century. The services needed may be any kind of supportive service, such as health care or income maintenance. The two factors which distinguish the protective service function from the function of other agencies are (1) the protective agency is willing to seek out the client who, because of his mental impairment, may not want the service: and (2) the agency is willing and able to initiate legal action in or intervention with the client's life pattern as a last resort technique in providing needed service [p. 53].

Burr (1970) described a three-year multidisciplinary demonstration project for social, health, and legal protective services for older adults who were "current, former, or potential" public assistance recipients. The program was designed for "aged, blind, and disabled . . . with serious physical and mental impairment" in order to produce the effects of "stabilizing them in their current environmental situation, helping them to secure appropriate protective placement, or reducing stress in crisis or emergency situation [p. 55]." This three-county program also demonstrated how a public service agency becomes "the community focal point for providing surrogate service . . . ."

Even where the community aged are not in need of such protective services, there are difficulties, as pointed out by Taylor and Gaitz (1968). As part of a rehabilitation program, medical regimens were prescribed for 38 elderly patients "living in settings where they were responsible for themselves; and 62 . . . were placed in settings ostensibly offering supervision of medical care [p. 24]." Evaluation on follow-up showed "deviations" and "disgressions" from the prescriptions, varying in "quality and effect." These included ignoring medication, giving it sporadically or to a point of toxicity or failure to meet a health goal, for example, control of blood pressure or behavior. "Although more likely to occur among self-care patients (54%), digression also occurs frequently when patients are allegedly under professional supervision (47%) [p. 24]."

To reverse the flow of elderly patients from the community to state mental hospitals, a number of experiments have been tried. An example is that reported by Cohen and Kraft (1968). From a state hospital in Pennsylvania where 700 elderly patients were destined to be "permanent residents [in] a system in which they enjoy the lowest priority," these men and women were transferred to a geriatric center and "a change to high priority status."

> The reports on the first 700 patients indicate that 70% have responded very favorably to restorative therapy and have improved sufficiently for return to community housing or to simplified care settings. In response to increased medical and nursing care, personal attention, and extensive involvement in various forms of corrective therapy, they improved in all spheres. . . . most of all [they] became enthusiastic about participating in arrangements for return to the community [p. 265].

Of the 700 patients transferred to the center, 16% have been readmitted to the mental hospital, 65 died in the center and 1 after placement, and 163 "have achieved substantial long-term placements in community housing or in less specialized care facilities." These facilities include commercial boarding homes (the majority of placements have been in this type of facility), foster homes, private nursing homes, and county homes. Cohen and Kraft emphasized the need for medical and social care, needs unmet in "low priority systems . . . careful preparation, matching, and selection [for placement] . . .

some form of support, if only minimal benign surveillance by a person in a position of supervision"; and the critical nature of the length of the rehabilitation and preparation period: "50% leave after five months or less and 85% leave after seven months or less. It appears that, when preparation extends beyond this length of time, the likelihood of discharge fades rapidly [p. 268]."

The average patient in this geriatric center program was 74 years old and had spent 19 years in the hospital. Sixty percent were women, 10% were nonwhite, 40% had never married, 90% had completed nine grades of school or less, 74% had little or no family interest, most "had employment histories which made them highly vulnerable in times of economic decline," and "except for a few, their lives had been marked by recurrent deprivation, difficult living situations, low income levels, inability to amass savings, and failure to keep apace with the changing patterns of society [p. 265]."

Less fortunate outcomes of returning elderly psychiatric patients to community facilities have been outlined by Butler (1970). He described the problems of placing these patients in the District of Columbia, where one naively might expect a model program for the Nation's Capitol, in "foster care homes." Unlike foster family care for children, a familiar model, Butler noted that

"community" placement is a euphemism in the District of Columbia for boarding house placement often [is] in impoverished and crime-ridden neighborhoods. Indeed, "boarding housing," in turn is often a euphemism for a flop house. Malnutrition was discovered. Some patients had been assaulted in these "homes" as well as while walking unattended on the streets. . . . Some patients received inadequate medical coverage. . . . Racial segregation was practiced. . . . Only $125 per month was paid . . . for each patient. . . . [There were] 180 to 200 such "foster care homes" with . . . 2 to 40 patients. Operators were given only six hours of training. . . . It must be stated that some of these homes were well run and that operators could have the best of intentions . . . [pp. 259–260].

There have been numerous suggestions for but only a few examples of a continuum of care for older citizens. Liebowitz and Brody (1970) have reviewed one such program which has evolved over the past two decades, beginning in 1952 with the opening of a 150-bed facility for the "well" in the model of the traditional "home for the aged" and expanding to include about 900 individuals in its present functions as a multiservice center. The first stage of change resulted from a study of applicants who were not well enough to be admitted, "to determine their fate and apparent needs." Later additions to the program came with understanding of "the role of advancing age and illness among adult children as precipitants or contributory factors to the aged parents' application . . . implications for clinical approaches to applicants and family members . . . need for family-focused services . . . (and) needed but unavailable supportive community-based services [p. 12]." What followed was

the center's decision to develop a variety of services such as day-care for impaired aged . . . outpatient psychiatric services, and temporary and emergency care. . . . Intermediate Houses . . . social service, and a "hot line" telephone to the Home for emergencies [p .13].

Burnside's (1970) report of community programs for the aged surveyed group work in a number of contexts. These included (a) "remotivation groups" in a nursing home; (b) an "internal visiting" program in a geriatrics institution for chronic brain syndrome patients; (c) group meetings of older patients in a veterans' hospital; (d) group experiences for the chronically hospitalized in a geriatric hospital; (e) a rehabilitation program for hemiplegic patients; (f) a geriatrics council in a veterans' hospital ward; (g) geriatric patients' group experience in a mental hospital and similar programs in general and convalescent hospitals; (h) group experiences for the "very old" (past 85); (i) health discussion groups of physically disabled aged led by visiting nurses; and (j) programs for "well-functioning members" in the older age range, in homes for the aged, recreation centers, community centers, and in various other institutional environments. The goals of these group experiences are summarized as resocialization and life-style reexpansion, sharing, and crisis intervention.

Gaitz (1970) emphasized the need for a professional "coordinator" in multidisciplinary, multiservice community programs, basing his recommendation upon his experience in a Texas state hospital. The primary aim of a project for older patients who had been admitted to a screening ward operated by the county and then committed to a state hospital was "to provide the community with a resource for comprehensive care of elderly persons, a resource which would improve the delivery of service. . . ." A follow-up evaluation during a one-year period demonstrated that "an elderly person needs someone who can explain, intercede, expedite, defend, and even fight for him when necesary . . . [for example] the coordinator [p. 218].

Similarly, but in another environment of the community, Carey (1970) described a four-year project, which included a two-year service period, evaluating a "senior advisory service" for 1,000 older tenants in public housing. The program consisted of in-service-trained workers of mature years who rendered circumscribed services—reach-out, information, advocacy and generally facilitative— under professional supervision . . . . [They] functioned competently as reach-out agents, expeditors, advocates and friendly supporters; less well as developers of mutual aid programs. The reluctance of older tenants to seek help, the volume of needs expressed and the paucity of resources called for great efforts to make accessible what was available. Measured by responses to pre- and post-service interviews of randomly selected populations of the four served and two other control projects, the program had a measurable impact on the emotional and physical functioning of tenants served, particularly those 75 years and older; a lesser and mixed effect on social functioning [p. 54].

For "community-based" aged not in the homogenous environment of public housing there is the study of a "friendly visitor" program by Bennett, Sanchez, Neary, and Halpin (1970). In order to reduce the social isolation of older individuals living independently, a pair of visitors (trained, Red Cross Volunteers) visited, interviewed, and tested each subject in two experimental and one control group (10 persons each). Visits to members of one experimental group were weekly, less often with the second experimental group, and the control group was seen only at the beginning and end of the 6-week service period. "Preliminary results in the form of behavioral observations and case reports indicate that those persons seen once a week during the past month have shown marked improvement in grooming, interest in the visitors, sociability, and communicativeness [p. 54]."

Visits by caseworkers for longer periods of time but with the same target population formed the basis for one of the programs of a neighborhood senior center. Booth (1970) also focused on the "isolated and disadvantaged elderly person unable to seek the help needed to sustain himself in the community" and to effectively function. This three-year demonstration project utilized the store-front center, caseworkers, and home visits to involve "hard-to-reach . . . apathetic and distrustful" senior citizens among the 3,000 served over the period of the project. "Individualized reaching-out activities, relevant program and most of all relationship to staff have proved to be the most successful techniques of involvement [p. 57]."

EVALUATION

The most critical yet, unfortunately, the least frequently explored dimension of community mental health and other health programs is the problem of evaluation of their services. Such evaluation requires criteria of performance, goals, and objectives specifically stated and testable, reliable measuring methods, and objective assessment of the process and outcome of intervention programs. The summary decriptions of the programs reported in the preceding section of this chapter, with few exceptions, illustrate the serious need for adequate evaluation. Overgeneralization and multiple methodological weaknesses mark many of the programs and studies reported in the gerontological and geriatric literature. It is no surprise then that confusion and contradiction is not uncommon. Anderson (1967) commented, for example, on the contradictions reported on the effects of institutionalization.

> Two methodological weaknesses may account for these contradictions. . . . (1) low self-esteem and poor adjustment are probably associated with the reasons for selecting institutional living. . . . the differences (between an institutional sample and a sample of community residents) may have existed before the former sample changed residence. . . . (2) institutionalization is too gross a contextual variable to explain any differences which might be found. Instead, elements having a direct effect on self-esteem must be isolated and tested for a relationship with the dependent variable [p. 313].

Bultena (1969) and Lieberman (1969) also evaluated the differential characteristics of persons moving to a different community or institutional setting.

Lawton, Ward, and Yaffe (1967) recognized the methodological problems of programs and their evaluation and, in attempting to reduce the difficulties, have specified the dimensions of their studies. By utilizing measures whose reliabilities may be assessed, and factor analysis to establish the basic dimensions of health behaviors and attitudes, this group developed 30 measures of physical health, self-reports of health status and its life-threatening quality, degree of functional disability, emotional status, and degree of pain, for annual periods. Factor analysis of the data gathered by the measures of about 150 66–90-year-old apartment-dwelling men and women yielded "basic health factors" of disability, self-perceived health, "consensual awareness" of health status, physician-rated health, "self-protective health behavior," and subjective discomfort. There were sex differences on the dimensions of disability, self-perceived health, apparent health decline, psychological adjustment, hospitalization, and number of signs and symptoms.

In another factor analytic study and another population sample, Fisher and Pierce (1967) used psychological tests and rating scales to gather data on 358 patients among 534 over the age of 60 admitted to the psychiatric wards of a general hospital. The cluster analysis of the responses to the tests and ratings indicated the factors of intellectual functioning and "social and cognitive accessibility"; and five "profile types based upon the average standard scores on each dimension [pp. 480ff]." These types were psychiatric patient (43%), intractable (7%), deteriorated accessible (13%), deteriorated and ill (29%), and deteriorated inaccessible (7%).

Although many investigators urge longitudinal studies in order to reduce the methodological weakness of cross-sectional studies, one of the major difficulties is in attrition, especially among older individuals. The attrition by mobility among younger persons yields a similar problem. In the study by Britton, Bergmann, Kay, and Savage (1967), an original sample of 297 respondents, aged 65 or older, seen initially in their homes were followed up four years later. Of the 297, 180 were still living (nearly 40% attrition) of whom 91 were selected for reevaluation. Data on 80 were obtained, the other 11 "unable or unwilling to complete the psychometric investigations." Thus, the latter comprised only 4% of the original sample, but 12% of the already attrited second sample. Variables associated with mortality and morbidity make it difficult to interpret or generalize data gathered from survivors of an initial cohort.

Changes on ratings and self-report measures have been used by many investigators, both to establish base-line values and as criterion changes associated with community program impact upon older individuals. "Life satisfaction" and morale scales developed in the Kansas City Study of Adult Life are among the most widely used criterion measures in a number of community studies. Wood, Wylie, and Sheafor (1969) and Adams (1969) used such measures in studies of rural and of small-town older, community-living individuals. Robertson and Banks (1970) in a senior citizens mobile service program and Wylie (1970) used life satisfaction and morale measures specifically as "program impact" criteria of a three-year demonstration effort in a rural town in Kansas. The program, designed to "mobilize the resources of community-residing aged individuals to work on problems affecting younger residents," also had as a goal the evaluation of this demonstration as it affected the lives of the "aged target population." The criterion measure, a modification of the Kansas-City-developed Life Satisfaction Index A (Neugarten, Havighurst, & Tobin, 1961), was seen as capable of describing both negative as well as positive effects and "social-psychological program effects." Responses to mailed questionnaires, sent prior to the demonstration and after its close two and one-half years later, were analyzed for 98 participants and 33 nonparticipants to evaluate changes in social participation in the demonstration programs. Wylie reported that "the increased morale associated with participant status did reflect a general fit with the attitudes of younger residents. . . . The unearthing of negative morale changes among nonparticipants was a sobering finding [p. 39]."

Graber (1965) emphasized a common difficulty in the distribution of state and local resources for health needs of the aging and aged." This evaluation is significant in the understanding of the network and patterns of community resources. Further, the lag in developing economic support for the aged in this country is illuminated by Randall's (1965) survey of the history of social welfare programs for the aging. She reported that, as recently as a generation ago (1928), only the United States, China, and India had no old age pensions or dependency support.

Several crucial observations were made by Kent (1965) in his evaluation of "friendly visiting, activity centers, and similar programs . . . ." He stated:

> I know of no large-scale study demonstrating the effectiveness of these approaches nor their influences on large numbers of persons. But this is not the point I wish to make. . . . Boredom and loneliness may be related to deep-seated personality characteristics. . . . Perhaps, something need be done much earlier in life . . . [p. 52].
>
> Opinions on the desirability or undesirability of retirement villages are rampant. But studies are virtually nonexistent. I challenge anyone to state that he knows for sure that such villages do or do not promote adjustment, do or do not contribute to mental health, do or do not lengthen life . . . [p. 53].
>
> The faith we have in untested and unproved concepts is enormous . . . [p. 54].

The need for dependable evaluation criteria was highlighted by Shanas (1965). In her analysis, although only 2% of those 65–75 year's of age are in institutions and 7% of those 75 and older, 8% of those living in the community are "bedfast and house-bound," 30% have difficulty in walking stairs, and another 18% find it difficult to attend to various parts of daily routine. Although about one-third of the community-living elderly had not seen a physician in a year or more, Shanas reported that "as long as old people can get about, they describe themselves as well. Indeed, some persons who are completely housebound and unable to leave the house without assistance, consider themselves 'well' [p. 240]." It is this wide range of coping behaviors which multipurpose gerontological programs often are intended to serve, target behaviors whose variability results in as great problems for program evaluation as for the programs themselves.

Lipman (1965), in studying a 50% sample of 1,500 older residents in public housing, evaluated community approaches in offering services in a major metropolitan area as "fragmented." He hypothesized that planning and coordination of services "in greater quantity, improved quality, and broader scope will be beneficial in prolonging independent living of the elderly resident in public housing . . . [p. 256]." This can be accomplished by utilizing the health, money, education, and race resources of the older person as well as his relationship to society and vice versa, the aged person's own idosyncratic integration of resources, and society's role in supporting these resources.

Frankel (1966) not only described in detail changes and their effects on older individuals, and community and other programs for them, but also summarized the status of evaluation of senior citizens' centers, as deplorable a situation as Kent (1965) reported for other programs for the aged. Frankel's summary evaluation stated that only "in a few cases, all too few, centers have developed with a sound social work philosophy, with a broad spectrum of services, and with a trained staff [p. 25]."

In the important area of housing for the aged, Walkley, Mangum, Sherman, Dodds, and Wilner (1966) extensively surveyed retirement housing and adjustments toward environments: physical, social, and psychological. These investigators reported that

There is . . . little information regarding expressed satisfactions or dissatisfactions with various features of group housing settings and little data about residents' general reactions to specific facilities. Nor is there yet systematic information about the effects of residence in such settings on a host of variables, including style of life, morale, expectations, aspirations, health and illness, etc.

[Significantly, the writers pointed out that] evaluation, and need for reorientation, fails or is inhibited by management, residents, professionals and the programs themselves. . . . the one basic and crucial problem . . . is that of potential availability of . . . [retirement] housing to older persons of low or limited economic means [p. 34].

Because of the extensive use of volunteers in many programs for the aged, it is of interest to review Pearse's (1966) study, one of the few attempts to evaluate a program designed to train volunteers (themselves in the 60–80+ age range) in a demonstration project. Of 46 trained in groups of 6 or 7 each, 14 still were serving one day weekly after three years and 6 others were assistants or substitutes. For those continuing, "the experience has been personally satisfying. The regularity with which they meet their commitments attests to this . . . [p. 158]." However, the disadvantages are static quality, the lack of effective recruitment measures for both volunteer leaders and for new participants, isolation from the main facility, measures that would stimulate active interest and support of those who house an activity of this kind, but do little more, are lacking, and, for the future, present leaders face a loss of strength and lessened ability to continue.

In evaluating an aging project in Boston associated with the development of six programs—housing, protective services, senior center, and so on—Cohen (1966) made explicit several major difficulties in "informing, mobilizing, strengthening, and coordinating existing and potential resources . . . in response to community need; involving the elderly themselves; selecting competent leaders; identifying problems, encouraging and supporting legislation, raising funds [p. 33]." Significantly, she concluded that the six programs

> were accompanied by frustrations and pitfalls arising from unpredicted community resistance. What appears on paper is orderly and logical, but factors, predictable and unpredictable, affect process. Miscalculations were made in judging importance of projects for the aging in competition with a variety of other life stresses, economic, social, political, of the community [p. 33].

As Clark (1969) has written about the "medieval mind," obviously little different from the "twentieth century mind": "They cared passionately about the truth, but their sense of evidence was different from ours [p. 41]."

More than a decade ago, at the Fifth International Congress of Gerontology in 1960, Randall (1962) observed that "nationally as well as locally our approaches have been sporadic . . . actually expedient and uncoordinated, rather than thoroughly planned . . . [p. 344]." More recently, Binstock reported (1967) that an evaluation program at Brandeis University, funded by the Ford Foundation, analyzed seven demonstration projects in social planning for the aged (four are reported in Morris & Binstock, 1966). After three years of planning and implementation of programs, the research staff's data were interpreted by Binstock (1967) as follows:

> While the planning councils were able to achieve some of their goals for the elderly, most goals evolved sporadically, expediently, and haphazardly. Very rarely was technical knowledge employed in order to allocate scarce resources for effectively enhancing the welfare of the aging. . . . in the vast majority of these cases, little technical knowledge was applied in the development of goals. The choices, in fact, were overwhelmingly political.
>
> The Brandeis staff found it analytically sound . . . to regard as goals only those objectives that embodied a proposal for changing the policy

of one or more organizations. . . . this criterion led to the identification of approximately 100 goals.

Less than half . . . were selected on the basis of sound evidence that their realization would actually enhance the welfare of older persons. The assumption made in a majority of cases that the establishment of a given program or service would help the elderly could, in some instances, have been supported by current research reports; in others, it could not. In either case, there was little attempt to conduct an extensive search for such evidence.

Less than 5% of the goals were chosen from among a set of alternative measures for improving the welfare of the elderly . . . data from basic and applied research indicate differences in the marginal benefits gained by the input of various welfare measures.

Less than a tenth of the projects' goals made substantial distinctions among the varying characteristics of older persons. . . . not one of the project goals even took account of the diverse requirements of persons in their sixties, seventies, eighties, and nineties.

Only about one-fourth of the goals were chosen on the basis of data with regard to the needs of older persons. Usually the need was assumed.

Only a handful of goals were developed with attention to the power variables that would be likely to determine the success or failure of an attempt to establish a program or service. When some goals proved to be feasible, it was not because the planning projects had carefully designed them with an eye to strategies of implementation.

Only limited data exist with regard to the effectiveness of certain types of programs, the comparative effectiveness of different types, and the differential needs of older persons. Unfortunately, even these data are not readily accessible to professionals engaged in planning for the elderly. Although political scientists . . . have analyzed power variables relevant to the achievement of planning objectives within analogous settings, for the most part their insights have not been drawn upon by the professionals who are planning for the welfare of the elderly.

The limited utilization of technical knowledge in community planning for the elderly has meant that the selection of goals has been primarily the outcome of community welfare politics, a politics characterized by an aversion to conflict. . . . conflict is avoided whenever possible. Objectives tend to be sought in the name of "the community," and only with the overwhelming consensus of influential persons and organizations. . . . these councils . . . [have] as their main interest . . . maintaining an image of neutral disinterested civic statesmanship. . . .

The training given to the social work professionals who staff welfare councils tends to reinforce this political culture. . . . Professional education tends to emphasize methods for achieving consensus, rather than techniques for enhancing the welfare of the elderly or other subgroups . . . .

The lay directors of planning councils, seeking status, tend not to generate planning proposals. They rely upon professional staff to supply them. The professionals, who have an aversion to conflict, prefer to submit proposals that are uncontroversial and fashionable. The fashions, in turn, are styled by "national experts," who are becoming increasingly influential as American society undergoes a professionalism of reform. . . . The evolving system of expertise in the United States warrants close examination, for it is these "national experts" (certainly not older persons) who shape the politics of aging in communities throughout the nation [pp. 44–46].[2]

The implicit suggestion by Binstock that older persons should have a greater, and significant, role in shaping "the politics of aging" must be examined against the background of Schmidhauser's political science analysis of political influence of the aged over the past two decades. Schmidhauser (1968) concluded his analysis by stating that

in the 1960's, as in the 1950's, the task of evaluating the poiltical role of elderly persons through use of modern research on political behavior and social psychology often raises more questions than answers. The evidence does serve to indicate that the political role of the elderly is a complex phenomenon, subject indeed to significant variations in different environments [p. 49].

Finally, Havighurst's (1969) report clearly reflected the present state of evaluation of community programs of social services for the aged and aging. Need for, rather than availability of, evaluative research characterized the Committee's suggestions for research priorities.

The majority of aging and aged adults in the United States do not live in institutions. Rather, they remain in their communities and manage without the help of organized services. When families and individuals require social intervention because of age-related needs, the capacity of communities to respond effectively and efficiently is often deficient. Flexible and alternative programs for providing income maintenance, health services, housing, and work and leisure activities are often either not apparent to the persons in need or are not, in fact, available.

Because of the varied and changing needs of individuals over the later year of life, social services need to be comprehensive, to provide services ranging from simple information to immediate direct service during a time of crisis. To achieve this goal it is necessary to clearly identify the elderly who require services, to ascertain their needs and requirements, and to learn how to deliver services to them most efficiently so that their lives can be permanently changed for the better.

Research is particularly needed to clarify . . . : (a) the effect of social services on the functional capacity of the individual; (b) the relative values of services offered on the basis of age segregation and those

---

[2]This material was reprinted by permission of the publisher, the Gerontological Society, from R. H. Binstock, "What Sets the Goals of Community Planning for the Aging?" *Gerontologist,* 1967, **7,** 44–46.

offered in a mixed-age situation; (c) the degree to which older persons may determine which services are best suited to meet their needs; (d) the special requirements of ethnic and economic sub-groups; (e) effects of possible amelioration of the aging process or changes in the social order upon requirements for community services; and (f) a basis for projecting the future service needs of the aged.

There is also a great need for the development of a variety of models to demonstrate, explore, and serve as guidelines for the provision of services. These models should focus both upon the provider of services and upon the consumer. In all cases, it is of extreme importance that evaluative research be designed into each model tested.

The major recommendations regarding research needs reflect a basic lack of information concerning the effectiveness of current methods of providing services for the elderly. In particular, we need research on:

1. How to organize and deliver adequate comprehensive services to the aged.

2. The psychological consequences of how services are offered and how this affects consumer usage.

3. The range of environmental situations which promote or hinder access to services.

4. Uses of public and private facilities, including schools and community centers, with demonstration programs, backed with evaluative research on how these institutions may be used more effectively.

5. Identification of the changes in need that accompany the move from late maturity to extreme old age. For this task, longitudinal research will be needed, both with representative samples and the samples from minority groups.

6. Development of a variety of instruments or social indicators to (a) appraise the effectiveness of service; (b) determine disability or functional capacity; and (c) identify individual service requirements.

7. The development and evaluation of systems for providing information concerning persons with need and for referring such persons to appropriate services. Such systems must have the function of evaluating the relevance and quality of service ultimately rendered, as well as that of evaluating the classifying needs.

8. Experimentation to determine the relationship of housing and other environmental factors to the ability of the elderly to manage on their own.

9. The development of new strategies and policy for gaining personnel to provide services to the elderly.

10. Operational research methods for organizing medical and health services and delivering care to the elderly. Attention must be given to the problem of ensuring that older people get their just share of such care [pp. 14–15].[3]

---

[3]This material was reprinted by permission of the publisher, the Gerontological Society, from R. J. Havighurst, "The Status of Research in Applied Social Gerontology." *Gerontologist*, 1969, **9** (Pt. 2), 1–90.

SUMMARY

Community concern and care for the mental and physical health of older individuals in society have been recorded over the centuries in oral and written history. During the past three decades, however, formal programs involving other than institutional care have developed, so that broadly-based community efforts have moved well beyond the traditional state hospital, chronic hospital, nursing home, or home for the aged patterns, for example, toward multipurpose, multidisciplinary, community programs such as senior citizens' centers.

Although this development appears to hold most promise among the many programs attempted, evaluation of these and other community mental health and other health programs is sadly lacking. A number of investigators have reported the lack of program evaluation and the serious need for such evaluations. Seldom are goals defined, even less often are these determined for other than political or other expedient reasons, and rarely are there systematic and comprehensive evaluations of the impact of the programs upon the aged population.

Difficult though it is, this important and necessary part of community programming for the psychological, social, economic, and other health variables in aging should be given maximum opportunity and support. These pages of review suggest highest priority for evaluation of the many community programs planned and in functional operation, if the aging and aged in our society are to realize both their potential and an optimal quality of life.

REFERENCES

Adams, D. L. Analysis of a Life Satisfaction Index. *Journal of Gerontology,* 1969, **24**, 470–474.

American Medical Association. *Commission on the Cost of Medical Care Report.* Chicago: Author, 1963–1964.

Anderson, N. N. Effects of institutionalization on self-esteem. *Journal of Gerontology,* 1967, **22**, 313–317.

Anderson, O. W. Influence of social and economic research on public policy in the health field. *Milbank Memorial Fund Quarterly,* 1966, **44**, 11–48.

Bates, F. L., & White, R. F. Differential perceptions of authority in hospitals. *Journal of Health and Human Behavior,* 1961, **2**, 262–267.

Bennett, R., Sanchez, E., Neary, J.-M., & Halpin, M. Development and evaluation of a Friendly Visitor Program for the community-based aged. *Gerontologist,* 1970, **10**, 54. (Abstract)

Binstock, R. H. What sets the goals of community planning for the aging? *Gerontologist,* 1967, **7**, 44–46.

Blenker, M. Environmental change and the aging individual. *Gerontologist,* 1967, **7**, 101–105.

Blenker, M., Bloom, M., & Nielsen, M. A research and demonstration project of protective services. *Social Casework,* 1971, **52**, 483–499.

Blenker, M., Jahn, J., & Wasser, E. *Serving the aging: An experiment in social work and public health nursing.* New York: Community Service Society, 1964.

Bloom, B. L., The ecology of psychiatric hospitalization for acute and chronic brain syndromes. *Journal of Gerontology,* 1969, **24**, 48–54.

Booth, F. E. Involving the "hard-to-reach" older person in social activities. *Gerontologist,* 1965, **5**, 25. (Abstract)

Booth, F. E. The Neighborhood Senior Center—The effective vehicle for the delivery of service. *Gerontologist,* 1970, **10**, 57. (Abstract)

Boulding, K. E. The concept of need for health services. *Milbank Memorial Fund Quarterly,* 1966, **44**, 202–223.

Britton, P. G., Bergmann, K., Kay, D. W. K., & Savage, R. D. Mental state, cognitive functioning, physical health, and social class in the community aged. *Journal of Gerontology,* 1967, **22**, 517–521.

Brodman, K., Erdmann, A. J., Lorge, I., & Wolff, H. G. The Cornell Medical Index—An adjunct to medical interview. *Journal of the American Medical Association,* 1949, **140**, 530–534.

Bultena, G. L., & Wood, V. The American retirement community: Bane or blessing? *Journal of Gerontology,* 1969, **24**, 209–217.

Burnside, I. M. Group work with the aged: Selected literature. *Gerontologist,* 1970, **10**, 241–246.

Burr, J. J. National plan for protective services to older adults. *Gerontologist,* 1970, **10**, 55. (Abstract)

Brush, F. R. Eleventh Annual Conference. *Transactions of the American Hospital Association,* 1909, **11**, 182.

Butler, R. N. Immediate and long-range dangers to transfer of elderly patients from state hospitals to community facilities. *Gerontologist,* 1970, **10**, 259–260.

Carey, J. W. Senior Advisory Service for public housing tenants. *Gerontologist,* 1970, **10**, 54. (Abstract)

Carp, F. M. Compound criteria in gerontological research. *Journal of Gerontology,* 1969, **24**, 341–347.

Chen, Y.-P. Economic poverty: The special case of the aged. *Gerontologist,* 1966, **6**, 39–45.

Clark, K. *Civilisation.* New York: Harper & Row, 1969.

Coe, R. M. Professional perspectives on the aged. *Gerontologist,* 1967, **7**, 114–119.

Cohen, D. Theory and practice are ,challenged when a voluntary planning agency in a large metropolitan area attempts to put social welfare plans for the aging into action. *Gerontologists,* 1966, **6**, 33. (Abstract)

Cohen, E. S., & Kraft, A. C. The restorative potential of elderly long-term residents of mental hospitals. *Gerontologist,* 1968, **8**, 264–268.

Comalli, P. E., Jr. Cognitive functioning in a group of 80–90-year-old men. *Journal of Gerontology,* 1965, **20**, 14–17.

Comalli, P. E., Jr., Krus, D. M., & Wapner, S. Cognitive functioning in two groups of aged: One institutionalized, the other living in the community. *Journal of Gerontology*, 1965, **20**, 9–13.

Cumming, E., & Henry, W. E. *Growing old*. New York: Basic Books, 1961.

Cumming, J., & Cumming, E. *Ego and milieu*. New York: Atherton Press, 1962.

Curtis, J., & Miller, D. Senior Citizens Club sponsored by municipal Department of Recreation and Parks and private nursing home. *Gerontologist*, 1966, **6**, 33. (Abstract)

Denney, D., Kole, D. M., & Matarazzo, R. G. The relationship between age and the number of symptoms reported by patients. *Journal of Gerontology*, 1965, **20**, 50–53.

Dunham, H. W. *Community and schizophrenia*. Detroit: Wayne State University Press, 1965.

Erikson, E. H. Childhood and society. (2nd ed.) New York: Norton, 1963.

Feldstein, P. J. Research on the demand for health services. *Milbank Memorial Fund Quarterly*, 1966, **44**, 128–165.

Fisher, J., & Pierce, R. C. A typology of mental disorders in the aged. *Journal of Gerontology*, 1967, **22**, 478–484.

Frankel, G. The multi-purpose Senior Citizens' Center: A new comprehensive agency. *Gerontologist*, 1966, **6**, 23–27.

Fraser, E. M. When someone needs you—You can't fail them: A report of the Metropolitan Referral Service for Aging. *Gerontologist*, 1965, **5**, 38. (Abstract)

Freeman, J. T. Geriatric education: A study of United States medical school catalogues. *Gerontologist*, 1970, **10**, 35. (Abstract)

Friedson, E., & Rhea, B. Knowledge and judgment in professional evaluations. *Administrative Science Quarterly*, 1965, **10**, 107–124.

Fuchs, V. R. The contribution of health services to the American economy. *Milbank Memorial Fund Quarterly*, 1966, **44**, 65–103.

Gaitz, C. M. The coordinator: An essential member of a multidisciplinary team delivering health services to aged persons. *Gerontologist*, 1970, **10**, 217–220.

Georgopoulous, B. S., & Mann, F. C. *The community general hospital*. New York: Macmillan, 1962.

Glidewell, J. C. Perspectives in community health. In C. C. Bennett (Chm.), Community psychology: A report of the Boston Conference on the Education of Psychologists for Community Mental Health, Boston University, 1966.

Goffman, E. *Asylums*. Chicago: Aldine, 1962.

Gold, J. G., & Kaufmann, S. M. Development of care of elderly: Tracing the history of institutional facilities. *Gerontologist*, 1970, **10**, 262–274.

Graber, J. B. Inventory of state and local resources to meet the health needs of the aging and aged. *Gerontologist*, 1965, **5**, 16–19, 48.

Hamilton, E. L. Hospital administration—One of a species. *Administrative Science Quarterly*, 1957, **1**, 460.

Havighurst, R. J. (Chm.) Committee on Research and Development Goals in Social Gerontology, the Gerontological Society: The status of research in applied social gerontology. *Gerontologist*, 1969, **9**(Pt. 2), 1–90.

Hiestand, D. L. Research into manpower for health service. *Milbank Memorial Fund Quarterly*, 1966, **44**, 146–181.

Hollingshead, A. B., & Redlich, F. C. *Social class and mental illness: A community study.* New York: Wiley, 1958.

Joint Commission on Mental Illness and Health. *Action for mental health: Final report of the Commission.* New York: Basic Books, 1961.

Kaplan, J., Ford, C. S., & Wain, H. Measuring the impact of a gerontological counseling service on a medical community. *Journal of Gerontology,* 1966, **21**, 27–30.

Kent, D. P. Aging—Fact and fancy. *Gerontologist,* 1965, **5**, 51–56, 111.

Kershaw, J. A. *Government against poverty.* (Research Report No. 107) Washington, D.C.: Brookings Institution, 1970.

Laumann, E. *Prestige and association in an urban community.* Indianapolis: Bobbs-Merrill, 1966.

Laverty, R. Nonresident aid—community versus institutional care for older people. *Journal of Gerontology,* 1950, **5**, 370–374.

Lawton, M. P., Ward, M., & Yaffe, S. Indices of health in an aging population. *Journal of Gerontology,* 1967, **22**, 334–342.

Lepkowski, J. R. The attitudes and adjustments of institutionalized and non-institutionalized Catholic aged. *Journal of Gerontology,* 1956, **2**, 185–191.

Lewin, K. *Principles of topological psychology.* New York: McGraw-Hill, 1936.

Lieberman, M. A. Institutionalization of the aged: Effects on behavior. *Journal of Gerontology,* 1969, **24**, 330–340.

Lieberman, M. A., Prock, V. N., & Tobin, S. S. Psychological effects of institutionalization. *Journal of Gerontology,* 1968, **23**, 343–353.

Liebowitz, B., & Brody, E. M. Integration of research and practice in creating a continuum of care for the elderly. *Gerontologist,* 1970, **10**, 11–17.

Lipman, A. The Miami Concerted Services baseline study. *Gerontologist,* 1965, **5**, 256–258, 277–278.

Lipman, A., & Smith, K. J. Disengagement, poor health, and poverty. *Gerontologist,* 1968, **8**, 26. (Abstract)

Lissitz, S. Theoretical conceptions of institutional and community care of the aged. *Gerontologist,* 1970, **10**, 298–304.

Llewelyn-Davies, L. Facilities and equipment for health services. *Milbank Memorial Fund Quarterly,* 1966, **44**, 249–272.

Loeb, M. B., Pincus, A., & Mueller, B. J. A framework for viewing adjustment in aging. *Gerontologist,* 1966, **6**, 185–187, 236.

MacDonell, J. A. The operation of geriatric day hospitals. *Gerontologist,* 1966, **6**, 25. (Abstract)

MacMahon, B., Pugh, T. F., & Ipsen, J. *Epidemiologic methods.* Boston: Little, Brown, 1960.

Mason, E. P. Some correlates of self-judgment of the aging. *Journal of Gerontology,* 1954, **9**, 324–337.

Matchar, J. C., Furstenberg, F. F., & Kalisch, H. P. Comprehensive medical care: Sinai Hospital's approach to medical care for the aged. *Gerontologist,* 1965, **5**, 125–128.

Miller, S. M., & Mishler, E. G. Social class, mental illness, and American psychiatry: An expository review. *Milbank Memorial Fund Quarterly Bulletin,* 1959, **37**, 174–199.

Morris, R., & Binstock, R. H. *Feasible planning for social change.* New York: Columbia University Press, 1966.

Neugarten, B. L., Havighurst, R. J., & Tobin, S. S. The measurement of life satisfaction. *Journal of Gerontology,* 1961, **16**, 134–143.

Office of Economic Opportunity. First four Foster Grandparents programs underway. *Gerontologist,* 1966, **6**, 54–55.

Pan, J. Factors in the personal adjustment of old people in Protestant homes for the aged. *American Sociological Review,* 1951, **16**, 379–381.

Parsons, T. *The social system.* Glencoe, Ill.: Free Press, 1951.

Pearse, D. T. Three years later—An evaluation of volunteer training. *Gerontologist,* 1966, **6**, 154–158.

Pollack, M., Karp, E., Kahn, R. L., & Goldfarb, A. I. Perception of self in institutionalized aged subjects: I. Response patterns of mirror reflection. *Journal of Gerontology,* 1962, **17**, 405–408.

Prock, V. N. Institutionalization as a stabilizing process. *Gerontologist,* 1965, **5**, 23. (Abstract)

Randall, O. A. A critique of the paper by Barbara Shenfield. In J. Kaplan & G. J. Aldridge (Eds.), *Social welfare of the aging.* New York: Columbia University Press, 1962.

Randall, O. A. Some historical developments of social welfare aspects of aging. *Gerontologist,* 1965, **5**(Pt. 2), 40–49.

Revans, R. W. Research into hospital management and organization. *Milbank Memorial Fund Quarterly,* 1966, **44**, 207–248.

Robertson, R. J., & Banks, O. L. Indirect measurement of results in a project for improving socialization among the elderly. *Journal of Gerontology,* 1970, **25**, 265–267.

Romney, L. S. Community co-ordination linking the hospital and the community. *Gerontologist,* 1966, **6**, 32. (Abstract)

Rosenberg, G. S. Age, poverty, and isolation from friends in the urban working class. *Journal of Gerontology,* 1968, **23**, 533–538.

Rosenblatt, D, & Taviss, I. The home for the aged—Theory and practice. *Gerontologist,* 1966, **6**, 165–168.

Rosenstock, I. M. Why people use health services. *Milbank Memorial Fund Quarterly,* 1966, **44**, 94–127.

Ross, H. A. Protective services for the aged. *Gerontologist,* 1968, **8**(Pt. 2), 50–53.

Safier, R. Homemakers for chronically ill and aged: A description. *Gerontologist,* 1966, **6**, 150–153.

Schmidhauser, J. The political influence of the aged. *Gerontologist,* 1968, **8**(Pt. 2), 44–49.

Schutz, A. *The phenomenology of the social world.* Evanston: Northwestern University Press, 1967.

Scott, F. G. Factors in the personal adjustment of institutionalized and non-institutionalized aged. *American Sociological Review,* 1955, **20**, 538–546.

Scott, W. R. Some implications of organization theory for research on health services. *Milbank Memorial Fund Quarterly,* 1966, **44**, 35–64.

Shanas, E. *The health of older people: A survey.* Cambridge: Harvard University Press, 1962.

Shanas, E. Health care and health services for the aged. *Gerontologist,* 1965, **5**, 240–276.

Simmel, G. *The web of group-affiliations.* Glencoe, Ill.: Free Press, 1955.

Srole, L., Langner, T. S., Michael, S. T., Opler, M. K., & Rennie, T. A. C. *Mental health in the metropolis: The midtown Manhattan study*. Vol. 1. New York: McGraw-Hill, 1962.

Taylor, J., & Gaitz, C. N. An obstacle in rehabilitation of geriatric patients: Errors in following regimen. *Gerontologist*, 1968, **8**, 24. (Abstract)

Tillich, P. The philosophy of social work. *Social Service Review*, 1962, **36**, 13–16.

Tuckman, J., Lorge, I., & Zeman, F. The self-image in aging. *Journal of Genetic Psychology*, 1961, **99**, 317–321.

Vickery, F. E. A multi-service Senior Center—Its unique role and function. *Gerontologist*, 1965, **5**, 246–249, 277.

Vidich, A., & Bensman, J. *Small town in mass society*. Princeton: Princeton University Press, 1958.

Walkley, R. P., Mangum, W. P., Jr., Sherman, S. R., Dodds, S., & Wilner, D. M. The California Survey of Retirement Housing. *Gerontologist*, 1966, **6**, 28–34.

Weinerman, E. R. Research into the organization of medical practice. *Milbank Memorial Fund Quarterly*, 1966, **44**, 104–145.

Wendel, R. F. The economic status of the aged. In, *Working with older people: A guide to practice*. Vol. 3. *The aging person: Needs and services*. Rockville, Md.: United States Public Health Service, 1970.

West, J. *Plainville, U.S.A.* New York: Columbia University Press, 1945.

Wood, V., Wylie, M. L., & Sheafor, B. An analysis of a short self-report measure of life satisfaction: Correlation with rater judgments. *Journal of Gerontology*, 1969, **24**, 465–469.

Wylie, M. L. Life satisfaction as a program impact criterion. *Journal of Gerontology*, 1970, **25**, 36–40.

Zampella, A. D. General principles of the medical team approach to care of the elderly. *Gerontologist*, 1966, **6**, 25. (Abstract)

The Social Environment
of Aging

Attitudes toward Aging: A Critical Examination of Recent Literature and Implications for Future Research

RUTH BENNETT and JUDITH ECKMAN

Attitudes toward aging may be critical for adjustment and survival. It is possible that attitudes contribute to observed maladaptive behaviors among the aged, some of which may result in premature death. Negative views of aging, life in general, and oneself may result in an old person's unwillingness or inability to seek needed services, health care, or other types of assistance. Negative attitudes of old people may affect others in their environs, who in turn may feel free to respond negatively to old people or to ignore them completely. Negative views toward aging among the aged may reinforce negative views toward aging in the young, resulting in a feedback loop that further reinforces negative views in both young and old. The short-range effects of this feedback process may be to

Ruth Bennett received her PhD in sociology from Columbia University in 1962. She is currently the Principal Research Scientist on the Gerontology Staff of the Biometrics Research Unit of the New York State Department of Mental Hygiene, as well as Adjunct Associate Professor in the Program in Gerontology and Leisure Education at Teachers College, Columbia University. Her major research interests concern the impact of environment and environmental manipulation on the adjustment of the aged in the community.

Judith Eckman received her PhD in social psychology from Columbia University in 1968. She is currently Senior Research Scientist on the Gerontology Staff of the Biometrics Research Unit of the New York State Department of Mental Hygiene, as well as a lecturer at the College of Physicians and Surgeons, Columbia University, and at the Center for Instruction in the Care of the Aged of the Jewish Home and Hospital for the Aged in New York City. In addition, she is Adjunct Assistant Professor in the Program widen the gulf between young and old; the long-range effects may be to cause the young to dissociate themselves from their own aging. The net result of these processes may be the observed responses in the United States today of neglect and rejection of the aged and a seeming inability or unwillingness to plan for one's own old age.

In 1954 Tuckman and Lorge concluded their paper, "Old People's Appraisal of Adjustment over the Life Span," with the following statement:

> The fact that any age period beyond the twenties, thirties or forties was considered unfavorably for the majority of the aspects not only by the older respondents but also by a younger group of graduate students supports the suggestion that cultural factors play an important part in the way older years are viewed. Replies such as these do suggest the need to change community attitudes toward aging so that individuals may approach the middle and later years with greater emotional security [p. 422].

The major purpose of this review of the literature, 1950–70, on attitudes toward aging in the United States was to determine how far we have come in studying, as well as changing, attitudes of the aged and to delineate gaps in our knowledge. The literature[1] reviewed consisted of studies of attitudes toward aging and the aged, self-image, and life in general, including morale and life satisfaction, as well as some studies of the traits of conformity and rigidity, which probably underlie the acceptance of or reluctance to change one's attitudes.

Brief definitions of these terms follow:

1. Attitudes toward aging consist of evaluations of the process of aging.

---

in Gerontology and Leisure Education at Teachers College, Columbia University. Her major research interests concern cross-national comparisons of attitudes toward the aging and behavior modification in the mentally ill aged.

The authors are indebted to Joseph Zubin, Chief of Psychiatric Research, Biometrics Research, New York State Department of Mental Hygiene, for reading several drafts of this chapter.

[1]Studies were selected according to the following criteria: (a) they were published in prominent journals or books and/or were regarded as "classics"; (b) they were conducted on a specified population or sample; and (c) they utilized standard, quantitative, reliable measures with at least "face validity." The studies reviewed in this chapter utilized five types of research design: (a) descriptive and/or correlational surveys in which no interage comparisons were made; (b) cross-sectional surveys in which the attitudes of the aged

2. Attitudes toward the aged are evaluations by any age group of aged people as a group.

3. Morale and life satisfaction are attitudes reflecting evaluations of one's surroundings and one's life circumstances.

4. Self-image is an attitude toward or evaluation of oneself.

5. Conformity and rigidity are seen as personality and/or behavioral traits which are more enduring than attitudes. Conformity may determine one's readiness to accept others' evaluations or opinions as one's own. Rigidity is the inability or unwillingness to change one's attitudes.

DEFINITION OF ATTITUDE

An attitude is a hypothetical construct usually defined as "an enduring organization of motivational, emotional, perceptual and cognitive processes, with respect to some aspect of the individual's world [Scott, 1968]." An attitude embodies both an affective component and an action tendency (conation), but is distinguished from other subclasses of motives by the presence of a cognitive (sometimes evaluative) component.

Values are designated as a subclass of attitude which according to some formulations includes the belief that the focal object is desirable or undesirable independent of the person's appraisal of it. Opinion usually refers to one kind of verbal manifestation of an attitude, namely, the expressing of an evaluative appraisal or prediction concerning the object (Scott, 1968). Attitudes are commonly distinguished from cognitions or beliefs by the presence of affect in the person who maintains the concept. Variable properties of attitudes suggested by recent theoretical formulations include the following:

---

were contrasted to those of the young; (c) cross-national studies in which the attitudes of the United States aged were compared to those of the foreign aged; (d) longitudinal descriptive studies in which one group was compared to itself over time; and (e) experimental or intervention studies in which attitudes of a group were measured before and after experiencing an intervening event, for example, institutionalization. As the studies are discussed, it will become clear that the descriptive survey and the cross-sectional comparison survey were used most frequently. The longitudinal descriptive and cross-national study designs occurred least frequently, and the incidence of experimental or interevention studies fell between the two.

1. Direction: attitudes are generally conceived as embodying a favorable or unfavorable component, representing positive feelings or negative feelings;

2. Magnitude (affective): the "degree" of favorableness or unfavorableness of an attitude;

3. Intensity: the "strength of feeling" associated with an attitude (this is correlated with magnitude);

4. Ambivalence: the equality of mixed positive and negative feelings toward an object;

5. Salience: the prominence of the attitude, or the readiness of the individual to express it;

6. Salience (affective, cognitive, or conative): the degree of contribution of each of the major components to the attitude constellation;

7. Cognitive complexity: the elaborateness of the cognitive component of an attitude—the "richness" of the ideational content or the number of ideas the person has about the object;

8. Overtness: the prominence of the conative component or "action" tendency;

9. Embeddedness: the degree of isolation versus connectedness of an attitude from other cognitive elements (e.g., beliefs, values, other attitudes); and

10. Flexibility: the ease or difficulty of modification of an attitude.

ATTITUDES TOWARD AGING AND THE AGED

The first type of attitude explored concerns aging and the aged. By and large, most of the studies in this area have utilized either a cross-sectional design or a descriptive survey design. In general in the United States, when the attitudes of the old are compared to those of the young, both groups seem equally negative in their outlooks, although the specific negative items selected sometimes differ.

The most extensive early research in this area was conducted by Lorge and associates. Tuckman and Lorge (1952a, 1954, 1956) investigated attitudes of both young and old samples using questionnaires containing what they considered to be negative stereotypes and common misconceptions of old people. Their results indicated that both young and old people look upon old age as a period characterized by economic insecurity, poor health, loneliness, resistance to change, and failing physical and mental powers. Tuckman and Lorge (1954) also found that a group consisting of institutional-

ized and noninstitutionalized aged had an even more negative attitude than did the young toward the later years. Axelrod and Eisdorfer (1961) raised questions about the validity of the Tuckman and
Lorge studies, wondering if young people adequately discriminated
in their responses to people in the wide age range of 35 and over.
They tested this idea by asking 280 students to respond to Tuckman-
Lorge stereotypes in relation to five stimulus groups: 35, 45, 55, 65,
and 75 years old. The mean number of negative stereotypes increased with the age of the stimulus group, confirming the Tuckman
and Lorge findings.

Bekker and Taylor (1966) utilized the Tuckman and Lorge
questionnaire as modified by Axelrod and Eisdorfer to study the
effect of "frame of reference" on perception of aging. One hundred
male and female undergraduates were asked to respond to the
questionnaire for a kind of "average grandparent" with several items
modified to "my grandparent." Biographical information enabled
the author to select 50 students who came from four-generation
families and match them for age and sex with 50 students from
three-generation families. The responses of the two groups were
found to differ primarily on four stereotype factors: physical characteristics, personality traits, mental deterioration, and insecurity.
Students of the four-generation group attributed fewer negative
characteristics to grandparents, perceiving them as having fewer
characteristics of "old age." Most of the "average grandparent"
items, especially of the last three traits, were expected to reflect attitudes rather than information, and the authors reported that 20-
year-olds with living great-grandparents saw their grandparents as
less elderly than did 20-year-olds without living great-grandparents,
although the grandparents were the same age in each group. Of
course, as the authors noted, there may have been subtle differences
in "youthfulness" communicated by the two groups of grandparents
due either to real emotional differences or differences in constitution
(since those with living parents might indeed be hardier).

More recently, Kogan and his associates conducted studies of
attitudes toward aging among old and young. Kogan (1961a, 1961b)
and Kogan and Shelton (1962a, 1962b) showed agreement among
young and old on most items, particularly negative ones.

Kogan (1961a) was first concerned with the development of a
Likert scale to facilitate the study of attitudes toward old people with
respect to both norms and individual differences. He noted that
Tuckman and Lorge made no use of scaling procedures to measure
attitudes or their psychological correlates. He asked the following

questions: (a) Taking research on minority groups as a model, are attitudes toward old people related to authoritarianism, anomie, and ethnic prejudice? (b) Are attitudes toward old people associated with attitudes toward people with various physical disabilities? (c) If mental deterioration is seen as an attribute of old age, is there a relationship between attitude toward mental illness and attitude toward old age?

Kogan also hypothesized a significant relationship between attitude toward old people and various personality dimensions. His original sample consisted of 401 males and 81 females, all members of introductory psychology courses in two different northeastern universities. The instrument (OP scale) devised consisted of 17 items expressing negative sentiments about old people and 17 items with positive content. These items were interspersed among items from the California F and the Anti-Negro scales (Adorno, Frenkel-Brunswick, Levinson, & Sanford, 1950), Srole's Antiminority and Anomie scales (Srole, 1956), a scale of attitudes toward mental illness, and a scale of attitudes toward blindness. Six response categories were available, ranging from strongly disagree to strongly agree. For the personality measures, 30 true–false items taken from Murray (1938) were included to measure needs such as achievement, autonomy, narcissism, and nurturance. In analyzing his results, Kogan reported that positive and negative items measuring attitudes toward old people correlated significantly in the direction of logical consistency of response. This is especially interesting considering that care had been taken by Kogan to build items that were logical opposites, rather than settling for opposite but identical wording. Thus, the content of the items in this battery was presumably more powerful than response set, although subjects disagreed more with statements commenting adversely on old people than they agreed with statements praising old people. Examination of item means revealed that college subjects in general tended to be more favorable than unfavorable in their attitudes toward old people as manifested by responses to the OP items in the battery.

Examination of the correlates of attitudes toward old people revealed another advantage of using both positively and negatively worded items. Statistically significant correlations were obtained between F scale scores for items worded in the authoritarian direction and the negatively worded OP items only, indicating that response set might have been responsible for the obtained relationship. While these correlations suggest that authoritarian persons are unfavorably disposed toward old people, this conclusion was not borne out when positively worded items were examined.

It was also found that subjects unfavorably disposed toward old people on both OP scales were more disposed toward anomie, as defined in Srole's items. Subjects unfavorably disposed toward old people tended also to hold unfavorable attitudes toward those with physical disabilities and, possibly, those with mental illness. A high score on nurturance, as defined from a factor analysis of the personality inventory, was associated with a favorable attitude toward old people on the OP scale.

Kogan concluded that attitudes toward old people are scalable. He discussed at some length the findings that attitudes toward old people are related to feelings of anomie but are unrelated to authoritarian tendencies. The lack of relationship of the OP scale to authoritarianism suggested that while old people may constitute a minority, their minority status may not necessarily mean that they are equated with ethnic minorities. When one considers the unique features of old people as attitudinal objects, it is clear they cannot be categorized in strictly outgroup terms; for most individuals encounter old people as family members, and, more important, old people constitute a minority to which most people will eventually belong. However, as Kogan noted, old people do not occupy an authoritative position in our society and are often, in fact, weak and vulnerable. He concluded that it may be such countervailing experiences with aged persons that are responsible for lack of clear-cut OP scale relationships with authoritarianism.

Of the relationship between anomie and unfavorable attitudes toward old people, Kogan noted that if agreement with anomic items implies that the subject has a precarious and threat-oriented view of life, old age may well represent for him that period of life when his pessimistic predictions are confirmed. Old people have no future, are helpless, and are awaiting death. Thus, the anomic subject may perceive the aged as symbolic of that period of life when the individual is least able to cope with a hazardous environment.

For subjects negatively disposed on the OP scale, physically disabled persons and possibly mentally ill persons are also groups to be avoided or rejected. While some parts of this broad complex of attitudes seem to be related to authoritarianism, other parts are not. There is some indication in Kogan's data that Srole's concept of anomie may be relevant to the formation of a wide range of attitudes. However, no definitive statement can be made until reversed scales are developed for the many variables in question, in order to control carefully for the effects of response set on the obtained significant relations.

As was noted above, some positive attitudes were found on the OP scale. Golde and Kogan (1959) suggested that since dependency is one of the salient qualities attributed to old people by the younger generation, it is not surprising that those people who have strong nurturance needs have positive attitudes toward old people.

When the same OP scale was administered to a sample of apparently healthy older adults (Kogan, 1961b), no differences between young and old respondents emerged for the OP negative scale, but there was a significantly greater tendency for old people to endorse the OP items worded positively. This suggests that an acquiescent response set exerted a stronger influence in the older sample. For old subjects as well as young, there was no clear relationship between attitudes toward old people and authoritarianism, since their correlations became nonsignificant or significant in the opposite direction when the reversed scales were used. Kogan asserted that the phenomenon of acquiescence can probably be considered an important personality correlate of aging and hypothesized a relationship between response acquiescence and "cognitive energy" level. He suggested that given the energy loss alleged to be associated with old age, it might well be expected that older persons would differ from their younger counterparts in willingness to endorse authoritative statements. Little content consistency on the OP scale (i.e., an almost zero correlation between positively and negatively worded statements) with old subjects was also found. The explanation offered is that for old persons, the matched statements are possibly logical but not psychological opposites, leading to the inference that this attitude domain is less likely to be unidimensional for old subjects than for young ones. The old person's ambivalence regarding aging and his direct exposure to individual differences among age peers may be contrasted with the overgeneralized view, positive or negative, that college-aged subjects are likely to form of a group relatively remote from them in age status. Future research could address itself to the aspects of attitudes toward old people in an aged sample that allow for consensus and, correspondingly, less ambivalence. This would pave the way for the development of unidimensional subscales to reflect specific attitudinal domains among the elderly.

Because of evidence that response set tendencies increase with age, Kogan and Shelton (1962a, 1962b) decided to use a sentence completion test to explore old people's attitudes toward old people compared with their attitudes toward "people in general." Twenty item stem pairs expressing an attitude toward old people and toward people in general were given to a sample of healthy old people consisting of males with a mean age of 70.7 and females with a mean age of 69.4. They found that individuals of advanced age definitely distinguished between old people and people in general. In addition, when their responses were compared with those of a younger sample, it was found that similarities between old and young subjects responses far outweighed the differences. The items on which old and young samples differed were those where a personal relationship with a specified old person was implied. In this case, young people described old people differently from the way they described the rest of the population, whereas old people regarded both groups as the same and as having the same interest in an interpersonal relationship. However, neither the old nor the young sample revealed in their responses any particular wish to become involved with old people in interpersonal relationships. In other words, old people understood the needs of other old people, but emphasized the gratification derived from relationships with "people in general." The authors noted that a simple "favorability–unfavorability" dimension of attitudes toward old people and people in general does not do justice to the complexity of the data.

When the sentence completion test was given to two additional samples of old and young people, six items yielded significant differences between old and young for both men and women. These were (a) *"In general, old people need . . . ."* Young subjects more often cited "assistance" as a major need of "old people" than did old people themselves, who cited a "positive response from others" as a dominant need. (b) *"One of the greatest fears of many old people is . . . ."* Young subjects more frequently considered "death and dying" as a greater fear, while old subjects more often stressed "lack of money" and "financial insecurity." The authors suggested that the relatively low salience of the financial concerns of the aged in the thoughts of the young subjects and the corresponding emphasis on the fear of death indicate the cross-generational differences distinguishing this problem area. (c) *"Old people's appearance . . . ."* Both old males and females stressed the importance of appearance, while young subjects cited this category rarely. (d) *"Old people tend to resent . . . ."* Young subjects of both sexes more frequently cited the rather diffuse category of "younger people" as the object of old people's resentments than did old people themselves, who were specific in their descriptions of what they resented. Implicit in the description of their resentments such as "rejection," "lack of concern," and "reference to age" was the likelihood of these conditions being caused by young persons, so that young persons were not entirely incorrect in their assessment. (e) *"One of the greatest pleasures of old people is . . . .*" Old subjects more frequently chose "companionship and love" as opposed to young people who favored "interest in family." The authors noted that the results of this question support the views of the disengagement theorists and run counter to observations of those who emphasize the close family relationships of later life. However, in no sense did the findings imply an absence of affectional needs which would ordinarily be gratified by the family. Finally, (f) *"When an old person I do not know sits down next to me on a train or bus, I . . . ."* Old subjects manifested a greater interest in the "old person" than did young subjects who indicated that they would remain indifferent. Since earlier research demonstrated that young subjects manifested more interest when the referent was "a person" rather than an "old person," Golde and Kogan (1959) thought that the young subjects wished to avoid direct personal contacts with old persons. Several additional items in Kogan and Shelton's (1962b) study differentiated the responses of old men from young men, and several differentiated the responses of old women from young women, but it is beyond the scope of this chapter to discuss them in detail, and the reader is referred to an excellent discussion by Kogan and Shelton.

The data were interpreted by the authors to indicate that there is a "meaningful psychological syndrome of cross-generational conflict." Old persons anticipate the feelings of young subjects and attempt to cope with them in some fashion. The old person emphasizes some of his own characteristics and suppresses others in order to achieve acceptance and ward off rejection by young persons. An example of this is the item on appearance, where young subjects give more negative and age-specific descriptions, and old persons are more likely to insist that it is important for old people to maintain a good appearance. The data reflect a concern on the part of old subjects about being set apart, considered different, or rejected. Since there is a basis for such feelings in light of the young people's responses, Kogan and Shelton concluded that old people are aware of the social context in which they find themselves. The parallel of these findings with research conducted on minority groups is striking, although they do not reflect the harsh sentiments that characterize racial prejudice. These findings suggest that in order to bring about attitude change, methods derived from extensive experience in altering attitudes toward minority groups might be applied to the aged.

Much attitude research of the descriptive type has been conducted. Since we are restricting our review to investigations that utilized objective and preferably scalar measures, we will not discuss descriptive studies in detail. While surveys conducted by Kutner,

Fanshel, Togo, and Langner (1956), Kuhlen (1959), and Riegel and Riegel (1960) indicated that most old people have negative views of old age, it is not clear whether (a) their attitudes about aging grew less positive as they aged, thus differentiating them from the young; (b) whether they maintained negative views of aging throughout life; or (c) whether they began each of life's stages with a negative view of it. The question that remains to be answered is whether it is the negative experiences associated with being old that are responsible for the findings reported. In a comparative study of the United States and five foreign countries, Arnhoff, Leon, and Lorge (1964) found that United States youth viewed aging less negatively than did their foreign counterparts, although all confirmed the negative stereotype to some degree. Tuckman and Lorge (1952b) found that old people in institutions had more negative views toward aging than those outside. These findings indicate that both cultural context and immediate environment affect the views the aged have of aging. Cross-sectional studies tend to maximize psychological differences between old and young, usually portraying the old as more negative on whatever measure is used. There are virtually no longitudinal studies of attitudes toward aging; thus it is difficult to state whether or not people's attitudes toward aging and the aged grow more negative as they themselves age. It is true that Hickey and Kalish (undated) and Hickey, Hickey, and Kalish (1968) found that adolescents have more negative views of aging than young children. However, their views may not continue to grow more negative as they age. In fact, a true longitudinal study of attitudes toward aging might possibly reveal peaks and troughs for different life stages. It is conceivable that views of the young toward aging could become more positive as they themselves approach old age.

SELF-IMAGE AND ATTITUDES TOWARD THE SELF

Turning now to the related area of self-image and attitudes toward the self, we find that studies in this area also are mainly of the cross-sectional survey type. Typically, in the descriptive survey, the self-image of the aged is measured and correlated with other factors. The findings seem divided as to whether self-image is found to be negative or positive in the aged.

Cross-sectional studies of the self indicate that old people have more negative views of themselves than young people have of themselves. Mason (1954) studied self-judgments of 604 institutionalized persons aged 55 and over, 30 middle-class community persons 60 and over, and 30 lower-class community young persons. Self-judgments were measured by a self-concept questionnaire and the Who Are You (WAY) technique. The three groups responded to 10 of the 26 items of the self-concept questionnaire in a significantly different fashion. Both aged groups reported similarly negative views concerning their present state of happiness and ability to contribute. However, the aged middle-class community group and the young lower-class community group held more positive views of themselves than the aged institutionalized group concerning skills in social interaction. The overall conclusion was that while old people view themselves more negatively than the young, there is evidence that socioeconomic status compensates to some degree for negative self-judgments.

Tuckman and Lorge (1954) studied the classification of self as young, middle aged, or old in four groups ranging in age from under 20 to 80 and over. Almost all persons under 30 classified themselves as young. The turning point to middle age was between 40 and 44. Only in those over 80 did a majority classify themselves as old, and even then only 53% did so. Similarly, Busse, Jeffers, and Obrist (1957) studied 134 white and 28 black subjects, aged 60 and over, who were retirees and volunteers from Golden Age clubs. Chronological age was found to be significantly related to feeling old in this age group. The older a person was, the more likely he was to think of himself as belonging to an old age group. A self-evaluation of being in poor health was correlated with feelings of being old. More blacks than whites thought of themselves as being old.

Jyrkila (1960) found that a majority of old people in Elmira, New York, did not have negative views of themselves and did not accept stereotypic views of aging. Those who accepted a negative view were found to be less active and more maladjusted. Pollack, Karp, Kahn, and Goldfarb (1962) studied perception of self in institutionalized and community aged subjects. The incidence of self-derogatory statements was higher for institutionalized than community subjects, and higher for women than men. Neither age nor mental status scores were related to self-image.

Kogan and Wallach (1961) found that young subjects rated the concepts of "myself" and "the ideal person" as more favorable than did old subjects, as measured by the semantic differential technique. They saw this as evidence of a decline in the favorability of the self-concept in old age. In one of the few longitudinal studies in this area, Britton (1963a, 1963b) found no negative changes in self-image with increased age over a period of six to seven years.

Cameron (1969) investigated perceived age stages by testing a random sample of 571 people, aged 14–100, including males and females and blacks and whites. He used a simple questionnaire with questions worded as follows: "What age do you think of when you hear or use the words 'young adults'?" He found that the adult life-span was divided into four parts by the terms he presented. "Young adulthood" was considered to be between 18 and 25; there was then a 15-year gap until age 40; "middle age" was the period between 40 and 55; this was followed by a 10-year gap. Finally, "old age" was the term applied to ages 65 to 80; after that, people were "aged."

Relocation is a potentially disruptive phenomenon that may occur in the lives of many aged people. In a study of the process of institutionalization using projective techniques (Lieberman & Lakin, 1963), self-image was found to be more negative after institutionalization. On the other hand, Anderson (1964) found no difference in self-image between nursing home residents and their waiting-list counterparts. Carp (1967), using a sentence completion procedure on subjects before and after their move into a new housing facility, found that attitude toward the self was not stable over time. On the second occasion, sentence completion scores on attitudes toward the self correlated with the proportion of favorable adjective checklist items and with other readministered scales, but did not correlate with sentence completion scores on the prior test; i.e., individual scores were highly unreliable. The author suggested that this may have been due to a reduction of the need to present a "good face" on the self score in order to be admitted to the facility. Attitude toward the self may induce relaxation of defensiveness in some cases, and hence lower self-image scores; in other cases, favorable self-attitudes may be evidenced directly in optimism and therefore higher self-image scores. Thus, the group mean may remain unchanged, though individual reliability is low.

It should be noted that to think of oneself as old does not necessarily reveal a negative self-image; it is, after all, an accurate perception of oneself in the United States after age 65. However, it is interesting to note that in at least two studies, those of Jyrkila (1960) and Busse et al. (1967), the findings indicated that old people who viewed themselves as old tended to be more maladjusted or sicker than those who viewed themselves as young. It appears that in the aged, "accurate" perception of one's own age does not seem indicative of good adaptation.

Although definitive conclusions are difficult to reach at this time, it appears that self-image grows more negative with age, although longitudinal studies are needed to substantiate this. However, it is not entirely clear whether it is aging per se or the negative concomitants of aging that produce the negative view. Clearly, low socioeconomic status, poor health, institutionalization, and other negative concomitants contribute in large measure to views the aged hold of themselves. Very large samples need to be studied, controlling for the effects of the negative concomitants of aging in order to determine the effects of age per se on attitudes toward the self.

ATTITUDES TOWARD LIFE IN GENERAL AND MORALE

Attitudes toward life in general among the aged have been investigated using measures variously termed morale scales, life satisfaction scales, and personal adjustment measures. Studies of attitudes toward life have been conducted using the descriptive survey technique, the descriptive correlational design, and the before-and-after intervention design.

Many descriptive surveys have examined morale and its corrrelates within a single setting and have been specifically concerned with the relationship between morale and activity. When the activity and morale studies are examined in terms of the context in which the population existed, the results do not fall into any congruent or easily interpretable pattern. In studies of large cities, findings varied enormously. In a large Massachusetts city, Schooler (1968) found that adjustment, as indicated by morale, was positively associated with participation. This was true for the subgroup of old men who lived in neighborhoods that were relatively distant from services such as transportation, the library, and major shopping centers. In Durham, North Carolina, Maddox and Eisdorfer (1962) found that activity did not significantly decrease with age, nor did morale; activity was, however, positively correlated with morale. Rosow (1967), studying apartment dwellers in Cleveland, also found no simple decline in activity among the aged; among the active aged only, old age density was associated with high morale. Contrast these findings with those of Cumming and Henry (1961) and Hink (1967) in Kansas City, who reported that activity decreased with age, but was negatively associated with personal adjustment. Havighurst, Neugarten, and Tobin (1964) elaborated on this work and made the compelling observation that personality rather than age per se was the determining factor in the relationship between activity and life satisfaction. Specifically, they found that the active person with an ego-integrated personality is more satisfied.

In studies conducted in Milwaukee low-cost public housing projects, Havens (1968) found that newly relocated elderly persons who moved into the projects were better adjusted if they continued to participate socially. However, in studying public housing in Chicago, Messer (1967) found that activity was not critical to morale in old-age-concentrated settings, where morale was high for both the active and inactive. Only in normal age-integrated housing projects was activity related to morale. He concluded that the presence of age-appropriate normative expectations and reference groups accounted for high morale in old-age-dense communities. Lipman (1967) studied adjustment in public housing in Miami and hypothesized that those aged living outside housing projects would be more disengaged and dissatisfied and have less faith in people, higher anxiety, and poorer morale than those aged living within them. He found that the only significant differences between tenants and nontenants were on morale scores. Activity did not differ significantly in the two groups. Lipman concluded, however, that old age density did not explain the higher morale of the public housing residents. Rather, he felt that the heightened feelings of independence achieved by living in government-sponsored housing accounted for their higher morale.

In studies of retirement housing, Sherman, Mangum, Dodds, Walkley, and Wilner (1968) found in California that participation and morale were higher in retirement housing than in apartments and hotels for the elderly. This implies that something other than old age concentration accounted for the findings. It has been tentatively suggested that old age density, congeniality, and homogeneity taken separately or in combination contribute to adjustment (Burgess, 1961; Proppe, 1968; Sheets, Pachawich, & Ullman, 1968).

There are few cross-sectional, longitudinal, or cross-cultural studies of morale or attitudes toward life in general among the aged. Maddox and Eisdorfer (1962) conducted a longitudinal study of morale and found that it did not decrease with age though the group was aged to begin with and was followed only for a few years. Neugarten, Havighurst, and Tobin (1961) found no relationship between age and life satisfaction, but the age range studied was fairly restricted. However, Kogan and Wallach (1961) conducted a cross-sectional study and found that old people had more negative views of life than the young had.

The findings from descriptive surveys of specific settings indicate that the aged are not a homogeneous group with respect to attitudes toward life. However, when context is defined, measured, and analyzed, it is clear that it plays an important role in determining both life satisfaction and social adjustment. While several contextual factors have been suggested, old age density seems to have emerged as a critical one which should not be omitted from any future environmental research.

An attenuated age range may account for some of the findings that indicate that morale is not lower in older age groups. When youths are compared to old people, differences do emerge. Canadians Schonfield and Trimble (1967) noted that old people in Calgary were happier than young ones. Variations in morale or life satisfaction over wide age ranges and subgroups should be systematically investigated in cross-sectional, longitudinal, and cross-cultural studies, to determine whether morale declines with age or whether any apparent decline is accounted for by negative concomitants of aging.

ATTITUDINAL UNDERPINNINGS: RIGIDITY AND CONFORMITY

We turn now from attitudes to the attitudinal underpinnings (a) rigidity and its seeming opposites, acquiescence/flexibility/persuasibility; and (b) conformity and its opposite, nonconformity. Attitudinal underpinnings are thought to be personality traits that determine the tenacity with which attitudes are held and that presumably are stable and therefore not easily changed. Needless to say, it has not been demonstrated conclusively that the traits of rigidity or conformity are properties of personality systems rather than of attitudes or some other psychological systems. The particular traits of rigidity and conformity were selected because of their relevance to the maintenance and change of attitudes. If old people hold negative views of themselves and of aging, it is important to determine the extent to which they are conforming to the views of others and the tenacity with which they hold their views. If these negative views are the views of others internalized by the aged, it is important to determine how necessary conformity is to the old person before suggesting that he reject the views held by those around him. There are very few personality studies of old people and virtually no studies of the traits that seem important for attitude change.

Clinical observations have been made on rigidity in the aged, but few scientific studies have been conducted on this trait. Taylor (1955), Schaie (1958), and Riegel and Riegel (1960) found that old people hold to their views more tenaciously than others. Chown (1960, 1961) supported this finding in English samples.

Nahemow and Bennett (1968) compared young and old tenants in a low-cost public housing project and found that old people were more persuasible in regard to their opinions than the young. Lack of social integration of the setting, as indicated by the frequency of social isolates, seemed to explain these findings. That is, the more isolates in the setting, the more persuasible its residents. The more isolated an old person, the more anxious he seemed to please or to acquiesce to the interviewer. Thus, persuasibility seemed less a correlate of age than of one of the concomitants of age, namely, social isolation. One question raised by this finding is whether a period of isolation or residence in a malintegrated setting may facilitate a change in attitude.

Kogan (1961b) found old people to be more acquiescent than young people. On the other hand, in a public opinion poll, Gergen and Back (1962) found that old people were less acquiescent than young people. It is difficult to argue that acquiescence, persuasibility, and flexibility are one and the same trait and that all are polar opposites of rigidity. They all seem like highly negative traits. Therefore, studies correlating the traits of acquiescence, persuasibility, and flexibility are needed, as are longitudinal, cross-national, and interventional studies of these traits.

As for conformity, there is no clear-cut evidence that there is more or less of it in old people. Our own research (Nahemow & Bennett, 1964, 1965, 1967, 1968) indicated that there is no relationship between the trait of persuasibility and that of conformity in old people. For these studies, conformity was defined as behavior enacted in accordance with social norms, while persuasibility was operationally defined as agreement with two opposite verbal statements dealing with the same issue. Those who conformed were active and well integrated in the "ingroup," and they evaluated their setting positively. Those who were persuasible were isolated, inactive, and held negative evaluations of their setting.

There is little to indicate that negative views of aging and the self held by old people derive from a tendency to simply conform with similar views held by young people. In fact as noted previously in the discussion of Kogan and Shelton's (1962b) study, negative views held by the aging seem related to feelings of rejection and neglect, conditions caused by but not necessarily advocated by the young. Nor is it obvious that conformity is any more characteristic of the aged than of the young. From the Nahemow and Bennett studies it seemed that old people pick and choose among norms of a residental setting and conform to some norms but not to others. Typically, they conform out of a sense of commitment to their group rather than out of the need to please others. Until more cross-sectional and longitudinal studies of the trait of conformity are conducted, little more can be said about whether or not it is found with greater frequency in the aged than in the young.

The evidence to date thus suggests that old people are no more rigid or conforming than young people. Therefore, it should be possible to change attitudes of the aged toward aging, the self, and life in general, and the job of changing these attitudes may be no more difficult than changing the attitudes of the young. Only experimental efforts focused on inculcating and changing attitudes, using both young and old samples, will reveal whether the old are differentially conforming or impervious to change.

CONCLUSIONS

Old people in the United States seem to hold negative views toward aging, toward the self, and toward life in general. However, it is not yet clear if this is in marked contrast to the young, the foreign aged, or to views the aged held earlier in life. Negative views of aging are shared by young and old alike, although in the 1950s Tuckman and Lorge found that the aged viewed aging even more negatively than the young. Due to the more advanced form of scaling used by Kogan and associates, more light has been shed on these questions, including the fact that old people exhibit a more acquiescent response set on attitude questionnaires than young people do. Also, they did not find strong evidence that old people viewed aging more negatively than young people did. In the area of self-image, about as many studies indicated that old people had positive views of themselves as indicated the converse. While cross-sectional studies did sometimes indicate that old people viewed themselves more negatively than young people, concomitants of aging such as illness and low socioeconomic status may explain this finding. Few longitudinal studies of either attitude or self-image were found.

Studies of attitudes toward life in general and morale seem to indicate that these attitudes are less affected by age than by some of the concomitants of aging, namely, isolation, inactivity, ill-health, and institutionalization. There is also some evidence as to how personality influences life satisfaction. Most studies were conducted in a single setting, and although comparisons across settings are difficult, they are necessary in order to obtain a comprehensive picture. Findings from the few cross-sectional and longitudinal studies do not yet allow firm conclusions.

As for changing negative attitudes in the aged, it is not obvious that this is either more difficult or easier to accomplish than in young people. Old people seem no more rigid or tenacious in their views; if anything, they seem more acquiescent. However, acquiscence does not seem to be related to aging per se.

The views of the aged do not seem to reflect blind conformity to the views of young groups. Sad as it may seem, some of their negative views of aging and the aged, themselves, and life in general seemed grounded in reality and based upon their experiences. It is possible that improvement in the life conditions of the elderly would lead to some change in their negative views about aging held by young people as well.

A few words should be said about methodology. Research methods in this field must be broadened and improved before any definitive conclusions can be drawn. Additional longitudinal studies are needed to determine what happens to all types of attitudes with age. More cross-cultural studies are needed to determine whether the attitudes of the aged in the United States are unique. Controlled experiments are needed to learn which concomitants of aging, if any, produce which negative attitudes and, correlatively, which, if any, negative attitudes produce the often-observed negative concomitants of aging. Finally, a set of reliable, valid, and standard measures needs to be developed and used in as many surveys and experiments as possible. There are several good scales of attitudes toward aging, the self, and life in general. However, no two studies seemed to use the same sets of measures; thus, contradictory results probably can be as easily attributed to differences in measures as to substantive factors.

If we think attitudes of the aged determine adjustment and possibly survival, then we must make a concerted effort to utilize the best research methods and measures available to obtain conclusive findings. If we think it necessary to change the attitudes of the aged or of younger members of our society, we shall need to determine experimentally the best ways of modifying these attitudes. If we can modify attitudes and behavior in and toward the aged, it will be possible to attract more young professionals and service workers into the gerontological field. When young professionals become aware that their efforts on behalf of the aged result in improved morale, self-image, and, possibly, chances for survival, a transformation of attitudes in society at large may result, akin to recent changes in attitudes of whites toward blacks.

A word must be said about material we have excluded from this chapter. Attitudes of the elderly toward war, politics, morality, and so on, were not covered although they may well be related to the attitudes reviewed. They were omitted for the following reasons:

(a) there was not a substantial literature on them, (b) methods used to study them were not especially sophisticated, and (c) they did not seem as relevant for adjustment or survival as did the attitudes studied in the research reviewed. Attitudes toward death and dying, on the other hand, require separate and extended treatment (see Kastenbaum's discussion in this volume, pp. 701–710) beyond the discussion in this chapter.

While the aged hold negative attitudes toward aging and the aged, life in general, and the self, it is not clear if these attitudes are a result of aging per se or of its concomitants. Therefore, research is needed to answer the following questions:

1. Do attitudes toward aging, the self, and life in general grow negative with age in all age groups, subgroups, and countries?

2. If aging brings on these negative attitudes, what, if anything, can be done to change them?

3. Do attitudes toward aging, life in general, and the self correlate with each other in the aged in all contexts? Do these attitudes correlate similarly with adjustment, mental illness, successful aging, and the will to survive?

4. Do the aged hold their views in order to conform to the views of the young? Are they held more tenaciously by the aged?

5. Are new methodologies necessary to provide answers for the above questions?

REFERENCES

Adorno, T. W., Frenkel-Brunswik, E., Levinson, A. S., & Sanford, R. N. *The authoritarian personality*. New York: Harper, 1950.

Anderson, N. N. Social activity, self conception and institutionalization of older people. Paper presented at the annual meeting of the Gerontological Society, Minneapolis, October 1964.

Arnhoff, F., Leon, H. V., & Lorge, I. Cross-cultural acceptance of stereotypes toward aging. *Journal of Social Psychology,* 1964, **63**, 41–58.

Axelrod, S., & Eisdorfer, C. Attitudes toward old people: An empirical analysis of the stimulus group validity of the Tuckman-Lorge questionnaire. *Journal of Gerontology,* 1961, **16**, 75–80.

Bekker, L. D., & Taylor, C. Attitudes toward the aged in a multi-generational sample. *Journal of Gerontology,* 1966, **21**, 115–118.

Britton, J. H. Dimensions of adjustment of older adults. *Journal of Gerontology,* 1963, **18**, 60–65. (a)

Britton, J. H. Change in adjustment of older community residents after six years. Paper read at the Sixth International Congress of Gerontology, Copenhagen, August 1963. (b)

Burgess, E. (Ed.) *Retirement villages.* Ann Arbor: Division of Gerontology, University of Michigan, 1961.

Busse, E. W., Jeffers, F. C., Obrist, W. D. Factors in age awareness. Paper presented at the 4th International Congress of Gerontology, Merano, Italy, July 1959.

Cameron, P. Age parameters of young adults, middle-aged, old, and aged. *Journal of Gerontology*, 1969, **24**, 201–202.

Carp, F. Attitudes of old persons toward themselves and toward others. *Journal of Gerontology*, 1967, **22**, 308–312.

Chown, S. M. A factor analysis of the Wesley Rigidity Inventory: Its relationship to age and nonverbal intelligence. *Journal of Abnormal and Social Psychology*, 1960, **61**, 491–494.

Chown, S. M. The effects of age on the relationship between different types of rigidity. *Bulletin of the British Psychological Society*, 1961, **44**, A12. (Abstract.)

Cumming, E., & Henry W. *Growing old*. New York: Basic Books, 1961.

Gergen, K. J., & Back, K. W. Communication in the interview and the disengaged respondent. Paper presented at the annual meeting of the American Psychological Association, St. Louis, September 1962.

Golde, P., & Kogan, N. A. sentence completion procedure for assessing attitudes toward old people. *Journal of Gerontology*, 1959, **14**, 355–363.

Havens, B. An investigation of activity patterns and adjustment in an aging population. *Geronotologist*, 1968, **8**, 201–206.

Havighurst, R. J., Neugarten, B. C., & Tobin, S. S. Disengagement, personality and life satisfaction in the later years. In R. J. Havighurst et al. (Eds.), *Age with a future*, Copenhagen: Munksgaard, 1964.

Hickey, T., & Kalish, R. A. Attitudes of children and teenagers toward adults and elderly. No date.

Hickey, L., Hickey, T., & Kalish, R. A. Children's perceptions of the elderly. *Journal of Genetic Psychology*, 1968, **112**, 227–235.

Hink, D. Styles of interaction among older persons. Paper presented at the annual meeting of the Gerontological Society, St. Petersburg, Florida, November 1967.

Jyrkila, F. *Society and adjustment to old age*. In *Transactions of the Westermarck Society*. Vol. 5. Turku, Munksgaard, 1960.

Kogan, N. Attitudes toward old people: The development of a scale and examination of correlates. *Journal of Abnormal and Social Psychology*, 1961, **62**, 44–54. (a)

Kogan, N. Attitudes toward old people in an older sample. *Journal of Abnormal and Social Psychology*, 1961, **62**, 616–622. (b)

Kogan, N., & Shelton, F. Images of "old people" and "people in general" in an older sample. *Journal of Genetic Psychology*, 1962, **100**, 3–21. (a)

Kogan, N., & Shelton, F. Beliefs about "old people": A comparative study of older and younger samples. *Journal of Genetic Psychology*, 1962, **100**, 93–111. (b)

Kogan, N., & Wallach, M. A. Age changes in values and attitudes. *Journal of Gerontology*, 1961, **16**, 272–280.

Kuhlen, R. G. Aging and life adjustment. In J. Birren (Ed.), *Handbook of aging and the individual*. Chicago: University of Chicago Press, 1959.

Kutner, B., & Fanshel, D., Togo, A. M., & Langer, T. S. *Five hundred over sixty*. New York: Russell Sage Foundation, 1956.

Lieberman, M., & Lakin, M. On becoming an institutionalized person. In R. H. Williams, C. Tibbetts, & W. Donahue (Eds.), *Processes of aging.* Vol. 1. New York: Atherton, 1963.

Lipman, A. The impact of subsidized public housing on the aged. Paper presented at the 20th annual meeting of the Gerontological Society, St. Petersburg, Florida, November 1967.

Maddox, G., & Eisdorfer, C. Some correlates of activity and morale among the elderly. *Social Forces,* 1962, **40,** 254–260.

Mason, E. P. Some correlates of self-judgments of the aged. *Journal of Gerontology,* 1954, **9,** 324–337.

Messer, M. Possibility of an age-concentrated environment becoming a normative system. *Gerontologist,* 1967, **17,** 247–251.

Murray, H. A. *Explorations in personality.* New York: Oxford University Press, 1938.

Nahemow, L., & Bennett, R. Conformity to social norms and persuasibility among residents of a home for the aged. Paper presented at the annual meeting of the American Psychological Association, Los Angeles, September 1964.

Nahemow, L., & Bennett, R. Social adjustment and persuasibility in two branches of a home for aged. Paper presented at the annual meeting of the American Psychological Association, Chicago, September 1965.

Nahemow, L., & Bennett, R. Conformity, persuasibility and counter-normative persuasion, *Sociometry,* 1967, **30,** 14–25.

Nahemow, L., & Bennett, R. Attitude change with institutionalization. Unpublished report, National Institute of Mental Health, Bethesda, Maryland, 1968. (Mimeo)

Neugarten, B. C., Havighurst, R. J., & Tobin, S. S. The measurement of life satisfaction. *Journal of Gerontology,* 1961, **16,** 134–143.

Pollack, M., Karp, E., Kahn, R. & Goldfarb, A. Perception of self in institutionalized aged subjects. *Journal of Gerontology,* 1962, **17,** 405–408.

Proppe, H. Housing for the retired and the aged in Southern California: An architectural commentary. *Gerontologist,* 1968, **8**(Pt. 1), 176–179.

Riegel, K. F., & Riegel, R. A study on changes of attitudes and interests during later years of life. *Vita Humana,* 1960, **3,** 177–206.

Rosow, I. *Social integration of the aged.* New York: Free Press, 1967.

Schaie, W. K. Rigidity–flexibility and intelligence: A cross-sectional study of the adult life span from 20 to 70 years. *Psychological Monographs,* 1958, **72**(9, Whole No. 462).

Schonfield, D., & Trimble, J. Advantages of aging. Paper presented at the annual meeting of the Gerontological Society, St. Petersburg, Florida, November 1967.

Schooler, K. Relation between social interaction and morale of the elderly as a function of environmental characteristics. Paper presented at the annual meeting of the Gerontological Society, Denver, November 1968.

Scott, W. A. Attitude measurement. In G. Lindzey & E. Aronson (Eds.), *Handbook of social psychology.* Reading, Mass.: Addison-Wesley, 1968.

Sheets, W. A. Pachawich, S. J., & Ullman, P. S. The aged: Satisfied or dissatisfied. *Journal of the American Geriatric Society,* 1968, **16,** 314–322.

Sherman, S., Mangum, W., Dodds, S., Walkley, R., & Wilner, D. Psychological aspects of retirement housing. *Gerontologist,* 1968, **8**(Pt. 1), 170–175.

Srole, L. Social integration and certain correlaries: An exploratory study. *American Sociological Review*, 1956, **21**, 709–716.

Taylor, C. Age differences in rigidity as revealed in attitude scale responses. Unpublished doctoral dissertation, Syracuse University, 1955.

Tuckman, J., & Lorge, I. The best years of life: A study in ranking. *Journal of Psychology*, 1952, **34**, 137–149. (a)

Tuckman, J., & Lorge, I. The effect of institutionalization on attitudes toward old people. *Journal of Abnormal Social Psychology*, 1952, **47**, 337–344. (b)

Tuckman, J., & Lorge, I. Old people's appraisal of adjustment over the life span. *Journal of Personality*, 1954, **22**, 417–422.

Tuckman, J., & Lorge, I. Perceptual stereotypes about life and adjustments. *Journal of Social Psychology*, 1956, **43**, 239–245.

Social Roles, Work, Leisure, and Education

ROBERT J. HAVIGHURST

In their research on adulthood and old age, psychologists and sociologists have found a major tool in the *social role construct*. There are three broad social role categories: *family, work, and community*. The work category appears to be the simplest of the three because it contains only the worker role. But this is such a pervasive role and it has so many ramifications when seen through the experiences of men and women from the ages of 40 to 80 that we soon cease to think of it as a simple category. The family roles that have been selected for study by social scientists are parent, grandparent, spouse, homemaker, member of a kin or extended family group, and adult child of aging parents. The community category includes about all role behavior beyond the family and work roles. Roles in this category that have been defined and studied are association member, church member, citizen, friend, and neighbor.

In addition to these three broad categories, which account for nearly all of the action and time of adults, there is *leisure activity*. This cannot be called a role unless the ordinary definition of a social role is stretched somewhat. Our society has not yet defined a set of expectations that are appropriate for the use of leisure time with the clarity that it has defined the behaviors and attitudes expected of the other roles on the list. However, with growing amounts of free time throughout adult life and especially after the demands of the

Robert J. Havighurst received his PhD in physical chemistry from Ohio State University in 1924. After about 10 years of teaching and research in physical science, he changed his field to that of social psychology and education. He has been a Professor of Human Development and Education at the University of Chicago since 1941. His major research interests are in the social psychology of human behavior and development at all age levels.

worker role decrease, a set of expectations and norms for free-time activity are in the process of developing. An ethics of leisure is evolving to parallel the ethics of work and of family that have dominated Western society during the past 100 years.

The social role construct has been useful in two ways. First, it facilitates thinking and discussion about the activities and the social adjustment of people. Probably 90% of our waking time is spent in one or another of a dozen social roles. These roles are grouped by people into characteristic clusters called life-styles. The second use of the social role construct is as the major set of variables for a research design that aims to study quantitatively the behavior of various groups of people and to relate this behavior to their social adjustment and life satisfaction.

A very large fraction of the social-psychological research on human behavior after age 40 consists of examination of these roles and their interactions and their relationships to life satisfaction. Participation in these various roles has been studied in relation to age, sex, and occupation or socioeconomic status. Most of these studies are cross-sectional in nature, reporting on role participation or role performance at a given point in time. Thus, the data are weak on age changes, since they compare people of different ages at a given time, but do not trace the changes for a given group of people through time. In general, we find that participation and performance in a given role have an age pattern. Such studies are well summarized by Riley and Foner (1968).

Leisure-time activities have been studied in relation to age, sex, and socioeconomic status and are reported in the book *Aging and Leisure* (Havighurst, 1961). Havighurst (Donald & Havighurst, 1959; Havighurst, 1957a; Havighurst & de Vries, 1969; Havighurst & Feigenbaum, 1959) made analytic studies of leisure activities and their significance to people.

Studies on the interrelationships of performances in the various roles have been done by Havighurst (1957b) and the Cross-National Study Group (Havighurst, Munnichs, Neugarten, & Thomae, 1969), as noted in Tables 1 and 2, but not to any substantial degree by others. The need for these studies is especially important in view of the growing salience of the concept of flexible life-styles. As people pass through adult life, they reorder and realign their social roles, partly through choice and partly through necessity. Some do this more readily than others. Preretirement counseling and education may have this kind of role flexibility as a goal.

TABLE 1

Intercorrelations between Role Performance Ratings for Males

Role	A. Kansas City males, ages 40-70							
	B	C	D	E	G	H	I	L
A. Worker	.19	.14	.01	.22	.36	.18	.19	.06
B. Association member		.41	.50	.24	.06	.15	−.02	.28
C. Citizen			.40	.22	.17	.01	.17	.27
D. Friend				.15	.04	.29	.16	.36
E. Church member					.22	.21	.15	.12
G. Parent						.33	.21	.23
H. Spouse							.39	.39
I. Homemaker								.33
L. User of leisure								−

Role	B. Cross-national males, ages 70-75									
	B	C	D	E	F	G	H	I	J	K
A. Worker	.13	.12	.11	.07	.04	−.02	−.09	−.08	−.07	−.01
B. Association member		.15	.09	.04	.13	.01	.02	.05	.20	−.08
C. Citizen				−.15	.07	−.08	−.02	.09	.05	−.12
D. Friend				.06	.18	.00	−.05	.02	.11	.02
E. Church member					.05	.15	.16	.16	.00	.12
F. Neighbor						.07	.14	.12	.17	.09
G. Parent							.07	.10	.13	.46
H. Spouse								.20	.10	.01
I. Homemaker									.14	.01
J. Kin										.08
K. Grandparent										−

Note. Figures represent partial correlation coefficients, holding socioeconomic status constant. Material appearing in the table has been taken with permission from R. J. Havighurst, "The Social Competence of Middle-Aged People," *Genetic Psychology Monographs,* 1957, **63,** 297-395; and from R. J. Havighurst, J. M. A. Munnichs, B. L. Neugarten, and H. Thomae (Eds.), *Adjustment to Retirement: A Cross-National Study.* New York: Humanities Press, 1969.

Scientific knowledge is also thin and inadequate concerning role performance in various countries as well as in various ethnic and socioeconomic subcultures in the United States. This inadequacy is being corrected partly by a set of papers on the elderly in minority groups (Havighurst, 1971a) and by current cross-national studies (Havighurst, 1957b, 1971a; Havighurst et al., 1969).

TABLE 2

Intercorrelations between Role Performance Ratings for Females

Role	Kansas City females, ages 40-70							
	B	C	D	E	G	H	I	L
A. Worker	.18	.38	.23	.08	−.11	.29	−.04	.38
B. Association member		.42	.42	.45	.18	.04	.08	.35
C. Citizen			.34	.21	.09	.21	.05	.45
D. Friend				.14	.38	.28	.30	.37
E. Church member					.17	.16	.21	.17
G. Parent						.55	.45	.35
H. Spouse							.31	.36
I. Homemaker								.35
L. User of leisure								−

Note. Figures represent partial correlation coefficients, holding socioeconomic status constant. Material appearing in the table has been taken with permission from R. J. Havighurst, "The Social Competence of Middle-Aged People," *Genetic Psychology Monographs,* 1957, **63**, 297-395.

WORKER ROLE STUDIES

The central role of adult life for men has traditionally been the worker role, while for women the axis of life has been the roles of wife, mother, and homemaker. Although these roles are losing some of their centrality during the latter half of the twentieth century, they remain the ones to which most attention is paid by social scientists.

The development of urban technology has made the work career much more complex than it was in a society with a simpler economy and technology. Men find their jobs disappearing due to changing technology. Some occupations require a relatively early age of retirement. Women are entering the offices and factories in great numbers.

Sheppard (1971) summarized the situation with respect to workers over 50 in a way that is useful to psychological research. Participation as a worker in the contemporary economic system is increasingly dependent upon the *attitudes* of workers and their employers. Increasing numbers of employees find it at least conceivable to retire at age 60 or even before and to make ends meet with social security and pension incomes. Therefore, they can weigh the pros and cons of continued working with greater income as compared with early retirement with reduced income. Employers, on the other hand, are in a position to ignore middle-aged or elderly applicants in favor of younger persons.

With the passage of the Manpower Development and Training Act (MDTA) of 1962, the federal government recognized a public responsibility for helping individuals obtain the training necessary for employment. However, in the first seven years of MDTA activity (1962–69), only 10% of all trainees were 45 or older, although 25% of all unemployed persons were in this age group. A variety of retraining programs are now being tried out, and the industrial psychologist is involved in this kind of research.

The movement of middle-aged women into the labor force is attracting the attention of psychologists. In 1970, more than half of all women aged 45–54 were in the labor force, and 43% of all women aged 55–64 were at work or seeking work. The causes of this phenomenon are complex: partly they reflect the desire for a higher material standard of living; partly, the desire to escape from boredom and idleness; and partly, a result of decreasing numbers of children.

What Sheppard called "the emerging pattern of second careers" is becoming a socially and economically significant phenomenon. The concept of an adult lifetime devoted to a single occupation has lost some of its earlier force. Not only are increasing numbers of people forced into seeking a second career due to the disappearance of an earlier job or to a practice of early retirement in certain occupations, but, more important, an increasing number of middle-aged people are deliberately looking for a different job. For example, Sheppard (1971) interviewed 140 white male union members in Pennsylvania and found that 35% of them were definitely interested in changing to a *new and different* type of occupation. These men are experiencing what has been called the "blue-collar blues."

A research team working under the auspices of the Gerontological Society (Havighurst, 1971b) produced an interview schedule for use with middle-aged people to find out what factors determine job change and job stability. They regarded the work career of a person as a resultant of the interaction of the *personality* of the individual and the *pressures* for *change* or *stability* in the work situation. They employed a schema (see Table 3) that gives four combinations of self-direction (a personality factor) and situational constraint directed toward change. The four combinations are the following:

1. *Low self-direction and low situational change constraint.* This combination tends to produce routine careers in stable organi-

zations such as public service and large commercial enterprises. It also allows for promotion up a clearly defined path of mobility within a job hierarchy.

2. *High self-direction and low situational change constraint.* This combination is made to order for the entrepreneurial type, who sees the work area as an open field in which he can exercise choice. He decides to change his career and takes the necessary steps, which may include training for a new job. He may also deliberately choose to change from a full-time to a part-time job.

3. *Low self-direction and high situational change constraint.* This combination requires the individual to change his work pattern, and he tends to take whatever job the situation presents. Unskilled workers are generally in this situation; it also includes those women who find themselves widowed or deserted by their husbands and who must take whatever jobs are available.

4. *High self-direction and high situational change constraint.* This combination requires the individual to adjust to a new situation (in family, in health, or in the job area), but he makes a deliberate choice of what kind of work he will do and trains for the new job, if training is desirable.

Examples of careers illustrating these four types are reported in the publication cited in Table 3.

TABLE 3

Personal and Situational Factors Interacting to Produce Career Patterns

Situational constraint forcing career change	Personal factor	
	Low self-direction	High self-direction
Low constraint	A. Routine career. Promotion as an organization man.	B. Flexible career. Deliberate change of type of work.
High constraint	C. Unskilled worker. Woman who goes to work because she needs money.	D. Job disappears. Worker selects and prepares for a new one. Woman who deliberately goes to work when family obligations decrease.

Note. For further development of the ideas in this schema, see J. Murray, E. Powers, and R. J. Havighurst, "Flexible Careers." (Final Report of the Committee on Research and Development Goals in Social Gerontology) *Gerontologist,* 1971, **11** (4, Pt. 2).

FAMILY ROLE STUDIES

The period from about 1925 to 1950 saw major changes in the structures and functions of families in the societies that were becoming urbanized and industrialized. In those countries there was a trend toward fewer children per family and toward the cessation of childbearing well before the age of 40 for women. Then, as the children grew up and left the home, the conjugal couple became the typical middle-aged family unit from the ages of 55 to about 70, after which the earlier mortality of men left about half of all once-married women as widows.

During this same period, the young adult children became more and more commonly a nuclear family unit with their young children, living independently of their middle-aged and elderly parents. It was thought that this would tend to reduce the strength of the ties between the families of the two generations. Elderly conjugal families would be increasingly "on their own," having tenuous relations with the nuclear families of their adult children.

However, this expectation was not confirmed in a number of studies made in northern Europe and the United States in the period from 1950 to 1970. Instead, it became clear that a vigorous extended family or kin structure existed, characterized by mutual economic assistance, active communication through visits and correspondence, and a strong sentiment of family loyalty and obligation. Troll (1971) summarized such studies for the decade 1960-70 and concluded that the research of this period had established the importance of extended kin relations and the continued contact between elderly individuals and their kin, particularly their children. Thus, the several family roles of middle-aged and elderly people came increasingly under study, not only the roles of parent, spouse, and homemaker, but also those of grandparent, child of aging parents, and member of an extended family.

The Grandparent Role

With the increasing numbers of four-generation families, many grandmothers in their 50s and early 60s are employed outside of the home, and others may be caring for an elderly parent in his 80s. Intrafamily relations have become more varied, and it seems useful to define four stages of the conjugal family of husband and wife from middle age on: late maturity, ages 45–54; preretirement, ages

55–65; early retirement, ages 65–74; and late retirement, age 75 plus. Relations of the conjugal family with other generations in the family vary from one stage to another. The numbers of families decrease from one stage to the next, mainly due to the death of the husband. Fifty percent of the once-married women aged 70–74 are widows, and this figure rises to 75% for women aged 75–79.

Studies of widows are just beginning to throw light on the lives and problems of this large group. Lopata (1971a, 1971b) identified a number of personal problems of widows, which are based partly upon poverty and partly upon loneliness.

More and more studies are being made of the relations of grandparents to the other generations in the extended family. The grandmother role seems to be more intensive and more valued by the younger generations than the grandfather role. The grandmother is more experienced in the details of child care and can share this experience usefully with the mother. Neugarten and Weinstein (1964) identified five categories of grandparenting: formal, funseeker, surrogate parent, reservoir of family wisdom, and distant figure. The value of the grandparent role has been observed outside of the biological family, through a number of foster grandparent programs with children who live in institutions or who need tutoring in school, etc.

Social Class, Sex, and National Differences in Family Roles

In studying the various family roles within the extended family, the research literature generally points to the greater importance of women than of men in kinship ties. This is due partly to the greater strength of the mother–daughter tie than the mother–son or father–son ties from early adulthood on. For a nuclear family of young and middle-aged adults, residence is generally closer to the wife's parents, interaction greater with the wife's relatives, and mutual aid more frequent along the female line.

Social class differences in kin relationships are generally present, but are not as large as the sex differences. Middle-class people visit their relatives more frequently than working-class people if geographic distance is taken into account. However, those in the working class do a higher *proportion* of their total visiting with kin, although middle-class people do more visiting altogether than working-class people. In middle-class families there is more flow of help from old parents to middle-aged children, while within the working class, more help goes from middle-aged children to their parents.

A study of cross-national differences in family roles of elderly people (Shanas, Townsend, Wedderburn, Friis, Milhoj, & Stehouwer, 1968) allowed for a comparison of the interaction of social class and national differences in three countries: England, Denmark, and the United States. Shanas summed up her chapter on "The Family and Social Class" as follows:

> Middle class, white collar persons in both Britain and the United States are more likely than working class persons to have only a few children and to live at a greater distance from their children. The married children of middle class families, both sons and daughters, tend to live apart from their parents, not only in separate households, but also at a greater distance from them. In some degree this physical separation of parents and children is compensated for by more overnight visiting on the part of white collar families. The average old person of white collar background maintains strong relationships with his children. He is more likely than his blue collar counterpart, however, to see his children infrequently or not at all. In the case of white collar parents, the patterns of help in old age flow from parents to children; in the case of blue collar parents, they flow from children to parents.
>
> In Denmark, different styles of family life in old age are reported by white collar and blue collar persons on the one side, and agricultural workers on the other. Middle class and working class appear to merge into a common classless pattern [p. 256].

Stehouwer, who focused attention on the national differences in this study, stated:

> The main difference between the family relations of elderly people in Denmark on one hand, and Britain and the United States on the other, is that although older people in Denmark, just as in the United States and Britain, report frequent contacts with children, there seems to be less involvement in the daily lives of their children and a greater independence. In other words, the relatively small amount of help and support between generations in Denmark seems to indicate less mutual dependence [p. 223].

Stehouwer ascribed these national differences to differences in social and fiscal legislation among the three countries. Denmark early established both a tradition of public care for the aged and a general pension system. In addition, Danish legislation does not make adult children responsible for the economic support of their parents, which is a responsibility of the state.

MAJOR RESEARCH AND CONCEPTUAL ISSUES

A major research problem is to answer a number of related questions concerning the sum total of social role performance. Does a pattern of role performance (a life-style) become fixed fairly early in adult life and give substantial continuity to a person's life? Do people change their role performance patterns very much, and under what conditions do they change? Can people deliberately change their patterns of role performance? Can such change be brought about by counseling and by educational experiences?

There are two broad hypotheses concerning these matters:

1. *Every individual has an equal quantum of time-energy, which he distributes over the various possible roles. If he places more of this quantum in one role, he must correspondingly reduce his activity in other roles.*

If this hypothesis is true, there should be some negative correlations between performance in some pairs of roles. There should be evidence of compensatory behavior—low performance in some roles to compensate for high performance in other roles.

2. *Each individual has his own supply of time-energy, and this varies from one person to another. The quantity depends upon his health, vigor, and motivation. These terms are used loosely to indicate the general and changeable nature of the entity. Some persons are active in a variety of roles; others are inactive in most roles.*

If this hypothesis is true, there should be positive correlations between a number of roles and not much evidence of compensatory behavior.

The data shown in Tables 1 and 2 on the intercorrelations among role performances tend to support Hypothesis 2. However, this hypothesis cannot be tested seriously without some measures of health, vigor, and motivation. If these were defined and measured at least semiquantitatively, we should expect the sum total of role performance scores to correlate with them.

Tables 1A and 2, taken from the Kansas City Studies of Adult Life, generally support Hypothesis 2, with some interesting and useful exceptions. In the data for women we find small negative correlations between the *worker* role and the roles of *parent* and *homemaker*. There is also a very low correlation between the roles of *citizen* and *homemaker*. These are to be expected when one thinks of possible conflicts between the demands of certain roles. The minority of women who were employed had relatively little time for homemaking and for parental behavior. Yet their attention and effort in the role of *spouse* were not cut down. (Those who were unmarried were not included in the computation of the correlation coefficient.)

The correlation coefficients for men in the Kansas City Studies of Adult Life show low or negative relationships between the following role pairs: worker–user of leisure, association member–parent, association member–homemaker, citizen–spouse, and worker–friend. Here it appears that the family roles and the community roles tend to have only a low relationship. The average coefficient for the pairs of mixed family and community roles is .14, while the average of family roles is .31, and the average of community roles is .32. For women, these average coefficients are .18, .44, and .33, respectively.

The relationship of age to role interaction may be seen crudely by comparing the correlation coefficients of Table 1A and 1B, where men over 70 are compared with men aged 40 to 70. The level of correlation coefficients goes down with increased age, although the relative size of the three groups of correlations is the same in the two age groups. Family roles have an average intercorrelation of .13, community roles, .08, and mixed family–community roles, .06. It would seem reasonable to interpret these data as an indication that older men have less energy for social role participation than they had when they were younger and that they tend to distribute their energy in more individualized ways, thus reducing the correlation coefficients among pairs of roles. But this must be a very tentative conclusion, since the Kansas City sample of men was not easily comparable to the international sample in the Cross-National Study of Retirement. Furthermore, the rating scales for the older men were somewhat different from those used with the Kansas City sample.

Wilensky (1961) distinguished between "orderly" and "disorderly" careers and found that men with orderly careers tended to be more active in the community roles. He stated:

Orderly experience in the economic system is associated with many social ties which range broadly and at the same time overlap. Men who have predictable careers . . . belong to more organizations, attend more meetings, and average more hours in organizational activity. Their attachments to the local community are also stronger—indicated by support of local schools and, to a lesser extent, by contributions to church and charity.

In both formal and informal contacts, the men of orderly career, more than their colleagues of chaos, are exposed to a great variety of people: the fellow-members they see in the clubs and organizations represent many social and economic levels; frequently-seen relatives and close friends are more scattered in space both social and geographical, cutting across neighborhoods, workplaces, occupations, or income brackets. Finally, the total participation pattern of the orderly is more coherent: close friends tend to form a circle and they overlap work contacts. . . . There is some indication that these friendships, anchored in workplace, forming a leisure-time clique, may also be longer-lasting [p. 535].

Others have also suggested that effective performance in one role tends to contribute to performance in other roles. Moberg (1965), studying the behavior of people as church members, said:

> It is not unreasonable to think that association with people in church-related activities and organizations contributes to their knowledge of other voluntary organizations; friendships in the church with persons who are members of other groups may lead to social participation in them [p. 83].

On the other hand, there may be a negative correlation between a pair of roles, as is illustrated in Table 1B. The correlation coefficient between the church member and the citizen roles is —.15. This is due to the fact that there were a number of avowed atheists in the European sample of retired men who were active in socialist party affairs. Thus, they scored quite high on the citizen role and zero on the church member role.

Disengagement Theory and Role Activity

The *disengagement theory* as proposed by Cumming and Henry (1961) implies that role performance should decrease with age, after about age 60–65. This is generally true. However, the disengagement theory also proposes that morale, or life satisfaction, is negatively correlated with quantity of role performance after this age period. A number of studies have tested this proposition, and most of them have failed to support this aspect of the disengagement theory (Havighurst, Neugarten, & Tobin, 1968; Havighurst et al., 1969; Kutner, Fanshel, Togo, & Langner, 1956; Maddox, 1963).

It has become clear that the personality (the "motivation" of Hypothesis 2) tends to determine the relationships among disengagement, role activity, and life satisfaction. A person with a passive-dependent personality may enjoy disengagement, while a person with a striving, achievement-oriented personality may dislike disengagement and may try to make up for losses in certain roles by a reformation of his role activity (Havighurst et al., 1968; Neugarten, Havighurst, & Tobin, 1968; Reichard, Livson, & Peterson, 1962; Streib, 1971).

Social Environment and Role Performance

The immediate social environment of a person gives him opportunities and stimulation and also restrictions on his role performance.

A number of studies deal with the social environment. For instance, Rosow (1967) and Carp (1969) reported on the relationship of role performance to the kind of living arrangements of elderly people. Those who live in retirement hotels or in public housing projects for the elderly are thrown into close contact with others of the same age group, and this enhances their performance in the roles of friend and neighbor, while it somewhat reduces their activities in family roles. The retirement communities (Leisure World, Sun City, St. Petersburg, etc.) create an environment of elderly people with a set of recreational, religious, and civic institutions that favor certain kinds of role performance and disfavor others.

Cross-National Studies

It is likely that role behavior differs among older people because of national cultural differences as well as social class and sex differences. The systematic comparisons of British, Danish, and American samples did provide useful information on cross-national differences, as has just been noted.

A more intensive study of role behavior for people of various national cultures was made by a team of researchers from eight different countries (Havighurst et al., 1969). They studied samples of retired male teachers and workers in heavy industry, aged 70–75, from the following large city and industrial areas: Chicago, Vienna, Warsaw, Milan, Bonn and the Ruhr in West Germany, Nijmegen in southern Holland, London, and Paris. An intensive open-ended interview with small but random samples of 25 men in each occupational category was used, although only teachers were involved in the London and Paris samples. The researchers could compare the social class factor with the nationality factor, although the "nationality" dimension was more nearly that of certain large metropolitan areas than of nations or countries. For instance, Vienna may not be representative of rural Austria, and Chicago may not be representative of the United States.

This was intended as a pilot study to work out methods of comparative study that take into account differences in languages and research methods and habits of social scientists in the various countries involved. Their basic instrument was the open-ended interview and a set of rating scales that were applied to the interviews. The research team hoped to secure reliable and comparable quantitative ratings on role activity in the following 12 roles: worker, parent, grandparent, kin, spouse, homemaker, club member, citizen, church member, friend, neighbor, and acquaintance. All but 2 of these roles were rated with a reasonable amount of agreement by judges or raters from six countries.

Thus, it was possible to compare the size of differences in role activity between upper-middle-class and upper-lower-class men with the size of differences between the various metropolitan areas (countries). By means of analysis of variance, it was found that the occupational (social class) differences were statistically significant in 5 roles, while the differences among countries were significant in 10 roles. Only in the citizen role and the grandparent role were there no significant differences among the national groups.

Studies of Leisure Activity

There have been many descriptive studies of the free-time activities of men and women at various points in the adult life-span. It is relatively easy to make a count of the kinds of activities and the amount of time spent by people in various kinds of leisure activity. It would be more difficult but more useful to analyze the values and meanings people find in their leisure and to relate these to the significance of their work and their community role participation. (Efforts along this line were described by the writers Kleemeier, 1961, brought together for the book he edited.) Kreps (1971) proposed research on the options open to people after age 50, when they may alter their worker role and at the same time change their leisure activity. A group working together under the Committee on Research Goals in Social Gerontology of the Gerontological Society in the summer of 1971 interviewed men and women who changed their work roles between the ages of 45 and 65 in order to find out how this change affected their performance in leisure and other roles (Murray, Powers, & Havighurst, 1971).

It seems clear that Americans as a rule do not take easily to leisure when it becomes available to them in the form of retirement. Only a small proportion (though perhaps a growing one) get as much satisfaction out of leisure activities as they get from work, if they are employed. For instance, Pfeiffer and Davis (1971) asked the men and women in the Duke University longitudinal study, "What is more satisfying to you, your work or leisure activities?" These people ranged in age from 46 to 71, with about one-fourth over 65. The majority (54%) said work was more satisfying, while 15% opted for leisure, and 31% said the two kinds of activity were equally satisfying. This was largely a middle-class group, and work is more highly regarded in that group than in the working class (Friedmann & Havighurst, 1954).

Still, leisure activities are very attractive to some people. In connection with the Kansas City Studies of Adult Life made by the University of Chicago group, intensive analyses were made of the significance of leisure activities to men and women aged 40 to 70. When the favorite leisure activities of the respondents had been rated on some 20 variables, a factor analysis brought out five factors that accounted for 71% of the variance among the variables (Havighurst, 1961). The first three factors, in order of the proportion of the variance they account for, are (a) challenging new experience; (b) expressive pleasure, activities that bring sheer pleasure; and (c) instrumental service, activities that serve the community.

The cross-national study of retired teachers and industrial workers provided useful data on the leisure activities of these men. Havighurst and de Vries (1969) found the following "patterns" of free-time activity, in decreasing order of frequency:

1. *Mildly active time filling:* routine leisure activity takes up two to three hours a day and requires some degree of initiative;

2. *Expressive pleasure:* the individual uses free time for sheer pleasure in an autonomous and energetic way;

3. *Ordinary routines expanded to fill the day and week:* the ordinary social relations are maintained but take much more time than formerly;

4. *Instrumental service:* the individual devotes a large portion of his free time and energy to doing useful things without pay;

5. *Challenging new experience:* the individual does new things for his own interest and pleasure, with energy and success; and

6. *Apathy:* the individual does nothing that requires initiative.

Life-Style Studies

The concept of life-style is a useful global construct to describe the patterns of role performance and leisure activity of a person or a group of people. This construct has been used rather differently by several researchers and research groups. Williams and Wirths (1965) examined the interview data on elderly people in the Kansas City Studies of Adult Life and discovered a number of patterns or life-styles that appear to combine the personality data with social role data in a useful way. In a more limited way, Havighurst and Feigenbaum (1959) and Havighurst and de Vries (1969) combined leisure activities and role performance into life-styles that can be used to compare people of different social classes and different nationalities. Maddox (1968) found life-styles to be persistent through time.

National Styles of Role Performance of the Elderly

From the pilot cross-national study described above (Havighurst et al., 1969), it is clear that there are characteristic life-styles for retired men that occur differentially among several of the countries (metropolitan areas) in the study. These are as striking as the social class life-styles. At the risk of oversimplification, it can be said that there are three visible life-styles: (a) family and church centered, as in southern Holland; (b) work and informal social relations, as in Bonn, Chicago, Warsaw, and Milan (for teachers but not for industrial workers); and (c) leisure centered, as in Vienna and probably Copenhagen.

These examples illustrate the proposition that a life-style is a result (and also a cause, to some extent) of the situation (facilities, economic circumstances, tradition, etc.) that a society maintains. Thus, the great social and political importance of the churches in Holland makes the church member role a focus for the life-style of retired men; the presence and the tradition of drama and music, together with a relatively favorable pension, make leisure activities the characteristic life-style feature in Vienna; the emphasis on work and professional activity in Europe and the United States leads to a work-centered life-style even after formal retirement for teachers, with a substantial element of social activity among friendship and neighborhood groups. Yet there are variant life-styles in all of these countries. For instance, the leisure-centered style probably dominates the "retirement communities" of the South and West in the United States. And rural communities in all modern societies probably have a different life-style for the elderly than the metropolitan areas.

Education: The Role of Student

Can older people fit comfortably into the role of student? There are many potential advantages to older people in this role, and adult education programs have been devised specifically for people in their 50s, 60s, and 70s. Many of these programs and projects looked very good when they were operating, and the people involved as students and teachers felt that they were successful. But few of these programs "took hold" and became institutionalized. Several surveys of adult education have shown that participation in educational projects of various kinds drops off sharply after age 45. Also, men participate less than women in general educational activities, though specific preretirement programs draw men in their 60s (cf. Jacobs, Mason, & Kauffman, 1970).

There are two broad categories of adult education programs for middle-aged and older people. One is a varied program of classes and activities that adults of all ages attend. Some older people enjoy these programs for the same reasons that younger people do. But only a limited number of people past age 50 participate under present conditions.

The other kind of program is beamed specifically at a given age group and generally at a subgroup of older people. It may be a study or discussion group at a senior center or in a church congregation. It may be a retraining program for middle-aged workers who must find new jobs. Of special interest is the growing movement toward *preretirement education and counseling*. Such programs are assessed in a background paper on retirement (Schulz, 1971) prepared for the White House Conference on Aging. Schulz summarized the situation as follows:

> Despite general interest in preretirement education programs, the development of such programs seems to be in a very early stage. Significant numbers of workers do not have access to such programs, sponsored by either employers, non-profit organizations, or the community. And there is still disagreement over the need for such programs and whose responsibility it is to provide them.
>
> Some companies have felt that it is the company's responsibility to prepare the employee for retirement, through a series of intensive counseling sessions. The logic for this kind of thinking goes something like this: The person has spent his entire working life, or at least the last ten to twenty years before retirement with the company. Thus, the company feels that they must not only provide for the financial adequacy after retirement but also that they have a responsibility to "re-program" the man so that he will be able to adjust psychologically in retirement.
>
> On the other hand, some companies have reviewed preparation for retirement as an individual responsibility. This is in keeping with the American tradition of saving for later security and the individualism which characterizes American industry. Thus, any company "counseling" program is seen as an interference in the employee's private life. Still other companies feel that the problems of retirement and aging are for the community, state, and federal governments to solve (Greene, Pyron, & Manion, 1969).

In addition, certain specific problems have been noted by persons studying existing programs.

(1) A large majority of programs do not invite or encourage the attendance of spouses, despite strong indications that this is desirable.
(2) Programs often do not begin till shortly before retirement.
(3) The majority of programs are limited—concerned primarily with the financial aspects of retirement and distribution of printed matter. A more comprehensive program is usually not available to those who desire it.
(4) Most adults today do little definite personal planning for retirement.
(5) What is the "best" or most effective type of program is not yet known. Some evidence indicates the need for more intensive counseling programs to increase effectiveness and postretirement follow-up [p. 41].

Recently, the report of the President's Task Force on the Aging (1970) took a broader view of the question.

Traditionally, America's schools have been for children and youth. Increasingly, they are recognized as essential, in a changing, technologically-advancing society, for ongoing job training. The Nation must see its schools also as places where people can be helped to continue to grow throughout their lives. In the broadest possible sense they must become centers for later life or "retirement" preparation [p. 46].

NEEDED RESEARCH

After about age 55 there is a slow decline, on the average, of physical vigor and health. However, many people retain their health and vigor with little or no decline until the mid-70s. These two variables should be introduced into studies of role performance. Until we have a reasonably good measure of health and vigor, we will not be able to do broadly effective research on the role performance of elderly people. Although physicians are loath to rate people on a scale of vigor or of health, they probably could be brought into a group as advisers on the choice of a few medical and physical measurements that could be combined into a rating scale. A self-checking inventory, such as the Cornell Medical Index (Brodman, 1951), might be used, but this gives a measure of poor health, not good health.

Cross-cultural and cross-national studies. It is this writer's conviction that we can learn the most in the area of social role performance by studying well-defined samples of people who represent a variety of national, ethnic, and social class subcultures. Each of these subcultures is likely to provide a social setting in which the process of growing old differs somewhat from the process in other subcultures. Within the United States there are a number of ethnic minorities that should be studied in this way. Research proposals made by a committee headed by Donald Kent have been published in *The Gerontologist* (Havighurst, 1971a). Cross-national studies are also needed and can be made with careful attention to the problems of method that have emerged in the few pilot cross-national studies that have already been done.

Longitudinal studies. Some of the most important problems have to do with questions of stability and continuity of life-style through the middle years and on into the later years. These can best be answered by longitudinal studies with subsamples overlapping in age, so that a sample aged 55 today can be compared with a sample aged 45 today; and the sample of 45-year-olds should be maintained and studied for 10 years, thus giving longitudinal data where today only cross-sectional data at two different ages are available.

Flexible careers studies. It has become clear that there is likely to be a growing amount of movement from one job to another in the age period 45–70. The most desirable situation is one that maximizes freedom of choice for the individual so that he can change jobs if he wants to, retire early or late, take a part-time job, and combine a changing work role with developing leisure and community member roles.

The interview schedule worked out by the Flexible Careers Study Group of the Gerontological Society (Havighurst, 1971b) promises to produce some useful information if it is used with a variety of middle-aged groups, and especially with people who are in situations where a change of job is mandatory or desirable from their point of view.

Service roles studies. There are likely to be a growing number of part-time service jobs or roles open to people in their later decades. Some of them will be paid for with public funds, such as Foster Grandparents, Project SERVE, Homemakers, and senior center staff. Others will be volunteer, unpaid jobs. These should be studied for their effect on the life satisfaction and morale of the people who fill these roles.

REFERENCES

Brodman, K. The Cornell Medical Index. *Journal of the American Medical Association,* 1951, **145,** 152–157.

Carp, F. M. *The retirement process.* Washington, D.C.: United States Government Printing Office, 1969.

Cumming, E., & Henry W. E. *Growing old: The process of disengagement.* New York: Basic Books, 1961.

Donald, M. N., & Havighurst, R. J. The meanings of leisure. *Social Forces,* 1959, **37,** 355–360.

Friedmann, E., & Havighurst, R. J. *The meaning of work and retirement.* Chicago: University of Chicago Press, 1954.

Greene, M. R., Pyron, C. H., Manion, U. V., & Winkelvoss, H. *Preretirement counseling, retirement adjustment, and the older employee.* Washington, D.C.: Administration on Aging, 1969.

Havighurst, R. J. The leisure activities of the middle-aged. *American Journal of Sociology,* 1957, **63,** 152–162. (a)

Havighurst, R. J. The social competence of middle-aged people. *Genetic Psychology Monographs,* 1957, **56,** 297–395. (b)

Havighurst, R. J. The nature and values of meaningful free-time activity. In R. J. Kleemeier (Ed.), *Aging and leisure.* New York: Oxford University Press, 1961.

Havighurst, R. J. (Ed.) The status of research in applied social gerontology. (First Report of the Committee on Research and Development Goals in Social Gerontology) *Gerontologist,* 1969, 9(4, Pt. 2).

Havighurst, R. J. (Ed.) Careers after 50. The elderly in minority groups. Research proposals in applied social gerontology. (Second Report of the Committee on Research and Development Goals in Social Gerontology) *Gerontologist,* 1971, 11(1, Pt. 2). (a)

Havighurst, R. J. (Ed.) Research plans and proposals in applied and social gerontology. (Third Report of the Committee on Research and Development Goals in Social Gerontology) *Gerontologist,* 1971, 11(4, Pt. 2). (b)

Havighurst, R. J., & de Vries, A. Life styles and free-time activities of retired men. *Human Development,* 1969, **12,** 34–54.

Havighurst, R. J., & Feigenbaum, K. Leisure and life style. *American Journal of Sociology,* 1959, **64,** 396–404.

Havighurst, R. J., Munnichs, J. M. A., Neugarten, B. L., & Thomae, H. (Eds.) *Adjustment to retirement: A cross-national study.* New York: Humanities Press, 1969.

Havighurst, R. J., Neugarten, B. L., & Tobin, S. S. Disengagement and patterns of aging. In B. L. Neugarten (Ed.), *Middle age and aging.* Chicago: University of Chicago Press, 1968.

Jacobs, H. L., Mason, W. D., & Kauffman, E. *Education for aging: A review of recent literature.* Washington, D.C.: Adult Education Association of the United States of America, ERIC Clearing House on Adult Education, 1970.

Kleemeier, R. W. (Ed.), *Aging and leisure.* New York: Oxford University Press, 1961.

Kreps, J. Career options after fifty: Suggested research. In R. J. Havighurst (Ed.), *Careers after fifty. Gerontologist,* 1971, 11,(1, Pt. 2).

Kutner, B., Fanshel, D., Togo, A. M., & Langner, T. S. *Five hundred over sixty: A community survey on aging.* New York: Russell Sage Foundation, 1956.

Lopata, H. Z. *Widowhood in an American city.* Cambridge, Mass.: Schenkman, 1971. (a)

Lopata, H. Z. Widows as a minority group. In R. J. Havighurst (Ed.), The elderly in minority groups. *Gerontologist*, 1971, **11**(1, Pt. 2). (b)

Maddox, G. L. Activity and morale: A longitudinal study of selected elderly subjects. *Social Forces*, 1963, **42**, 195–204.

Maddox, G. L. Persistence of life style among the elderly. In B. L. Neugarten (Ed.), *Middle age and aging*. Chicago: University of Chicago Press, 1968.

Moberg, D. O. Religiosity in old age. *Gerontologist*, 1965, **5**, 78–87.

Moberg, D. O., & Taves, M. J. Church participation and adjustment in old age. In A. M. Rose & W. A. Peterson (Eds.), *Older people and their social world*. Philadelphia: Davis, 1965.

Murray, J. R., Powers, E. A., & Havighurst, R. J. Flexible careers. (Third Report of the Committee on Research and Development Goals in Social Gerontology) *Gerontologist*, 1971, **11**(4, Pt. 2).

Neugarten, B. L., & Weinstein, K. The changing American grandparent. *Journal of Marriage and Family Living*, 1964, **26**, 199–204.

Neugarten, B. L., Havighurst, R. J., & Tobin, S. S. Personality and patterns of aging. In B. L. Neugarten (Ed.), *Middle age and aging*. Chicago: University of Chicago Press, 1968.

Pfeiffer, E., & Davis, G. C. The use of leisure time in middle life. *Gerontologist*, 1971, **11**, 187–195.

President's Task Force on the Aging. *Toward a brighter future for the elderly*. Washington, D.C.: United States Government Printing Office, 1970.

Reichard, S., Livson, F., & Peterson, P. G. *Aging and personality*. New York: Wiley, 1962.

Riley, M. W., & Foner, A. *Aging and society: An inventory of research findings*. New York: Russell Sage Foundation, 1968.

Rosow, I. *Social integration of the aged*. New York: Free Press, 1967.

Schulz, J. H. Retirement. Paper presented at the White House Conference on Aging, Washington, D.C., 1971, Brandeis University.

Shanas, E., Townsend, P., Wedderburn, D., Friis, H., Milhoj, P., & Stehouwer, J. *Older people in three industrial societies*. New York: Atherton Press, 1968.

Sheppard, H. L. *New perspectives on older workers*. Kalamazoo, Mich.: Upjohn Institute for Employment Research, 1971.

Streib, G. F. Retirement roles and activities. Paper presented at the White House Conference on Aging, Washington, D.C., 1971, Cornell University.

Troll, L. E. The family in later life: A decade review. *Journal of Marriage and the Family*, 1971, **33**, 263–290.

Wilensky, H. Orderly careers and social participation. *American Sociological Review*, 1961, **26**, 521–530.

Williams, R. H., & Wirths, C. G. *Lives through the years*. New York: Atherton Press, 1965.

Ecology and the Aging Process

M. POWELL LAWTON and LUCILLE NAHEMOW

Ecology refers to the study of natural systems, emphasizing the interdependence of one element in a system upon every other element. Darwin's and Wallace's theories of natural selection were originators of ecological theories. Darwin referred to the "web of life," indicating that in the struggle for existence every species must adapt to both the demands of the physical environment and every other species. Thus, as one species changed the others changed and produced systems in which each island had different life forms. In like manner, human ecology has a wholistic framework. Ecologists argue than one cannot understand one element in nature without considering its surroundings.

According to Klausner (1971), "Adaptation is the most important dynamic concept in human ecology [p. 27]." It is with regard to this quality that the writings of such diverse individuals as Webber, Darwin, Skinner, and many others are seen as containing a unifying element and becoming integrated into theories of human ecology. We will consider the ecology of aging in terms of the adaptation of man to his environment and his alteration of the environment as part of the process of human adaptation. The aging process itself can be seen as one of continual adaptation: adaptation both to the external

M. Powell Lawton received his PhD in clinical psychology from Columbia University in 1952. He has worked in clinical practice and clinical research for the Veterans Administration and the Commonwealth of Pennsylvania. He is presently Director of Behavioral Research at the Philadelphia Geriatric Center. His major research interests are in social gerontology and ecological psychology. He is Secretary of the Gerontological Society, Past-President of the Division on Adult Development and Aging of the American Psychological Association, and Associate Editor for Social Gerontology for the *Journal of Gerontology*.

Lucille Nahemow received her PhD in social psychology from Columbia University. She helped to establish the environmental psychology program at

environment and to the changes in internal capabilities and functioning which take place during the life cycle.

Recently, the word "ecology" has become a slogan in addition
to a field of inquiry. Both the avant garde and the mass media warn
of the impending ecological catastrophe due to many years of disregard for the maintenance of existing natural systems. Less obvious,
but no less important, are the frequently unanticipated behavioral
and social consequences of changes in the man-made environment.
Thus, when we spend our tax dollars on road building rather than
on public transportation, we may critically affect the ability of older
persons to maintain themselves in the community. The fact that the
connection is not obvious does not negate its seriousness. In like
manner, the way old people are cared for in nursing homes has a
distinct impact on the cost of governance for all of the members of
a society, not merely those with a direct relationship to the aged.
Klausner (1971) pointed out that

> the older use of ecology as a scientific term refers in a value-neutral way
> to the functional connectedness of parts of the system. Current usage
> carries a warning that the system is becoming imbalanced and may be
> entering its death throes—an ominous eschatology. Such a slogan term,
> though, is a morally useful reminder that holding constant experimental
> conditions while varying a limited phenomenon is a figment of the labora-
> tory. When man builds dams or applies insecticides, nature holds nothing
> constant [p. 170].

Change is inevitable and it is occurring at an accelerated rate.
Toffler (1970) called the consequent confusion and anxiety "future
shock." According to him, it is necessary that man learn to adapt to
more and more rapid change. However, the question is being asked
more often and more loudly: Change to what and toward what end?
Dubos (1965) pointed out that so-called successful adaptations
might well be harmful in the long run. Since environments may
change and man is very adaptable, he may adapt to situations that
destroy his values. The high degree of persuasibility found in patients
who have "adjusted" to nursing homes suggests that this may be the
case (Nahemow & Bennett, 1967).

---

the Graduate Center of the City University of New York, the first such program in the United States. She has conducted research with the elderly in such
diverse settings as ghetto communities, homes for the aged, a state mental
hospital, and various apartment residences. She is currently a Research Psychologist at the Philadelphia Geriatric Center and also teaches at New York
University.

"Adaptation" is both a key concept in ecology and a key concept in the aging process. Aging can be conceptualized in many ways. The least explanatory way is to see aging as an accrual of years. One can also talk of mental age, physiological age, and so on (Fozard, 1971). The authors see aging as a dynamic process in time and space. Every day of his life each person interacts with the objects, the people, and the ideas that he perceives in his environment, and in that process he changes, "matures," if you will, or "ages." We define the ecology of aging as a system of continual adaptations in which both the organism and the environment change over time in a nonrandom manner; either environment or the organism is capable of initiating a cycle of action, or of responding. The environmental component of the ecological chain has been rediscovered in the behavioral sciences, due partly to our recent biologically oriented concern over a clean physical environment, but in no small measure due also to the sustained, persistent voices of a few people like Lewin (1935), Heider (1959), Chein (1954), Barker (1968), and the urban social ecologists. None of these dealt explicitly with the physical or man-made environment; each was concerned primarily about the behavior of the individual or a social group. Lewin (1935) and Heider (1959) admitted the environment primarily in its social form. The "life space" was the world of social institutions, objects, and other people that were salient to the behavior of the individual. Barker's "behavior setting" is the interface of the physical environment and the individual, but the "standing pattern of behavior," that is, the defining feature of a setting, is an organismic activity. For good theoretical reasons, Barker (1968) has not attempted to separate environmental components from individual components in the behavioral equation. He and the social area analysts have concerned themselves with behavior in the aggregate, in the one case predicting from knowledge of the man-made rules defining the behavior setting, and, in the other, from knowledge of the economic rules that define the existence of urban neighborhoods.

Durkheim (1933) introduced the concept of social space to refer to the "group framework" or social environment in which the individual lives and works, as contrasted with the physical environment. The work of Sorre (1943), a geographer, described by Buttimer (1969), provided many obvious examples of the interrelationship between the social and the physical environment and objected to Durkheim's separation of the two. He envisioned social space as a collection of physical areas that were subjectively defined by those who lived in that area. According to Sorre, social space was typically perceived in terms of visible features of the environment such as theaters, schools, and so on. In this he was a forerunner of Lynch (1960) who found that such landmarks play an important role in people's perceptions of cities. Chombart de Lauwe (1966) further delineated the concept of social space and pointed out that there was a multiplicity of such environments for each individual: geographic, economic, cultural, religious, and legal space. Thus, an individual's economic space does not necessarily coincide with his religious space. There is both a subjective and an objective component to social space.

Evidence is beginning to accumulate suggesting that selected groups of people show particular sensitivity to certain aspects of the environment. De Long (1968) argued that the impaired older person receives different visual signals than others as a consequence of his greater reliance on macular and peripheral, as compared to foveal, vision. Thus, the aged person would be more attuned to movement than to color. Pastalan (1971) investigated the experience of the environment reported by students of architecture who wore diffusing lenses, ear plugs, and fingertip film designed to simulate the modal impairment of the average 80-year-old person. This procedure directly affected the mood of the student volunteers, at least one of whom became so depressed that he quit the experiment. The authors had the opportunity to experience the lenses and can attest to the fact that the world does, indeed, take on a different aspect through the "old age" lenses, particularly in its apparent separation from the self. Try as we might we could not get "close" to things. Hall (1966) suggested that physical distance between people engaged in social interaction is a function of cultural expressive habits, the immediate situation, and the characteristics of the individual. Possibly the tendency for older people to stand close to one another when engaging in conversation is as much a function of their impaired sensory capacities as their cultural heritage (De Long, 1970). Environments that are primarily occupied by older people most certainly have a different ambience for the occupants than for younger observers. Younger people typically view such environments with distaste. This may be one explanation for the difficulty experienced in recruiting professionals to work with the aged.

There appears to be a rapidly increasing amount of empirical investigation relating to the environment of older people. This has developed new liaisons between gerontologists, architects, planners, and engineers. In the past our links with medicine, psychology, and sociology have always been, close, and we have shared the medical and academic thinking of these fields. In contrast, transportation engineers, designers, builders, architects, etc., are all engaged in work with strong practical components. As a consequence they think in terms of solutions to concrete problems. Alexander (1964), who was concerned with principles of good design, noted that there may be an infinite number of environmental solutions to a problem. Consequently, a particular solution can be seen as better or worse than other solutions in dealing with a particular situation. When we consider such issues as how to house and occupy the growing population of elderly persons, for example, solutions must be found. Here we mean "solution" in the sense in which Alexander uses the term, that is, as a *series* of alternative solutions, some of which are more creative or functional than others.

DEVELOPMENTAL ASPECTS OF THE INDIVIDUAL AND THE ENVIRONMENT

Both the individual and the environment have a past, a present, and a future. Much of the present volume revolves around the developmental aspects of human life. Several authors call attention as well to the developmental aspects of environment. New methodologies for isolating cohort effects, as contrasted with age effects (Baltes & Nesselroade, 1970; Schaie, 1965), have led to the question of specifying the content of cohort differences. Riegel (see pp. 37–68, this volume) calls for a recognition of the "cultural-historical direction" of the environment. Baltes mentioned how the environmental resources offered by society are age graded: the aged are given less opportunity for learning new skills, and the continued practice of old skills may be rendered impossible. Some time ago, Demming and Pressey (1957) recognized this possible specificity of cognitive performance to environmental experience and devised some intellectual tests that might be less foreign to older people than standardized tests like the Wechsler scales. Similarly, Neugarten (pp. 311–335) and Lowenthal (pp. 281–310) call attention to the differing receptivity of the individual to environmental experience as he ages and to his change from an active to a passive orientation to the environment. Charles Taylor, in his unpublished discussion of Neugarten's and Lowenthal and Chiriboga's chapters, gave as an example of the determining content of historical experience the possible effect of the school milieu of the end-of-century on the social behavior of today's aged. Being on time for appointments and starting meetings on schedule are overlearned behaviors entirely understandable when one remembers the authoritarian teacher-centered classroom of 1900.

Neugarten and Lowenthal deal extensively with the adaptive mechanisms utilized by the individual as he copes with the environment in different life stages. Cultural anthropology and human geography are examples of fields that deal with the developmental aspect of environment. Attention to the enduring values of a culture, the social practices for transmitting and changing these values, and the artifacts used in the service of these goal pursuits allows us to compare cultures and to view their evolution. On the societal level, similar changes occur swiftly enough to allow us to view the individual as he ages in terms of the degree to which he responds to the changing society and the way it responds to him. Historical events become assimilated into social norms and cultural values, but the experiencing of an event in history may frequently maintain its motivating power through the lifetime of the individual. Today's elderly have lived through the abolition of child labor, the immigration era of the United States, the rise of labor unionism, the mechanization of industrial production, and the giant extension of the educational system. The explicit interiorization of such major societal changes has never been adequately studied in gerontological research. The more specific environmental experiences of subgroups of the elderly may greatly condition their present response to their environment. One psychologist (R. Kalish, personal communication, 1970), perhaps with only mild exaggeration, has noted that much of what is known about the psychological functioning of the aged may really be describing the elderly European-born Jewish immigrant, because of the repeated use of such people as research subjects. Conceivably, childhood exposure to a rigidly stratified society, to pogroms, and to American anti-Semitism of the early century may be environmental-historical experiences that retain their motivating power into old age, just as different experiences may for other subgroups. Though we have little empirical knowledge at hand, we can hope that the future will bring more investigation of the behavioral consequences of changing environments.

THE DIMENSIONS OF ENVIRONMENT

A major task of planning has been that of matching individuals with environments meeting their needs. A necessary first step in this process is the ability to describe environments. While we do not yet have a satisfactory taxonomy of environments, there have been some beginning efforts to classify them in both a priori and empirical fashions.

A Priori Classification

Some time ago Anderson (1963) classified environments in terms of their resources, incentives, and constraints. Resources represent the material and symbolic content of the environment. Incentives are group-induced behavioral reinforcers, and constraints are physical and social barriers to self-fulfillment.

Lawton (1970a) described the behavioral system as composed of (a) the individual, (b) the interpersonal environment (the world of significant others), (c) the suprapersonal environment, which is determined by the modal characteristics of those in physical proximity to the individual (i.e., for the child, the "adult world"; for the black in the business community, the "white" world, etc.), (d) the social environment (institutions and social norms), and (e) the physical environment.

Sells (1963) developed an elaborate listing of stimulus types. Approximately 250 entries are grouped under the major categories of (a) natural aspects of the environment; (b) man-made aspects of the environment; (c) description of task, problem, situation, and setting; (d) external reference characteristics of the individual (status, role); and (e) individuals performing relative to others (i.e., as a group member). While this listing is in taxonomic form, many of the entries seem so nomothetic as to constitute a dead end for further development of research and theory.

Probably one reason for the obvious difficulty experienced in these and other environmental classifications lies in the absence of basic theoretical material available from the study of perception. Ittelson (1970) pointed out that in the history of experimental psychology the study of environmental perception has most frequently been indirect. Most experimental work has used object perception, rather than large-scale environmental perception, as its base. Thus, even to talk about environmental perception, he found it necessary to define the characteristics of the environment. Ittelson defined a basic distinction between the environment and an environmental object: the defining property of the environment is that it surrounds the perceiver; it enfolds. No one can be isolated and identified as standing outside of and apart from it. Perceptual objects may be quite large, such as New York City seen from an airplane, but they are not environments unless the perceiver is embedded in them. In addition, they always contain a surplus of information, some of which is redundant, some contradictory, and some inadequate or ambiguous. They are multimodal, stimulating all the senses simultaneously.

They always contain peripheral as well as central information. At the level of abstract meaning, we cannot even contemplate the environment without thinking in terms of the meaning it has for the particular person who is perceiving that environment. Environments always have an ambience, an atmosphere which is of central concern to the person within them.

Empirical Classifications

In the search for empirical environmental dimensions, several investigators have turned to factor-analytic techniques. Schooler (1970) interviewed a national probability sample of 4,000 older people and obtained information regarding a number of aspects of their possessions, dwelling unit, and neighborhood. A principal-component analysis of these discrete characteristics yielded five environmental factors: (a) distance to services; (b) condition of dwelling unit; (c) convenience to services, friends, and relatives; (d) characteristics of structure; and (e) availability of social services. Lawton and Kleban (1971) factored characteristics of the neighborhood environment of 115 elderly Jewish residents of an urban slum and obtained factors that were named central location, distance from facilities, independent household, busy location, well-kept neighborhood, and nonresidentional block. In a study of age and poverty as determinants of social isolation, Rosenberg (1970) studied over 1,000 working-class people age 45 and over. To describe the "neighborhood context" in which they lived he used aggregate measures of suprapersonal environmental characteristics such as the mean age of the block residents, mean income, number of household members, proportion of males, etc. A component analysis resulted in three major factors: comfortable young white working class, neighborhood extensivity, and work-oriented neighborhood. Taietz (1970) conducted an investigation of 144 communities. Factor analysis of 79 economic, social, demographic, and physical characteristics of the communities yielded four factors serving as measures of community structure: structural complexity, socioeconomic status, political and educational homogeneity, and professional and white-collar concentration.

Each investigator used a set of variables that was uniquely suited to his investigation. The idiosyncrasies of the area studied, the researcher's theoretical orientation, and the vicissitudes of empirical investigation all contribute to the researcher's selection of variables. The variables included in the matrix determine what the emergent factors will be. The factor's predictive meaning is very much a function of the specifics of the people to whom the factors were related. Similarities in the factors obtained by these investigations are nonetheless in evidence, however. Distance to needed services and socioeconomic status factors occur repeatedly. Replication of studies like these over more communities, more variables, and more people should produce results that eventually converge on stable, replicable environmental dimensions at least no less predictive than factors of the intellect. In general, early attempts at taxonomy are lacking in either a firm theoretical basis or empirical refinement. Once environmental dimensions are identified, it will be much easier to investigate individual responses to the environment.

INDIVIDUAL EXPERIENCE OF THE ENVIRONMENT

Among people in general, there appear to be wide differences in responsiveness to the physical environment. The aesthetic quality of one's dwelling unit, the arrangement of objects in one's personal space, or the natural environment may evoke strong affect in one person and hardly exist in the life space of another. On the other hand, under many conditions for all people, awareness of the environment is minimal—an adaptive mechanism allowing us to go about our goal-directed activity without the intrusion of extraneous stimuli. In Helson's (1964) terms, people are normally at adaptation level with respect to their environment. This usual state of filtering out consciousness of our physical surroundings is probably what makes it so difficult to study response to the environment. The experience of the environment will be discussed in terms of environmental cognition and its evaluative aspect, environmental preference.

Environmental Cognition

The individual's link to what is "outside" is mediated by his internal representation of the external world. Much of the early effort of environmental psychology has been devoted to understanding how the individual perceives and structures the physical environment. Tolman's (1948) concept of the "cognitive map" has been adopted by ecological psychologists and given a more explicitly geographic meaning than Tolman gave it. Stea (1969) suggested that what has been called "environmental perception" by such workers as Lynch (1960) in his work on "the image of the city" is a complex cognitive rather than perceptual process. We agree, and shall refer to "environmental cognition" and to the "apprehended environment" as its end product.

There is relatively little research giving any picture of how the older person conceives of his environment. Some common methods of obtaining such information from younger subejcts have involved drawing, map reading or map drawing, and responding to semantic differential adjective lists. Each of these methods involves response difficulties for older people. One of the authors explored the older person's image of New York City. The imagery reported during the interview was similar to that reported by Lynch (1960), in that landmarks were frequently mentioned as characterizing the city. For example, Rockefeller Center and Radio City Music Hall were frequently mentioned as features of the city. This was true despite the fact that these people, most of whom lived in Brooklyn, Queens, or the Bronx, rarely went into Manhattan. Most older New Yorkers made almost exclusive use of facilities existing in their own neighborhoods. Nevertheless, their image of the city focused on Manhattan.

Inkblot projective tests may be viewed as one route to the cognitive representation of the external world. There have been relatively few studies of the Rorschach responses of older people that have adequately controlled health and institutional status. Judging from several studies (Ames, 1960; Eisdorfer, 1963; Light & Amick, 1956; Singer, 1963) increasing age has been shown to be associated with lowered productivity, a lesser likelihood of venturing beyond the actual contours of the blots to produce responses (lessened tendency to use human movement and color), greater stereotyping, and a lessened tendency to articulate the stimulus accurately (an increased number of vague or poor-form whole responses). The traditional meaning of these patterns is well in accord with findings from experimental psychology of reduced sensory acuity, response withholding, and the tendency toward perceptual assimilation found in aged as compared to young subjects. On the other hand, such changes did not take place in Ames' originally most intact group and were not observable cross-sectionally in Eisdorfer's highest-IQ group. These restrictions of one's perceptual world are thus not inevitable consequences of aging; the decrements may reflect the poor health or the institutional status of some of the subjects.

Size and distance seem to be major dimensions of the apprehended environment. Gelwicks (1970) discussed home range as a behavioral phenomenon. Does the perceived size of one's personal space, his local area, or his total life space also change intrinsically with age, or with the various factors associated with aging? The complexity and level of abstraction with which one views one's environment is another dimension with possible age-related changes. If sensory and physical deficits limit the fineness of the detail with which one can differentiate his environment, internal representations of it should be less complex—emphasizing the larger aspects that are most critical to adaptive behavior. Similarly, in light of some demonstrations that age decrements in conceptual thinking occur (Bromley, 1956, 1957), one might expect increasingly greater reliance on concrete descriptors of one's environment with age. Perhaps more interesting than simple age functions are variations in the perceived environment that are associated with other personal and situational factors. Gutmann, Gottesman, and Tessler (1968) asked elderly patients on a special treatment ward and patients on a custodial ward of a mental hospital to take the examiner on a "tour" of their ward. The treatment ward patients' environment was more differentiated, in terms of the number of spaces shown and named and the number of activities mentioned as occurring in them. Data from studies of younger subjects suggest that the physical environment is frequently judged along dimensions such as evaluation, potency, friendliness, and coherence, as judged by semantic differential responses to environmental stimuli. However, older subjects had difficulty with such response formats in similar work now in progress by the authors.

Environmental Preference

Environmental preferences have been studied more than other aspects of environmental cognition, probably because it is very simple to ask about likes and dislikes. While the link between enduring affective states and environmental evaluation is by no means established, people do exhibit affective responses to their environment, and their measurement is of great potential interest. Environmental features may be evaluated for (a) their aesthetic quality, (b) their objective functional quality, or (c) their subjective functional quality. Perrin (1970) suggested that *aesthetic qualities* (usually visual) are relatively insignificant determinants of most people's evaluation of environmental features, despite the preoccupation of people in the design professions with this aspect. Our own unpublished research supports this view: only a very small percentage of tenants in housing for the elderly responded to an aesthetic feature when asked what they like most or least about their building. No direct attempt to scale the aesthetic preferences of older people has been made. An investigation of such issues as the effect of earlier-life experience on aesthetic judgments of neighborhoods and dwelling units, the process of adaptation to environmental beauty and ugliness, or late-life standards of personal beauty would add an important dimension to our understanding of older people.

Objective functional quality. Given a norm for quality of performance, one may choose to evaluate an environmental feature in terms of the behavior it elicits. Lawton (1971) suggested that behavioral competence be defined as a combination of quality of performance and level of complexity achieved by the individual in a variety of tasks of living. Environments that foster competent behavior would thus be high in functional quality. An institutional environment whose structure encourages continence would be evaluated more positively than one where patients of equal competence were incontinent. Or, a neighborhood whose security afforded greater mobility for its aged residents would be evaluated highly. These quality criteria are viable only as long as one accepts the value judgments upon which the norms are based, however. The more complex the behavior, such as "meaningful leisure time activity" or "prosocial behavior," the more difficult it is to establish a behavioral evaluation criterion.

Subjective functional quality. Perrin (1970) argued that the major basis for people's environmental evaluations is the degree to which the environment facilitates the individual's sense of competence. This basis for evaluation is the inner aspect of objective functional quality. Most frequently, important instrumental and expressive roles are performed with the environmental aspects of the situation taken for granted; the environmental assumes prominence primarily when it functions as a barrier to the competent performance of a valued role. An individual may evaluate positively an environment seen as very negative by most people, such as an urban ghetto, because his familiarity and sense of orientation to the neighborhood give him competence that would be lost should he try to adapt to a new environment.

THE INDIVIDUAL AND HIS LINKS TO THE ECOLOGICAL SYSTEM

Environmental cognition is a mediator between the individual and his environment. Environmental cognition faces outward in the sense that its focus is the representation of what is outside the individual. A corollary set of mediating processes face inward, toward the individual and how his sensory, perceptual, and cognitive processes themselves function as they deal with environmental information.

Try as we may to reinforce the idea of an open system a heuristic focus on one element or another is frequently necessary. The search for intraindividual elements that link environment and behavior is one such point. Theoretically, much of the subject matter of individual psychology concerns itself with such links, but there are some areas at the individual level that are more salient to the environment than others. This section will consider some intrapersonal receptor and stimulus-processing variables that have been investigated in the general psychological literature and that may be of potential value in predicting behavior, in combination with knowledge of the context of the behavior. For the most part, this section will be speculative, since relatively little is known about such variables as evidenced in older people.

Sensory processes. There is a reduction in the amount of environmental information received as one ages. Each sensory element by itself appears to show an age decrement: visual acuity (Chapanis, 1950), dark adaptation (Birren, Bick, & Fox, 1948), auditory threshold (Schaie, Baltes, & Strother, 1964), and olfactory sensitivity (Kimbrell & Furchtgott, 1963).

Perception. Similar changes occur at higher levels of perceptual functioning such as flicker fusion threshold (Coppinger, 1955), perception of verticality (Comalli, Wapner, & Werner, 1959), and susceptibility to optical illusions (Wapner, Werner, & Comalli, 1960), though most of these presumptive "age changes" have not been tested out in terms of longitudinal intraindividual change, or their relationship to the health of the individual. Viewed in terms of Werner's (1961) developmental psychology, the responses of older people appear to be characterized by diffusion, or failure to differentiate discrete aspects of the stimulus field. Thus, the heightened response of older people to the Müller-Lyer illusion is interpreted as "assimilation," or nondifferentiation. On the other hand, the decreased susceptibility to the Titchener circles illusion during old age was interpreted as failure to respond to the "contrast" effect (Wapner et al., 1960). The U-shaped age curve in each of these perceptual tasks supports the curvilinear age regression hypotheses of Werner (1961).

Cognition and cognitive styles. Environmental information appears to be processed at a slower rate as age progresses, although evidence seems to be piling up to indicate that, given time, the healthy older subject's performance quality may be the equal of the younger person's in many tasks (Eisdorfer, 1968).

What are the implications of such knowledge for the ecological psychology of later life? First, it seems clear that decisions and behavior are sometimes based upon less environmental information for the older person. Occasionally, as in the case of an automobile accident consequent to inadequately registered or processed environmental signals, the resulting behavior is disastrously maladaptive. For the most part, however, the everyday behavior of people with lowered receptivity is either only mildly impaired, or not impaired at all. What are the adaptational processes that apparently make it possible for the molar units of behavior to maintain quality while the molecular units diminish in quality?

Withholding a response, in preference to risking errors, appears to be one such mechanism (Eisdorfer, 1968). If we accept humor as reflecting folk knowledge, the saying, "Older people appear to be wise when they are just being careful [Palmore, 1971]" suggests that this may be an effective technique. Stimulus amplification, whether self-initiated or environmentally engineered (Lindsley, 1964) is another technique, for example, the habit of sitting closer to a sound source than one might have done as a younger person. Birren (1970) hypothesized a further process that may have compensatory value. Given the situation of a slower rate of information processing in old age, a counteracting adaptation may take place in an older person's capacity to utilize increasingly larger chunks of information, thus, a heightened quality of "mature judgment," that is, the ability to discern the implications of environmental stimuli, or to plan.

Where compensatory adaptational styles are not adequately developed, the input deficit is likely to be expressed in behavior. In some situations, too great a proportion of the determinant of behavior may be intraindividual, leading to the classical types of distortion: oversimplification, compression, projection, self-reference, overinclusion, reification, and so on. The subject may appear to be reacting to an environmental situation other than the one that others might perceive. In the search for cues to behavior, he may perceive an environment as he perceived it at an earlier point in his life, as in the instance of estimating the time needed to cross a highway on the basis of car speeds of 40 years ago. In the deteriorated aged person this may constitute a severe problem. In a nursing home the question arose as to why residents never left the premises. A staff member recalled an instance of a patient who had gone out and walked the streets in search of her family in a house they had lived in before moving out of the state some 20 years ago.

There has, in fact, been very little research regarding age changes in the intrapsychic mechanisms used by individuals to organize their environment. Following the developmental theory of Werner (1961), Rochwarg (1954) analyzed Rorschach protocols of 40 presumably healthy aged subjects and 40 adults between the ages of 23 and 45 in terms of the complexity of organization and the indications of primitive thought shown in their responses. The elderly subjects showed a lower developmental level by these indices. This study suffers, of course, from all the disadvantages of cross-sectional research and from a failure to analyze the effect of physical health. Taken at face value, however, it appears to indicate a lessened degree of precision in articulating environmental stimuli and particularly in integrating them into combinatory larger concepts.

Witkin, Lewis, Hertzman, Machover, Meissner, and Wapner (1954) described a variety of personality and behavioral differences related to a basic disposition to find behavioral cues within oneself ("field independence") as contrasted to finding them in the environment ("field dependence"). The field independent person is usually better able to deal analytically with both aspects of the self and the environment. Criteria for the definition of field dependence include perception of verticality and performance on the Gottschaldt figures, where the aged were found to be more field dependent than younger people (Schwartz & Karp, 1967).

Gardner, Holzman, Klein, Linton, and Spence (1959) worked with "cognitive styles," manners of structuring knowledge so as to make an understandable and manipulable world out of the oversupply of available information. One such style is the leveling versus sharpening dimension, that is, the tendency of the individual to minimize or maximize differences among environmental stimuli. In a line-length judging task, the leveler will fail to perceive differences as successive pairs of originally identical lines suffer increasing discrepancies in length, while the sharpener will tend to perceive differences between lines at or below threshold level. Within limits, both styles may be adaptive. In a task involving ambiguous figures, older subjects were slower to perceive the change as a series of drawings moved serially from the representation of one object to another (Korchin & Basowitz, 1956); they were also slower to perceive closure in a Gestalt completion test (Basowitz & Korchin, 1957). This behavior is akin to leveling, or reducing the amount of perceptual discrimination required.

In other theoretical frameworks, affective personality dimensions of "repression" versus "sensitization" have been studied at length in younger populations (Ericksen & Pierce, 1968), as has the conceiving of one's behavior as being reinforced from within or from without the self, that is, internal versus external control (Rotter, 1966). Age changes during later life in locus of control have not been studied. However, Kuypers (1971) contrasted elderly "externals" and "internals," finding that subjects who perceived control as coming from within were more active, reality oriented, differentiated, and adaptive. These traits clearly imply greater competence in environmental manipulation. A personality dimension involving the active seeking out of environmental stimulation—curiosity, stimulus seeking, effectance, or need for novelty—has been described (Fiske & Maddi, 1961). Risk taking has been studied as a general personality dimension (Kogan & Wallach, 1964) and in its change with age (Botwinick, 1966, 1969). The latter studies determined that older subjects were more likely to withhold responses in all situations, but when forced to respond, they did not necessarily choose the response involving less risk.

While the predictive and discriminant validities of these cognitive styles are not clearly established, they do attempt to describe how environmental input is organized in terms of enduring personality dispositions. As applied to the psychology of adult life, there is no implication that one pole of a cognitive style is necessarily more adaptive than the other. Theoretically, at least, unless he is at the extremes of either pole, a person may live competently as a leveler or a sharpener, as field dependent or field independent. We urgently need to examine whether these qualitative forms persist into old age and whether their correlates in behavior and attitude are similar to those found among younger people. Thus, one direction of inquiry would explore individual differences in cognitive styles—the behavioral results of an individual with a particular cognitive style interacting with a specific stimulus environment.

An exogenous developmental change occurs with the change in social and economic input. Consequently, corresponding endogenous changes in the functioning of these processing variables might be expected in order to minimize maladaptation. On this basis, one would expect to find perceptual and cognitive mechanisms being used to reduce the complexity of the environment, so that objects and situations come to be of manipulable proportions. There is, of course, an inevitable loss of fineness of discrimination and the possibility of maladaptive behavior inherent in such minimization. One would thus need to test whether, or for whom, or under what environmental conditions, there are also quantitative age changes in cognitive style that lead to changes in the competence of behavior. That is, the following hypotheses might be advanced:

1. Within the middle range of any dimension of cognitive style, the adequacy of behavior resulting from the aged individual's environmental transactions is not predictable from his cognitive style per se.

2. Extreme values of any cognitive style lead to less adaptive behavior.

3. As a consequence of biological age changes, cognitive styles are likely to change in a direction that will tend to simplify the apprehended environment or make more immediately apparent to the individual how he should respond.

These points will be considered again in the final, theoretical section of this chapter.

TOPICAL AREAS IN THE ECOLOGICAL PSYCHOLOGY OF LATER LIFE

With housing programs for older people being one of the largest and most successful national programs, it is not surprising that this area has attracted more research than other areas. In addition to housing, this section will discuss relocation, migration, institutionalization and institutional life, transportation, and the community.

Housing for the Elderly

The large number of descriptive and analytic findings relating to housing for the elderly cannot possibly be reviewed here. A substantial amount of descriptive information may be found in the Cornell studies of 1957–60 (Beyer, 1961; Beyer & Wahl, 1963; Beyer & Woods, 1963; Langford, 1962), which reported on a survey of 5,000 social security recipients living in normal age-integrated communities of varying size. Similar descriptive data about tenants in government-supported British housing may be found in Hole and Allen (1962, 1964). By far the most intensive study and complete report on a planned housing environment for the elderly is the story of one of the country's first public projects for the elderly, Victoria Plaza, in San Antonio, Texas (Carp, 1966). Another volume edited by Carp (undated) contains a collection of reports of completed and partially completed studies by a number of researchers. Finally, Rosow's (1967) study of apartment dwellers in Cleveland examined carefully a large number of questions about the social adjustment of older people that relate directly or indirectly to ecological parameters.

Not all studies using planned housing tenants as subjects are ecological studies. However, it seems worthwhile to examine research that has contrasted older people living in normal age-integrated communities to those living in planned environments, in search of leads to the understanding of transactional phenomena. The impact of new housing is of interest both because of its implications for improving the lives of older people and because of its meaning for the science of ecology. However, new housing obviously represents not only a physical change, but a major social one as well; as an independent variable, change of residence of any kind is a mélange of processes that vary greatly among individuals and among situations. Thus, no housing impact study may be viewed as a test of the causal effect of a new physical environment.

Carp (1966) showed that from the standpoint of the tenants who moved into a model residence, their situation was improved. There were major positive changes after one year of residence in housing satisfaction, satisfaction with life-sustaining resources, morale, level of activity participation, social interaction, and perceived health, as compared to a group of unsuccessful applicants for the same housing. These results contrast somewhat with the much less marked effect demonstrated by Lipman (1968), who compared matched pairs of tenants and unsuccessful applicants interviewed on only one occasion. His tenants showed higher morale and perceived independence, but no advantage in activity level, social interaction, or in several self-rated indices of well-being.

Carp's (1966) study was conducted in the atmosphere of an experiment on which national attention was focused, and there was undoubtedly an esprit among the first group of occupants that maximized the beneficial effects. Lipman's study, on the other hand, was less definitive in that it was not longitudinal, and even his very careful matching may not have removed all confounding variables. The tenants were from several locations and had lived for varying lengths of time in their planned housing. Thus, his modestly positive effects may well reflect the more usual type of gain to be expected. In any case, impact studies are needed utilizing data that do not depend solely upon the tenants' report and that contrast the effects of differing environments.

The selection of tenants, whether by the housing sponsor or by self-selection is of interest. Lawton (1969) suggested that tenants tend to match their competencies with the resources of the environments in which they choose to live; empirical data from three sites supported the hypothesis that less competent individuals choose housing with more services. In order to make a firm determination of the bases for self-selection, housing groups would have to be compared with random or matched samples of nonapplicant groups, which has not to our knowledge been done extensively. However, some information suggests that middle-income retirement village dwellers are younger, healthier, better educated, and more likely to be married, still working, have fewer children and see them less frequently than the older population at large (Bultena & Wood, 1969; Hamovitch, undated; Mangum, 1971; Sherman, Mangum, Dodds, Walkley, & Wilner, 1968). Carp (1966) and Jackson (1970) found that applicants chosen by housing authorities were more active socially and rated as more intact mentally and as more socially acceptable than unsuccessful applicants. However, Carp's white San Antonio tenants expressed a greater housing need than unsuccessful applicants, while Jackson's southern blacks tended to be chosen so that those with greatest need were rejected: her unsuccessful applicants were older, expressed greater housing need, and felt less secure financially.

It is clear that any impact assessment must take into account both external and self-imposed selection processes. The needs of people for differing locations, physical settings, on-site services, age integration, neighborhood contexts, and social contexts vary widely, and undoubtedly enter into housing choice. Hamovitch, Peterson, and Larson (1969) reported early findings of their attempt to sort out the bases for housing preferences and satisfactions. Rather than utilizing simple preference questions, they asked subjects in different housing situations to state the importance of a number of attributes of the physical and social environment, the type of attribute they prefer, the extent to which their present housing possessed such attributes, and the extent of their satisfaction with their housing. Thus, they assess the reality, the salience, the congruence of reality and ideal, and the relationship between any of these factors and stated satisfaction.

In general, older people tend to be satisfied with their current housing. Estimates vary: 83% of 5,000 social security beneficiaries indicated unwillingness to move from their neighborhoods (Langford, 1962); 75% in Los Angeles did not wish to move (Goldscheider, 1966); and about two-thirds of relatively large samples of people living in the community and in planned housing in California indicated a high degree of satisfaction with their housing (Hamovitch et al., Sherman et al., 1968). Only 4% of Rosow's (1967) apartment-dweller sample indicated that they had serious complaints about their housing, and he presented some evidence suggesting that the "housing problem" is primarily an income problem. In contrast, only 19% did not wish to move from an urban slum (Lawton, Icleban, & Singer, 1971). The radical departure of the urban slum group from the general pattern attests to the responsivity of the elderly individual to his environmental circumstances and to the need for knowing both the actual circumstance and the degree of satisfaction with it.

Preferences regarding age segregation vary with one's present circumstances; Lawton (1968) found that 30% of community residents would prefer living with age peers, while only 9% of older people already living in age-segregated housing objected to living this way. A positive association between living among age peers and morale was found in a group of midwestern migrants to retirement areas (Bultena & Wood, 1969). Public housing tenants living in age-segregated settings were less dependent on social interaction to maintain morale (Messer, 1967) than were similar tenants in age-integrated housing. The morale of socially oriented apartment dwellers was directly related to the concentration of age peers in their apartment buildings (Rosow, 1967). Rosow also demonstrated clearly that the amount of social interaction of his apartment dwellers was a function of the proportion of age peers in the subject's social environment. Furthermore, high age-peer density was particularly useful in maintaining the social interaction level of the very old, of women, and of nonmarried people, especially from the middle class.

If congruence of personal need with environmental resource is important, not all tenants and housing will be perfectly matched, particularly where housing options are limited. Carp (1966) found that adjustment and happiness one year after occupancy could be predicted on the basis of information provided by the subject and by ratings made by an interviewer prior to occupancy. Positive self-attitude, engagement in group and other social relations, and mental alertness were some successful predictors. Mangum (1971), using the same data as Sherman et al. (1968), tested the congruity hypothesis. The adjustment of the individual was hypothesized to be a function of the degree of consonance between the individual's activity level and the activity-inducing properties of each of six housing settings, indexed as a composite of the Kleemeier (1959) dimensions of congregate, segregate, and institutional quality. In general, the hypotheses were not borne out, but taking account of the small number of environments (six) and the fact that they were not originally chosen to contrast these dimensions, some individual findings were consonant with the hypothesis, and the method does offer some promise. Mangum also investigated the relative variance-accounting power of status characteristics, environmental characteristics, and personality characteristics on a single-occasion measurement of adjustment. In general, environmental characteristics accounted for more variance in sites serving lower socioeconomic groups, and personal characteristics accounted for more variance among residents of higher economic class communities. High self-esteem, low anxiety, and high activity level were associated with adjustment (a composite of morale, liking for environment, and acceptance of age-segregated living).

There have been relatively few studies focusing explicitly on physical environmental dimensions. Carp (1966) found no relationship between floor of residence or distance from elevator and popularity. Lawton and Simon (1968) found a marked tendency for tenants of five housing environments to choose near neighbors as friends, a tendency that did not change over time. The tendency to choose friends from a smaller geographic range was on occasion increased by poor health, eastern European birth, nonmarried status, and low income. More active patterns of space traversal for the purpose of social interaction were reported by people who were more competent on a variety of indices. Lawton (1970c) also reported wide variations among 12 sites in the percentages of their populations observable in common spaces or engaged in social activity. Lesser proportions of the populations of sites with healthy tenants, and sites with few services, were observable in common spaces than in sites with less healthy tenants and many services. The greater the number of people observed in common spaces, the greater the number there were engaging in social interaction. More social interaction was observed in buildings with least common space, but this latter spatial factor was confounded with socioeconomic class: public housing sites contained least common space and had a higher proportion of publicly observed people interacting. Thus, one does not know whether the crucial element was the amount of space or the economic level of the tenants.

The tenant as an active manipulator of the environment was studied in his tendency to leave his apartment door open. Over 10 sites, the aggregate proportion of open doors was highly correlated with the building's mean number of sociometric choices made per tenant and the proportion of observed people who were engaging in social behavior (Lawton, 1970c). There was also a relationship between the number of sociometric choices made by an individual and his frequency of leaving his door open (Lawton & Simon, 1968). Thus, there do appear to be some predictable relationships between spatial variables and the older person behaving in both active and passive roles.

A major issue awaiting further study in the area of housing is the joint variation of individual and environment in determining outcome. Almost nothing is known about the specifics of neighborhood, siting, architecture, suprapersonal environment, on-site services, and administrative milieu as they influence satisfaction, morale, and other aspects of well-being.

Studies of Relocation

A number of studies of mortality and morbidity presumably attributable to the physical relocation of older people have now been conducted; this issue was reviewed extensively by Blenkner (1967). Since there are basic similarities in structure among many of them, they are most easily summarized in tabular form, as in Table 1. Section A lists studies that have found some evidence of excess mortality among relocated groups, as compared to nonrelocated groups. The Jasnau (1967) study is very gross in comparing only the total hospital's over-65 population death rate during the year of many transfers with the rate during the year before such transfers. Otherwise, all studies utilize some comparison with nonrelocated groups— either the previous institutional mortality experience or the death rate among nonrelocated control subjects. It is worth noting that the admission policies of many institutions have changed considerably over the past 10 to 15 years, so that sicker individuals are now being admitted. Accordingly, we must keep in mind that making the comparison between mortality among earlier years' less ill people and the mortality of the sicker contemporary relocatees would inflate the chance of demonstrating relocation mortality.

While there does seem to be a recurrent finding of excess mortality, the special-risk groups identified by the different studies (see column labeled "Excess mortality rate" in Table 1) appear to vary considerably. For example, Killian (1970) found almost 10 years' age difference between his subjects who died and those who lived, while only scattered age effects, if any, have been reported by others. It would seem fairly clear from looking at the same column that patients with psychosis, brain syndrome, poor mental status, and poor physical functioning were subject to the relocation mortality effect. However, as Markus (1970) pointed out, in any of the studies using earlier mortality experience as the control condition, the characteristics predicting mortality among relocatees (when not also compared in nonrelocated control groups) may be only those that predispose to death in all populations, relocated or not, unless the same characteristics were known and measured at two points in time for both relocated and comparison subjects. Age and sex are likely to be the only modifier variables identifiable from past records; most comparisons in such studies were made for age- and sex-specific mortality rates. The sufficiently controlled predictors of excess mortality (see Footnote a, Table 1) all suffer from failure to be replicated in more than one study or by being contradictory to findings in other studies, except for the one predictor physical status. This predictor was to some extent validated by both Shahinian, Goldfarb, and Turner (1966) and Killian (1970) in his "ambulation" variable.

Added significance to the physical health variable is provided in Section B, which summarizes the three relocation studies that showed no excess mortality. The relocated subjects of Miller and Lieberman (1965) and Lawton and Yaffe (1970) were in considerably better health than those in studies showing a mortality effect, and those of Lieberman, Tobin, and Slover (1971) were especially chosen for their rehabilitation potential. There is no doubt that the preponderance of the data favors the risk hypothesis, especially among physically and mentally vulnerable people. However, methodology improvements such as substituting the longitudinal control-group design for institutional mortality experience are necessary to establish firmly the existence of the relocation effect. Subgroup risks plainly require more exploration also.

The studies in Sections B and C of Table 1 point to other issues worthy of exploration. Almost all identify possible negative changes other than death to which relocated groups may be subject. Miller and Lieberman (1965) found depression prior to the move to be associated with further negative change after relocation. Kral, Grad, and Berenson (1968), using relocated subjects as their own controls, found biochemical changes that followed relocation and were more marked in men and in psychotics. Lieberman et al. (1971) found environmental characteristics that were differentially associated with decline among 26 nursing and boarding homes to which mental patients were discharged. Reimanis (1967) showed that the mere expectation of change may occasion a negative psychological reaction. His hospitalized veterans' responses on an anomie scale rose after an announcement of their old age center's closing and subsided significantly following the rescinding of that order.

One of the major types of involuntary relocation to which older people are subject has been occasioned by urban and highway renewal programs. The major work in this area (Niebanck, 1965) unfortunately presents change data only on income and rental, both of which worsen considerably after relocation. The Kasteler, Gray, and Carruth (1968) study, noted in Table 1, is the only source of empirical evidence regarding the impact of this type of relocation; it suffers from being cross sectional rather than longitudinal, and

TABLE 1

Studies of Relocation of Older People: Designs and Results of Empirical Studies

Study	Type of experimental subjects	Type of control subjects	Type of relocation	Postrelocation interval	Excess mortality rate	Diminished mortality rate
Studies showing excess Mortality rate						
Aleksandrowicz (1961)	Aged mental hospital patients	Institutional mortality rate re 3-month prelocation	Ward fire forcing transfer to another ward	3 months	All subjects—no subgroup analysis	
Aldrich and Mendkoff (1963); Aldrich (1964)	Nursing home patients	Institutional 10-year mortality rate	Closing of institution, transfer to other nursing home	12 months	All subjects, psychotics more so, no clear age effect[a]	
Jasnau (1967)	Aged mental hospital patients	Institutional mortality rates, year before transfer versus year of transfer	Transfer from one ward to another, same hospital	Not specified	Not a longitudinal study—gross death rates for all patients 65+ compared	
Shahinian, Goldfarb, and Turner (1968)	Nursing home patients	Nontransferred and normally transferred patients (not matched) in other institutions	Closing of institutions, transfer to other nursing home	12 months	Poor mental status, physically impaired,[a] CBS,[a] motor impaired,[a] no sex or age effect[a]	Physically well[a]

Markus, Blenkner, Bloom, and Downs (1970, 1971)	Home for aged patients	Institutional 15-year mortality	Move to new building	9 months and 12 months	Males 75+,[a] females 75-79,[a] physically dependent subjects under age 75, poor mental status	Field-independent,[a] physically unlimited, females 80+[a]
Killian (1970)	Aged mental hospital patients	Nontransferred matched on four relevant characteristics	Transfer to other hospital, transfer to community	4 months	Older subjects and nonambulatory older subjects[a]	Ambulatory[a]
Markus (1970)	Home for aged patients	Institutional 15-year mortality	Move to new building		Females,[a] males over 80,[a] low physical functioning	
Studies showing no relocation mortality effect						
Miller and Lieberman (1965)	Healthy home for aged patients	Institutional 15-year mortality rate	Closing of institution, transfer to other home for aged	18 weeks	Depression at premove interview predicted rated "negative change"	
Lawton and Yaffe (1970)	Apartment building tenants	Matched community residents, matched tenants of 18+-months residence	Community residents voluntarily moving to new building	12 months	Relocated subjects more likely both to improve and decline in health, more control subjects unchanged	

TABLE 1

Studies of Relocation of Older People: Designs and Results of Empirical Studies (Continued)

Study	Type of experimental subjects	Type of control subjects	Type of relocation	Postrelocation interval	Excess mortality rate
Lieberman, Tobin, and Slover (1971)	Aged mental hospital patients, selected as "manageable" in community	Nondischarged aged patients short-term effects. No control group for 12-month relocation effect	Discharge to nursing or boarding homes	15 weeks	Decline in composite index of behavioral adequacy and in health.
				12 months	Low (2%) death rate, but no control comparisons.
					Decline predicted by cold, dehumanized, dependency-fostering environments
Miscellaneous relocation studies					
Reimanis (1967)	Male Veterans Administration domiciliary residents	None	Announcement of institution's closing (threat, not actual)	Up to 5 years	Anomie scores rose after announcement of closing, dropped after order rescinded
Kasteler, Gray, and Carruth (1968)	Relocated community residents 55 and over	Probability sample of nonrelocated community residents 55 and over	Involuntary relocation for highway building in past 5 years	23 months	Personal adjustment on Activities and Attitudes (Burgess et al., 1948), better for nonrelocated
Kral, Grad, and Berenson (1968)	Home for aged residents	None	"Relocation" unspecified		Adrenocortical signs of stress and high death rate among males and psychotics, no control comparisons

Note. Last two columns indicate results.
aCharacteristic was measured for both relocated and control subjects.

from including in one small experimental group subjects who had experienced relocation at any time during the past five years.

Finally, some comment is indicated on the possibility of a positive relocation effect. Less than the expected mortality rate was found for the relocation subjects, as compared to nonrelocated, who were rated with good prognosis for remaining life-span (Shahinian et al., 1966). The females over age 80 of Markus, Blenkner, Bloom, and Downs (1971) had a lower than expected mortality rate, as did the ambulatory patients of Killian (1970). Lawton and Yaffe (1970) found that more of their new housing tenants experienced an increase in health after the first year than comparison groups (though more also declined). This subgroup was initially no healthier than those who declined. These, at present, merely suggestive findings are consistent with the idea that the stimulation provided by a new environment may facilitate, rather than impede, adaptive behavior in people able to cope with the new situation.

Institutions for the Aged

Institutionalization represents a major total change in one's pattern of living, certainly a more radical change than does new housing. We are no nearer to unraveling which effects may be ascribed to physical and which to social changes than we are in the case of housing. Although only a small percentage of aged individuals are housed in institutions, no review of the ecology of the aging process would be complete without a consideration of this specialized setting. The following brief section will consider the impact of institutionalization on residents and discuss some specific effects of environmental factors. More comprehensive reviews of the social-psychological aspects of institutions may be found in Bennett and Nahemow (1965a), Lieberman (1969), and Lawton (1970b).

Lieberman (1969) discussed in depth the issue of impact of institutionalization on the individual. He reviewed the large amount of data showing institutionalized older people to be less competent than those in the community. However, he found no studies satisfactorily separating negative institutional impact from either self-selection or administrative selection as explanations of the poorer status of the resident of institutions. Lieberman, Prock, and Tobin (1968) compared matched groups of (a) community residents who had not applied to institutions, (b) applicants on the waiting list to enter institutions, and (c) people who had lived in the institution from one to three years. They found, as others have, that those in institutions were significantly poorer in various cognitive, affective, and social functions than community residents of similar demographic and health status. The waiting-list group was similarly impaired in relation to the community group. This negative effect could have been due either to the anxiety consequent to the process of applying and waiting for admission, or to selective factors determining their application to the institution but not controlled in the matching. The other comparison, between the waiting-list and the institutionalized subjects, revealed an interesting pattern of greater anxiety in the waiting-list subjects, but greater cognitive impairment, body preoccupation, and less emotional reactivity in the institutionalized subjects. The authors concluded that at least some of the effects generally thought to be produced by institutionalization are characteristic of people during the process of waiting to enter the institution. Further, at least for those who survive the first year, some adaptation occurs so as to decrease anxiety, though other negative features persist and may increase after institutionalization. It is important to note, however, that the necessary longitudinal data have not yet been reported that would enable us to state conclusively that these differences represent changes due to institutionalization. Nor do we have a satisfactory answer to the question of whether lifelong adaptational style or earlier stress experiences may differentiate those who enter institutions from those who do not. Lieberman (1969) reviewed a few studies suggesting this possibility. Bennett and Nahemow (1965b) conducted a two-year follow-up of the adjustment of residents in a home for the aged. They found that even after two years there was a marked continuity of personal style. Those who had participated in groups and had had frequent contact with relatives and friends before they entered were found to participate more in the life of the home two years after entry. Thus, we find, not surprisingly, that different people respond differently to institutions.

Of even greater potential meaningfulness to treatment technology is the definition of institutional qualities associated with favorable or unfavorable patient outcomes. Gottesman, Quarterman, and Cohn (see pp. 378–427, this volume) review particular institutional treatment programs that have significantly affected the well-being of residents. Other stimulus qualities of institutions have been defined (reviewed by Lawton, 1970b), but have not been put to a definitive test of impact: "milieu" (Beattie & Bullock, 1963; Bennett & Nahemow, 1965a); physical structure (Pincus & Wood, 1970; size (Anderson, Holmberg, Schneider, & Stone, 1969; Beattie & Bullock, 1963; Greenwald & Linn, 1970); and administrator's characteristics

(Anderson et al., 1969). Gottesman and his associates are at present conducting a multi-institution study that will relate these and other institutional characteristics to a presumed indicator of quality, the amount and type of services received by patients. Definitive information on differential impact, however, requires longitudinal patient evaluation in order to control for the initial characteristics of patients being treated in different institutions.

Exactly this issue was attacked by Turner, Tobin, and Lieberman (1972) in an attempt to predict whether some personal adaptational styles would be more congruent with life in a set of three institutions than others. They followed waiting-list subjects through a year of institutional life and determined that those who were more "intact" at follow-up were those who had been predicted to adjust well in terms of several personality similarities to "successfully" adapted old-timers. The strongest predictor of intactness was a "vigorous, hostile-narcissistic" personality style.

This study dealt with the matching of personality to a single-dimensional environment. The same group in another study of the placement of elderly mental hospital patients into nursing homes (Lieberman, Tobin, & Slover, 1971) took into account both individual and environmental variation in predicting behavioral and psychological outcome. Site visits by a skilled judge to the 26 placement institutions resulted in nine ratings of their environments in terms of such qualities as warmth, physical attractiveness, cue richness, etc. Overall, personal characteristics did not predict outcome significantly, while environmental characteristics did. Decline was associated with low environmental warmth, fostering of dependency, and health care adequacy. The interactive quality of personal and environmental characteristics in determining decline could not be tested because there were relatively few mismatchings, as defined by pairings of personal and environmental characteristics of high versus low congruity. On the basis of the test data, however, they classified their subjects as responsive or unresponsive to their environments. They hypothesized that the high-responsive subjects' well-being would be predicted better by environmental characteristics than would that of low-responsive subjects. This was, in fact, the case: the best-predicting variables for high responders were environmental, and the best-predicting variables for low responders were personal characteristics.

Kahana (1971) tested directly several congruence hypotheses among residents of three homes for aged. Congruence was related to morale in two of the three, though the particular aspects of congruence differed among homes. The dimensions of person–environment congruence showing the most relationships to morale were the domains of needs/opportunities for privacy and needs/opportunities for impulse expression.

Relatively few studies have been made of explicitly spatial characteristics of institutions. Kahana and Kahana (1970) manipulated experimentally the age homogeneity of mental hospital wards to which newly admitted aged patients were assigned. Patients placed on age-integrated wards improved more by cognitive and social interaction criteria than those placed in age-segregated wards.

Social relationships among residents in a home for the aged were found to be facilitated by proximity of rooms (Friedman, 1966). Lawton, Liebowitz, and Charon (1970) examined the effects of the experimental renovation of a small area for chronic brain syndrome patients from a situation of two four-person rooms to that of private bedroom areas opening onto a small social space with an open view of the hall. The effect was to increase the range of movement of patients, but to decrease the amount of staff–patient interaction. Sommer and Ross (1958) found that social interaction among geriatric mental hospital patients was increased by rearranging the seating in a dayroom from traditional perimeter style to the sides of square four-person tables.

In mental hospitals the provision of privacy through single-occupancy bedrooms was found, paradoxically, to be associated with increased social behavior (Ittelson, Proshansky, & Rivlin, 1970). The expressed need for privacy, that is, preference for single or double rooms in a home for aged, was found to be determined by a variety of conditions (Lawton & Bader, 1970). Greater wish for a private room occurred among older, as opposed to younger, community residents; middle-class institutional residents; those already occupying single rooms; and under the hypothetical condition of good, as contrasted with poor, health. Pincus and Wood (1970) defined and measured four dimensions of institutions (privacy, freedom, integration, and resources), each of which had a physical aspect. The privacy and resources dimensions of eight institutions were related to residents' perceptions and self-reported behavior related to these two dimensions. The satisfaction reported by patients in relation to the privacy, freedom, and integration of their institutions paralleled the patients' reports of their behavior in availing themselves of these institutional qualities.

One can thus easily see that only a bare beginning has been made in exploring the inner responses of patients, or variations in their behavior, as a consequence of institutional features. The system properties of functioning institutions have been described (Harel,

1970, Lawton, 1970b); multivariate analytic techniques are necessary to the analysis of the relationship between institutional characteristics and patient outcome.

Migration

The move into specialized housing for older people, institutionalization, and urban renewal are three special cases involving the
physical relocation of older people. The general phenomenon of
migration is usually studied from a sociological perspective. Such
moves obviously may have psychological motivations and consequences, and the total phenomenon is clearly transactional and
therefore relevant to the ecological psychology of later life.

Most of our information on migration is derived from census
data (the latest available at the time of writing being from 1960).
As summarized by Lenzer (1965), the aged population is less mobile
than the general population. Sixty-four percent of the aged respondents lived in the dwelling where they had lived five years previously,
as compared to only 50% of the young people. However, for those
age 75 and over, mobility sharply increased to 46%, reflecting at
least partially disruptions due to decline in health, changes in family
composition due to marriages and death, etc. In a single year, about
10% of older people change residence.

Relatively few older people move to remote locations. Only
4% moved to another state between 1955 and 1960, a rate less than
half that of the entire population. Florida, California, Arizona, and
Texas had the largest net gains of older people through interstate
moves, although these same states gained similarly from the migration of people of all ages.

Lenzer (1965) noted that high mobility was seen among
unemployed people still in the labor force, low-income families,
separated or divorced people, and household members who are not
heads of household or their spouses. A study of the mobility of
residents of the Los Angeles area (Goldscheider, Van Arsdol, &
Sabagh, undated) suggested that mobility in this area was also high
among those in lower status occupations, those with less education,
among renters, and among those with an earlier history of mobility.

Considerably less is known about the reasons why older people
move, their feelings about moving, and the extent to which moves
are anticipated. If severe dislocation may be associated with death,
there is every reason to ask the question as to whether other types
of moves have less severe psychological and behavioral consequences.

Only one study has followed a substantial number of the same individuals over a one-year period to ascertain the extent to which their housing plans were realized. Goldscheider et al. (undated) determined that the older people, as compared to younger, in a sample of almost 1,000 respondents were less likely to express either the wish to move or plans to move within the coming year. In their one-year follow-up of actual behavior, their general conclusion was that younger people were much more successful (61%) in realizing their wishes and plans to move (fulfillment rate) than were older people (37%). Another report from this study (Goldscheider, 1966) shows that among their small sample of nonwhites, the desire to move was greater than among whites, but the latter were three times as successful in actually moving. However, among people with neither the wish nor a plan to move, both younger and older people were highly successful in maintaining stability (around 90%). Goldscheider (1966) reported that dissatisfaction with neighborhood and dwelling unit were the major reasons for older people's moves, as compared with the predominantly economic and occupational reasons characterizing the moves of the population at large (Rossi, 1955). Lawton, Kleban, and Carlson (1971) studied the wish to move and actual moving in residents of an urban slum. In general, the most adequate people wished to move, but very few predictors of actual change of residence over a two-year period were found. A very low fulfillment rate was found, as compared to the sample reported by Goldscheider et al.

One gets the impression that while most people are satisfied with their housing, the options open for older people who wish to change are very few. Since relatively few older people do realize their wishes and plans, it is reasonable to assume that many of them will accept new living and housing arrangements that are less than satisfactory. Thus, there are two problem segments:

1. Those who wish and need badly to move and are faced with undesirable alternatives. These people include those relocated by urban renewal, those who are forced to move because of role losses or changes in household composition, or those who live in deteriorating neighborhoods. Since economic factors frequently limit the available options, vulnerable groups such as blacks, the rural poor, and the physically ill frequently end up in worse environments after moving.

2. Those who do not wish to move and who adapt to undesirable and ultimately self-defeating living situations. Their lack of desire to move may easily be an expression of low competence or

dependence (as suggested by Lawton et al., 1971) or a compulsion to avoid wishing for something that is unlikely to eventuate.

On the other hand, the results of the migration of relatively competent people moving of their own volition into environments of their choice seem to be relatively positive, as reviewed in the housing section. The psychological and behavioral results of moves into normal age-integrated communities rather than specialized housing have not been studied, however.

Transportation

As the process of aging continues into later years, the availability of transportation becomes more critical for continuing maintenance in the community. According to Taves and Shmelzer (1970), "Transportation is still mistaken for other problems. Problems labeled nutrition or health delivery or social withdrawal are often really a lack of transportation [p. 1]." Carp (1970) found that many older persons in San Antonio who mentioned the need for medical, recreational, instructional, or religious services explained that the problem was not the absence of such services but the lack of transportation. She maintained that part of the social isolation of which retired persons complain is due to the unavailability or high cost of transportation which would enable them to get where other people are. She found that the elderly were more likely to be driven by others than to drive themselves and this left many dependent upon others for their participation in activities. In San Antonio the bus is the only form of public transportation available; fully 40% of the retired persons studied never rode a bus. Those who had many complaints about the transportation system were precisely those who used buses the most. The buses were not within easy access from their homes, did not go where they wanted to go, and ran infrequently. Consequently, public transportation was grossly underutilized.

Bourg (1970) studied mobility patterns of the elderly in Nashville, Tennessee. He found that easy access to transportation was a critical link in the ability of elderly persons to remain functioning members of society. Because transportation was inadequate, dependence upon others was fostered. Bourg concluded that "the elderly with low income tend to have smaller behavioral maps than those with high income if we control for living alone and assistance from family [p. 17]."

Nahemow and Kogan (1971) found that older people who wished to make use of the facilities of New York City were almost totally dependent upon mass transportation. Automobiles were made available for visits to children and other relatives, but for little else. Consequently, most activities that older people engaged in were local. Most people walked a good deal both to run errands and to "get out." The average person rarely left the immediate neighborhood, living within a constricted social space.

Transportation systems have usually been considered the exclusive province of transportation engineers and others with little interest in human behavior. However, interest in the impact of the physical environment on behavior has been developing rapidly. A focal point has been concern by social scientists with the transportation system as well as a new humanistic orientation on the part of builders and traffic managers (Craik, 1969; Hammel, 1970; Markowitz, 1970; Nash & Hille, 1968).

In a paper submitted to the Committee on Science and Astronautics of the United States House of Representatives, Webber and Angel (1970) stated:

> Transportation facilities, like cities, have almost no value that is intrinsic to the facilities themselves. Insofar as they are positively valued, their values are instrumental to the accomplishment of purpose other than transport. . . . If transport has value only as it facilitates the transactional business of the social economy and as it satisfied other social purposes—then it must follow that the tests for transport goodness must be external, social effects [p. 25].

This is a critical point which is often overlooked. Cost accounting criteria are necessary but not sufficient. In a complex, urban society, transportation is the key to social integration (Irwin, 1970; Webber, 1963).

Community and Neighborhood Studies

Ecological studies using the community as the unit of analysis date back to the work of the Chicago group of sociologists (Park, Burgess, & McKenzie, 1925) who developed a body of theory and new methodologies. Typically, though, they did not consider the elderly as the primary focus. For example, Gist and Fava (1964) listed "population change" among their five ecological elements that may produce changes in the natural areas of the city. While they see the proportion of elderly persons in a community as having a critical impact on that community, they do not deal with the community's impact on the elderly individual.

Schooler (1969), in a national survey, hypothesized that environment was related to psychological adjustment by way of the intervening variable of social behavior. That is, environment affects the amount of social interaction engaged in by the older person, which in turn affects his morale. In a large multivariate analysis of factor dimensions representing these three classes of variables, morale was found to be correlated with amount of social interaction. However, when environmental factors, such as distance to facilities, judged convenience of location, and accessibility to supportive services, were partialed out, the relationship between social behavior and morale decreased. Low but significant relationships between environmental variables and morale remained after partialing out social factors. The author suggested that environmental factors may be related to morale through perceptual and cognitive processes, rather than through their facilitating or obstructing of social behavior. The environmental variables used by Schooler were defined in terms of their relevance to the individual, rather than in spatial terms such as community, neighborhood, census tract, block, etc. In this section we will consider those investigations that relate the characteristics of the community or the neighborhood to the characteristics of the individuals living there.

Studies of community characteristics. Barker and Barker (1961) conducted an ecological study comparing the elderly in two communities, "Midwest" in America and "Yoredale" in England. Each community was described in terms of its behavior settings, that is, settings defined by the locations where people congregate outside of their homes and the standing pattern of behavior that occurs in them. The authors obtained the following measures: (a) the number of behavior settings occupied by individuals 65 years or over, (b) the number of hours a person spent in these settings in the course of a year, and (c) the capacity in which a person occupied a behavior setting, that is, the centrality of his role (leaders were considered more central to a particular behavior setting than onlookers).

The two towns were compared on these dimensions. It was found that the Midwest elderly were involved in more behavioral settings than those in Yoredale. Midwest residents of all ages spent more time in the town's public behavior settings than did Yoredale residents. They noted, however, that in both communities the environments of older persons "regress" in the sense that older people are less active in town life than persons in their middle years. The Barkers (1961) attributed the differences in the rate of regression in the two communities to the different social dynamics of the communities in question. Midwest citizens, they feel, are under more pressure than their English counterparts to participate. They feel that this difference in pressure is exhibited with special clarity in deviant groups, such as old people and children. Thus, the Barkers found a strong and predictable relationship between the expectational system of a town and the behavior of its inhabitants.

Taietz (1970) examined the relationships between the structural properties of incorporated communities and the social involvement and morale of individuals residing in them. Taietz considered the community the most viable unit of analysis to use for such an examination. He stated:

One of the distinctive features of the present study is the manner in which it makes use of the community as a variable and as a unit of analysis. We assumed that the community was particularly important in the study of the role and status of the aged, for with advancing age there is a displacement of attachment to work to an attachment to other institutions. We defined the community as a territorially based social organization which is organized for the production of goods, services, facilities, and gratifications [p. 9].

According to this conceptualization, a community is a unit that has primarily economic relevance. A city neighborhood would thus not qualify as a community. The neighborhood was rejected as a unit of analysis because it can be indexed only by overlapping and sometimes conflicting criteria and because of the difficulties experienced by investigators who attempted to measure neighborhood boundaries.

Starting with a sample of 144 communities in New York State, Taietz (1970) selected a sample of communities differing in size and complexity. Seventy-eight variables were selected for inclusion in a factor analysis. These included such variables as population size, median age, mobility, quality of housing, variety of medical specialists in practice, types of physical structures, and transportation.

Four major factors were found that described these communities: (a) structural complexity (in general, large communities were high in structural complexity and small communities low), (b) socioeconomic status, which related primarily to income, (c) political and educational homogeneity, and (d) professional concentration. Dependent variables were derived from individual interviews with elderly persons in a subsample of 32 communities; subjects were asked about their participation in formal voluntary organizations, knowledge about them, morale, and community integration.

The data were analyzed by means of a stepwise regression analysis technique in which communities were first classified into

(a) rural, (b) small urban places, (c) independent cities, and (d) central cities and suburbs. Regression analysis techniques were applied separately for each type of community. Clusters of variables were added successively, beginning with individual background characteristics such as education and marital status, followed by social behavior, attitudes and morale, and finally the community structure factors. Thus, the increment in variance attributable to each successively added group of variables was ascertained.

Separate analyses were performed for each size of community, with complex relationships being found between environmental factors and the dependent variables. For example, it was found that community structure variables increased the explained variance in participation in formal voluntary organizations slightly more in rural communities than in others. However, looking at the cognitive element (knowledge of senior citizen centers), Taietz found that structural variables had little impact in rural communities (after individual characteristics were accounted for), but a considerable impact in both small urban places and central cities. Thus, the importance of environmental factors was demonstrated, although understanding the pattern of their effects requires further study.

Studies of neighborhood characteristics. To be sure, the concept of neighborhood is ambiguous, and yet firmly resists other better-definable substitute concepts. We feel that the neighborhood is a very important ecological unit for the study of the elderly. Lee (1970) delineated the concept of a neighborhood in a number of planning surveys in Great Britain. He said of the social scientist studying a neighborhood:

> He cannot capture it (the neighborhood) whole in the net of a single concept. If he isolates it as a piece of territory, he often finds little or no correspondence with human behavior; if he concentrates instead on social relationships he finds that these do not synchronize with geography. Yet he persists in thinking that the two components are somehow crucially interdependent [p. 349].

Lee found some consensus among residents' conceptions of "neighborhood," and some correspondence between conception and geography. He concluded:

> Neighborhood . . . remains a highly salient phenomenon of urban living. people move about the local urban environment to satisfy a wide range of needs with minimum effort. . . . Each neighborhood schema is unique, but is related in lawful ways to the physical environment and to the personality of its possessor. . . . More friendships, club memberships and shopping links are formed in the locality than elsewhere and their number is correlated with the physical span of schemata [p. 367].

Lee found that there was substantial agreement concerning the dimensions of the neighborhood schemata and that the area generally encompassed in the "neighborhood" was usually less than a half mile radius.

The study of the travel of the elderly by Nahemow and Kogan (1971) showed that the urban elderly spend most of their time in the immediate neighborhood. When 780 New Yorkers over 65 years of age were asked about what they did each time they left the house during a two-day interval, 56% of the trips mentioned were walking trips, particularly for local shopping. Trips that necessitated leaving the neighborhood were infrequently undertaken. Relatives, for example, were likely to be visited only once a month, whereas friends, who more often lived nearby, were likely to be visited more frequently. The average person estimated that he could walk about nine blocks to the store without becoming tired. We find it particularly interesting that the radius an older person can walk to the store without becoming tired is roughly equivalent to the area that Lee found corresponding to "neighborhood." It seems that after retirement many people become more neighborhood and less community oriented.

Rosenberg's (1970) study of age and poverty used a narrow and geographic definition of neighborhood—the city block. He was interested in the relationship between poverty and social isolation, predicting that those individuals who were in congruent environments, that is, surrounded by people like themselves, would be less isolated than those who were cut off from "their own kind." He found that the poor and the solvent were differentially sensitive to separate aspects of their neighborhoods. The solvent were more responsive in their social behavior to the socioeconomic aspects of the neighborhood context than the poorer older men were. In contrast, the social isolation of the poor seemed to be more affected by the personal characteristics of the residents of the neighborhood, such as the age of the people living there or the presence of married people in the neighborhood. Thus, it appears that the effect of neighborhood context is critically dependent upon the salience to the individual of the particular characteristic of neighborhood studied.

Lawton, Kleban, and Singer (1971) interviewed 115 elderly Jewish residents of a deteriorating neighborhood in Philadelphia. The area had changed markedly over a 30-year period, so that these elderly people were a distinct racial minority; for the older Jewish residents there was a high degree of what Rosenberg (1962) called "contextual dissonance." Predictor variables for feelings of well-being were obtained from three domains: demographic, health, and environmental factors. Stepwise multiple-regression analyses showed a significant independent contribution of environmental factors to the prediction of neighborhood motility and interviewer ratings of alertness (Lawton & Kleban, 1971). These aged residents were also compared with similar residents of other communities and were found to have lower morale, less money, poorer health, and less contact with friends and neighbors than residents of other areas. While their low state of well-being may have been due to unfavorable neighborhood factors, it might also have been due to self-selection, inasmuch as these subjects constituted a residual group who had not moved out with the Jewish majority.

Rosow's (1967) well-known study of friendship patterns of older people in Cleveland defined the subject's immediate neighborhood as the apartment building where he lived. He found that a relatively high concentration of older people in the apartment building was a critical variable in determining the amount of social interaction the elderly tenant has. The effect was more marked in working-class than in middle-class people. That is, middle-class tenants were more likely to have friends living distant from them and were therefore more independent of the local context.

In conclusion, we find studies of the elderly in the community few but important in demonstrating the effects of environmental context on variables such as social interaction and morale. In general, the more easily interpretable results were obtained from studies of smaller analytic units such as the neighborhood. Further exploration of the interaction of the individual with the community and other larger structures is clearly needed.

AN ECOLOGICAL THEORY OF ADAPTIVE BEHAVIOR AND AGING

Having examined environmental dimensions, the apprehended environment, individual environmental information-processing characteristics, and the results of a number of studies of older people behaving in specifiable environments, it is clear that a theoretical framework is required to encompass the growing body of information in this field. The following section is the skeleton of a theory of man–environment transactions. We have sketched the model rather broadly with the full expectation of substantial revision.

Reduced competence, a frequent concomitant of aging, is the occasion for retrenchment. The attempt to conserve resources leads to the utilization of more primitive cognitive styles: field dependence, leveling, repression, external control, homeostasis seeking, and preference for simplicity. Field dependence and an external perceived locus of control relieve the individual of the task of searching for appropriate behavioral modes within himself. Leveling, repression, routinization, and simplistic cognition have the effect of reducing the number of external cues to be discriminated. Thus, stability is achieved through cognitive styles that reduce the internal and external demands on the individual for complex response.

There appears to be an attempt to reduce tension through simplification—taking the path of least resistance. While minimization of internal and external cues for action may be adaptive in that it prevents the individual from involving himself in problems too complex to handle, the behavior may also be maladaptive. A response can be withheld to the point where the individual has no control over the environmental forces impinging on him. His vulnerability is thus increased by both his inability to discriminate adequately among environmental cues and his tendency to minimize those that he does perceive. The coping mechanisms that the individual falls back on to permit environmental mastery no longer work; in fact, they may increase his vulnerability. Thus, tension-reducing response patterns now become tension increasing.

Lawton and Simon (1968) suggested the "environmental docility" hypothesis as a way to conceptualize differential changes in vulnerability. As the competence of the individual decreases, the proportion of behavior attributable to environmental, as contrasted with personal, characteristics increases. That is, the less competent are more vulnerable—not vulnerable in terms of receptor sensitivity, but in terms of their behavior being controlled by environmental, rather than intrapersonal, forces. This hypothesis was formulated on the basis of their findings that decreased health and lower social status increased dependence on proximate neighbors. Rosow's (1967) findings are interpretable within the same framework, including the important fact that local dependence is less among middle-class than among working-class people. Mangum's (1971) contrast between higher and lower income subjects in predicting adjustment from environmental factors is totally consistent with this suggestion.

The motivational theories of Berlyne (1960) and Fiske and Maddi (1961) have called attention to the inadequacy of tension reduction as an explanation of all behavior and have led to a productive search for evidence of tension-creating behavior in humans. Some of the cognitive response styles (e.g., scanning, sharpening, sensitization, and preference for novelty or complexity) appear to be stimulus-processing catalysts leading to activation, or to change from a previously established adaptation level (Helson, 1964). The great missing link in psychological knowledge about the ecology of aging is knowledge of the conditions under which continuing states of homeostasis, as contrasted with activation, (a) are sought by the aged individual, (b) are facilitated by the contemporary environment of the aged person, and (c) lead to adaptive behavior and internal states of well-being.

The transactional model that we are presenting in order to relate the aging individual to his environment uses the following components:

1. *Degree of individual competence.* This is conceived as a diverse collection of abilities residing within the individual, which differ among themselves and vary over time between minimum and maximum limits that are specific to the individual. Theoretically one could assess a person's degree of general competence, but it is much more in accord with the facts of human nature to characterize competence in terms of seperate aspects such as cognitive ability, psychological adjustment, physical health, or other qualities.

2. *Environmental press.* Environmental press were defined by Murray (1938) as forces in the environment that together with an individual need evoke a response.[1] Press may be fruitfully differentiated, characterized, and scaled in terms of their normative stress-producing properties, problematic qualities, demand character, supportive character, and so on. Press are neutral, in that their positive or negative quality is defined by the interacting individual, rather than residing intrinsically in the environment. Environmental press will fluctuate from time to time, as the environment itself alters momentarily; similarly, the individual's need and competence vary over time.

3. *Adaptive behavior.* This is what is usually thought of as the outer manifestation of individual competence, although in our view it is one resultant of the individual–environment transaction. What is adaptive is defined both by social norms and by values based upon self-actualization criteria.

4. *Affective responses.* These are the inner aspect of the individual–environment transaction. While affective responses include aesthetic and other evaluative attitudes toward the environment, they

---

[1]Murray (1938) distinguished between alpha and beta press: alpha referring to the objective aspect of environmental demand and beta referring to the subjective aspect. We are here referring to what Murray called "alpha press."

are meant to include much more broadly any internal emotional states that are involved in the environment–behavior transaction.

5. *Adaptation level.* According to Helson (1964), individual receptor processes tend to establish an adaptation level to external stimuli such that a stimulus of a given magnitude is perceived as neither strong nor weak; the magnitude of the stimulus perceived as indifferent depends not only upon its contemporary value, but also upon the context in which it appears and upon the weighted mean of all the perceiver's previous experiences with similar stimuli. While the adaptation level concept was initially formulated to deal with psychophysical phenomena, we intend that it refer more generally to affective, perceptual, and cognitive experience.

Wohlwill (1966) suggested an extension of adaptation level theory that states the "optimization principle." According to this theory, stimuli that deviate *in either direction* from the adaptation level are experienced with positive affect up to a limiting point beyond the adaptation level; positive affect then decreases and again becomes negative as the stimulus increases or decreases further beyond the adaptation level.

Figure 1 presents this model in schematic form. The strength of press is shown on the abscissa and the degree of individual competence is shown on the ordinate. A point on the schema locates an individual of a given level of competence coping with environmental press of a given magnitude. This point's location also implies behavior and affect that may be characterized in terms of adaptiveness and positiveness, respectively. The far left- and right-hand areas of Figure 1 denote areas where no combination of personal competence and press can result in positive affect or adaptive behavior.

The diagonal line labeled AL represents a theoretical mean adaption level for all individuals at a given level of competence, averaged over the particular environmental press at issue. Individuals of a given level of competence would be distributed normally to the right and left of the AL point for that level; their AL at different points in time would fluctuate according to the conditions elaborated in Helson's theory.

Positive affect, a feeling of comfort within one's environment, occurs near adaptation level. This is true for the region in which the environmental demands are both slightly lower and slightly higher than adaptation level. Wohlwill's (1966) theory would add a symmetrical gradient whereby positive affect would increase as the stimulus departed from adaptation level, but begin to decrease as it approached the "tolerable affect-marginal behavior" segment.

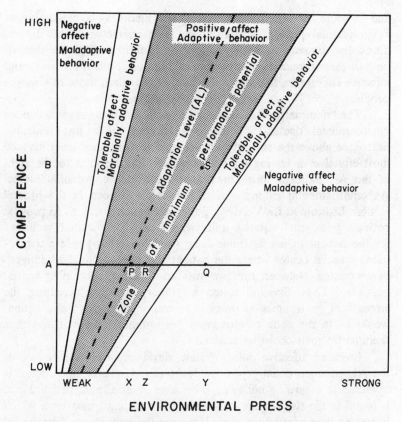

Fig. 1. Diagrammatic representation of the behavioral and affective outcomes of person–environment transactions.

The low point of environmental demand might occur in sensory deprivation situations, the high point in many types of stressful or overloading situations. Figure 1 makes clear that individuals of high competence have a wide latitude of capacity to interact with the environment in ways that maximize adaptive behavior and positive affect, as indicated in the upper areas of the two shaded segments. Relatively few high-competence individuals will show the breakdowns in behavior or affect that occur beyond adaptation threshold, which are represented by areas to the left and right of the two cross-hatched segments, in the face of excessively low or high environmental demands.

On a behavioral level, it seems clear that the environment of many older people is reduced in complexity, in terms of lowered role demands, less economic freedom, dwindling interpersonal worlds, and in some cases deprived physical surroundings—a weakening of environmental press. Concomitantly, their competence may be reduced by comparison with younger or healthier people. Either or both of these processes may lead to adaptation levels for sensory and affective experience that are significantly lower than those of younger people.

The "minimal goals" approach to rehabilitation suggests that an environmental demand in the neighborhood of a just noticeable difference above the subject's accustomed performance level may be most effective in raising his performance. The segment to the right of the AL indicates this "maximum performance potential" zone. An environmental example of this principle is seen in the Marcel Rivière Institute at La Verriere, designed in such a way as to provide patients with small spatial units which enhance "spatial security" for the patient to use as home base (Sivadon, 1970). He also provided a social center where the patient was exposed to the "danger" of encounter. Between the two was an "insecurity-inducing spatial obstacle." Thus, Sivadon tested his theory that by increasing the strength of environmental press in tolerably small units, the patient would be in the zone of maximum performance potential and thus therapeutic goals could be attained.

From an affective point of view, deviations from either side of the AL produce equally positive responses. However, the region is asymmetric regarding behavior. The zone of maximum performance is found to the right of the AL at an environmental press level which is greater than adaptation level. If we see the individual as motivated to maximize positive affect (Thorndike's law of effect), this may occur by lowering environmental demands. Thus, the individual may accept a situation in which his maximal behavioral potential is not realized.

The dynamic aspects of this system may be illustrated by an individual of Competence A whose AL in terms of Press X is represented by the Point P. Her personal resources (competence) and environmental demands (press) are thus in equilibrium, and her affect and behavior reflect her resultant well-being. Now let us suppose that she has a stronger press imposed on her (forced relocation, for example), which may be represented by the new level of Press Y. The new transactional balance, given no change in competence, is represented by Point Q, which is out of the range of adaptive behavior and positive affect. According to adaptation level theory, a new AL should move to the right from P along the line AQ. However, the Demand Level Y is beyond adaptation threshold, and a new AL cannot be established within the adaptive range. How can the subject's behavior be brought again within the positive outcome zone? Structurally this can be done either by lowering the level of environmental press or by raising the subject's competence. Each of these maneuvers (and their interactions) may be approached either actively or passively from the point of view of the subject. Theoretically, there are four adaptive maneuvers, as indicated in Table 2. Let us take examples of each possibility. Environmental change with the subject assuming a relatively passive role might involve societal intervention, such as agency assistance in finding a new home or in moving. Active effort by the subject to produce environmental change might consist of the individual trying to create a new household consistent with her needs, or in leaving her front door open to signal that she was open to visitation. However, it is clear in the example given that active effort on the part of the individual is only possible when the environmental demand is within the range of potential adaptation. Thus, should relocation force the person to a completely new area in which she has no family or friends available for assistance or social interaction, the likelihood of active effort by the individual is decreased (Fried, 1963). Both active and passive approaches would be meant to reduce environmental stress and assist in reestablishing an adaptation level within the positive outcome range, where ordinary coping is relatively effortless.

Rather than changing the environment, elevation of the subject's competence might be sought. An example where the subject is relatively passive would be an environmental educational program to assist the person to become rapidly socialized to the new environment. Elevation of competence through the subject's own effort would be self-therapy (see pp. 378–427 by Gottesman, Quarterman, & Cohn), or the discovery of new potential within oneself that would enable a positive outcome to emerge even though environmental press remained elevated. Clearly, change and mutual feedback in both competence and environmental press would be the rule, although in

TABLE 2

Adaptive Maneuvers with Active or Passive Individual Roles and Individual or Environmental Points of Application

Point of application	Passive responder	Active initiator
Environment	Social and environmental engineering	The individual redesigns his environment
Individual	Rehabilitation, prosthesis	Self-therapy, growth

general, the environment may be more plastic than individual competence.

If a socially or self-engineered intervention scheme reduced the level of press from Y to Z, the individual with Competence Level A would now be operating at Point R. Point R is within the subject's zone of maximum performance. In this situation, the subject "rises to the occasion." If the environmental press vary within relatively narrow limits around Point Z for a period of time, the individual will establish a new adaptation level. This is more difficult to accomplish than the schema shows, however. Should the variation around Z be too great, the individual will be thrown into his zone of maladaptive behavior from time to time and this will serve to counter the adaptation process.

A newly achieved adaptation level will correspond to a level of performance that is above the previous one. This new level of performance now characterizes the individual's average level and, thus, his level of competence increases. Schematically, he can be represented as occupying a higher level of competence. If this process is repeated by gradual stages, the individual's competence level can ultimately be raised considerably. A carefully engineered series of interventions with controlled timing could ultimately raise the individual to Point B. Now Environmental Press Y would no longer be outside of his range of positive outcome.

The above example began with an environmentally imposed change, although responses to this change were examined with the subject playing both an active and a passive role. The individual at Point P, without major external stimulation, may also initiate change away from AL, as implied by the dual motivational bases for behavior, need reduction and stimulus seeking. A move toward weaker or stronger level of environmental press may be initiated by either the individual or an environmental circumstance.

Tension reduction as a goal of behavior would account to some extent for the active effort sometimes expended by the individual to achieve a state of dependency, or comfort, if we think of positive affect's being engendered by moving toward the left from AL. This process would, for instance, account for a person's tendency to assume a stance of dependence if tempted by an environment with too many supports, or to actively create such an environment.

Stimulus seeking, or tension creation, would begin at AL. At a point far to the left on Line AQ, the cumulative effect of weak environmental press would have discouraged stimulus-seeking behavior. At AL, however, in the absence of competing motivation, the optimization principle may account for the phenomenon of a subject's exploring his environment in search of change. The AL may thus be experienced as mild boredom, while extreme left-hand portions of Line AQ represent pathological boredom, and the central portion of the segment AP represents lassitude.

Looking at lower levels of competence, Figure 1 illustrates a number of phenomena:

1. As individual competence decreases, the area for maladaptive behavior and negative affect increases.

2. Negative outcomes are more likely with excessively strong than with weak environmental press.

3. Positive affect and adaptive behavior are possible only at relatively low levels of environmental demand for the person of low competence.

4. Small changes in level of environmental press in people of low competence may evoke gross changes in quality of affect or behavior. This statement illustrates the environmental docility principle, contrasting the low-competence individual with the high-competence one, who may deal with major changes in press while still functioning adequately.

5. For every individual including those with low competence there is a band in which environmental press are associated with positive outcome, and conversely, a band in which self-initiated or externally initiated action may increase or decrease the environmental demand in his behavioral world.[2]

6. Both stimulus-seeking and self-initiated dependency striving may occur at low levels of competence as well as at high levels.

7. The amount of variation in press permitted around Z to raise adaptation level and simultaneously level of competence is much smaller at the low-competence end of the scale than at the high-competence end.

This model is obviously deficient in its dependence on global concepts such as "competence" or "environmental press." For example, there are all varieties of environmental press, and it makes a great deal of difference whether the stimulus dimension to which the individual reacts is one of intensity, stability, complexity, extensiveness, or patterning. On a macroenvironmental level, the dynamic relationships between individual competence, environment, and behavior will also clearly be different depending upon exactly what

---

[2]This illustrates the minimal goals principle so important to performing good rehabilitative work with groups that have low treatment—effect ceilings, such as the brain damaged.

type of competence or what type of environment one is concerned with. However, the model should assist in the definition of both research ideas and intervention schemes.

One can ascertain that for most levels of supportive environmental services, there are people who are too well and people who are too impaired to function adequately in them. Thus, planners must take into account how wide a range of competence in the potential inhabitants of an environment there can be so as to provide maximum motivation for exercise of skills without overstepping the individual's limits of tolerance for stress. According to this model, other factors being equal, moderate degrees of segregation by competence seem indicated in housing or institutions. Environmental programming is seen as an effective means of elevating behavior and affect, particularly if it is carefully adjusted in its demand quality to the functional level of the people who utilize it. Conversely, "downward" environmental programming, or increased support, is seen to be appropriate as poor health, social rejection, or emotional distress intrude. Just as a stimulating environment may be programmed by either the professional or the active effort of the individual himself, an overly provident environment that decreases function may be offered as a "service" or promoted by the individual. No person is immune to the seductive power of the too-easy life, no matter on what level of competence he is operating. There is no question that it is possible to discourage independent behavior in the name of service to the elderly. The major emphasis of most planning in geriatric settings has been in the direction of augmenting the supportive, rather than the demand aspects of environment. This direction is appropriate, to the extent that decrements are more frequent among the elderly and their world more apt to be deprived than glutted. However, the net balance of positive outcome may be maximized only by careful assessment of the individual, his environment, his active and passive needs, and the potential behavior and affective states that may eventuate from the transaction.

REFERENCES

Aldrich, C. K., & Mendkoff, E. Relocation of the aged and disabled: A mortality study. *Journal of the American Geriatrics Society*, 1963, **11**, 185–194.

Aleksandrowicz, D. Fire and its aftermath on a geriatric ward. *Bulletin of the Menninger Clinic*, 1961, **25**, 23–32.

Alexander, C. *Notes on the synthesis of form.* Cambridge, Mass.: Harvard University Press, 1964.

Ames, L. B. Age changes in the Rorschach responses of a group of elderly individuals. *Journal of Genetic Psychology*, 1960, **97**, 257–285.

Anderson, J. E. Environment and meaningful activity. In R. H. Williams, C. Tibbitts, & W. Donahue, (Eds.), *Processes of aging*. Vol. 1. New York: Atherton, 1963.

Anderson, N. N., Holmberg, R. H., Schneider, R. E., & Stone, L. B. *Policy issues regarding nursing homes*. Minneapolis: American Rehabilitation Foundations, 1969.

Baltes, P. B., & Nesselroade, J. R. Multivariate longitudinal and cross-sectional sequences for analyzing ontogenetic and generational changes. *Developmental Psychology*, 1970, **2**, 163–168.

Barker, R. G. *Ecological psychology*. Stanford, Calif.: Stanford University Press, 1968.

Barker, R. G., & Barker, L. S. The psychological ecology of old people in Midwest, Kansas, and Yoredale, Yorkshire. *Journal of Gerontology*, 1961, **61**, 231–239.

Basowitz, H., & Korchin, S. J. Age differences in the perception of closure. *Journal of Abnormal and Social Psychology*, 1957, **54**, 93–97.

Beattie, W. M., & Bullock, J. Preface to a counseling service. St. Louis, Mo.: Health and Welfare Council of Metropolitan St. Louis, 1963. (Mimeo)

Bennett, R., & Nahemow, L. Institutional totality and criteria of social adjustment in residences for the aged. *Journal of Social Issues*, 1965, **21**, 44–78. (a)

Bennett, R., & Nahemow, L. A two-year followup study of the process of social adjustment in residents of a home for the aged. In M. P. Lawton & F. G. Lawton (Eds.), *Mental impairment in the aged*. Philadelphia: Philadelphia Geriatric Center, 1965. (b)

Berlyne, D. E. *Conflict, arousal, and curiosity*. New York: McGraw-Hill, 1960.

Beyer, G. *Economic aspects of housing for the aged*. Ithaca, New York: Cornell University Center for Housing and Environmental Studies, 1961.

Beyer, G., & Wahl, S. *The elderly and their housing*. (Bulletin 989) New York: Cornell University Agricultural Experiment Station, December 1963.

Beyer, G., & Woods, M. E. *Living and activity patterns of the aged*. Ithaca, New York: Cornell University Center for Housing and Environmental Studies, 1963.

Birren, J. E. Toward an experimental psychology of aging. *American Psychologist*, 1970, **25**, 124–135.

Birren, J. E., Bick, M. W., & Fox, C. Age changes in the light threshold of the dark adapted eye. *Journal of Gerontology*, 1948, **3**, 267–271.

Blenkner, M. Environmental change and the aging individual. *Gerontologist*, 1967, **7**, 101–105.

Botwinick, J. Cautiousness ni old age. *Journal of Gerontology*, 1966, **21**, 347–353.

Botwinick, J. Disinclination to venture response vs. cautiousness in responding: Age differences. *Journal of Genetic Psychology*, 1969, **115**, 55–62.

Bourg, C. Life styles and mobility patterns of older persons. Paper presented at the Interdisciplinary Workshop on Transportation and the Aging, Administration on Aging, Washington, D.C., May 1970.

Bromley, D. B. Some experimental tests of the effect of age on creative intellectual output. *Journal of Gerontology*, 1956, **11**, 74–82.

Bromley, D. B. Some effects of age on the quality of intellectual output. *Journal of Gerontology*, 1957, **12**, 318–323.

Bultena, G. L., & Wood, V. The American retirement community: Bane or blessing? *Journal of Gerontology*, 1969, **24**, 209–217.

Burgess, E. M., Cavan, R., & Havighurst, R. *Your activities and attitudes scale*. Chicago: Science Research Associates, 1948.

Buttimer, A. Social space in interdisciplinary perspective. *Geographical Review*, 1969, **59**, 417–426.

Carp, F. M. *A future for the aged*. Austin: University of Texas Press, 1966.

Carp, F. M. Public transit and retired people. In E. J. Cantilli & J. L. Shmelzer (Eds.), *Transportation and aging: Selected issues*. Washington, D.C.: Administration on Aging, 1971.

Carp, F. M. *Patterns of living and housing of middle-aged and older people*. (USPHS Publ. No. 1496) Washington, D.C.: United States Department of Health, Education, and Welfare, undated.

Chapanis, A. Relationships between age, visual acuity, and color vision. *Human Biology*, 1950, **22**, 1–31.

Chein I. The environment as a determinant of behavior. *Journal of Social Psychology*, 1954, **39**, 115–127.

Chombart de Lauwe, P. H. *Paris essais de sociologie, 1952–1954*. Paris: Editions Ouvrieres, 1966.

Comalli, P. E., Wapner, S., & Werner, H. Perception of verticality in middle and old age. *Journal of Psychology*, 1959, **47**, 259–266.

Coppinger, N. W. The relationship between critical flicker frequency and chronological age for varying levels of stimulus brightness. *Journal of Gerontology*, 1955, **10**, 48–52.

Craik, K. Transportation and the person. *High Speed Ground Transportation Journal*, 1969, **3**, 86–91.

De Long, A. J. The administrator and the environmental language of the older person. In, *Directions '68*. Washington, D.C.: American Association of Homes for the Aging, 1968.

De Long, A. J. The microspatial structure of the older person: Some implications of planning the social and spatial environment. In L. A. Pastalan & D. H. Carson (Eds.), *Spatial behavior of older people*. Ann Arbor: University of Michigan Institute of Gerontology, 1970.

Demming, J. A., & Pressey, S. L. Tests "indigenous" to the adult and older years. *Journal of Counseling Psychology*, 1957, **4**, 144–148.

Dubos, R. *Man adapting*. New Haven: Yale University Press, 1965.

Durkheim, E. *The division of labor in society*. New York: Free Press, 1933. (Originally published: Paris: Alcan, 1893.)

Eisdorfer, C. Rorschach performance and intellectual functioning in the aged. *Journal of Gerontology*, 1963, **18**, 358–363.

Eisdorfer, C. Arousal and performance: Experiments in verbal learning and a tentative theory. In G. Talland (Ed.), *Human aging and behavior*. New York: Academic Press, 1968.

Ericksen, C. W., & Pierce, J. Defense mechanisms. In E. F. Borgatta & W. W. Lambert (Eds.), *Handbook of personality theory and research*. Chicago: Rand McNally, 1968.

Fiske, D. W., & Maddi, S. R. (Eds.) *Functions of varied experience.* Homewood, Ill.: Dorsey, 1961.

Fozard, J. L. Psychological functional age. Paper presented at the annual meeting of the Gerontological Society, Houston, Texas, October 1971.

Fried, M. Grieving for a lost home. In L. J. Duhl (Ed.), *The urban condition.* New York: Basic Books, 1963.

Friedman, E. P. Spatial proximity and social interaction in a home for the aged. *Journal of Gerontology,* 1966, **21**, 566–570.

Gardner, R. W., Holzman, P. S., Klein, G. S., Linton, H. B., & Spence, D. P. Cognitive control: A study of individual consistencies in cognitive behavior. In, *Psychological issues.* Pt. 4. New York: International University Press, 1959.

Gelwicks, L. E. Home range and use of space by an aging population. In L. A. Pastalan & D. H. Carson (Eds.), *The spatial behavior of older people.* Ann Arbor: University of Michigan Institute of Gerontology, 1970.

Gist, N. P., & Fava, S. *Urban society.* (5th ed.) New York: Thomas Cromwell, 1964.

Goldscheider, C. Differential residential mobility of the older population. *Journal of Gerontology,* 1966, **21**, 103–108.

Goldscheider, C., Van Arsdol, M. D., & Sabagh, G. Residential mobility of older people. In F. Carp (Ed.), *Patterns of living and housing of middle-aged and older people.* (USPHS Publ. No. 1496) Washington, D.C.: United States Department of Health, Education, and Welfare, undated.

Greenwald, S. R., & Linn, M. W. Intercorrelation of data on nursing homes. Paper presented at the annual meeting of the Gerontological Society, Toronto, Ontario, October 1970.

Gutmann, D., Gottesman, L., & Tessler, S. A comparative study of ego functioning in geriatric patients. Paper presented at the annual meeting of the Gerontological Society, Denver, October 1968.

Hall, E. T. *The hidden dimension.* New York: Doubleday, 1966.

Hammel, L. Regional planning and its implications for the elderly. In E. J. Cantilli & J. L. Shmelzer (Eds.), *Transportation and aging: Selected issues.* Washington, D.C.: Administration on Aging, 1971.

Hamovitch, M. B. Social and psychological factors in adjustment in a retirement village. In F. M. Carp (Ed.), *The retirement process.* Bethesda, Md.: National Institute of Child Health and Human Development, undated.

Hamovitch, M. B., Peterson, J. A., & Larson, A. E. Perceptions and fulfillment of housing needs of an aging population. Paper presented at the Eighth International Congress of Gerontology, Washington, D.C., August 1969.

Harel, Z. A theoretical model for the organizational analysis of residential care settings for the aged. Paper presented at the annual meeting of the Gerontological Society, Toronto, Ontario, October 1970.

Heider, F. On perception, event structure, and psychological environment. In *Psychological issues.* Pt. 3. New York: International Universities Press, 1959.

Helson, H. *Adaptation level theory.* New York: Harper & Row, 1964.

Hole, W. V., & Allen, P. G. A survey of modern dwellings for old people. *Architects Journal,* 1962, **135**, 1017–1024.

Hole, W. V., & Allen, P. G. The rehousing of old people: Some planning implications. *Architects Journal,* 1964, **139,** 75–82.

Irwin, N. Public transit and the quality of urban living. *Ekistics,* 1970, **29,** 47–57.

Ittelson, W. H. The perception of the large-scale environment. Paper presented to the New York Academy of Sciences, New York, April 1970.

Ittelson, W. H., Proshansky, H. M., & Rivlin, L. G. Bedroom size and social interaction of the psychiatric ward. *Environment and Behavior.* 1970, **2,** 255–270.

Jackson, J. J. Social impacts of housing relocation upon urban, low-income black aged. Paper presented at the annual meeting of the Gerontological Society, Toronto, Ontario, October 1970.

Jasnau, K. F. Individualized versus mass transfer of nonpsychotic geriatric patients from mental hospitals to nursing homes with special reference to the death rate. *Journal of the American Geriatrics Society,* 1967, **15,** 280–284.

Kahana, B., & Kahana, E. Changes in mental status of elderly patients in age-integrated and age-segregated hospital milieus. *Journal of Abnormal Psychology,* 1970, **75,** 177–181.

Kahana, E. Effects of matching institutional environments and needs of the aged. Paper presented at the annual meeting of the Gerontological Society, Houston, Texas, October 1971.

Kasteler, J. M., Gray, R. M., & Carruth, M. L. Involuntary relocation of the elderly. *Gerontologist,* 1968, **8,** 276–279.

Killian, E. C. Effect of geriatric transfers on mortality rates. *Social Work,* 1970, **15,** 19–26.

Kimbrell, G. M., & Furchtgott, E. The effect of aging on olfactory threshold. *Journal of Gerontology,* 1963, **18,** 364–365.

Klausner, S. Z. *On man in his environment.* San Francisco: Jossey-Bass, 1971.

Kleemeier, R. W. Behavior and the organization of the bodily and the external environment. In J. E. Birren (Ed.), *Handbook of aging and the individual.* Chicago: University of Chicago Press, 1959.

Kogan, N., & Wallach, M. A. *Risk taking: A study in cognition and personality.* New York: Holt, Rinehart & Winston, 1964.

Korchin, S. J., & Basowitz, H. The judgment of ambiguous stimuli as an index of cognitive functioning in aging. *Journal of Personality,* 1956, **25,** 81–95.

Kral, V. A., Grad, B., & Berenson, J. Stress reactions resulting from the relocation of an aged population. *Canadian Psychiatric Association Journal,* 1968, **13,** 201–209.

Kuypers, J. Internal–external locus of control and ego functioning correlates in the elderly. Paper presented at the annual meeting of the Gerontological Society, Houston, Texas, October 1971.

Langford, M. *Community aspects of housing for the aged.* Ithaca, New York: Cornell University Center for Housing and Environmental Studies, 1962.

Lawton, M. P. Social and medical services in housing for the elderly. (Progress report) Philadelphia, Philadelphia Geriatric Center, 1968. (Mimeo)

Lawton, M. P. Supportive services in the context of the housing environment. *Gerontologist,* 1969, **9,** 15–19.

Lawton, M. P. Ecology and aging. In L. A. Pastalan & D. H. Carson (Eds.), *The spatial behavior of older people*. Ann Arbor: University of Michigan Institute of Gerontology, 1970. (a)

Lawton, M. P. Institutions for the aged: Theory, content, and methods for research. *Gerontologist*, 1970, **10**, 305–312. (b)

Lawton, M. P. Public behavior of older people in congregate housing. In, *Proceedings of the Environmental Design Research Association*, Pittsburgh: Environmental Design Research Association, October 1970. (c)

Lawton, M. P. Assessment of the competence of older people. In D. Kent, R. Kastenbaum, & S. Sherwood (Eds.), *Research, planning, and action for the elderly*. New York: Behavioral Publications, 1972.

Lawton, M. P., & Bader, J. The wish for privacy among young and old. *Journal of Gerontology*, 1970, **25**, 48–54.

Lawton, M. P., & Kleban, M. H. The aged resident of the inner city. *Gerontologist*, 1971, **11**, 277–283.

Lawton, M. P., Kleban, M. H., & Carlson, D. The inner city resident: To move or not to move. Paper presented at the annual meeting of the Gerontological Society, Houston, Texas, October 1971.

Lawton, M. P., Kleban, M. H., & Singer, M. The aged Jewish person and the slum environment. *Journal of Gerontology*, 1971, **26**, 231–239.

Lawton, M. P., Liebowitz, B., & Charon H. Physical structure and the behavior of senile patients following ward remodeling. *Aging & Human Development*, 1970, **1**, 231–239.

Lawton, M. P., & Simon, B. B. The ecology of social relationships in housing for the elderly. *Gerontologist*, 1968, **8**, 108–115.

Lawton, M. P., & Yaffe, S. Mortality, morbidity, and voluntary change of residence by older people. *Journal of the American Geriatrics Society*, 1970, **18**, 823–831.

Lee, T. Urban neighborhood as socio-spatial schema. In H. M. Proshansky, W. H. Ittelson & L. G. Rivlin (Eds.), *Environmental psychology*. New York: Holt, Rinehart & Winston, 1970.

Lenzer, A. Mobility patterns among the aged, 1955–1960. *Gerontologist*, 1965, **5**, 12–15.

Lewin, K. *Dynamic theory of personality*. New York: McGraw-Hill, 1935.

Lieberman, M. Institutionalization of the aged: Effects on behavior. *Journal of Gerontology*, 1969, **24**, 330–340.

Lieberman, M. A., Prock, V. N., & Tobin, S. S. Psychological effects of institutionalization. *Journal of Gerontology*, 1968, **3**, 343–353.

Lieberman, M., Tobin, S., & Slover, D. *The effects of relocation on long-term geriatric patients*. (Final Rep. Proj. No. 17–1328) Chicago: Illinois Department of Health and Committee on Human Development, University of Chicago, 1971.

Light, B. H., & Amick, J. H. Rorschach responses of normal aged. *Journal of Projective Techniques*, 1956, **20**, 185–195.

Lindsley, O. R. Geriatric behavioral prosthetics. In R. Kastenbaum (Ed.), *New thoughts on old age*. New York: Springer, 1964.

Lipman, A. Public housing and attitudinal adjustment in old age: A comparative study. *Journal of Geriatric Psychiatry*, 1968, **2**, 88–101.

Lynch, K. *The image of the city*. Cambridge, Mass.: MIT Press, 1960.

Mangum, W. P. Adjustment in special residential settings for the aged: An inquiry based on the Kleemeier conceptualization. Unpublished doctoral dissertation, University of Southern California, 1971.

Markowitz, J. The transportation needs of the elderly. In E. J. Cantilli & J. L. Shmelzer (Eds.), Transportation and aging: Selected issues. Washington, D.C.: Administration on Aging, 1971.

Markus, E. J. Post-relocation mortality among institutionalized aged. Cleveland: Benjamin Rose Institute, 1970. (Mimeo)

Markus E., Blenkner, M., Bloom, M., & Downs, T. The impact of relocation upon mortality rates of institutionalized aged persons. Journal of Gerontology, 1971, 26, 537–541.

Messer, M. The possibility of an age-concentrated environment becoming a normative system. Gerontologist, 1967, 7, 247–251.

Miller, D., & Lieberman, M. A. The relationships of affect state and adaptive capacity to reactions to stress. Journal of Gerontology, 1965, 20, 492–497.

Murray, H. A. Explorations in personality. New York: Oxford, 1938.

Nahemow, L., & Bennett, R. Conformity, persuasibility and counternormative persuasion. Sociometry, 1967, 30, 14–25.

Nahemow, L., & Kogan, L. S. Reduced fare for the elderly. New York: Mayor's Office for the Aging, 1971. (Mimeo)

Nash, A., & Hille, S. Public attitudes toward transport modes: A summary of two pilot studies. Highway Research Record, 1968, 233, 33–46.

Niebanck, P. L. The elderly in older urban areas. Philadelphia: University of Pennsylvania Institute for Environmental Studies, 1965.

Palmore, E. Attitudes toward aging as shown by humor. Gerontologist, 1971, 11, 181–186.

Park, R. E., Burgess, E. W., & McKenzie, R. D. (Eds.), The city. Chicago: University of Chicago Press, 1925.

Pastalan, L. A. Toward an empathic model in architecture. Ann Arbor: Department of Architecture, University of Michigan, 1971. (Mimeo)

Perrin, C. With man in mind. Cambridge, Mass.: MIT Press, 1970.

Pincus, A., & Wood, V. Methodological issues in measuring the environment in institutions for the aged and its impact on residents. Aging & Human Development, 1970, 1, 117–126.

Reimanis, G. Increase in psychological anomie as a result of radical and undesirable change expectancy. Journal of Personality and Social Psychology, 1967, 6, 454–457.

Rochwarg, H. Changes in the structural aspects of perception in the aged: An analysis by means of the Rorschach test. Unpublished doctoral dissertation, Michigan State College, Ypsilanti, 1954.

Rosenberg, G. S. The worker grows old. San Francisco: Jossey-Bass, 1970.

Rosenberg, M. The dissonant religious context and emotional disturbance. American Journal of Sociology, 1962, 68, 1–10.

Rosow, I. Social integration of the aged. New York: Free Press, 1967.

Rossi, P. Why families move. New York: Free Press, 1955.

Rotter, J. B. Generalized expectancies for internal versus external control of reinforcement. Psychological Monographs, 1966, 80(1, Whole No. 609).

Schaie, K. W. A general model for the study of developmental problems. Psychological Bulletin, 1965, 64, 92–107.

Schaie, K. W., Baltes, P., & Strother, C. R. A study of auditory sensitivity in advanced age. *Journal of Gerontology*, 1964, **19**, 453–457.

Schooler, K. S. The relationship between social interaction and morale of the elderly as a function of environmental characteristics. *Gerontologist*, 1969, **9**, 25–29.

Schooler, K. S. *Residential physical environment and health of the aged*. (Final Rep. USPHS Grant EC 00191) Waltham, Mass.: Florence Heller School for Advanced Studies in Social Welfare, Brandeis University, 1970.

Schwartz, D. W., & Karp, S. A. Field dependence in a geriatric population. *Perceptual and Motor Skills*, 1967, **24**, 495–504.

Sells, S. B. (Ed.) *Stimulus determinants of behavior*. New York: Ronald Press, 1963.

Shahinian, S. B., Goldfarb, A. I., & Turner, H. Death rate in relocated residents of nursing homes. Paper presented at the annual meeting of the Gerontological Society, New York, November 1966.

Sherman, S. R., Mangum, W. P., Dodds, S., Walkley, R. P., & Wilber, D. M. Psychological effects of retirement housing. *Gerontologist*, 1968, **8**, 170–175.

Singer, M. T. Personality measurements in the aged. In J. E. Birren et al. (Eds.), *Human aging*. (USPHS Publ. No. 986) Washington, D.C.: United States Department of Health, Education, and Welfare, 1963.

Sivadon, P. Space as experienced: Therapeutic implications. In H. M. Proshansky, W. H. Ittelson, & L. G. Rivlin (Eds.), *Environmental psychology*. New York: Holt, Rinehart & Winston, 1970.

Sommer, R., & Ross, H. Social interaction in a geriatrics ward. *International Journal of Social Psychiatry*, 1958, **4**, 128–133.

Sorre, M. *Les fondements de la geographie humaine*. Paris: Colin, 1943. 3 vols.

Stea, D. Environmental perception and cognition: Toward a model for "mental maps." In G. J. Coates & K. M. Moffett (Eds.), *Response to environment*. Raleigh, N.C.: School of Design, North Carolina State University, 1969.

Taietz, P. Community structure and aging. Ithaca, N.Y.: Department of Rural Sociology, Cornell University, 1970. (Mimeo)

Taves, M., & Shmelzer, J. Mobility, transportation, and aging. Washington, D.C.: Administration on Aging, 1970.

Toffler, A. *Future shock*. New York: Random House, 1970.

Tolman, E. C. Cognitive maps in rats and men. *Psychological Review*, 1948, **55**, 189–208.

Turner, B. F., Tobin, S. S., & Lieberman, M. A. Personality traits as predictors of institutional adaption among the aged. *Journal of Gerontology*, 1972, **27**, 61–68.

Wapner, S., Werner, H., & Comalli, P. E. Perception of part-whole relationships in middle and old age. *Journal of Gerontology*, 1960, **15**, 412–416.

Webber, M. Order in diversity: Community without propinquity. In L. Wingo (Ed.), *Cities and space*. Baltimore: Johns Hopkins University Press, 1963.

Webber, M., & Angel, S. The social context for transportation policy. *Ekistics*, 1970, **29**, 25–28.

Werner, H. *Comparative psychology of mental development.* (4th ed.) New York: Scientific Editions, 1961.

Witkin, H. A., Lewis, H. B., Hertzman, M., Machover, K., Meissner, P. B., & Wapner, S. *Personality through perception.* New York: Harper, 1954.

Wohlwill, J. F. The physical environment: A problem for a psychology of stimulation. *Journal of Social Issues,* 1966, **22,** 29–38.

The Aged in an Affluent Economy

BURKHARD STRÜMPEL

How well off are old Americans? The economic situation of a person is determined by his means and his needs. It depends upon his motivation as well as his state of health, physical and psychic stamina, and skills, and on his ability to provide for the future by saving or education, by occupational mobility or retraining. Old people differ in important respects from young people in that their abilities and opportunities to earn are extremely limited; their retirement income is modest on the average while their financial needs are not reduced to the same extent through smaller household size; moreover, they are more frequently confronted with the costs and loss of earning brought about by major illnesses. While young people can more easily translate their material goals and motivations into behavior (decide to work more, save for the future, etc.), old people tend to be "locked into" their circumstances. The choices of youth tend to be the inescapable constraints of the old. If they abstained earlier from saving or being educated or establishing pension rights in time, they are stuck later with their own failure to do so. Old age is the stage in the life cycle most likely to exhibit poverty as well as a cumulation of the causes of poverty. In 1969, 21% of the households headed by a person of 65 years or older were among the poorest 10% of all households.[1]

Burkhard Strumpel received his doctorate in economics from the University of Cologne, West Germany, in 1962. He is a Program Director in the Institute for Social Research and Associate Professor of Economics at the University of Michigan. He is currently involved in research in analyzing economic motivation, values, and well-being.

The author acknowledges the skillful assistance of M. Susan Schwartz and the valuable advice of Richard E. Barfield, George Katona, and James N. Morgan.

[1]Households were ranked according to a means/need ratio. As to the definition of this ratio, see Morgan and Smith (1969, pp. 140–142).

Since old age cuts across all social and income strata and psychological or personality types, there is, of course, vast variation in the material situation of the aged. Old age security and comfort depend upon past provisions. Those who were better off during their working years had more opportunity and leeway to accumulate pension rights and to build up liquid and other assets. Not only were they more likely to save, but if they did so, they also saved more in proportion to their income than their less fortunate contemporaries.[2] Thus, we would expect people who received higher incomes during their working years to have higher assets in proportion to their working incomes than people in lower income groups.

It can be stated fairly that the socioeconomic situation of the aged is changing faster than that of the population as a whole. Thus, any stock-taking to be relevant will have to be accompanied by an assessment of changes.

The most powerful trends underlying changes over the last 10 years are the following:

1. In the United States, life expectancy at birth was 54 years in 1920, 63 years in 1940, and 71 years in 1967.

2. The growing preference for retirement or even early retirement. The proportion of workers wanting to work as long as they are able is steadily declining. Old age financial security provides older people with additional discretion in determining the time of their retirement.

3. The emergence of a separate subculture for the aged, reflecting the two aforementioned phenomena as well as completing the triumph of the nuclear family as the primary social unit. The average number of persons per household declined from 3.33 in 1960 to 3.17 in 1970. The number of persons 65 and older who were living alone (or with others who were not related) increased from 3.2 million in 1960 to 5.2 million in 1970—an increase of 61%. "Senior citizen" clubs, recreational activities, and retirement towns, etc., are only the most recent expressions of this trend.

On the one hand, these developments are creatures of affluence; on the other hand, they create needs and aspirations. The proportion

---

[2]According to repeated empirical findings and theoretical considerations, the proportion of money saved out of income at a given time and within a given society increases with rising income.

of national income and production to be spent for the nonproductive part of the population is increasing rapidly. More complete retirement benefits are accumulated by more extensive OASDHI (social security) coverage, both in terms of proportion of individuals covered and of amount of coverage and benefits, by more extensive participation in supplementary claims, particularly private pension plans and life insurance, and by a much-improved liquid asset position. The number of retired OASDHI beneficiaries rose from 1.7 million in 1950 to 8.1 million in 1960 and 12 million in 1967. In 1950, 9.8 million workers were covered by some type of private pension or deferred profit-sharing plan; in 1965, more than 25 million workers were covered (Kolodrubetz, 1967). At the same time, the number of private pension beneficiaries rose from .45 million to 2.75 million.

Finally, individuals have responded by increasing their saving activity. The proportion of aged having liquid assets increased from 72 to 80% during the 1960s. The average amount of savings held increased even more (see Table 10). In 1969, 25% of the 62 million American family units owned common stock. The proportion among the aged was close to this figure. Twenty years earlier, the proportion had been as low as 6 to 8% of the then less than 50 million family units (Katona, Strümpel, & Zahn, 1971).

These changes, in turn, can be traced to changes in occupational structure and education. The more highly educated white collar and service occupations (including professions) are accounting for an increasing share of the nation's population and income. They tend to entertain longer time horizons and to attach more value to building up assets and old age security.

How do these trends—conflicting in the effect on the well-being of the aged—add up to an integrated picture? The next section will deal with the economic situation of the aged and its changes. It will be followed by a discussion of how older people react to changes in their material situation by adjusting their retirement age and working and consumption behavior; the last section will deal in detail with the "problem cases," that is, with a more-detailed identification of the aged poor.

Another problem area highly pertinent to the thrust of this volume is indicated by the terms "quality of life" and "subjective well-being." How do the aged perceive their economic situation and its changes? How do they cope with financial difficulties? The author is at present developing measures of well-being and adaptation that, however, have not yet been applied to the population as a whole (Strümpel, 1971b).

THE ECONOMIC SITUATION OF THE AGED

During the period 1960 to 1969, the proportion of people 65 or older changed only insignificantly from 9.1 to 9.9% of the total population (Census Bureau data). Calculated as the proportion of the adult population, there were 13% aged both in 1960 and 1969. However, the percentage of families headed by someone 65 or older increased from 15 to 21%.[3] Whereas the number of all families increased by 14%, the increase in families with a head 65 or older was 40%.

Table 1 documents the changes in family structure of the aged that have taken place during the last decade. The "undoubling" of the aged, that is, the maintenance of a separate household, is, of course, a trend perceptible for several decades. It gained further momentum in the 1960s, particularly among single aged women. In 1960, 41% of the females 75 years or older and 18% of the younger aged women (65 to 74) were living with their relatives. Nine years later, the respective figures were 28 and 15%.

In 1968, about half of the families headed by a person over 65 received less than $2,000 in annual income, and 55% of the aged household heads were in the lowest quintile (20%) of the family income distribution (see Table 2). The percentage figures for 1960 were the same within sampling error. The unsatisfactory relative income position of the aged household hardly improved during that period.

While we are interpreting these findings, several observations are in order. First, although the *income* gains of the elderly households did not exceed those of all families, the *asset position* of the

---

[3]These and the following figures and tables are extracted from four national surveys conducted by the Survey Research Center of the University of Michigan, two in 1960 and two in 1969. Data on the asset position of the aged were obtained from the 1960 and 1969 Surveys of Consumer Finances, an annual study of the Survey Research Center. The remainder of the data were results of the 1960 Low-Income Study (see Morgan, Martin, Cohen, & Brazer, 1962) and the 1969 interviewing year of the Panel Study of Income Dynamics. Some of the quantitative information obtained in these surveys relate to the calendar years 1959 and 1968. Each of these surveys covers a representative cross section of families in the continental United States. Interviews were taken with the head of the household, defined as the husband in complete families. The surveys exclude people living in institutions. People with very low incomes were overrepresented in the 1969 Panel Study. All results from this study, therefore, had to be weighted.

TABLE 1

Family Structure of the Aged Population 1960 and 1969

Family structure	1960				1969			
	All aged	Age 65-74	Age 75 or older	Number of cases[a]	All aged	Age 65-74	Age 75 or older	Number of cases
Proportion of aged who are—								
Head of family or wife of head	83	87	73	520	86	89	80	661
Living with relatives	17	13	27	117	14	11	20	163
Proportion of the female aged who are—								
Heads; single, widowed, or divorced	35	35	36	119	43	39	51	186
Wife of head	40	47	23	136	37	46	21	156
Living with relatives	25	18	41	92	20	15	28	121
Proportion of the male aged who are—								
Head of family	92			265	93			319
Living with relatives	8			25	7			42

Note. Figures are given in percentages with the exception of Ns.

[a] Unweighted N; the Ns do not reflect the proportions in the universe.

TABLE 2

Family Income of the Aged Population in 1959 and 1968

Group	Median income in constant dollars[a] (1957−1959 = 100)		Percent in lowest income quintile		Percent in highest income quintile		Number of cases[b]	
	1959	1968	1959	1968	1959	1968	1959	1968
All families	5309	6510	20	20	20	20	2800	4452
Age of head of family								
Under age 65	5800	7322	13	13	22	23	2416	3947
65 or older	1946	2696	57	55	9	4	384	505
65 to 74	2320	3116	50	48	12	6	261	326
75 or older	1400	2328	72	68	2	2	123	179

[a]Gross income.
[b]Unweighted N.

elderly improved both absolutely and relatively.[4] Second, the proportion of *households* with a head 65 years or older has increased while
the proportion of *individuals* of the same age range has remained
constant. As more of the elderly now have somewhat more resources,
fewer feel forced to move in with their children, thus increasing the
number of small lower income households headed by an aged person.
Many more of these households now are one-person households;
they are relatively not as needy as they appear to be if only household
income is being considered.

To get a clearer picture of what the insistence of many older
people on maintaining their own households does to their material
well-being, it is necessary to look at the distribution of "welfare
ratios." The welfare ratio relates the income available to the household's needs as computed on the basis of family size.[5] Social statis-

---

[4]The proportion of older families with liquid assets increased eight
percentage points (from 72 to 80%) between 1960 and 1969, and the real
median assets value of asset holders (i.e., dollar amounts adjusted for inflation) increased 25%. The respective figures for all families are 6 and 12
(Table 10).

[5]The welfare ratio definitions and measurements were derived from the
Low-Income Study of 1960 (Morgan et al., 1962, pp. 188–189) and the
Panel Study of Income Dynamics (Morgan et al., 1969, pp. 140–142). The

ticians agree that needs as well as actual living expenses per capita are higher for small than for large households. It is mainly the needs for housing and consumer durables that do not rise at an equal pace with the number of persons in a family. A one-person household is in need of a bathroom, a kitchen, a living room, a vacuum cleaner, and a car hardly any less than a three- or four-person household. This means that "undoubling" has a price and entails material sacri-

TABLE 3

Median Welfare Ratios of Aged in 1959 and 1968

Group	1959		1968	
	Welfare ratio as percent of overall median	Number of cases[a]	Welfare ratio as percent of overall median	Number of cases[a]
All persons	100	5464	100	8767
Persons age 65 or older	79	637	80	824
Married heads				
65 or older with wife	90	207[b]	89	252[b]
Unmarried heads				
65 or older	56	177[c]	63	253[d]
Dependent persons				
65 or older	94	117	88	163
Persons age 65-74	84	434	87	548
Persons age 75 or older	68	203	67	276

Note. The figures represent welfare ratios for individuals computed on the basis of the ratios of the families to which they belong. It is thus assumed that all members of the household enjoy the same standard of living.

The table should be read as follows: In 1959, the median welfare ratio of persons 65 or older was 79% of the median welfare ratio of all adults; that is, the median welfare ratio of persons 65 or older was 21% lower than the welfare ratio of all adults.

[a]Unweighted *N*.
[b]Figure represents number of households headed by a married aged male.
[c]Among those, 33% were male (*n* = 58); 67% were female (*n* = 119).
[d]Among those, 28% were male (*n* = 76); 72% were female (*n* = 186).

measure of income used in both studies includes estimates of income in kind: imputed rental on own home, nonmoney transfers, and money saved on home production. The standard of need used in the 1960 study was estimated for each family according to data derived from a schedule prepared by the Community Council of Greater New York. Family needs in the 1969 study were based on the food needs standard of the Department of Agriculture, which is scaled according to age and sex. To estimate the cost of all needs, food needs were multiplied by an adjustment factor based on family size.

fice. Both in 1960 and 1969, the median welfare ratio of all individuals 65 or older was about 20% lower than the median of the
entire population (see Table 3). However, proportionately more aged
in 1969 than in 1960 (17 versus 14%) were in the lowest welfare
decile, that is, among the lowest tenth of the households if ranked
according to their welfare status. Thus, even if the lower needs of
smaller households are being considered, the situation of the poorest
of the elderly, although absolutely improved during the 1960s,
seems to have stagnated relatively. We will consider this point further
in a later section.

There are significant differences in welfare and welfare changes
between subgroups of the aged. Table 3 suggests (and here the situation in 1969 was slightly improved compared to 1960 without
changing the basic picture) that unmarried, that is, mostly widowed,
aged are by far the worst off. This reflects the failure of our welfare
system to support survivors, mainly female, adequately. Interestingly,
the relative economic position of the households of the dependent
aged (i.e., those who double up with their relatives) deteriorated;
this is probably due to the fact that, given the preference for "undoubling," very many of the relatively well-off elderly with higher
incomes (mainly increased social security benefits) have left the
household to establish their own, and those who remain tend to add
to the family needs at a faster rate than to its means. Since the group
of dependent aged consists predominantly of single females, it is
useful to compare them with female household heads who by definition are single. As our survey data show, the most striking difference
between the two groups is that while only 14% of female household heads received no transfer income in 1960, almost 50% of
dependent individuals had no income from this source. The respective figures for 1969 were 5 and 25%. These data clearly identify
the female aged, whether dependent or independent, as the primary
soft spot within the aged population. Moreover, there is a spill-over
effect of poverty from those who are dependent upon their relatives,
an obviously disadvantaged subgroup of the population as a whole.

The younger aged (heads 65 to 74 years old) are considerably
better off than the older aged (74 years or older), and the differences between both groups have absolutely and relatively widened
during the 1960s. The most obvious but by no means sufficient
explanation for these significant differences is the lower educational
attainment of older Americans, as shown in Table 4. This trend is
strong enough to be perceptible even if income differences of age
groups only 10 years apart are being compared. We will take up

TABLE 4

Distribution of Retired People by Age and Educational Level in 1966

Education of head	Younger than 60	Age 60-64	Age 65-69	70 and older	All retired
0-5 grades	10	13	18	23	19
6-11 grades	44	50	52	49	48
12 or more grades	37	27	25	20	25
College degree or more	9	10	4	6	6
Not available	0	0	1	2	2
Total	100	100	100	100	100
Number of cases	114	68	149	344	675

Note. This table has been taken from G. Katona and J. N. Morgan, "Retirement in Prospect and Retrospect." (Joint Economic Committee. *Old Age Income Assurance. Part 2: The Aged Population and Retirement Income Programs.* 90th Congress, 1st session) Washington, D.C.: United States Government Printing Office, 1967. The figures are derived from survey data and are given in percentages.

this point again in a later section. Moreover, the "older aged" are hurt by the erosion of their pension rights through inflation and, even more severely, by the failure of the social security and pension systems to have the retired participate in the secular increase in income and welfare. The American system of old age security, unlike, for example, the German system, is not designed to let the aged share the fruits of rising prosperity. It does little more than adjust social security benefits to changes in the consumer price index. This leaves the older aged, once they have retired, with a number of handicaps that sharply increase the welfare differentials emerging between themselves and younger cohorts of aged people as well as the working population. In a world of continuously rising real incomes, the aforementioned trends—education, inflation, "non-dynamic" pension rights—condemn most of the aged, once they have retired, to a gradual erosion of their welfare position relative to the rest of the population and to later-retiring aged cohorts.

Finally, the questions arise: How does the income or welfare distribution of the population as a whole compare with that of the aged? Is old age a period in life where everybody is poorer but more equal? Quite to the contrary, as our data show. At least in economic terms, inequality among the aged is more pronounced than among the rest of the population. This is true particularly for the income distribution. In other words, income differences of the working years are more than perpetuated in old age. The Gini coefficients presented in Table 5 suggest that the distribution of money income (net of payroll taxes), of gross disposable income, and of welfare ratios is and has been for 10 years more unequal for households headed by an aged person than for the rest of the households. The leveling impact of the prevailing social security legislation is not sufficient to compensate for the striking differences in the accumulation of other sources of income: assets, private pension rights, more frequent part or full-time work of higher status workers. This little-noticed phenomenon no doubt accentuates the welfare problem of the aged if described only in *average* terms.

TABLE 5

Lorenz Coefficients of Inequality for Various Measures of Income,
by Age of Family Head

Measure	All family heads	Family heads under 55	Family head 55-64	Family head 65 and older
Total family money income				
1959	.39	.33	.44	.50
1968	.37	.32	.40	.43
Disposable money income plus estimates of income in kind[a]				
1959	.35	.30	.39	.44
1968	.34	.30	.36	.38
Welfare ratio				
1959	.33	.30	.35	.39
1968	.32	.29	.35	.36
Number of cases[b]				
1959	2800	1941	475	384
1968	4452	3273	674	505

Note. The Lorenz coefficient (or Gini Index) derives from the Lorenz curve, which plots the cumulated fraction of aggregate income against the cumulated proportion of families when families are arranged in ascending order by income. The line of perfect equality is a 45° line from the origin. The Lorenz coefficient is defined as the proportion of the triangular area between the curve and the line of perfect equality. Higher coefficients are descriptive of less equality.

[a]Imputed rental on own-home, nonmoney transfers and money saved on home production.

[b]Unweighted *N.*

REACTIONS TO CHANGES IN THE MATERIAL SITUATION
OF THE AGED

There are conflicting hypotheses among social scientists about the relationship between progress or affluence and the amount of work chosen and preferred by man. The incentive hypothesis holds that work effort will increase with rising remuneration. There are others who claim that well-being and wages, as a rule, have a "disincentive" effect; most people are primarily oriented toward reaching a certain target level of income. Whenever they can attain this level with less effort, they will gladly trade more leisure for potential additional income.

Extensive studies in behavioral economics demonstrate that both reactions are encountered in reality. Very frequently there is third case: for many people, marginal changes in the level of wages are not as important for their working choices as "nonmaterial" considerations like interest in and satisfaction from their job (Katona et al., 1971). Moreover, some people have more, some less, freedom of action. Social norms in all Western societies prescribe full-time paid work for adult men prior to retirement age and also, although somewhat less rigidly, for unmarried women. There are no such norms for married women, and their participation in the labor force thus shows striking international differences. Americans tend to raise their aspirations with accomplishment. The margin of unsatisfied income aspirations usually remains well ahead of actual income. Thus, even well-off middle-aged married women desire additional income and therefore, as well as for other reasons, return to work in great numbers. In contrast, in Europe, particularly West Germany, saturation and indifference toward a higher level of consumption is more prevalent, and participation of women in the labor force is largely confined to those with young families with urgent needs.

Men sometimes have the chance to increase their effort at the margin, that is, to work overtime or in second jobs. Increasingly in recent years the *age of retirement* has become a matter of choice. The American social security system, as well as many private pension arrangements, allows for a flexible retirement age, adjusted to the needs and wants of both employee and employer. Both the improvements in old age security and the prosperity during the 1960s, making it easier for aging people to retain their jobs or even find new full or part-time jobs, have brought about more freedom to the individual to shift his retirement age forward or backward.

The prosperity of the 1960s as well as changes in social security legislation unleashed a strong momentum toward earlier retirement. In 1960, 23% of heads 65 years or older were employed full time as opposed to only 14% in 1969.[6] Table 6 shows the working status of elderly household heads. Interestingly, the number of aged doing *no paid work* at all increased only insignificantly, if at all. However, the substantial decrease in the average number of hours worked is the more remarkable since unemployment was much higher in 1960 than in 1969.

These rapid behavioral changes are clearly reflected in the goals, aspirations, and plans of somewhat younger cohorts of workers. Between 1963 and 1968, the number of workers 55 to 64 years old planning to retire early increased from 21 to 26% (Barfield & Morgan, 1969).[7] The proportion of workers aged 45 to 54 years old who were planning to retire before age 65 rose from 23 to 35%. Whereas previously early retirement was often associated with very

TABLE 6

Labor Force Participation and Hours Worked for Aged Family Heads in 1959 and 1968

Hundreds of hours worked per year	Distribution of those who worked					
	All family heads 65 and older		Family heads 65-74		Family heads 75 and older	
	1959	1968	1959	1968	1959	1968
1-5	28	38	27	37	26	41
6-10	17	22	16	21	29	24
11-15	12	11	13	10	7	14
16-20	15	15	14	17	25	11
21 or more (full time)	28	14	30	15	13	10
Total	100	100	100	100	100	100
Proportion working	35	33	46	42	10	16

Note. Figures represent percentages.

[6]Unpublished Survey of Consumer Finances, Institute for Social Research, University of Michigan.

[7]The question: "When do you think you will retire from the work you do; I mean at what age?" (wording insignificantly changed in 1968).

low earnings, health handicaps, chronic unemployment, obsolescence of job skills, or earnings that had dropped off substantially in later years (Epstein, 1966),[8] data from the study by Barfield and Morgan (1969) modify this picture considerably. Their data show a newly emerging brand of early retirees who are stimulated to plan for early retirement mainly by the prospect of acquiring a satisfactory retirement income at a fairly early age. Financial factors, primarily expected retirement income, are of principal importance in the retirement decision, with attitude toward work having less influence. A "threshold" level of retirement income that most people seem to consider necessary to insure a reasonably adequate postretirement standard was found. In 1969, this level was about $4,000 per year. Of those rated as having a relatively favorable outlook toward their economic future, 46% planned to retire early; among those with an average outlook, 38%, and of those with a relatively unfavorable economic outlook, only 22.5% expressed plans of early retirement. Reasons connected with health, work satisfaction or dissatisfaction, or concrete plans for leisure time activities, although of perceptible impact, proved to be much less powerful than financial considerations.

All this is in line with the thrust of this chapter. The aged in their economic preferences and behavior differ in several important respects from the rest of the adult population. In addition to a decent standard of living, their behavior expresses two apparent overriding wishes: reducing their work load and maintaining their own household, apart from their children. The 1960s saw an improvement in the income and asset position of the aged reaching retirement age; this period also provided them with more extensive employment opportunities. Unlike their younger contemporaries, the aged did fail to translate their more favorable "terms of trade" (real wage rates and extended employment opportunities) into more participation in the labor and commodity markets. They reduced their work load earlier and more rapidly than previous cohorts approaching retirement age. And they insisted more frequently on retaining their own living quarters even where a genuine sacrifice of living standards was involved.

---

[8]Social Security Administration earnings records show that men who had elected to begin drawing social security benefits at age 62 were only half as likely as age 65 retirees to have had covered earnings of $4,800 in the year with the largest earnings and that early retirees were almost four times as likely to have earned less than $2,400 in their best years since 1950.

Excursus: The Aged Consumer and Saver

Old age tends to reduce market participation not only on the output but also on the input side; it affects not only working behavior but also saving and spending. Some of the most characteristic features of the mass consumption society (e.g., high rate of durable purchases, particularly automobiles; incurrence of installment debt) are distinctly less frequent among the aged.

Installment debt has a high negative correlation with age (see Table 7). In 1969, 49% of all households reported to be without installment debt, 77% of those 65 to 74 years old reported no installment debt, and 93% of those 75 and over had no installment debt. This age correlation is apparent also in the amount of debt. Of those with debts outstanding, the mean amount among all people is about one and one-half times that of heads 65 to 74 and about six times that of heads 75 or older. Among the older population, heads who are still employed are more willing to incur debt. Almost 30% of the employed 65 or older have debts, with a mean value of $1,514,

TABLE 7

Installment Debt by Age of Family Head in 1969

Amount of outstand-ing installment debt	Distribution of families with outstanding installment debt				
	All families	Head, age 55-64	Head, age 65 and older	Head, age 65-74	Head, age 75 and older
$1-99	6	10	14	5	57
$100-199	7	5	7	5	14
$200-499	16	20	35	42	0
$500-999	20	22	14	11	29
$1000-1999	25	25	21	26	0
$2000-2999	13	10	5	5	0
$3000-4999	9	5	2	3	0
$5000 or more	4	3	2	3	0
Total	100	100	100	100	100
Mean value	$1437	$1166	$696	$970	$250
Number of cases[a]	2317	382	268	165	103
Proportion with no installment debt	49	61	83	77	93

Note. Figures represent percentages.
[a]Unweighted N.

TABLE 8

Purchasing Behavior and Plans to Purchase by Age of Head, 1969

Behavior	All families	Age of head				
		Under 25	55-64	65 and older	65-74	75 and older
Bought car within last 12 months	32	40	23	12	16	5
Expect to buy car within 12 months	14	32	9	3	4	1
Bought other durables within last 12 months	38	44	32	22	23	20
Expect to buy other durables within 12 months	22	32	16	7	10	2
Number of cases[a]	2317	188	382	268	165	103

Note. Figures represent percentages.
[a]Unweighted N.

whereas 15% of the retired have debts, with a mean value of no more than $560. Older families are not as active in purchasing and planning to purchase consumer durables as younger families are (see Table 8). Not surprisingly, this is most pronounced with respect to automobiles, which account for a very large fraction of the volume of durable purchases.

Seventy-four percent of nonfarm family units with a head 65 or older own their home as compared to 63% of all family units (see Table 9). However, the reported value of housing is far lower among the older population. Among family units headed by a person 65 or older owning a home, 36% reported a house value greater than $15,000 as compared to 54% of all nonfarm homeowners. Although the frequency of homeownership among the aged is impressive, the value of homeownership to their total material situation is subject to reservations. First, the aged are immobile; they tend to hang on to their living quarters even after they become too large, too expensive, and too demanding in terms of upkeep. Second, the present system of property taxation makes the appreciation of real estate for the aged a mixed blessing: given their inertia, their current expenditure burden is rising at rates reaching far beyond the increase in their incomes.

TABLE 9

Home Ownership and House Value for Nonfarm Family Units for 1969

House value	Distribution of home owners	
	All families	Family head, age 65 and older
$1-9,999	24	42
$10,000-14,999	22	22
$15,000 or more	54	36
Total	100	100
Mean value	$18,920	$13,850
Number of cases[a]	2,317	268
Proportion owning home	63	74

Note. Figures represent percentages.
[a]Unweighted *N*.

Finally, a few words about other assets of the aged are in order. The proportion of family unit heads reporting liquid assets is relatively constant among all age groups of the population—approximately 80% (see Table 10). However, there is a strong correlation between the value of assets and age. Among family heads 65 and older with financial assets, the mean asset value is twice that of all family heads and about 25% higher than family units with a head aged 55–65. However, between 35 and 40% of the aged families have no liquid assets beyond $1,000.

POVERTY AMONG THE AGED

The dominant theme under which we have looked at the economic aspect of old age has been that of welfare: Do the means available to old people conform to their needs as well as to society's norms of a decent and appropriate standard of living? Our conclusions may be summarized as follows:

1. The aged are worse off, on the average, than the rest of the population.

2. The income inequality during people's working years tends to be accentuated in old age. Some public transfers counteract but cannot compensate for the striking differences of various subgroups of the population in building up old age security and for the unequal opportunities to do so.

TABLE 10

Asset Position by Age of Family Head in 1960 and 1969

Value of liquid assets	All families		Head, age 55-64		Head, age 65 and older		Head, age 65-74		Head, age 74 and older	
	1960	1969	1960	1969	1960	1969	1960[a]	1969	1960[a]	1969
$1-99	11	10	8	5	6	2		2		3
$100-199	8	8	3	2	3	3		4		5
$200-499	16	14	14	10	11	8		9		6
$500-999	16	15	12	8	7	10		8		11
$1,000-1,999	15	13	13	16	16	10		9		10
$2,000-4,999	18	18	24	21	24	22		22		19
$5,000-9,999	9	10	14	15	14	17		16		19
$10,000 or more	7	12	12	23	19	28		30		27
Total	100	100	100	100	100	100		100		100
Mean value		$4,671		$7,440		$9,576		$10,888		$7,446
Number of cases	2,136	2,317[b]	308	382[b]	286	268[b]		165[b]		103[b]
Proportion having liquid assets	77	83	77	81	72	80		82		78

Note. Assets include savings in checking accounts, savings accounts, certificates of deposit, and bonds. Figures represent percentages.
[a]Data not available.
[b]Unweighted N.

3. Although their retirement income rose at least at an equal pace with the rest of the population, the aged during the 1960s had to satisfy to a substantial degree a pent-up demand in nonmaterial forms of welfare, such as retaining their own household and reducing the pace of work. To satisfy these aspirations, however, required substantial financial sacrifices. This means that the material situation of the aged did not improve parallel to the increase in their retirement benefits.

This concluding section looks at the welfare of the aged in a different manner. We will single out the economic problem cases—the poorest among the aged—and try to locate as well as to describe them and to trace the basis of their unfavorable situation to causally related circumstances and characteristics.

It rarely happens in social research and reality that a phenomenon as complex and varied as poverty can be satisfactorily explained by a small number of related variables. The analysis of the aged poor appears to be one of these complex cases. (Table 11 shows the differential distribution of poverty according to various background variables). Here disability, past educational attainment, region and size of community, race, and age (within the retired population) are all powerful explanatory variables. In this section, we define the aged poor as those people over 65 who fall into the lowest welfare ratio decile of *all persons*. In 1960, 15% of the aged belonged in this category; in 1969, 17% belonged.

The information in Table 11 is largely self-explanatory. The following conclusions deserve to be stressed. In 1969, 66% of the poor aged suffered from some sort of physical or mental disability, which had affected only 41% of all aged. It is disturbing that our welfare system and our health, accident, and disability insurance system during the 1960s have allowed disability to become a more powerful determinant of poverty among the aged than it was in 1960. Here an obvious area for political intervention is indicated.

In 1960, 35% of the aged poor individuals were 75 years or older. By 1969, very old people were somewhat less likely to be poor than previously, although the poor were still overrepresented within their ranks.

In 1960, more than half of the aged poor lived in the South (including Texas and border states) as opposed to one-third of all aged. In 1969, the South accounted for no less than 60% of the poor aged. Both in 1960 and 1969, between 40 and 50% of the aged poverty cases were found in rural areas whose population accounted for less than half of this percentage. No doubt the welfare ratio measured and analyzed has a strong bias in favor of monetary income. Thus, it may appear unjustified to classify two families with the same money income, one of which is living in rural Alabama, the other in New York City, in the same welfare category. It can be expected that the aspirations and expectations of people in poor areas remain lower than those of states with substantially higher per capita income. Yet this society is concerned about establishing equal living conditions all over the country; this is reflected quite clearly, for example, in the welfare legislation introduced by the Nixon administration. Thus, strong regional differences in aged poverty are of problematic significance and call for political remedy.

In 1969, 27% of the poor aged were black in contrast to only 11% of all aged. No significant change in this proportion has occurred during the 1960s.

In 1969, 79% of the aged poor household heads, but only 56% of all aged heads, had eight years or less formal education. The overriding importance of education may be of relatively recent origin. In 1960, there were more low-educated aged (61%) but less low-educated aged poor (75%). Because of small group size, the differences between the two years, although suggestive and plausible, are not statistically significant.

Figure 1 makes use of the Automatic Interaction Detector Program (AID), a search strategy for analyzing the structure between a number of variables from survey data (Sonquist, Baker, & Morgan, 1971). This technique, unlike stepwise regression or analysis of variance, does not assume the impact of the predictor on the dependent variable to be additive throughout the whole sample. Rather, it identifies subgroups by splitting the sample. To do so, the most powerful predictor is chosen so as to maximize the difference between two subgroups with respect to the dependent variable. Then it proceeds to do the same thing for each of the remaining subgroups until the subgroup differences on the dependent variable are no longer significant.

Figure 1 illustrates an analysis of a cross section of aged American heads of households in 1969. The dependent variable is poverty according to the specified definition (see top-center box of Figure 1). Of the whole sample 20.7% are poor. The most drastic differences (in terms of variance maximization) are between whites (17% poor) and nonwhites (51% poor). For the whites (comprising 89% of the sample) education proves to be the next most powerful discriminator, contrasting the 25% of the poor among the low educated (0–8 grades) with only 8% of the poor among the better educated. Furthermore, in accordance with Table 11, variables

TABLE 11

Correlates of Poverty of the Aged

Variable	All persons	All poor persons	All aged	Poor aged
Disability[a]				
1969				
Disabled	14	34	41	66
Not disabled	86	66	59	33
Not ascertained	0	0	0	1
1960				
Disabled	12	21	31	37
Not disabled	86	74	64	52
Not ascertained	2	5	5	11
Age				
1969				
65-74	11	19	65	59
75 and older	6	13	35	41
1960				
65-74	10	14	68	55
75 and older	5	12	32	45
Region[b]				
1969				
Northeast	21	9	21	11
North Central	36	39	31	24
South	30	45	36	60
West	13	7	12	5
1960				
Northeast	23	11	26	21
North Central	30	21	32	23
South	32	62	31	53
West	15	6	11	4
Type of community				
1969				
SMSA, largest city, 500,000 or more	33	21	22	14
SMSA, largest city, 100,000-499,999	21	11	16	8
SMSA, largest city, 50,000-99,999	11	14	10	7
Non-SMSA, largest place, 25,000-49,999	7	6	13	8
Non-SMSA, largest place, 10,000-24,999	10	15	12	18
Non-SMSA, largest place, under 10,000	18	33	27	45
1960				
Urban	30	19	34	23
Suburban	29	9	19	14
Adjacent	20	22	24	21
Outlying	21	50	23	42

TABLE 11

Correlates of Poverty of the Aged (Continued)

Variable	All persons	All poor persons	All aged	Poor aged
Race				
1969				
White	87	57	89	73
Black, other	13	43	11	27
1960				
White	90	64	90	71
Black, other	10	36	10	29
Number of cases[c]				
1969	8754	1873	823	163
1960	5464	856	637	108

	All family heads	Poor family heads	Aged family heads	Poor aged family heads
Education				
1969				
0-8 grades	28	59	56	79
9-11 grades	17	19	15	15
12 grades	27	13	13	3
College (with or without degree)	27	8	16	2
Not ascertained	1	1	0	1
1960				
0-8 grades	33	69	61	75
9-11 grades	21	14	14	18
12 grades	24	11	12	13
College (with or without degree)	22	6	13	4
Number of cases[c]				
1969	4452	501	505	110
1960	2800	464	384	75

Note. SMSA = Standard metropolitan statistical area.

[a]The questions were as follows:

For 1969: "Do you (HEAD) have any physical or nervous condition that limits the amount of work you can do?" "Is there anyone [else] in this family who is not working or going to school because of poor health?"

For 1960: "Have you had an illness, physical condition or nervous condition which limits the type of work or amount of work you can do?" "Is there anyone else living here whose work or schooling is limited by some illness, physical condition or nervous condition?"

[b]See Department of Commerce, Bureau of the Census, *1960 Census of Population*, Vol. 1, for census definition of the four major regions. The South includes Texas, the border states, and Delaware.

[c]Unweighted *N*.

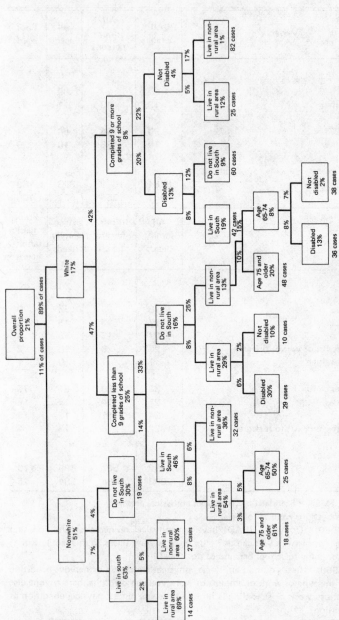

Fig. 1. Automatic Interaction Detector Analysis of the proportion of the poor among family heads age 65 or older for 1969. (Rural area is defined as a county or group of counties in which the largest city has a population of less than 10,000. Percentages within boxes refer to the proportion of poor within the particular subgroup. Percentages outside of the box refer to the proportion of the particular subgroup out of all the aged.)

like region, disability, rural/urban residence, and age (under 75 years, or over) are repatedly used for further splits.

Even though race is heavily interwined with living in the South, rural residence and, low education, the black–white difference is the most important contributor to the poverty variable. In other words, the analysis shows clearly that blacks, even in comparison with those whites who, like them, live in the South, or even in the rural South, are more likely to be poor.

The other variable of overriding importance for the explanation of poverty is education. The correlation between low educational attainment and poverty among the aged, already high in 1960, has been strengthened further during the subsequent decade (see Table 11). The educational revolution is an expression of the peculiar, highly aspirative American culture (Katona et al., 1971). While creating immense opportunities for young people of virtually all backgrounds and social strata, it reduces the chances for success of those who do not further their education. The very momentum of educational expansion made for a generation gap in training and skills that could not help but relegate the lesser-educated older people to second-rate economic status. The antiegalitarian impact of much of today's higher education has moved a long way from the function mass education (and higher education has become mass education) accorded by the founding fathers of the American educational philosophy (Strümpel, 1971a). With the educational revolution leveling off, intergenerational differences of educational attainment and earning power will narrow down. This trend will certainly strengthen the relative economic position of the aged now suffering from these differences. However, barring a radical restructuring of our system of income maintenance, the economic situation of the dropouts will no doubt constitute a serious social problem, not only during their working years but throughout their period of old age.

REFERENCES

Barfield, R., & Morgan, J. N. *Early retirement: The decision and the experience*. Ann Arbor: Institute for Social Research, University of Michigan, 1969.

Epstein, L. A. Early retirement on work life experience. *Social Security Bulletin*, 1966, **29**, 3–10.

Katona, G., Strümpel, B., & Zahn, E. *Aspirations and affluence*. New York: McGraw-Hill, 1971.

Kolodrubetz, W. W. Growth in employee benefit plans, 1950–1965. *Social Security Bulletin*, 1967, **30**, 10–27.

Morgan, J. N., Martin, D., Cohen, W. J., & Brazer, H. E. *Income and welfare in the United States.* New York: McGraw-Hill, 1962.

Morgan, J. N., & Smith, J. D. *A panel of income dynamics: Study design, procedures, and forms, 1969 interviewing year.* (A report on research in process under contract to the Office of Economic Opportunity) Ann Arbor: Institute for Social Research, University of Michigan, 1969.

Sonquist, J. A., Baker, E. L., & Morgan, J. N. *Searching for structure.* Ann Arbor: Institute for Social Research, University of Michigan, 1971.

Strümpel, B. Higher education and economic behavior. In S. B. Withey (Ed.), *A degree and what else.* New York: McGraw-Hill, 1971. (a)

Strümpel, B. (with R. T. Curtin & M. S. Schwartz) Economic life styles, values, and subjective welfare—An empirical approach. In E. Sheldon (Ed.), *Understanding economic behavior.* New York: Lippincott, in press.

Epilogue

Loving, Dying, and Other Gerontologic Addenda

ROBERT J. KASTENBAUM

Sleeping, dreaming, imaging, fantasizing, meditating, creating, loving, grieving, dying. These activities have something in common: lack of coverage by the American Psychological Association's Task Force on Aging. It is hard to work up a grumble about omissions when so much material has been explored with so much scholarship and skill. However, it would also be remiss to conclude this volume without at least a brief discussion of some of the questions that remain in search of a task force.

THE INNER SANCTUM

Sleeping, dreaming, imaging, fantasizing, meditating, creating, loving, grieving, and dying are processes that involve the inner core of human experience. Even the willing and articulate person may find it difficult to convey these experiences to others. Anybody who has made a serious attempt to study private experience could compile a formidable list of methodological problems. No matter how formidable the methodological challenge, however, old people do

---

Robert J. Kastenbaum received his PhD in clinical psychology from the University of Southern California in 1959. He is currently Professor and Chairman of the Department of Psychology, College I, University of Massachusetts, Boston. His major research interests center around aging, death, and time perspective. He is Editor of two professional journals, *Aging & Human Development* and *Omega,* and is President-Elect of the American Association of Suicidology.

have their inner lives, and we do not have a comprehensive gerontology unless we know something about this realm.

Approaches to private experience can be classified roughly into "outer" and "inner." Detection of rapid eye movements in an old person would provide one kind of information about his sleep and dream life. Maintenance of a sleep-and-dream diary or intensive analysis of a dream series would provide another kind of information. Those who shy away from an inner approach to inner experience could make valuable contributions with physiological, behavioral, or "unobtrusive" (Webb, Campbell, Schwart, & Sechrest, 1966) measures. It is doubtful that methodological problems alone account for our disinclination to visit the inner sanctum. It might be useful to examine other reasons for neglecting this general realm before delving into specific areas.

Clinical observations have stimulated some of the most productive theory and research in the behavioral sciences. This source of stimulation has been grossly underdeveloped in gerontology. As Lawton (1970) has shown, very little cross-referencing traffic exists between clinical psychology/psychiatry and gerontology. The reluctance of clinicians to enter into intensive relationships with the aged is of primary importance for its mental health implications. But it is also a factor in the lack of impetus for studying the phenomenologic and psychodynamic side of aging.

Sociopolitical pressure on gerontologists has placed a premium on two kinds of data: the "hard" and the "fast." For a long time there was very little information either available or desired about aging and the aged. When the information need finally burst to the surface, it did so with an imperious call for a sort of "instant gerontology." Descriptive information was an obvious place to begin: how many old people, where, doing what? The need for "fast" descriptive data to guide planning and program development encouraged attention to the relatively external and countable aspects of human functioning. In-depth studies were too slow and did not seem to meet specifications for the types of information needed. Another slower-moving current of interest generated itself around the extension of basic psychological and physiological information through the later years of life. The emphasis was on hard data that could be obtained through experimental techniques already familiar in the field. If topics with a heavy emphasis on phenomenology were neglected, one has only to recall that these concerns were temporarily out of fashion in psychology in general. Certain areas, such as creativity or bereavement and dying, had not yet become recognizable specialties.

However well justified the initial patterning of research interests may have been, it is unfortunate that the patterns have remained more or less frozen during the last two decades. Take dreaming, for example. None of the landmark volumes on aging nor any of the existing textbooks even hint at the fact that old people dream, much less that these dreams might tell us something we should know. Psychologists have been responsive to sociopolitical pressures for information. Only sporadically, however, have we exercised leadership in demonstrating that certain topics *should* be of interest to government, industry, and other information consumers. Must psychological gerontology wait until outsiders insist it is important to learn about the creative process or love-sex-intimacy dynamics in old age?

We are not completely immune to the old age stereotypes prevalent in our culture. Ask gerontologists to examine their own development and aging (Kastenbaum, Derbin, Sabatini, & Artt, in press)! It seems to be a soul-wrenching experience. We sometimes assume that old people do not have sexual thoughts. A somewhat parallel line of reasoning prevails on the topic of death, in addition to the assumption that death is especially "natural" in old age (hence, especially "unnatural" for the not-so-old). We assume that "old people live in the past" is both an accurate and adequate characterization of fantasy life and meditation in the elderly. All these assumptions tend to dampen the inquisitive spirit and thereby perpetuate themselves.

It is possible that there are some things we really do not want to know about old men and women. Feifel (1959) and others have suggested that the aged cue off our own death-related anxieties. Face to face with the old man's vulnerability we are reminded of our own mortality. Even more broadly, we may resist the prospect of being enveloped by the old person's world that one day will be our own. Why let ourselves in for vicarious suffering? Why borrow misery from the future? Aversion from intimate contact with the aged is common.

These are some of the reasons, along with the methodological difficulties, that may have inhibited attention to the private experience of older men and women. Perhaps more attention should be devoted to the private experience of those who study aging. How many gerontologic researchers have been encouraged to take a guided tour of their own attitudinal structures? Might a self-discovery component add much to the training of psychologists and others preparing for careers with the aged? Should we perhaps reconsider the recruitment and selection processes as well as the training programs themselves? Possibly there is a subtle bias in favor of bringing along new researchers who will remain within the mold of the past.

SLEEPING

Advances in sleep research during the past two decades have been notable. Although a few studies have focused on the elderly, one cannot say that psychological gerontology has shown an inclination either to contribute or utilize information on this topic. Greater attention to sleeping patterns would almost certainly lead to advances on both the theoretical and applied fronts. Consider, if you will, the following points:

1. Sleep disturbances sometimes anticipate and often accompany a variety of disorders (Luce & Segal, 1966). Depressive reactions, for example, almost invariably involve an alteration in sleep patterns.

2. Available data suggest not only that sleep patterns tend to change with advancing adult age, but that these changes are for the worse (Kahn, 1970). On the average, it takes us longer to fall asleep, we awaken more frequently during the night, and we spend less time in Stage 4 slumber (the deepest phase of the sleep cycle).

3. Older people themselves often complain that they are not sleeping well. These complaints sometimes are brushed aside as being (a) just one more element in a hypochondriacal picture, (b) inconsistent with the assumption that the elderly do not require much sleep, or (c) contradicted by the observation that they have in fact spent many hours in bed. That the old person may actually be suffering sleep deprivation and that this deprivation could be partially responsible for decrements in cognition and performance are possibilities often overlooked.

4. Effects of sleep deprivation at any age level show more than a faint resemblance to the behavior syndrome displayed by people who are "just old." A chronic fatigue state leads to inattentiveness, loss of memory, irritability, resistance to novelty, decreased vigor, etc.

5. There are impressive individual differences in sleep patterns just as there are impressive individual differences in level and style of coping with old age.

Implications for psychology spark off in every direction:

1. *Interventions.* Could the elderly person learn to maintain or extend his Stage 4 sleep through a conditioning/EEG-feedback system? Would sleep problems be responsive to desensitization or other

therapeutic procedures aimed at relieving anxieties elders sometimes feel as they lie abed?

2. *Research.* Sleeping patterns might provide useful dependent variables in studies of treatment effects. Conversely, these patterns could also be used as independent variables from which we might try to predict a wide variety of phenomena: number and types of social roles enacted, cognitive performance, vulnerability to accidents, etc. We might attempt to discover possible relationships between "good" and "poor" elderly sleepers and their retirement, disengagement, morale, and health status. Perhaps knowing how well an old person sleeps would prove a powerful source of information for predicting many other things about him.

DREAMING, IMAGING, FANTASIZING, MEDITATING

These phenomenological states will be considered together, not because they are indistinguishable, but because we know so little about any of them in old age.

Do the aged have more dreams or fewer? What functions are served by these dreams? Is it possible that anticipatory "death work" takes place chiefly through dreams? To what extent, if any, might dreams of the aged "compensate" for the limitations and frustrations of their present life situation?

What does an old person see when he closes his eyes? What sounds can he recall to his ears, and with what degree of "presence"? Do odors and tastes, perhaps even kinesthetic "ghosts," waft back to him over a distance of years? In general, do people tend to grow stronger or weaker in their processes of imagery? Is there a return to childlike freshness and concreteness of imagery, or a gradual dulling away of all images? Does the preferred mode of imagery change with the years?

How much of an older person's time is spent in fantasy or meditative activities? How purposive are these thoughts? Under what conditions are these thoughts directed to the remote or immediate past, remote or immediate future? Butler (1963) called attention to the "life review" process in old age. What other adaptational processes might be discovered? Granted that old people often do seem to dwell upon the past, are there important differences in how they use the past and in the manner they link the past with the present and future? When does ruminative thought nourish and sustain? When does it contribute to psychobiological decline in the aged? Singer (1966) suggested that "the aged person who now has the leisure and inclination for at least a reminiscent form of fantasy may soon find himself bored at his own self-recounting of his past, and the apathy and depression that presages senile withdrawal sets in [p. 191]." Like the rest of us, Singer can offer hypotheses and suggestions but little data on the aged even though daydreaming is his field of expertise.

The lack of attention to a distinctively psychological level of functioning—the dreaming, imaging, fantasizing, meditating processes—astounds and puzzles students who expect to learn about these topics when they start looking into gerontology. Their puzzlement is all the more emphasized by the cultural tradition that imputes (if ambivalently) a special quality of "wisdom" to the old.

CREATING, LOVING, GRIEVING

Creativity is something more than the productivity figures for older workers. Loving is not encompassed by the frequency of reported sexual interests and activities. We do not understand grieving in old age by counting the number of widows and computing their economic or even their social adjustment. We are indebted to those gerontologists who have taken the trouble to investigate worker productivity, sexual interests, and the role of widowhood. These topics are important in their own right, and they may also be important as correlates of intimate psychological processes. Still unmet, however, is the challenge of studying creating, loving, and grieving on their own terms.

Do people become more or less "creative" with advancing age? If "it depends," then, what does it depend on: previous experience, current opportunity, what? Are certain types of creativity more likely to flower in old age than in earlier times? Should we look for distinctive creativity in materials used, themes, style, or in the nature of the "creative act" itself? Should a sterility–creativity dimension be added to our assessment of intellectual functioning in adults? Can an old person think and act creatively even when impaired in certain ways (e.g., short-term memory deficit or fluctuating levels of awareness)?

As we move up close to study creativity in later life we will also learn about curiosity behavior, flexibility, self-discipline, openness to experience, information-retrieval mechanisms, and other topics. Chances are that the better we become as students of creativity, the more creativity we will see. Our categories and conceptions will probably become more varied, more subtle. We might, for example, learn to appreciate those creative acts that unfold over a long period of time.

All the "dirty old men" jokes in the world do not dilute the poignancy of love and sex in later life. And yet once again, our limited data tend to be at several removes from the heart of the matter. Consider just one line of possible inquiry: what does an older person lose if and when he no longer has a loving sexual partner? (It might be more accurate to turn convention aside and employ the female pronoun, considering the greater likelihood of women outliving their men.) Is it possible that the loss of intimate sharing may prove more critical than the orgasm deprivation? Where else is the old man or woman to receive immediate proof that his body can be a source of pleasure both to himself and others? In what other context than the boudoir will he have the opportunity for the whisperings, the nonverbal communications, the private world of people very close to each other? Strangers and young people may tend to stereotype him as Another Old Man. They see him with all his clothes on, more or less playing the public role. They do not fathom that he has been lover and beloved. When the identity-enhancing intimacy of loving sex has terminated, where is the elder to turn for a convincing reminder that there is more to him than his new and skimpy public role?

Grieving is an experience that most of us undergo sooner or later. For the old person it may be a central and virtually continuous experience. In fact, it has been suggested that much of the behavior that we take as hallmarks of "bad aging" can be understood in terms of bereavement overload (Kastenbaum & Aisenberg, 1972). One death (or other loss) sometimes follows another before the elder can pull through his mourning process. There are seldom opportuities to replenish or substitute for what or who has been lost (how can one really replace a middle-aged child who has died?). The energy-draining, inward-luring grief reaction may not be as temporary in the older as in the younger adult. And any circumstance that leads an old person to break step with the world around him tends to mitigate against his subsequent reintegration. He may have to cope not only with the suffering inherent in the grieving process, but also with the increased alienation that often follows in the wake.

Psychologists might take the lead in helping to differentiate between changes in later life that are related to grief (postbereavement or anticipatory states) and those associated with other causes. We might also encourage a go-easy approach with psychotropic drug administration that is intended to subdue grief. The same might apply to superficial efforts to jolly the bereaved person into "resocialization" status without due regard for the most essential and positive aspects of his experience.

DYING

Death is the unspoken variable in many gerontological studies and discussions. The limited direct reference to death in psychogerontologic theory and research seems disproportionate to the magnitude of the topic. References in the mainstream of research tend to cluster into a few categories. We are reminded, for example, that differential death rate is a factor influencing the interpretation of longitudinal studies, or that men tend to die earlier than women, leading to a preponderance of widows. Despite the gradual increase in clinical and research contributions to the topic of death in old age, the field as a whole seems to keep these at arm's length as of "special interest" only.

One could argue for a complete reversal of emphasis. Death is a central fact in human existence. Failure to confront death on a broad research, action, and conceptual front is failure to recognize the most critical sector of content matter in gerontology. We know comparatively little about the psychosocial causes of premature death in later life and why, for that matter, some people do not survive long enough to become subjects for our gerontological investigations.

How do our sociophysical environments maintain life or hasten death in the elderly? Precisely how do old men and women meet their deaths? How would they prefer to live out their remaining months, weeks, days, and hours? Although the quantity and quality of available information on these topics leave much to be desired, there is a larger gap yet: that between knowledge and its application. Practical efforts do not have to wait indefinitely for the "more research [that] needs to be done." Perhaps some day gerontologists will have as much skill and understanding to offer concerning the dying situation as some of our colleagues have on the topic of prenatal care and birth.

THE MISSING FOOTNOTE

Most research reports in gerontology, including those authored by psychologists, require the reader to supply his own footnote, something like this: "The findings reported here do not necessarily apply to 'nonwhite' or other minority subpopulations." Neglect of aging in blacks, Indians, Spanish-speaking Americans, and Oriental-Americans has also characterized the federal and most local governments. The White House Conference on Aging, for example, had virtually no provisions to come to terms with minority group aging until pressures were brought to bear by the newly created National Caucus on the Black Aged (Jackson, 1971). The government has not been asking psychogerontologists for information about minority aged, and we, by and large, neither have been developing this information nor expressing concern about its lack.

What are we really missing? For one thing, we have already missed the opportunity to gather comparative information on the psychology of minority group aged up to this point in time. The most painstaking study that begins tomorrow is unlikely to reveal what has been going on during the past quarter century of neglect. Obviously, we are missing the breadth required to develop a true psychogerontology, not merely a psychogerontology of easily available whites.

A moment's reflection tells us that we are also missing whatever may be particularly distinctive to growing old from a given minority group position. Fewer blacks than whites survive into the later years of life, for example. Do the black survivors have something special going for them? If so, what? We miss the opportunity for stimulation from psychogerontologists who themselves represent other racial or ethnic groups. We miss the opportunity to apply psychological knowledge in some of the places where it might help, for example, reduction of tensions between minority aged and "the Establishment."

Real progress in the study of minority group aging in the United States may not come about until we have played our part in establishing training programs for indigenous researchers and practitioners. There are the usual "do-gooder" errors to be made in the meantime, but perhaps some of us have already had the opportunity to get these errors out of the way in other contexts. Action groups seeking to advance minority causes seldom step forward with emphasis on, or even mention of, the aged. As we dialogue with APA colleagues who are advocating programs in the area of "black psychology" or "Mexican-American psychology," we might attempt to see that the aged in these minorities receive their share of the attention. It is not only the middle-class white who tends to forget his elders in the heat of rhetoric and the cool of strategy.

And so this writer has had his opportunity to point up a few topics that were not accommodated by the original task force structure. No doubt if these topics had been included, other omissions would have been detected by other observers. In fact, there is no reason now why the reader cannot set forth as his own task force. As psychologists, perhaps we can represent in our thinking, methods, and actions the richness of human experience that men and women bring with them to their last years of life.

REFERENCES

Butler, R. N. The life review: An interpretation of reminiscence in the aged. *Psychiatry*, 1963, **26**, 65–76.

Feifel, H. Attitudes toward death in some normal and mentally ill populations. In H. Feifel (Ed.), *The meaning of death*. New York: McGraw-Hill, 1959.

Jackson, H. National Caucus on the Black Aged: A progress report. *Aging & Human Development*, 1971, **2**, 226–231.

Kahn, E. The effects of age on sleep. In E. Hartmann (Ed.), *Sleep and dreaming*. Boston: Little, Brown, 1970.

Kahn, E., & Fisher, C. The sleep characteristics of the normal aged male. *Journal of Nervous and Mental Disease*, 1969, **148**, 477–493.

Kastenbaum, R., & Aisenberg, R. B. *The psychology of death*. New York: Springer, 1972.

Kastenbaum, R., Derbin, V., Sabatini, P., & Artt, S. "The ages of me": Toward definitions of personal and interpersonal age. *Aging & Human Development*, 1972, **3**, in press.

Lawton, M. P. Gerontology in clinical psychology and vice-versa. *Aging & Human Development*, 1970, **1**, 147–160.

Luce, G. G., & Segal, J. *Sleep*. New York: Lancer Books, 1966.

Singer, J. L. *Daydreaming*. New York: Random House, 1966.

Webb, E. J., Campbell, D. T., Schwart, R. D., & Sechrest, L. *Unobtrusive measures: Nonreactive research in the social sciences*. Chicago: Rand McNally, 1966.

Subject Index

710

711

714

715

716

717